Perl for Web Site Management

Perl for Web Site Management

John Callender

O'REILLY®

Beijing · Cambridge · Farnham · Köln · Paris · Sebastopol · Taipei · Tokyo

Perl for Web Site Management
by John Callender

Copyright © 2002 O'Reilly & Associates, Inc. All rights reserved.
Printed in the United States of America., 1005

Published by O'Reilly & Associates, Inc., 1005 Gravenstein Highway North, Sebastopol, CA 95472.

O'Reilly & Associates books may be purchased for educational, business, or sales promotional use. Online editions are also available for most titles (*safari.oreilly.com*). For more information contact our corporate/institutional sales department: 800-998-9938 or *corporate@oreilly.com*.

Editors:	Linda Mui and Richard Koman
Production Editor:	Colleen Gorman
Cover Designer:	Hanna Dyer
Interior Designer:	David Futato

Printing History:

January 2002:	First Edition.

ISBN: 1-56592-647-1
[M]

Table of Contents

Preface

This book is about getting your job done. More specifically, it's about getting your job done more quickly, effectively, and enjoyably, especially if your job includes building and maintaining useful collections of information on the World Wide Web. Finally, and most importantly, it's about getting these things done using the Perl programming language.

What this book is *not* about is everything else; it's not about how to write HTML well, design professional-looking images, or create an effective navigation scheme for your web site. Nor is it about how to configure your web server software, perform basic system administration tasks, or maintain your web site's Internet connection. I assume you already know those things, can find out about them somewhere else, or can find someone else to do them for you. Finally, this book is not about how to create a large web site using some sort of point-and-click web authoring application. Instead, my assumption is that you want to learn how to build your own web publishing solutions using the simple, flexible, and freely available tools that have built many of the most useful sites on the Web today.

On the most fundamental level, this book is about learning to move beyond the world of the computer *user,* and to begin moving toward the world of the computer *programmer*. That's a big journey, with many stages, and this book does not pretend to take you all the way to the end. Instead, it concentrates on the first few steps, doing its best to guide you past the more obvious pitfalls. How far you end up going depends on your particular needs and aptitude. This book is about helping you make a good start.

Intended Audience

This book assumes that you are experienced with computers, though not necessarily with Unix, or with programming. You are enthusiastic about the Web as a communications medium, and know the basics (at least) of creating web sites, but would like to take your efforts to the next level. You might be responsible for a small-business web site, or be part of a team working on larger-scale web projects. Perhaps you are putting content on a company intranet. Maybe you are a hobbyist, building a web site for the local soccer league. You might be educated in a traditional computer science discipline, but you're just as likely to have a noncomputer background as a teacher, writer, artist, or *anything*, really.

This book grows from my own experience. A few years ago I made my own transition from a career as a writer and editor to a much more rapidly moving career at the center of an expanding collection of commercial web projects. It has been an exciting journey, involving a nonstop learning process. When I think about the last few years, I don't feel that I've been climbing a learning *curve* so much as scaling a near-vertical learning *cliff*, and when I look down at my starting point the difference between here and there is sobering (just as it is sobering for me to look upward, to the heights where the *real* experts reside).

I thought about this the other day, as I was explaining to a co-worker how I used a 30-line Perl script to create several hundred web pages based on a page design of hers, doing in a few minutes what it would have taken her (or me, not long ago) many days, even weeks, to accomplish with manual HTML coding. "How did you *learn* this stuff?" she asked. It reminded me of the Arthur C. Clarke saying: for the uninitiated, "Any sufficiently advanced technology is indistinguishable from magic."

If you'd like to work that kind of magic—writing programs to automate repetitive tasks, updating page designs throughout your site in just a few seconds, and building vast arrays of web-based information from arbitrarily formatted source data—this book is for you.

Programmers by Accident

Traditionally, a wide gulf has separated computer users from computer programmers. Users traditionally see computers as a means to an end, and learn only as much about them as they need to in order to solve their immediate problem. Users tend to use trial-and-error, or outright guesswork, rather than reading the documentation. Programmers, on the other hand, tend to see mastery of the computer as an end in itself. They abhor guessing, and think nothing of absorbing hundreds of pages of documentation at a single sitting. They spend years perfecting their craft, training themselves to think logically, to break down problems into manageable tasks, to code cleanly and clearly.

Because of the Web, though, those traditional distinctions between users and programmers have been blurred. The Web makes it easy for someone who isn't a programmer to create useful collections of computer-based information. It also creates an upgrade path, a sequence of manageable steps that a programming novice can follow, with real benefits achieved at each stage. This is very different from the traditional route to becoming a programmer, in which one had to learn a great deal before being able to do anything useful.

A major factor in this upgrade path is Perl, the programming language of choice for web content creators. Perl is designed to be usable by mere mortals, people who haven't spent years in a computer science lab. One of the design criteria that guided Perl's creator, Larry Wall, was that with Perl, "Easy things should be easy, and hard things should be possible." In this sense Perl is modeled on the natural languages that Larry, who was educated as a linguist, appreciated for their ability to efficiently express both simple ideas ("Give me the red ball") and complex ones ("When in the course of human events, it becomes necessary for one people to dissolve the political bands which have connected them with another. . .").

Like natural languages, one of the ways in which Perl makes easy things easy is that it is designed to let you get by using only a small subset of the language. As Larry puts it, Perl lets you talk baby talk, and in Perl such baby talk is officially okay. While there are those who argue that Perl makes a poor choice for a 1st programming language, it clearly makes a spectacular choice for a 0th programming language. By that I mean that Perl is an ideal language to learn if you are not now, and may never be, a full-time programmer because Perl, unlike other languages, will actually let you accomplish useful things almost from the outset.

There are some who believe that such amateurs, who are sometimes referred to as *accidental programmers,* have no business playing around with programming. A metaphor they sometimes trot out is that of surgery: "You wouldn't want an amateur heart surgeon operating on you, would you?" This misses the point of the latest wave in computing, however. Delivering useful and interesting information via computer has become so easy in the age of the Web that the pool of content creators has expanded well beyond the ranks of professional programmers. Whatever purists may say, this is a good thing, just as it is a good thing that lots of non-physicians have been trained to perform CPR. The sloppy, unprofessional care these people provide saves hundreds of lives each year. In the same sense, even sloppy, unprofessional programming can do wonderful things on the Web. If some obscure piece of content you are interested in is available online, it's probably there because someone who is not a professional programmer chose to make it available, and didn't ask permission before he did so.

Of course, many tasks are beyond the capabilities of accidental programmers (just as there are many situations in which CPR, in and of itself, is an insufficient remedy). As Tolkien wrote in *The Two Towers,* "Perilous to us all are the devices of an art deeper than we possess ourselves." As accidental programmers we must always be mindful of our own limitations, and should not hesitate to call in a professional if we seem to be getting in over our heads. That doesn't mean we need to let the professionals have all the fun, however. We just need to do our best, as Larry Wall advises, to have "the *appropriate* amount of fun" (emphasis added).

What This Book Offers

The bulk of this book consists of examples of the behind-the-scenes programming used to create and maintain large web sites. Most of the programming is in Perl, with the remainder consisting of Unix command-line utilities and shell scripting.

Accompanying the examples are in-depth explanations intended for an audience that is technically adept, but not expert at programming. Along the way are pointers to more detailed explanatory material, whether in manpages (more about those in the next chapter), on the Web, or in other books. The overall approach is that of a tutorial, progressing from simple concepts in the early chapters to more complex ones later on.

All of the examples are based on actual, in-the-trenches programming. Although some have been rewritten to make them suitable as teaching devices, at the core each represents a particular solution for a particular set of circumstances—and not necessarily the only solution, or even the best one. "There's more than one way to do it" is the Perl community's motto. There is no "correct" way to do anything in Perl, except in the sense that Larry Wall described in the preface to *Programming Perl*, where he wrote that "A Perl script is 'correct' if it gets the job done before your boss fires you."

All of the examples in this book have met that standard successfully, at least for certain values of *job* and *boss* and *fires,* but beyond that you probably shouldn't assume too much. In particular, do not think of these examples as being general solutions that you can apply directly to your own situation. Instead, you should see them as demonstrations of the kind of tools that can be developed quickly to solve particular problems. With some work, you will be able to use them as starting points for your own solutions.

Organization

Here's a brief description of what you'll find in each of this book's chapters:

Chapter 1, *Getting Your Tools in Order*
> Explains how to evaluate web-hosting providers, log into a Unix shell session, use some basic shell commands, and locate a suitable editor for creating text files.

Chapter 2, *Getting Started with Perl*
> Introduces the Perl programming language and explains how to run simple Perl scripts, including an overview of Unix file permissions, Perl variable types, quoting operators, and an explanation of how to run Perl-based CGI scripts.

Chapter 3, *Running a Form-to-Email Gateway*
> Shows how to run a simple CGI script to bundle up the output of an HTML form and email it to an appropriate address.

Chapter 4, *Power Editing with Perl*

Gives an example of some simple Perl programming that can automate repeated editing changes to HTML documents.

Chapter 5, *Parsing Text Files*

Demonstrates how to use Perl to take arbitrarily formatted source data (in this case, text prepared for publishing via a page layout program) and convert it into an in-memory data structure.

Chapter 6, *Generating HTML*

Continuing the example from Chapter 5, shows how an in-memory data structure can be output as HTML files, producing a web-based directory of trade-show exhibitors.

Chapter 7, *Regular Expressions Demystified*

Explains how to use regular expressions to construct patterns for matching and, optionally, changing strings of text.

Chapter 8, *Parsing Web Access Logs*

Shows how to use regular expressions to extract individual entries from a web server's access log, incorporating them into an in-memory data structure for later output.

Chapter 9, *Date Arithmetic*

Continuing the example from Chapter 8, discusses techniques for working with date/time strings inside a program.

Chapter 10, *Generating a Web Access Report*

Completing the example begun in Chapters 8 and 9, shows how to output custom reports from a web server's access logs.

Chapter 11, *Link Checking*

Demonstrates how to use Perl to create a series of increasingly intelligent tools for identifying broken web links. Includes an explanation of installing and using LWP (libwww-perl), a powerful library for requesting and manipulating web pages from within a Perl script.

Chapter 12, *Running a CGI Guestbook*

Shows how to create a CGI script that allows web users to post comments in a guestbook file on the server.

Chapter 13, *Running a CGI Search Tool*

Shows how to use SWISH-E, a free search engine, along with a simple CGI script, to allow full-text search capability on a web site.

Chapter 14, *Using HTML Templates*

Shows how to use a simple template system to enforce design consistency across a large collection of HTML pages.

Chapter 15, *Generating Links*
> Continuing the example begun in Chapter 14, shows how to construct navigational links that tie a large web site together.

Chapter 16, *Writing Perl Modules*
> Continuing the example begun in Chapters 14 and 15, shows how to construct modules for sharing code between multiple Perl scripts.

Chapter 17, *Adding Pages via CGI Script*
> Completes the example begun in Chapters 14, 15, and 16, showing how to use a CGI frontend to add well-formed HTML pages to a document collection.

Chapter 18, *Monitoring Search Engine Positioning*
> Shows how to use Perl and the WWW::Search module to automate the checking of a site's position in the results returned from third-party search engines.

Chapter 19, *Keeping Track of Users*
> Begins the presentation of a system for letting users sign themselves up for access to a resource protected by HTTP's basic authentication, using a user-supplied email address for a verification step.

Chapter 20, *Storing Data in DBM Files*
> Continues the example begun in Chapter 19, showing how DBM files (optionally with the MLDBM Perl module) can be used to store persistent user data on the web server.

Chapter 21, *Where to Go Next*
> Describes other areas that readers who have finished this book might wish to explore next.

Online Examples

All the numbered code examples in this book are available for download from *http://www.elanus.net/book/*. You may also get them, along with errata listings, from the official O'Reilly page for the book at *http://www.oreilly.com/catalog/perlwsmng/*.

Conventions Used in This Book

We use the following font and format conventions:

Italic
> Used for new terms where first defined, domain names, and filenames.

`Constant width`
> Used for code listings and command output.

`Constant width bold`
> Used for command-line input and for highlighting sections of code.

Indicates a tip, suggestion, or general note.

Indicates a warning or caution.

How to Contact Us

Please address comments and questions concerning this book to the publisher:

O'Reilly & Associates, Inc.
1005 Gravenstein Highway North
Sebastopol, CA 95472
(800) 998-9938 (in the United States or Canada)
(707) 829-0515 (international/local)
(707) 829-0104 (fax)

There is a web page for this book, which lists errata, examples, and any additional information. You can access this page at:

http://www.oreilly.com/catalog/perlwsmng/

To comment or ask technical questions about this book, send email to:

bookquestions@oreilly.com

For more information about books, conferences, software, Resource Centers, and the O'Reilly Network, see the O'Reilly web site at:

http://www.oreilly.com

Acknowledgments

I owe a deep debt to Larry Wall. Whether he knew he was creating such a wonderful tool for accidental programmers like me, or whether that was just a happy side-effect of his creating a uniquely useful tool for people like himself, I will always be grateful to him for Perl.

Others in the Perl community who loom large in my personal list of heroes are Tom Christiansen, Mark-Jason Dominus, Tom Phoenix, Larry Rosler, and Nathan Torkington. I'd like to thank them on behalf of newbies everywhere. Even more than their prodigious knowledge of Perl, I'm in awe of the dedication they display in using their knowledge to help those just starting out.

At O'Reilly & Associates, I want to thank Tim O'Reilly, both for greenlighting this book, and for his vision in creating a series of books, conferences, and web sites that make learning about these technologies so much fun. I also would like to thank Richard Koman, Andy Oram, Paula Ferguson, and Linda Mui for their editorial assistance, and the following technical reviewers for their comments on the initial draft: Elaine Ashton, Scott Davenport, Joe Johnston, Nathan Patwardhan, Bill Peña, and Tom Phoenix.

I am very grateful to William Cobert and John Bethune at Canon Communications for giving me a chance to change careers. Among many others who helped me during that time, I want to single out Jennifer Field and Kate Leachman, graphic designers who joined me in making a breakneck transition to a new medium.

Among a long list of online acquaintances, I'd like to give special thanks to Dave Ewers, Ron Underwood, and Mark Thompson, for the many lessons they taught me in using the computer as a communications tool. Among the residents of the Ishar MUD (*http://www.ishar.com/*), I want to thank Clayton Bittle, Scott Book, John Brady, Sue Wen Chiao, Conner, James Crumpton, Cymoril, Jeremy Dewar, Dylan Hart, Matthew Hine, Aaron Hopkins, Dan Porter, Jayson Shenk, Jason Snyder, Jason Stone, and Jason Sylvester. Without them this book would almost certainly have been finished sooner, but it wouldn't have been nearly as good a book.

At Cyberverse Inc. (*http://www.cyberverse.com/*), the best ISP I have ever found or ever expect to find, I want to give special thanks to Jay Smith and Greg Domeno. I'm sure that Greg, in particular, never dreamed how much handholding, late night support, and general education was included in a monthly $24.95 dial-up fee.

I'd also like to thank Dr. Jim Campos, principal of Main Elementary School in Carpinteria, California, and technology teacher Julie Cole. Working with them and their students on Main School's entry in the 2000 International CyberFair competition (which forms the basis of the material presented in Chapters 14 through 17) was truly inspirational.

Finally, I want to thank my mom, who has waited a long time to be acknowledged in a book of mine. I'd also like to give an extra-special thanks to my wife Linda, and to my children Julia and William, for the many sacrifices they made so that I could write this book.

## CHAPTER 1

Getting Your Tools in Order

As I explained in the Preface, this book is intended for readers who have some experience creating web sites and now want to move to the next level, using the Perl programming language to create larger, more useful sites. In this first chapter, though, we won't be discussing Perl. Instead, we'll talk about some of the other things you'll be using as you make that transition: a good hosting provider, the Unix shell environment, and a text editor for writing your programming code.

If you were setting out to climb a mountain (or even to take a short hike in the backcountry), you'd want to make sure you had everything squared away before you left the trailhead. That's what this chapter is about: getting you set up properly with gear and supplies before you head into the wilderness.

If you already have a web-hosting provider you're happy with, are familiar with using an ssh or Telnet client to log into a Unix shell session, and have a programmer's text editor you're happy with, congratulations! You should probably skip right to the next chapter, where I introduce the Perl programming language. Otherwise, read on.

Open Source Versus Proprietary Software

I assume in this book that you work in a Windows or Macintosh environment for your day-to-day computing. Much of the material I present, however, focuses on learning to work in a very different environment, that of the Unix and Unix-like systems upon which much of the Internet has been built. In particular, I focus on learning to work with Linux, a Unix-like operating system that is especially popular with Internet service providers (among others) for running web servers.

Learning to work with Linux means learning to work in the world of *open source software*. Open source software (*http://www.opensource.org/*) is a relatively new name for a relatively old phenomenon. It refers to software whose original instructions, or *source code,* are made freely available to anyone who uses that software. The opposite of open source is *proprietary* (or *closed source*) *software,* in which users have access only to the compiled binary form of the program—that is, the *executable* that actually runs on the computer.

Advocates of the open source development model claim many advantages for this approach. Open source developers are part of a voluntary, collaborative effort. Their goal is the creation of simple, flexible tools that are as useful as possible. Standards are open, and interfaces well documented. New features are added according to genuine need. Releases come early and often; bugs are identified and fixed in a matter of days, or even hours.

With proprietary software, say the open source crowd, one is dependent on a closed team of programmers who labor out of sight, insulated from the healthy effects of peer review and massively parallel debugging. Direction is determined by marketing committee. The goal is the maximization of profit, with user needs a sometimes-distant second. Standards that promote flexibility and user choice may be ignored, or even actively subverted.

At this point you may be thinking, who cares? I know I used to think that way. In my former existence as a nonprogramming user of DOS (and later, Windows and Macintosh computers), I dealt strictly with closed source software. Much of it was commercial software, some of it was shareware or freeware, but none of it came with source code included, and frankly, I didn't care. I didn't know how to program, so I wouldn't have known how to modify it even if I'd had the source code, and I didn't have a compiler to turn modified source code into an executable, anyway, so what was the point?

I could probably have gone on like this quite happily for the rest of my life, except for one thing: the Internet. While we Windows and Mac users were poking along contentedly in our proprietary, closed source world, a bunch of wild-eyed zealots in the research and academic community used the strengths of open source software to build a global computer network with mind-boggling capabilities. One especially impressive creation to come out of that effort was the World Wide Web, the largest open source development project in the history of computers.

Because I fell in love with the Web, and because I wanted to add my own creations to it, I found myself drawn increasingly into the world of open source software. In those days no one was selling closed source web publishing solutions. Instead, people were building their own solutions using things like the Unix shell and the Perl programming language. I wasn't exercising a moral choice in following in their footsteps; I just wanted to put lots of useful information on the Web, and these were the tools people were using to do that.

For those embarking on that same journey today, though, there is a choice (or at least the appearance of one). In one camp are commercial vendors trying to convince you that you can do everything you need with proprietary, user-oriented applications. In the other camp are people like me, telling you that you don't need to use shrink-wrapped software, that you can go further, and have more fun, by learning to build your own solutions with open source tools.

To return to the trailhead metaphor that began this chapter, the creation of a large-scale web site is like climbing a mountain. The proprietary software approach is like a shiny aerial tram: you buy your ticket, climb on board, and enjoy the view as you ride to the top. The open source approach is more like a rope, a hammer, and some pitons: the destination is the same, and you still get to enjoy the view along the way, but the experience is fundamentally different.

Consider the following: the tram passenger might see a lovely spot for a picnic on the way up, but only the climber can actually stop there. Once at the peak, when it becomes clear that this is actually only an outlying foothill, the tram passenger can only gaze wistfully at the real mountains looming beyond, while the self-sufficient climber can lace up the crampons and go. And of course, if you can't afford the tram ticket, or if the tram breaks down halfway to the top. . .

Ultimately, you will have to make your own decision. I encourage you to give the open source approach a try, though. It is an approach that leads to empowerment and self-sufficiency. It sounds silly to say that open source software changed my life, but that's basically what happened. It can do the same for you.

OS X and Darwin: Apple's Foray into Open Source

Apple's recently introduced OS X operating system has an interesting open source underpinning: the heart of the system is something called Darwin, a version of the BSD Unix operating system that Apple makes available in source code form. Although some provisions of the license under which Apple makes the source code available have been criticized by leaders of the traditional free software community, Darwin still represents a promising development in terms of merging the traditionally separate worlds of proprietary and open source software.

Philosophical issues aside, OS X offers an exciting combination for someone like me, who has had to get used to shifting gears from a consumer-oriented graphical user interface (GUI) on my desktop to a Unix command-line interface on the remotely hosted web servers I use. With OS X, I can have my cake and eat it, too: a well-integrated, user-friendly GUI, running on top of a real Unix system, with all the power and flexibility that go along with that. Time will tell, but in the meantime, readers of this book who use OS X should be aware that many of the features I describe using on a Unix-based (technically, Linux-based) web server will work similarly (or even identically) under Darwin.

Evaluating a Hosting Provider

I'm assuming in this book that you are already experienced with HTML and with the basics of setting up a web site. That means you probably already have a hosting arrangement of some sort: a web server either within your own company or at an outside Internet Service Provider (ISP). To keep things simple, I'm going to assume that you're hosting with an outside ISP, but in a large company it is quite possible that your "provider" will be an internal company department. This is especially likely if you are developing content for a company intranet, rather than the public Internet. It really doesn't matter, though. The only question is, can your hosting partner, wherever that partner is located, deliver what you need?

As your web efforts grow more ambitious, you need to think carefully about your hosting arrangements. One of the things I've learned as I've gone from maintaining a personal home page to maintaining multiple commercial sites is the number of ways in which a site can outgrow its hosting environment. After a fair amount of (sometimes painful) experience, I've come up with the following list of attributes that I now look for when evaluating a hosting provider for my own web projects.

The first four items in the following list (Unix environment, shell access, *cron* capability, and CGI scripting/server-side includes) represent the minimum needed to implement the examples in this book. The remaining items may be more or less important depending on what you're trying to do.

Unix environment
> The examples in this book assume that your web server is running Unix (loosely defined); specifically, the open source variant of Unix called Linux. Linux web servers are quite popular with ISPs because they deliver powerful, stable performance at a minimal cost in terms of hardware and software.

Shell access
> The ability to log into a Unix shell session will also be necessary for running the examples in this book. You will use the Unix shell to run Perl scripts and various command-line utilities. This book assumes you will be using the *bash* shell (which is the default shell in Linux), but most of the examples will work more or less the same under other shells.

Cron capability
> Along with the ability to log into the Unix shell, you should look for a hosting setup that allows you access to the Unix *cron* facility, which lets you run programs on the server at specified times, regardless of whether you are logged on. Such cron jobs are extremely useful for making backups, analyzing log files, checking various aspects of server operation, automatically notifying you if there is a problem, and so on.

CGI scripting/server-side includes

The ability to generate pages dynamically is an important feature of many high-end web sites. Because the CGI scripting or server-side includes (SSIs) used to achieve this effect can consume a lot of resources on the server (and can also represent significant security risks), inexpensive hosting packages often do not include access to them. Some of the examples in this book assume you will be able to use them, though.

Disk space

When you are creating all of your HTML pages manually, 10- or 20MB of disk space can seem like a lot of room. If you are going to have a lot of graphics or multimedia files, though, you'll use it up in a hurry. Using Perl to generate web pages from large data files, which we'll be doing later on, also burns through disk space like there's no tomorrow. Log files, reports, backups; all of them take space—and disk space is cheap compared to the time and effort that go into filling it up. Plan accordingly.

Secure server capability

The ability to support encrypted web transactions is important if your site is going to be exchanging sensitive information, such as credit card numbers, with its users. Hosting packages that include such "secure servers" tend to be significantly more expensive than those that don't. None of the examples in this book require secure web server capability.

Root access

The ability to log into the *superuser,* or *root,* account on your web server is sometimes necessary for things like configuring the server, installing software, and so on (though none of the examples in this book assume that you have such access). Because the root account can do pretty much anything on a Unix server, ISPs aren't likely to give access to it to just anyone. You almost certainly won't have access to it if you are in a shared hosting environment. Even then, though, there may occasionally be times when a little superuser help at the right time can make a big difference. This is one reason why it's a good idea to take your ISP's tech support people to lunch once in a while (or at least send them something yummy at holiday time). People are a lot more likely to drop what they're doing to solve your silly problem if their stomachs think kindly toward you.

CPU load

One of the hidden costs of using an inexpensive web hosting package is that you'll be sharing the server with a lot of other users. Assuming you all have the ability to do interesting things like use CGI scripts and server-side includes, the server might end up doing a lot of work—which can slow things down unacceptably. If your ISP is pursuing a business strategy of adding users as quickly as possible and falls even a little bit behind in terms of upgrading the infrastructure, the situation can go from bad to worse very quickly.

Uptime/reliability/disaster recovery

Another hidden cost of inexpensive web hosting packages is the low level of staffing and disaster preparation that you may encounter. How often do problems (say, a hard-disk failure on the server) occur? When they happen, how long is it before the ISP's technical staff becomes aware of it? How long before the problem is corrected? Even if you're confident in your ISP's abilities to stay on top of issues like this (and especially if you're not), inquiring about their backup systems and keeping your own independent backup copies of all important data is a very good idea.

Connectivity

Network slowdowns and outages are a fact of life on today's Internet. Depending on what sort of connectivity your site has, such outages can be either a continuing headache or an occasional annoyance. Does your ISP have multiple, independent pipelines to the Internet backbone? Does it have connections with smaller, regional networks so that it can bypass the major routes in case of congestion?

Bandwidth

Closely related to the question of connectivity is that of bandwidth: how big are the pipes through which your web traffic will be flowing? Depending on how busy your site is, a single T1 line (which carries data at 1.5 megabits/second) may be more than enough—but depending on your hosting situation you may be sharing that bandwidth with a dozen or a hundred or a thousand other web sites.

Data transfer limits

Some ISPs offer unlimited data transfer, others say your site can deliver only so much data in a given period of time before they shut you down or charge you extra. You'll have to know how much traffic your site normally generates in order to evaluate what this means to you; as an example, the most popular commercial site I work on (which is not really all that popular by web standards) currently pushes about a gigabyte of traffic on a good day.

Environmental stability

A good ISP is always working to keep its web hosting platform current: installing new software versions, fixing bugs, tweaking the caching technology, and so on. The downside to this, though, is that you may have built something that relies on some aspect of the old environment. Ideally, your ISP will not change things out from under you without giving you prior warning. In reality, though, depending on your hosting situation, you may not get that kind of notice.

You've probably detected a consistent theme in this list: for the most part you get what you pay for in web hosting. A package that seems like a really good deal in one area may be a ticking time bomb in another. For a medium- to high-profile commercial project, you should be prepared to pay for appropriate hosting.

Web Hosting Alternatives

The following is a rough hierarchy of web hosting alternatives, arranged from lowest cost (and capabilities) to highest.

Free Hosting

A number of providers offer free web space in return for things like the ability to run ad banners on your site. While they may be suitable for a low-end site, such arrangements are unlikely to offer things like shell access, CGI scripting, or server-side includes. Most also limit disk space fairly severely, requiring you to pay if you want to use more. For the examples in this book, such free web hosts probably will not be sufficient.

Shared Hosting (Low Grade)

Many Internet providers offer personal web space as part of a basic dial-up access package. Others offer relatively inexpensive web hosting without dial-up access. Although most of these providers do not include shell access or CGI scripting/server-side includes as part of the basic package, some do. An account with such a provider would probably be a good choice for someone on a strict budget looking to practice the examples in this book. With some searching, you can find providers that offer this level of access for $20 to $30 per month. For a site that represents a hobby, or a nonprofit community service project, or a demo of something you hope to turn into a commercial site later on, this may be sufficient—but be aware that things like load, reliability, and bandwidth can come back to haunt you.

Shared Hosting (High Grade)

For a cost ranging from $50 per month to about $250 per month, you can find providers willing to sell you a significant chunk of space on a web server with full CGI scripting, server-side includes, and shell access. You'll still probably be in a shared-server environment, but significantly fewer customers will probably be sharing that space with you. You should hopefully see better server performance, and a better response time on frantic calls to tech support asking why the server's down. For many low-end commercial web sites, this represents a good balance of cost and capability.

Dedicated Hosting/Co-Location

As your site grows, and especially as you find yourself providing some sort of service for which advertisers or customers are actually paying you, you will begin to hanker for your own, dedicated web server. This gives you the ultimate in flexibility and performance, while also helping to protect you from the environment changes and other hassles that sometimes make life in a shared environment more interesting than you'd like. Costs typically range from several hundred dollars per month to $1,500 per month or more.

A popular variation on this theme is the *co-located server*. A co-located server is a machine that you own, but which sits at your ISP, where it can enjoy your provider's fat connection to the Internet and be looked after by the ISP's technical staff. Again, the cost for this kind of hosting typically ranges from several hundred dollars per month to $1,500 or more, with the additional up-front expense of actually paying for the computer.

Getting Started with SSH/Telnet

You're probably already familiar with the process of making a dial-up PPP connection to the Internet from your Windows PC or Macintosh. Once connected, you then run client software to access various Internet services: a *web client* (like Netscape Navigator) to access web sites, a *mail client* (like Netscape's mail reader, or Eudora) to send and receive email, or an *FTP client* (like WS_FTP or Fetch) to transfer files. Traditionally, a *Telnet client* is just another piece of software that runs on top of your Internet connection. You use Telnet to log into a *shell session* on a remote server. Once you're in the shell session, you type text commands into the Telnet window, and those commands are then executed on the remote server and the results sent back to you.

We'll talk more about shell sessions. For now, let's talk a bit more about Telnet.

There's an inherent problem with using Telnet to connect to a remote server. Because Telnet traffic is sent across the network unencrypted, a malicious user located on a network somewhere along the path between you and the web server could easily obtain your username and password and use them to connect to the server as you. For that reason, a growing number of ISPs don't allow customers to make Telnet connections to their servers. Instead, they require customers to use something called *ssh* (for *secure shell*), an encrypted protocol that makes it much harder for bad guys to get hold of your login information. Once you've established the connection, an ssh session looks the same from the user perspective as a Telnet session: you get a shell window, where you type in commands and see the results of those commands printed out afterward.

I strongly encourage you to use ssh instead of Telnet. If your ISP doesn't support ssh connections you may have no choice but to use straight Telnet, but in that case you'd probably be well-served to start looking for another ISP.

In order to use ssh (or, if you must, Telnet), you will need a suitable client program. If you're running Windows, you already have one because Windows comes with a Telnet client preinstalled. I've never been happy with the Windows Telnet client, though, and can't recommend it (even without considering the security implications). Instead, I suggest you to go to your favorite software-download site (like TUCOWS, at *http://www.tucows.com/*), and get something better. I've had good luck with a shareware Telnet program called CRT, and likewise have had good experiences with a slightly more expensive but ssh-capable version of it called SecureCRT (*http://www.vandyke.com/products/securecrt/*). For Windows users on a budget, a free ssh client program called PuTTY is also available (*http://www.chiark.greenend.org.uk/ ~sgtatham/putty/*).

For Macintosh users, a third-party program called NiftyTelnet (*http://andrew2. andrew.cmu.edu/dist/niftytelnet.html*) gets high marks from my Mac-using friends (among its other attributes, it supports ssh). For Mac users running OS X, a command-line ssh client (called ssh, cleverly enough) comes with the operating system.

The following discussion presents a simple, idealized example of how you log into a Unix shell session. The specifics of your own login process may be different, depending on what client program, protocol, and connection method you are using. Consult your client program documentation and proceed accordingly.

Once you have your ssh (or Telnet) client software, you need three pieces of information, most likely provided by your ISP:

- The hostname of the computer you'll be logging into (e.g., *andros.example.com*)
- Your username
- Your password

Whichever client program you're using, start it up. Once you're running the client program, some poking around in the menus should reveal a command that lets you Connect... or Connect to remote host... or words to that effect. Choose that command, and in the dialog box that comes up enter the hostname of the computer you want to connect to. Hit the Connect button (or whatever it's called), and in a few seconds you should see something like the following:

    login:

Type your login name (taking note of the fact that on Unix systems, login names, along with most other things you're going to be typing in, are case sensitive, so jbc is different from Jbc, which is different from JBC). Anyway, type in your login name, and press the Enter key. The next thing you see should be:

    password:

Now type in your password (to protect you from shoulder-surfing snoops, the characters won't display on your screen, so type carefully) and press the Enter key. With any luck, you'll see something like the following:

    Last login: Wed Feb 24 23:32:24 1999 from pm4-37.sba1.avtel.net
    [jbc@andros jbc]$

That cryptic-looking last line is called a *shell prompt*. Yours may look different to a greater or lesser extent, depending on how your server and user account have been configured; it may be as simple as a single percent symbol or dollar sign:

```
$
```

Regardless, you're now in business.

Meet the Unix Shell

The Unix *shell* is the program that interprets the things you type at the command-line prompt. It is called the *shell* because it forms a shell around the computer's lower-level functions so that you, the user, don't have to deal with them directly.

If you've been using personal computers long enough to remember poking around in the DOS command-line environment, guess what? That experience is going to prove useful. In many ways working in DOS is similar to working in a Unix shell session (though Unix fans will say it's similar in the same sense that driving a soapbox racer is similar to driving a Ferrari).

If your computing experience has been limited to using a graphical environment like Windows or the Mac OS, this is going to seem a bit strange at first. If you stick with it, though, you'll come to appreciate the power and flexibility of the command-line interface.

It's a bit like LEGO blocks. The command-line interface is like the LEGOs I grew up with 30 years ago: you got the little square one and the slightly bigger rectangle and the *really* big rectangle and so on. The individual components were basic, but if you put them together with sufficient imagination you could make a spaceship, or a fire engine, or a skyscraper, or whatever you wanted. Unix commands are designed to be put together with each other in the same way, and before you know it you've got a custom tool to solve whatever your particular problem is.

A graphical interface is more like those fancy LEGO sets you can buy today: pre-molded plastic pieces that go together in just one way. You get a much snazzier-looking spaceship, but that's all you get. If you want a fire engine you have to buy another kit—and if you want something unusual you're out of luck. As Net user and Unix convert Peter J. Schoenster has written, "With a PC [meaning a Windows PC], I always felt limited by the software available. On Unix, I am limited only by my knowledge."

The hardest thing about working in command-line mode is that, well, you have to learn a lot of commands. You can't rely on being able to click through menus to discover the one you need, or having a dialog box pop up to request more specifics when you need to invoke a command with a particular set of options. It's very much the "open sesame" school of computing: you *must* know the magic words in order to get anywhere. Without them, your shell prompt will just stare at you, mocking you for your lack of clue.

It's really not that bad, though; with a little practice you'll soon by tapping away like a pro (or at least like a rapidly progressing amateur). Also, the folks who pioneered the Unix wilderness realized that no one wants to carry around a bunch of printed documentation, so they put a very complete set of documentation for all these commands right there in the computer, in the form of *manpages*. We'll talk about them in the next section. Accessing the manpages for a particular command is as easy as entering man *command_name* at the shell prompt, which is great—except that you still have to know the name of the command in order to call up its manpage.

Like I said, you *must* learn the magic words. But only a few at a time, and if you jot them down on a piece of paper and keep them by the computer you'll be up to speed in no time.

man, more, and less

Unix manpages take some getting used to. Often written by the author of the program being documented, they tend to assume a fairly high level of familiarity with Unix and programming concepts. They also tend to vary quite a bit in terms of style and content. As you read more of them, though, they begin to make sense.

When you enter the command man *command_name*, with *command_name* being replaced by the name of a Unix command you want to learn more about, you should get a print-out on your screen explaining everything you wanted to know (and a good deal more, probably) about the command in question. Normally this output will be automatically displayed for you a screenful at a time using something called a *pager* program. One popular pager program is called *more;* perhaps inevitably, there is an updated version of it called *less*. Both of them work pretty much the same. When your screen fills up with output a special prompt appears at the bottom of it, and when you're ready to go on you press the Enter key to advance a single line, or the spacebar to advance a whole screenful. Depending on the vintage of your pager software, you may be able to type b to go back up a screen, and a forward slash (/) to enter a case-sensitive search term, after which the pager will scroll forward to the first appearance of that term. Enter q to exit from the pager and return to your shell prompt.

So, what is it that you'll be paging through? The accompanying sidebar, "Making Sense of Manpages" gives an overview of the contents of a typical manpage.

A few other interesting facts about manpages:

You will often see commands, or their manpages, referred to with a parenthetical number after the command name. For example, "*less* is a program similar to more (1). . ." What's going on with that parenthetical number?

Making Sense of Manpages

Although Unix manpages (the online documentation you access by entering man *program_name* at the shell prompt) are not always consistently formatted, most of them adhere to the following format to some degree:

NAME
: The name of the command, along with a one-line explanation of what it does.

SYNOPSIS
: A highly condensed cheat sheet showing how to use the command, including the possible *command-line arguments*. Optional arguments are typically shown inside square brackets. Don't worry; you can become quite proficient at Unix without ever learning most arguments.

DESCRIPTION
: A general explanation of what the command does.

OPTIONS
: A detailed description of what each command-line option does.

EXAMPLE
: A section with actual examples of how the command might be used. Sadly, this section is missing from many manpages.

ENVIRONMENT
: A description of how the command interacts with so-called environment variables. Don't worry about this for now.

BUGS
: Any known bugs.

AUTHOR
: The person who wrote the command.

What's going on is that manpages are grouped into numbered sections. Section 1 contains manpages describing user commands, so most of the time when you read a manpage you will be reading a "section 1" manpage. When a command is referred to as command (1), that means you can read about the command in its section 1 manpage. Another commonly used section is section 5, which gives file formats for various configuration and administration files.

To explicitly read a manpage from a particular section, you give the section number as an argument to the man command, before the name of the command itself. For example, entering the command man 1 crontab will let you read the section 1 manpage for the *crontab* command, which lets you automatically run commands at timed intervals. Entering man 5 crontab will let you read the section 5 *crontab* manpage, which describes the format of the file you use to control these timed commands.

In practice, you don't have to worry about supplying the section number because the man program will search through all the sections until it finds a manpage for the command whose name you entered. The only time you need to worry about it is when there are entries in different sections with the same name, as there are with crontab.

Two more options you may sometimes want to use with man are the -a option, which causes all the manpages for a particular command to be displayed, and the -k option, which searches all the one-line command descriptions for a keyword you supply. The -k option is the same thing you get with the separate, standalone command apropos. You can sometimes use this to find the name of a command when you don't actually know it. For example, if you know that there is a command that displays a calendar, but can't remember what it is, try using man -k to search for the word calendar:

```
[jbc@andros jbc]$ man -k calendar
cal (1)              - displays a calendar
```

Directories and the pwd Command

Let's get started with our first Unix command: pwd. Type it at your shell prompt, and press the Enter key:

```
[jbc@andros jbc]$ pwd
/u1/j/jbc
[jbc@andros jbc]$
```

pwd stands for "print working directory." Entering that command at the shell prompt causes the Unix server to print out the full path of the directory you are currently "in." After that it prints out your prompt again, letting you know that it's ready for you to enter your next command.

If that comment about a working directory made sense to you, congratulations! This is the part where you get to rest on your DOS-era laurels while the Johnny-come-latelies do some catching up.

You must understand a simple but extremely important concept in order to work effectively with computers: the concept of a *directory structure*. GUIs sometimes obscure this underlying reality with user-friendly metaphors like desktops and icons and trashcans, but to work comfortably in the world of the command-line interface you're going to need to come to grips with this.

Computers store information in files. A large hard drive can have many thousands of files. To make it easier to name and keep track of them, they are organized into a system of directories, with related files kept together in the same directory and the directories themselves arranged into a hierarchical structure.

At the top (or bottom, depending on how you like to picture things) is the *root directory*. This is the directory that contains all of the other directories and files.

Within that root directory can be various files, as well as other directories. Within those directories can be more files, and more directories, and so on, for as many levels as you need. When all is said and done, you have a hierarchy of branching directories similar to the branches of a tree, with the files in those directories corresponding to the leaves of the tree. Except that in this case, the root directory would probably correspond most closely to the tree's trunk, which both sounds odd and conjures up a weird image of a tree that potentially has a bunch of leaves (files) growing out of its trunk and major branches.

Oh, well. Metaphors can take you only so far. If you like, you can substitute the other popular metaphor for a directory structure (the metaphor that GUIs use): a filing cabinet, with the file folders corresponding to directories and the individual documents inside them corresponding to individual computer files. To each his own. The important thing is to keep track of where you are (in other words, what directory you are currently working in, and what directories your files are in).

In the previous example, where we typed in pwd, and the computer responded with /u1/j/jbc, the directory we were currently in was a directory called jbc, which was contained within a directory called j, which was contained within a directory called u1, which was contained within the root directory. This form of writing the name and "parentage" of a directory is called a *path*, and as you can see, the forward slash character (/) is used to divide the directory names within the path. When it is at the very beginning of a path the slash character has a special meaning: there (and only there) it refers to the root directory.

This particular directory (/u1/j/jbc) happens to be my home directory on the machine *andros.lies.com*. This means it is the directory I start off in when I first log into a shell session on that machine. Depending on how the administrator of your server has set things up, your home directory will be called something else, possibly /home/*username*, with *username* being replaced by your actual username.

The accompanying sidebar, "Designating a Path and Filename" explains the various ways you can describe a file's location within the computer's directory structure.

The ls Command: List Directory Contents

So, with the pwd command you can see what your current working directory is. What about looking at the contents of that directory?

For this you use the ls command. By entering it at the shell prompt, you can get a list of the files and directories contained in the current directory:

```
[jbc@andros jbc]$ ls
[jbc@andros jbc]$
```

Hmm. In this case, we didn't get anything (except another shell prompt). That doesn't necessarily mean there's nothing in the directory, however. In Unix systems,

Designating a Path and Filename

When you are logged into the Unix shell and you type in the name of a file in order to specify it to the computer, you can specify the file's name in any of the following ways:

- The filename all by itself—for example, walnuts.txt. In this case, the computer will typically look for a file with that name in the current *working directory* (that is, in the directory whose name would be printed to your screen if you used the pwd command).

- The filename listed along with the *full,* or *absolute, path* of the directory where it resides—for example, /u1/j/jbc/walnuts.txt. You can tell this is an absolute path because it begins with an initial slash character, which is used to indicate the root directory. The nice thing about using an absolute path is that you can use it from any directory you like, and the computer will know exactly what file you're talking about.

- The filename listed along with a *partial,* or *relative, path*—for example, u1/j/jbc/walnuts.txt. Notice that this is exactly the same as the last example, except that it's missing that initial slash. In this case, the computer will assume that this path begins in the current *working directory.* If your current working directory happens to be the root directory, it will point to the same file as the last example. Otherwise, it will point somewhere else: starting in the current working directory, it will look for a directory within it called u1, then a directory in that called j, then one called jbc, and finally for a file called walnuts.txt.

files can be hidden by naming them with an initial period character (usually pronounced "dot"). The basic version of ls doesn't display these files. But by supplying a *switch* to the command, you can cause it to display them. In this case, the switch is -a, which stands for "all," such that entering ls -a can be read as "list files (all)".

```
[jbc@andros jbc]$ ls -a
.               .Xdefaults    .bashrc    .screenrc
..              .bash_logout  .profile
[jbc@andros jbc]$
```

So, there are some things in that directory, but all of them happen to have names that begin with a dot. It turns out this is a common method in Unix to name configuration files and other administrative stuff in a way that keeps them out of sight most of the time. Most of these files are used simply to configure your environment, which is why they're kept hidden—so they don't clutter directory listings.

Actually, though, they're not all files. Two of them happen to be directories. In Unix, directories are treated just like another file in ls listings. With the ls -a listing, you can't tell (unless you happen to know already) which of those listed items are actually directories. To find out, you need to use another switch: -l (a lowercase letter "L").

You can shove both the -a and -l switches together with a single hyphen character in front of them, yielding the following form of the ls command: ls -al. Let's try it:

```
[jbc@andros jbc]$ ls -al
total 14
drwxr-xr-x 2 jbc   jbc   1024 Feb 10 23:25 .
drwxr-xr-x 9 root  wheel 1024 Feb 10 22:04 ..
-rw-r--r-- 1 jbc   jbc   3785 Aug 22 1996 .Xdefaults
-rw-r--r-- 1 jbc   jbc     24 Jul 13 1994 .bash_logout
-rw-r--r-- 1 jbc   jbc    124 Aug 23 1995 .bashrc
-rw-r--r-- 1 jbc   jbc    220 Aug 23 1995 .profile
-rw-r--r-- 1 jbc   jbc   3166 Mar 25 1997 .screenrc
```

There's a lot of information there, but most of it you can safely ignore for now. Each line of the ls -al command's output describes a different file; the file's name is given in the far righthand column. The very first character in each line is what tells you whether the file is a directory: a d means the file is, in fact, a directory, while a hyphen (-) means it is a regular file.

From the ls -al listing, therefore, you can see that two files are contained in this directory that are not regular files, but are actually directories: one called . (a single period character, pronounced "dot") and the other called .. ("dot dot"). These, it turns out, are special. They show up in every ls -al listing you ever do. The . directory is just a shorthand way of referring to the *current directory* (that is, the directory whose contents you're looking at, the one whose name is printed out when you enter the pwd command). The .. directory is a shorthand way of referring to the current directory's *parent directory;* that is, the directory that the current directory branches off from (or is contained within, depending on whether you picture your directory hierarchy as a tree or a bunch of nested file folders).

It may seem odd to you at this point to list the directory itself and the directory's parent in the ls -al listing, but it actually turns out to be fairly handy at times.

The mkdir Command: Make a New Directory

Here's a command that is pretty straightforward: mkdir, which you use to create a directory. You invoke it with the name of the directory you want to create, and the command creates the directory for you, as a *subdirectory* of (that is, as a directory that branches off from, or is contained within) the current directory.

Why might you want to create a directory? In general, you would do this to create a new storage location to help you keep your various files organized. Just like in the real world, it's a lot easier to keep track of things on a computer if you take the time to develop a system for what goes where, and then make a point of putting things where they belong.

Let's try creating a directory called walnuts (for no particular reason; you can call yours foo or rutabagas or whatever strikes your fancy):

```
[jbc@andros jbc]$ mkdir walnuts
[jbc@andros jbc]$
```

Well, that wasn't very exciting. But this is typical of Unix, which assumes that you know what you're doing and don't need feedback unless you specifically ask for it, or unless something goes wrong.

Entering our old friend ls -al, we get the following:

```
[jbc@andros jbc]$ ls -al
total 14
drwxr-xr-x 2 jbc   jbc    1024 Feb 10 23:25 .
drwxr-xr-x 9 root  wheel  1024 Feb 10 22:04 ..
-rw-r--r-- 1 jbc   jbc    3785 Aug 22  1996 .Xdefaults
-rw-r--r-- 1 jbc   jbc      24 Jul 13  1994 .bash_logout
-rw-r--r-- 1 jbc   jbc     124 Aug 23  1995 .bashrc
-rw-r--r-- 1 jbc   jbc     220 Aug 23  1995 .profile
-rw-r--r-- 1 jbc   jbc    3166 Mar 25  1997 .screenrc
drwxr-xr-x 2 jbc   jbc    1024 Mar 13 10:35 walnuts
```

And there it is, in the last line: our new directory, walnuts.

The cd Command: Change Directories

Here's another easy one: the cd command, which, if invoked with the name of another directory as its argument, switches you to that directory so that it becomes your new working directory. Let's switch to the walnuts directory we just created:

```
[jbc@andros jbc]$ cd walnuts
[jbc@andros walnuts]$
```

Because my prompt is configured to show the name of the current working directory inside those square brackets, I can see right away that I've switched to that directory. If your prompt doesn't show your working directory, you can verify that you've moved by using the pwd command:

```
[jbc@andros walnuts]$ pwd
/u1/j/jbc/walnuts
[jbc@andros walnuts]$
```

A couple of useful shortcuts with the cd command: entering cd by itself will return you to your *home directory* (the directory you start off in when you first log in). Also, entering cd with an argument of - (a hyphen all by itself) will (in some shells, bash being one of them) return you to the directory you were last in. This can prove handy for popping back and forth between one directory and another.

CTRL-C (^C): Cancel a Command in Progress

Sometimes when you enter a command at the shell prompt your cursor will jump to the next line, indicating that the command has been entered, but nothing more will appear on your screen. You will see neither the output that you might have been expecting nor the new shell prompt that tells you the command has completed. You've got what's known as a *hung terminal*.

This may have happened for several reasons:

- Your Internet connection may have become bogged down somewhere between you and the server.
- You may have entered a command that will take a really long time to complete.
- The server may be running slowly because of some other command or commands currently running on it.
- You entered a command that expects some sort of extra input, and the server is waiting for you to supply it.

A quick solution to most of these problems is to hold down the Ctrl key on your keyboard and simultaneously tap the C key. This key combination (which you will frequently see abbreviated as Ctrl-C or ^C), will cancel the current command. Unless there's some sort of problem with your Internet connection, this should return you to the shell prompt.

The exit Command: End Your Shell Session

So, you now know how to log into a shell session, list the contents of a directory, create a new directory, change directories, and cancel a command in progress to fix a hung terminal. You also know how to use man to find out more about shell commands, and how to use a *pager* to help you read a long manpage. Those are probably enough magic words for your first introduction to the Unix shell. Except that you'll need one more: the exit command. Entering this at the prompt will end your shell session, logging you out from the remote server:

```
[jbc@andros jbc]$ exit
logout
```

Network Troubleshooting

One of the really cool things about the Internet is the way you, or anyone, can see how your traffic is being routed across the Net, and what's happening to it along the way. This comes in very handy when you're experiencing some sort of problem connecting to another site. With just a few seconds of research, you can often tell exactly where the problem lies, and this in turn can tell you if it's something you need to fix yourself, something you need to complain to somebody else about, or something that's essentially out of your control. It also comes in very handy for evaluating the quality of the explanations you get when you bug your ISP about network outages, which in turn can be an important factor in deciding where to host your web site.

ping and traceroute

The first network utilities we're going to talk about are the ping and traceroute commands. These utilities let you probe a TCP/IP network (like the Internet) to see where your data packets are going, how long it's taking them to get there, and whether any of them are getting lost along the way. (See the accompanying sidebar, "Packet-Switching 101," if these concepts are new to you.)

The ping command sends a bunch of test packets to a particular hostname or IP address and measures how long it takes for them to come back. When you've sent enough packets to satisfy your curiosity, you type Ctrl-C, and the program prints out a brief summary and exits. Here's an example:

```
[jbc@andros jbc]$ ping www.yahoo.com
PING www.yahoo.com (204.71.200.74): 56 data bytes
64 bytes from 204.71.200.74: icmp_seq=0 ttl=248 time=19.5 ms
64 bytes from 204.71.200.74: icmp_seq=1 ttl=248 time=18.5 ms
64 bytes from 204.71.200.74: icmp_seq=2 ttl=248 time=21.4 ms
64 bytes from 204.71.200.74: icmp_seq=3 ttl=248 time=24.4 ms
64 bytes from 204.71.200.74: icmp_seq=4 ttl=248 time=19.5 ms
64 bytes from 204.71.200.74: icmp_seq=5 ttl=248 time=18.5 ms
64 bytes from 204.71.200.74: icmp_seq=6 ttl=248 time=18.5 ms
64 bytes from 204.71.200.74: icmp_seq=7 ttl=248 time=19.5 ms
64 bytes from 204.71.200.74: icmp_seq=8 ttl=248 time=19.5 ms
64 bytes from 204.71.200.74: icmp_seq=9 ttl=248 time=19.5 ms

--- www.yahoo.com ping statistics ---
10 packets transmitted, 10 packets received, 0% packet loss
round-trip min/avg/max = 18.5/19.8/24.4 ms
```

That's a very respectable set of ping statistics: I sent 10 packets, got them all back (for 0% packet loss), and had an average round-trip time of 19.8 milliseconds. The various people responsible for the route between the machine where I entered this command and *www.yahoo.com* are doing a fine job.

Now let's try pinging some other site in a more-distant part of the Net:

```
[jbc@andros jbc]$ ping www.ontas.com.au
PING www.ontas.com.au (203.60.16.17) from 209.151.249.42 : 56(84) bytes of data.
64 bytes from vws1.southcom.com.au (203.60.16.17): icmp_seq=0 ttl=243 time=277.8 ms
64 bytes from vws1.southcom.com.au (203.60.16.17): icmp_seq=1 ttl=243 time=275.4 ms
64 bytes from vws1.southcom.com.au (203.60.16.17): icmp_seq=2 ttl=243 time=281.6 ms
64 bytes from vws1.southcom.com.au (203.60.16.17): icmp_seq=3 ttl=243 time=294.1 ms
64 bytes from vws1.southcom.com.au (203.60.16.17): icmp_seq=4 ttl=243 time=288.1 ms
64 bytes from vws1.southcom.com.au (203.60.16.17): icmp_seq=5 ttl=243 time=280.7 ms
64 bytes from vws1.southcom.com.au (203.60.16.17): icmp_seq=6 ttl=243 time=275.1 ms
64 bytes from vws1.southcom.com.au (203.60.16.17): icmp_seq=7 ttl=243 time=273.4 ms
64 bytes from vws1.southcom.com.au (203.60.16.17): icmp_seq=8 ttl=243 time=282.5 ms
64 bytes from vws1.southcom.com.au (203.60.16.17): icmp_seq=9 ttl=243 time=271.6 ms

--- www.ontas.com.au ping statistics ---
10 packets transmitted, 10 packets received, 0% packet loss
round-trip min/avg/max = 271.6/280.0/294.1 ms
```

Packet-Switching 101

The Internet runs on *TCP/IP,* which stands, if you're into acronym expansion, for *Transmission Control Protocol/Internet Protocol.* TCP/IP is a form of networking based on *packet switching.* I've assumed in this book that you've been using the Internet and making web pages for a while, so you've probably already picked up a smattering of how TCP/IP networking works. If not, here's a very high-level overview.

First, though, we'll talk about what TCP/IP networking *isn't*: it isn't a telephone call. When you make a traditional telephone call, you are establishing a circuit between your phone and the phone at the other end. This is the equivalent of having a pair of wires running all the way from your phone to that other phone. When you say "hello" into the mouthpiece the sounds are transformed into electrical impulses that travel through the circuit and make the speaker on the other end vibrate in just the right way so that your voice will be heard. The circuit is analogous to having a very long tube connecting you to the other party, like the speaking tubes they used to use on big ships to let the captain on the bridge talk to the engineer down in the boiler room.

When your computer talks to another computer over the Internet, a fundamentally different process takes place. First, the information that is going to be sent is broken up into smallish chunks, and those chunks are stuck into little virtual envelopes inscribed with the address of the sender, the address of the recipient, and instructions on how the chunks should be put back together at the other end. Then those chunks (which are called *packets)* are sent out onto the Net, where they are routed from one machine to another (these machines are called *routers*) until they reach their destination. The packets don't all necessarily follow the same route, or reach the destination in the same order that they were sent out; some of them might not even get there at all. But that's okay because the computer on the receiving end can use the instructions on the envelopes to put them all back together the right way, or send a message back to the originating computer asking it to re-send the ones that got lost.

In analogy terms, this is like having a network of runners between the captain on the bridge and the engineer down in the boiler room. The captain writes instructions on little bits of paper and hands them off to the nearest runner, who takes them part of the way to their destination and hands them off to someone else, and so on.

It's instructive to think about what happens as each system is subjected to a greater load than it can handle gracefully. The circuit-based phone system works fine for a while, but when it reaches the point where there is no more capacity for additional circuits, it breaks completely (i.e., no additional calls can be made). The people who were lucky enough to get one of those circuits can still communicate just fine, but the others get a recording asking them to try again later.

A packet-switching network will let you continue to dump packets into it until the cows come home, but its performance will gradually degrade as it exceeds its capacity. Certain routers will be revealed as weak links in the chain; they will begin to deliver packets more slowly, or not at all. For the user, this will make the whole process appear to take longer; web pages will load more slowly, or, as things worsen, not at all.

It takes a little longer (280 milliseconds on average), but this still looks pretty healthy, considering that all of my packets are successfully making it to Tasmania and back (from California) in about a quarter second.

How do I know my packets are going to Tasmania? Well, I don't, technically. But it seems like a good guess, based on the output of another essential network debugging utility: traceroute. The traceroute command lets you traverse the route that your data follows between your machine and some other machine, sending three test packets to each router along the way. Let's try it on *www.ontas.com.au*:

```
[jbc@andros jbc]$ traceroute www.ontas.com.au
traceroute to www.ontas.com.au (203.60.16.17), 30 hops max, 38 byte
packets
 1  chancy-colocate.hq.cyberverse.net (209.151.233.1)  5.843 ms  3.555 ms  0.619 ms
 2  216.246.13.129 (216.246.13.129)  6.868 ms  7.195 ms  5.374 ms
 3  newDuke-bb.softaware.com (207.155.0.34)  5.414 ms  7.280 ms  7.684 ms
 4  aar1-serial6-1-1-0.Anaheim.cw.net (208.172.39.33)  8.603 ms  10.074 ms  8.562 ms
 5  acr2-loopback.Anaheim.cw.net (208.172.34.62)  7.325 ms  9.941 ms  8.773 ms
 6  optus-networks.Anaheim.cw.net (208.172.33.142)  241.478 ms  245.452 ms
      241.621 ms
 7  POS4-0-0.rr2.optus.net.au (192.65.89.213)  241.389 ms  269.195 ms  251.966 ms
 8  GigEth3-0.sg2.optus.net.au (202.139.191.2)  243.714 ms  252.133 ms  240.937 ms
 9  POS2-0.mg1.optus.net.au (202.139.124.82)  254.781 ms  263.256 ms  258.124 ms
10  GigEth1-0-0.mb1.optus.net.au (202.139.188.4)  254.089 ms  255.718 ms  255.304 ms
11  202.139.130.94 (202.139.130.94)  271.595 ms  278.407 ms  273.950 ms
12  Ether2-2.fra-core1.hbt.southcom.com.au (203.31.212.161)  279.584 ms  284.519 ms
      295.090 ms
13  vws1.southcom.com.au (203.60.16.17)  280.207 ms  299.295 ms  293.986 ms
```

Reading down from the top of the traceroute command's output, I see my packets go:

- Through a router owned by Cyberverse, my ISP
- Through a machine that doesn't have a hostname, just an IP addresses (216.246.13.129)
- Through the network of a company called Softaware (my ISP's upstream provider on this route), with routers whose hostnames end in softaware.com
- Through the network of Cable & Wireless (cw.net)
- Through the network of Optus (an Australian ISP), via routers whose names end with optus.net.au.
- To the network of a company called Southern Internet Services (at hosts whose names end with southcom.com.au), which has a web page describing the company as "Tasmania's Premier ISP" (*http://www.southcom.com.au/*)

Now you know what good ping and traceroute results look like. What do bad results look like? Typically you'll see longer round-trip times, perhaps greater than 1000 ms (that is, greater than 1 second). You'll also probably see lost packets, which show up in the ping command's output as missing numbers in the ICMP sequence and are summarized in the results printed at the end. With traceroute, lost packets show up as asterisks where the round-trip time for that test packet should be.

Another thing you might see in the results of a traceroute command is !H in place of a particular packet's round-trip time; this stands for "host unreachable," and is usually a sign of a fairly serious routing problem.

mtr

The traditional way you use ping and traceroute to troubleshoot a misbehaving TCP/IP connection is to first use traceroute to figure out where the packets are going, then systematically ping the hosts along the route to identify where the problem is. At some point a clever guy named Matt Kimball created a tool to carry out both of those steps simultaneously, naming the program mtr (for *Matt's traceroute*) (see *http://www.bitwizard.nl/mtr/*).

If the mtr utility is installed on your Unix server, you can run it by entering mtr followed by the name of the host you are interested in tracerouting and pinging:

    [jbc@andros jbc]$ mtr www.ontas.com.au

When you do, your shell window will display a list of hosts (the same as that shown by the traceroute command) down the left side of the window, with the rest of the window taken up by constantly updating statistics on the results of repeatedly pinging each host. The longer you leave mtr running, the more data it will gather (see Figure 1-1). When you are done, type q to quit back to the shell prompt.

A Suitable Text Editor

You'll need one more tool in order to begin working magic with Perl: a *text editor*.

Actually, you'll probably want two of them because you will be writing your Perl scripts in two different places. Sometimes you will write them on your desktop PC (or Mac), then will transfer them to your ISP's Unix server using an FTP program (like WS_FTP for the PC, or Fetch for the Mac). Other times you will create your scripts right there on the Unix machine using a Unix text editor.

> Because FTP is an unencrypted protocol, it is prone to the same security problems as Telnet is. For that reason, you may wish to investigate using an encrypted protocol for your file transfers. Martin Prikryl's WinSCP (*http://winscp.vse.cz/eng/*) offers a nice Windows implementation of the secure scp protocol (which uses ssh for security) to do file transfers. For Mac users, the aforementioned NiftyTelnet (*http://andrew2.andrew.cmu.edu/dist/niftytelnet.html*) also does scp file transfers. (Mac users running OS X can also use the scp command-line program directly.)

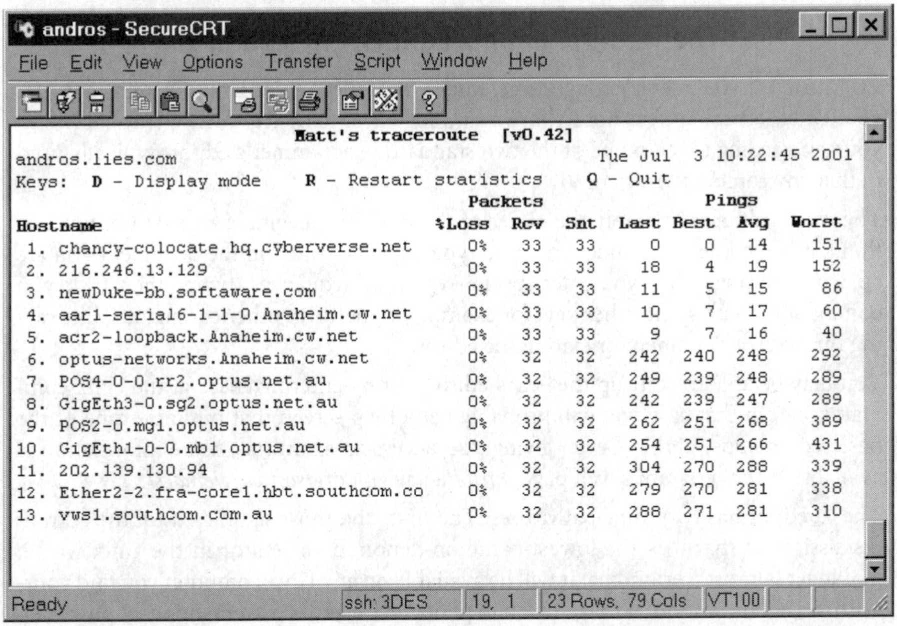

```
andros - SecureCRT

File   Edit   View   Options   Transfer   Script   Window   Help

                    Matt's traceroute    [v0.42]
andros.lies.com                              Tue Jul  3 10:22:45 2001
Keys:  D - Display mode    R - Restart statistics    Q - Quit
                              Packets                    Pings
Hostname                   %Loss  Rcv  Snt   Last Best  Avg  Worst
  1. chancy-colocate.hq.cyberverse.net   0%   33   33      0    0   14    151
  2. 216.246.13.129                      0%   33   33     18    4   19    152
  3. newDuke-bb.softaware.com            0%   33   33     11    5   15     86
  4. aar1-serial6-1-1-0.Anaheim.cw.net   0%   33   33     10    7   17     60
  5. acr2-loopback.Anaheim.cw.net        0%   33   33      9    7   16     40
  6. optus-networks.Anaheim.cw.net       0%   32   32    242  240  248    292
  7. POS4-0-0.rr2.optus.net.au           0%   32   32    249  239  248    289
  8. GigEth3-0.sg2.optus.net.au          0%   32   32    242  239  247    289
  9. POS2-0.mg1.optus.net.au             0%   32   32    262  251  268    389
 10. GigEth1-0-0.mb1.optus.net.au        0%   32   32    254  251  266    431
 11. 202.139.130.94                      0%   32   32    304  270  288    339
 12. Ether2-2.fra-core1.hbt.southcom.co  0%   32   32    279  270  281    338
 13. vws1.southcom.com.au                0%   32   32    288  271  281    310

Ready                    ssh: 3DES    19, 1    23 Rows, 79 Cols   VT100
```

Figure 1-1. The mtr utility displaying network troubleshooting information

The traditional text editors used in the Unix environment are emacs and vi (the latter pronounced "vee-eye"). Both are extremely powerful and full-featured. Both can also be a bit intimidating for beginners. Because of that, I'm actually going to focus on a simpler (albeit less powerful) editor called pico for this book's text-editing-under-Unix examples. If pico is not available on your system, you may need to buckle down and learn emacs or vi whether you want to or not. In that case, see the sidebar later in this chapter, "The Traditional Unix Editors: emacs and vi."

Whichever tools you end up using, the bottom line is that you're going to need some way to edit text on both your desktop computer and the Unix server. Editing in each environment will have its pluses and minuses. Writing scripts on your PC will probably feel more familiar to you, at least at first. You can use your mouse for selecting text, and can work on your script when you're not actually connected to the Internet. The downside is that you'll have to use an FTP program to move your script to the Unix server every time you make a change to it. Writing your scripts directly on the Unix machine lets you avoid the file-transfer step. You'll have to gain at least a passing familiarity with a Unix text editor, though, which means learning a bunch of keyboard commands to move around within the file, since you won't be able to do things with your mouse.

I edit on the Unix server for small scripts and on my local PC for larger projects. You may have already dealt with this issue when deciding how to create HTML files for your web site, assuming you are coding your HTML by hand, rather than using an

The Traditional Unix Editors: emacs and vi

Eventually, if you spend enough time editing text files under Unix (or right away, if your Unix server happens not to have a simpler editor like pico) you will probably find yourself needing to learn one of the two standard programmer's editors typically used in that environment: emacs or vi.

The emacs editor is arguably the easier of the two for a beginner to pick up. For one thing, it is *modeless*, meaning what you type appears as text in the document you are currently editing, while you enter special keystroke sequences (typing the Ctrl key in combination with some other key, for example) to perform other commands, like saving the current document or exiting the editor.

You may be able to start up the emacs editor just by entering emacs at the Unix command line. In that case you will probably get a help screen that outlines some of the basic commands, perhaps even giving you access to a tutorial. More information is available at the program's web page, *http://www.gnu.org/software/emacs/*.

The vi editor has two principal virtues. The first, and most significant for the current discussion, is that it is the lowest-common-denominator editor in the Unix world, making it (almost) certain that it will be available on any Unix computer you find yourself using. The second is that, for an experienced user, it is tremendously powerful, allowing very rapid text editing.

The main downside to vi is that it achieves this power via a *moded* approach, in which particular keystrokes do different things depending on what *mode* the program is currently in (command mode, insert mode, or ex mode). This ends up being relatively difficult to learn, and even once learned, relatively awkward to use until you've practiced a fair amount.

A nice vi tutorial is available at *http://www.eng.hawaii.edu/Tutor/vi.html*.

HTML authoring program. There's one important difference, though: if you're creating the scripts on your local PC or Mac, then uploading them to your Unix server via FTP, you must make the FTP transfer in *text mode* (sometimes called *ASCII mode*, depending on your FTP program). This typically doesn't make any real difference when uploading HTML files, but it matters a lot for Perl scripts: if you upload your Perl scripts in *binary mode,* they probably won't work. This is because each type of computer (Unix, PC, and Macintosh) uses a different sequence of characters to mark the end of a line of text. Transferring in ASCII mode causes the FTP program to convert the line endings for you on the fly.

You may be inclined to try to use a word processor program (like Microsoft Word) to create and edit your Perl scripts when you're working on the local PC, but I would advise against it. Because they have been optimized for the specific task of outputting attractive paper-based documents, modern word processors are a poor choice for editing straight ASCII text. You'll be much happier with something that doesn't try to convert all your straight quotes to curly quotes and flag all your Perl syntax as misspelled and ungrammatical. On the Windows side, I've been very happy with a freeware program called EditPad (available at *http://www.editpadpro.com/ editpadclassic.html*); a shareware program called UltraEdit (*http://www.ultraedit.com/*) is also very good. On the Mac side, a program called BBEdit Lite (see *http://www. barebones.com/*) is very popular.

This chapter has presented only a shallow introduction. If you are anything like me, you will be able to continue to learn more about choosing web hosting vendors, working in the Unix shell, troubleshooting network problems, and using text editors for many years to come. With the information presented here, though, you should be able to take your first steps and begin doing useful work. In particular, you should now be ready for the next chapter, in which you get your first exposure to the Perl programming language.

## CHAPTER 2

Getting Started with Perl

Now we're ready to add the centerpiece of your information toolkit: Perl, the "Swiss army chainsaw" for web content creators. This chapter explains how to locate Perl on your system, and walks you through running a very simple Perl script. Along the way it explains command paths, and gives a quick lesson on Unix file permissions. Next it covers Perl variables, quoting, and then finishes by explaining how to run a Perl CGI script (which means running a script via your web server, with the output of the script being returned to your web browser).

Finding Perl on Your System

The first thing we need to do to get you running Perl scripts is to verify that Perl has already been installed on your server, find out where it is, and check to see what version it is.

Log into a shell session and enter the command which perl. The which command prints out the full path to the program that will run when you enter the program's name by itself:

```
[jbc@andros jbc]$ which perl
/usr/bin/perl
```

So, in this case, I now know that the perl interpreter is located at /usr/bin/perl. Your copy of perl may be located somewhere else. Wherever it is, write down the location. You'll need to know it later.

 If your web server doesn't have the which command, you can try finding the location of Perl using the similar command whereis, giving it the -b option to limit its output to binary files, as in:

```
[jbc@andros jbc]$ whereis -b perl
perl: /usr/bin/perl /usr/local/bin/perl
```

What if the which command doesn't give you any output, and just dumps you back to the shell prompt?

```
[jbc@andros jbc]$ which perl
[jbc@andros jbc]$
```

Or what if it gives you an error message?

```
[jbc@andros jbc]$ which perl
which: no perl in (/usr/bin:/bin:/usr/local/bin)
```

These tell you that Perl hasn't been installed on your server, or its location is not in your search path, or you don't have permission to run it, or something equally annoying. Contact your ISP's tech support staff and find out what's going on.

Let's assume you *did* find a copy of perl when you used the which command. The next thing to do is to figure out what version it is. To do that, you run the perl program itself with a -v command-line switch:

```
[jbc@andros jbc]$ perl -v

This is perl, v5.6.1 built for i586-linux

Copyright 1987-2001, Larry Wall

Perl may be copied only under the terms of either the Artistic License
or the GNU General Public License, which may be found in the Perl 5
source kit.

Complete documentation for Perl, including FAQ lists, should be found
on this system using `man perl' or `perldoc perl'.  If you have access
to the Internet, point your browser at http://www.perl.com/, the Perl
Home Page.
```

Hopefully you have a version number of at least 5.005 because earlier versions of Perl (among other shortcomings) have some significant security problems. If you find that you are dealing with an older version of Perl, contact your ISP's tech support staff to find out what's going on.

Creating the "Hello, world!" Script

It's some kind of unwritten law that the first program you create in a new language should print out the message Hello, world! I'm not sure who originated the practice, but far be it from me to violate it. If you want to modify the following instructions to make your first Perl script say Hello, sailor! or Hey, bignose! or something else you find equally (or probably more) amusing, go right ahead.

For this demonstration I'm going to assume that you'll write this script on the Unix server using the pico text editor. (If your Unix server does not have pico available, you will probably need to look into using emacs or vi; see Chapter 1.) If you want to write the script on your local PC or Mac, that's fine, too; just remember that you'll have to upload it to the Unix server via FTP (ASCII upload, please) before you can test it.

Running Perl on a Non-Unix Computer

Because many Internet providers' web servers are Unix-based, this book focuses on running your Perl scripts in that environment, even if you actually create them on your PC or Macintosh. Although Perl was originally created for Unix, though, the language has been successfully ported to many non-Unix platforms. For example, if you want to install a copy of Perl on your desktop Windows machine or Macintosh in order to test and run your Perl scripts right there, you can easily do so. Indeed, the more you learn about Perl, the more you will want to have it available on every computer you use.

Rather than trying to compile your own local copy of the perl program from the source code, you will probably want to use one of the freely available, already compiled binary distributions of Perl. At the time of this writing, the best such distribution for the Windows environment is the one from ActiveState Tool Corp., called ActivePerl. More information about how to obtain and install ActivePerl can be found at the ActiveState web site, at *http://www.activestate.com/*.

For Macintosh users not using OS X, the distribution you want is called MacPerl. More information about it, including links to suitable download sites, can be found on the MacPerl pages at *http://www.macperl.org/*. If you run OS X, guess what? You already have a real, live Unix version of Perl pre-installed with your operating system.

You will need to know about various minor tricks and gotchas in order to use Perl in a non-Unix environment. For example, you will not be able to use a *shebang line* to tell your computer where to find the perl interpreter in order to run your script. (You'll be learning about shebang lines in just a minute.) In Windows, you will run your scripts by associating the .plx filename extension with the Perl interpreter, or by entering a command of the form perl scriptname.plx in the DOS shell.

This book does not go into detail on how to use Perl in non-Unix environments, but there is plenty of information available for those who wish to do so. As a starting point, I encourage you to check out Frequently Asked Questions files maintained at the ActivePerl and MacPerl sites mentioned previously. You also can browse the information on these and other Perl ports at CPAN, the Comprehensive Perl Archive Network, at *http://www.cpan.org/ports/*.

You start up pico by entering the command pico in the Unix shell (clever, eh?). There are some special features of pico you can turn on with command-line options, and we'll be using three of them: -d (which makes your keyboard's Delete key erase the character under your cursor, rather than the character to the cursor's left), -w (which turns off automatic word wrapping), and -z (which allows you to *suspend* the pico program by typing Ctrl-Z; more about that later).

 Although I show pico's command-line options merged together with a single leading hyphen (-dwz), older versions of pico may require you to enter them separately, as -d -w -z.

Let's get started. Enter `pico -dwz hello.plx` at the command line. This begins your pico editing session, with your cursor at the beginning of a new file called `hello.plx`:

```
[jbc@andros jbc]$ pico -dwz hello.plx
```

I typically give `.plx` filename extensions to my Perl scripts, even on Unix machines, where the filename extension has no formal significance (unlike on DOS/Windows machines, where it is used to indicate the file's type). This is a legacy of my originally learning Perl on a DOS computer. I left the extension on in these examples for two reasons:

- If used routinely, it can make locating and identifying your Perl scripts a bit easier.
- It can help you avoid accidentally giving a script a name already used by another program.

If you prefer your scripts to have clean, sensible names (like `hello`, as opposed to `hello.plx`), feel free to use that approach instead, and adjust the examples in this book accordingly.

After entering this command you'll see the pico screen, which has a titlebar at the top, a blank area with a blinking cursor where you enter and edit your text, and a brief help screen at the bottom (see Figure 2-1).

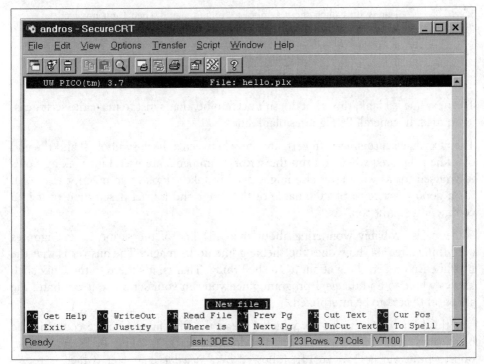

Figure 2-1. The Unix text editor pico, ready to begin editing a new file

The pico help screen shows various commands; all of them have the form Ctrl-*something*, (that is, you hold down the Ctrl key and press another key at the same time), with Ctrl indicated by the ^ character in the help screen. Now type Example 2-1 into your new file.

Example 2-1. Your first perl script

```
#!/usr/bin/perl

# hello.plx -- my first perl script

print "Hello, world!\n";
```

Some important points about what's going on here:

The first line is some special magic that will make it easier for you to run your scripts. This needs to be the very first line of your script, and it needs to take the following form: a hash symbol (#), then an exclamation point (!), then the path on your system to the perl program itself, which you figured out earlier when you did the which perl thing. Just put it there and forget about it. (Unix users sometimes call this a *shebang line,* which for some reason strikes me as funny.)

 I grew up calling the # symbol a "pound sign." Then I got involved with the Internet and started running into people from other parts of the world who insisted I was using that term incorrectly. I tried to explain that it was actually they who were mistaken, but this seemed to upset them, so I let the matter drop.

The next line is blank, though it doesn't need to be; that's just to make the script easier to read. In general, Perl ignores blank lines.

The next line is a *comment.* In Perl, anything between a hash symbol (#) and the end of a line is ignored when you run the script. Comments are useful for making notes to yourself (or to whomever else might need to take a look at your script later on). It's a good practice to put the name of the script and a brief description of it in a comment up at the top.

Someone is probably wondering about that first line of the script: if perl ignores everything after a #, how does the shebang line do its magic? The answer is that the first line isn't a Perl thing at all. It's a shell thing. That is, it's there so the Unix shell knows where to find the perl program when you run your script, so it can hand the script off to perl to be interpreted.

The third line of the script (by which I mean the fifth line, if you're counting the blank lines, too) is the part that actually does the work: invoking Perl's print function to print out Hello, world!, followed by a *newline* character (which is represented by the sequence \n). Note the semicolon (;) that terminates the Perl statement. Most Perl statements need to be terminated by a semicolon; accidentally leaving one off is a common way for new Perl programmers to mess up their scripts. Also note the double-quotes—please note that these are "straight" quotes (""), not "curly" quotes ("")—surrounding the *string* of text to be printed. When you want to give Perl a string of text (as opposed to a *number,* or a *variable* all by itself) and have it do something with that text, you usually will need to put quotes around the string.

We'll be covering quoting in more detail later in this chapter. For now, just make sure you copy this script exactly as given. Perl is probably the best computer language in the world at trying to figure out what you really mean when you make a mistake, but that's not saying much. It's still a computer language, which makes it extremely literal-minded by human standards.

Here's how Perl thinks about this line: you've got a *function* (print), followed by an *argument* to that function. In the case of the print function, the argument supplies the stuff that is going to be printed. In this particular case, the argument consists of a double-quoted string of text. And then there's a semicolon, terminating the statement.

Now let's save the script. In pico, I do that by typing Ctrl-X, then answering y when it asks me if I want to save the modified buffer, and then just hitting the Enter key to accept the filename hello.plx.

If you wrote the script on your local PC, you'll now need to save it and FTP it to your home directory on the Unix server.

Is It a Perl Script or a Perl Program?

The short answer, from the official Perl Frequently Asked Questions list: it doesn't matter.

Historically, a *program* was something written in a programming language, while a *script* was written in a scripting language. Programming languages were big, brawny things that took years of professional training to understand. Scripting languages were simple little things designed to let ordinary users automate a limited selection of tasks, often within the context of a particular application. Programs were created by writing source code that got run through a compiler to produce machine-readable code (an *executable*) that could then be distributed and run over and over again. Scripts were created by writing ASCII text that had to be *interpreted* to create the machine-readable form each time the script was run.

Today these distinctions have become fairly meaningless, at least in the case of Perl. Perl scripts can do pretty much anything that programs written in full-fledged programming languages can do. In this book, when talking about things written in Perl, I use the terms *script* and *program* interchangeably.

The Dot Slash Thing

The next step is to try running the script by entering its name at the Unix command prompt. You may be able to do this by just entering the name of the script (hello.plx) all by itself. Or you may need to precede its name by a period and a forward slash (./). What decides this is whether the dot (.), which you will recall is a shortcut for the current working directory (meaning the directory you are currently in), is in your *command path*.

The command path is just a list of directories that the shell looks in to find the command whose name you entered. On a DOS system, the current working directory is in your command path by default, but not so under Unix.

If the current working directory isn't in your command path, entering hello.plx by itself at the shell prompt will not work because the Unix shell will not be able to find the script, even though it's right there. Instead, you'll have to enter ./hello.plx, with that initial dot slash (./) telling the Unix shell to look in the current working directory for the command whose name you're typing in.

> Having to explicitly enter the ./ before your program's name can actually be a good thing because it makes it less likely that you will accidentally run a different program with the same name in some other directory that is in your command path.

You can check to see if the current working directory is in your command path with the printenv command, as follows:

```
[jbc@andros jbc]$ printenv PATH
/usr/local/bin:/bin:/usr/bin:/usr/sbin:.
```

If you don't have access to the printenv command, you can also try using the echo command to display the contents of the $PATH shell variable:

```
[jbc@andros jbc]$ echo $PATH
/usr/local/bin:/bin:/usr/bin:/usr/sbin:.
```

Using either method should cause the Unix server to print out a colon-separated list of directories that will be searched when you type in a command. If the current working directory (.) isn't in there, you'll need to put ./ at the beginning of your script name when you try to run it from the command line.

If you get sufficiently annoyed by this, ask your local expert (system administrator, tech support person, or a knowledgeable acquaintance) to tell you how to modify your command path by editing the startup files (the .login or .cshrc file, perhaps) in your home directory. More information about this is probably available in the manpage for your shell (e.g., man bash).

In this book, I assume you do *not* need to enter the ./ before your script names when running them from the command line. If you do, though, just remember to type it in.

Unix File Permissions

Back at my Unix command prompt, I try typing the name of the script to run it:

```
[jbc@andros jbc]$ hello.plx
hello.plx: Permission denied.
```

Hmm. Welcome to the world of *Unix file permissions*. This is one of the trickier parts of making the transition to Unix. If you're an impatient person, just type the following command:

```
[jbc@andros jbc]$ chmod 700 hello.plx
```

and go on to the next topic. If you want to know what's really going on, though, (which I strongly recommend, since it will save you much trouble later), keep reading.

In Unix, you can have three different types of permissions with respect to a particular file: read permission, write permission, and execute permission. *Read permission* lets you read the file (you need me to tell you that?), *write permission* lets you make changes to the file, and *execute permission,* in the case of a script or program, lets you actually run it.

So, that's the first half of the permissions story. The second half is this: the three types of permission can be set to "on" or "off" for each of three different sets of people: the file's *owner* (you, in the case of the scripts you've created), members of the file's *group* (which we're going to ignore for now), and *everyone else in the world* (which we're also going to ignore for now).

Check the permissions on a file by entering ls -l *filename*, with *filename* being replaced by the name of the file. To look at the permissions on my hello.plx script:

```
[jbc@andros jbc]$ ls -l hello.plx
-rw-r--r-- 1 jbc jbc 42 Sep 5 06:55 hello.plx
```

The first column in the ls -l listing (the -rw-r--r-- part) is what tells you what permissions the file has. That -rw-r--r-- thing can be decoded as follows:

The initial - means it's a *file* rather than a *directory* or a *link* (see Figure 2-2).

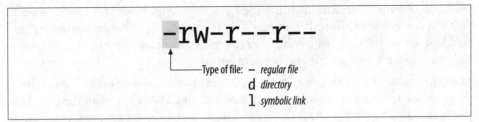

Figure 2-2. Decoding permissions: the type of file

The next three characters (rw-) mean that the file's *owner* (me, in this case) has read and write but not execute permissions (Figure 2-3).

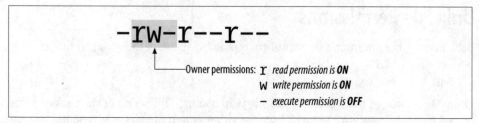

Figure 2-3. Decoding permissions: the file's owner

The next three characters mean that members of the file's group have read permission but not write or execute permission (Figure 2-4).

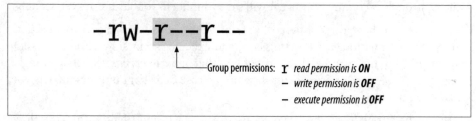

Figure 2-4. Decoding permissions: the file's group

Finally, the last three characters mean that everyone else in the world has read permission, but not write or execute permission (Figure 2-5).

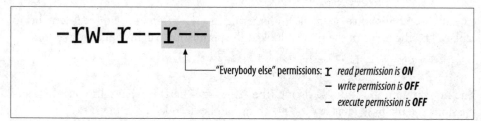

Figure 2-5. Decoding permissions: everyone else

You change a file's permissions using the Unix command chmod (for *change mode)*. You can use either of two different methods to supply the chmod command's arguments: if you use the *symbolic mode,* you say things like chmod u+x to mean "for the file's *user* (owner), turn on the execute permission."

The other method for supplying chmod arguments is the *numeric mode*. You express the permissions you want as a three-digit number, like 644 or 755, with the first digit giving the owner's permissions, the second digit giving the group permissions, and the last digit giving the everybody else permissions. You arrive at the numbers by addition, using the following formula:

```
4 = read permission
2 = write permission
1 = execute permission
```

You just add the numbers corresponding to the permissions you want to allow. For example, for *read plus write* you use the number 6 (because 4 + 2 = 6). *Read, write, and execute* is 7 (because 4 + 2 + 1 = 7). No permissions at all is 0 (zero).

Now, remember that the first digit gives the owner's permissions, the second digit gives the group permissions (which we're going to ignore), and the third digit gives the everybody else permissions. Thus, 644 means the file's owner gets read and write permission (4 + 2 = 6), and the group and everyone else get read permission (4).

These are the permissions that new files get by default when I create them in my Unix shell session, and they are, in fact, the permissions represented by the -rw-r--r-- I saw in the ls -l listing we were looking at a moment ago.

 I find the numeric chmod arguments to be the easiest to use, so that's what I presented here, but you may prefer to use the symbolic arguments. If you would rather use something like chmod u+x hello.plx instead of chmod 700 hello.plx, feel free to go ahead and do things that way. More details on the symbolic chmod arguments are available by entering man chmod at the command line.

In order to run hello.plx as a script, we're going to need to turn on the execute permission for the file's owner. While we're at it, we may as well turn off all the group and everyone else permissions, since no one else needs to do anything with this script. We can accomplish all of that with the following command:

```
[jbc@andros jbc]$ chmod 700 hello.plx
```

Now, checking the permissions we get:

```
[jbc@andros jbc]$ ls -l hello.plx
-rwx------   1 jbc  jbc   42 Sep  5 06:55 hello.plx
```

which is what we want. Now the file's owner (me) has execute permission, as indicated by the x in -rwx------, and the file's group and everyone else have no permissions at all, as indicated by the ------.

Running (and Debugging) the Script

Now that we've made hello.plx executable by its owner, let's try running it again:

```
[jbc@andros jbc]$ hello.plx
Hello, world!
```

Congratulations! You've just run your first Perl script.

The Joy of Debugging

What if your script *didn't* run, though, but instead died with some sort of error message? Or what if it successfully ran, but didn't produce the output you were expecting? Then you get to experience the joy of *debugging*.

You're going to be experiencing a lot of this particular joy. As a novice programmer, the bulk of your time is going to be spent in the debugging phase: tracking down and squashing the silly mistakes that keep your script from running as you intended. (Actually, my understanding from the experienced programmers I know is that they, too, spend a good chunk of their time debugging.)

Sometimes the mistake is obvious: you left off a semicolon, or the closing quotation mark in a quoted string. Other times the mistake is maddeningly obscure (at least until you identify it, at which point it, too, will become obvious): you gave the wrong arguments to a function, or were confused about some aspect of how Perl behaves.

Debugging is a specialized skill, and it takes practice to get good at it. It's somewhat like car repair. An experienced mechanic can ask a few questions, listen to the engine for a second, and immediately tell you what's wrong with your car and what it will take to fix it. Meanwhile, a novice mechanic will be pulling apart the transmission when the only problem is a broken light on the dashboard.

As you learn about debugging you're sometimes going to feel like that novice mechanic, banging your head against the keyboard for what seems like hours, then finding out the problem was actually in some completely different part of your script.

This is okay. It's a good thing. It's how you learn.

With that said, I'd like to offer some debugging tips gleaned from my own experience, in the hope that they will help you learn somewhat more quickly than you otherwise would.

Pay close attention to error messages

Perl does its best to give you useful feedback when something goes wrong. Listen to that feedback. When your script dies with some sort of error message, read the message carefully. It will usually report a line number in your script where the problem occurred, so go to that line number and see if you can figure out what's going on. (But be aware that the problem might actually be on an earlier line, since sometimes you can make a mistake that still looks like valid Perl code, and that doesn't trigger an error until later on in the script. Forgetting to properly terminate quoted strings is a good example of this. Similarly, some sorts of mistakes will produce a whole bunch of error messages. In that case, it's usually the first error message you want to pay the most attention to, because the subsequent ones may well go away once the first problem is fixed.)

Use the -w switch to turn on Perl's warnings feature

By putting a space and -w at the end of the shebang line that starts off your Perl script, you tell Perl to give you warnings about things it thinks might be problems in your script. You will be seeing examples of this later on.

Use perl -c *scriptname to do a compile check before running your script for real*

By entering the command perl -c *scriptname* or perl -wc *scriptname* (with *scriptname* replaced by the actual name of your script), you cause Perl to try to compile your script without actually running it. The -c version compiles the script without invoking the warnings feature; the -wc version compiles it with warnings turned on. In either case, you can get feedback on any problems your script might have, without having to actually run it.

Take a step back

Vary your mental perspective. Try to consider the problem in a larger context. Perhaps the problem is not in the chunk of code where you think it is, but in some untested assumption elsewhere in your script.

Try to isolate the problem

By commenting out chunks of code, then re-running the script, you can often narrow down where in the script the problem is occurring. Even better is to avoid the need for this by building and debugging the script in small increments. Create a simple framework first, get it working, then add on increasingly complex features, testing each component before going on the next. In this way you will uncover bugs as you go, and it usually will be obvious where the bug resides: it is in the small section of code you just added. While it may seem as if it would be faster to code up the whole thing first, then do all the debugging at the end, in practice it rarely works out that way.

Use print *statements to test your assumptions*

By sprinkling temporary print statements here and there in your script, you can often track down just where a problem is occurring. For example, if you think that at a certain point in the program a variable should contain one value, but the script seems to be acting as if it contains something else, add a statement to print out the contents of the variable at that point, then re-run the script.

Resist the temptation to attribute the problem to some previously undiscovered bug in Perl

Every novice Perl programmer eventually comes up against a bug that defies all efforts to identify and eradicate it. As the programmer's frustration level mounts, an idea begins to creep into his or her head: it must not be a problem in the script, but instead is something broken in Perl itself. I've thought this at least a dozen times, and I was always wrong. Take my word on this one: it's almost certainly a bug in your script, not in Perl.

One thing that I'm not going to talk about much in this book is the *Perl debugger*, but I would be remiss if I didn't mention it. You run the debugger by running perl with the -d command-line switch—for example by entering the following at the shell prompt, with *scriptname.plx* replaced by your actual script name:

```
[jbc@andros jbc] perl -d scriptname.plx
```

This will place you in a special debugging mode, where you can step through your program one statement at a time, doing interesting things like examining the current contents of variables. It's very useful, but somewhat overwhelming for a beginner, which is why I suggest you stick with things like embedded print statements for the time being. Still, if you're curious, or if you have a really thorny debugging problem and you think the debugger might help, see the `perldebug` manpage for more information. If your version of Perl is recent enough, the `perldebtut` manpage, which gives an introduction geared more toward beginners, will also be available.

Perl Documentation

This mention of the `perldebtut` man page is a good place to talk about the official Perl documentation. There is a very complete set of documentation that comes free with Perl. If everyone was tied down and forced to read every word of it, we'd all know a lot more about Perl.

Unfortunately, the sheer quantity of the Perl documentation, along with the fact that much of it is written for people who are already experienced programmers, can make things tough for accidental programmers. There is a subset of the Perl documentation, though, that you should definitely try to familiarize yourself with now—if only so you'll know where to look for answers later on, when those answers will make more sense to you.

man perl, perldoc perl

You can read the Perl documentation by entering `man perl` at the Unix command line. If you are on a system that doesn't have the `man` command (for example, because you installed Perl locally on your PC or Mac), you can use a utility called `perldoc` that comes bundled with Perl by entering `perldoc perl`. (Also, the ActiveState version of Perl installs the Perl documentation as HTML pages accessible under the Start menu.)

The Perl documentation has been split up into numerous sections; you access the appropriate section by entering `man` *sectionname* or `perldoc` *sectionname*. More about this, including the list of section names, in that first `man perl` page.

Some of those Perl manpages are going to be over your head for now, but among the ones you should at least skim through are `perl`, `perlfaq`, `perltoc`, `perldata`, `perlsyn`, `perlop`, `perlre`, `perlrun`, and `perlfunc`. The others are useful, too; it's just that you probably will need to learn some more before you can get much out of them.

Function Documentation with perldoc -f

You also should know about a neat trick you can do with `perldoc`: If you enter `perldoc -f`, followed by the name of a particular Perl function, you will get the part of the `perlfunc` manpage that describes that function. For example:

```
[jbc@andros jbc]$ perldoc -f join
join EXPR,LIST
    Joins the separate strings of LIST into a single
```

```
string with fields separated by the value of EXPR,
and returns that new string.  Example:

    $rec = join(':', $login,$passwd,$uid,$gid,$gcos,$home,$shell);

Beware that unlike "split", "join" doesn't take a
pattern as its first argument.  Compare the split
entry elsewhere in this document.
```

The Perl FAQ

A really useful part of the Perl documentation is the Perl FAQ (for "Frequently Asked Questions") file. You access it by entering man perlfaq at the command line. That manpage will in turn refer you to manpages called perlfaq1, perlfaq2, and so on, with each of those FAQ files containing a different set of questions and answers. Unlike some other FAQ listings you may have encountered, Perl's really is incredibly complete and useful; most of the Perl questions you're likely to come up with are covered.

Indeed, the Perl FAQ is so complete, it can be hard to find the specific part that deals with your particular question. So now, if your version of Perl is recent enough, there's another neat trick you can do with perldoc: perldoc -q *something* will search through the Perl FAQs and print any entries whose titles contain the word "something." For example:

```
[jbc@andros jbc]$ perldoc -q 'cgi form'
Found in /usr/local/lib/perl5/5.6.1/pod/perlfaq9.pod
    How do I decode a CGI form?

    You use a standard module, probably CGI.pm.  Under no
    circumstances should you attempt to do so by hand!
```

And so on.

Perl Variables

It's time for you to get acquainted with the idea of a *variable*. Variables are very important in programming. They provide containers that you use to store information for later retrieval and manipulation. You choose a name for your variable (hopefully picking a nice, descriptive name that will make sense to you later on), then stick a value in it (or a bunch of values, or pairs of values; more on that in a minute). Later, you can get that value (values, pairs of values) back by referring to the variable by name. This actually sounds more complicated than it is. The following examples should help clear things up.

There are three types of variables in Perl. In increasing order of niftiness, they are *scalar, array,* and *hash variables.* You'll be using them all, so let's get to know them.

Scalar Variables

Replace the `print` statement in your *"Hello, world!"* script with the following:

```
$greeting = "What are you looking at?\n";

print $greeting;
```

This new form of the script uses a variable to hold the string that will be printed. First the string is assigned to the variable using the assignment operator, an equal sign (=). Then we feed the variable (called `$greeting`) to the `print` function.

In Perl, variables whose names begin with a dollar sign ($) are used to store a single something: a single number or a single string of text. Programmers call these single-something containers *scalar variables*.

 When I say scalar variables hold a single string of text, I don't mean they necessarily hold only a single letter or word. Except for a very large limit based on the computer's available memory, a scalar variable can hold as long a text string as you like. You could put the entire text of the *Encyclopedia Britannica* in a scalar variable if you wanted to. It's just that from Perl's perspective, it would just be one thingy.

A good trick for remembering that the dollar sign refers to a scalar variable is to remember that a dollar sign looks sort of like a letter s, for *scalar* (or *singular)*.

In real life, of course, there wouldn't be much point in storing a string in a variable just so you could turn around and print it out; you could just as easily feed the double-quoted string directly to the `print` function and be done with it. In real-life scripts, though, scalar variables turn out to be really handy because you can update the contents of the variable in one place, and have that change take effect in lots of different places where the variable is used.

Array Variables

Now, replace the lines you just put in `hello.plx` with the following:

```
@greeting = (
    "Hello, world!\n",
    "Hey. What's up?\n",
    "Excuse me, but your pants are on fire.\n",
);

print $greeting[0];
```

Here's your first exposure to the second of Perl's three main variable types: the *array variable*. Indicated here by the @ sign in front of the variable name `@greeting` (think @ for the *a* in *array* to help you remember), an array variable doesn't hold a single thing, like a scalar variable; instead, it holds a whole *list* of things. In this case, we're assigning three strings to it, using the assignment operator (=). This works just like it did when we assigned the greeting to the scalar $greeting variable; the variable name goes on the left side of the equal sign, and the stuff we're assigning to it goes on the right. When you're assigning a list of things to an array variable, you enclose the list in parentheses, and use commas to separate the individual elements. The extra line breaks and indenting I used in this example are just cosmetic flourishes designed to make the script easier to read. Perl doesn't care; as with most line breaks and extra spacing, Perl ignores it.

Did you notice how I stuck an extra comma after the last element? That comma wasn't needed, strictly speaking, because there were no more elements coming after it. But Perl lets you put an extra comma there if you want, and that turns out to be a useful habit. Later, if you want to add another element to the list, you can just do a copy-and-paste to duplicate the last line, then edit the pasted copy to suit your needs. Likewise, you can use cut-and-paste to rearrange the elements in the list, without having to worry about cleaning up the commas afterward.

You access individual elements in the array by *position*; that is, you say to Perl, "Give me the third element in the array," and Perl gives you the third element. Actually, Perl counts array positions starting with zero, so you say "give me array element 0" to mean "give me the first element in the array," and "give me array element 1" to mean "give me the second element in the array," and so on.

You communicate these requests to Perl by giving the name of the array, followed by a pair of square brackets ([ ]), with the number of the array element you want inside the square brackets. For example, $greeting[0] would give you the "Hello, world!\n" element from the @greeting array. Notice how we revert to using the dollar sign (Perl's symbol for a *single* something) when we want to refer to a single element of an array. It is important to realize that $greeting and $greeting[0] are two completely different things. $greeting is the scalar variable named $greeting, and $greeting[0] is the first element (that is to say, the element at position 0) in the array variable named @greeting.

You should be aware, too, that we commonly build up array variables one element at a time, rather than in one fell swoop like we did here. For example, in the previous script we could have replaced the assignment section with the following:

```
@greeting = (); # empties the array, if it previously held anything

$greeting[0] = "Hello, world!\n";
$greeting[1] = "Hey. What's up?\n";
$greeting[2] = "Excuse me, but your pants are on fire.\n";
```

and the variable would have ended up containing the exact same elements.

Try running the script now in order to print out the first greeting ($greeting[0]), and then try changing the number in the square brackets to print out the second greeting (that is, $greeting[1]) and the third greeting ($greeting[2]). See how it works?

You're now an expert at array variables.

Hash Variables

We've saved the best for last. If you ask an experienced programmer what he likes most about Perl, *hash variables* will probably be mentioned near the top of the list.

Go ahead and modify hello.plx to contain the following in place of all that array variable stuff:

```
%greeting = (
    traditional => "Hello, world!\n",
    terse       => "Hi.\n",
    surfer      => "How's the break?\n",
);

print $greeting{traditional};
```

Hash variables are a lot like array variables, but instead of containing a bunch of individual elements that you access according to their position within the array, a hash variable contains pairs of elements, with each pair consisting of a key (which is a string) and a corresponding value. You access the individual elements in the hash by saying "give me the value that corresponds to this particular key."

A way to remember that the percent sign (%) represents a hash variable is to think of the two little circles in the percent sign as representing the key-value pairs that make up a hash. (Thanks to Jason Holland for suggesting this one.)

Because the value associated with a particular key is a singular sort of thing, we use the dollar sign ($) when accessing individual hash elements, just like we did when accessing individual array elements. Instead of the square brackets, though, we use curly braces ({}). You can remember this by remembering that hash variables are a bit fancier than array variables, so it makes sense that the brackets used to access an individual hash element are a bit fancier, too.

Anyway, try running the script to see what happens when you print out $greeting{traditional}. You should get the value associated with that key: Hello, world! followed by the newline character. Now try modifying the script to instead print out the terse greeting (by using $greeting{terse}) and the surfer greeting (by using $greeting{surfer}). That's all there is to it.

It's fairly uncommon to assign all a hash variable's key-value pairs in one fell swoop like we did in this example. Usually you will build up your hashes by assigning one key-value pair at a time, as in the following code:

```
%greeting = (); # empty out any existing key-value pairs in %greeting

$greeting{traditional} = "Hello, world!\n";
$greeting{terse}       = "Hi.\n";
$greeting{surfer}      = "How's the break?\n";
```

You probably were wondering about those things that looked like arrows (=>, an equal sign followed by a greater than symbol) in the original assignment of the hash variable's elements. Perl lets you use => (sometimes referred to as a "fat arrow") as a replacement for the comma when assigning hash elements because it's easier to read, making it clear which keys go with which values. You may also have noticed that even though the keys to the hash are strings, we haven't bothered to put quotation marks around them. We can get away with this because using => has the effect of automatically quoting the word to the left of it. As long as our keys consist of a single word, we don't need to worry about using quotation marks on the left side of => (though we still need them on the right side, if we want the value to be a string).

This means that we could have written the assignment of %greeting like this:

```
%greeting = ("traditional", "Hello, world!\n", "terse", "Hi.\n",
    "surfer", "How's the break?\n");
```

and it would have worked just the same as the way we actually did write it.

We also left off the quotation marks inside the curly brackets, as with $greeting{traditional}. As long as the key consists of a single word with no internal spaces, this is fine; it's just Perl working hard to save you from extra typing.

Please note, though, that you don't *have* to use single words for your hash keys; you can make the keys as long as you want, including sticking space characters into them. You could use the entire Gettysburg Address for a hash key if you wanted to. You would just need to be sure to enclose it in quotation marks.

There is one last bit of trivia you should know about hashes: the key-value pairs in a hash are not stored in any particular order. Each key always stays with its associated value, but the different pairs get jumbled up into an essentially random order. If you need to access them in a particular order you'll have to sort them, using techniques you'll be learning about shortly.

A Bit More About Quoting

So far, whenever we've needed to quote a string we've used *double quotes* (as in, "this is a double-quoted string"). In fact, Perl also supports the use of *single quotes* (as in, 'this is a single-quoted string'). It's important for you to understand the difference between the two.

The difference is just this: when it processes a double-quoted string, Perl looks in it for things that look like variables and replaces them with the contents of those variables.

This process is called *variable interpolation*. It also looks for certain sequences beginning with a backslash (\) and replaces them with special characters. The sequences are called *backslash escapes,* and the process of replacing them with special characters is called *backslash interpretation*.

When it's processing a single-quoted string Perl doesn't bother doing this. You get the string, just like it's written. (Actually, Perl processes two backslash escapes within a single-quoted string: \', which it interprets as a literal single quote, and \\, which it interprets as a literal backslash. This lets you put literal single quotes and literal backslashes inside your string, which would otherwise be difficult to do.)

Let's create a new script called quotes.plx (Example 2-2) to see how this works.

Example 2-2. A script to test how Perl treats single- and double-quoted strings

```
#!/usr/bin/perl

# quotes.plx -- test handling of single- and double-quoted strings

$veggies = 'rutabagas';

print "I like to eat $veggies.\n";
```

When you save this script and run it in the shell you should get this:

```
[jbc@andros jbc]$ quotes.plx
I like to eat rutabagas.
```

Now modify the script to replace the double quotes in the print statement with single quotes, so the last line becomes:

```
print 'I like to eat $veggies.\n';
```

Now when you run the script you should get:

```
[jbc@andros jbc]$ quotes.plx
I like to eat $veggies.\n[jbc@andros jbc]$
```

See what happened? The $veggies variable was not interpolated, and the \n was not interpreted as a newline. As a result, you just got the literal string $veggies (instead of the contents of that variable) and the literal string \n (instead of a newline) printed out to your screen.

"Hello, world!" as a CGI Script

Before ending this brief introduction to Perl, I want to show you one more thing: the "Hello, world!" script rewritten to run as a CGI script.

I've assumed in this book that you already have a certain amount of web authoring experience, so you may have encountered CGI scripts before, and may even have run a few yourself. In case they're completely new to you, though, here's the lowdown: In simplest terms, a *CGI script* is a separate program that a web server runs in order to produce a customized page to show to a web user. CGI stands for *Common Gateway Interface*, which is just a description of a set of relatively simple rules for how the communication between the web server and the separate program will be conducted. CGI scripts can be written in any language that can produce the appropriate sort of output, but Perl is by far the most popular choice because of how easy it is to create CGI scripts in Perl.

CGI scripts are something of a gateway drug for Perl use. Many accidental programmers first come to Perl not because they've decided to learn Perl programming *per se*, but because they want to create a CGI script (probably to process the output of a web form), and someone has told them that Perl is the way to go. That's okay; Perl doesn't mind. It happily does the task at hand, biding its time until the user is ready for more.

Content-Type Headers

Let's modify hello.plx so that it will run as a CGI script. Every CGI script needs to output a *CGI header* as the first thing the script outputs. This header, which consists of one or more lines of text followed immediately by a blank line, is checked by the web server, then passed on to the remote user's browser in order to tell that browser what type of document to expect. Most of the time, your script is going to output an HTML document, which means you'll need to output your script's header using something like the following snippet of Perl:

```
print "Content-type: text/html\n";
print "\n";
```

Please note the blank line being output by the second print statement. CGI novices tend to forget that, but it's really important because the header needs to be followed by that blank line. Now that I've impressed that point on you, here's a more compact way to output the header, with the two print statements combined into one:

```
print "Content-type: text/html\n\n";
```

So, adding that line to the hello.plx script you created earlier in the chapter gives you the following:

```
#!/usr/bin/perl

# hello.plx -- my first perl script!

print "Content-type: text/html\n\n";

print "Hello, world!\n";
```

Here-Document Quoting

As long as you're claiming this is HTML that you're outputting, you should probably go ahead and make the output a valid HTML document. That's easy enough to do, and while you're doing it you can also learn a handy trick for quoting an extended string of text: *here-document quoting*. Take a look at Example 2-3, a modified version of the hello.plx script.

Example 2-3. The hello.plx script modified to run as a CGI script and to output an HTML document

```
#!/usr/bin/perl

# hello.plx -- my first perl script!

print <<"EOF";
Content-type: text/html

<HTML>

<HEAD>
<TITLE>Hello, world!</TITLE>
</HEAD>

<BODY>
<H1>Hello, world!</H1>
</BODY>

</HTML>
EOF
```

Take a careful look at the stuff that comes immediately after the print function. That <<"EOF"; thing, and the EOF all alone on a line by itself at the end, are being used to quote a multiline string. Basically, they're being used to indicate what the print command should print. Notice, also, how we've gone ahead and included the CGI header, and the all-important blank line following it, right in the here-document string.

There's nothing special about the EOF string being used to delimit the here-document string's output, by the way; you can use anything you like, as long as it's the exact same at the beginning and end of the quoted string (including capitalization). You could have said:

```
print <<"Walnuts";
Some stuff
to be printed...
Walnuts
```

and it would have worked fine. Just make sure, again, that Walnuts is all by itself on the last line. Even a space character before or after it will mess things up. It needs to be right at the left margin, with nothing after it but a newline. And, obviously, it will help to pick a string that isn't likely to occur in the multiline string you're quoting.

If the line terminating your here-document quoting is the very last line of your script, some text editors will leave off the newline at the end of that line. This can cause the here-document quoting to fail. You can avoid the problem by making sure you enter an explicit newline immediately after the EOF string (or whatever string you're using to end the here-document quoting).

File Locations/Extensions for Running CGI Scripts

You need to do one more thing in order to run hello.plx as a CGI script: you need to let the web server know it's a CGI script. How you do this depends on how your ISP has configured their web server. The two most common ways are to change the file's name so that it ends with a .cgi extension, or to place the file in a special directory on the server called /cgi or /cgi-bin. Ask your ISP how the server is configured, and proceed accordingly.

For this discussion, I'm going to assume that you can run a CGI script in any directory in your web space, as long as the script has a .cgi extension. Let's copy the script to an appropriate directory, and change its extension to .cgi:

```
[jbc@andros jbc]$ mkdir /w1/e/elanus/begperl
[jbc@andros jbc]$ chmod 755 /w1/e/elanus/begperl
[jbc@andros jbc]$ cp hello.plx /w1/e/elanus/begperl
[jbc@andros jbc]$ cd /w1/e/elanus/begperl
[jbc@andros begperl]$ mv hello.plx hello.cgi
```

Did you follow that? First I used the Unix mkdir command to create a new directory called begperl in my web space, which in my case is located at /w1/e/elanus. I used chmod to change the directory's permissions to 755, which are typical permissions for a directory that a web server needs to have access to. Then I used the cp command to copy hello.plx from my home directory to the new directory in my web space. Then I used the cd command to change to that directory, and used the Unix mv (for "move") command to change the file's name from hello.plx to hello.cgi, so the web server will know that it's a CGI script.

Many ISPs, by the way, require users to put their web stuff in a directory called public_html beneath their home directory. If that's the case with your ISP, you'll need to substitute directory names accordingly in the preceding example.

Testing from the Command Line

Before you try to run a CGI script via the web server, you should always try running it from the command line. This is important to remember because it lets you use a divide-and-conquer strategy in your battle with the forces of darkness. A whole class of things can go wrong with your script and prevent it from running from the command line; another whole class of things can go wrong when you try to run it via the web server. By testing from the command line first you allow yourself to deal with one set of problems at a time, rather than both together. That's a big win when you're debugging.

If everything is working properly, you should get something that looks like this when you run the script from the command line:

```
[jbc@andros begperl]$ hello.cgi
Content-type: text/html

<HTML>

<HEAD>
<TITLE>Hello, world!</TITLE>
</HEAD>

<BODY>
<H1>Hello, world!</H1>
</BODY>

</HTML>
```

Did you get that? Great! If not, what happened? Did you get a "permission denied" error, by any chance? Then check your permissions: you probably lost the "execute" permission somewhere along the way.

Testing from the Web Server

Assuming your script did print out from the command line, let's go to the final step: testing the script via the web server. In my case, that means typing the following into my web browser's Location box: *http://www.elanus.net/begperl/hello.cgi*. In your case, it might be something like *http://www.your_isp.com/~your_username/hello.cgi*. Whatever it is, go ahead and try it.

When I tried testing my copy of the hello.cgi script, my browser displayed the screen displayed in Figure 2-6.

You will see error messages like this a lot when you are learning to run CGI scripts. Here, the error message delivered by the server (the 403 error message) is pretty descriptive: you don't have permission to access that resource. It's a file-permissions problem.

But what if the error message isn't as informative? Much of the time you'll get the infamous 500 (that is, internal server) error message. That happens, for example, in cases where for some reason the script dies without outputting the required CGI header. In those cases, it can be really helpful to be able to check the web server's error log, since the script hopefully spat out some sort of helpful error message before it died, and the web server's error log is where those CGI script errors typically get recorded. Fortunately, since your ISP is enlightened enough to let you run

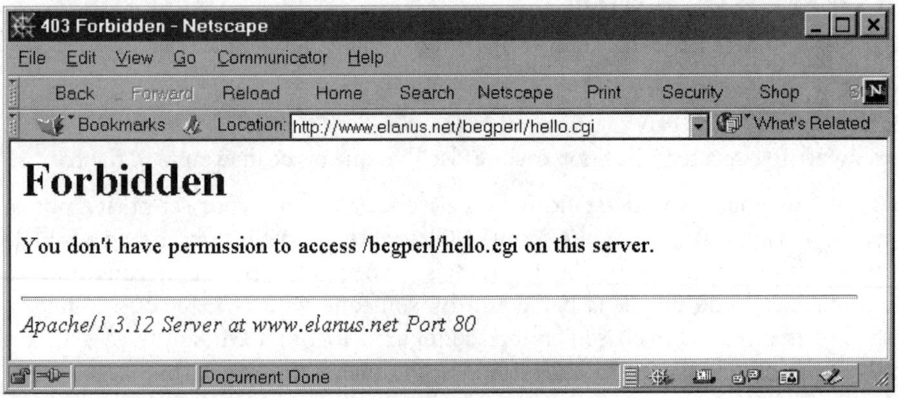

Figure 2-6. A server error resulting from CGI script file permissions

your own CGI scripts, they're probably enlightened enough to give you access to the web server's error log. In my case, it's at `/w1/e/elanus/.logs/error.log`.

One way to check that error log is to open up a second Telnet window, log into a second shell session on your Unix server, and enter the command `tail -f /path/to/error.log`. This will cause that window to display new entries in the error log as they are added. Then you can just pop back and forth from one window to the other to check the error log as you work on your script.

> If you don't have access to your web server's error log for some reason, you can try adding the following line at the top of your script:
>
>   use CGI::Carp 'fatalsToBrowser';
>
> This will cause your script to try to output a valid CGI header, followed by the error message that otherwise would have gone to the error log, so you can see the error message in your browser.

In this case, I'm just going to use my existing shell session, and issue the `tail` command without the `-f` switch to print out the last 10 lines of the error log, looking for an explanation of the problem that caused the script to fail. Lo and behold, there it is:

```
[jbc@andros begperl]$ tail /w1/log/e/elanus/error.log
(stuff deleted)
[Sun Feb 18 11:44:45 2001] [error] [client 209.151.241.118] file
permissions deny server execution: /w1/e/elanus/begperl/hello.cgi
```

So, again, it was a file-permissions problem. But wait; the script ran fine when you ran it from the command line. What gives?

CGI Script File Permissions

When you ran it from the command line you ran it as you, the file's owner. But when you ran it as a CGI script using the web server, you ran it as somebody else. The permissions you assigned to the original hello.plx file (-rwx------, or 700) allow the file's owner to execute it, but not anyone else. No one else can even *read* the file.

This is a key point to understand: when a web server runs your script, it's not the same thing as you running your script. CGI scripts, by definition, are accessible to every person with access to the Internet, so when the web server runs one, the assumption is made that it is being run by someone who is malicious, stupid, or both. For this reason, web servers are configured to run CGI scripts as a special, underprivileged user (often called "nobody", another quaint Unixism that strikes me as funny) in order to minimize any damage that might be done.

This particular script can't do any real harm, so we don't need to worry about the security implications of letting John Q. Public run it. To let him do so, though, we need to turn on the "read" and "execute" permissions for the "everybody else in the world" category of user. And we may as well turn on the same permissions for the file's group while we're at it, yielding a permissions setting of 755, which is the setting we're going to use for most of the CGI scripts we create from here on out. Here's how that looked when I did it in my shell session:

```
[jbc@andros begperl]$ chmod 755 hello.cgi
[jbc@andros begperl]$ ls -l hello.cgi
-rwxr-xr-x   1 jbc      www            217 Sep 11 23:42 hello.cgi
```

Now try running hello.cgi via the web server again, either by hitting the Reload button in your browser, or just typing the script's address into the Location box again and hitting the Enter key. Figure 2-7 shows the result in my web browser.

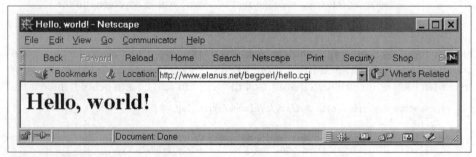

Figure 2-7. The output of successfully running "Hello, world!" as a CGI script

All right! Take a break, and treat yourself to something you like. You've earned it.

## CHAPTER 3

Running a Form-to-Email Gateway

Now that you're able to run real, honest-to-goodness CGI scripts, let's make something useful: a web-form-to-email gateway. This is probably one of the most common uses of CGI scripts, since it satisfies a very common need: you have an HTML form that you want visitors to your web site to fill out, and you want the contents of that form sent to you as an email message.

My goal with this chapter is to get your form-to-email gateway script up and running as quickly as possible. Along the way I explain foreach loops, if blocks, and how Perl evaluates conditional statements for "truth." I also touch on how to open a pipe to another program and print output to that program, as well as how to use the die function to make your script stop dead in its tracks if it notices something unusual happening.

Because you still are at a fairly early stage in your Perl education, I'm going to ask you to take more or less on faith some other Perl features demonstrated in this chapter. I'll explain what they're doing in terms of this chapter's example, but I will stop short (for now) of giving a complete explanation of how you would use them in other circumstances. This is the case with this chapter's treatment of the substitution operator, and the CGI.pm module, for example. Don't worry, though. We'll be covering them more thoroughly in the chapters ahead.

Checking for CGI.pm

We're going to make life easy for ourselves by writing this script using something called CGI.pm. CGI.pm is a *Perl module*, which is basically a chunk of prewritten Perl code that you can pull into your script to do lots of useful magic. CGI.pm, as you might guess, is a module specifically designed to do CGI sorts of things. It was created by Lincoln Stein, one of the real heroes of the Perl community, especially for anyone who uses Perl for web work. In this script, we'll be using CGI.pm primarily to decode data submitted from an HTML form. Although it's possible to do that form decoding without using CGI.pm, I encourage you not to try to do that. See the accompanying sidebar, "Using CGI.pm Versus Manual Form Decoding," for an explanation.

Using CGI.pm Versus Manual Form Decoding

There are a lot of freely available form-processing CGI scripts out there. Many of them don't use the `CGI.pm` module, and instead do their form decoding with a chunk of code that looks something like this:

```
foreach $pair (@pairs) {

    ($name, $value) = split(/=/, $pair);

    # Un-webify plus signs and %-encoding
    $value =~ tr/+/ /;
    $value =~ s/%([a-fA-F0-9][a-fA-F0-9])/pack("C",
            hex($1))/eg;
    $name  =~ tr/+/ /;
    $name  =~ s/%([a-fA-F0-9][a-fA-F0-9])/pack("C",
            hex($1))/eg;

    $FORM{$name} = $value;
}
```

Variations of that code have been floating around on the Net at least since 1994. Unfortunately, it contains a subtle bug, one that will cause your script to lose data if it is asked to handle a form submission featuring a multivalued form element (like a checkbox group with more than one item checked).

CGI form decoding is one of those programming tasks that seems simple enough, but actually turns out to be fairly complex once you account for all the special cases that can crop up. That's why I, and most other experienced Perl CGI programmers, use the `CGI.pm` module to handle it instead of the manual form decoding represented by this example. `CGI.pm` has been debugged and improved for many years by some of the best minds in the Perl community. It won't let you down.

First, let's check to see if `CGI.pm` is already installed on your ISP's machine. Open up `hello.plx` (your "Hello, world!" script from earlier) and add a line so that it looks like this:

```
#!/usr/local/bin/perl

# hello.plx - my first perl script!

use CGI;

print "Hello, world!\n";
```

The line that says use CGI; (without a trailing .pm) pulls in the CGI.pm module for you. Save the script (which means saving it and then FTPing it to your Unix machine if you're writing it on your local PC), then run it from the command line. If you see:

```
[jbc@catlow jbc]$ hello.plx
Hello, world!
```

CGI.pm is already installed, and you're in good shape. But if you see something like this:

```
[jbc@catlow jbc]$ hello.plx
Can't locate CGI.pm in @INC at hello.plx line 5.
BEGIN failed--compilation aborted at hello.plx line 5.
```

CGI.pm is not installed as part of your copy of Perl, and you need to get it installed.

One approach to this is to ask your ISP to do it, and if they won't, get another ISP. (Isn't it great how glibly I offer that advice?) Alternately, you can download and install CGI.pm somewhere under your own user directory or in your own web space, and then add the following line to all your scripts:

```
use lib '/home/your/private/dir';
```

with /home/your/private/dir being replaced with the full pathname of the directory where you installed CGI.pm. I provide more specifics on how to install and use modules in a later chapter. You can also learn more about how to do this by reading the installation section of Lincoln's excellent CGI.pm documentation, at *http://stein.cshl. org/WWW/software/CGI/cgi_docs.html*, or by reading the perlmodinstall manpage.

The fact is, though, that CGI.pm has been distributed along with Perl by default for some time now, so you probably will find it already available.

Besides the CGI.pm documentation, by the way, which you can access at the URL just given, or by entering man CGI or perldoc CGI at the shell prompt (assuming CGI.pm is already installed), another excellent source of information on CGI.pm is Lincoln Stein's book, the *Official Guide to Programming with CGI.pm* (Wiley & Sons).

Creating the HTML Form

Among the things Lincoln explains in his documentation is how you can use CGI.pm not only to process the output of HTML forms, but to actually produce those forms in the first place. With this approach, you just send a user to your CGI script, and the first time the user invokes the script it delivers an HTML form with all the values set to their defaults. Then, when the form is submitted back to the same script, it takes the data supplied by the user and does whatever you want it to do.

CGI.pm has lots of nifty features like that, but they tend to be a bit overwhelming for beginners, so in this case we're going to take a more straightforward approach and simply create our form as a standard HTML page, then submit it to our CGI script for processing.

Example 3-1 shows an HTML form you can use for this demonstration. I'm not going to bother explaining what's going on with the table tags and form elements in this web page; again, I'm assuming you already know about those things, or can learn about them elsewhere.

You can download your own copy of this web page from this book's online example repository, at *http://www.elanus.net/book/.* Or you can just create your own copy of it.

Example 3-1. A page with an HTML form for testing a CGI form-to-email gateway

```
<HTML>

<HEAD>
<TITLE>Sample Form</TITLE>
</HEAD>

<BODY>

<H1>Sample Form</H1>

<P>Please fill out this form and submit it. Thank you.</P>

<FORM ACTION="mail_form.cgi" METHOD="POST">

<TABLE>

<TR>
<TD ALIGN="right"><STRONG>My name:</STRONG></TD>
<TD><INPUT NAME="name" SIZE=30></TD>
</TR>

<TR>
<TD ALIGN="right"><STRONG>Address:</STRONG></TD>
<TD><INPUT NAME="address" SIZE=30></TD>
</TR>

<TR>
<TD ALIGN="right"><STRONG>City:</STRONG></TD>
<TD><INPUT NAME="city" SIZE=30></TD>
</TR>

<TR>
<TD ALIGN="right"><STRONG>State:</STRONG></TD>
<TD><INPUT NAME="state" SIZE=2></TD>
</TR>

<TR>
<TD ALIGN="right"><STRONG>Zip:</STRONG></TD>
<TD><INPUT NAME="zip" SIZE=10></TD>
</TR>

<TR>
<TD ALIGN="right"><STRONG>Country:</STRONG></TD>
```

```
<TD><INPUT NAME="country" SIZE=10 VALUE="USA"></TD>
</TR>

<TR>
<TD ALIGN="right"><STRONG>My email:</STRONG></TD>
<TD><INPUT NAME="email" SIZE=30></TD>
</TR>

<TR>
<TD ALIGN="right"><STRONG>My favorite color:
</STRONG></TD>
<TD>
<TABLE BGCOLOR="#CCCCFF" BORDER><TR><TD>
<TABLE>
<TR>
<TD><INPUT NAME="color" TYPE="radio" VALUE="red">
</TD>
<TD>Red</TD>
</TR>
<TR>
<TD><INPUT NAME="color" TYPE="radio" VALUE="green">
</TD>
<TD>Green</TD>
</TR>
<TR>
<TD><INPUT NAME="color" TYPE="radio" VALUE="blue">
</TD>
<TD>Blue</TD>
</TR>
</TABLE>
</TD></TR></TABLE>
</TD>
</TR>

<TR>
<TD ALIGN="right"><STRONG>Movies I liked:</STRONG>
</TD>
<TD>
<TABLE BGCOLOR="#CCCCFF" BORDER><TR><TD>
<TABLE>
<TR>
<TD><INPUT NAME="movies" TYPE="checkbox"
VALUE="Blade Runner"></TD>
<TD><EM>Blade Runner</EM></TD>
</TR>
<TR>
<TD><INPUT NAME="movies" TYPE="checkbox"
VALUE="Pulp Fiction"></TD>
<TD><EM>Pulp Fiction</EM></TD>
</TR>
<TR>
<TD><INPUT NAME="movies" TYPE="checkbox"
```

```
VALUE="Full Metal Jacket"></TD>
<TD><EM>Full Metal Jacket</EM></TD>
</TR>
</TABLE>
</TD></TR></TABLE>
</TD>
</TR>

<TR>
<TD ALIGN="right"><STRONG>When I grow up I want
to be a(n):</STRONG></TD>
<TD>
<SELECT NAME="grow_up">
<OPTION>Astronaut
<OPTION>Fireman
<OPTION>CGI programmer
</SELECT>
</TD>
</TR>

<TR>
<TD ALIGN="right"><STRONG>My opinion on cucumber
sandwiches is:</STRONG></TD>
<TD>
<TEXTAREA NAME="sandwiches" ROWS=5 COLS=20 WRAP="virtual">
</TEXTAREA>
</TD>
</TR>

<TR><TD COLSPAN=2> </TD></TR>
<TR>
<TD> </TD>
<TD><INPUT TYPE="submit"> <INPUT TYPE="reset">
</TD>
</TR>
</TABLE>

</FORM>
</BODY>
</HTML>
```

When displayed in a web browser, the form should look something like Figure 3-1.

The <FORM> Tag's ACTION Attribute

When an HTML form is submitted, the contents of all the form's fields are bundled up and handed off to whatever script is specified in the ACTION attribute of the <FORM> tag. In the previous example page, the form is handed off to a script called mail_form. cgi located in the same directory as the form itself.

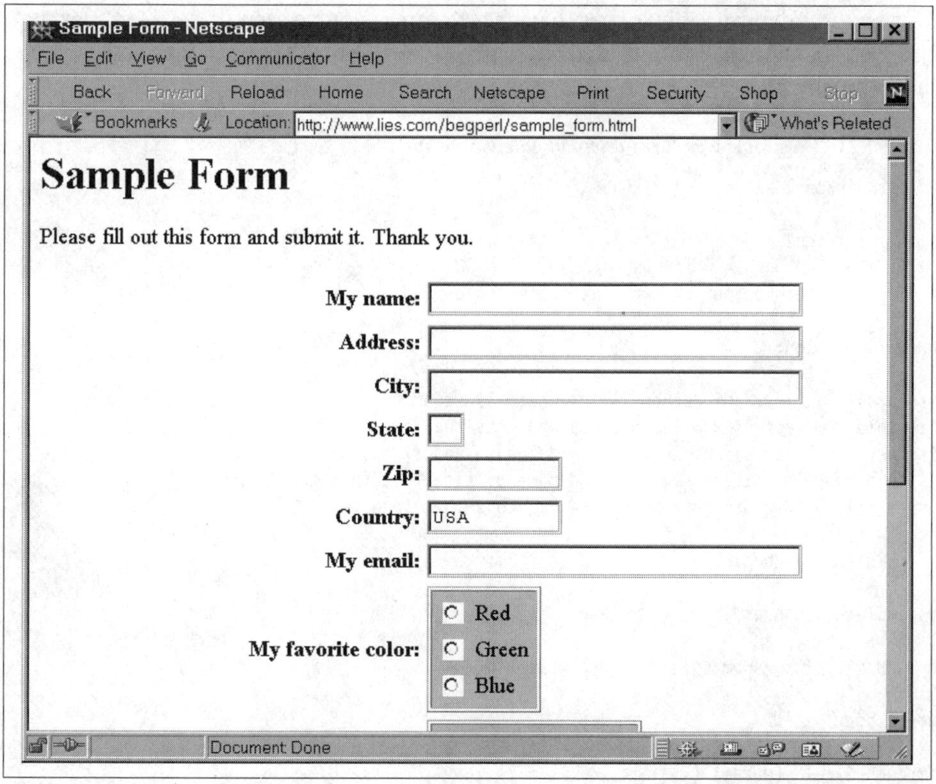

Figure 3-1. A form for testing a CGI form-to-email gateway

If you wanted to, you could have put some path information into the ACTION attribute and handed the form off to a script in a different directory. You could even have given a full URL (*http://www.somewhere.com/somepath/somescript.cgi*) and handed the form's contents off to a script on a completely different server. But I'm digressing. The point is, the ACTION attribute of the <FORM> tag is what determines where the form data goes when the form is submitted.

The mail_form.cgi Script

Example 3-2 shows a simple script that will take the output of a web form, bundle it up into an email message, and mail it off to someone. Go ahead and download this script from the book's online example repository, at *http://www.elanus.net/book*, and stick it in a suitable location on your web server. If you can execute CGI scripts anywhere, you can stick it in the same directory as your HTML form. If you need to put your scripts in a special location, stick it there, and then be sure to modify the ACTION attribute of the <FORM> tag to point to it properly. For example, if you needed to put the script in a top-level directory on your server called cgi-bin, you would edit the <FORM> tag to read: <FORM ACTION="/cgi-bin/mail_form.cgi" METHOD="POST">.

This script is considerably longer than the examples you've seen so far. Don't let that bother you, though. It's all relatively simple Perl, and I'll be explaining the whole thing, line by line.

Example 3-2. A simple web form-to-email gateway script

```perl
#!/usr/bin/perl -w

# mail_form.cgi

# bundle up form output and mail it to the specified address

# configuration:

$sendmail  = '/usr/sbin/sendmail'; # where is sendmail?
$recipient = 'forms@example.com';  # who gets the form data?
$sender    = 'forms@example.com';  # default sender?
$site_name = 'my site';            # name of site to return to after
$site_url  = '/return/path/here/'; # URL to return to after

# script proper begins...

use CGI qw(:standard);

# bundle up form submissions into a mail_body

$mail_body = '';

foreach $field (param) {
    foreach $value (param($field)) {
        $mail_body .= "$field: $value\n";
    }
}

# set an appropriate From: address

if ($email = param('email')) {
    # the user supplied an email address
    $email  =~ s/\n/ /g;
    $sender = $email;
}

# send the email message

open MAIL, "|$sendmail -oi -t" or die "Can't open pipe to $sendmail: $!\n";

print MAIL <<"EOF";
To: $recipient
From: $sender
Subject: Sample Web Form Submission

$mail_body
EOF
```

Example 3-2. A simple web form-to-email gateway script (continued)

```
close MAIL or die "Can't close pipe to $sendmail: $!\n";

# now show the thank-you screen

print header, <<"EOF";
<HTML>
<HEAD>
<TITLE>Thank you</TITLE>
</HEAD>

<BODY>

<H1>Thank you</H1>

<P>Thank you for your form submission. You will be hearing
from me shortly.</P>

<P>Return to
<A HREF="$site_url">$site_name</A>.</P>

</BODY>
</HTML>
EOF
```

Warnings via Perl's -w Switch

Let's go through the script section by section. First comes the usual top-of-the-script stuff, with one change—the shebang line now has a trailing -w:

```
#!/usr/local/bin/perl -w
```

As mentioned in Chapter 2 in the discussion of debugging, -w turns on Perl's *warnings* feature, which causes the script to complain to standard error if certain suspicious-looking things appear to be going on. We haven't bothered with it before this, since the other scripts so far have been so short and simple, but this one is complex enough that it's worth turning it on.

With that said, you should realize that Perl's warnings feature is mainly a tool to help you while you're writing the script. Once the script is written and working properly, there shouldn't be any warnings.

> Beginning with Perl Version 5.6.0, you can enable warnings by putting a statement that says use warnings; near the beginning of your script instead of using the -w shebang-line switch. If your version of Perl is recent enough to support it, the use warnings approach has some minor advantages over the -w switch, so you should probably use it. In this book I'll just be using the -w switch.

The Configuration Section

Next comes the script's configuration section:

```
# configuration:

$sendmail  = '/usr/sbin/sendmail'; # where is sendmail?
$recipient = 'forms@example.com';  # who gets the form data?
$sender    = 'forms@example.com';  # default sender?
$site_name = 'My Site';            # name of site to return to after
$site_url  = '/~myname/';          # URL to return to after
```

Each line stores some text in a scalar variable. Later on in the script, we will use these variables to plug the text they contain into various places. We do the initialization of the variables up at the top of the script, though, because that makes it easy to modify the script later on if something needs to be changed.

And in fact, you need to do some modifying of this section right now because each value is just for illustration purposes. You will need to replace the strings inside the single quotes on the right side of each assignment with a string that makes sense for your own web server. I'll be walking you through each configuration variable in turn.

The first line in the configuration section is where you give the location on your system where the Unix sendmail program can be found. The script will use this information later on to send the message containing the form data. Use the which command in the shell to find out where on your system sendmail is located (or the whereis command, if which is not supported on your system; see Chapter 2):

```
[jbc@catlow jbc]$ which sendmail
/usr/sbin/sendmail
```

Once you've located sendmail, you can put the full path inside the single quotes on the right side of the equal sign to assign it to the $sendmail variable:

```
$sendmail = '/usr/sbin/sendmail';
```

Calling the variable $sendmail doesn't do anything special within Perl, by the way. Perl doesn't know how you are planning to use this variable, and just treats it as a storage location. You could call it $mail_program_location or $walnuts or anything else you wanted (as long as the variable began with a $ followed by a letter or an underscore character), but $sendmail is concise and easy to remember, which will make life simpler later on. In general, you should work on choosing good names for your variables, with "good" defined as "likely to make sense to a future maintainer of the code."

A growing number of ISPs are replacing sendmail on their systems with qmail, a program that has some distinct advantages over sendmail in the areas of security and reliability. qmail typically includes a drop-in sendmail replacement that allows existing programs written to use sendmail to continue working properly.

The next configuration line lets you set the email address you want the form contents mailed to. If you have an email address specifically for receiving the submissions of this form, use that. Otherwise, just use your own email address. Stick the address inside the single quotes on the righthand side of the assignment, replacing the forms@example.com from the example.

Some form-to-email-gateway scripts that I've seen, by the way, let you set this address in the form itself, where it is stored as a hidden form field. The thinking with this is that it will be easier for nonprogrammers to adapt the script for their own use because they won't have to monkey with the script itself in order to send the form output to their particular email address. But this turns out to be a really bad idea from a security standpoint because anyone on the Internet can then hijack your script by invoking it with a form that has a bogus email address stored in it. This is how unsuspecting webmasters find themselves getting visits from the Secret Service after some practical joker uses their script to send threatening email to the President.

The next configuration line lets you set a default value for the email's From: header. Assuming that the user filling out the form supplies an email address, the script will replace the variable's contents with that address later on, but you put a default value in it for now in case the user doesn't supply one. It probably makes sense to fill in the same address here as you filled in for the $recipient variable.

Finally, you have two variables ($site_name and $site_url) that are used to construct a link for the user to click on in the "Thank You" page displayed after the form submission has been processed. Typically, you would replace this with an appropriate link label and an appropriate path (from the web server's perspective) to take the user to whatever page you think would make sense. For example, if you were to leave these two configuration lines as given in the example, the script would construct a link in the "Thank You" page that looked like this:

```
Return to <A HREF="/~myname/">My Site</A>.
```

Note that if $site_url contains a relative rather than an absolute path, the resulting link will be relative to the location of the script (which is what delivers the "Thank You" page) rather than the form. This wouldn't make any difference if both form and script were in the same directory, but if the script was somewhere else (in a cgi-bin directory, for example), it *would* make a difference.

Invoking CGI.pm

After the configuration section of the script comes the following line:

```
use CGI qw(:standard);
```

This is where you work the CGI.pm magic. In effect, what you are doing with this line is adding a whole bunch of prewritten Perl code to your script. That code arrives in the form of some new functions that your script now has access to for doing various

CGI-related things. As I mentioned earlier, I'm not going to explain that process in detail here. In a few minutes, though, you'll see how easy this makes it to process the submitted form elements received by the script.

foreach Loops

The next part of the script introduces one of those things that seem really obvious to programmers, but can cause nonprogrammers some confusion until they figure out what's going on. I'm talking about *loops*. In this case, a loop created with Perl's foreach function.

The idea with a loop is to make a block of programming code that performs a specific set of actions, then feed it a series of thingies for processing. It's somewhat like an assembly line, and like an assembly line it's really efficient for the programmer because she has to write the code block only once, but can easily make the program run thousands or millions of thingies through it. The illusion of power this produces is part of why people become addicted to programming and stay up all night debugging code.

Anyway, here's the next chunk of code from the script, showing the foreach loop in action:

```
# bundle up form submissions into a mail_body

$mail_body = '';

foreach $field (param) {
    foreach $value (param($field)) {
        $mail_body .= "$field: $value\n";
    }
}
```

First off, we assign the empty string (that is, nothing) to a scalar variable called $mail_body. You're probably thinking that's a somewhat silly thing to do, and you're right, it is rather silly, at least from the perspective of the behavior of the script. If the $mail_body variable had previously existed in the script and had contained something already, this line would actually do something because it would empty out the contents of the variable. But this is the script's first mention of the $mail_body variable. Why bother assigning the empty string to it?

It's a question of style. I didn't always appreciate this point when I was just starting out as a programmer, but it's an important one. As a beginning programmer, you're often going to feel like it takes everything you've got just to get the darn program to work, and that you can't spare any extra energy making it pretty or elegant. But the fact is, when you are writing a program you are writing it not just for the computer that will run it. You are writing it for the human beings who will have to read it and make sense of it down the road. That's what comments are for, but it goes beyond comments. For a human being reading your script, that line where you assign the empty string to the $mail_body variable is useful because it makes it clear, without requiring a scan back through the script, that this variable is starting off empty as we enter the foreach loop that follows.

Let's look at that loop now. The next line in the script looks like this:

```
foreach $field (param) {
```

The (param) in that line is a bit of CGI.pm magic that produces a list of the names of all the form fields submitted to the script. You'll learn more about this magic later; for now, just be sure to invoke it exactly as given here, and you should be okay.

Putting foreach $field in front of all that means we're going to step through the block of code that follows for each field name, with the name being stored in the $field variable each time through the block. This sets up our assembly line.

The opening curly brace ({) at the end of that line matches up with the closing curly brace (}) four lines later to define the block of code that's going to be executed each time through the loop. That is, all the code inside that pair of curly braces is where the assembly-line action takes place.

I encourage you to indent your scripts carefully when defining blocks of code, to help you keep track of your curly braces. Making all your curly braces match up correctly is one of the hardest things about programming. Programmers won't tell you that, though, because they want you to think that what they do is much darker and more mysterious.

To make things more interesting, there's another foreach loop nested inside the first one. It takes each field name and uses another bit of CGI.pm magic (param($field)) to produce a list of the submitted values corresponding to that field name.

I did it this way, by the way, instead of assuming that each field name would have only a single corresponding value because of the possibility of multivalued form fields. If the form has a checkbox group, for example, one field name can have several different values associated with it. Using this "inner" foreach loop, I can process each value individually.

Finally, at the heart of all this foreach'ing, we have the one line of Perl that does the actual work:

```
$mail_body .= "$field: $value\n";
```

At first glance it looks like you're just assigning the current field name and value (followed by a newline: \n) to a variable called $mail_body. That's true; that's what you're doing, but with a difference. Instead of using the normal assignment operator (=), you're using the concatenation assignment operator (.=), which means that you're appending the stuff inside the quotes to the end of whatever is already in the $mail_body variable. If you used the = operator, you would actually be replacing whatever was in the $mail_body variable each time you assigned to it, and when you got done looping through all your `foreach`'s all you would have in $mail_body would be the last "$field: $value\n" pair. With the .= operator, you're building up a $mail_body variable that contains all your submitted form data, with each "field: value" pair on a separate line.

if Statements

The next section of the script introduces another common programming construct: the `if` statement. An `if` statement is similar to the `foreach` loop we just looked at, in that it allows you to do something special with a block of code. An `if` statement allows you to make execution of the code conditional upon the outcome of a test.

Another term for an `if` statement is a *conditional statement*. Conditional statements in Perl look like this:

```
if (test) {
    do something...
}
```

Other, fancier versions of Perl's conditional statements look like this:

```
if (test) {
    do something...
} else {
    do something else...
}
```

or this:

```
if (test) {
    do something...
} elsif (another test) {
    do something else...
} elsif (yet another test) {
    do some other something else...
} else {
    do still some other something else...
}
```

and so on. The trickiest part for beginners (besides getting all those curly braces in the right place) is understanding how Perl evaluates those (test) statements for "truth." To understand that, see the accompanying sidebar titled "True or False?"

Here are some examples that demonstrate conditional tests in action. The following chunk of Perl will print true! because the test evaluates to the number 1, a true value:

```
if (1) {
    print "true!\n";
} else {
    print "false!\n";
}
```

True or False?

The basic rule Perl uses for figuring out whether the *logical test* inside the parentheses at the beginning of an if block is true is as follows.

If the stuff inside the parentheses evaluates to (in programmer-speak, *returns*) the number 0, or the string "0", or the *empty string* (which you'll sometimes see written as ''), or an *undefined value*, it's *false*. In all other cases, it's *true*.

If you put a scalar variable inside the parentheses, it just returns whatever value (if any) it contains, and the expression's truth value is determined based on that. If you stick an *array* variable inside your logical test, however, something interesting happens. A logical test, it turns out, supplies something called a *scalar context*. You'll be learning more about scalar context later on, but for now all you need to know is that when you evaluate an array variable in a logical test, what ends up being evaluated for "truth" is not the list of elements that the array contains. Instead, what gets evaluated is the *number* of elements the list contains. This in turn means that if your logical test contains an array variable, and if that array variable contains any elements at all, it's going to return a positive number, which will be *true*.

This leads to the following (possibly counter-intuitive) result:

```perl
$walnuts = 0;      # scalar variable containing the
                   # number 0

@rutabagas = (0); # array variable containing a
                   # single list element:
                   # the number 0.

if ($walnuts) {
    print "Scalar was true.\n";
}

if (@rutabagas) {
    print "Array was true.\n";
}
```

If you run this chunk of code, it will print out:

```perl
Array was true.
```

This happens because although the $walnuts scalar variable returns the number 0, which is false, the @rutabagas array contains a single element, which means that in a logical test it returns the number 1, which is true.

The following chunk of Perl will print false! because the test evaluates to the number 0, a false value:

```perl
if (0) {
    print "true!\n";
} else {
    print "false!\n";
}
```

The following chunk of Perl will print true! because Perl evaluates the test ($walnuts) by replacing the variable with whatever has been assigned to it (the number 1, in this case):

```
$walnuts = 1;
if ($walnuts) {
    print "true!\n";
} else {
    print "false!\n";
}
```

Likewise, the following chunk of Perl will print false! because $walnuts evaluates to the number zero (0), which is false:

```
$walnuts = 0;
if ($walnuts) {
    print "true!\n";
} else {
    print "false!\n";
}
```

The following chunk of Perl will print false! (as long as the $rutabagas variable has not had something assigned to it previously in the code) because $rutabagas has not been defined yet, and so it evaluates to the undefined value, which is false:

```
$walnuts = 1;
if ($rutabagas) {
    print "true!\n";
} else {
    print "false!\n";
}
```

Here's a tricky one. This next example demonstrates a bug I've accidentally introduced into my own scripts at least a dozen times. See if you can spot it:

```
$rutabagas = 0;
$walnuts = 1;
if ($rutabagas = $walnuts) {
    print "true!\n";
} else {
    print "false!\n";
}
```

Did you fall for it? This chunk will print true! It does so because what is happening inside the parentheses is an assignment operation, in which the contents of the $walnuts variable is being assigned to the $rutabagas variable. When an assignment takes place inside the (test) parentheses, Perl evaluates to true or false based on the value of whatever it was that got assigned. In this case, the number 1, which had been previously assigned to $walnuts, was assigned to $rutabagas, and therefore the test evaluated to true.

The trick here was that you might have thought that the line:

```
if ($rutabagas = $walnuts) {
```

means the same thing that it does when you read it in English; i.e., "if the contents of the $rutabagas variable is equal to the contents of the $walnuts variable, then…" There is a way to do that sort of test, returning true if two values are equal to each other, but that's not what we actually did here. Remember, the = operator in Perl is the assignment operator; it just takes whatever is on the right side of it and sticks it into whatever is on the left side of it.

The way to write a test to see if two things are numerically equal is to use the special logical operator: ==. That's right: two equal signs next to each other. This tests for *numeric equality*. You would use it like this:

```
$rutabagas = 0;
$walnuts = 1;
if ($rutabagas == $walnuts) {
    print "true!\n";
} else {
    print "false!\n";
}
```

which, this time, would print false! because the value in $rutabagas is not numerically equal to the value in $walnuts.

You can use lots of other logical operators to do lots of other nifty sorts of tests, but we don't need them for the current script, so I'm going to give you a rest and not explain them in detail. If you're curious, though, Table 3-1 gives a brief summary of the more commonly used ones.

Table 3-1. Commonly used logical operators

==	!=	Numeric equality, inequality
eq	ne	String equality, inequality
<	>	Numeric less than, greater than
lt	gt	String less than, greater than
<=	>=	Numeric less than or equal to, greater than or equal to
le	ge	String less than or equal to, greater than or equal to
and, or, not		Mean more or less what you think they do
(	)	Can be nested inside the test parentheses to group logical elements. For example:
		`if (($john eq 'smart') or (($john eq 'rich') and ($fred eq 'smart')))` `{ do something }.`

Anyway, let's return to the form-to-email script. Now we're going to look for a submitted form field named email, and if it's there, use it for the From: address that we'll stick on the emailed copy of the submitted form contents:

```
# set an appropriate From: address

if ($email = param('email')) {
    # the user supplied an email address
```

```
    $email =~ s/\n/ /g;
    $sender = $email;
}
```

Notice how we've used the CGI.pm magic of param('email'), which returns the contents of the submitted form field named email, and assigned the returned value to a variable named $email. That assignment is performed inside a logical test's parentheses, so if we assigned something with a true value, the test will return true. In that case, we replace the default value previously assigned to the $sender variable with whatever the user supplied. This will be used to construct a From: address on the mailed copy of the submitted form contents, allowing the recipient to reply to that email in order to send a message back to the person who filled out the form.

An experienced programmer would probably notice the following subtle problem in this code: it assumes that the submitted email parameter, if it is there at all, will be true. It's possible, though, that the user could submit the number 0 in that field, which would evaluate to false. Later, you will learn ways to construct fancier logical tests to avoid problems like that. For now, though, in the interest of simplicity, we're just going to use this version, and accept that practical jokers will be able to trick the script into treating their submitted email address as nonexistent, even if they did, in fact, submit something.

One other bit of cleverness appears in the following line:

```
    $email =~ s/\n/ /g;
```

This line causes any newlines in the submitted email parameter to be replaced by space characters. Doing that is a good idea because otherwise someone could trick your script into sending email to the President after all, by submitting an email address that consisted of their actual email address, followed by a newline, and then a string like CC: president@whitehouse.gov.

Anyway, the =~ operator in the previous line is a way to connect a variable to a *substitution* operation. The substitution operation (s/\n/ /g) in turn is based on Perl's *regular expressions*, which I'm not going to talk about now, but which will figure quite prominently in later chapters. For now, trust me that it does what I said it does.

Filehandles and Piped Output

Now take a look at the next section of the script:

```
# send the email message

open MAIL, "|$sendmail -oi -t" or die "Can't open pipe to $sendmail: $!\n";

print MAIL <<"EOF";
To: $recipient
From: $sender
Subject: Sample Web Form Submission
```

```
$mail_body
EOF
```

```
close MAIL or die "Can't close pipe to $sendmail: $!\n";
```

Previously, when you wanted to have your program output something, you just used Perl's print function. When you use print from within a Perl program, whatever you print goes to your screen (if you were running the script from the shell) or to the remote user's web browser (if you were running the script as a CGI script, and had output a suitable CGI header beforehand). In each case you were printing to what Unix users call *standard output*, or STDOUT, which is the default destination that the print command prints to.

You don't have to print to STDOUT, however. You can also send our output somewhere else using something called a *filehandle*. Doing so is a three-step process:

1. Open the filehandle.
2. Print to the filehandle.
3. Close the filehandle.

The most common use for printing to a filehandle is to let your script store its output in a file. What we're doing here involves a less-common use: using a filehandle to send the script's output to another program so that the other program can do something special with it. In this case, your script is sending its output to the Unix sendmail program, so sendmail can, well, send some mail.

Programmers call this *piping* your output to another program, and the symbol that represents it in the command for opening the filehandle is the vertical bar (which on my keyboard is the character I get when I type a shifted backslash, above the keyboard's Enter key). The character (|) looks something like a pipe, which I assume is where the name comes from. Here's the command in which you "open a pipe" to sendmail:

```
open MAIL, "|$sendmail -oi -t"
    or die "Can't open pipe to $sendmail: $!\n";
```

Here you have Perl's open function, then the name of the filehandle (by convention, filehandle names should be ALL CAPS), followed by a comma and a quote-delimited string containing the pipe symbol, and then the name of the command you want to pipe your output to. In this case, you're piping to the path and command name you previously stored in the $sendmail variable, along with some -oi -t command-line switches that you need to supply to sendmail. You can use man sendmail to find out what those command-line switches do if you're curious. Otherwise, just be sure to include them, and don't worry about it.

die Statements

Oh, and that or die... thing. It's a really, really good idea to stick an or die... statement like this in your Perl script every time the script is trying to open a filehandle or execute an external command of some sort. You should do this because these sorts of actions represent weak links in your script, where something can easily go wrong even though the script itself is functioning properly. Let's say you get your script working and everything's going great, but then someone comes along and moves the sendmail program on your Unix server, such that Perl can't find it when it tries to open this pipe. Without an or die... statement, Perl will try to open the pipe, fail, and continue on as if nothing had happened. You, and the users of your CGI scripts, will never know there's something wrong—except that you won't be getting any emailed form submissions.

With the or die... statement there, however, the script will try to open the pipe, and when it fails the script will execute whatever comes after the or, which in this case means the die statement. The die statement makes the script stop dead in its tracks and print an error message. That message is printed to a special place called *standard error*, which actually means it prints to your screen in the case of scripts you run from the command line, or to the web server's error log in the case of a CGI script. The error message that gets printed there is whatever comes after the die statement, so by making it a meaningful message like Can't open pipe to sendmail you make life a lot easier for whomever has to track down and fix the problem. The $! you have included in the error message, by the way, is a special Perl variable that contains the text of whatever specific error message was returned by your system when Perl tried to do whatever it was that failed.

A CGI script that "dies" in this fashion can cause the user at the other end to receive an error message (a 500 error, for example, if the script hasn't output its CGI header yet), which you might think is a bad thing. Realistically, though, it's better for your script to blow up in a dramatic fashion, rather than pretending everything is okay when it really isn't.

You can't count on web users to let you know about problems like this, by the way, even if your 500 error message displays an email address and a request that they contact you. In my experience at least 90–95% of web users will just leave if they encounter an error like this. It's really up to you to scan through your server's error log from time to time to make sure nothing weird is showing up in there.

Outputting the Message

We open the pipe to sendmail, then print to that filehandle by using the print function followed by the name of the filehandle we want to print to (MAIL). (Notice, by the way, how you don't use a comma after the name of the filehandle. Sticking a comma there is a common mistake.)

```
print MAIL <<"EOF";
To: $recipient
From: $sender
```

```
Subject: Sample Web Form Submission

$mail_body
EOF
```

Here we are printing out some header fields that sendmail expects to see. We use the value from the script's configuration section (as stored in the $recipient variable) for the To: header, and either the value from the configuration section, or the submitted form data we replaced it with, for the From: header. We print a blank line, then finish up with the message body that was previously stored in the $mail_body variable.

Finally, we close the filehandle:

```
close MAIL or die "Can't close pipe to $sendmail: $!\n";
```

I threw an or die... statement on the close statement, by the way, more out of habit than because this script is ever likely to fail at that point. I never used to bother doing the or die... thing on close statements, until the day my ISP's disk filled up and a script I had created to automatically rewrite a big chunk of my web site went happily about its business, opening filehandles to all the site's files and printing updated content to them, then failing (silently) when it tried to close the filehandle and got a "disk full" error. The end result: a site full of empty (that is to say, deleted) files and a new habit of mine of checking the success or failure of my close statements.

The last part of the script just delivers a "Thank You" HTML page that will display to the user after the form has been processed. The code for that part looks like this:

```
# now show the thank-you screen

print header, <<"EOF";
<HTML>
<HEAD>
<TITLE>Thank you</TITLE>
</HEAD>

<BODY>

<H1>Thank you</H1>

<P>Thank you for your form submission.
You will be hearing from me shortly.</P>

<P>Return to <A HREF="$site_url">$site_name</A>.</P>

</BODY>
</HTML>
EOF
```

There are three interesting things about this. The first interesting thing is how we've used the header function (which was imported from CGI.pm) to produce the CGI header for the script, rather than typing out all that Content-type: text/html stuff. A simple print header handles that task, including printing out the required blank line.

The second interesting thing is how we're giving the print function more than one thing to print, using a comma to join the elements into a list. I'm embarrassed to tell you how long I had been using the print function before I realized you could do that.

The final interesting thing we've done here is to use the `$site_url` and `$site_name` variables defined at the beginning of the script to create a link that can be used to leave the "Thank You" page. As mentioned previously, if you use a relative path in the `$site_url` variable, that path will end up being evaluated relative to the directory where the CGI script resides, not the HTML form that submitted to it.

Testing the Script

Once you have created the HTML form, created the script, and checked the permissions on everything, there's nothing left to do but fill out the form and submit it. If everything works right, you should get the "Thank You" screen, which in my case looked like Figure 3-2.

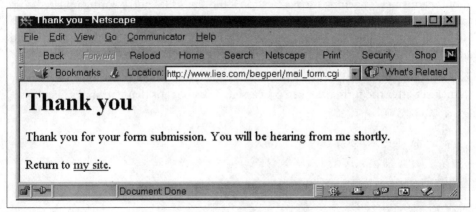

Figure 3-2. The "Thank You" page delivered by mail_form.cgi

A few minutes later, if you check your email, you should have a message like this waiting for you at whatever email address you specified in the configuration section's `$recipient` variable:

```
Subject: Sample Web Form Submission
   Date: Wed, 23 Sep 1998 15:00:34 -0700
   From: "John Callender" <jbc@west.net>
     To: forms@example.com

name: John Callender
address: 1234 Any St.
city: Anytown
state: CA
zip: 91234
```

```
country: USA
email: jbc@west.net
color: blue
movies: Blade Runner
movies: Pulp Fiction
movies: Full Metal Jacket
grow_up: CGI programmer
sandwiches: They're actually not bad if you use lots of peanut butter.
```

The body of that email, again, will consist of the names and values of all the fields in the HTML form submitted by the web user, which the script stored in the $mail_body variable before printing it out to the email message.

If this doesn't work for you (and it probably won't the first time), get busy checking your error logs and testing your script from the command line and doing all the other things you need to do to track down and eliminate your bugs.

There's one more thing I should mention about trying to run mail_form.cgi from the command line. Once you've got the script in good shape, such that the Perl interpreter is happy with the syntax (that is, you've got all the curly braces in the right place and so on), you might see this weird-looking message:

```
[jbc@andros begperl]$ mail_form.cgi
(offline mode: enter name=value pairs on standard input)
```

What's that offline mode:… message? It is a CGI.pm debugging tool. CGI.pm is written to detect if it is being run from the command line, rather than from a web server. In that situation, it gives you a chance to input data on the command line to correspond to the data that would have been received from an HTML form if the script were being run as a CGI script. In other words, after getting the preceding message, you could type the following into your shell window:

```
Name=John Callender
Address=1234 Any St.
City=Anytown
```

And so on. When you finished inputting name=value pairs, you would type Control-D (which you might see abbreviated as ^D in some places), after which your script would go ahead and run the way it would have if it had received all that data via a form submission.

 If you are testing a CGI.pm-using script on a Windows machine, the key sequence to signal the end of your input would be Control-Z (^Z), as opposed to the Control-D (^D) you use under Unix.

And there you have it: a simple CGI script that actually does something useful. Namely, bundling up and emailing the contents of a web form submission.

CHAPTER 4

Power Editing with Perl

This chapter presents an example of how powerful Perl is at automating repetitive tasks. It features a pair of scripts designed to rename, and then make minor editing changes to, a collection of HTML pages. Along the way, this chapter discusses how to use the shell's globbing feature to create a list of filenames matching a wildcard pattern, how to read and manipulate a file's contents from within a Perl script, and how to write a modified version of a file back out to disk. It also gives you your first detailed look at Perl's pattern matching and substitution operators, and the powerful regular expressions that are at their heart.

Being Careful

Science-fiction author and programmer Neal Stephenson has written a great essay called "In the Beginning Was the Command Line" (*http://www.cryptonomicon.com/beginning.html*). The most memorable part of the essay is Stephenson's description of the Hole Hawg, a drill made by the Milwaukee Tool Company. The Hole Hawg is strictly for professionals; it apparently is capable of boring a hole through almost anything, and bears the same relation to the standard homeowner's electric drill that such a tool bears to a preschooler's plastic toy. In Stephenson's metaphor, the Hole Hawg represents Unix, the operating system that does exactly what you tell it to, swiftly and mercilessly, regardless of whether you know what you're doing.

Perl takes this principle even further, which is where its characterization as the "Swiss Army chainsaw" of programming comes from. In this early phase of your work with Unix and Perl, try to remember that you're working with the Hole Hawg and the Swiss Army chainsaw. To the extent that you can cultivate some healthy paranoia, you'll save yourself lots of trouble later on. Look carefully at the command you are about to execute before you press the Enter key. As you are building your programs, have them start small, doing simple, nondestructive things, and do your best to verify that they actually are doing what you intended them to do, *before* you unleash their full power.

Another piece of advice that bears repeating is: keep good backups. Using the techniques described in this chapter without having a recent backup on hand is like doing a high-wire act without a net: definitely not recommended, especially for beginners.

Renaming Files

In this chapter, we're going to pretend we're working on a web site that was developed by someone working in a Windows environment (where filenames are case-insensitive, and HTML files typically get .htm filename extensions). Now, however, that site has been moved to a Unix web server, and you wish to make the following changes:

- Rename all the .htm files so that the filenames end with .html.
- Change the filenames (some of which feature uppercase letters) so that they are uniformly lowercase.
- Modify all the HREF attributes contained in those pages so that they match your changes to the filenames.

If you had only a few files to deal with, you could just do all this manually. Filenames could be changed one at a time using the Unix mv (for "move") command, which has the effect of renaming the file whose name is given in its first argument to the name given in its second argument:

```
[jbc@andros testsite]$ mv Index.HTM index.html
```

You could then edit the HREF attributes of each file in a text editor, changing <A HREF="Index.HTM"> to <A HREF="index.html">. And so on.

But what if you have a *lot* of files that you want to manipulate? At a certain point, the effort of manually making all those changes (and policing the errors that will inevitably creep in as you grind your way through this boring task) is going to be less than the effort of writing a tool to make the changes for you. At this early stage in your education that break-even point will come later (since creating the tool will be a slower process than it will be later on), but you can think of the effort involved as an educational investment that will pay you back many times over in future productivity gains. The plodding, manual approach offers no such promise of future rewards.

In any event, let's get started.

Globbing

Here's an ls listing of a directory containing some of those mixed-case filenames:

```
[jbc@andros testsite]$ ls
Clinton.JPG         Hello_CGI.htm      Sample_Form.htm
Form_to_Email.HTM   Hello_Command.HTM  guestbook_email.htm
Guestbook.HTM       NEXT.HTM           index.htm
```

The first thing to do is figure out how you're going to feed all those filenames to your Perl script so that it can do its modifying. There are many ways to do that, but the method you're going to use here is a feature of the Unix shell called *pathname expansion*, or, more colloquially, *globbing*.

If you come from a Windows background, you're probably familiar with the use of an asterisk (*, pronounced "star") as a wildcard character when specifying a filename. The asterisk stands for "any number of characters, including no characters" when specifying a filename. This legacy of the DOS command-line environment shows up in dialog boxes' `Filename` fields, where you sometimes see things like *.doc to represent "all filenames ending with the characters .doc", or *.* to represent "all filenames whatsoever."

DOS/Windows filenames are divided into two parts: the filename itself and a three-character extension, with the period character (., pronounced "dot") serving as the separator between the two parts. Unix filenames don't feature the notion of a filename extension, at least not in the formal sense that DOS filenames do. You're free to stick a .plx or .txt or .walnuts on the end of your Unix filenames, but the operating system doesn't care that you've done so. You can also stick multiple periods in a filename, so you could have a file called this.filename.has.lots.of.dots.

Why am I carrying on about this? For only one reason: in DOS or Windows, the wildcard sequence that allows you to specify "every filename whatsoever" is *.*. In Unix, it's just *. Let's try it out now.

> The statement that * stands for "every filename whatsoever" in Unix and Unix-like systems isn't quite accurate. Files whose names begin with a single period are "hidden," and won't be matched by a * wildcard sequence. To match those names, you would need something like .* ("dot star").

You may not have realized it before this, but you can supply a filename as an argument to the `ls` command, in which case `ls` will list information about that file only:

```
[jbc@andros testsite]$ ls index.htm
index.htm
```

In fact, you can give a whole bunch of filenames, and `ls` will dutifully list just those filenames (or, more precisely, just those of the names that correspond to files in the current directory):

```
[jbc@andros testsite]$ ls index.htm Hello_Command.HTM guestbook_email.htm
Hello_Command.HTM  guestbook_email.htm  index.htm
```

Now, the tricky and cool part is that you can use an asterisk as a wildcard character, and it will be interpreted as "any character, or any number of characters, including no characters, that will match a filename in the current directory." So, as mentioned before, a * all by itself means "match any filename in the current directory at all" (except those starting with dots):

```
[jbc@andros testsite]$ ls *
Clinton.JPG        Hello_CGI.htm       Sample_Form.htm
Form_to_Email.HTM  Hello_Command.HTM   guestbook_email.htm
Guestbook.HTM      NEXT.HTM            index.htm
```

That's the same output we got with ls all by itself because ls's default behavior is to list all the files in the current directory, and that's (almost) the same thing as saying ls *.

> I said "almost" in the preceding sentence because of subdirectories. In this example no subdirectories were contained within the current directory. If there had been one or more subdirectories, and if those subdirectories' names did not begin with a dot (.), the output of ls * would have included the contents of those directories, which invoking ls by itself would *not* have done. That happens because the * matches the names of those subdirectories, which means the ls command would have received those subdirectory names as explicit command-line arguments, and when ls gets a subdirectory name as an argument, it displays the contents of that directory. If that sounded confusing, just ignore it until later, when it will make more sense.

But let's say we want to list only the filenames ending in .htm. We can just do this:

```
[jbc@andros testsite]$ ls *.htm
Hello_CGI.htm  Sample_Form.htm  guestbook_email.htm  index.htm
```

Hmm. There's that Unix case-sensitivity thing again: we only got the files with lowercase .htm filename endings. But what about those uppercase .HTM files? How can we list those along with the .htm ones? Well, one easy way to do it is by just adding *.HTM to the command's arguments, like this:

```
[jbc@andros testsite]$ ls *.htm *.HTM
Form_to_Email.HTM  Hello_CGI.htm       NEXT.HTM         guestbook_email.htm
Guestbook.HTM      Hello_Command.HTM   Sample_Form.htm  index.htm
```

If you think this wildcard-expansion thing is fun, see the accompanying sidebar, "More Fun with Shell Expansion," for even niftier tricks.

Now, a subtle but potentially very powerful point about all this is that it isn't actually the ls command that is expanding that * into a list of matching filenames. In fact, it's the shell that is doing so, and it is only after the shell has done the expansion that it hands off that list of filenames as the argument to ls. In other words, the ls command never sees the literal star (*) character. It only sees the list of filenames that are the result of the shell's expansion of *. This is powerful because you are not limited to using filename expansion only in the arguments to the ls command. You can also use it in the arguments to *any* command, including your own custom Perl programs.

In still other words, you can use the shell's wildcard expansion as a convenient, flexible way to hand off a list of specific filenames to your Perl program for processing.

More Fun with Shell Expansion

The accompanying text describes the use of the asterisk character (*) as a wildcard that stands for "any character whatsoever, including no characters" when doing pathname expansion in the arguments to a bash shell command. This is only one of many types of expansions that the bash shell can perform on your command-line arguments, though.

For example, a question mark (?) will be interpreted as a wildcard that matches exactly one character in a filename. That means you could list all the files in a directory that had names ending with a period followed by exactly three letters using something like this:

```
[jbc@andros jbc]$ ls *.???
```

Square brackets can be used to create something called a *character class*, which is a list of characters, any one of which can match at that point in a filename. Thus, to list all the files in a directory whose names begin with a lowercase a, b, or c, you could do something like this:

```
[jbc@andros jbc]$ ls [abc]*
```

If you put a hyphen inside a character class, you create a *range* of characters that includes all the characters from the one on the left side of the hyphen to the one on the right side of the hyphen. Thus, the following would list all the files whose names begin with a lowercase letter:

```
[jbc@andros jbc]$ ls [a-z]*
```

while the following would list all the files whose names begin with an uppercase letter:

```
[jbc@andros jbc]$ ls [A-Z]*
```

If you put a caret symbol (^) at the beginning of your character class, you turn it into a *negated character class*, which means it becomes a list of all the characters that *can't* match at that location. So, for example, the following would list only those files whose names do not begin with a lowercase letter:

```
[jbc@andros jbc]$ ls [^a-z]*
```

This is different from using the character class [A-Z] because there are many other characters besides the uppercase letters that the negated class [^a-z] would match (all the numerals, for example).

All the examples so far relate only to *pathname expansion*, or *globbing*, which is the shell's expansion of your command-line arguments to match existing filenames. The shell also does several other sorts of expansion, of which I'm going to mention two.

The first is *tilde expansion*. If you stick a tilde character (~) in your command-line arguments, the shell will try to expand it into the path to your home directory. Thus, the following would use the more command to print out to your screen the contents of the .bash_profile file in your home directory (assuming you have such a file), regardless of what directory you were in when you issued the command:

```
[jbc@andros testsite]$ more ~/.bash_profile
```

—continued—

The lone tilde expanding into the path of your home directory is actually a special case of the general way tilde expansion works, which is to expand the string ~username into the path of the home directory for username. Thus, if there is a user named joe on your system, and he has a file named walnuts.txt in his home directory, you can display that file by entering the following at the shell prompt (assuming joe has given you read permission to that file):

```
[jbc@andros jbc]$ more ~joe/walnuts.txt
```

The last sort of shell expansion I'm going to mention is called *brace expansion*. Brace expansion lets you create arbitrary strings of text that don't have to match any existing filename (though they can if you want; the shell doesn't care). To do brace expansion, you give an optional *preamble*, then a list of strings separated by commas and surrounded by curly braces, then an optional *postamble*, and the shell turns that into a list of words created by sticking each string inside the braces between the preamble and the postamble.

This is easier to demonstrate than it is to describe, so here's an example that uses the echo command (which is simply a shell command that prints its arguments out to your screen, followed by a newline):

```
[jbc@andros jbc]$ echo before{a,b,c}after
beforeaafter beforebafter beforecafter
```

This may seem fairly pointless, but in fact brace expansion can save you a lot of typing in certain situations. For example, suppose you want to use the more command to print out to your screen the contents of three files, all of which reside in the same directory, without having to switch to that directory first. You could type out the full pathname of each file in the arguments to more, or you could just type the pathname once, and use brace expansion to do the rest:

```
$ more /etc/httpd/conf/{access,httpd,srm}.conf
```

The shell will dutifully expand the command's arguments into the three full pathnames you wanted, separated by spaces:

```
/etc/httpd/conf/access.conf
/etc/httpd/conf/httpd.conf
/etc/httpd/conf/srm.conf
```

A Simple Renaming Script

Let's see a Perl program that renames all the files for you. We'll build the script from scratch, modifying things as we go along; see Example 4-1 for the final script:

```perl
#!/usr/bin/perl -w

# rename.plx - rename files so they end in '.html'

foreach $file (@ARGV) {
    print "got $file\n";
}
```

Let's look at this line by line. The first line is just the usual shebang line, with warnings turned on via the -w switch. As mentioned before, if you are using a Perl version equal to or later than 5.6.0, you can do the same thing with a use warnings statement at the beginning of your script. Next is a comment giving the name of the script and a brief description of what it does (or will do, once we're done creating it).

The next three lines contain a foreach loop. A foreach loop, you will recall, processes each element of an array variable or list, sticking the current item into the scalar variable whose name is given between the foreach keyword and the list, so that item can be accessed during the current trip through the loop.

In this case, the array being processed by the foreach loop is the special array @ARGV. What is the @ARGV array variable, you ask? Well, it turns out to be something special: every script gets it automatically every time it runs, and it contains a list of whatever words came after the script's name on the command line. We call these additional words *arguments*. So this foreach loop will run once for each of the script's arguments, storing the current argument in the variable $file and printing out each element in @ARGV via the print "got $file\n" statement. (Later, we'll stick the code for renaming the files inside this loop. But for right now, we'll print a message just to inform us that the foreach loop works.)

Now, remember that the argument list in @ARGV will reflect the result of wildcard expansion by the shell. So, running rename.plx in the directory from our earlier example and giving it an argument of *.htm results in the following output:

```
[jbc@andros testsite]$ rename.plx *.htm
got Hello_CGI.htm
got Sample_Form.htm
got guestbook_email.htm
got index.htm
```

Likewise, running it with an argument of *.htm *.HTM gives this:

```
[jbc@andros testsite]$ rename.plx *.htm *.HTM
got Hello_CGI.htm
got Sample_Form.htm
got guestbook_email.htm
got index.htm
got Form_to_Email.HTM
got Guestbook.HTM
got Hello_Command.HTM
got NEXT.HTM
```

Now that we've seen how to feed a list of filenames to a script and run a foreach loop that processes each filename, here's a modified version of rename.plx that actually renames files. (If you are creating this script yourself, though, please don't run it yet; we still need to add some safety features to it.)

```
#!/usr/bin/perl -w

# rename.plx - rename files so they end in '.html'
```

```
foreach $file (@ARGV) {
    $new = lc $file;
    $new = $new . 'l';
    rename $file, $new or die "couldn't rename $file to $new: $!";
}
```

The script is the same, except for the part inside the foreach loop's block. Let's look at that line by line.

First comes this:

```
$new = lc $file;
```

This takes the name of the current file being processed through the foreach loop, makes a lowercase version of it using Perl's lc function, and assigns that lowercase filename to a new scalar variable called $new.

```
$new = $new . 'l';
```

The next line takes that new, lowercase version of the filename and adds a lowercase letter l to the end of it, using the . ("dot") operator, which is also called the *string concatenation operator* because it joins, or *concatenates*, the string on its left with the string on its right, returning the concatenated string.

Because all we're doing with that concatenated string is storing it back into the $new variable, we can actually write this line a little more concisely using the special operator .= (which I guess you could pronounce "dot equals"). The .= operator has the effect of appending a string to the string currently stored in a variable, and then sticking the concatenated string back into that variable:

```
$new .= 'l';
```

Shortening $new = $new . 'l' into $new .= 'l' is a bit like using a contraction when speaking (e.g., saying "won't" instead of "will not"), and is one of those natural-language-inspired shortcuts in Perl.

Next comes the line that does the actual work:

```
rename $file, $new or die "couldn't rename $file to $new: $!";
```

Here, Perl's rename function is used to take the file named by $file and rename it to $new. If that rename operation fails, the or die part of the line kicks in, terminating the script and printing an error message that includes $!, the special variable containing the error message returned by the system when the operation failed. If the rename function succeeds, everything after the or gets skipped, so the script continues happily to the next pass through the foreach block.

Sanity Checking

Your assembly line appears to be ready to go. If you're impatient, you're probably anxious to run your script right now. Resist that impulse. This is the time to look things over carefully with a pessimistic eye, asking yourself what could possibly go wrong and trying to prevent any nasty accidents. Measure twice, cut once, and all that. Swiss Army chainsaw. Hole Hawg.

One potential concern with this script is that the assembly line doesn't have a quality control inspector. Every item mentioned in @ARGV gets an l appended to it, and then the script tries to rename a file from the old name to the new one. Now, we already discussed how you were planning to run this script with a carefully crafted argument of *.htm *.HTM, which would be expanded by the shell into a list of just the files you wanted, but consider what would happen if you accidentally invoked the script like this:

```
[jbc@andros testsite]$ rename.plx *
```

You could accidentally glob up files other than the ones you wanted, appending l's to their names, too. Bad idea. The answer (one answer, at least) is to put some new code in the foreach block that skips to the next file without doing the renaming if something doesn't look right. This is a simple example of a common programming practice called a *sanity check*.

For example, you might want to add a sanity check that excludes files from being renamed if an existing file already has the new name. You could do that by adding the following code just before the line where you rename the file:

```
if (-e $new) {
    warn "$new already exists. Skipping...\n";
    next;
}
```

This uses Perl's -e file test operator, which returns true if the filename given after it corresponds to an existing file. In this case, that means it returns true if $new (which contains the version of the filename with the 'l' added to the end) already exists. If that happens, this if block will execute, causing a warning to be printed via the warn function. The warn function is similar to the die function, in that it causes your script to complain to standard error (printing a message to your screen in the case of a script run manually, or to the web server's error log for a CGI script). Unlike the die function, though, warn lets your script continue running after that point.

After issuing the warning, the if block uses the next function to make your script jump immediately to the next item in the foreach loop, without executing the rest of the statements in the loop. In other words, it causes the script to skip the rename operation for this file.

Another sanity check would skip files that were anything other than "plain" files. This would prevent the script from renaming a file that actually was a directory, for example, or a *symbolic link*. (In Unix, a symbolic link is a special file that actually just points to some other file.) Here's how you could implement that sanity check:

```
unless (-f $file) {
    warn "$file is not a plain file. Skipping...\n";
    next;
}
```

This check uses Perl's -f file test operator, which returns true if the filename given in its argument corresponds to a plain file. We used unless here instead of if because we wanted to reverse the sense of the logical test. In other words, we wanted to execute the statements in the block only if the conditional test returned false rather than true. This is precisely what you get with unless.

We're on quite a roll with these sanity checks, but let's add two more before we stop. First, let's prevent files from being renamed if the original name doesn't end in .htm (or .HTM, or any other case-insensitive variation of that three-letter filename extension). Also, let's prevent files from being renamed if their names contain forward slashes. That way, at least on a Unix system (where forward slashes are used to separate the directory names in a path), the renaming will be confined to the current directory. To add these features, insert the following before the rename:

```
unless ($file =~ /\.htm$/i) {
    warn "$file doesn't end in .htm or .HTM. Skipping...\n";
    next;
}

if ($file =~ /\//) {
    warn "$file contains a slash. Skipping...\n";
    next;
}
```

These logical tests are very interesting. Both of them use the =~ operator to tie the $file variable to a pattern matching operator based on Perl's regular expressions feature. In each case, the pattern matching operator checks the name stored in the $file variable to see if it matches a particular search pattern, and returns a true value if it does or a false value if it doesn't.

Before continuing, let's talk about regular expressions and the associated pattern matching operators a bit more.

Regular Expressions

Regular expressions (which you'll sometimes hear me refer to as *regexes*) are extremely powerful. For a beginning programmer, though, they're almost *too* powerful; they can seem weird and scary and needlessly complicated. Still, you need to stick with them because they're important.

As I've said, regular expressions are a tool for matching (and, potentially, replacing) specific patterns in a string of text. If you've used the "Find" or "Search and Replace" function in a word processor, you have some idea of what regular expressions do, but Perl's regular expressions are much more powerful than that. Their rich (that is to say, confusingly complex) syntax allows you to specify with astonishing precision exactly what patterns you are looking for and what you want done to them.

In later chapters I'll be explaining more about regular expressions. For now, let's just look at a few examples to get an idea of how they work.

We'll start with the one that looks for filename extensions like .htm (or .HTM, etc.). The whole expression looks like this: /\.htm$/i. The first thing you need to be able to do is break the expression down into its component parts. As Figure 4-1 shows, there are four different parts to this expression: the opening delimiter (/), the search pattern (\.htm$), the closing delimiter (/), and an optional modifier (i).

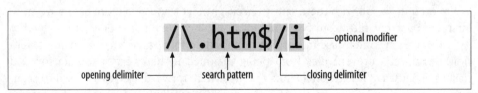

Figure 4-1. Parts of a simple regular expression

The delimiters are pretty straightforward: a slash to mark the beginning of the expression, and a slash to mark the end. The trailing modifier is easy to understand, too: this particular modifier (which you'll typically see referred to as the /i modifier) simply makes the expression match case-insensitively.

It's the regular expression pattern itself, the part between the delimiters, where the powerful magic hangs out. Regular expression patterns use their own specialized language, with lots of special rules and symbols. This pattern is actually fairly simple: \.htm$. Let's go through it piece by piece, from left to right.

First, the leading backslash-plus-a-period (\.) matches a literal period character. That should give you a hint: a period *without* a leading backslash does something special in a regular expression. I'm not going to tell you what that something special is until later, because I'd rather you used that part of your brain to remember the following helpful rule about regular expression patterns. An alphanumeric character (the characters A through Z, a through z, and 0 through 9) always just stands for itself. A nonalphanumeric character, though, can sometimes mean something special. About a dozen of these nonalphanumeric characters have special meanings inside a regex; I'll be introducing them as we go along.

Stick a backslash (\) in front of a nonalphanumeric character in your regex, though, and that special character will always revert to having its ordinary, literal meaning for matching purposes. That's what we've done in this pattern: we wanted to match a literal period, so we put a backslash in front of it.

The next three characters (htm) just match themselves. That is, they will match the literal characters h, and t, and m, one right after the other, in that order. Also, because of that trailing /i modifier, each will also match the uppercase version of itself, such that HTM (and hTM, and Htm, etc.) would all match, too.

Alphanumeric characters work in the opposite way from nonalphanumeric characters. What I mean is, an alphanumeric character always stands for itself, unless you put a backslash in front of it, in which case it gets some special meaning (like \n, which gives you a newline in a regex pattern, just like it does in a double-quoted string).

All of which brings us to the last thing in this pattern: the trailing $. It's not an alpha-numeric character, and it doesn't have a leading backslash, so that should give you a hint that it might be doing something special. And in fact it is: when a dollar sign ($) is used at the very end of a regular expression pattern, it means that the pattern that precedes it can match only if it occurs at the end of the string. In other words, the $ doesn't match anything itself, but it makes it so that the rest of the pattern can match only if it comes at the very end of the string being matched against.

So, in this particular example, our pattern will match a string only if that string ends with the literal sequence .htm (or .HTM, .HtM, or whatever). A string like this: 'this string has an .htm, but not at the end' would *not* produce a match with this particular pattern (but take out the $ at the end of the pattern, and it would).

Now let's look at the regex in the don't-allow-any-slashes sanity check: /\//. This expression is actually a good deal simpler than the first one. There's just an opening delimiter (/), the pattern itself (\/), and the closing delimiter (/). The pattern itself just matches a literal slash character, courtesy of the backslash in front of it. Without that backslash, Perl would think the slash in the pattern was actually the closing delimiter.

But for a simple pattern it sure *looks* confusing. The slash character doesn't have any special meaning in the regex pattern itself; it only has to be backslashed because of its role as the pattern's delimiter. It would be really nice if there was a way to use some other character to delimit the search pattern in this case, so we didn't have to backslash the slash. And, as it turns out, there is a way to do that: put an m (for "matching operator") in front of the expression, and then choose whatever we want for the delimiter. So, for example, that same regex could have been written as m#/#, or m|/|, either of which is arguably more readable than the original version. We also could choose a paired delimiter, like parentheses or braces, in which case the closing delimiter would be the closing member of the pair: m{/}. That one's my personal favorite, so let's update the code in fix_links.plx to use that version.

Summing up, the first of our regex-using sanity checks, which begins with this line:

```
unless ($file =~ /\.htm$/i) {
```

will fire off only if the filename in $file fails to end in the literal string .htm (or .HTM, etc.). The second of our regex-using sanity checks, which now begins with this line:

```
if ($file =~ m{/}) {
```

will fire off only if the filename in $file contains a slash character.

Running the Renaming Script

We could go on adding sanity checks all day, but I think we've been sufficiently paranoid for now. Now that the rename.plx script is finished, it should look like

Example 4-1 (which you can download from this book's script repository, at *http://www.elanus.net/book/*, if you want to play around with it).

Example 4-1. A script for renaming listed files to have lowercase filenames ending in .html

```
#!/usr/bin/perl -w

# rename.plx - rename files so they end in '.html'

foreach $file (@ARGV) {
    $new  = lc $file;
    $new .= 'l';

    if (-e $new) {
        warn "$new already exists. Skipping...\n";
        next;
    }

    unless (-f $file) {
        warn "$file is not a plain file. Skipping...\n";
        next;
    }

    unless ($file =~ /\.htm$/i) {
        warn "$file doesn't end in .htm or .HTM. Skipping...\n";
        next;
    }

    if ($file =~ m{/}) {
        warn "$file contains a slash. Skipping...\n";
        next;
    }
    rename $file, $new or die "couldn't rename $file to $new: $!";
}
```

Running it in our directory full of wackily named files, and using `ls` to look at the filenames before and after, results in the following:

```
[jbc@andros testsite]$ ls
Clinton.JPG         Hello_CGI.htm      Sample_Form.htm       rename.plx
Form_to_Email.HTM   Hello_Command.HTM  guestbook_email.htm
Guestbook.HTM       NEXT.HTM           index.htm
[jbc@andros testsite]$ rename.plx *.htm *.HTM
[jbc@andros testsite]$ ls
Clinton.JPG         guestbook_email.html  index.html  sample_form.html
form_to_email.html  hello_cgi.html        next.html
guestbook.html      hello_command.html    rename.plx
```

All the files whose names ended in .htm or .HTM have been renamed so that their filenames are uniformly lowercase and have .html extensions.

Modifying HREF Attributes

We're halfway there: we've modified all our filenames to be consistently lowercase and to end in .html. Now we just need to edit the HREF attributes of the links inside those HTML files to reflect those changes. To do that, we will need to write a new script that can open up each member of a list of files that is passed to it, make changes to that file, and save the changes back to disk.

Even more than the renaming-files example we just finished, this one exposes us to a real risk of accidentally doing bad things to our data. Again, please make sure you have a good backup before proceeding. Also, see the accompanying sidebar, "Parsing HTML with Regexes Considered Harmful," for a discussion of some of the limitations of the approach presented here.

Parsing HTML with Regexes Considered Harmful

The accompanying example shows how to use a simple regular expression to manipulate a collection of HTML files (specifically, to alter the HREF attributes in the files' <A> tags). Although I think it's a useful example (or I wouldn't be presenting it here), you should be aware of the inherent limitations of this approach.

In short, regular expressions, for all their power, simply can't do a good job of breaking down an HTML document into its component parts (a process called *parsing*). Among the things that are perfectly valid in an HTML document, but which tend to give simple regex-based parsers fits, are:

- Tags that continue across multiple lines
- Tag attributes that contain quoted angle brackets
- Tags "hidden" inside HTML comments

The accompanying example avoids some of these issues by simply looking for strings of the form HREF="something", but this opens an even larger can of worms because it simplistically assumes that any such string is actually part of an <A> tag, which, obviously, need not be the case. Further, real-world HREF attributes often have spacing on either side of the =, which this script doesn't account for.

As perlfaq9 (that is, the Perl documentation file you can read by entering man perlfaq9 in the shell) points out, in the section headed, "How do I remove HTML from a string?", the most correct way to parse an HTML document in a Perl script is to install and use the HTML::Parser module from CPAN. Unfortunately, you won't be learning how to do things like that until somewhat later in this book. For now, just be aware that the approach presented here, while it offers some distinct advantages compared to manually editing dozens or hundreds of HTML files, falls well short of being an ideal solution and could, in fact, result in accidental mangling of your data. Please be careful.

First Version of the fix_links.plx Script

Here is a script that represents a first step in altering this example site's HTML documents to match the filename changes made in the first half of the chapter:

```
#!/usr/bin/perl -w

# fix_links.plx

# this script processes all the *.html files whose names are supplied
# to it on the command line, replacing all HREF attributes
# that point to local resources in the current directory
# with rewritten versions that have:
#
# 1) '.htm' extensions changed to '.html', and
# 2) VaRiEnT captialization uniformly downcased.

foreach $file (@ARGV) {

    unless (-f $file) {
        warn "$file is not a plain file. Skipping...\n";
        next;
    }

    unless ($file =~ /\.html$/) {
        warn "$file doesn't end in .html. Skipping...\n";
        next;
    }

    if ($file =~ m{/}) {
        warn "$file contains a slash. Skipping...\n";
        next;
    }

    open IN, $file or die "can't open $file for reading: $!";
    while ($line = <IN>) {
        print $line;
    }
    close IN;
}
```

This script actually looks a lot like rename.plx, the last example we worked on. After an initial comment explaining what it does, it has a foreach loop that processes each filename passed to it in the command-line arguments. Inside that loop come some sanity checks that should look pretty familiar because they're based on those in rename.plx. You'll notice two slight differences in the second sanity check's regular expression pattern compared with the corresponding one in rename.plx: a literal l (the letter "L") has been added (so it looks for files ending in .html rather than .htm), and the /i modifier has been removed, such that only lowercase .html extensions will qualify.

Next comes the following line, which opens the $file currently being processed through the foreach loop, so the script can read it:

```
open IN, $file or die "can't open $file for reading: $!";
```

This is the standard Perl idiom for opening up a file in order to read its contents into your script. Perl's open function takes two arguments: a filehandle name (by convention, it should be ALL CAPS), and a string specifying both the name of the file you want to open and, optionally, a symbol specifying how you want to open it.

You saw in the last chapter how putting a pipe symbol (|) at the beginning of the filename string opened a pipe to an external program, such that printing to the filehandle sent the printed output to that program's standard input. Because the default behavior of the open function is to open the file for reading, though, and because opening the file for reading is exactly what you want to do in this case, you can dispense with the symbol and just give the filename, which is what this line does.

After the open statement is the all-important or die clause, to have the script die with an error message if the file can't be opened.

Reading from a File with a while Loop

So, we have a filehandle opened for reading. In order to actually read from it, we put the filehandle inside a pair of angle brackets, which causes Perl to return a line of data from the file. The way you typically do that in your Perl script is with a while loop, like the one that comes next in this script:

```
while ($line = <IN>) {
    print $line;
}
```

A while loop is sort of a cross between an if block and a foreach loop. Its general form is:

```
while (something) {
    do something;
    do some other something;
    do still some other something;
}
```

Like an if block, the part inside the parentheses is tested, and the block fires off only if the thing being tested returns a true value. Like a foreach loop, though, the script can execute the block multiple times. What happens is, after the conditional test (that is, the part inside the parentheses) returns a true value and the script makes its first trip through the block, the conditional test is evaluated again, and if it's still true, the block is executed again. And so on, *ad infinitum*.

Obviously, it could be a problem for your script if you put something in your while loop's conditional test that never became false. The number 1, for example, is always "true," so the following loop would in effect be a trap from which your script could never escape:

```
while (1) {
    print "hello, world!\n";
}
```

If you put this code in your script, it would simply print `hello, world!\n` over and over again, forever (or until you remembered that you can kill your script in mid-execution by typing `Ctrl-C` in the shell).

Let's take another look now at the line that begins this `while` loop, looking particularly at the logical test:

```
while ($line = <IN>) {
```

Perl looks at the return value of whatever is inside the parentheses in order to determine truth or falseness for the purpose of controlling the `while` loop. In this case, what is inside the parentheses is an assignment to the scalar variable `$line`. As Perl sees things, the return value of an assignment operation (that is, the thing that will be tested for truth) is whatever is assigned. So, what's being assigned? The output of `<IN>`, which, as I mentioned a few moments ago, is simply a line from the file previously opened for reading and associated with the filehandle `IN`.

Specifically, the line that is assigned is the "next" line because that is how the `<IN>` input operator works. The first time it is evaluated it returns the first line of the file, the next time it is evaluated it returns the next line, and so on, until the end of the file is reached, at which point it returns the undefined value, which is false, thereby terminating the loop.

In simpler language, the particular `while` loop shown here will run once for each line in the file, with the current line being stored in `$line` for each trip through the loop. In that sense it is somewhat analogous to running a `foreach` loop on an array consisting of all the lines in the file.

But wait. Some extremely clever and attentive reader out there is wondering about a special case. What if the file being read from contains a blank line, or a line consisting solely of the number 0? When a line like that is read and assigned to the `$line` variable, the `while` loop's test will be evaluating the empty string, or the number 0. Either of those will evaluate to false (because the empty string and the number 0 are both false, according to Perl), thereby terminating the loop before the entire file has been read. Won't that be a problem?

Well, no. That doesn't happen, and it doesn't happen because of a subtle fact about the input operator that you should try hard to remember because if you are anything like me you will fail to remember it many times during your Perl education, leading to some subtle bugs in your code. The reason an empty line, or a line containing only the number 0, doesn't cause the `while` test to fail is that the input operator doesn't just read and return the line itself. It also returns the newline that marks the end of the line. Or, more precisely, it considers that newline to be part of the line, and so returns it along with whatever came before it.

So you see, an empty line in the file isn't really empty. It consists of a newline, which is not the empty string, and isn't 0, and so is true, according to Perl. The same is true of a line containing just the number 0: it isn't just the number 0 (or the string `"0"`) that gets returned by the input operator; it's the 0 followed by a newline, and hence (again) is true.

If you run this new `fix_links.plx` script in the directory containing your HTML files, it will print out to your screen the contents of all the files specified in its arguments (or at least, all those that make it past the sanity checks). Pipe the command's output to the `more` command, and you can page through that output a screenful at a time until you get tired of doing so, when you can just type q to quit from the pager and return to your shell prompt:

```
[jbc@andros testsite]$ fix_links.plx *.html | more
<HTML>
<HEAD>
<TITLE>This is the title</TITLE>
</HEAD>
<BODY>
```

And so on.

Modifying Data with a Substitution Operator

Now that our script is successfully reading in the contents of the HTML files, we just need to assign those contents to a variable, rewrite any links in them that point to the newly renamed files, and print the rewritten contents back out to the file. To do that, we begin by adding the following line just before the line where we open the file for reading:

```
$content = '';
```

This sets a $content variable to contain the empty string, such that it will be emptied for each trip through the enclosing foreach loop.

Then, we delete the print statement from inside the while loop, and modify it so that it looks like this:

```
while ($line = <IN>) {

        # for HREF attributes pointing to the current directory,
        # downcase attribute, and rename '.htm' to '.html'

        $line =~ s/HREF="([^"\/]+\.htm)"/HREF="\L$1\El"/gi;

        $content .= $line;
    }
```

This new version of the while loop adds a search-and-replace operation, courtesy of Perl's *substitution operator*. The substitution operator, as you saw briefly in the previous chapter, has a search pattern just like a "regular" regular expression, except that it adds a *replacement string*, which is used to replace the part of the string that matched the search pattern. Figure 4-2 breaks this particular substitution operator down into its component parts.

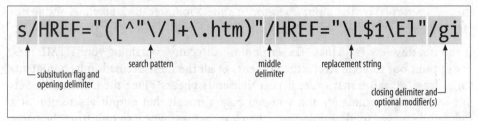

Figure 4-2. Components of a substitution operator

Notice how a delimiter is in the middle, between the search pattern and the replacement string. Notice also how any optional modifiers go after the final delimiter (that is, after the replacement string). When this substitution operator is run against the $line variable, which holds the current line being read from the current file, whichever part of the string in $line matches the search pattern will be replaced by the replacement string.

This substitution operator is designed to find all the strings of the form HREF="Something.HTM" in the file, and replace them with strings of the form HREF="something.html" (that is, downcasing the attributes and sticking an "l" on the end of the filename extension). So, let's see how it achieves that. After the initial s (which flags this as the substitution variety of regex) and the opening delimiter, we have the following search pattern:

```
HREF="([^"\/]+\.htm)"
```

This pattern looks a bit mind-boggling at first, but don't let that throw you. Like any regular expression pattern, it will eventually yield its secrets to a determined analysis. You just have to be patient and go through it carefully, one character at a time.

This pattern begins by matching the literal string HREF=". You'll notice that the non-alphanumeric characters = and " don't need to be backslashed; they don't mean anything special by themselves in a regex pattern. You *could* backslash them if you wanted to, just to be safe, and nothing bad would happen, but I haven't bothered.

Next comes a left parenthesis, which *is* a special character in a regex search pattern. It doesn't match anything in the string being matched against. Instead, it, along with its paired right parenthesis that comes later, serves to mark off a part of the expression for a *capturing* operation. This means that part of the string being matched against (the part corresponding to the part of the pattern enclosed by the parentheses) is going to be remembered and will be available later (in this case, in the replacement string we'll be looking at in just a moment).

The next part of the pattern is the following interesting-looking construct: [^"\/]. Those square brackets create something called a *character class* in the pattern. (If you read the sidebar titled "More Fun with Shell Expansion" earlier in this chapter, you might remember reading about character classes there. Perl's regex character classes work the same way.)

In essence, a character class is a list of characters, any one of which can match at this point in the pattern. For example, the class [abc] would allow any of the characters a, b, or c to match. Except that, just to make things interesting, this particular character class begins with a caret symbol (^). When a character class begins with a caret symbol, it becomes a *negated character class*. That is, it becomes a list of characters that *can't* match at that point in the pattern. To put it another way, using a negated character class is the same thing as using a normal character class containing all the characters except the ones actually listed in the negated class. So, this particular character class says, in effect, "match any character except a double quote or a forward slash." (The forward slash, you will notice, is escaped by a leading backslash, so it isn't interpreted as the end of the regex pattern. The double quote, though, doesn't need to be backslashed because it has no special meaning in a regex search pattern.)

After this negated character class comes a plus sign (+), which is a regular expression *quantifier*. A quantifier doesn't match anything by itself. Instead, it tells the expression how many of the immediately preceding item to match. The plus sign quantifier says "match one or more of the preceding item." Because the quantifier is "greedy," it will match as many characters as it can. In this case, the immediately preceding item is the negated character class, which means that this plus sign says, "match any of the characters allowed by the preceding character class. You have to match at least one of them in order for the expression as a whole to successfully match, but you should keep matching until you have matched as many as you can."

The next part of the pattern says to match a literal period (escaped by a backslash, to turn off its special meaning), then the literal characters htm. Then comes a closing parenthesis, which again is not meant to be matched literally, but instead ends the capturing operation begun earlier. Finally, at the end of the pattern is a literal double quote (which doesn't have to be escaped, though you could throw a backslash in front of it just to be safe if you weren't sure).

So much for the search pattern of this substitution regex. The second part, the replacement string, looks like this:

```
HREF="\L$1\E1"
```

This works pretty much like a regular double-quoted string. We've used a couple of interesting twists in this case, though. The first interesting thing is that we've used a special scalar variable, $1. This variable holds the part of the text string being matched against that was matched by the part of the regex pattern enclosed by parentheses. (If we had more than one pair of capturing parentheses in the search pattern, we could access the part captured in the leftmost-starting pair via $1, the next via $2, and so on.) Because the replacement string works like a double-quoted string, that variable will be interpolated, meaning it will be replaced by whatever is stored in the variable.

The second interesting thing we've done is to use the \L string escape sequence (which works in any double-quoted string, not just the replacement part of a substitution operator) to force all the text that comes after it to be lowercase. The \E escape sequence that comes later tells Perl to stop doing the lowercase thing; that is, it turns off the lowercasing previously turned on by \L. In this case that \E isn't really necessary because the only remaining characters in the string at that point are the lowercase l (an "L", not to be confused with the earlier numeral 1 in $1), and a double quote ("), neither of which would have been changed by \L's lowercasing behavior. Still, I figured it was good form to explicitly end the lowercasing with \E, so you'd see how that was done.

After the replacement string comes the final delimiter and the trailing modifiers, of which there are two in this case: the /g modifier and the /i modifier, both shoved together (the order doesn't matter). The /i modifier does the same thing it does in a normal, nonsubstituting regex: it makes the search pattern's alphabetic characters case-insensitive. The /g modifier does something interesting: it makes the substitution operation *global*, in the sense that after the first substitution has taken place, the substitution operator will continue looking for more places that match, and making more substitutions, until it has gone through the entire string. Without the /g modifier the substitution operator would perform its search and replace operation only once, at the first point in the string where it found a match, leaving the rest of the string untouched.

So, to review this substitution operation as a whole, here's what it does: it searches through the current line of the current file, looking for HREF attributes of the form: HREF="(something that includes no double quote or slash characters, and ends with .htm)". When it finds one, it captures everything from the double quote at the beginning of the attribute value to the one at the end of the attribute value, then replaces the entire thing with a version of itself that has a lowercase l appended to the end of the attribute value.

The requirement that the captured sequence contain no double quotes is just a way of making sure to capture the entire HREF attribute value (which this script assumes will always be delimited by double quotes), and nothing more. The requirement that the captured sequence contain no slash characters is a way of restricting this replacement operation to working only on HREF attributes that point to HTML files in the current directory. That is, the substitution operator will only modify attributes that don't contain a full URL (with a leading http://), and don't have any sort of path component pointing to a different directory. This way, your fix_links.plx script will not try to rewrite HREF attributes that point to files in other directories, or on other web sites. (Note that this will break on non-Unix systems that use something other than a forward slash as a directory separator.)

Returning to the disclaimers offered at the beginning of this chapter, this script is designed to work only in a particular set of circumstances. We've assumed that we only want to modify links pointing to files in the current directory. We've further assumed that all the links we are interested in rewriting are in HREF attributes delimited by double quotes, with no space, tab, or newline characters on either side of the = joining the HREF to the attribute value. Finally, we've assumed that there are no strings of this form in the files in question other than those actually in <A> tags. That's a lot of assuming, granted, but in these particular (hypothetical) circumstances, the script is good enough to get the job done.

Writing the Modified Files Back to Disk

Just one more component is needed in our power-editing script: the part where it takes the modified content from the HTML file and writes it back out to disk, replacing the previous version of the file. Before doing that, though, let's run a test by having the script print out the modified files to our screen, so we can check to make sure the correct changes are being made. Once we're satisfied with that, we can make the final modifications to the script that will cause it to actually update the files on disk.

Below the while loop that cycles through the reading of each file's contents, and below the close IN statement but before the right curly brace that ends the larger foreach loop that cycles through each file, we'll add the following to the script:

```
# print $content, to check the changes
print "File $file, after changes:\n\n$content\n";
```

Now you can run the script at the command line, piping its output to more, and page your way through the output, checking to make sure that only the changes you intended are being made:

```
[jbc@andros testsite]$ fix_links.plx *.html | more
File form_to_email.html, after changes:

<HTML>
<HEAD>
<TITLE>This is the title</TITLE>
</HEAD>
<BODY>
(etc.)
```

Once you're happy with the way that output looks, you can comment out that print statement and add the following lines just below it:

```
open  OUT, "> $file" or die "can't open $file for writing: $!";
print OUT $content;
close OUT            or die "can't close $file after writing: $!";
```

These three lines are very important. They represent the most commonly used method for taking data you have in your Perl program and printing it out to a file on disk.

The first line shows how to use the open function to create a new filehandle for writing to a file. The first argument to the open function is the name for the filehandle (by convention, ALL UPPERCASE); the second argument is a string containing the name of the file that you want to open, preceded by the > character.

The > character in the string is the part that tells Perl to open the file for writing. If the filename you specify in that string does not already exist, a new, empty file will be created as a result of the open statement. If the filename specified *does* already exist, any data it contains will be erased. (Unix folks say that the file's contents will be *clobbered*.) This clobbering happens as soon as the open operation is performed, before any data has actually been written to the file. So, obviously, you need to be very careful about opening files in this fashion, especially when those files contain data you care about.

Once you've opened the file for writing, printing data to the file is easy: you just use the print function, followed by the filehandle name, followed by the data you want to print. Again, as with the printing-to-sendmail example from the previous chapter, you need to remember not to put a comma after the filehandle name when printing to it.

Finally, we close the filehandle. Notice how we're checking for failure and having the script die with an informative error message if either the open or close operation fails.

The final version of this script is given in Example 4-2.

Example 4-2. A script for modifying HREF attributes

```
#!/usr/bin/perl -w

# fix_links.plx

# this script processes all the *.html files whose names are supplied
# to it on the command line, replacing all HREF attributes
# that point to local resources in the current directory
# with rewritten versions that have:
#
# 1) '.htm' extensions changed to '.html', and
# 2) VaRiEnT captialization uniformly downcased.

foreach $file (@ARGV) {

    unless (-f $file) {
        warn "$file is not a plain file. Skipping...\n";
        next;
    }

    unless ($file =~ /\.html$/) {
        warn "$file doesn't end in .html. Skipping...\n";
        next;
    }

    if ($file =~ m{/}) {
        warn "$file contains a slash. Skipping...\n";
        next;
    }

    $content = '';
    open IN, $file or die "can't open $file for reading: $!";
```

Example 4-2. A script for modifying HREF attributes (continued)

```
    while ($line = <IN>) {

        # for HREF attributes pointing to the current directory,
        # downcase attribute, and rename '.htm' to '.html'

        $line =~ s/HREF="([^"\/]+\.htm)"/HREF="\L$1\El"/gi;

        $content .= $line;
    }

    close IN;

    # print $content, to check the changes
    # print "File $file, after changes:\n\n$content\n";

    open OUT, "> $file" or die "can't open $file for writing: $!";
    print OUT $content;
    close OUT          or die "can't close $file after writing: $!";
}
```

And that's it! If you run this script in the directory containing the files to be modified, using a command-line argument of *.html, it will process each file in that directory whose names end with .html, checking all the HREF attributes and converting those that need it to using lowercase filenames ending in .html.

## CHAPTER 5

Parsing Text Files

If you've been working through the examples in this book in order, congratulations. You've now built up enough of a Perl vocabulary to begin doing really useful work. The extended example covered in the next two chapters is your reward: we're going to use Perl to build a potentially large collection of HTML pages from a set of structured text files. This chapter explains how to take the text files containing our source data and *parse* that data into its component pieces. The next chapter shows how to take that parsed data and use it to output a collection of HTML pages.

To keep things in perspective, we're still using pretty simplistic Perl. Many advanced Perl features are covered later in the book that will let us do this particular job faster, with the resulting code being shorter and cleaner. Just because we're still using baby talk, though, doesn't mean that what we're doing isn't extremely powerful. It is.

My toddler son has been working hard over the last 18 months to pick up a useful subset of English. At the time of this writing he can express preferences for different foods (saying "cacka?" to ask for a cracker, for example), choose among different leisure options ("pah?" to go to the park), and so on. To point out that he's not speaking in complete sentences or using a William F. Buckley vocabulary misses the point: he has made a huge leap from the nonverbal world he used to inhabit. In the same sense, the little bit of Perl you've picked up so far, plus the little bit more we cover in the next two chapters, is sufficient to give you a huge leap in the area of web content creation.

The "Dirty Data" Problem

Throughout my brief career creating commercial web sites, I've had to contend with the "dirty data" problem. There will be some sort of resource that a client or employer wants to put on the Web, and it's too big a job for the HTML to be coded manually (or rather, the potential payoff is too small to justify the required effort). Unfortunately, the source data isn't "clean" enough to be fed through one of those spreadsheet- or database-driven web authoring products that purport to relieve you of the hassle of hand-coding your HTML.

Perhaps the source data is in the form of a big, glossy marketing brochure with dozens of pages of product descriptions. Or maybe it's a product catalog, or an organization's member directory, or an archive of magazine articles. There's some sort of structure to the data, but not in the sense that it resides in or can be easily imported into a database. It may have started life in such a format, but it has since grown beyond that, getting additional information added to it, corrections made, and so on. Often, the most current version of the data is stored as a collection of word processing or desktop publishing documents; extracting a text-only version of the information is relatively easy, but that still leaves it a long way from being a useful collection of web pages.

Making things more complicated is the fact that the internal structure of the documents may be more of a guideline than a hard-and-fast rule. When you get your data from a real database, you can be reasonably sure that the structure is consistent. With word processing or desktop publishing documents, though, you depend on human beings for the consistency of the document structure, and human beings are notoriously fallible in that regard.

If you speak Perl, even Perl baby talk, however, the solution is easy. Because Perl excels at extracting information from arbitrarily formatted text files, it is a very efficient tool for parsing dirty source data. Perl's hash variables let you quickly build a data structure to hold the information you've extracted. Perl also makes it easy to recognize and flag problems in the data, so they can be corrected. Once everything is being read cleanly, Perl makes it easy to output the information as a series of HTML pages.

This chapter leads you through the creation of a web-based exhibitor directory for a fictional trade show: SprocketExpo 2000. Like many trade shows, SprocketExpo has a printed show directory that is distributed at the event, with each exhibitor getting a listing with contact information and a short descriptive blurb. Elsewhere in this exhibitor's directory are a brief alphabetical index and a list of exhibitors by product category. Our task is to create a web-based version of that directory.

Here's the sequence of steps we will follow to complete that task:

1. Meet with the trade show organizers to outline, in broad terms, the required features of the finished web-based directory.

2. Obtain a sample of the data files we will be parsing, examine the files carefully, and discuss their structure with the show organizers.

3. Create a Perl script to parse those data files, assembling the parsed data into a suitable data structure for use in producing the HTML pages later on.

4. Output a sample version of the parsed data, to confirm that everything is, in fact, being parsed correctly.

5. Make improvements to the script (or corrections to the data files) to fix problems with data being parsed incorrectly.

6. Modify the script so it outputs the actual HTML pages of the web-based directory.

Steps 1 through 5 in that list will be described in this chapter. Step 6 will be described in the next chapter.

Required Features

The organizers of SprocketExpo, as befits their role as fictional constructs intended only to provide a useful programming example, are unconcerned about the graphic design of their web site. A simple headline with the name of the show, and a few links along the left side of each page, will be sufficient for "branding" purposes.

They explain that the completed directory will need the following features:

- A top-level page displaying the total number of exhibitors, and the date and time when the directory was generated. This page will also need links to the alphabetical and category pages described next.

- A page for each letter of the alphabet, listing all the exhibitors whose names begin with that letter. The exhibitors' names on these pages will actually be links pointing to each exhibitor's detailed listing page.

- A page for each product and service category under which exhibitors have been classified. Each page will have a list of exhibitor names (with links to their detail pages) similar to those on the alphabetical pages.

- A detailed listing page for each exhibitor, showing the exhibitor's name, booth number, address, phone, fax, email, URL, and description. Also, each page needs to display a list of product and services categories this exhibitor is associated with, with that list consisting of links to the corresponding category pages.

Obtaining the Data

The data we will be working with is in the form of two text files used by Sprocket-Expo's production staff to create the directory's print version. The first data file, called exhibit.txt, contains the individual exhibitor listings (see Example 5-1). You can download this file (like all the examples in this book) from the book's web site, at *http://www.elanus.net/book/*.

 The example files given here contain fictional information for only a handful of companies. This will be sufficient to demonstrate how to use Perl to construct a web-based version of the listings. In the real world, of course, the source files would be considerably larger, with information on many more companies.

Example 5-1. The source data file exhibit.txt

```
ACME Fittings
Booth 104
1234 Industrial Way
```

Example 5-1. The source data file exhibit.txt (continued)

```
Carpinteria, CA 93013
(805) 555-4567
(805) 555-4568 (fax)
ACME Fittings has been manufacturing precision machined fittings for
more than 25 years. No job is too large, or too small.

Arlington Adhesives
Booth 724
7890 Avenue A
Washington, DC 20007
(202) 555-3456
(202) 555-3457 (fax)
Arlington is the right choice for all your adhesive needs.
The company offers a full line of medical-grade adhesive products,
including the patented Stick-Tight Sealant.

Best Glue Products
Booth 903
789 Windy Way
Suite 765
Chicago, IL 60608
(312) 555-2345
(312) 555-2346 (fax)
sales@bestglueprods.com
http://www.bestglueprods.com/

New York Fasteners
Booth 876
345 6th St.
New York, NY 10036
(212) 555-0987
(212) 555-0988 (fax)
sales@ny-fasten.com
http://www.ny-fasten.com/
Introducing the latest line of fastener products for today's widget
assembly market, New York Fasteners is the premium source for
connection technology.

Premium Parts Company
Booth 654
1234 Main St.
Anytown, CA 91234
(213) 555-1234
(213) 555-1235 (fax)
Premium Parts is a leading supplier of sprockets and zippers.
Specialties include green, red, and blue sprockets.

Very Small Parts Co., The
Booth 1278
4567 Western Way
New York, NY 10036
(212) 555-6789
```

Example 5-1. The source data file exhibit.txt (continued)

```
(212) 555-8765 (fax)
sales@verysmallparts.com
http://www.verysmallparts.com
The Very Small Parts Company will be exhibiting their full line of
sprocket technology, including the recently introduced AlsoSprachMaster
2000.
```

The second text file, category.txt, contains the information used to produce the directory's category listings. You can view category.txt in Example 5-2.

Example 5-2. The category.txt file

```
[[Adhesives]]
Arlington Adhesives, 724
Best Glue Products, 903
New York Fasteners, 876

[[Sprockets]]
Acme Fittings, 104
Premium Parts Company, 654
Very Small Parts Co., The, 1278

[[Zippers]]
New York Fasteners, 876
Premium Parts Company, 654
```

Before we start writing the Perl script that will process these data files, it is crucial that we have a good understanding of what is in them. In particular, it is important that we know about any exceptions to the rules governing the files' structure. Especially when we are dealing with very large data files, it is easy to make assumptions about their structure that occasionally turn out to be mistaken.

In our meetings with the SprocketExpo organizers, we listen carefully when they describe how the information is formatted, then restate what we know about it, giving the organizers a chance to correct us. We ask whether the information is going to be updated or modified in the future because we may be able to write our script in a way that minimizes the extra work involved in updating the web-based version.

Parsing the Data

Taking a look at exhibit.txt, we can see that it consists of individual company listings separated by blank lines. Within each company's listing, the same sequence of lines occurs: the first holds the company name, the next holds the booth number, the next holds the street address, and so on. By splitting up the file wherever we see a blank line, we can isolate individual companies' information. By counting lines within those sections, we should be well on our way to extracting the relevant data from the file. We can then use pattern-matching operators to help us identify the data contained in lines that otherwise would be ambiguous.

Example 5-3 shows our first version of make_exhibit.plx, the script that will do this parsing and HTML-page creation. It features several new Perl features you haven't seen before, but not to worry; we'll be going through them all one by one.

Example 5-3. First version of make_exhibit.plx

```perl
#!/usr/bin/perl -w

# make_exhibit.plx

# this script reads a pair of data files, extracts information
# relating to a group of tradeshow exhibitors, and writes
# out a browseable web-based directory of those exhibitors

use strict;

# configuration section:

my $exhibit_file = './exhibit.txt';

# script-wide variable:

my %listing; # key:   company name ($co_name).
             # value: HTML-ized listing for this company.

# read and parse the main exhibitor file

my @listing_lines = ( ); # holds current listing's lines for passing
                         # to the &parse_exhibitor subroutine

open EXHIBIT, $exhibit_file
    or die "Can't open $exhibit_file for reading: $!\n";

while (<EXHIBIT>) {
    if (/^\s*$/) {
        # this line is blank (or has nothing but space chars)
        if (@listing_lines) {
            &parse_exhibitor(@listing_lines);
            @listing_lines = ( );
        }
    } else {
        # this line actually has data
        push @listing_lines, $_;
    }
}

# process last batch of lines, if the file didn't have a trailing
# blank line to trigger it already.

if (@listing_lines) {
    &parse_exhibitor(@listing_lines);
}

close EXHIBIT or die "Can't close $exhibit_file after reading: $!\n";
```

Example 5-3. First version of make_exhibit.plx (continued)

```perl
# output parsed data for debugging

print "LISTINGS:\n\n";

foreach my $co_name (sort keys %listing) {
    print $listing{$co_name}, "\n";
}

# script proper ends. subroutine follows.

sub parse_exhibitor {

    # extract the relevant information about a particular
    # exhibitor and store it in the appropriate hash.
    #
    # invoked with an array of lines read from $exhibit_file.
    # has no return value, but instead modifies the following
    # script-wide variable:
    #
    # %listing

    my @lines = @_;

    my($co_name, $booth, $address, $address2, $phone, $fax, $email,
        $url, $description);

    my $line_count = 0;

    foreach my $line (@lines) {

        chomp $line;
        ++$line_count;

        if ($line_count == 1) {
            $co_name = $line;
        } elsif ($line_count == 2) {
            $booth = $line;
        } elsif ($line_count == 3) {
            $address = $line;
        } elsif ($line_count == 4) {
            $address2 = $line;
        } elsif ($line_count == 5) {
            $phone = $line;
        } elsif ($line_count == 6){
            $fax = $line;
        } elsif ($line =~ /^\S+@\S+$/) {
            $email = $line;
        } elsif ($line =~ /^http:\S+$/) {
            $url = $line;
        } else {
            $description .= "$line\n"; # append so that multiline
                                       # descriptions work right
```

Example 5-3. First version of make_exhibit.plx (continued)

```
        }
    }

    # done cycling through @lines.
    # create the %listing entry.

    $listing{$co_name} = <<"EOF";
co_name:   $co_name
booth:     $booth
address:   $address
address2:  $address2
phone:     $phone
fax:       $fax
email:     $email
url:       $url

description:
$description
EOF
}
```

Using strict and Scoping Variables

The first new-to-you Perl feature we've put in this program is found right up at the top, after the opening shebang line and comments:

```
    use strict;
```

This looks something like the use statements you've previously used to pull in an external module (like CGI.pm). In this case, though, the use is doing something slightly different: it's pulling in a *pragma*, which is basically a way for you to tell the perl interpreter that you'd like it to treat your program in some special way. By invoking the strict pragma, you're telling Perl that you are willing to be held to a higher standard than you otherwise would. In particular, you're saying that you are willing to *declare* all your variables before using them, rather than just having them spring into existence the first time they're mentioned.

This is an important step in your journey from Perl toddler to full-fledged programmer. Real Perl programmers use the strict pragma in all but the shortest scripts. Having to declare your variables before you use them seems like a bit of a pain, but it turns out to be a huge time-saver in terms of protecting you from subtle bugs.

The way you usually declare your Perl variables when working under strict is to put the word my in front of them the first time you mention them. It's like issuing a press release: here's my $walnut variable that I'll be using from now on. One of the ways this is helpful is that later on, when you accidentally refer to $walnuts, Perl will catch your mistake. Under the strict pragma, trying to access a variable that hasn't been declared yet is illegal; your script won't even run, but instead will die during the compilation phase with a message like `Global symbol "$walnuts" requires explicit package name at ./rutabagas.plx line 42`.

The other way in which my declarations are helpful is that they allow you to limit the visibility of your variables. Instead of being *global variables* visible from anywhere in your program, variables declared with my are visible only from the point of their declaration to the end of the *innermost enclosing block* (the stuff between a pair of curly braces). In other words, you work your way outward in your program from the point of the my declaration, and stop when you hit the first enclosing pair of curly braces. The point from the my declaration to the closing curly brace is the only part of the program where that variable will be visible. (It actually can get a bit more complicated than this. See the section headed "Private Variables via my()" in the `perlsub` manpage if you're curious.) Programmers call this the variable's *scope*.

Our first example of a my variable is the next thing in the `make_exhibit.plx` script:

```
# configuration section:

my $exhibit_file = './exhibit.txt';
```

Here we've got a configuration variable where we give the name of the data file holding the exhibitor information. We declare the variable with my here, at the variable's first mention, which satisfies the `strict` pragma's sense of propriety. Because we haven't actually entered any enclosing block at this point, the variable's scope is just the rest of the enclosing file; that is, it will be visible throughout the rest of the script.

Next we declare a hash variable named `%listing` that we will use to hold the formatted listing for each exhibitor in the trade show:

```
# script-wide variable:

my %listing; # key:   company name ($co_name).
             # value: HTML-ized listing for this company.
```

This variable will need to be visible throughout the whole script, which is why we've made a point of declaring it up here. And because it will be playing such an important role in the data structure we'll be creating, we give it a big comment, explaining that its keys will be company names, and its values the HTML-ized listings for those companies. (Actually, we're not going to bother adding HTML to the listings until a later stage of the script, but we've cheated in this case by writing a comment that won't have to be updated later.)

In naming hash variables, it's generally a good idea to name the variable for the *values* being stored, rather than for the *keys*. This ends up sounding more natural when using the hash. If you then stick the word "of" between the variable name and the key when reading something like $hash{key}, it helps to make the relationships clear. For example, the hash element `$listing{'ACME Fittings'}` can be read as "the listing of ACME Fittings".

The choice of company names for the keys to this hash (and for some other hash variables we'll be adding in a later version of the script) represents a crucial decision. We're going to be in big trouble later if it turns out that two exhibitors in the show both want to use the same name, or if slight variations exist in different occurrences of the same company's name in the data files. Fortunately, we made a point of discussing this with the show's organizers beforehand, and they assured us that such things absolutely will not happen.

Next comes the part of the script where we read in the contents of the file whose name is stored in $exhibit_file. But before we do that, we declare an array variable called @listing_lines:

```
# read and parse the main exhibitor file

my @listing_lines = (); # holds current listing's lines for passing
                        # to the &parse_exhibitor subroutine
```

As the accompanying comment indicates, this variable will hold the chunk of lines from the file that corresponds to a particular exhibitor. Once we've accumulated all of a particular exhibitor's lines in that array, we're going to pass it off to a *subroutine* for processing. More about that in just a moment.

Now we open the exhibitor file for reading, associating it with the EXHIBIT filehandle, and telling the script to die with an error message if the file can't be opened:

```
open EXHIBIT, $exhibit_file
    or die "Can't open $exhibit_file for reading: $!\n";
```

Nothing new there.

Using the Default Variable $_

Next, though, is a chunk of code that we're going to need to spend some time on. The code consists of a while loop that cycles through each line being read from the EXHIBIT filehandle, accumulating them in the @listing_lines array variable. When it encounters a blank line, the while loop hands the @listing_lines array off to the previously mentioned &parse_exhibitor subroutine for processing, then empties the array in order to begin the cycle again with the next company. Take a look at the code now, and then we'll talk about it in detail:

```
while (<EXHIBIT>) {
    if (/^\s*$/) {
        # this line is blank (or has nothing but space chars)
        if (@listing_lines) {
            &parse_exhibitor(@listing_lines);
            @listing_lines = ();
        }
    } else {
        # this line actually has data
        push @listing_lines, $_;
    }
}
```

The first thing you'll notice here is that the `while (<EXHIBIT>)` line doesn't actually assign the current line being read from the file to a variable (at least, not visibly). Previously, you would have used something like `while ($this_line = <EXHIBIT>)` to store the current line in a variable, so it would be accessible inside the loop. But in fact, Perl does that for you automatically, using a special scalar variable called `$_`. We haven't used this feature before because it can make things a little more confusing for beginners, but it's handy enough that I think it's worth confusing you with it now.

What makes it so handy is that Perl uses `$_` as the default variable for lots of operations, meaning you can write things very concisely if you play your cards right. That's what we're doing in the next line:

```
if (/^\s*$/) {
```

Here we're using a regular expression to test whether the current line being processed is blank. But as you can see, we haven't bothered to tie the search pattern to a variable with the `=~` operator. Instead, we've just put the regex inside the conditional test all on its lonesome, and Perl cleverly figures out that we actually want to run the regex against the contents of the `$_` variable.

This regex has a few interesting things going on in its own right. The initial `^` symbol is a special character that means whatever comes after it can match only if it occurs at the very beginning of the string. It's the opposite, so to speak, of the trailing `$` symbol, which means, as you may recall from the previous chapter, that whatever comes *before* it can match only at the very *end* of the string.

Please don't be confused by the fact that the `^` symbol means something completely different here, at the beginning of the search pattern, than it did the last time you saw it, when it occurred at the beginning of a square-bracket-delimited character class inside the pattern. Here it does the beginning-of-the-string anchor thing. At the beginning of a character class it does the negating-the-character-class thing. (The scary thing is, these sorts of hair-splitting distinctions will eventually seem quite natural to you.)

Now, the only thing inside that search pattern except for the `^` beginning-of-string anchor and the `$` end-of-string anchor is this: `\s*`. That backslashed s is a special symbol that matches any of several kinds of *whitespace*: a space, a tab, or a newline, basically. The asterisk (*) after it is a quantifier; it means the preceding item (the `\s`, in this case) can match any number of times from 0 to infinity. Like the 1-or-more plus-sign quantifier (+) that you saw in the previous chapter, the * is greedy. That means it will match as many times as it can, but unlike the +, the * lets its preceding item successfully match even when it's not there at all (that is, when the preceding item is present zero times).

So, putting the whole pattern together, `/^\s*$/` will match the current line from the file if and only if it is either completely blank, or consists only of whitespace characters like spaces and tabs. We could have used `/^$/` for our pattern, which, because it has the beginning- and end-of-string anchors together, would match only a truly blank line, with no whitespace. But we know from painful experience that so-called "blank" lines in human-edited text files have a way of accumulating sneaky little whitespace characters. As a result, we've chosen to use the more permissive /^\s*$/ pattern, so our script will have a better chance of recognizing the boundaries between different companies' data in the source file.

If that regex successfully matches, it means we've hit such a boundary, so we need to send the accumulated lines in @listing_lines to the &parse_exhibitor subroutine for processing. But first we check to make sure some lines actually are accumulated in @listing_lines, via the following if statement:

```
if (@listing_lines) {
```

Who knows; maybe the very first line of the file is blank, and we'll hit this code before we've actually accumulated any lines to process. If we *have* accumulated some data, though, that test will return a positive number (because, again, a logical test puts an array variable into a scalar context, causing it to return the number of elements it contains). That will make the if test true, which will cause the block to execute, meaning we'll run the following two lines:

```
&parse_exhibitor(@listing_lines);
@listing_lines = ( );
```

That first line is where we run the subroutine, which we'll be discussing in greater detail in just a minute. The second line empties out the @listing_lines array, which we need to do so that we're ready to start accumulating lines for the next company in the file.

The push Function

Finally, the last part of the while loop features an else block, which executes in cases where the earlier "is this line blank?" regex returned false. In other words, it executes for all lines that actually have data, and what it does is this:

```
push @listing_lines, $_;
```

This is your first exposure to Perl's very cool push function. You give push an array variable in its first argument, and then a list of one or more items in its subsequent arguments, and those items are added onto the end (or bottom, depending on how you visualize things) of the array. It's somewhat analogous to the .= operator we've been using to append text to the end of a scalar variable, in that it lets you take an existing array variable and add new items to it.

That's it for the while loop that reads data from the file. There's an interesting chunk of code that comes after it, though:

```
# process last batch of lines, if the file didn't have a trailing
# blank line to trigger it already.

if (@listing_lines) {
    &parse_exhibitor(@listing_lines);
}
```

As the comment explains, this will check after the file has been read in completely to see if any unprocessed lines are still hanging around in @listing_lines. This would happen if the file didn't have a blank line at the very end of it to trigger the submission of the last company's data to the &parse_exhibitor subroutine. I wish I could say I was smart enough to think of that without needing to spend a few minutes first, scratching my head over what was happening to the last company's data, but alas, I wasn't, at least not in this case. Live and learn.

In any event, the next thing in the script is the closing of the EXHIBIT filehandle:

```
close EXHIBIT or die "Can't close $exhibit_file after reading: $!\n";
```

There's nothing especially novel about that. Immediately following that is a section we've thrown in just for debugging purposes to print out the data accumulated in the %listing hash and to make sure the script is actually parsing that data correctly:

```
# output parsed data for debugging

print "LISTINGS:\n\n";

foreach my $co_name (sort keys %listing) {
    print $listing{$co_name}, "\n";
}
```

This uses a foreach loop to cycle through all the elements in the hash, using the keys function, which you haven't seen previously, to return a list of all the hash's keys. And we're using the sort function in front of the keys function to sort those keys into an appropriate order. By default sort puts the list of items in its argument into a case-sensitive alphabetical order, with uppercase letters sorting first, which works fine for our current purposes. Later, you'll learn how to use a fancier version of the sort function to do other kinds of sorting.

That's basically it for the main body of the script, as the next comment indicates:

```
# script proper ends. subroutine follows.
```

All that's left is the script's subroutine. Before we look at it in detail, though, let's talk about what a subroutine is and why you might want to use one. And in order to talk about *that*, we're first going to talk about the issue of *complexity*.

Managing Complexity

I said in an earlier chapter that making all your curly braces match up properly was the single hardest thing about programming. I was half joking, of course (you knew that, right?), but I was also half serious. I'm going to return to that issue now, but instead of talking about curly braces (which were really just a symptom), I'm going to talk about the underlying problem.

The underlying problem is *complexity*. To write a program that works, you need to build a model of it in your head, then re-create that model in functional form in your code. When the model gets too complex for you to hold all the pieces in your head at one time, you start to have problems. You have to pause, go back, and reacquaint yourself with what was going on in some other part of it. You have to check to see what name you used for a variable, or what untested assumptions might have been implicit in a regular expression you wrote. Parts of your code that you didn't think would interact with each other do interact, with unexpected consequences.

As a beginning programmer, things are made worse by the fact that you are juggling lots of extra complexity by virtue of your inexperience. Seasoned programmers don't have to devote their attention to remembering what open or keys or while does; they've internalized the meanings of those terms through long practice.

There is no "magic bullet" for solving the complexity problem. As you gain experience you will continue to struggle with it, although, to paraphrase Woody Allen, you will hopefully find yourself failing with a better class of problem. Managing complexity is a combination of many things: using the right approach to solve a particular problem (programmers call this "choosing the right algorithm"), making appropriate use of comments to document your code, and selecting appropriately descriptive variable names, for example. Another extremely helpful technique is the one we'll be discussing next: using *subroutines*.

Subroutines

The idea with a subroutine is to take a portion of your program that performs some particular task and separate it from the rest of your code. The subroutine becomes, in effect, a mini-program within the larger program. Whenever you want to run the subroutine you invoke it from the main program as if it were your own custom Perl function, possibly passing the subroutine some arguments that it needs in order to perform its particular task. If the same subroutine is going to be used more than once within your program, you get a big gain; you have to create the subroutine only once, as opposed to copying-and-pasting the same code all over your program. Even better, future changes to the subroutine's code have to be made in only one place.

Even if the subroutine is going to be called only once from within your program, though, it can still represent a gain in the battle against complexity if it helps make the main program cleaner, and hence more easily understood. In effect, you are taking a chunk of your program's complexity and stuffing it into a black box. As long as the black box does what it's supposed to do, and its *interface* (that is, the way your program interacts with it) is simpler than what's inside it, you come out ahead in the complexity battle.

A subroutine starts off with the word sub, then the name of the subroutine, and then a curly-brace-delimited block. The code inside the block is what will be executed when the subroutine is invoked. For example, here's a subroutine to perform a familiar task:

```
sub hello {
    print "hello, world!\n";
}
```

If you had that subroutine in your script, you could print a greeting by using the following line:

```
&hello;
```

A slightly fancier version of the &hello subroutine might look like this:

```
sub hello {
    my $greeting = $_[0];
    unless ($greeting) {
        $greeting = "Hello, world!\n";
    }
    print $greeting;
}
```

This version gives you the option of passing it an argument to customize the greeting that is printed. You could do that by invoking the subroutine like this:

```
&hello("Hey. What's new?\n");
```

That argument arrives in the subroutine via the special @_ array. In this case the subroutine was invoked with a single argument, which you access via $_[0], but if there had been more arguments (passed as a comma-separated list, normally) they would all be available in @_.

> Experienced Perl programmers frequently invoke their subroutines without a leading ampersand character (&), typically adding an empty argument list (as in hello( )) in cases where the subroutine isn't being given any arguments. This approach makes their code look a bit cleaner, along with having some other fairly subtle effects on how the subroutine behaves. For now, though, I'll be invoking subroutines using the & to help you tell the difference between user-defined subroutines (which will always have the ampersand) and built-in Perl functions (which won't).

You can put your subroutine definitions anywhere you like in your script, though it's common practice to put them down at the end in order to leave the main program uncluttered. Even if a subroutine isn't defined until the end of your script, it will still be visible and useable before that point. This happens because the perl interpreter sees the subroutine definition during the compile phase, which happens before your script is actually run.

The other thing I should mention about subroutines is this. Besides giving you the option of invoking them with one or more arguments, subroutines also can pass back one or more return values. Basically, the return value of the last expression evaluated in the subroutine is returned to the point where the subroutine was invoked. As a result, the following code would print out hellohellohello:

```
my $returned = &times_three('hello');
print $returned;
```

```
sub times_three {
    my $arg = $_[0];
    $arg . $arg . $arg;
}
```

We'll be seeing plenty of examples of using a subroutine's return values in later chapters. In this chapter, though, we won't be bothering with our subroutines' return values.

The &parse_exhibitor Subroutine

Now that you know how subroutines work, let's take a look at this &parse_exhibitor subroutine you've been hearing so much about. This is a fairly long subroutine, so I'm going to give it to you all at once, then go back over it line by line to explain what it's doing:

```
sub parse_exhibitor {

    # extract the relevant information about a particular
    # exhibitor and store it in the appropriate hash.
    #
    # invoked with an array of lines read from $exhibit_file.
    # has no return value, but instead modifies the following
    # script-wide variable:
    #
    # %listing

    my @lines = @_;

    my($co_name, $booth, $address, $address2, $phone, $fax, $email,
        $url, $description);

    my $line_count = 0;

    foreach my $line (@lines) {

        chomp $line;
        ++$line_count;

        if ($line_count == 1) {
            $co_name = $line;
        } elsif ($line_count == 2) {
            $booth = $line;
        } elsif ($line_count == 3) {
            $address = $line;
        } elsif ($line_count == 4) {
            $address2 = $line;
        } elsif ($line_count == 5) {
            $phone = $line;
        } elsif ($line_count == 6){
            $fax = $line;
        } elsif ($line =~ /^\S+@\S+$/) {
            $email = $line;
```

```
        } elsif ($line =~ /^http:\S+$/) {
            $url = $line;
        } else {
            $description .= "$line\n"; # append so that multiline
                                       # descriptions work right
        }
    }

    # done cycling through @lines.
    # create the %listing entry.

    $listing{$co_name} = <<"EOF";
co_name:   $co_name
booth:     $booth
address:   $address
address2:  $address2
phone:     $phone
fax:       $fax
email:     $email
url:       $url

description:
$description
EOF
}
```

It's good practice to start off subroutines, at least big ones, with a detailed comment explaining what the subroutine does, so that's what we've done here:

```
# extract the relevant information about a particular
# exhibitor and store it in the appropriate hash.
#
# invoked with an array of lines read from $exhibit_file.
# has no return value, but instead modifies the following
# script-wide variable:
#
# %listing
```

You're trying to let this subroutine act as a black box, which means you don't want to have to examine its guts later on if you can avoid doing so. That opening comment is your last line of defense against having to examine the subroutine's guts. At some point in the future you're going to be reading this script trying to figure out what this subroutine does. So give your future self a break by writing a detailed description now, so you won't have to figure it all out again later.

The first thing after the comment is the assignment of the @_ variable, containing the subroutine's arguments, to the @lines variable:

```
my @lines = @_;
```

These lines we're assigning are a chunk of lines from the exhibitor file, with all of them corresponding to a particular company. In general, it's a good idea to copy your subroutine's arguments into a named variable up at the top of the routine.

Notice, by the way, how this @lines variable has been scoped, via its my declaration, so it will be completely invisible outside of the subroutine.

As long as we're scoping variables, let's scope a bunch more, for use in holding the various pieces of information we're going to be parsing from the lines in @lines:

```
my($co_name, $booth, $address, $address2, $phone, $fax, $email,
    $url, $description);
```

Again, all these variables will be completely invisible outside of the subroutine, so there's no need to worry about accidentally using the same name as some other variable being used elsewhere in the script. Notice, by the way, how we can enclose the list of variables in parentheses, and just use a single my declaration outside the parentheses to declare the whole list.

Next, we declare a $line_count variable, set it to 0, and begin cycling through the lines in @lines with a foreach loop:

```
my $line_count = 0;

foreach my $line (@lines) {
```

Nothing unusual here, except for one thing: notice how we're using a my declaration on the $line variable, which will hold the current item from @lines for the current trip through the loop. If we use that "innermost enclosing block" rule to determine the $line variable's scope, we would think that the variable would be visible all the way to the end of the subroutine (since the my declaration comes before the foreach loop's initial curly brace).

Fortunately, Perl is smart enough to know that in this case, we actually want the variable to be scoped to the foreach loop. So that's the way it works: if you put a my declaration on the variable that will hold the current element for each trip through a foreach loop, the variable's scope extends only from the declaration to the end of the loop.

Next, the subroutine uses Perl's chomp function on $line. The chomp function removes the trailing newline from a string.

```
chomp $line;
```

 An older Perl function called chop removes the last character from a variable regardless of whether that character is a newline. chomp was introduced to avoid the problem of accidentally removing a character you actually cared about in cases where you tried to use chop on a line that was already missing its newline.

Next comes an interesting little operator: ++, the *auto-increment* operator. Stick that in front of a variable and it causes the variable's contents to have 1 added to them:

```
++$line_count;
```

Saying ++$line_count is the same thing as saying $line_count = $line_count + 1. In this case, bumping up the number stored in the $line_count variable by 1 is letting us keep track of which line we're on in the sequence of lines we're currently processing.

Next is an extended if-elsif section. You learned about this slightly fancier version of an if block back in Chapter 3, but this is the first time we've used it. In this case we're using it with the == operator (which is used to test for numeric equality) to assign the current value in $line to whichever variable seems to be appropriate, based on our earlier inspection of the sequence of lines in the exhibitor.txt file:

```
if ($line_count == 1) {
    $co_name = $line;
} elsif ($line_count == 2) {
    $booth = $line;
} elsif ($line_count == 3) {
    $address = $line;
} elsif ($line_count == 4) {
    $address2 = $line;
} elsif ($line_count == 5) {
    $phone = $line;
} elsif ($line_count == 6){
    $fax = $line;
```

So far so good. But after the fax line, we run into a problem. Our inspection of exhibit.txt has revealed that for the last three pieces of information in each company's section (email, URL, and description), we can't just count lines to tell what type of data we're getting. Some companies don't include an email address or URL in their information. Others don't include a description.

Perl to the rescue. Once we get past a $line_count of 6, we can use regular expressions to figure out what the current line contains. Here's the part of the if-elsif chain that does that:

```
} elsif ($line =~ /^\S+@\S+$/) {
    $email = $line;
} elsif ($line =~ /^http:\S+$/) {
    $url = $line;
} else {
    $description .= "$line\n"; # append so that multiline
                               # descriptions work right
}
```

We use the following pattern to check for email addresses: /^\S+@\S+$/. Reading the pattern from left to right, it anchors to the beginning of the string with ^, then uses \S, which is a special sequence that means "anything other than a whitespace character."

It was \s, with a lowercase s, you'll recall, that meant "any whitespace character" in a regex. You'll see more examples of this later, in which regexes use a backslashed lowercase letter to mean one thing, and the corresponding backslashed uppercase character to mean the opposite.

Continuing with this email-address-matching regex, there is a plus sign (+) quantifier on the \S, which makes it match one or more times. Next there is an "at" sign (@), which has no special meaning in this regex, and so doesn't require a backslash. Then comes another one-or-more-nonwhitespace-characters construct (\S+), and finally a dollar sign (\$) as the end-of-string anchor. Taken together, the regex will match any line that begins with one or more nonwhitespace characters, has a literal @, then one or more nonwhitespace characters, with nothing else before the end of the line.

Now, that's a pretty naïve way of trying to match email addresses. There are plenty of perfectly valid ways of specifying an email address that would not be matched by that expression, and plenty of other data lines that might show up at this point in the file (a URL, for example), that *could* match the expression. In the real world, you might well want to spend some more time making this expression smarter so as to exclude those possibilities.

For now, though, we're going to leave it as is, and go on to the next expression, the one intended to match URLs: /^http:\S+\$/. This one requires that the string being matched against begin with a lowercase http:, then have one or more non-whitespace characters going all the way to the end of the line. Again, it's a pretty naïve approach to matching URLs, and could easily run afoul of something like a multiline description that happens to have a URL on its last line. But again, it's good enough for the current example, with the proviso that in the real world you might want to spend some more time on it.

After the two elsif blocks that use those regexes to look for email addresses and URLs, the extended if-elsif section ends with a final else block that simply takes any lines that haven't matched any of the previous conditions and appends their contents to the \$description variable. This reflects our analysis of the exhibit.txt file, where we saw that companies' descriptions tend to run for several lines. We make sure to add the chomped \n back on at the end when doing this appending, so we don't end up accidentally joining the last word of one line to the first word of the next. And that's it (for now) for our parsing operation. We end the subroutine by taking the data gathered during that if-elsif block and assigning it to the script-wide %listing array, keyed by the company's name:

```
    # done cycling through @lines.
    # create the %listing entry.

    $listing{$co_name} = <<"EOF";
co_name:   $co_name
booth:     $booth
address:   $address
address2:  $address2
phone:     $phone
fax:       $fax
email:     $email
url:       $url

description:
$description
EOF
```

Eventually we'll be making that \$listing{\$co_name} entry prettier with HTML markup so that it can be used on the individual listing pages for the companies, but we can leave that step for later. For now we just store a plain-text version of each listing to help us in debugging the script.

Outputting Sample Data

It's time to run this first version of the script to find out how it does in parsing the exhibitor.txt data file:

```
[jbc@andros sprocketexpo]$ make_exhibit.plx | more
```

Figure 5-1 shows our ssh window just before we enter the command, and Figure 5-2 shows the window just after we enter the command. Strangely, even though we're piping the command to more (which is supposed to stop the output at one screenful), we get more than a screenful of text appearing in our window. The text scrolls by so fast that we can't read the first part. What's going on?

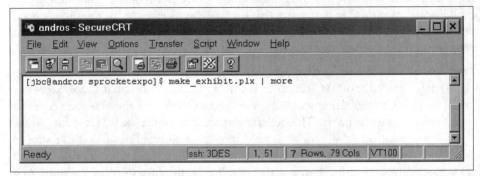

Figure 5-1. Preparing to enter the command make_exhibit.plx | more

What's going on is that reality is more complex than the mental model we were using. In brief, both the script's warnings and its conventional output are printed to our window, but the more command only sees the part that prints to standard output (the part from the print statements in the script). As a result, it pauses that output too late for us to see the stuff being printed to standard error (the part from the warn statements in the script). The accompanying sidebar, "Fun with Output Streams," explains how to use a little shell magic to make the merged output streams interact with more the way we were expecting them to. (Another solution, since the Secure-CRT ssh client has the capability to scroll back to see previous output, is to just scroll back to see the information that scrolled off the screen.)

However you manage to read the output, here's the first part of what make_exhibit.plx will print to your screen:

```
[jbc@andros sprocketexpo]$ make_exhibit.plx | more
Use of uninitialized value in concatenation (.) or string at
./make_exhibit.plx line 108, <EXHIBIT> line 9.
Use of uninitialized value in concatenation (.) or string at
./make_exhibit.plx line 108, <EXHIBIT> line 9.
```

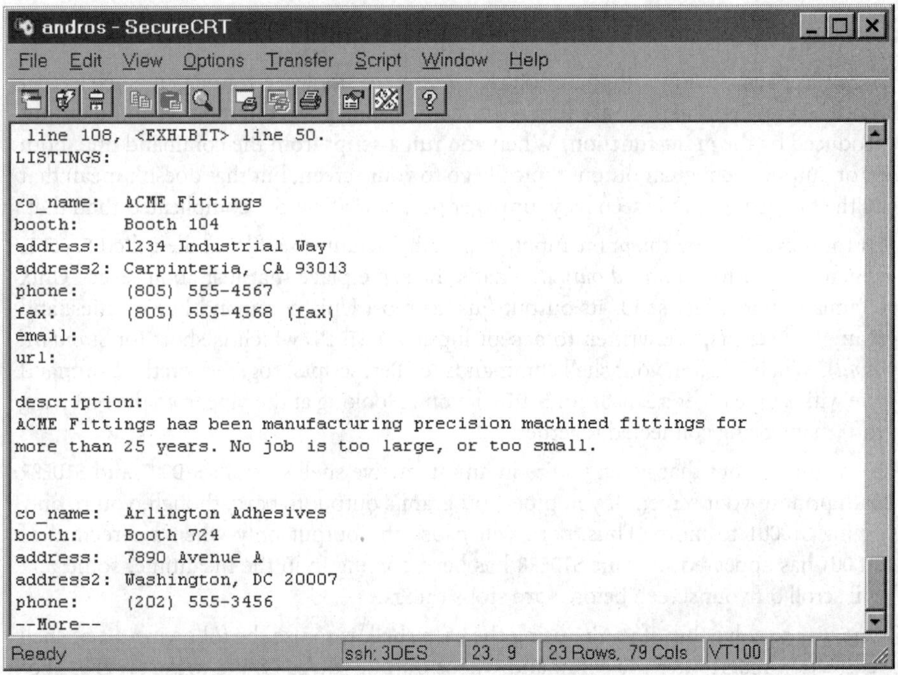
andros - SecureCRT
File Edit View Options Transfer Script Window Help
line 108, <EXHIBIT> line 50.
LISTINGS:
co_name: ACME Fittings
booth: Booth 104
address: 1234 Industrial Way
address2: Carpinteria, CA 93013
phone: (805) 555-4567
fax: (805) 555-4568 (fax)
email:
url:
description:
ACME Fittings has been manufacturing precision machined fittings for
more than 25 years. No job is too large, or too small.
co_name: Arlington Adhesives
booth: Booth 724
address: 7890 Avenue A
address2: Washington, DC 20007
phone: (202) 555-3456
--More--
Ready
ssh: 3DES
23, 9
23 Rows, 79 Cols
VT100

Figure 5-2. After entering the command shown in Figure 5-1, several lines of error output scroll off the top of the terminal window before more pauses the output

```
Use of uninitialized value in concatenation (.) or string at
./make_exhibit.plx line 108, <EXHIBIT> line 19.
```

We're getting these warnings courtesy of the script's `-w` shebang line switch. Checking the script to see what's on line 108, we see that that's the place in the `&parse_exhibitor` subroutine where we assign the multiline here-document-quoted string to `$exhibit{$co_name}`. Basically, Perl is complaining that some of the variables we're trying to interpolate into that string have not had any value assigned to them yet. This actually makes sense because some of the companies don't have an email address or URL that we can parse. When we go to store those listings, the attempt to interpolate `$email` and `$url` produces the previous warnings, since nothing has been assigned to those variables yet.

Notice, by the way, how the `my` declaration on those variables helps us. When we declare a variable with `my` inside a subroutine, Perl gives us a fresh version of that variable, completely invisible to the outside world *and* invisible to any other invocation of that same subroutine, each time the subroutine is invoked. Without this scoping behavior, we might have had old values, parsed from a previous company, when it came time to interpolate the `$email` and `$url` variables for a company that didn't provide those pieces of information.

Fun with Output Streams

As you've seen already with this book's CGI script examples, error output (such as that produced by Perl's `warn` or `die` functions) can go someplace different from the output produced by the `print` function. When you run a script from the command line, both error output and regular output typically go to your screen, but that doesn't mean that all the merged output is seen by your pager program. It's more complicated than that.

Output produced by the `print` function goes by default to a filehandle called STDOUT, which is short for *standard output*. That's the same place that just about every Unix command-line utility sends its output (just as most Unix command-line utilities, and many Perl scripts, are written to accept input via STDIN, which is short for *standard input*). When you join your shell commands (or Perl scripts) together on the command line with a pipe (|), it's STDOUT (or STDIN, if you're looking at the pipe from the receiving end) that's being connected together.

Now, it turns out that when you're in an interactive shell session, STDOUT and STDERR both print to your screen. If you pipe a program's output to more, though, you're only piping STDOUT to more. Thus, more will pause the output only when a screenful of STDOUT has appeared. If some STDERR has been coming in in the meantime, some text will scroll off your screen before more stops things.

One way to solve this, if you're using the bash shell, is to use the following bit of shell redirection magic after the command whose output you're piping to more: `2>&1`. For example, the command in the accompanying text could have been issued as:

`[jbc@andros sprocketexpo]$ make_exhibit.plx 2>&1 | more`

This takes STDERR (which is indicated by the numeral 2 here) and duplicates it to STDOUT (indicated by the numeral 1). In effect, anything sent by the script to STDERR will end up going to STDOUT, such that more will see the merged output stream and can pause the output before anything scrolls off your screen.

If you are using a C shell, like tcsh, you could try this alternative, which will accomplish more or less the same thing:

`andros:/u1/j/jbc/sprocketexpo/> make_exhibit.plx |& more`

We can ignore the warnings for now. The script's current method of storing listing data in the %listing hash is intended only as a quick debugging tool; it's not worth making it smart enough to avoid generating such warnings. When we create the version of the script that produces the actual HTML output, we can pay more attention to this issue.

Let's look now at the parsed company listings that are printed out after the warnings. All of them look as we expected, until we come to the one for Best Glue Products:

```
co_name:  Best Glue Products
booth:    Booth 903
address:  789 Windy Way
```

```
address2: Suite 765
phone:    Chicago, IL 60608
fax:      (312) 555-2345
email:    sales@bestglueprods.com
url:      http://www.bestglueprods.com/

description:
(312) 555-2346 (fax)
```

Examining this output carefully, we can see that there is a problem. Best Glue Products' portion of the exhibit.txt file was formatted differently, with an additional address line displaying the Suite 765 information. The extra line meant that our line counting was off in the rest of that section, such that we parsed what should have been address2 as the phone number, the phone number as the fax number, and the fax number as the description.

Making the Script Smarter

Once we know about it, it's an easy matter to modify the original data file to fix the Best Glue Products listing. But it would be nice if we could make the &parse_exhibitor subroutine smart enough to spot those sorts of problems on its own. By adding some sanity checks and having the script output appropriate error messages if they fail, we can make the process of policing the data file for these sorts of errors much easier.

For example, &parse_exhibitor uses the following lines to parse the company's name:

```
if ($line_count == 1) {
    $co_name = $line;
```

What if that line somehow ended up being blank? The code in the main body of our script shouldn't allow that to happen, but it doesn't hurt to program defensively. Let's modify those lines to look like this:

```
if ($line_count == 1) {
    unless ($co_name = $line) {
        warn <<"EOF";
line_count=1, but got a false co_name. skipping exhibitor.
($exhibit_file line number $.)
EOF
        return;
    }
```

By placing the assignment to the $co_name variable inside a logical test, we can test the value being assigned for truth. In the event that a false company name is assigned, we issue a warning, including the name of the file we were parsing ($exhibit_file) and the special variable $., which gives the line number of the file-handle most recently read from. (This will help us locate the problematic listing in $exhibit_file.) Then we use the return function, which causes a subroutine to stop whatever it's doing and returns program execution to the point in the script where the subroutine was invoked. In this case, that means the company that elicits this warning will not be added to the %listing hash.

Yes, this block will fire off if a company should happen to have a false name, like "0". We'll just have to live with that prospect for now. (In a future chapter, though, we'll learn how to avoid such problems.)

Let's add a similar sanity check to the lines that parse the booth number, modifying them to look like this:

```
} elsif ($line_count == 2) {

    if ($line =~ /^Booth (\d+)/) {
        $booth = $1;
    } else {
        warn <<"EOF";
line_count=2, but couldn't parse booth. skipping exhibitor.
(co_name '$co_name'. $exhibit_file line number $.)
EOF
        return;
    }
```

Here we've used a regular expression to parse the booth number from line 2 only if the line starts with the literal string Booth, followed by a space, and then one or more digits (courtesy the special regex sequence \d, which matches a single digit, and the + one-or-more quantifier). While we're at it, we've used a pair of capturing parentheses to grab just the digits from this line and assign them to $booth (via the special $1 variable, which you'll remember contains whatever was captured in a successful regex match's leftmost capturing parentheses). Before we were just assigning this whole line to $booth. This change will make things a little simpler when we produce the finished version of the listings.

This sanity check also aborts the subroutine via the return function if the line doesn't look right.

Line 3 (with the address information) and line 4 (with the city, state, and Zip information) both look a little tougher from the standpoint of devising suitable sanity checks. We might be tempted to use a regex to look for an appropriate structure in line 4, but then we think about the possibility of non-U.S. companies, with their variations in address format, and decide against it. As a result, we'll just keep assigning lines 3 and 4 to the $address and $address2 variables, respectively.

Line 5, with the company's phone number, offers a more fruitful opportunity for sanity checking. Here's what we come up with for that block:

```
} elsif ($line_count == 5) {

    if ($line =~ /^\((\d{3})\)/) {
        $phone = $line;
    } else {
        warn <<"EOF";
```

```
line_count=5, but couldn't parse phone number. skipping exhibitor.
(co_name '$co_name'. line '$line'. $exhibit_file line number $.)
EOF
            return;
        }
```

The regex in this new conditional test is an interesting one: /^\(\(\d{3}\)\)/. In order, from left to right, we've got:

- A ^ beginning-of-string anchor
- A literal left parenthesis, courtesy of the leading backslash in \(
- A series of exactly three digits, courtesy of the \d (standing for "any digit character") and the {3} after it, which is a quantifier specifying that the preceding item must match exactly three times
- A literal right parenthesis, courtesy of the \)

We use a similar sanity check for line 6, which should contain the company's fax number:

```
} elsif ($line_count == 6){

    if ($line =~ /^(\(\d{3}\).+) \(fax\)$/) {
        $fax = $1;
    } else {
        warn <<"EOF";
line_count=6, but couldn't parse fax number. skipping exhibitor.
(co_name '$co_name'. line '$line'. $exhibit_file line number $.)
EOF
        return;
    }
```

The regular expression in this one is /^(\(\(\d{3}\)\).+) \(fax\)$/. That breaks down as follows:

- The ^ beginning-of-string anchor.
- A left parenthesis to begin a capturing operation.
- A literal (noncapturing) left parenthesis, courtesy of the \(.
- Three digits, courtesy of the \d{3}.
- A literal right parenthesis, courtesy of the \).
- A period (.), with a + one-or-more quantifier after it. In a regex, a period stands for any single character whatsoever, so this part of the expression will match anything it possibly can, as long as the rest of the expression matches.
- A right parenthesis to end the capturing operation begun earlier.
- A literal space.
- The literal sequence (fax), courtesy of the backslashed parentheses on either side of the literal string fax.
- The $ end-of-string anchor.

The idea here is to look for lines that start off with three digits inside parentheses, then have a bunch of anything, then have a space and the string (fax) at the very end of the line. Everything before the trailing ' (fax)' gets captured into $1 for assignment to the $fax variable.

There's one more sanity check that would be good to add to the &parse_exhibitor routine. Even though the show organizers assured us that it wouldn't be possible for two companies to share the same name, it would be really smart to check for that anyway. Because we're using the company's name as the key in the %listing hash, a subsequent appearance of the same name would create problems. We can modify the last part of the &parse_exhibitor routine to check for that, and issue a warning if needed, by adding the following code just before we store the new listing in the %listing hash:

```
    if ($listing{$co_name}) {

        # we already have an entry in %listing for this $co_name,
        # so give an error message that we're going to be
        # writing over the old data.

            warn <<"EOF";
Parsed duplicate listing for co_name '$co_name'. Overwriting
previous data. ($exhibit_file line number $.)
EOF
    }
```

And that should do it for the sanity checks.

Parsing the Category File

The next step is parsing the information contained in the category file, category.txt. Since that file has a simpler structure than exhibit.txt, this part of the script will be easier.

In terms of a data structure to store the information, though, there's a complication. If you look at category.txt, you'll see that it contains lines with category names, formatted with double square brackets surrounding them, like this:

```
[[category name]]
```

Then, for each category, there are one or more lines containing company names and booth numbers, formatted like this:

```
company name, booth number
```

So, we might initially think we want a hash, with keys consisting of the different category names. For values, though, we won't be able to use a simple scalar value, because what we want to store for each category is a *list* of exhibitors.

The ideal data structure would be a *hash of lists*—that is, a hash where each key would be a category name and the corresponding value would be a list (or an array) containing the company names that go with that category. Unfortunately, we don't know how to do that yet. For now, we can fake it by using hash values that consist of a list of company names separated by newline characters. That is, the value associated with each category name key will still be a scalar value, but that scalar value will be a string containing company names on separate lines, like this:

```
first company name
second company name
third company name
```

And so on. Once we've created that multiline scalar value, it will be easy to split it up into an array of individual company names, as we'll see in the next chapter.

So, let's make our modifications to the make_exhibit.plx script. First, we need to add another line to the configuration section at the top of the script, specifying the name of the file holding the category data:

```
my $category_file = './category.txt';
```

Next, we add the following code to the section just below that, where we declare the script-wide variables of our data structure:

```
my %companies_by_category; # key:   category name.
                           # value: $co_name\n$co_name\n$co_name...
```

Next we add the following to the main body of the script, after the part that parses the exhibitor file but before the section that outputs the debugging version of the exhibitor listings. This block of code, which handles the reading of blank-line-separated chunks from the category file, is nearly identical to the section that reads the exhibitor file, except that it invokes a different subroutine, called &parse_category, to process each batch of lines:

```
# read and parse the category file

my @category_lines = (); # holds current category's lines for passing
                         # to the &parse_category subroutine

open CATEGORY, $category_file
    or die "Can't open $category_file for reading: $!\n";

while (<CATEGORY>) {
    if (/^\s*$/) {
        # this line is blank (or has nothing but space chars)
        if (@category_lines) {
            &parse_category(@category_lines);
            @category_lines = ();
        }
    } else {
        # this line actually has data
        push @category_lines, $_;
    }
}
```

```
    # process last batch of lines, if the file didn't have a trailing
    # blank line to trigger it already.

    if (@category_lines) {
        &parse_category(@category_lines);
    }

    close CATEGORY or die "Can't close $category_file after reading: $!\n";
```

Next we need to create the &parse_category subroutine, which will be very similar to the &parse_exhibitor routine. I'll show it to you first, and then we'll go over the few tricky parts:

```
sub parse_category {

    # extract the relevant information about a particular
    # category and store it in the appropriate hashes.
    #
    # invoked with an array of lines read from $category_file.
    # has no return value, but instead modifies this script-wide
    # variable:
    #
    # %companies_by_category

    my @lines = @_;
    my $category;
    my $line_count = 0;

    foreach my $line (@lines) {

        chomp $line;
        ++$line_count;

        if ($line_count == 1) {
            if ($line =~ /^\[\[(.+)\]\]$/) {
                # line looks like '[[category name]]'
                $category = $1;
            } else {
                warn <<"EOF";
line_count=1, but couldn't parse category name. skipping this category.
($category_file line number $.)
EOF
                return;
            }

        } elsif ($line =~ /^(.+), \d+$/) {

            my $co_name = $1;

            if ($listing{$co_name}) {
                $companies_by_category{$category} .= "$co_name\n";
            } else {
                warn <<"EOF";
parsed co_name '$co_name' from category file, but couldn't find a
```

```
corresponding company listing. ($category_file line number $.)
EOF
            }

    } else {

            warn <<"EOF";
line '$line' from category file doesn't appear to be either a
category or a company ($category_file line number $.)
EOF
        }
    }
}
```

Just a few lines here require explanation. First, you'll notice the regex pattern used to check line number 1 in each chunk of lines being processed: /^\[\[(.+)\]\]$/. That pattern matches two literal opening square brackets at the beginning of the line, then a bunch of anything (courtesy of the match-any-single-character period, and the match-one-or-more plus sign quantifier that follows it), then two closing square brackets at the end of the line. In doing so, it captures the stuff between the double square brackets using a pair of capturing parentheses. This matches the formatting of the category names in the category.txt file.

You'll also notice, a few lines later, a nice sanity check. After we capture a $co_name from those lines that come after line 1, we append the string "$co_name\n" to the value associated with the current category in the %companies_by_category hash. But we do that only if the captured company name matches one of those already present as a key in the %listing hash. Otherwise, we output a suitable warning:

```
if ($listing{$co_name}) {
    $companies_by_category{$category} .= "$co_name\n";
} else {
    warn <<"EOF";
parsed co_name '$co_name' from category file, but couldn't find a
corresponding company listing. ($category_file line number $.)
EOF
}
```

We'll make just one more change to make_exhibit.plx before running it again to test the category-file parsing (and all the new sanity checks): adding an extra section to the printing of debugging output to show the parsed category information. That code will go at the very end of the script proper, just before the subroutine definitions:

```
print "\nCATEGORIES:\n\n";

foreach my $cat (sort keys %companies_by_category) {
    print "$cat:\n\n$companies_by_category{$cat}\n";
}
```

As you saw previously in this chapter, we're using the keys function to return the category names from %companies_by_category, and sticking a sort function to the left of keys in order to sort them alphabetically. Because each value in the %companies_by_ category hash is already a newline-separated list of companies, we can just print them out as is for debugging purposes.

Testing the Script Again

The current version of make_exhibit.plx, with all the sanity checks and category-parsing code added, is given in Example 5-4.

Example 5-4. Updated version of make_exhibit.plx

```perl
#!/usr/bin/perl -w

# make_exhibit.plx

# this script reads a pair of data files, extracts information
# relating to a group of tradeshow exhibitors, and writes
# out a browseable web-based directory of those exhibitors

use strict;

# configuration section:

my $exhibit_file  = './exhibit.txt';
my $category_file = './category.txt';

# script-wide variables:

my %listing;                 # key:   company name ($co_name).
                             # value: HTML-ized listing for this company.


my %companies_by_category;  # key:   category name.
                            # value: $co_name\n$co_name\n$co_name...


# read and parse the main exhibitor file

my @listing_lines = (); # holds current listing's lines for passing
                        # to the &parse_exhibitor subroutine

open EXHIBIT, $exhibit_file
    or die "Can't open $exhibit_file for reading: $!\n";

while (<EXHIBIT>) {
    if (/^\s*$/) {
        # this line is blank (or has nothing but space chars)
        if (@listing_lines) {
            &parse_exhibitor(@listing_lines);
            @listing_lines = ();
        }
    } else {
        # this line actually has data
```

Example 5-4. Updated version of make_exhibit.plx (continued)

```perl
        push @listing_lines, $_;
    }
}

# process last batch of lines, if the file didn't have a trailing
# blank line to trigger it already.

if (@listing_lines) {
    &parse_exhibitor(@listing_lines);
}

close EXHIBIT or die "Can't close $exhibit_file after reading: $!\n";

# read and parse the category file

my @category_lines = ( ); # holds current category's lines for passing
                          # to the &parse_category subroutine

open CATEGORY, $category_file
    or die "Can't open $category_file for reading: $!\n";

while (<CATEGORY>) {
    if (/^\s*$/) {
        # this line is blank (or has nothing but space chars)
        if (@category_lines) {
            &parse_category(@category_lines);
            @category_lines = ( );
        }
    } else {
        # this line actually has data
        push @category_lines, $_;
    }
}

# process last batch of lines, if the file didn't have a trailing
# blank line to trigger it already.

if (@category_lines) {
    &parse_category(@category_lines);
}

close CATEGORY or die "Can't close $category_file after reading: $!\n";

# output parsed data for debugging

print "LISTINGS:\n\n";

foreach my $co_name (sort keys %listing) {
    print $listing{$co_name}, "\n";
}

print "\nCATEGORIES:\n\n";
```

Example 5-4. Updated version of make_exhibit.plx (continued)

```perl
foreach my $cat (sort keys %companies_by_category) {
    print "$cat:\n\n$companies_by_category{$cat}\n";
}

# script proper ends. subroutines follow.

sub parse_exhibitor {

    # extract the relevant information about a particular
    # exhibitor and store it in the appropriate hash.
    #
    # invoked with an array of lines read from $exhibit_file.
    # has no return value, but instead modifies the following
    # script-wide variable:
    #
    # %listing

    my @lines = @_;

    my($co_name, $booth, $address, $address2, $phone, $fax, $email,
        $url, $description);

    my $line_count = 0;

    foreach my $line (@lines) {

        chomp $line;
        ++$line_count;

        if ($line_count == 1) {
            unless ($co_name = $line) {
                warn <<"EOF";
line_count=1, but got a false co_name. skipping exhibitor.
($exhibit_file line number $.)
EOF
                return;
            }

        } elsif ($line_count == 2) {

            if ($line =~ /^Booth (\d+)/) {
                $booth = $1;
            } else {
                warn <<"EOF";
line_count=2, but couldn't parse booth. skipping exhibitor.
(co_name '$co_name'. $exhibit_file line number $.)
EOF
                return;
            }

        } elsif ($line_count == 3) {
```

Example 5-4. Updated version of make_exhibit.plx (continued)

```perl
            $address = $line;

        } elsif ($line_count == 4) {

            $address2 = $line;

        } elsif ($line_count == 5) {

            if ($line =~ /^\(\d{3}\)/) {
                $phone = $line;
            } else {
                warn <<"EOF";
line_count=5, but couldn't parse phone number. skipping exhibitor.
(co_name '$co_name'. line '$line'. $exhibit_file line number $.)
EOF
                return;
            }

        } elsif ($line_count == 6){

            if ($line =~ /^(\(\(\d{3}\).+) \(fax\)$/) {
                $fax = $1;
            } else {
                warn <<"EOF";
line_count=6, but couldn't parse fax number. skipping exhibitor.
(co_name '$co_name'. line '$line'. $exhibit_file line number $.)
EOF
                return;
            }

        } elsif ($line =~ /^\S+@\S+$/) {

            $email = $line;

        } elsif ($line =~ /^http:\S+$/) {

            $url = $line;

        } else {

            $description .= "$line\n"; # append so that multiline
                                       # descriptions work right
        }
    }

    # done cycling through @lines.

    if ($listing{$co_name}) {

        # we already have an entry in %listing for this $co_name,
        # so give an error message that we're going to be
        # writing over the old data.
```

Example 5-4. Updated version of make_exhibit.plx (continued)

```
            warn <<"EOF";
Parsed duplicate listing for co_name '$co_name'. Overwriting
previous data. ($exhibit_file line number $.)
EOF
    }

    # create the %listing entry

    $listing{$co_name}  = <<"EOF";
co_name:  $co_name
booth:    $booth
address:  $address
address2: $address2
phone:    $phone
fax:      $fax
email:    $email
url:      $url

description:
$description
EOF
}

sub parse_category {

    # extract the relevant information about a particular
    # category and store it in the appropriate hashes.
    #
    # invoked with an array of lines read from $category_file.
    # has no return value, but instead modifies this script-wide
    # variable:
    #
    # %companies_by_category

    my @lines = @_;
    my $category;
    my $line_count = 0;

    foreach my $line (@lines) {

        chomp $line;
        ++$line_count;

        if ($line_count == 1) {
            if ($line =~ /^\[\[(.+)\]\]$/) {
                # line looks like '[[category name]]'
                $category = $1;
            } else {
                warn <<"EOF";
line_count=1, but couldn't parse category name. skipping this category.
($category_file line number $.)
EOF
```

Example 5-4. Updated version of make_exhibit.plx (continued)

```
                return;
        }

    } elsif ($line =~ /^(.+), \d+$/) {

        my $co_name = $1;

        if ($listing{$co_name}) {
            $companies_by_category{$category} .= "$co_name\n";
        } else {
            warn <<"EOF";
parsed co_name '$co_name' from category file, but couldn't find a
corresponding company listing. ($category_file line number $.)
EOF
        }

    } else {

        warn <<"EOF";
line '$line' from category file doesn't appear to be either a
category or a company ($category_file line number $.)
EOF
        }
    }
}
```

Running `make_exhibit.plx` now should produce output looking very much like it did before, except with some extra warnings courtesy of the new sanity checks:

```
line_count=5, but couldn't parse phone number. skipping exhibitor.
(co_name 'Best Glue Products'. line 'Chicago, IL 60608'. ./exhibit.txt
  line number 29)
```

There's our sanity check catching the fact that Best Glue Products' entry in the exhibit.txt file has that extra address line, which throws off the line count in the &parse_exhibitor routine. This time, though, Best Glue Products won't appear with incorrectly parsed information in the debugging output; instead, because of this sanity check, it never makes it into the %listing hash.

The fact that Best Glue Products isn't in that hash leads to another warning, when the &parse_category routine reads its name for one of the categories but can't find that name as a key in %listing:

```
parsed co_name 'Best Glue Products' from category file, but couldn't
find a corresponding company listing. (./category.txt line number 5)
```

There's another warning from the &parse_category routine, this one because there's another inconsistency in the data files:

```
parsed co_name 'Acme Fittings' from category file, but couldn't find a
corresponding company listing. (./category.txt line number 10)
```

Some research turns up the explanation: different capitalization of the company name in exhibit.txt and category.txt: ACME in the former and Acme in the latter. Remember, with Perl (as with most things Unix) text comparisons are *case-sensitive*.

The rest of the output from make_exhibit.plx looks like it did before, except (again) that Best Glue Products is missing from the %listing output, and we get the following category information at the end:

```
CATEGORIES:

Adhesives:

Arlington Adhesives
New York Fasteners

Sprockets:

Premium Parts Company
Very Small Parts Co., The

Zippers:

New York Fasteners
Premium Parts Company
```

Armed with the warnings from our script, we manually correct the problems in the source data files. Best Glue Products gets its entry in exhibit.txt changed to look like this, with the extra address line moved to the line before it:

```
Best Glue Products
Booth 903
789 Windy Way, Suite 765
Chicago, IL 60608
(312) 555-2345
(312) 555-2346 (fax)
sales@bestglueprods.com
http://www.bestglueprods.com/
```

Also, in the category.txt file, we change Acme Fittings' name to ACME Fittings, to match the entry in exhibit.txt:

```
[[Sprockets]]
ACME Fittings, 104
Premium Parts Company, 654
Very Small Parts Co., The, 1278
```

We're finished parsing the data files. All that's left is to modify the script to print out our web pages. We'll do that in the next chapter.

## CHAPTER 6

Generating HTML

Continuing the example begun in the previous chapter, it's time for us to modify our script, make_exhibit.plx, to output the HTML pages for the SprocketExpo 2000 exhibitor's directory.

The Modified make_exhibit.plx Script

The final version of make_exhibit.plx is given in Example 6-1. It features a fair number of changes from the previous version, but don't worry; we'll be going through those changes one by one, explaining them all.

Example 6-1. The final version of make_exhibit.plx

```perl
#!/usr/bin/perl -w

# make_exhibit.plx

# this script reads a pair of data files, extracts information
# relating to a group of tradeshow exhibitors, and writes
# out a browseable web-based directory of those exhibitors

use strict;

# configuration section:

my $exhibit_file  = './exhibit.txt';
my $category_file = './category.txt';
my $base_path     = '/w1/s/sprocketexpo/exhibit';
my $base_url      = '/exhibit';
my $show_name     = 'SprocketExpo 2000';

# scriptwide variables:

my %listing;              # key:   company name ($co_name).
                          # value: HTML-ized listing for this company.
```

Example 6-1. The final version of make_exhibit.plx (continued)

```perl
my %letter_count;          # key:   lowercase letter.
                           # value: count of exhibitors starting with
                           #        that letter (for creating entries
                           #        in %listing_path).

my %listing_path;          # key:   company name ($co_name).
                           # value: path (relative to $base_path) of
                           #        this company's HTML listing page.
                           #        takes the form 'listings/a/a1.html'.

my %index_line;            # key:   company name ($co_name).
                           # value: HTML-ized <LI> link to listing page.

my %companies_by_category; # key:   category name.
                           # value: $co_name\n$co_name\n$co_name...

my %companies_by_letter;   # key:   lowercase letter.
                           # value: $co_name\n$co_name\n$co_name...

my %categories_by_company; # key:   company name ($co_name).
                           # value: $category_name\n$category_name...

# read and parse the main exhibitor file

my @listing_lines = ( );   # holds current listing's lines for passing
                           # to the &parse_exhibitor subroutine

open EXHIBIT, $exhibit_file
    or die "Can't open $exhibit_file for reading: $!\n";

while (<EXHIBIT>) {
    if (/^\s*$/) {
        # this line is blank (or has nothing but space chars)
        if (@listing_lines) {
            &parse_exhibitor(@listing_lines);
            @listing_lines = ( );
        }
    } else {
        # this line actually has data
        push @listing_lines, $_;
    }
}

# process last batch of lines, if the file didn't have a trailing
# blank line to trigger it already.

if (@listing_lines) {
    &parse_exhibitor(@listing_lines);
}

close EXHIBIT or die "Can't close $exhibit_file after reading: $!\n";
```

Example 6-1. The final version of make_exhibit.plx (continued)

```perl
# read and parse the category file

my @category_lines = ( ); # holds current category's lines for passing
                          # to the &parse_category subroutine

open CATEGORY, $category_file
    or die "Can't open $category_file for reading: $!\n";

while (<CATEGORY>) {
    if (/^\s*$/) {
        # this line is blank (or has nothing but space chars)
        if (@category_lines) {
            &parse_category(@category_lines);
            @category_lines = ( );
        }
    } else {
        # this line actually has data
        push @category_lines, $_;
    }
}

# process last batch of lines, if the file didn't have a trailing
# blank line to trigger it already.

if (@category_lines) {
    &parse_category(@category_lines);
}

close CATEGORY or die "Can't close $category_file after reading: $!\n";

# append the category information to the company listings

foreach my $co_name (keys %listing) {

    if ($categories_by_company{$co_name}) {

        my @categories = split /\n/, $categories_by_company{$co_name};

        $listing{$co_name} .= <<"EOF";
<P><STRONG>Categories listed under:</STRONG></P>
<UL>
EOF
        foreach my $category (sort @categories) {
            my $cat_cleaned    = &clean_name($category);
            my $path           = "$base_url/cats/$cat_cleaned.html";
            $listing{$co_name} .=
                "<LI><A HREF=\"$path\">$category</A>\n";
        }
        $listing{$co_name} .= "</UL>\n";
    }
}
```

Example 6-1. The final version of make_exhibit.plx (continued)

```perl
=comment the following debugging code has been commented out

print "LISTINGS:\n\n";

foreach my $co_name (sort keys %listing) {
    print $listing{$co_name}, "\n";
}

print "\nCATEGORIES:\n\n";

foreach my $cat (sort keys %companies_by_category) {
    print "$cat:\n\n$companies_by_category{$cat}\n\n";
}

=cut

# make sure all the directories we'll need exist

my @dirs = ($base_path, "$base_path/alpha", "$base_path/cats",
            "$base_path/listings");

foreach my $letter ('a' .. 'z') {
    push @dirs, "$base_path/listings/$letter";
}

umask 022;
foreach my $dir (@dirs) {
    if (-e $dir) {
        unless (-d $dir) {
            die "$dir already exists, and isn't a directory.";
        }
    } else {
        mkdir $dir, 0777 or die "couldn't mkdir $dir: $!";
    }
}

# write out each company listing

foreach my $co_name (sort keys %listing) {

    my $path   = "$base_path/$listing_path{$co_name}";
    my $title  = "$co_name ($show_name exhibitor listings)";

    my $content = <<"EOF";
<P ALIGN="center"><STRONG><A HREF="$base_url/">Exhibitor Listings
Index</A></STRONG></P>

$listing{$co_name}
EOF

    &write_page($path, $title, $content);
}
```

Example 6-1. The final version of make_exhibit.plx (continued)

```perl
# write out the alphabetical index pages

foreach my $letter ('a' .. 'z') {

    my $cap_letter = uc $letter;
    my $title      =
        "$show_name - Exhibitors starting with '$cap_letter'";
    my $path       = "$base_path/alpha/$letter.html";
    my $alpha_bar  = &make_alpha_bar($letter);

    my $content    = <<"EOF";
<P ALIGN="center"><STRONG><A HREF="$base_url/">Exhibitor
Listing Index</A></STRONG></P>

$alpha_bar

<H2 ALIGN="center">$show_name - Exhibitors starting with
'$cap_letter'</H2>
EOF

    if ($companies_by_letter{$letter}) {

        # there is at least one listing for this letter

        $content .= "<UL>\n";
        my @co_names = split /\n/, $companies_by_letter{$letter};
        foreach my $co_name (sort {lc $a cmp lc $b} @co_names) {
            $content .= $index_line{$co_name};
        }
        $content .= "</UL>\n";

    } else {

        # there are no listings for this letter

        $content .= <<"EOF";
<P ALIGN="center"><STRONG>(There currently are no listings
for this letter)</STRONG></P>
EOF
    }

    &write_page($path, $title, $content);
}

# write out the category pages

my $cat_list = ''; # to hold the HTML-ized list of categories
                   # for the top-level page

foreach my $category (sort keys %companies_by_category) {

    my $cat_cleaned = &clean_name($category);
```

Example 6-1. The final version of make_exhibit.plx (continued)

```perl
    my $path        = "$base_path/cats/$cat_cleaned.html";
    my $title       =
        "$category Exhibitors ($show_name Exhibitor Listings)";

    my $content = <<"EOF";
<P ALIGN="center"><STRONG><A HREF="$base_url/">Exhibitor
Listings Index</A></STRONG></P>

<H2 ALIGN="center">$show_name Exhibitor Listings - $category</H2>

<UL>
EOF

    my @companies = split /\n/, $companies_by_category{$category};
    my $count      = @companies; # how many companies in this category?

    $cat_list .= <<"EOF";
<LI><STRONG><A
HREF="$base_url/cats/$cat_cleaned.html">$category</A></STRONG>
<EM>($count exhibitors)</EM>
EOF

    foreach my $co_name (sort {lc $a cmp lc $b} @companies) {
        $content .= $index_line{$co_name};
    }

    $content .= "</UL>\n";

    &write_page($path, $title, $content);
}

# write out the top-level page

my $path        = "$base_path/index.html";
my $title       = "$show_name Exhibitor Listings";
my $alpha_bar   = &make_alpha_bar;
my $date        = localtime;
my $count       = keys %listing; # how many exhibitors, total?

my $content     = <<"EOF";
<H2 ALIGN="center">$show_name Exhibitor Listings</H2>

<P ALIGN="center"><EM>Last updated $date<BR>
$count exhibitors total</EM></P>

<P><STRONG>Alphabetical Index:</STRONG></P>

$alpha_bar

<P><STRONG>Category Index:</STRONG></P>

<UL>
```

Example 6-1. The final version of make_exhibit.plx (continued)

```
$cat_list
</UL>
EOF

&write_page($path, $title, $content);

# script proper ends. subroutines follow.

sub parse_exhibitor {

    # extract the relevant information about a particular
    # exhibitor and store it in the appropriate hashes.
    #
    # invoked with an array of lines read from $exhibit_file.
    # has no return value, but instead modifies the following
    # scriptwide variables:
    #
    # %listing
    # %index_line
    # %companies_by_letter

    my @lines = @_;

    my($co_name, $booth, $address, $address2, $phone, $fax, $email,
        $url, $description);

    my $line_count = 0;

    foreach my $line (@lines) {

        chomp $line;
        ++$line_count;

        if ($line_count == 1) {
            unless ($co_name = $line) {
                warn <<"EOF";
line_count=1, but got a false co_name. skipping exhibitor.
($exhibit_file line number $.)
EOF
                return;
            }

        } elsif ($line_count == 2) {

            if ($line =~ /^Booth (\d+)/) {
                $booth = $1;
            } else {
                warn <<"EOF";
line_count=2, but couldn't parse booth. skipping exhibitor.
(co_name '$co_name'. $exhibit_file line number $.)
EOF
```

Example 6-1. The final version of make_exhibit.plx (continued)

```
                return;
            }

    } elsif ($line_count == 3) {

        $address = $line;

    } elsif ($line_count == 4) {

        $address2 = $line;

    } elsif ($line_count == 5) {

            if ($line =~ /^\(\d{3}\)/) {
                $phone = $line;
            } else {
                warn <<"EOF";
line_count=5, but couldn't parse phone number. skipping exhibitor.
(co_name '$co_name'. line '$line'. $exhibit_file line number $.)
EOF
                return;
            }

    } elsif ($line_count == 6){

            if ($line =~ /^(\(\d{3}\).+) \(fax\)$/) {
                $fax = $1;
            } else {
                warn <<"EOF";
line_count=6, but couldn't parse fax number. skipping exhibitor.
(co_name '$co_name'. line '$line'. $exhibit_file line number $.)
EOF
                return;
            }

    } elsif ($line =~ /^\S+@\S+$/) {

        $email = $line;

    } elsif ($line =~ /^http:\S+$/) {

        $url = $line;

    } else {

        $description .= "$line\n"; # append so that multiline
                                   # descriptions work right
    }
}

# done cycling through @lines.
```

Example 6-1. The final version of make_exhibit.plx (continued)

```
    if ($listing{$co_name}) {

        # we already have an entry in %listing for this $co_name,
        # so give an error message that we're going to be
        # writing over the old data.

                warn <<"EOF";
Parsed duplicate listing for co_name '$co_name'. Overwriting
previous data. ($exhibit_file line number $.)
EOF
    }

    # create the %listing entry

    $listing{$co_name}  = <<"EOF";
<H2>$co_name</H2>
<P><STRONG>Booth $booth</STRONG></P>
EOF
    $listing{$co_name} .= "<P><EM>";
    $listing{$co_name} .= $address                  if $address;
    $listing{$co_name} .= "<BR>\n$address2"          if $address2;
    $listing{$co_name} .= "<BR>\n$phone"             if $phone;
    $listing{$co_name} .= "<BR>\n$fax (fax)"         if $fax;
    $listing{$co_name} .=
        "<BR>\nEmail: <A HREF=\"mailto:$email\">$email</A>"
                                                     if $email;
    $listing{$co_name} .= "<BR>\nWeb: <A HREF=\"$url\">$url</A>"
                                                     if $url;
    $listing{$co_name} .= "\n</EM></P>\n\n";

    if ($description) {
        $listing{$co_name} .= "<P><STRONG>Description:</STRONG><BR>\n";
        $listing{$co_name} .= "$description</P>\n";
    }

    # create the %listing_path entry

    my $first_char = lc substr $co_name, 0, 1;
    unless ($first_char =~ /[a-z]/) {
        $first_char = 'a';
    }
    ++$letter_count{$first_char};

    $listing_path{$co_name} =
      "listings/$first_char/$first_char$letter_count{$first_char}.html";

    # create the %index_line entry

    $index_line{$co_name} = <<"EOF";
<LI><A HREF="$base_url/$listing_path{$co_name}">$co_name</A>,
<EM>Booth $booth</EM>
EOF
```

Example 6-1. The final version of make_exhibit.plx (continued)

```
    # append to the %companies_by_letter entry for this letter
    $companies_by_letter{$first_char} .= "$co_name\n";

}

sub parse_category {

    # extract the relevant information about a particular
    # category and store it in the appropriate hashes.
    #
    # invoked with an array of lines read from $category_file.
    # has no return value, but instead modifies these scriptwide
    # variables:
    #
    # %companies_by_category
    # %categories_by_company

    my @lines = @_;
    my $category;
    my $line_count = 0;

    foreach my $line (@lines) {

        chomp $line;
        ++$line_count;

        if ($line_count == 1) {
            if ($line =~ /^\[\[(.+)\]\]$/) {
                # line looks like '[[category name]]'
                $category = $1;
            } else {
                warn <<"EOF";
line_count=1, but couldn't parse category name. skipping this category.
($category_file line number $.)
EOF
                return;
            }

        } elsif ($line =~ /^(.+), \d+$/) {

            my $co_name = $1;

            if ($listing{$co_name}) {
                $companies_by_category{$category} .= "$co_name\n";
                $categories_by_company{$co_name}  .= "$category\n";
            } else {
                warn <<"EOF";
parsed co_name '$co_name' from category file, but couldn't find a
corresponding company listing. ($category_file line number $.)
EOF
            }
```

Example 6-1. The final version of make_exhibit.plx (continued)

```
        } else {

            warn <<"EOF";
line '$line' from category file doesn't appear to be either a
category or a company ($category_file line number $.)
EOF
        }
    }
}

sub clean_name {

    # accepts a scalar, returns it with whitespace converted
    # to underscores and nonword chars deleted

    my $name = $_[0];
    $name =~ s/\s+/_/g;
    $name =~ s/\W+//g;
    $name;
}

sub write_page {

    # write out an HTML page based on three arguments:
    # a path (including the filename at the end) where the
    # page is to be written, the title of the page, and
    # the content of the page. this subroutine incorporates
    # a template for the SprocketExpo 2000 exhibitors directory;
    # the template will need to be modified for future shows.

    my($path, $title, $content) = @_;

    open OUT, ">$path" or die "can't open $path for writing: $!\n";
    print OUT <<"EOF";
<HTML>
<HEAD>
<TITLE>$title</TITLE>
</HEAD>
<BODY>
<TABLE>
<TR>
<TD VALIGN="top" WIDTH=150>
<H3 ALIGN="center">SprocketExpo<BR>2000</H3>
<P><A HREF="/">Home</A><BR>
<A HREF="/regform.html">Register</A><BR>
<A HREF="/exhibit/">Exhibitors</A><BR>
<A HREF="/contact.html">Contact Us</A></P>
</TD>
<TD VALIGN="top">

<!--begin content-->
```

Example 6-1. The final version of make_exhibit.plx (continued)

```
$content

<!--end content-->

</TD>
</TR>
</TABLE>
</BODY>
</HTML>
EOF
    close OUT or die "can't close filehandle for $path: $!\n";
}

sub make_alpha_bar {

    # this makes an HTML alphabet navigation tool and
    # returns it. it takes one (optional) argument: a
    # letter of the alphabet. that letter (if supplied) is
    # not turned into a link in the resulting chunk of HTML,
    # but instead is enclosed in a <STRONG></STRONG> tag to
    # indicate that that's the page the user is currently on.

    my $unlink_letter = lc $_[0];
    my $alpha_bar = "<P ALIGN=\"center\">";
    foreach my $letter ('a' .. 'z') {
        my $cap_letter = uc $letter;
        if ($letter eq $unlink_letter) {
            $alpha_bar .= "<STRONG>$cap_letter</STRONG> | ";
        } else {
            $alpha_bar .=
"<A HREF=\"$base_url/alpha/$letter.html\">$cap_letter</A> | ";
        }
        if ($letter eq 'm') {
            # split the alpha_bar
            $alpha_bar =~ s{ \| $}{<BR>\n};
        }
    }
    $alpha_bar =~ s{ \| $}{</P>\n};
    $alpha_bar;
}
```

The first change you'll notice in make_exhibit.plx is the number of new variables added to the configuration section:

```
    # configuration section:

    my $exhibit_file  = './exhibit.txt';
    my $category_file = './category.txt';
    my $base_path     = '/w1/s/sprocketexpo/exhibit';
    my $base_url      = '/exhibit';
    my $show_name     = 'SprocketExpo 2000';
```

The first of the new variables is $base_path. This tells the script where to write the files it will be creating, in terms of the server's filesystem. The second of the new variables, $base_url, tells the script how to construct HTML links that point to that directory, from the web server's perspective. The third new variable, $show_name, will be used to add the name of the show in appropriate locations throughout the generated pages.

The next new material in the script comes immediately after the configuration section, in the section that describes the sitewide variables of the script's data structure. Several new variables have been added here, along with extensive commenting describing them:

```
# scriptwide variables:

my %listing;                    # key:   company name ($co_name).
                                # value: HTML-ized listing for this company.

my %letter_count;               # key:   lowercase letter.
                                # value: count of exhibitors starting with
                                #        that letter (for creating entries
                                #        in %listing_path).

my %listing_path;               # key:   company name ($co_name).
                                # value: path (relative to $base_path) of
                                #        this company's HTML listing page.
                                #        takes the form 'listings/a/a1.html'.

my %index_line;                 # key:   company name ($co_name).
                                # value: HTML-ized <LI> link to listing page.

my %companies_by_category; # key:   category name.
                                # value: $co_name\n$co_name\n$co_name...

my %companies_by_letter;   # key:   lowercase letter.
                                # value: $co_name\n$co_name\n$co_name...

my %categories_by_company; # key:   company name ($co_name).
                                # value: $category_name\n$category_name...
```

The first new variable here is %letter_count. We'll be using this hash from within the &parse_exhibitor subroutine to keep track of how many companies we've seen beginning with each letter of the alphabet. We'll use that count, in turn, to construct the unique filename for each company's detailed listing page.

Next is a hash called %listing_path. This will hold the unique pathname for each company's detailed listing page, keyed by the company name. As the comment explains, those paths will take the form listings/a/a1.html. More on that soon.

The next new sitewide variable is a hash named %index_line. This one is also keyed by the company name, with the values consisting of lines suitable for use in the lists of companies that will be displayed on the alphabetical and category pages. Again, you'll see what those lines look like in just a moment, when we look at how the %index_line hash is used in the script.

The next new variable is named %companies_by_letter. Like the %companies_by_category hash we used in the last chapter, each value in this hash is a list of company names separated by newlines. The corresponding keys, in this case, are lowercase letters of the alphabet ('a', 'b', 'c', etc.). We'll use this to construct the alphabetical index pages.

The last new variable in our sitewide variables section is called %categories_by_company. This is similar to the %companies_by_category variable you already saw, except in this case the keys are company names and the values are newline-separated category names. We'll use this variable for constructing the links to appropriate category pages at the bottom of each exhibitor's detailed listing page.

Changes to &parse_exhibitor

The next changes in the program, at least in terms of the sequence in which commands are actually executed, are down toward the bottom, in the &parse_exhibitor subroutine. The opening comment for that routine has been updated to reflect the additional scriptwide variables the routine will now be updating:

```
# extract the relevant information about a particular
# exhibitor and store it in the appropriate hashes.
#
# invoked with an array of lines read from $exhibit_file.
# has no return value, but instead modifies the following
# scriptwide variables:
#
# %listing
# %index_line
# %companies_by_letter
```

Toward the end of the subroutine, where it is adding the current exhibitor's listing to the %listing hash, it now includes HTML markup:

```
# create the %listing entry

$listing{$co_name}  = <<"EOF";
<H2>$co_name</H2>
<P><STRONG>Booth $booth</STRONG></P>
EOF
```

Also, as subsequent parts of that listing are added to $listing{$co_name}, the subroutine uses if statements to avoid adding an element if that particular element isn't present for this particular company. Notice, though, how we're using a one-line version of the if test that you haven't seen before:

```
$listing{$co_name} .= "<P><EM>";
$listing{$co_name} .= $address                if $address;
```

```
$listing{$co_name} .= "<BR>\n$address2"              if $address2;
$listing{$co_name} .= "<BR>\n$phone"                 if $phone;
$listing{$co_name} .= "<BR>\n$fax (fax)"             if $fax;
$listing{$co_name} .=
    "<BR>\nEmail: <A HREF=\"mailto:$email\">$email</A>"
                                                     if $email;
$listing{$co_name} .= "<BR>\nWeb: <A HREF=\"$url\">$url</A>"
                                                     if $url;
$listing{$co_name} .= "\n</EM></P>\n\n";

if ($description) {
    $listing{$co_name} .= "<P><STRONG>Description:</STRONG><BR>\n";
    $listing{$co_name} .= "$description</P>\n";
}
```

These one-line if tests work great when you need to make only a single line of code conditional on the outcome of the test. The following two blocks of code do the same thing:

```
if (test) {
    do something;
}

do something if test;
```

The same thing works for unless:

```
unless (test) {
    do something;
}

do something unless test;
```

The next new thing in the &parse_exhibitor routine is the part where we determine the path and filename for this exhibitor's detailed listing page and store it in %listing_path. The first step in doing that is extracting, and lowercasing, the first letter of the company's name, which we do by putting the lc function in front of a Perl function called substr:

```
# create the %listing_path entry

my $first_char = lc substr $co_name, 0, 1;
```

The substr function extracts a substring from a string and returns it. The arguments to substr are, in order, the string you wish to do the extracting from, the position in the string where you want to start extracting, and the length of the substring you want to extract. In this case, we're extracting a substring from the string stored in $co_name, we're starting at position 0 (which means the very beginning of the string), and we're extracting a substring 1 character long. We could have accomplished the same thing using a regular expression match, but when you know the precise position in a string where you want to extract a substring, the substr function works fine and is perhaps a little easier to understand.

Next, we check that first character extracted from the company's name to make sure it really is a letter, using the character class [a-z] inside a regex. (Maybe 3M is exhibiting at SprocketExpo.) For companies whose names fail that test, we go ahead and assign them to the letter a for alphabetical-index purposes:

```
unless ($first_char =~ /[a-z]/) {
    $first_char = 'a';
}
```

Now add 1 to the current value in the scriptwide %letter_count hash for that particular letter, using the ++ auto-increment operator that you learned about already:

```
++$letter_count{$first_char};
```

Notice that the first time we encounter a company whose name begins with a particular letter of the alphabet, this line of code will be trying to add 1 to a previously unseen hash value. You might think that would cause Perl's warnings feature to complain about using an uninitialized value, as it did when we tried to interpolate undefined scalar variables into a string, but in fact Perl is okay with this, and doesn't issue any warnings. It just adds 1 to the undefined value, gets 1 for an answer, and stores that in the hash.

Now that we've added 1 to $letter_count{$first_char}, we use the resulting value in order to construct a unique filename for this company's detailed listing page, storing the path to that page in the %listing_path scriptwide hash:

```
$listing_path{$co_name} =
    "listings/$first_char/$first_char$letter_count{$first_char}.html";
```

Notice that this will result in the first company seen for the letter a getting the path listings/a/a1.html, the second company for the letter a getting listings/a/a2.html, and so on.

Next we add a suitable entry, keyed on this company's name, to the %index_line scriptwide variable. This entry will be used to construct the <UL></UL> list of company names on the alphabetical and category pages:

```
# create the %index_line entry

$index_line{$co_name} = <<"EOF";
<LI><A HREF="$base_url/$listing_path{$co_name}">$co_name</A>,
<EM>Booth $booth</EM>
EOF
```

Notice how we use the $base_url configuration variable from the top of the script for the first part of the HREF attribute in this company's link, and the entry we just stored in $listing_path{$co_name} for the last part.

 We might want to separate the two components of the path because this way we can customize the script for use at SprocketExpo 2001, or WidgetWorld 2002, just by modifying the configuration section, leaving most of the script unchanged.

Finally, the last change to the &parse_exhibitor routine is to append this company's name to the %companies_by_letter entry for this letter of the alphabet. We'll be using that shortly to create the alphabetical index pages:

```
# append to the %companies_by_letter entry for this letter
$companies_by_letter{$first_char} .= "$co_name\n";
```

That does it for the changes to &parse_exhibitor.

The &parse_category subroutine gets only a few small changes in this final version of the script. First, we update its opening comment to mention that it is now updating a second sitewide variable, %categories_by_company:

```
# extract the relevant information about a particular
# category and store it in the appropriate hashes.
#
# invoked with an array of lines read from $category_file.
# has no return value, but instead modifies these scriptwide
# variables:
#
# %companies_by_category
# %categories_by_company
```

Then, we modify the chunk of code that handles company-name lines from category.txt to update that new variable. That only requires a single new line:

```
} elsif ($line =~ /^(.+), \d+$/) {

    my $co_name = $1;

    if ($listing{$co_name}) {
        $companies_by_category{$category} .= "$co_name\n";
        $categories_by_company{$co_name}  .= "$category\n";
    } else {
        warn <<"EOF";
parsed co_name '$co_name' from category file, but couldn't find a
corresponding company listing. ($category_file line number $.)
EOF
    }
```

Adding Categories to the Company Listings

The next step is to use that %categories_by_company hash that was populated in the &parse_category routine to add category links to the individual company listings, as stored in the %listing hash. Back in the main body of the script, after the part that reads through the category.txt file and runs the &parse_category routine on the lines read from it, we've added the following:

```
# append the category information to the company listings

foreach my $co_name (keys %listing) {

    if ($categories_by_company{$co_name}) {
```

Here we've got an outer foreach loop that cycles through all the company names in %listing (not bothering to put a sort in front of the keys function, since we don't care about the order in which we process the companies). Inside that, we begin an if block that executes only if we have one or more categories listed in the %categories_ by_company hash for this particular $co_name. In other words, we run the if block only for those companies that actually have categories.

Next, we use a function called split to turn the newline-separated list of company names stored in $categories_by_company{$co_name} into an actual list, and assign it to an array variable called @categories:

```
my @categories = split /\n/, $categories_by_company{$co_name};
```

The split function takes a first argument that is a regular expression pattern, and a second argument that is a string to be split. Then it splits the string wherever that regex matches and returns everything that didn't match as a list of elements, suitable for assigning to an array.

The result, in this case, is that we get a @categories array that consists of all the individual category names previously appended (with trailing newlines) to $categories_ by_company{$co_name}.

You can use perldoc -f split to read the perlfunc manpage's entry for split, and if you do you'll learn lots of other interesting things about the split function, including variations in its behavior that you can trigger by giving it different arguments. Those variations aren't relevant here, but another fact from the documentation *is* relevant: by default, split will not return trailing null elements. That is, if the pattern in split's first argument happens to match one or more times at the end of the string, split will *not* return the empty list elements it would if it encountered those matches elsewhere in the string.

This is really helpful in the current case, since we do in fact have a trailing newline at the very end of the string in $categories_by_company{$co_name} (because the last category name appended to the list had a newline after it). Without this special behavior of split's, the array assigned to @categories would end up looking like ('category one', 'category two', 'category three', ''), with an empty entry at the end. We don't want that empty category, and Perl is smart enough not to give it to us. That's cool.

Now that we have a list of categories corresponding to this particular company, we need to add category links to the end of the company's entry in the %listing hash. First, we append some HTML to that entry to get things ready:

```
        $listing{$co_name} .= <<"EOF";
<P><STRONG>Categories listed under:</STRONG></P>
<UL>
EOF
```

Then, we sort through the category names in @categories, turning each one into a link to the appropriate category page, and then finish up by closing the <UL> list with the </UL> tag. We do all that with this next block of code:

```
foreach my $category (sort @categories) {
    my $cat_cleaned    = &clean_name($category);
    my $path           = "$base_url/cats/$cat_cleaned.html";
    $listing{$co_name} .=
        "<LI><A HREF=\"$path\">$category</A>\n";
}
$listing{$co_name} .= "</UL>\n";
```

All of this Perl should be self-explanatory for you by now, except for that &clean_name subroutine, which is invoked with the current category name for an argument, and has its return value assigned to the $cat_cleaned scalar variable. That subroutine converts the category name into a form that will be suitable for a filename, with whitespace characters turned into underscores (_) and nonalphanumeric characters removed. Let's take a quick look at that subroutine, which we've added down toward the bottom of the script, in the part reserved for subroutine definitions:

```
sub clean_name {

    # accepts a scalar, returns it with whitespace converted
    # to underscores and nonword chars deleted

    my $name = $_[0];
    $name =~ s/\s+/_/g;
    $name =~ s/\W+//g;
    $name;
}
```

The only thing new to you in that subroutine is the special sequence \W in the second substitution operator's regex pattern; it stands for any nonalphanumeric character. There is a corresponding sequence, \w, with a lowercase w, that stands for any alphanumeric character. In each case, Perl's definition of *alphanumeric character* is any character in the ranges A-Z, a-z, or 0-9, or the underscore character (_). So, taken together, this subroutine would take a string like Red, Blue, and Green Widgets and return it as Red_Blue_and_Green_Widgets, making it easy for us to construct a filename for each category.

After we are done appending the category links to the entries in %listing, we're pretty much finished with the new code in make_exhibit.plx, except for the code that actually creates the finished HTML pages. We need to make one more change before we get to that, though: we need to get rid of the debugging code that we used in the last chapter to print out the contents of the %listing and %companies_by_category hashes. One way to get rid of it would be to just delete it, but we might want it back at some point for some future debugging. Better would be to comment it out temporarily, then uncomment it later if needed.

There are two schools of thought on how best to comment out an extended block of Perl. One approach is to just put an if (0) { } block around the whole thing. Because 0 will never be true, any code contained in the block will be disabled.

My own preference is to use something called POD, which is Perl's means of embedding documentation inside scripts. I'm not going to talk about how to use POD to do documentation in this book, but it's easy to use it to disable a chunk of code. You just put a line like this above the section you want to disable:

```
=comment this code has been commented out
```

And then you put a line like this below the section you want to disable:

```
=cut
```

Both lines need to be at the left margin, with no whitespace to the left of them. To my way of thinking, this approach makes the commented-out section more obvious than the if (0) { } approach. Also, if you're an obsessive if-block indenter, like I am, you don't have to worry about indenting the entire commented section, or "outdenting" it back when you re-enable the code.

With POD-based commenting, the old debugging section of make_exhibit.plx ends up looking like this:

```
=comment the following debugging code has been commented out

print "LISTINGS:\n\n";

foreach my $co_name (sort keys %listing) {
    print $listing{$co_name}, "\n";
}

print "\nCATEGORIES:\n\n";

foreach my $cat (sort keys %companies_by_category) {
    print "$cat:\n\n$companies_by_category{$cat}\n\n";
}

=cut
```

All that's left now is to have make_exhibit.plx actually output its finished HTML pages.

Creating Directories

The first step in writing our HTML files is to make sure that all the directories our script is going to be writing to already exist. If they don't, the script won't be able to open files in them for writing. So, we'll need to check for any of those directories that might be missing and create them if necessary.

In the script, that happens right after the (now-commented-out) debugging section:

```
# make sure all the directories we'll need exist

my @dirs = ($base_path, "$base_path/alpha", "$base_path/cats",
            "$base_path/listings");
```

We start by creating a @dirs array that contains a list of all the directories that we want to make sure exist already. As you can see, we're including in that list the $base_path directory from the script's configuration section, as well as subdirectories of that directory named alpha, cats, and listings.

Next, we need to add a directory under listings for each letter of the alphabet. We do this with the following block of code:

```
foreach my $letter ('a' .. 'z') {
    push @dirs, "$base_path/listings/$letter";
}
```

This uses a foreach loop, but the parentheses have something unusual inside them: Perl's very cool range operator, which consists of two dots (..) with something on either side of them. The normal way the range operator is used is to return a list of numbers, as in 1 .. 10, which would return a list of the numbers 1 through 10. But it also can return a range of strings, which means the 'a' .. 'z' used in this example returns a list consisting of all the lowercase letters of the alphabet. See the section on "Range Operators" in the perlop manpage for more details.

Next we need to check for the existence of the directories in @dirs and create those that don't exist already. We do that with the following chunk of code:

```
umask 022;
foreach my $dir (@dirs) {
    if (-e $dir) {
        unless (-d $dir) {
            die "$dir already exists, and isn't a directory.";
        }
    } else {
        mkdir $dir, 0777 or die "couldn't mkdir $dir: $!";
    }
}
```

A few new things need explaining in this code. First, we've used Perl's umask function to explicitly set the *umask* to 022. What's a umask, you're wondering? Just this: an octal number (like the numbers you use when giving an argument to the chmod command in the shell) that specifies the permissions you want *not* to give when creating a new directory or file. This script may already have been running with a umask (because it might have inherited one from its parent process when it was started up), but by setting it explicitly here we know exactly what we're dealing with. We'll come back to this in just a second, when we talk about the mkdir function.

Next we enter a foreach loop, setting $dir to the name of the current directory from @dirs. If that directory already exists (which we find out by running the -e "does this file exist?" file test on it), we check to make sure it really is a directory (via the -d file test), and if it isn't, we die with an error message. If the directory *doesn't* already exist, we create it using Perl's mkdir function, supplying the name of the directory in the first argument and the permissions mode 0777 in the second argument. Because of our explicit setting of the umask to 022 a few lines before, the permissions the new directory will actually end up with are 0755, which is what we wanted.

That 0777 mode needs the extra 0 in front of it in the argument to mkdir, by the way, because that's how Perl recognizes it as an octal (that is, a base-eight) number. And be sure not to put quotation marks around it or you'll get the string '0777', which isn't the same thing.

Generating the HTML Pages

We're finally ready to actually create our HTML pages. It's taken a lot of work to get to this point, but if you're like me and can remember grinding through the creation of lots of individual HTML pages by hand, this part is going to seem pretty cool.

Generating the Individual Company Listings

First, we'll output each individual company listing, which we do with the following chunk of code:

```
# write out each company listing

foreach my $co_name (sort keys %listing) {

    my $path  = "$base_path/$listing_path{$co_name}";
    my $title = "$co_name ($show_name exhibitor listings)";

    my $content = <<"EOF";
<P ALIGN="center"><STRONG><A HREF="$base_url/">Exhibitor Listings
Index</A></STRONG></P>

$listing{$co_name}
EOF

    &write_page($path, $title, $content);
}
```

No new Perl features in there at all. We use a foreach loop to cycle through all the company listings in the %listing hash, and for each company create three scalar variables:

- A $path variable, consisting of an appropriate filesystem path for this page, based on the $base_path configuration variable and the entry for this company from the %listing_path hash

- A $title variable, with a suitable title for this listing's HTML page
- A $content variable, containing the part of the finished HTML page that will be specific to this company's listing page

Once we've populated these three variables, we use them as arguments to a subroutine named &write_page, which writes out those pages to disk. Here's what that &write_page routine, which is located down toward the end of the script with the other subroutines, looks like:

```
sub write_page {

    # write out an HTML page based on three arguments:
    # a path (including the filename at the end) where the
    # page is to be written, the title of the page, and
    # the content of the page. this subroutine incorporates
    # a template for the SprocketExpo 2000 exhibitors directory;
    # the template will need to be modified for future shows.

    my($path, $title, $content) = @_;

    open OUT, ">$path" or die "can't open $path for writing: $!\n";
    print OUT <<"EOF";
<HTML>
<HEAD>
<TITLE>$title</TITLE>
</HEAD>
<BODY>
<TABLE>
<TR>
<TD VALIGN="top" WIDTH=150>
<H3 ALIGN="center">SprocketExpo<BR>2000</H3>
<P><A HREF="/">Home</A><BR>
<A HREF="/regform.html">Register</A><BR>
<A HREF="/exhibit/">Exhibitors</A><BR>
<A HREF="/contact.html">Contact Us</A></P>
</TD>
<TD VALIGN="top">

<!--begin content-->

$content

<!--end content-->

</TD>
</TR>
</TABLE>
</BODY>
</HTML>
EOF
    close OUT or die "can't close filehandle for $path: $!\n";
}
```

The &write_page subroutine is refreshingly simple. It just does the following:

- Takes the three arguments it was invoked with and copies them to variables named $path, $title, and $content.
- Opens a filehandle for writing to the supplied $path.
- Prints out an HTML page to that filehandle, interpolating the supplied $title and $content into that page.
- Closes the filehandle.

When this portion of the script runs, it will create an individual listing page for each company in the exhibitor directory, with the pages looking like the one shown in Figure 6-1.

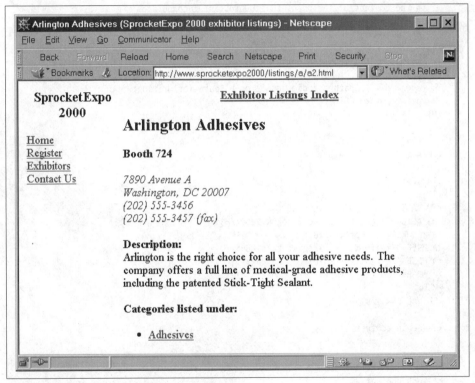

Figure 6-1. An exhibitor's individual listing

Generating the Alphabetical Index

The next thing the script does is to create the pages for the exhibitor directory's alphabetical index. These pages, one for each letter of the alphabet, will reside in the $base_path/alpha directory. The page for the letter "A" will have a list of all the companies whose names start with "A" (or with a nonalpha character), the page for "B" will have all the companies whose names start with "B", and so on. The code that creates those pages starts off like this:

```
# write out the alphabetical index pages

foreach my $letter ('a' .. 'z') {

    my $cap_letter = uc $letter;
    my $title      =
        "$show_name - Exhibitors starting with '$cap_letter'";
    my $path       = "$base_path/alpha/$letter.html";
```

Here we've used the range operator (..) again to create a list of all the lowercase letters of the alphabet so that we can iterate over them in a foreach loop. Inside the loop, we use Perl's uc function, a close relative of the lc function you already know about, to store an uppercase version of that letter in a variable called $cap_letter. Then we use $cap_letter to make a suitable title for our page (e.g., "SprocketExpo 2000--Exhibitors starting with A"), and follow that by creating a suitable path where this page will reside.

Next we invoke a new subroutine, called &make_alpha_bar, to create and return one of those alphabetical navigation thingies (which I'm going to call an "alpha bar") that you may have noticed on web sites before. What we're building is basically just a little chunk of HTML, with links for each letter of the alphabet. Each letter's link points at the corresponding alphabetical index page from our exhibitor directory. We use a subroutine to create the HTML, rather than just storing a single version of it in a scalar variable, so we can customize the alpha bar for each letter of the alphabet. In other words, we want to have the alpha bar on the "A" page to not have a link to itself, but instead to have the letter A rendered in bold text in order to give the user visual feedback as to what page she is on.

Here's what the &make_alpha_bar subroutine looks like:

```
sub make_alpha_bar {

    # this makes an HTML alphabet navigation tool and
    # returns it. it takes one (optional) argument: a
    # letter of the alphabet. that letter (if supplied) is
    # not turned into a link in the resulting chunk of HTML,
    # but instead is enclosed in a <STRONG></STRONG> tag to
    # indicate that that's the page the user is currently on.

    my $unlink_letter = lc $_[0];
    my $alpha_bar = "<P ALIGN=\"center\">";
    foreach my $letter ('a' .. 'z') {
        my $cap_letter = uc $letter;
        if ($letter eq $unlink_letter) {
            $alpha_bar .= "<STRONG>$cap_letter</STRONG> | ";
        } else {
            $alpha_bar .=
```

```
"<A HREF=\"$base_url/alpha/$letter.html\">$cap_letter</A> | ";
            }
        if ($letter eq 'm') {
            # split the alpha_bar
            $alpha_bar =~ s{ \| $}{<BR>\n};
        }
    }
    $alpha_bar =~ s{ \| $}{</P>\n};
    $alpha_bar;
}
```

The only tricky thing about this routine is the way we've used substitution regexes to tidy up the end of each of the two lines that constitute the alpha bar. As we go through the alphabet, we append a link for each letter, followed by the string " | ", to the $alpha_bar variable we're building up until we reach the letter M, which is where we want the alpha bar to break onto its second line. There, we use the substitution variety of regex s{ \| $}{
\n}, which replaces the trailing space-pipe-space sequence with a <BR> tag and a newline. Later, after completing the alpha bar with the letter Z, we use the similar substitution s{ \| $}{</P>\n}, which replaces the second line's trailing space-pipe-space sequence with a </P> tag and a newline.

Notice, by the way, how we had to backslash the literal pipe characters in these two regexes' search patterns. The pipe character means something special in a regex (you'll learn what in the next chapter), so we had to backslash it to get the literal character. Also, notice how we chose to use braces ({}) instead of the normal slashes (/) for our delimiters, and how when you use a paired delimiter like braces in a substitution-variety regex you get *two* delimiters, not one, in the middle of the expression. (I chose to go with braces for these regexes because I thought the end result was more readable that way, what with all the slashes and pipes and backslashes these expressions had already.)

So, returning to the main body of the script, where we were creating the alphabetical index pages, we follow up the part where we created this letter's particular alpha bar with the following code:

```
    my $content   = <<"EOF";
<P ALIGN="center"><STRONG><A HREF="$base_url/">Exhibitor
Listing Index</A></STRONG></P>

$alpha_bar

<H2 ALIGN="center">$show_name - Exhibitors starting with
'$cap_letter'</H2>
EOF
```

This creates the top part of this particular alphabetical index page's content, incorporating the $alpha_bar variable returned by the &make_alpha_bar routine.

Next comes an if-else block, which we use to create a customized "Hmm—there currently aren't any companies for this letter of the alphabet" page if there happen not to be any companies in the directory whose names begin with this letter. This is a rather cruel trick to play on a web user who unsuspectingly clicks through to the Q page, only to find nothing of interest there, but it lets us keep the code relatively simple for this example.

Anyway, here's what that block looks like:

```
if ($companies_by_letter{$letter}) {

    # there is at least one listing for this letter

    $content .= "<UL>\n";
    my @co_names = split /\n/, $companies_by_letter{$letter};
    foreach my $co_name (sort {lc $a cmp lc $b} @co_names) {
        $content .= $index_line{$co_name};
    }
    $content .= "</UL>\n";

} else {

    # there are no listings for this letter

    $content .= <<"EOF";
<P ALIGN="center"><STRONG>(There currently are no listings
for this letter)</STRONG></P>
EOF
}
```

The else block, which appends the "Yes, we have no bananas" message to the $content variable, should be self-explanatory. The if block, though, which executes in cases where there actually are companies for this letter, is more interesting. It gives another example of using the split function—in this case splitting this letter's entry in the %companies_by_letter hash into its component company names, just like you saw previously when we split the entries in %categories_by_company. Once we have the @co_names array that is the result of this split, we cycle through each company name with a foreach loop, appending the appropriate link to that company's individual listing page (as stored in the %index_line hash) to this page's list of companies.

Using an Explicit Sort Block

There's something you haven't seen before in the line that begins the foreach loop, though. After the sort function, but before the @co_names array that is actually being sorted, is the following curly-brace-delimited block: {lc $a cmp lc $b}. That's something called a *sort block*, and it lets us specify a customized sorting behavior for the sort function that precedes it. In this case, we've specified that we want to do a case-insensitive sort, so companies that wish to use lowercase company names (like "e.e. cummings enterprises") won't find themselves sorted to the end of the list by Perl's default ASCII-order sorting (in which all the uppercase letters come first).

The $a and $b variables are special variables that are specific to the sort block. (They're not actually my variables, though, as it turns out. Instead, they're something you haven't learned about yet called *local variables*. But the point is, you don't have to worry about them interacting with the rest of your script.) The $a and $b variables represent two items from the list of values being sorted, and the way they're treated in the sort block determines what sort of sorting behavior we'll get. In this case, we're lowercasing them by putting an lc function in front of each, then comparing them with the cmp operator, which is an operator specifically for sorting strings in ASCII order.

In fact, if we left out the lc functions so that our sort block looked like {$a cmp $b}, there would have been no point in having a sort block at all. That's because that particular sort block specifies the same sorting behavior that the sort function gives by default. We'll see lots more cool ways to sort things in future chapters, but that's enough for now.

Anyway, once we've finished creating the $content for this letter of the alphabet, we write out the resulting HTML page using the same &write_page routine we used for the individual company pages, invoking it with the following line:

```
&write_page($path, $title, $content);
```

Once we're done looping through the foreach loop for each letter of the alphabet, our alphabetical index is finished. The resulting pages will look something like the example shown in Figure 6-2.

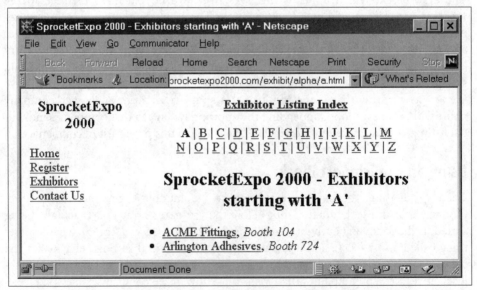

Figure 6-2. A page from the exhibitor directory's alphabetical index

Generating the Category Pages

The next step is to generate the page for each of SprocketExpo's product and service categories, with a list of all the companies included in that category. There are no new Perl concepts in this part of the script, so I'm going to just show the whole section here, then mention the high points after:

```perl
# write out the category pages

my $cat_list = ''; # to hold the HTML-ized list of categories
                   # for the top-level page

foreach my $category (sort keys %companies_by_category) {

    my $cat_cleaned = &clean_name($category);
    my $path        = "$base_path/cats/$cat_cleaned.html";
    my $title       =
        "$category Exhibitors ($show_name Exhibitor Listings)";

    my $content = <<"EOF";
<P ALIGN="center"><STRONG><A HREF="$base_url/">Exhibitor
Listings Index</A></STRONG></P>

<H2 ALIGN="center">$show_name Exhibitor Listings - $category</H2>

<UL>
EOF

    my @companies = split /\n/, $companies_by_category{$category};
    my $count     = @companies; # how many companies in this category?

    $cat_list .= <<"EOF";
<LI><STRONG><A
HREF="$base_url/cats/$cat_cleaned.html">$category</A></STRONG>
<EM>($count exhibitors)</EM>
EOF

    foreach my $co_name (sort {lc $a cmp lc $b} @companies) {
        $content .= $index_line{$co_name};
    }

    $content .= "</UL>\n";

    &write_page($path, $title, $content);
}
```

First, you'll notice that we declare a scalar variable named $cat_list at the beginning of this section, before we enter the foreach loop that cycles through each category. As the accompanying comment explains, we'll be using this variable to hold the list of categories that will go on the exhibitor directory's top-level page.

Then we begin the foreach loop, cycling through all the category names stored as keys in the %companies_by_category hash. We run each category name through the same &clean_name subroutine that we used when creating the category-page links for the individual company listings, and construct a filesystem path for that category page using a copied-and-pasted version of the same code we used there.

 Beware using copy-and-paste to duplicate code like this. Having two separate pieces of identical code to construct paths to our category pages is an invitation to trouble. If this code lives long enough, someone will modify one of these pieces of code and not the other, leading to broken links. A better solution in this case probably would have been to use a subroutine to create the category-page paths, and have both pieces of code use the subroutine. Or we could have created a %category_path hash, with keys of category names and values of the corresponding paths, populated it once, and then used the hash in both places. Oh, well. No program is perfect, I guess.

We then create a suitable title for this category page and generate its list of companies by splitting the value stored in $companies_by_category{$category}. We get a count of the number of companies in the category by the clever method of simply assigning the @companies array to the scalar variable $count. This has the effect of putting @companies in a scalar context, which means it returns the number of elements it contains, just like it would if we put it inside the conditional test of an if block.

Next, we cycle through the list of companies with a foreach loop. Again, when cycling through the company names, we use a custom sort block to avoid case-sensitive sorting problems. Inside the foreach loop, we use the entries in the %index_line hash, keyed by the company names, to generate the links to the individual company pages. Finally, we output the resulting category page, which will end up looking something like the example shown in Figure 6-3.

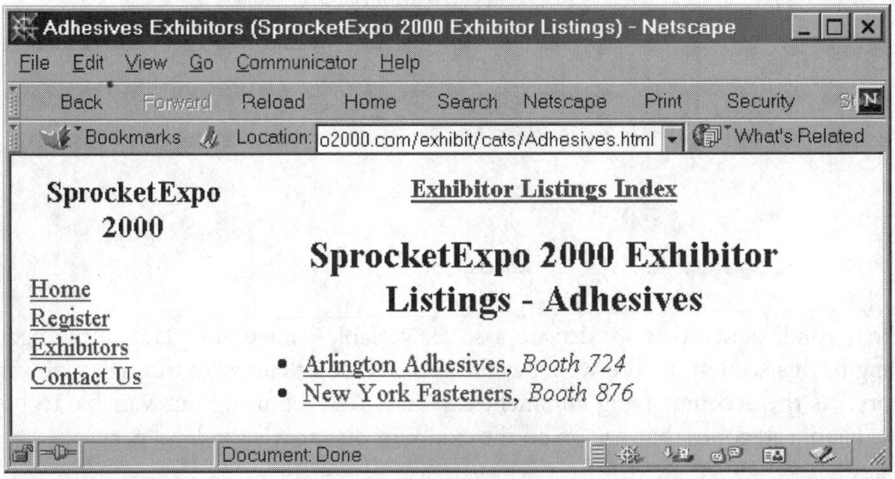

![Netscape browser window titled "Adhesives Exhibitors (SprocketExpo 2000 Exhibitor Listings) - Netscape" showing Location: o2000.com/exhibit/cats/Adhesives.html. The page shows "SprocketExpo 2000" with navigation links Home, Register, Exhibitors, Contact Us, an "Exhibitor Listings Index" header, a heading "SprocketExpo 2000 Exhibitor Listings - Adhesives", and a bulleted list: Arlington Adhesives, Booth 724; New York Fasteners, Booth 876.]

Figure 6-3. A page from the exhibitor directory's category index

Generating the Top-level Page

We're almost done. All that's left is to generate the site's top-level page. Here's the code that does that:

```
# write out the top-level page

my $path      = "$base_path/index.html";
my $title     = "$show_name Exhibitor Listings";
my $alpha_bar = &make_alpha_bar;
my $date      = localtime;
my $count     = keys %listing; # how many exhibitors, total?

my $content   = <<"EOF";
<H2 ALIGN="center">$show_name Exhibitor Listings</H2>

<P ALIGN="center"><EM>Last updated $date<BR>
$count exhibitors total</EM></P>

<P><STRONG>Alphabetical Index:</STRONG></P>

$alpha_bar

<P><STRONG>Category Index:</STRONG></P>

<UL>
$cat_list
</UL>
EOF

&write_page($path, $title, $content);
```

There are just a few new tricks here. First, we make an alpha bar for the top-level page, but we don't pass the subroutine a letter as an argument, so the alpha bar we get back does not have any unlinked letters.

Next, we populate the $date variable, which we'll use to put a timestamp on the top-level page, by assigning the output of Perl's localtime function to it. The localtime function is interesting because it behaves differently depending on whether it is in a scalar or an array context. If you put it in an array context (by assigning its output to an array variable, for example), it will return a list of various elements relating to the current date and time. If you put it in a scalar context, though (as we've done here, by assigning its output to a scalar variable), it returns a string describing the current date and time, like this: Mon Jul 9 17:46:53 2001.

Another trick showing how clever Perl's functions can be is in the very next line. We obtain a count of the total number of exhibitors by putting keys %listing, which in an array context would have returned a list of all the keys in %listing into a scalar context, causing it to return instead the number of keys in the hash.

The creation of the $content for the top-level page is straightforward: we just stick in our alpha bar and the list of category-page links stored in $cat_list while we were creating all the category pages. Then we run the &write_page routine, producing a page like the one shown in Figure 6-4.

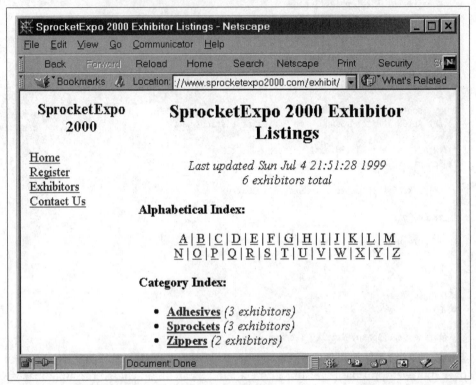

Figure 6-4. The top-level page for the exhibitor directory

The final version of the script weighs in at more than 500 lines, which is a lot of baby talk in anyone's book. Was it worth all that effort? If the directory we were creating included only six companies, as this example did, the answer would certainly be no; we could have created the HTML pages manually in a fraction of the time it took to create this script. Somewhere around a dozen or two dozen companies, though, Perl scripting starts to look like a much more attractive approach. The real-life tradeshow that this example was based on had more than 900 exhibitors. Manually marking up that many pages simply wasn't an option. It was the Perl way, or no way. I chose Perl.

## CHAPTER 7

Regular Expressions Demystified

So far, we've been treating regular expressions like unexploded bombs: dangerous, complicated things to be approached with extreme caution. It's time now to learn how they really work so that you can take them apart and put them back together and understand what's going on. It's not terribly difficult once you get the hang of it, and there's a big payoff once you do, but there's a fair amount of detail to learn along the way. We'll start with the outside of the expression (the delimiters and trailing modifiers), then spend most of our time looking at the search pattern syntax itself.

Delimiters

At the beginning and end of every regular expression is a *delimiter* (and if you're talking about a substitution variety of regular expression, there will be one or two more in the middle). The delimiter is a special character that indicates the boundaries of the expression. By default, the delimiter is a forward slash (/), but as you learned previously, you can choose another delimiter if you like in order to make the expression more readable.

As you also saw previously, if you choose as your custom delimiter an opening parenthesis (or one of the other paired delimiters: curly braces, square brackets, or angle brackets), the closing delimiter will be the corresponding closing character from that pair. Additionally, if you do this with a substitution variety of regular expression, you won't have a single delimiter in the middle of the expression, but instead will have a closing delimiter followed immediately by another opening delimiter. What this means is that all of the following mean exactly the same thing to Perl:

```
/walnuts/
m(walnuts)
m{walnuts}
m[walnuts]
m<walnuts>
```

Likewise with the following:

```
s/walnuts/rutabagas/
s(walnuts)(rutabagas)
s{walnuts}{rutabagas}
s[walnuts][rutabagas]
s<walnuts><rutabagas>
```

Regular expression delimiters are actually special cases of Perl's quoting operators, and they behave in a quotish sort of way. In particular, regular expressions act like double-quoted strings, in that they do variable interpolation. Because of this, this chunk of Perl:

```
$walnuts = 'rutabagas';
if (/$walnuts/) {
    # do something
}
```

works more or less the same as this chunk of Perl:

```
if (/rutabagas/) {
    # do something
}
```

I say "more or less the same" because there is, it turns out, one important difference. If the regular expression is going to be evaluated many times (because it is inside a loop, for example), the version without the variable inside it will run faster than the version with the variable. That is because Perl compiles regular expressions into an executable form before running them, and that compilation takes a certain (small, but measurable) amount of time. In the case of a regular expression that contains a variable, the expression must be recompiled before each execution because Perl doesn't know if the contents of the variable have changed since the last time the expression was executed.

We'll look at how you might solve this problem in just a moment, when we talk about the /o modifier.

Trailing Modifiers

After the last delimiter in your regular expression you can place a number of optional modifier characters that affect how the expression operates. Table 7-1 lists the more commonly used ones.

Table 7-1. Regular expression modifiers

Modifier	Description
/g	Make the match global; that is, keep looking for additional matches after the first one has been found.
/i	Match case-insensitively, such that the search pattern /walnuts/i would successfully match Walnuts and WALNUTS and so on.

Table 7-1. Regular expression modifiers (continued)

Modifier	Description
/m	Treat the string as multiple lines. More specifically, let the ^ beginning-of-string anchor and the $ end-of-string anchor match at the beginning or end (respectively) of internal lines within the search string. Without the /m modifier, these anchors would match only at the beginning or end of the entire string.
/o	Compile the regular expression search pattern only once. If the search pattern contains any variables whose contents change after the first time the expression is compiled, those changes won't be reflected in the regular expression. In effect, the /o modifier is a promise by you to Perl that any variables in the search pattern are not going to change during the time the script is running.
/s	Treat the string as a single line, even if it isn't. Specifically, let the special character . (dot), which normally matches any character except a newline, match newline characters embedded in the string.
/x	Allow the use of regular expression *extensions*. This lets you embed comments and whitespace in your regular expressions in order to make them more readable.

We'll cover these modifiers in more detail as they're used for specific regular expressions later on.

The Search Pattern

You've come to the heart of the regular expression: the search pattern itself. This is the string of text between the opening and closing delimiters (with a substitution expression, between the first and second delimiters). You've already seen a fair number of these, so you should have a rough idea of what they look like. Now, though, you're going to learn how Perl's regular expression engine actually processes them.

There are two kinds of characters in a regular expression search pattern. First, there are the *conventional* characters, including all the alphanumeric characters plus the underscore (A-Z, a-z, 0-9, and _), as well as a number of nonalphanumeric characters. All of these conventional characters just match themselves. A regular expression consisting entirely of these characters is easy to understand; it just matches itself. For example, the regular expression /walnuts/ simply matches any string that contains the literal substring walnuts.

 Although it's not a regular expression metacharacter, strictly speaking, the @ character also might need to be backslashed in order to give its literal meaning, if Perl otherwise might be confused about whether it was an array variable whose contents you were trying to interpolate into the regex pattern.

Besides the conventional characters, there are a number of "unconventional" characters, called *metacharacters*, which normally don't match themselves but instead convey some sort of special meaning. The entire list of regular expression metacharacters in Perl is:

```
\ | ( ) [ ] { } ^ $ * + ? .
```

Table 7-2 summarizes the metacharacters' special meanings. (Don't worry if this seems terribly complicated at this point; it will make much more sense once you've had a chance to work with some examples.)

Table 7-2. Regular expression metacharacters

Character	Type	Description
\	Escaping	Used immediately before a nonalphanumeric character, "escapes" the special meaning of that character (if any), causing the character to match literally. Used before an alphanumeric character, does just the opposite: converts that character from a literal character to a sequence with a special meaning (see Table 7-3).
|	Alternation	Used to separate two or more alternatives, any one of which can match at that point in the expression.
( )	Grouping	Used to group part of the search pattern together, for alternation or quantifying purposes. Also, parentheses can be used to capture parts of the matched string for later *backreferencing* via the special variables $1, $2, etc.
[ ]	Character class	Used to define a class of characters, any one of which can match at that point in the expression. Most regular expression metacharacters cease to act as metacharacters inside a character class. Instead, they just stand for themselves—that is, they are viewed as literal characters. One exception is the caret (^); if it is the very *first* character inside the square brackets of a character class, it transforms that character class into a *negated* character class, meaning any character can match *except* the characters listed inside the square brackets. For example, [^abcd] means "match any single character except a, b, c, or d." (Elsewhere in a character class, ^ just stands for itself.) Another special case is the hyphen (-). Outside a character class, it is a literal character. Inside the class, it is used to represent a range of characters that are considered to be part of the class. For example, [a-z] says "match any single lowercase letter of the alphabet."
{ }	Quantifier	Used to enclose a number (or a pair of numbers separated by a comma) that indicates how many times the preceding item in the expression must be repeated in order for the expression to match. {3} means "the preceding item must be repeated exactly 3 times". {3,5} means "the preceding item may be repeated between 3 and 5 times". {3,} means "the preceding item must be repeated at least 3 times." Each of the last two types of quantifiers is *greedy*, meaning it will normally attempt to match as many characters as it can.
^	Anchor	Beginning-of-string anchor. What follows will match only if it appears at the very beginning of the string (or line, if the /m modifier is used). (As described previously, when used as the first character inside a square-bracketed character class, ^ negates the class, making it a list of characters *not* allowed to match at that point.)
$	Anchor	End-of-string anchor. What comes before it will match only if it appears at the very end of the string (or line, if the /m modifier is used).
*	Quantifier	Zero-or-more quantifier. The item that comes before * may be repeated any number of times from zero to infinity. The * is normally greedy, meaning it will match as many characters as it can (as long as the expression as a whole matches). The * can be thought of as a shorthand form of {0,}.
+	Quantifier	One-or-more quantifier. Like *, except the preceding item must occur at least once in order for the match to succeed. Like *, the + is normally greedy and causes the preceding item to match as many times as it can. Shorthand for {1,}.

Table 7-2. Regular expression metacharacters (continued)

Character	Type	Description
?	Quantifier	Zero-or-one quantifier. The preceding item in the expression is optional, in the sense that it can match either zero or one times. Like other quantifiers, the ? is greedy, meaning it prefers to match a character if it can, rather than not matching it. Shorthand for {0,1}. Used immediately after another quantifier, the ? character does something different: it converts the preceding quantifier to nongreedy behavior, in which only the minimum number of items will be matched (as long as the overall expression matches successfully). The ? is also used for various other arcane purposes in regular expressions that you don't need to worry about for now.
.	Wildcard	Matches any single character whatsoever (except a newline). With the /s modifier, matches a newline, too.

As Table 7-2 mentions, the way to make a metacharacter match literally is to precede it by a backslash. Thus, to match a literal backslash in your expression you would use the sequence \\. To match a literal opening parenthesis you'd use \(. And so on. It turns out that even though many punctuation symbols have no special meaning, and hence would match literally if used by themselves, you'll always be safe putting a backslash in front to get their literal meaning. This is a helpful trick when you're still learning regular expression syntax because you can always just backslash your punctuation symbols if you want them to match literally, without worrying about whether that particular symbol is a true metacharacter.

But you do need to be careful not to backslash alphanumeric characters, at least not if you want to use them for their literal meaning. Used before an alphanumeric character, the backslash has the opposite effect: it creates a two-character sequence that has some special meaning. Table 7-3 lists some of the most commonly used two-character sequences:

Table 7-3. Special two-character sequences for regular expressions

Sequence	Description
\b	Word boundary. The expression containing this sequence can match only if the position where \b occurs corresponds to the boundary between a word character (A-Z, a-z, 0-9, and _) and a nonword character.
\B	Nonword-boundary. The expression can match only if \B is *not* at the boundary between a word character and a nonword character.
\d	A digit. Matches any single digit from 0 to 9. \d is shorthand for the character class [0-9].
\D	A nondigit. Matches any single character *except* the digits 0-9. Shorthand for the character class [^0-9].
\n	A newline. Matches the current operating system's line-ending sequence.
\r	A carriage return.
\s	A whitespace character. Matches any of space, tab, newline, carriage return, or formfeed. Same thing as the character class [\t\n\r\f].
\S	A nonwhitespace character. Matches any character *except* space, tab, newline, carriage return, and formfeed. Same thing as the character class [^ \t\n\r\f].
\t	A tab character.

Table 7-3. Special two-character sequences for regular expressions (continued)

Sequence	Description
\w	A word character. Matches all upper- and lowercase letters, numbers, and the underscore character. Same thing as the character class [A-Za-z0-9_].
\W	A nonword character. Matches any character *except* letters, numbers, and the underscore character. Same as the character class [^A-Za-z0-9_].

Taking It for a Spin

That's a lot of information to digest at one sitting. Let's put some of this into practice to help you get a better grasp of it. For this test drive, we'll be using the script shown in Example 7-1.

Example 7-1. A simple script to demonstrate regular expression behavior

```
#!/usr/bin/perl -w

# regex.plx

# test regular expression behavior

$string = 'Walnuts are very nutritious.';

if ($string =~ /Walnuts/) {
    print "Match!\n";
} else {
    print "No match!\n";
}
```

Running this script should yield the following output:

```
[jbc@andros regex]$ regex.plx
Match!
```

This shouldn't be terribly surprising. We're looking for the literal string Walnuts, which occurs inside the string, so we have a match.

Let's try out that fancy word-boundary backslash sequence \b. We can do that by modifying the line containing the regular expression in regex.plx to look like this:

```
if ($string =~ /Wal\bnuts/) {
```

Now when we run the script we should get the following:

```
[jbc@andros regex]$ regex.plx
No match!
```

The \b makes it so that the expression can no longer match, since it doesn't have a word boundary between Wal and nuts.

Now change that \b to a \B (which says there isn't a word boundary at that location):

```
if ($string =~ /Wal\Bnuts/) {
```

When we run the script it should give us:

```
[jbc@andros regex]$ regex.plx
Match!
```

Notice how the \B sequence doesn't actually take up any space in the match. That is, /Wal\Bnuts/ can still match the string Walnuts, even though it has that \B sequence stuck in the middle of it. The \B sequence (like \b, and the anchor metacharacters ^ and $) is what is called a *zero-width assertion*, meaning it simply asserts something about that particular point in the string, without actually taking up any space in the match itself.

Let's get rid of the Wal and go back to using the \b word-boundary assertion before nuts:

```
if ($string =~ /\bnuts/) {
```

As we would probably expect, the match fails because that \b word-boundary assertion still isn't true:

```
[jbc@andros regex]$ regex.plx
No match!
```

Suppose we stick a question mark (?) at the end of nuts, though, so that the line in the script ends up looking like:

```
if ($string =~ /\bnuts?/) {
```

Now when we run the script, we should get:

```
[jbc@andros regex]$ regex.plx
Match!
```

Can you figure out why the addition of the question mark made the expression match? It did so because the ? metacharacter, which is the zero-or-one quantifier, made the letter s in the search pattern *optional*. If you look carefully at the whole string you'll see that there is a place where the expression can match without the s: at the beginning of the word nutritious, where we have nut after a word boundary.

Thinking Like a Computer

The preceding example hints at an important principle of regular expressions (and of programming in general): computers are extremely literal-minded. Even when it looks as if they are thinking the same way a human thinks, they aren't. They are simply carrying out a specific sequence of instructions, very swiftly and very thoroughly.

Nowhere is the difference between human and computer thinking more apparent than in the area of pattern matching. When you use your eyes and brain to search a page for occurrences of a particular string of text, you might find yourself doing something like the following:

1. You think about the thing you're looking for, and stick a conceptual image of it in some sort of special mental holding area.

2. You scan quickly and superficially over the contents of the page, processing the text as words and multiword phrases, letting potential matches "pop out" through some obscure subconscious process.

3. You investigate each potential match more carefully to see if it represents a real match.

Computers do something very different. In the case of Perl's regular expression matching, there is no such thing as scanning "quickly and superficially," no recognition of words or phrases as conceptual units. Perl sees only a string consisting of individual characters in a linear sequence, and only knows one way to scan through it: one character at a time, from beginning to end.

The differences between how you and Perl do pattern matching have been mostly irrelevant in the examples we've looked at so far. When we start throwing in things like quantifiers and alternation, though, it quickly becomes important to have a better understanding of how Perl's regular expressions work.

So far we've just been looking at whether a particular expression matched a particular string. Now let's get a bit fancier and use capturing parentheses to explore just where in the string the expression is matching.

For this step we're going to modify regex.plx to look like Example 7-2. This version uses capturing parentheses around the regular expression, then prints out the contents of $1 using a here-document-quoted string. Notice, by the way, how we use a backslash to escape a literal dollar sign ($) in the here-document (which, with the double quotes in the opening <<"EOF", works like a double-quoted string), allowing us to print the string '$1' rather than having the variable interpolated.

Example 7-2. Regular expression test-bed script modified to use capturing parentheses

```
#!/usr/bin/perl -w

# regex.plx

# test regular expression behavior

$string = 'Walnuts are very nutritious.';

if ($string =~ /(\bnuts?)/) {

    print <<"EOF";
Match!
\$1 got: '$1'
EOF

} else {

    print "No match!\n";

}
```

When we run this new version of the script, it should print out the following:

```
[jbc@andros regex]$ regex.plx
Match!
$1 got: 'nut'
```

Notice how the capturing parentheses capture whatever it was that actually matched in the string. The zero-width word-boundary assertion \b, and the optional s that didn't match, don't show up inside $1.

Now we modify the line containing the regular expression to look like this:

```
if ($string =~ /(nut.*)/) {
```

When we run the script, it should give output like the following:

```
[jbc@andros regex]$ regex.plx
Match!
$1 got: 'nuts are very nutritious.'
```

This does a good job of demonstrating the "greediness" of the star (*). The dot (.) after nut is a wildcard matching any character, and the star says for it to keep on matching as many times as it can. In this case, that means matching all the way to the end of the string.

Bumping Along and Backtracking

Now we modify the regex.plx script to contain the following lines:

```
if ($string =~ /(nut.*)(.*)/) {

    print <<"EOF";
Match!
\$1 got: '$1'
\$2 got: '$2'
EOF
```

Here we've added a second pair of capturing parentheses after the first, with another .* "match as many of anything as you can" sequence inside it. Which raises an interesting question: in the greediness competition between these two greedy stars, which will win? That is, which one will get what? Run the script to find out:

```
[jbc@andros regex]$ regex.pl
Match!
$1 got: 'nuts are very nutritious.'
$2 got: ''
```

Obviously, the first greedy quantifier won. This behavior is typically described as "the leftmost quantifier is greediest," but Perl isn't really thinking in those terms. It is just carrying out a specific sequence of actions that end up producing that result.

Let's explore those actions in more detail. To do so, we modify the regular expression in regex.plx to look like the following:

```
if ($string =~ /(nut.*)(nut.*)/) {
```

As you can see, we are now requiring that the text that matches inside each pair of capturing parentheses must begin with the string 'nut'. When we run this version of the script, we get:

```
[jbc@andros regex]$ regex.plx
Match!
$1 got: 'nuts are very '
$2 got: 'nutritious.'
```

This is probably pretty close to what we expected to see, but it's instructive to consider the specific steps Perl went through to arrive at this result. They're probably a bit different from what we as human beings would have done.

Perl begins by taking the regular expression search pattern (/(nut.*)(nut.*)/) and trying to make it match at the very beginning of the string (by which I mean, the point immediately before the first character in the string). Perl does this by going through the search pattern from left to right, giving up only when it knows that the search pattern as a whole cannot match at that point. In this case, that happens pretty fast because the first thing in the search pattern (once we get past the opening parenthesis, which is just there for capturing purposes) is a literal 'n' character. Since the first character in the string is 'W', the expression as a whole cannot match at that location. Perl doesn't bother checking the rest of the search pattern; it abandons that first location and "bumps along" to the next possible location where the pattern could match: one character later, at the point between the first and second characters in the string. Again, there's no possibility of a match (because the literal 'n' in the pattern can't match the 'a' in the string), so Perl bumps along again, and once again fails right away at the 'l'.

Then something interesting happens: Perl tries matching at the point in the string between the 'l' and 'n' in Walnuts, and finds that the first item in the pattern (the literal 'n') does indeed match at that point in the string. Perl goes on to try the next item in the pattern, which is a literal 'u', and finds that it successfully matches the next character in the string, and then the same thing happens again with the 't'.

So far Perl has been proceeding through the search pattern one literal character at a time. The next item in the pattern (the dot) has a quantifier (the star) associated with it, so Perl considers that whole thing (.*) as one item for matching purposes.

In regular expression circles, such an item is referred to as a *quantified atom*. (The three literal characters nut that came before can be thought of as quantified atoms, too; they just happen to be quantified with a default quantity of one, the same as if each one had a {1} after it.)

The dot, you remember, is a wildcard that matches anything, and with the star after it, it can match zero or more times. The first thing Perl tries, therefore, is to match it zero times, which of course succeeds. You might think this is a silly thing to do, and it is, at least as far as the stuff being captured into $1 is concerned, but it still is important because Perl is working its way through the search pattern, making sure each item in it successfully matches. This item (the .*) has now successfully matched, even before any more of the string has been captured into $1, such that Perl could go on with the rest of the pattern from this point in the string if it had to. But it doesn't have to, yet, because it's not finished with .*. Being greedy, the .* wants to continue grabbing as many characters as it can, which it will do in a second. But first, Perl makes a mental note, so to speak, that there was a successful match here, with the .* matching nothing at all, so it can come back to this point later on if it needs to in order to make the entire pattern match. The official way to say this is that Perl *saves a state* at this point in the attempted match. Having saved that state, it then goes on to match another character with .*, then saves state again, then matches another character, saves state, and so on all the way to the end of the string, where the .* can't match anything more.

So far so good. Now Perl goes on to the next item in the search pattern, which, after the closing and opening capturing parentheses, is the literal n in the second nut.*. That fails because the previous .* sucked up the rest of the string, so there's nothing left to match. Perl therefore says, okay, this particular attempt to match the entire expression has failed, but I've got all those saved states to examine still. So, it begins *backtracking*, returning first to the most recently saved state (in which the .* had matched everything except the string's last character, the period). It still can't match the literal n there, so it keeps on backtracking (and failing) until it reaches the beginning of the word nutritious, where the n *does* match, and then the u, and the t, and then, finally, the second .* gets the rest of the string. At this point the entire pattern has matched, so Perl declares victory and stops.

Alternation

Next we modify the regular expression in regex.plx to look like this:

```
if ($string =~ /(nutritious|Walnuts)(.*)/)
```

Here we've used the vertical bar (|), which you'll remember is the *alternation metacharacter*, to say that the first pair of capturing parentheses in the regular expression can capture either the string nutritious or the string Walnuts. In evaluating a set of alternatives like this, Perl will begin with the leftmost alternative and go on to try subsequent alternatives only after the first one has been shown conclusively to fail at the current position in the string. You'll notice that the word nutritious, which comes later in the string, has been given as the first alternative to look for.

Here's a pop quiz: what will be captured into $1, nutritious or Walnuts? We can run the script to find out:

```
[jbc@andros regex]$ regex.plx
Match!
$1 got: 'Walnuts'
$2 got: ' are very nutritious.'
```

Did you fall into the trap? As a human being looking at the pattern / (nutritious|Walnuts)(.*)/, you might interpret it as, "Look for the word nutritious, and look for Walnuts only if that fails." Because of that, you might have been tempted to think that nutritious would be captured into $1, even though it starts to the right of Walnuts. But Perl doesn't think that way. It just follows the rules of regular expression matching. Those rules state that it will begin by trying every possible way of matching in the first position (that is, before the first character of the string), and bump along to subsequent positions only if the match fails at that first position. This means it tries the first alternative (in fact, just the first letter of that alternative), has it fail, and then jumps immediately over the | and tries the second alternative, which succeeds.

Let's try one more example. We begin by modifying regex.plx's search expression to look like this:

```
if ($string =~ /(nut)*(.*)/) {
```

Can you guess what will be captured by the two sets of parentheses? Run the script to find out:

```
[jbc@andros regex]$ regex.pl
Use of uninitialized value at ./regex.pl line 9.
Match!
$1 got: ''
$2 got: 'Walnuts are very nutritious.'
```

A quantifier (like *) placed immediately after a pair of parentheses quantifies whatever is inside those parentheses. In this case, the star after (nut) has the effect of saying "match the string nut zero or more times." This means nut would match, as would nutnut, and nutnutnut, and so on. But it also means that the empty string matches, which is what happened here: the empty string matched, and the following (.*) got the rest of the string, so the entire search pattern had matched, and Perl declared victory and quit. We need to be careful about this effect when using *: the zero-quantity match will always succeed, and may well end up short-circuiting some other behavior we were expecting. You can think of this as an exception to the "leftmost is greediest" rule; in this case, the left quantifier ended up with less than it could have had if it held out for a later match.

Oh, about that warning: even though the match succeeded, nothing was captured in the first set of capturing parentheses, so we got an "uninitialized value" warning when we tried to print out $1. For some strange reason, my version of Perl reported the problem as occurring on the line number corresponding to the if statement that started the block, rather than the line where the variable was actually used.

We could learn a lot more about regular expressions, things like *non-capturing parentheses* and the impressively named *zero-width negative lookahead assertions*, but with what we've learned so far we'll be able to handle 90% of the situations we'll encounter in day-to-day programming. In any event, we're going to declare victory ourselves at this point and move on.

 Find out more about regular expression delimiters and modifiers in the section on "Regexp Quote-Like Operators" in the perlop manpage, and more about search pattern syntax in the perlre manpage.

## CHAPTER 8

Parsing Web Access Logs

Web server access logs are an excellent source of information about what your site's visitors are up to. The information on separate visitors is all mixed together, though, and for all but the smallest sites the raw access logs are too large to read directly. What you need is log analysis software to make the information in the log more easily accessible. You can buy commercial log analysis software to do this, but Perl makes it easy to write your own. The next three chapters describe how to build such a home-grown log-analysis tool.

This chapter focuses on the first part of the process: extracting and storing the information we're interested in. We talk about log file structure, converting IP addresses, and creating regular expressions capable of parsing web access logs. We also talk about creating a suitable data structure for storing the extracted data, so we can answer interesting questions about what our site's visitors have been doing. Along the way we discuss the difficulty of identifying those visitors in the web server's log entries and devise an approach for extracting at least an approximate version of that information.

The example continues in Chapter 9, which focuses on how to do computations involving dates and times, and finishes in Chapter 10, which covers the specifics of how we manipulate the "visit" information from our logs, as well as the actual output of the finished report.

Log File Structure

Most web servers store their access log in what is called the "common log format." Each time a user requests a file from the server, a line containing the following fields is added to the end of the log file:

host

> This is either the IP address (like 207.71.222.231) or the corresponding hostname (like pm9-31.sba1.avtel.net) of the remote user requesting the page. For performance reasons, many web servers are configured not to do hostname lookups on

the remote host. This means that all you end up with in the log file is a bunch of IP addresses. A bit later in this chapter, you'll develop a Perl script that you can use to convert those IP addresses into hostnames.

identd result

This is a field for logging the response returned by the remote user's *identd* server. Almost no one actually uses this; in every web log I've ever seen, this field is always just a dash (-).

authuser

If you are using basic 'ecHTTP authentication (which we'll be talking about in Chapter 19) to restrict access to some of your web documents, this is where the username of the authenticated user for this transaction will be recorded. Otherwise, it will be just a dash (-).

date and time

Next comes a date and time string inside square brackets, like: [06/Jul/1999:00: 09:12 -0700]. That's the day of the month, the abbreviated month name, and the four-digit year, all separated by slashes. Next come the time (expressed in 24-hour format, so 11:30 P.M. would be 23:30:00) and a time-zone offset (in this example, -0700, because the web server this log was from was using Pacific Daylight Time, which is seven hours behind Universal Time/Greenwich Mean Time).

request

This is the actual request sent by the remote user, enclosed in double quotes. Normally it will look something like: "GET / HTTP/1.0". The GET part means it is a GET request (as opposed to a POST or a HEAD request). The next part is the path of the URL requested; in this case, the default page in the server's top-level directory, as indicated by a single slash (/). The last part of the request is the protocol being used, at the time of this writing typically HTTP/1.0 or HTTP/1.1.

status code

This is the status code returned by the server; by definition this will be a three-digit number. A status code of 200 means everything was handled okay, 304 means the document has not changed since the client last requested it, 404 means the document could not be found, and 500 indicates that there was some sort of server-side error. (More detail on the various status codes can be found in RFC 1945, which describes the HTTP/1.0 protocol. See *http://www.w3.org/ Protocols/rfc1945/rfc1945*.)

bytes sent

The amount of data returned by the server, not counting the header line.

An extended version of this log format, often referred to as the "combined" format, includes two additional fields at the end:

referer

The referring page, if any, as reported by the remote user's browser. Note that *referer* is consistently misspelled (with a single "r" in the middle) in the HTTP specification, and in the name of the corresponding environment variable.

user agent

The user agent reported by the remote user's browser. Typically, this is a string describing the type and version of browser software being used.

Assuming you have control over your web server's configuration, or can get your ISP to modify it for you, the combined format's extra fields can provide some very interesting information about the users visiting your site. The log analysis script described in this chapter will work with either format, however.

Converting IP Addresses

Before we jump into log-file analysis, let's return briefly to the problem of doing hostname lookups on the IP addresses that most likely comprise the "host" entries in our web access logs. Example 8-1 gives a script, clf_lookup.plx, that does just that. (Like all the examples in this book, it is available for download from the book's web site, at *http://www.elanus.net/book/*.)

Example 8-1. A script to do hostname lookups on IP addresses in web access logs

```perl
#!/usr/bin/perl -w

# clf_lookup.plx

# given common or extended-format web logs on STDIN, outputs
# them with numeric IP addresses in the first (host) field converted
# to hostnames (where possible).

use strict;
use Socket;

my %hostname;

while (<>) {
    my $line = $_;
    my($host, $rest) = split / /, $line, 2;
    if ($host =~ /^\d+\.\d+\.\d+\.\d+$/) {
        # looks vaguely like an IP address
        unless (exists $hostname{$host}) {
            # no key, so haven't processed this IP before
            $hostname{$host} = gethostbyaddr(inet_aton($host), AF_INET);
        }
        if ($hostname{$host}) {
            # only processes IPs with successful lookups
            $line = "$hostname{$host} $rest";
        }
    }
    print $line;
}
```

The script itself is pretty simple, but it introduces some new concepts that are definitely worth learning about. The first new thing is this line:

```perl
use Socket;
```

Here we are importing a module called Socket.pm. Just as we did earlier, when we pulled in the CGI.pm module, we're doing this in order to let some more experienced programmers do our dirty work for us. Specifically, the use Socket declaration in this script means we'll be able to do *DNS lookups* (converting numeric IP addresses to hostnames) using just a few lines of code.

Thousands of Perl modules are available. Some are distributed as part of the Perl language itself; these are usually referred to as being in the *standard distribution*, or as the *standard module* Walnuts.pm. (CGI.pm and Socket.pm are in the standard distribution.) Others can be found at CPAN, the Comprehensive Perl Archive Network, which we'll be learning more about in Chapter 11. If you can't wait until then, though (which I can totally understand, CPAN being something like the world's biggest toy store for a Perl programmer), see the accompanying sidebar, "Using CPAN," for details on how you can jump the gun and start exploring CPAN on your own.

Using CPAN

CPAN, the Comprehensive Perl Archive Network, is the official place to (among other things) get Perl modules that are not included in the standard distribution (that is, that are not distributed automatically along with all recent versions of the language). The hardest part about dealing with CPAN, at least for a beginning programmer, is that it is so extensive. With user contributions from all over the world, it has grown like kudzu, spreading organically in all directions, defying efforts to organize its contents usefully for anyone unwilling to spend a significant amount of time studying it.

Of course, if you are spending much time at all programming with Perl, the time spent learning what's in CPAN will be repaid many times over by the time you save using other people's code to perform common tasks rather than reinventing the wheel.

In any event, the following resources will help you get started with CPAN:

http://www.cpan.org/README.html
> The top-level overview of what's in CPAN, with links to more-specific starting points

http://www.cpan.org/modules/
> The top-level page within the modules portion of CPAN, with pointers to various views of the modules

http://www.cpan.org/modules/00modlist.long.html
> A long, annotated list of all the modules in CPAN

http://search.cpan.org/
> The CPAN search engine

The next thing in clf_lookup.plx is a my variable declaration for the %hostname hash. This is going to be used to cache hostname lookups while the script is running. That way, each IP address will have to be looked up only once rather than every time it appears in the log. It is important to initialize the %hostname hash out here, before the while loop that actually processes each line from the log file, because putting my %hostname inside the loop block would make it so that a new copy of the hash was created each time through the loop.

Let's get to the loop now. The beginning of the loop takes the form:

```
while (<>) {
```

Here we're beginning a while loop, which you'll remember means we're going to run a block of code repeatedly as long as whatever is inside those parentheses evaluates to a true value. But what a weird thing we've got inside that logical test. It looks somewhat like the angle-input operator we use to read lines from a filehandle, but there's no filehandle inside it.

What the <> (which is sometimes called the *diamond operator*) is doing is this: it looks at the @ARGV array (which you'll remember from Chapter 4 is the special variable holding your script's command-line arguments) and assumes that those arguments represent the names of one or more text files. The <> operator then returns the text from those files, one line at a time, so you can work with those lines in the body of your while block. It keeps feeding you lines of text until it has exhausted all of the first file mentioned in @ARGV, then goes on to the second file, and so on, until it has exhausted all the files mentioned in @ARGV. After the last line from the last file has been delivered, it returns undef (the *undefined value*), which is false, ending the loop.

You get an interesting extra feature with the <> operator. If you don't give your script any command-line arguments, such that there are no files mentioned in @ARGV, <> instead will read from *standard input* (that is, from the STDIN filehandle your script gets by default when it is started up). This in turn lets you do cool things like use your script in a shell pipeline to process the input or output for another program. In fact, we'll be using that feature with this script a little later.

Where does the <> operator put each line of text as it is working its way through the files mentioned in @ARGV? In the special scalar variable $_. As I mentioned previously, many of Perl's operators and functions are designed to work with $_ by default, and this ends up being really handy because it lets you write certain common operations very quickly.

In this case, though, we're going to go ahead and stick the contents of $_ into something a little more memorable. That happens in the next line:

```
my $line = $_;
```

Next comes the following:

```
my($host, $rest) = split / /, $line, 2;
if ($host =~ /^\d+\.\d+\.\d+\.\d+$/) {
    # looks vaguely like an IP address
```

Here you are using the `split` function to take the current line from the log file and separate it into everything before the first space character (which goes into the scalar variable $host) and everything after the first space character (which goes into $rest). This takes advantage of an optional third argument to the `split` function, with that argument being a number telling `split` how many fields to split the string into (in this case, two, because we don't need to keep splitting once we've split off the first field).

Next comes an `if` statement with a regular expression in the logical test. With your new understanding of regular expressions it should be pretty easy to decipher the meaning of /^\d+\.\d+\.\d+\.\d+$/: it matches a string consisting of four sets of one or more numbers each, separated by periods. This is not the exact same thing as an IP address (in which the component numbers can fall only within a certain range); this pattern is naïve, in that it would accept as IP addresses things like 98765.1234.1.1, but it's close enough for our current purpose.

Next come these two lines:

```
unless (exists $hostname{$host}) {
    # no key, so haven't processed this IP before
```

As discussed earlier, we're going to use $hostname{$host} to keep track of the IP addresses we've already looked up. Sometimes, though, we will attempt to look up an IP address and find that it can't be resolved to a hostname. In such cases, we'll stick undef into the value corresponding to $hostname{$host}. The hash will still have a key corresponding to that IP address, but there won't be an associated value. By testing for the existence of a particular hash key (which is what the exists function lets us do), we can avoid entering this `if` block if we come across those hosts again.

Next comes the actual looking up of the hostname, which is quite simple, thanks to the `Socket.pm` module:

```
    $hostname{$host} = gethostbyaddr(inet_aton($host), AF_INET);
}
```

gethostbyaddr is a Perl function that provides an interface to the computer's underlying hostname lookup function. The two arguments of inet_aton($host) and AF_INET are a little bit of magic provided courtesy of `Socket.pm`.

Next comes this:

```
    if ($hostname{$host}) {
        # only processes IPs with successful lookups
        $line = "$hostname{$host} $rest";
    }
}
```

If the gethostbyaddr returned a false value for this particular $hostname{$host} (meaning this IP address couldn't be resolved to a hostname), the script will skip over this block. Otherwise, it will re-create the $line variable (which corresponds to the current line from the log file) by interpolating the looked-up hostname in

`$hostname{$host}` into a string, along with the `$rest` variable (which you will recall holds the rest of the line).

The two closing curly braces end the two `if` blocks we were in, after which we print out just the current value of `$line`:

```
    print $line;
}
```

This script jumps through a number of hoops in the interest of cutting down the actual work it does—caching the lookups and avoiding rebuilding `$line` unless it has to make the script a little more involved—but it is worth taking that sort of care with a program like this because it may end up having to process some very big log files. Even with these tricks, because the `gethostbyaddr` function normally takes a certain amount of time to give up on an IP address that can't be resolved, this script will tend to take a long time to process large log files.

One use of `clf_lookup.plx` that is kind of fun is to put it in a pipeline to convert your log file's IP addresses into hostnames on the fly. For example, if your log file is called `access.log`, you could use the `tail` command with the `-f` switch to watch that log growing in real time, piping the output through `clf_lookup.plx` to convert the hostnames, like this:

```
[jbc@andros .logs]$ tail -f access.log | clf_lookup.plx
```

The Log-Analysis Script

Now that the hostname lookups are taken care of, it's time to write the log-analysis script. Example 8-2 shows the first version of that script.

Example 8-2. log_report.plx, a web log-analysis script (first version)

```perl
#!/usr/bin/perl -w

# log_report.plx

# report on web visitors

use strict;

while (<>) {
    my ($host, $ident_user, $auth_user, $date, $time,
            $time_zone, $method, $url, $protocol, $status, $bytes) =
/^(\S+) (\S+) (\S+) \[([^:]+):(\d+:\d+:\d+) ([^\]]+)\] "(\S+) (.+?)
 (\S+)" (\S+) (\S+)$/;

    print join "\n", $host, $ident_user, $auth_user, $date, $time,
        $time_zone, $method, $url, $protocol, $status,
        $bytes, "\n";
}
```

This first version of the script is simple. All it does is read in lines via the <> operator, parse those lines into their component pieces, and then print out the parsed elements for debugging purposes. The line that does the printing out is interesting, in that it uses Perl's join function, which you haven't seen before. The join function is the polar opposite, so to speak, of the split function: it lets you specify a string (in its first argument) that will be used to join the list comprising the rest of its arguments into a scalar. In other words, the Perl expression join '-', 'a', 'b', 'c' would return the string a-b-c. And in this case, using \n to join the various elements parsed by our script lets us print out a newline-separated list of those parsed items.

The Mammoth Regular Expression

The real juicy part of this script, though, is that giant regular expression used to parse each log file line into its component parts. Here's that part of the script again:

```
    my ($host, $ident_user, $auth_user, $date, $time,
            $time_zone, $method, $url, $protocol, $status, $bytes) =
/^(\S+) (\S+) (\S+) \[([^:]+):(\d+:\d+:\d+) ([^\]]+)\] "(\S+) (.+?)
    (\S+)" (\S+) (\S+)$/;
```

There are a couple of important things to note here. The first is that it is actually fairly tricky to represent this regular expression, which is meant to be on a single line, within the limited width of this book's pages. It's particularly tricky in this case because the spaces between the various elements are important, but it's hard to keep track of those spaces when the expression is broken to fit onto multiple lines. If you are going to test this script yourself, be sure that your version of the expression is all on one line, with a single space character between the right parenthesis that ends the first line and the begin parenthesis that begins the second line. (Or you can just download the example from the book's web site, at *http://www.elanus.net/book/*, since the downloadable example doesn't feature those problematic line breaks.) You also can refer to the version of this expression created using the /x modifier, which is described in the accompanying sidebar, "Regular Expression Extensions," and use that version instead of the one-line version given here.

The second interesting thing about this chunk of code is how we're taking advantage of the fact that a regular expression that contains capturing parentheses, if you place it in a list context, returns a list of all the elements captured by those parentheses. This means you can stick a list of scalar variables inside parentheses on the left side of the assignment operator, and a regular expression containing capturing parentheses on the right, and assign all the captured substrings in one fell swoop.

Let's go through the regular expression search pattern one chunk at a time:

```
/^(\S+) (\S+) (\S+)
```

The first thing in the expression is the beginning-of-string anchor (^). Next comes one or more nonwhitespace characters (\S+), which will match only if they are the first thing on the line (thanks to that beginning-of-string anchor). Because they are

Regular Expression Extensions

Putting the /x modifier at the end of a regular expression lets you use regular expression "extensions." This means that you can put *whitespace* characters (like spaces, tabs, and newlines) into the expression, and they will be ignored by Perl when trying to make a match. (The one exception to this is inside a square-bracketed character class, where literal whitespace characters will still count.) To get a literal whitespace character outside a character class you need to precede it by a backslash. Also, you can embed comments in the expression by preceding them with the hash symbol (#), just like you can with regular Perl statements. The idea is that you can break your expression across multiple lines and use indenting and comments in an effort to make it more easily understood.

With a substitution expression, by the way, the /x modifier applies only to the search pattern (the first half of the expression). The replacement part (the second half) still treats whitespace and the # sign as literal characters.

Here's how you might use the /x modifier to represent the regular expression in Example 8-2:

```
my ($host, $ident_user, $auth_user, $date, $time,
    $time_zone, $method, $url, $protocol, $status,
    $bytes) =

    /                # regexp begins
    ^                # beginning-of-string anchor
    (\S+)            # assigned to $host
    \                # literal space
    (\S+)            # assigned to $ident_user
    \                # literal space
    (\S+)            # assigned to $auth_user
    \                # literal space
    \[([^:]+)        # assigned to $date
    :                # literal :
    (\d+:\d+:\d+)    # assigned to $time
    \                # literal space
    ([^\]]+)         # assigned to $time_zone
    \]\ "            # literal string '] "'
    (\S+)            # assigned to $method
    \                # literal space   .
    (.+?)            # assigned to $url
    \                # literal space
    (\S+)            # assigned to $protocol
    "\               # literal string '" '
    (\S+)            # assigned to $status
    \                # literal space
    (\S+)            # assigned to $bytes
    $                # end-of-string anchor
    /x;              # regexp ends, with x modifier
```

enclosed by parentheses, whatever matches will be captured into the $host variable in the corresponding list on the left side of the assignment (and into $1, too, though we're not doing anything with that).

Next comes a literal space, then another sequence of one or more nonwhitespace characters, which is captured into $ident_user. Next comes another literal space, and (again) one or more nonwhitespace characters, which are captured into $auth_user.

After that comes another literal space, then the following interesting chunk:

```
\[([^:]+):(\d+:\d+:\d+) ([^\]]+)\]
```

This part of the pattern starts off by matching a literal left bracket ([). Next it captures one or more characters that are anything but colons (:). Then comes a colon, and then it captures a string consisting of three sets of one or more digits separated by colons. Next there is a space, after which the pattern captures one or more characters that are anything but a right bracket (]). Finally, the pattern matches a right bracket. In other words, it matches a date string that looks like:

```
[06/Jul/1999:00:09:12 -0700]
```

and in doing so captures the date, time, and time zone offset into the $date, $time, and $time_zone variables, respectively.

After that part of the pattern comes another literal space, and then this:

```
"(\S+) (.+?) (\S+)"
```

This part matches the request as sent by the web browser to the server. As mentioned earlier, that request typically looks something like this:

```
"GET / HTTP/1.0"
```

The tricky thing about this part of the pattern is the stuff inside the middle set of capturing parentheses. That's where you match the path of the actual page requested. At first glance you would probably be tempted to use (\S+) to match that part, on the theory that the requested path is unlikely to contain spaces, but occasionally a space will creep into the path, if only because a user accidentally typed one in when manually specifying the URL.

You could use something like ([^"]+) to match the URL part of the request, which would match all the way out to the double quote, and count on the fact that Perl would then backtrack to match the time zone, which needs to have a double quote after it. The problem with this, though, is that it would be relatively inefficient because you'd be making Perl do a lot of backtracking on almost every line.

The solution given here is better. By using .+? to match the URL, you say "match one or more of anything, but don't be greedy." This means the expression will match only as much as it has to in order to make the rest of the expression match. Once it has matched all of the requested URL, the rest of the expression should match, meaning you'll get what you were looking for without a lot of backtracking.

The last part of the regular expression is fairly simple, capturing the next two one-or-more-nonwhitespace chunks into $status and $bytes, with an end-of-string anchor at the end.

And that's it. The only remaining part of the script is the debugging print statement that outputs each captured item on its own line, with an extra newline at the end to put a blank line after each line's data has been printed out:

```
print join "\n", $host, $ident_user, $auth_user, $date, $time,
    $time_zone, $method, $url, $protocol, $status,
    $bytes, "\n";
```

Notice, by the way, how we've just stuck a print function in front of the join function. This chaining together of two or more functions, where the function on the right returns something that serves as the argument for the function on the left, is a handy shortcut you'll see experienced Perl users using all the time.

Before we test the script, we should think for a minute about what will happen in the case where a line from the log file doesn't match that monster regular expression. There's a fairly good chance that *all* the lines will fail to match the first time we try it because that expression is big and complicated, and one typo will mess the whole thing up. Even after we have it working properly, though, there's always the chance that a screwy line will show up in the log and fail to be parsed properly. What will happen in that case?

What will happen is that the match will fail, and nothing will be assigned to all those variables. If they were global variables, and we were counting on the successful match to replace whatever was already in them from processing the previous line, our script would now go on to print out the previous line's data all over again, which would be a problem. Since we are using my to give us a fresh batch of variables each time through the loop, though, we don't have to worry about that. Even so, we still have a problem. Since none of the variables were successfully assigned for this trip through the loop, the -w switch will cause our script to emit a bunch of "Use of uninitialized variable" warnings as soon as it comes to that print statement.

Perhaps the best thing to do in cases where a line doesn't match is to just bail out and go on to the next line. This behavior turns out to be very easy to add to the script: we just put or next at the end of the line containing the regular expression assignment:

```
($host, $ident_user, $auth_user, $date, $time,
            $time_zone, $method, $url, $protocol, $status, $bytes) =
/^(\S+) (\S+) (\S+) \[([^:]+):(\d+:\d+:\d+) ([^\]]+)\] "(\S+) (.+?)
 (\S+)" (\S+) (\S+)$/
            or next;
```

How does this work? The next function tells Perl to go on to the next iteration of the loop we're in. Putting or something at the end of a line of a Perl expression causes everything to the left of the or to be evaluated in a *Boolean context* (that is, evaluated to see if it yields a true or false value). If our regular expression fails to match, it will return an empty list. That not only means that all those variables will get undef assigned to them; it also means the whole expression will be false, which means the stuff to the right of the or will be executed. In general, you can put or (something) on the right side of the regular expression, and whatever you put there will fire off only in cases where the expression fails to match.

Different Log File Formats

It's fairly easy to modify this script to accept either the common or the extended log format. We do that by adding a configuration variable near the top of the script that looks like this:

```
my $log_format = 'common'; # 'common' or 'extended'
```

Then we modify the part of the script where the regular expression parsing occurs to include some logic to check that $log_format variable, along with a second version of the regular expression to be used on logs that are in the extended format:

```
    if ($log_format eq 'common') {

        ($host, $ident_user, $auth_user, $date, $time,
            $time_zone, $method, $url, $protocol, $status, $bytes) =
/^(\S+) (\S+) (\S+) \[([^:]+):(\d+:\d+:\d+) ([^\]]+)\] "(\S+) (.+?)
  (\S+)" (\S+) (\S+)$/
            or next;

    } elsif ($log_format eq 'extended') {

        ($host, $ident_user, $auth_user, $date, $time,
            $time_zone, $method, $url, $protocol, $status, $bytes,
            $referer, $agent) =
/^(\S+) (\S+) (\S+) \[([^:]+):(\d+:\d+:\d+) ([^\]]+)\] "(\S+) (.+?)
  (\S+)" (\S+) (\S+) "([^"]+)" "([^"]+)"$/
            or next;
    } else {
        die "unrecognized log format '$log_format'";
    }
```

I think this probably qualifies as the ugliest block of code in this entire book. This is not the sort of code that anybody wants to have to make sense of more than once, but fortunately, once we get it right, we aren't likely to need to modify it.

Anyway, you'll notice that the new regular expression for extended-format logs has a couple of new chunks at the end, both of which look like "([^"]+)". By now that should be an easy one for you: it means "match a literal double quote, then capture one or more characters that are anything but a double quote, then match another literal double quote." These two new chunks capture into the new $referer and $agent variables that we've added at the end of the parenthetical list being assigned to.

We've also added an else block, which just does a quick sanity check, dying with an error message if the $log_format variable was inadvertently set to an unexpected value.

You may have noticed that there is no my declaration before the list of variables in either branch of the if-elsif construct. That's because declaring those variables as my variables here, inside the curly braces of the if-elsif block, would limit their visibility later on in the while block, where they need to be visible. As a result, we've moved the my declaration for the variables above the if-elsif construct, just after the while (<>) line:

```
my ($host, $ident_user, $auth_user, $date, $time,
    $time_zone, $method, $url, $protocol, $status, $bytes,
    $referer, $agent);
```

We should also add the $referer and $agent variables to the list of variables that the debugging print statement should print out. This will give us some extra blank lines in the output if our log file is actually in the common format, but that print statement is just a quick debugging tool anyway; the real output that the script produces later will be implemented more intelligently:

```
print join "\n", $host, $ident_user, $auth_user, $date, $time,
    $time_zone, $method, $url, $protocol, $status,
    $bytes, $referer, $agent, "\n";
```

The entire script as it should look at this point is given in Example 8-3.

Example 8-3. Second version of the log_report.plx script

```
#!/usr/bin/perl -w

# log_report.plx

# report on web visitors

use strict;

my $log_format = 'common'; # 'common' or 'extended'

while (<>) {

    my ($host, $ident_user, $auth_user, $date, $time,
        $time_zone, $method, $url, $protocol, $status, $bytes,
        $referer, $agent);

    if ($log_format eq 'common') {

        ($host, $ident_user, $auth_user, $date, $time,
            $time_zone, $method, $url, $protocol, $status, $bytes) =
/^(\S+) (\S+) (\S+) \[([^:]+):(\d+:\d+:\d+) ([^\]]+)\] "(\S+) (.+?)
(\S+)" (\S+) (\S+)$/
            or next;

    } elsif ($log_format eq 'extended') {
```

Example 8-3. Second version of the log_report.plx script (continued)

```
        ($host, $ident_user, $auth_user, $date, $time,
            $time_zone, $method, $url, $protocol, $status, $bytes,
            $referer, $agent) =
/^(\S+) (\S+) (\S+) \[([^:]+):(\d+:\d+:\d+) ([^\]]+)\] "(\S+) (.+?)
 (\S+)" (\S+) (\S+) "([^"]+)" "([^"]+)"$/
            or next;
    } else {
        die "unrecognized log format '$log_format'";
    }

    print join "\n", $host, $ident_user, $auth_user, $date, $time,
        $time_zone, $method, $url, $protocol, $status,
        $bytes, $referer, $agent, "\n";
}
```

Now we're ready to test the log_report.plx script on a real log file, to make sure the regular expression is actually parsing the way we think it should. We set the $log_format variable to the appropriate value for our log files, then try using something like this in the shell (substituting appropriate pathnames as needed) to redirect the log file into the script's standard input and then pipe the script's output to more:

    [jbc@andros .logs]$ **log_report.plx < access.log | more**

If our log file has only IP addresses and no hostnames, we can put the clf_lookup.plx script we created earlier at the beginning of the pipeline with something like this:

    [jbc@andros .logs]$ **clf_lookup.plx < access.log | log_report.plx | more**

This makes use of a new shell redirection symbol that we haven't used before, the left angle bracket (<). The < character tells the shell to redirect the contents of a file into a command's standard input.

If we enter the command line given here and nothing prints out, we need to make sure we've got the log file path and filename correct. If that's not the problem, we need to double-check the configuration variable to make sure it has the appropriate value for our log file format (and take a careful look at the log file, too, to make sure it really is in the common or extended format).

If the script still doesn't output anything, the problem is probably in our regular expression. We need to make sure it is all on one line and has the appropriate spacing between the various elements. As a last resort, we can try shortening it a little bit at a time (or building it up from nothing a little bit at a time), getting it so that it successfully matches and captures something, at least, then adding additional elements until the whole thing is working.

Storing the Data

Now that we're successfully parsing out the individual elements from each line in the log file, what are we going to do with them? It's time to think about what sorts of things we want to keep track of, and how to represent them in our data structure.

One good thing to keep track of is the time of the first and last access processed. When printed out in our report, this will let us see what range of time is covered by the analyzed log file lines.

Another obvious thing to keep track of is how many raw hits are in the log file. Similarly, we can track the total amount of data (in megabytes) sent out by the server, and the number of HTML page views.

We'll begin implementing these features by adding the following to the top of the log_report.plx script, just before the start of the while loop that parses the log file lines:

```
my($begin_time, $end_time, $total_hits, $total_mb, $total_views);
```

This establishes a number of scalar variables that will be visible throughout the script, and will be used to store the various categories of information we're interested in tracking.

Now, at the end of the while loop, we'll comment out that debugging print statement and add the new lines shown here in order to store those various pieces of data:

```
#    print join "\n", $host, $ident_user, $auth_user, $date, $time,
#        $time_zone, $method, $url, $protocol, $status,
#        $bytes, $referer, $agent, "\n";

unless ($begin_time) {
    $begin_time = "$date:$time";
}
$end_time = "$date:$time";

++$total_hits;
$total_mb += ($bytes / (1024 * 1024));

next if $url =~ /\.(gif|jpg|jpeg|png|xbm)$/i;
# don't care about these for visit-tracking purposes

++$total_views;
&store_line($host, $date, $time, $url, $referer, $agent);
}
```

We stick the assignment to $begin_time inside an unless block that checks to see if the variable has been assigned already, so it only gets assigned when the first line of the log file is processed. The $end_time variable is just overwritten with the current values of $date and $time for every line, such that we end up with the date and time of the last access when we're done parsing the log file.

Adding one to $total_hits each time through the loop using the auto-increment operator (++) is easy enough to understand. $total_mb is assigned using the interesting += operator, which does what you would probably guess it does: it takes whatever number is on the right and adds it to the contents of the variable on the left, storing the new sum in the variable. It is thus the equivalent of:

```
$total_mb = $total_mb + ($bytes / (1024 * 1024));
```

except it's a bit easier to write. Dividing $bytes by the product of 1024 * 1024 simply converts that number to megabytes.

The next line uses that handy condensed form of an if statement: do something if something else. In this case, it says to bail out and go to the next cycle through the while loop (which in this case means going to the next line in the log file) if the contents of $url end in .gif, .jpg, .jpeg, .png, or .xbm. This reflects the fact that we're only interested in actual "page views" at this point, and don't care about the image files whose requests also end up in the log file. We could instead have used something like:

```
next unless $url =~ /\.html?$/;
```

which would skip to the next line from the log file unless the current line's $url ended in .htm or .html, but this would skip requests for CGI scripts and for directories that return a default page such as index.html. It probably makes sense to count those requests in $total_views.

Next, now that we've gotten rid of those extraneous log file entries, it's time to add one to the contents of $total_views. And finally, we invoke a subroutine called &store_line with the arguments $host, $time, $url, $referer, and $agent. We'll be using that subroutine in an effort to generate statistics on something more interesting: the activities of the individual visitors to our site.

The "Visit" Data Structure

Trying to track individual visitors via the entries in a web server's access log is something of an exercise in futility. With things like proxy servers and client-side caching getting in the way, the series of accesses that show up in the log from a particular hostname or IP address can give only an approximate picture of what individual visitors are doing. Multiple users sharing the same IP address can have their activity merged into what looks like a single, very active visitor. Conversely, a single visitor can show up in the logs via a different IP address on each request, defying efforts to abstract those requests into a meaningful "visit." A proxy server at a major ISP can cache the site's pages, then satisfy hundreds of requests that never get recorded in the server's logs.

Even so, it's hard not to wonder what a log file would reveal if we could pluck out the requests corresponding to specific hosts and string them together to see what patterns emerge. Many users still browse from individual host addresses without intervening proxy servers; for these users, at least, the resulting "visit" tracking provides a fascinating look at the paths being followed through the site. It's also interesting to see how many incoming requests are actually being generated by robot "spider" programs, and to study the behavior of those programs as they interact with the server. Finally, it's an interesting programming exercise to see how we can assemble and present information on these "visits."

As with the data structure we used to create the SprocketExpo exhibitor directory in Chapters 5 and 6, we could really benefit in this case by taking advantage of Perl's support for multilevel data structures. A *hash of hashes* (that is, a hash whose values are themselves hash variables) would make the task of storing and accessing information on these visits significantly easier. As it is, though, we won't be learning how to use multilevel data structures for several more chapters. That's okay; we can fake it by using the conventional variables we've been using already, just as we did for the SprocketExpo example.

For the purposes of this script, we're going to define a "visit" as a series of one or more requests received from the same host, with no more than 15 minutes elapsing between one request and the next. If we get another request from the same host but more than 15 minutes has elapsed since the last one, we will treat the new request as the start of a new "visit," counting it separately in our statistics.

We may as well make that 15-minute visit timeout a configuration variable up at the top of the script and store it in seconds to make our computations easier:

```
my $expire_time       = 900; # seconds of inactivity to consider a
                             # "visit" ended (0 = forever)
```

Notice how the comment tells us we can set the $expire_time variable to 0 to make the expiration time "forever." We'll see how this works in a minute.

A number of other variables, visible throughout the script and declared with my near the beginning, will be used to store the information on individual visits:

$total_visits
> This scalar will be incremented by one for each new visit processed. Besides being used in the script's report to tell us how many visits there were in all, this count will be used to generate a unique *visit number* for each visit.

%visit_num
> This hash will have keys consisting of hostnames or IP addresses, and values consisting of the currently "working" visit number corresponding to that host.

All of the following hash variables will have keys consisting of the visit number described previously:

%host
> Key is visit number, value is the hostname or IP address corresponding to that visit number.

%first_time
> Key is visit number, value is the date and time of that visit's first access.

%last_time
> Key is visit number, value is the date and time of that visit's last (that is to say, most recent) access.

%last_seconds

Key is visit number, value is the number of seconds returned by the &get_seconds subroutine for the date and time of that visit's last access.

%referer

Key is visit number, value is the HTTP_REFERER environment variable supplied for that visit's first access.

%agent

Key is visit number, value is the user-agent string supplied for that visit's first access.

We'll add all these new variables to the big my declaration up at the top of the script:

```
my($begin_time, $end_time, $total_hits, $total_mb, $total_views,
    $total_visits, %visit_num, %host, %first_time, %last_time,
    %last_seconds, %page_sequence, %referer, %agent);
```

The &store_line Subroutine

We previously saw how the &store_line subroutine was being invoked to process each line from the log file that didn't represent an image request. Now let's skip down to the bottom of the script and see what that &store_line subroutine actually does:

```
# script proper ends. subroutines follow.

sub store_line {

    # store one line's worth of visit data

    my($host, $date, $time, $url, $referer, $agent) = @_;
    my $seconds = &get_seconds($date, $time);

    if ($visit_num{$host}) {
        # there is a visit currently "working" for this host
        my $visit_num = $visit_num{$host};
        my $elapsed = $seconds - $last_seconds{$visit_num};
        if (($expire_time) and ($elapsed > $expire_time)) {
            # this visit has expired, so start a new one
            &new_visit($host, $date, $time, $url, $seconds,
                $referer, $agent);
        } else {
            # this visit has not expired, so add to existing record
            &add_to_visit($host, $date, $time,
                $url, $seconds, $elapsed);
        }
    } else {
        # there is no visit currently "working" for this host
        &new_visit($host, $date, $time, $url, $seconds,
            $referer, $agent);
    }
}
```

Most of the Perl in this subroutine should look pretty familiar by now. In essence, this routine is functioning as a traffic cop, using the host and the time of this access to figure out if this request represents a new visit, or another request in a previously started visit.

First, it checks to see if a key exists for the current line's $host in the %visit_num hash. If there is, it means we've previously processed a request from this host, so the script checks to see if the currently working visit for this host has "expired." That is, it looks to see if the time difference between this host's last access and the current access is greater than the value stored in the $expire_time configuration variable. If it is, it means enough time has gone by that this access needs to be considered the beginning of a new visit, and the script invokes the &new_visit subroutine. If it isn't, the script invokes the &add_to_visit subroutine instead. Finally, if there wasn't any key for the current $host in the %visit_num hash, if means this host hasn't been seen before at all. Accordingly, the &new_visit subroutine is invoked to create a new entry for it.

Here's where we've implemented the feature of turning off visit expiration for cases where the $expire_time configuration variable has been set to 0. We've done that by making the logical test that determines whether a visit has ended actually contain *two* logical tests, both of which must be true for the "true" branch to be invoked:

```
if (($expire_time) and ($elapsed > $expire_time)) {
```

This works because joining two logical tests with and requires both of them to be true for the expression as a whole to be true. If $expire_time is set to 0, which is a false value, the test can never return true.

So, again, three subroutines are invoked from within this &store_line subroutine: the &get_seconds subroutine, which accepts as arguments the date and time strings from the current log file line and converts them to something called *Unix seconds*. That routine, and the *date arithmetic* it performs, is the subject of the next chapter. The &new_visit and &add_to_visit routines, which handle the updating of the script's data structure, will be covered in Chapter 10.

## CHAPTER 9

Date Arithmetic

This chapter continues the example begun in Chapter 8. In that chapter, we created a script to extract information from each line of our web server's access log, and began work on the code to assemble "visit" statistics from that information. We had just reached the point where we wanted to use a subroutine called &get_seconds to convert from the date and time string included in our log file entries to something called the *Epoch seconds*. This &get_seconds subroutine is our first real exposure to the notion of *date arithmetic*. Let's take a brief detour to look at that subject in more detail.

Date/Time Conversions

The idea with date arithmetic is that it's much easier to do things like finding the interval between two date/time strings if you first convert those strings into a common format. The format of choice in this case is the Epoch seconds, which is the number of seconds since some specific point in time, called the *Epoch*. (On most Unix systems, the Epoch is 00:00:00 GMT/UTC on January 1, 1970.)

If you want to get the number of Epoch seconds corresponding to the current time, you can get it by using Perl's time function, as in:

```
$seconds = time;
```

Two other Perl functions called localtime and gmtime can be used to convert Epoch seconds into human-readable local time or GMT (respectively). You may recall looking at localtime briefly in Chapter 6; now we're going to look at it in more detail. Example 9-1 shows localtime and gmtime in action. (As usual, you can download this example from the book's web site, at *http://www.elanus.net/book/*.)

Example 9-1. time_demo.plx

```
#!/usr/bin/perl -w

# time_demo.plx - demonstrate some date arithmetic in Perl
```

Example 9-1. time_demo.plx (continued)

```
$seconds_now  = time;
$localtime    = localtime($seconds_now);
$gmt          = gmtime($seconds_now);

# compute time 2 days, 3 hours, 36 minutes and 12 seconds from now

$seconds_then = $seconds_now
    + (2 * 24 * 60 * 60)      # adding 2 days' worth of seconds
    + (3 * 60 * 60)           # and 3 hours
    + (36 * 60)               # and 36 minutes
    + 12;                     # and 12 seconds

$localtime_then = localtime($seconds_then);
$gmt_then       = gmtime($seconds_then);

print <<EndOfText;
Current Epoch seconds: $seconds_now
Current local time: $localtime
Current GMT: $gmt

In 2 days, 3 hours, 36 minutes and 12 seconds it will be:
Epoch seconds: $seconds_then
Local time: $localtime_then
GMT: $gmt_then
EndOfText
```

Running this script in the shell should give you something like this for its output:

```
[jbc@andros chap_09]$ time_demo.plx
Current Epoch seconds: 994876353
Current local time: Wed Jul 11 11:32:33 2001
Current GMT: Wed Jul 11 18:32:33 2001

In 2 days, 3 hours, 36 minutes and 12 seconds it will be:
Epoch seconds: 995062125
Local time: Fri Jul 13 15:08:45 2001
GMT: Fri Jul 13 22:08:45 2001
```

The localtime and gmtime functions are interesting examples of Perl's *context sensitivity*. Invoked in a *scalar context* (as we did in that example, when we assigned their return values to scalar variables), localtime and gmtime return a string of the form Fri Jul 13 15:08:45 2001. Invoked in a *list context* (which you could do by assigning the function's return value to an array or list), each function returns a nine-element list of numbers corresponding to various pieces of information about the current date and time (see Table 9-1 for details). This is typically used as follows:

```
($sec,$min,$hour,$mday,$mon,$year,$wday,$yday,$isdst) =
                                        localtime(time);
```

Table 9-1. Elements returned by the localtime and gmtime functions when invoked in a list context

Index	Name	Range	Comments
0	sec	0–59	Seconds since last full minute.
1	min	0–59	Minutes since last full hour.
2	hour	0–23	Hours since midnight.
3	mday	1–31	Day of the month.
4	mon	0–11	Number of months since January. Note: the number is one less than you may be thinking (e.g., Jan is 0, Dec is 11).
5	year	N/A	The number of years since 1900. Note that this is a three-digit number (100, 101, etc.) beginning in 2000.
6	wday	0–6	The number of days since Sunday (Sunday = 0, Saturday = 6).
7	yday	0–365	The number of days since January 1.
8	isdst	+,0,-	A numeric flag indicating if daylight savings is in effect. If it is in effect, the number is positive. If it isn't, the number is 0. If the daylight savings information is unavailable, the number is negative.

 If you leave out the argument to either localtime or gmtime (that is, you just invoke localtime or gmtime by itself rather than feeding it some number of Epoch seconds), it will use the current time in Epoch seconds for its argument. In other words, localtime with no argument works the same as localtime(time).

Using the Time::Local Module

All this information about obtaining the current number of Epoch seconds and converting it to a human-readable time string is fine, but in this case we actually need to go in the opposite direction. That is, we start with human-readable time strings from the log file, and we want to convert them to Epoch seconds so that we can easily determine the elapsed time between accesses. There is no built-in Perl function to do this, but there is a *standard module* (that is, a module that comes with the standard Perl distribution) called Time::Local that lets you do it.

To see how it works, let's return to the log_report.plx script begun in Chapter 8. The first thing we need to do is to pull in that Time::Local module with the following line added up near the top of the script:

```
use Time::Local;
```

Next, we'll add the following %month_num hash just below it, to let us easily translate from the three-letter month names in the log ('Jan', 'Feb', etc.) to the corresponding offset numbers used by localtime:

```
my %month_num = (
    Jan => 0,
    Feb => 1,
```

```
            Mar => 2,
            Apr => 3,
            May => 4,
            Jun => 5,
            Jul => 6,
            Aug => 7,
            Sep => 8,
            Oct => 9,
            Nov => 10,
            Dec => 11,
        );
```

Now we're ready to create the &get_seconds subroutine, which we do by adding the following down at the bottom of the script:

```
sub get_seconds {

    # this subroutine accepts a date string of the form
    # '06/Jul/1999' and a time string of the form '12:14:00'
    # and returns the number of seconds since the Unix
    # epoch, as determined by Time::Local's timelocal
    # function.

    my ($date, $time)    = @_;
    my ($day, $mon, $yr) = split /\//, $date;
    my($hr, $min, $sec)  = split /:/, $time;
    $mon                 = $month_num{$mon};
    $yr                  = $yr - 1900;

    my $seconds = timelocal($sec, $min, $hr, $day, $mon, $yr);
}
```

This subroutine should look pretty straightforward to you by now. Given the date and time portions of a log file line (which look like 06/Jul/1999 and 00:09:12, respectively), it splits them into their component parts using two invocations of the split function. It then converts $mon (which arrives as an abbreviation, like Jan or Feb) into an offset number using the %month_num hash we just created up at the top of the script. It also subtracts 1900 from $year.

All this is necessary in order to put the arguments in the proper form for feeding to the timelocal function, which is provided by the Time::Local module and which returns the appropriate number of Epoch seconds in the last line of the subroutine. In that sense, the Time::Local module's timelocal function is the opposite of the built-in localtime function. The Epoch seconds are assigned to a scalar variable called $seconds, and since that is the last thing assigned in the subroutine, that becomes the return value for the subroutine as a whole. (The assignment to $seconds isn't strictly necessary, since the subroutine would also return the Epoch seconds if you just put the timelocal function on the last line by itself, without assigning anything. To my way of thinking, though, explicitly assigning timelocal's return value to $seconds makes it a little clearer what's going on.)

Caching Date Conversions

This is probably the most straightforward way to implement the &get_seconds subroutine, and it works perfectly well. It's not very efficient, though. Beginning programmers normally are too busy worrying about making their programs run at all to worry about making them run faster. But this is a special case. Unlike a lot of our scripts, which take no appreciable time to run, this one could end up crunching some pretty big log files and taking a significant amount of time to do so. It also might end up being run day after day. A little extra effort spent on making it more efficient will pay dividends in the long run.

The Time::Local module's timelocal function involves a fair amount of behind-the-scenes computation, and the approach used here invokes that function once for each log file line that makes it as far as the &get_seconds subroutine. When you think about it, though, the only tricky part of the timelocal function is the part where it figures the appropriate number of seconds for the current date. The part where it adds the appropriate number of seconds for the current time of day is relatively simple; it just involves adding the seconds, plus the minutes times 60, plus the hours times 3600.

But for every access on a given day, the date part of the log file entry is going to be exactly the same. Which leads to this idea: why not use timelocal only for the date part, and run it only once for each day represented in the log file? You can then save the results of running timelocal for that date, and use those results for all the subsequent log file lines that have the same date. You can do the time-of-day part of the computation yourself, without using the timelocal function.

The Perlish way to do this sort of saving, or caching, of the values returned by a function is to use a hash. We can do that by modifying the &get_seconds subroutine to look like this:

```
sub get_seconds {

    # this subroutine accepts a date string of the form
    # '06/Jul/1999' and a time string of the form '12:14:00'
    # and returns the number of seconds since the Unix
    # epoch, as determined by Time::Local's timelocal
    # function. the subroutine caches conversions of the
    # date part in %date_seconds in order to improve
    # performance.

    my ($date, $time) = @_;
    my $seconds;
    if ($date_seconds{$date}) {
        $seconds = $date_seconds{$date};
    } else {
```

```
        my ($day, $mon, $yr) = split /\//, $date;
        $mon  = $month_num{$mon};
        $yr = $yr - 1900;
        $seconds = $date_seconds{$date} =
            timelocal(0, 0, 0, $day, $mon, $yr);
    }
    my($hr, $min, $sec) = split /:/, $time;
    $seconds += ($hr * 3600) + ($min * 60) + $sec;
}
```

This checks to see if we've looked up the current line's $date value already, and if we have, it just uses whatever value is already stored in the %date_seconds hash. Otherwise (that is, if we haven't already seen a log file line with this date during this script run), it uses the timelocal function to get it. It invokes timelocal using only the values for $day, $mon, and $yr, however. The $hr, $min, and $sec fields are left at zero, which is another way of saying that timelocal is being asked to give the Epoch seconds for midnight on the date in question.

The Epoch seconds value returned by timelocal is stored in both the $seconds scalar variable and the $date_seconds{$date} hash value, courtesy of a nifty two-assignments-in-one construct:

```
$seconds = $date_seconds{$date} = timelocal(0, 0, 0, $day, $mon, $yr);
```

Then, having exited the if-else block with $seconds set to the current date's Epoch seconds, we split the $time variable into its components and tack on the number of seconds corresponding to the current time of day using the += addition-plus-assignment operator:

```
$seconds += ($hr * 3600) + ($min * 60) + $sec;
```

One more thing needs to be done to make the &get_seconds subroutine work properly: you need to declare the %date_seconds hash with my, giving it an appropriate scope. Given the whole subroutine-as-a-black-box concept, it would be nice if we could put the my %date_seconds declaration inside the subroutine itself, where it will be invisible to the rest of the script. But that won't work because when we declare a my variable inside a subroutine, each invocation of the subroutine gets its own private copy of the variable. Other invocations' copies of the variable are invisible. This obviously won't do because the whole point of having the %date_seconds hash is to be able to cache the timelocal lookups in it so that subsequent invocations of the subroutine can get them without doing the lookup themselves.

We could deal with this the way we dealt with the %mon_num hash previously—by putting a my %date_seconds declaration up at the top of the script so that it becomes in effect a global variable visible from everywhere. But again, that's a poor solution because it adds to the script-wide namespace complexity we're trying to avoid. There must be a better way.

Scoping via Anonymous Blocks

And there is. The solution is to stick something called an *anonymous block* around the subroutine (which just means a pair of curly braces with no associated subroutine name), with the `my %date_seconds` declaration inside that block but outside the subroutine proper. That is, something like:

```
{   # start of anonymous block
    my %date_seconds;
    sub get_seconds {
        # subroutine definition goes here
    }
}   # end of anonymous block
```

This way, the same `%date_seconds` hash is visible to every invocation of the `&get_seconds` subroutine, and thus is available for caching `timelocal` lookup results, but the hash remains invisible for the rest of the script.

Remember that `%month_num` hash we initialized up at the top of the script? Since the `&get_seconds` subroutine is the only thing in the script that uses it, it would be nice to limit its scope, too, by putting it inside the anonymous block. (Putting it inside the subroutine itself would work, but it would be inefficient because the initialization of the hash would have to be repeated each time the subroutine was invoked.)

There is a problem with putting the `%month_num` initialization inside the anonymous block, though. You will recall that Perl goes through two phases when it runs a script. The first phase, called the *compilation phase*, is the time when things like subroutine definitions are processed. After that comes the *runtime phase*, when the sequential commands in the script are actually executed. This is why we can successfully invoke a subroutine from any point in a script, including points prior to the subroutine's definition: the subroutine will always be available because it was defined during the compilation phase, before the script's execution phase started.

The assignment of the various key/value pairs to the `%month_num` hash, though, is not like a subroutine definition. It doesn't happen at compile time, but at runtime, during the script's normal execution. That means we can count on the `%month_num` hash being available to the `&get_seconds` subroutine only if we can make sure that the hash assignment is executed *before* anything invokes the subroutine. We can't put the `%month_num` initialization in the anonymous block surrounding the `get_seconds` subroutine because it won't be available if the subroutine is invoked from a previous point in the script.

Using a BEGIN Block

Does that mean we're stuck with putting the `%month_num` assignment up at the top of the script, such that it will be visible everywhere, not just in the subroutine where it's needed? No, we're not stuck with that. We can use a special trick to make part of our script execute immediately after the compilation phase, before the normal runtime stuff happens. That trick is to put that part of our script inside a block labeled with the special word BEGIN (in all caps).

Let's modify that anonymous block enclosing the &get_seconds subroutine to be a BEGIN block, and move the %month_num hash definition from the top of the script to the inside of that BEGIN block. The final version of the &get_seconds subroutine, including its enclosing BEGIN block, will then look like this:

```
BEGIN {
    my %date_seconds;
    my %month_num = (
        Jan => 0,
        Feb => 1,
        Mar => 2,
        Apr => 3,
        May => 4,
        Jun => 5,
        Jul => 6,
        Aug => 7,
        Sep => 8,
        Oct => 9,
        Nov => 10,
        Dec => 11,
    );

    sub get_seconds {

        # this subroutine accepts a date string of the form
        # '06/Jul/1999' and a time string of the form '12:14:00'
        # and returns the number of seconds since the Unix
        # epoch, as determined by Time::Local's timelocal
        # function. the subroutine caches conversions of the
        # date part in %date_seconds in order to improve
        # performance.

        my ($date, $time) = @_;
        my $seconds;
        if ($date_seconds{$date}) {
            $seconds = $date_seconds{$date};
        } else {
            my ($day, $mon, $yr) = split /\//, $date;
            $mon  = $month_num{$mon};
            $yr = $yr - 1900;
            $seconds = $date_seconds{$date} =
                timelocal(0, 0, 0, $day, $mon, $yr);
        }
        my($hr, $min, $sec) = split /:/, $time;
        $seconds += ($hr * 3600) + ($min * 60) + $sec;
    }
}
```

Now we're all set. The &get_seconds subroutine, along with its enclosing BEGIN block, can go anywhere we like and will function as a tidy little black box, efficiently returning Epoch seconds while keeping all its variables hidden from the rest of the script.

To measure the difference in efficiency between the first version of the &get_seconds subroutine and this one, I compared the execution time of each when processing a log file with about 100,000 lines in it. The improved version allowed the lines to be processed in less than half the time (138 CPU seconds versus 387 CPU seconds).

Now we're ready to leave the &get_seconds subroutine and get back to the rest of the log_report.plx script. We'll do that in the next chapter.

## CHAPTER 10

Generating a Web Access Report

This chapter completes the example begun in Chapters 8 and 9. We've reached the final stage in creating our log analysis script, where we store the information about the individual "visitors" whose activities we are attempting to reconstruct, and use that data to print out the actual report. In describing these final enhancements to the log_report.plx script, we will look first at the &new_visit and &add_to_visit routines used to store our visit data. Then we will learn about a very useful pair of functions for producing formatted output: printf and sprintf. We'll talk about how to produce our report, and then how to embellish it with information about the site's more popular pages, as well as information regarding the referral strings and user-agent data available from combined-format logs. Finally, we'll talk about how to make the script email its report to our email address, and how to schedule it to run at periodic intervals using the Unix cron facility.

The &new_visit and &add_to_visit Subroutines

In Chapter 8 we looked at the log_report.plx script's &store_line subroutine, which served as a "traffic cop," directing the data from each line to either the &new_visit or &add_to_visit subroutines. Now let's take a look at those two subroutines in detail.

We'll start with the &new_visit subroutine, which we use to store information about a visit that has just started (either because the current log file line relates to an entirely new host that the script hasn't seen before, or because that host's previous visit or visits have already "expired").

```
sub new_visit {

    # record an entry for an access line that has been
    # determined to represent a new visit (either because
    # this is the first time this host has been seen,
    # or because the host's previous visit has expired).
```

```perl
    my ($host, $date, $time, $url, $seconds,
        $referer, $agent) = @_;

    my $visit_num               = ++$total_visits;
    $visit_num{$host}           = $visit_num;
    $host{$visit_num}           = $host;
    $first_time{$visit_num}     = "$date:$time";
    $last_time{$visit_num}      = "$date:$time";
    $last_seconds{$visit_num}   = $seconds;
    $page_sequence{$visit_num}  = $url;
    if ($log_format eq 'extended') {
        $referer{$visit_num} = $referer;
        $agent{$visit_num}   = $agent;
    }

}
```

There's nothing terribly clever here. All we're really doing is incrementing the script-wide $total_visits scalar by 1, then using the resulting number as a key to store information about this visit in a number of script-wide hash variables. Notice, by the way, how we use an if block to isolate the assignment to the %referer and %agent hashes, so that part is done only if the configuration section lists the log format as extended, meaning this is a "combined" format log with those two additional fields.

Now let's look at the &add_to_visit subroutine, which is where we update the information stored about a currently "working" visit:

```perl
sub add_to_visit {

    # append to an existing visit record because it has been
    # determined that the current line contains more data to
    # be added to a currently "working" visit

    my($host, $date, $time, $url, $seconds, $elapsed) = @_;
    my $visit_num               = $visit_num{$host};
    $last_time{$visit_num}      = "$date:$time";
    $last_seconds{$visit_num}   = $seconds;

    my $elapsed_string =
        (int ($elapsed/60)) . ':' . sprintf "%02u", $elapsed % 60;
    $page_sequence{$visit_num} .= " $elapsed_string, $url";
}
```

After copying its arguments into a number of scalar variables, this subroutine gets the $visit_num corresponding to this particular $host by doing a lookup in the script-wide %visit_num hash. Then it uses that $visit_num to add information to the various hashes in the visit record's data structure.

The only really new thing here is the part where we use the number of seconds since this visit's last access (supplied in the arguments by the traffic-cop &store_line subroutine) to create a string of the form 1:07. The part of that string to the left of the colon is the number of full minutes since the last access, and the part to the right is the number of seconds since the last full minute. Here's the code that produces that:

```
my $elapsed_string =
    (int ($elapsed/60)) . ':' . sprintf "%02u", $elapsed % 60;
```

There are three new things here, all of them useful and well worth learning about.

One new thing is the use of the int function. Given one argument (a number), this returns the integer portion of it (that is to say, the whole-number part of it, the part to the left of the decimal point). In this case, the argument given to it is the result of dividing the elapsed seconds by 60; taking the integer portion of that gives you the number of full minutes represented by that number of seconds.

Another new thing here is the use of the modulus operator (%). This is one of those things that never seemed to get covered in the math courses I took en route to my liberal arts degree, but which professional programmers consider so obvious as to hardly deserve mentioning. Anyway, the modulus operator divides two integers and returns the remainder—that is, the part left over that didn't divide evenly. Thus, 4 % 3 returns 1, 23 % 7 returns 2, and, in this case, $elapsed % 60 returns the number of seconds left in $elapsed after all the full minutes have been extracted.

The last new thing in this chunk of code is the sprintf function; see the accompanying sidebar "Formatting with printf and sprintf" for details on how to use it. In this case, sprintf is being used with the format string "%02u", which takes the argument that comes after it and formats it as a type of number called an *unsigned integer* (meaning an integer that will never be negative). That integer is padded with a leading 0, if necessary, to make the whole thing two digits long. Thus, the number 2 would be formatted as the string "02". Table 10-1 shows a list of commonly used formatting codes.

Table 10-1. Formatting codes for use with printf and sprintf

Code	Behavior
%%	Produces a literal percent sign (%).
%s	Formats argument as a string.
%d	Formats argument as a signed decimal integer.
%u	Formats argument as an unsigned decimal integer.
%f	Formats argument as a decimal floating-point number.
-	Inserted between the % and the code letter (for example, '%-4s'); causes the argument to be left-justified within the field.
0	Inserted between the % and the code letter (for example, '%04u'); forces the use of zeros rather than spaces to right-justify.
number	Inserted between the % and the code letter (for example, '%4s'); gives the minimum field width.
.number	Inserted between the % and the code letter (for example, '%1.2f'); gives the digits after the decimal point for a floating-point number, the maximum length for a string, and the minimum length for an integer.

Formatting with printf and sprintf

sprintf (and the closely related function printf) are extremely useful tools for producing formatted output. You can do things like left and right justification, padding a given string (or number) to a certain length with zeros or spaces, rounding off a number to a certain number of decimal places, and so on. You use sprintf when you want to return a formatted string (to assign to a variable, typically). You use printf in place of print to print formatted output to a filehandle (or to the default filehandle, STDOUT).

Both printf and sprintf are used in the same way. First, you give the function name (either printf or sprintf). In the case of printf, you can also give a filehandle. Then you give a *format* (which is a string that can contain both literal text and special formatting codes). Finally, you give a list of one or more arguments to be plugged into the format string and converted according to its formatting codes.

In the format string, the percent sign (%) is used to indicate the formatting codes. Everything else just gets printed (or returned, with sprintf) as it would with a normal single- or double-quoted string (depending on which sort of quoting you use around the format string). See Table 10-1 for a list of the more commonly used formatting codes. Here are some examples demonstrating their use:

```
printf '%4u', 4;            # prints '   4'
printf '%04u', 4;           # prints '0004'
printf '%-4u', 4;           # prints '4   '
printf '%1.1f%%', 12.73;    # prints '12.7%'
printf 'Cost: $%1.2f', 14.5; # prints 'Cost: $14.50'

printf '%10s %10s', 'walnuts', 'acorns';
# prints '   walnuts     acorns'

printf '%-10s %10.3s', 'walnuts', 'acorns';
# prints 'walnuts           aco'

$item = 'bread';
$cost = 1.59235;
printf 'The cost of %s is $%1.2f', $item, $cost;
# prints 'The cost of bread is $1.59'
```

Generating the Report

Now that the data is extracted from our log file and stored in an appropriate data structure, we're ready for the fun part: generating useful information from all that data.

Generating the Summary Line

We start by adding a new configuration variable, up at the top of the script, to give the name of our web site as we want it to appear in the script:

```
my $site_name       = 'My Web Site';
```

Now we add the following to the middle of the script, after the main while loop is finished but before the subroutine definitions:

```
# done processing log file. begin output.

my $report = <<EndOfText;
$site_name Access Report -- $end_time

        From                 To            Hits   Views Visits   Mb
==================== ==================== ====== ====== ====== ======
EndOfText
```

This is just printing out a suitable header for the summary line, which comes next:

```
my $summary_line = sprintf
    "%s %s %6u %6u %6u %6u\n", $begin_time, $end_time,
    $total_hits, $total_views, $total_visits, $total_mb;

$report .= $summary_line;

print $report;
```

This uses sprintf to print out a nicely formatted line summarizing the totals we kept track of during the while loop's processing of the log file lines. The format string starts off with the formatting code %s (twice). This just formats its argument as a string; in this case, it drops in $begin_time and $end_time, which will always be 20 characters wide due to the standardized format of the log file's date/time strings.

You might be wondering why we even need a formatting code for the $begin_time and $end_time strings. Since the format is enclosed in double quotes (needed to interpret the \n at the end as a newline character), it does variable interpolation, meaning you could just stick $begin_time and $end_time into the format string directly and leave them out of the list of arguments. In this case that would work fine, but in general it's probably a bad idea. Because a double-quoted format string undergoes variable interpolation before sprintf sees it, a variable whose contents include a literal percent sign could confuse sprintf into thinking it was seeing a formatting code. It's better to avoid that possibility by using a %s formatting code and passing the arguments in explicitly.

Next we use the formatting code %6u to print each of $total_hits, $total_views, $total_visits, and $total_mb as right-justified integers, with spaces used to pad them out to six digits each. (If your site is popular enough to require more than six digits in any of these fields, just adjust the sprintf formatting codes and modify the header line given earlier to make everything line up nicely.)

Saving Previous Summary Lines

If we run the script in its current form, we will get a single summary line printed out to our screen. It would be handy to be able to save those summary lines in a file from one script run to the next so that each report can give the latest results along with some historical context.

To do that, we begin by adding the following to the configuration section at the top of the script:

```
my $summary_file    = './summary.txt';
my $summary_count   = 7;   # how many script runs to summarize
```

Here we're specifying a suitable filename to use for storing the summary lines between invocations of the script, and telling the script how many summary lines to keep in that file before we start throwing the oldest ones away.

Now we modify the part of the script where we produce the report (that is, the part we just added that comes after the while loop and before the subroutine definitions) to look like this:

```
# done processing log file. begin output.

my @summary_lines;

if (-e $summary_file) {
    open SUMMARY, $summary_file or
        die "can't open $summary_file for reading: $!\n";
    @summary_lines = <SUMMARY>;
    close SUMMARY or die "can't close $summary_file after reading: $!\n";
}
```

Most of this should look familiar by now. First, we're declaring a new my variable called @summary_lines. It is declared in the script's outermost scope and might have been put in the big my declaration up at the top of the script, but since it is only used in this one part of the script, I suggest declaring it down here for clarity's sake.

Next, we check to see if the summary file exists already, and if it does we open a file-handle for reading. Then we do something cool: @summary_lines = <SUMMARY>. This reads all the lines from the filehandle at once, storing them in the @summary_lines array. Up until now, we've always used something like while (<SUMMARY>) to do this sort of thing. In this case, though, since we want all those lines in an array and we aren't worried about the file being so large that the resulting array will consume all our computer's memory, this works better. Next comes the following:

```
my $summary_line = sprintf
    "%s %s %6u %6u %6u %6u\n", $begin_time, $end_time,
    $total_hits, $total_views, $total_visits, $total_mb;

unshift @summary_lines, $summary_line;
```

First, we build the current $summary_line using the same sprintf format we used previously. Then we use a Perl function called unshift to add that summary line to the beginning of the @summary_lines array we just read in from the summary file.

The unshift function works just like the push function we learned about previously, except that it adds entries to the front (or left, or top, depending on how you visualize things) of an array instead of adding them to the end (or right, or bottom), as push does. See the sidebar, "push and pop, unshift and shift," as well as Figure 10-1, for details.

---

push and pop, unshift and shift

Two important functions for adding elements to a Perl array are push (which adds new elements to the end of an array) and unshift (which adds new elements to the beginning of an array). Each function has a complementary function that does just the opposite: removing an element from the array and returning it.

The opposite of push is pop. The pop function pops an entry off the end (right, bottom) of the array and returns it. The opposite of unshift is shift. The shift function shifts an entry off the beginning (left, top) of the array and returns it. Here are some examples:

```
@a = (1, 2);
push @a, 3;      # @a has (1, 2, 3)
unshift @a, 4;   # @a has (4, 1, 2, 3)
$p = pop @a;     # $p has 3, @a has (4, 1, 2)
$q = shift @a;   # $q has 4, @a has (1, 2)
push @a, $p, $q; # @a has (1, 2, 3, 4)
```

You unshift elements onto the beginning (or top, or left end) of an array and shift elements off from there. You push elements onto the end (or bottom, or right end) of an array and pop elements off from there. See the perlfunc manpage for details.

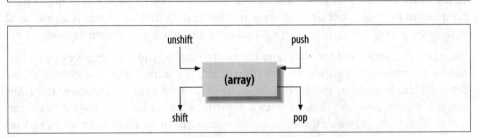

Figure 10-1. The four functions for manipulating either end of an array

So, now we have the current summary line at the beginning of the @summary_lines array. Next, we check to see if we've gone over the limit specified in the configuration variable $summary_count:

```
if (@summary_lines > $summary_count) {
    $#summary_lines = $summary_count - 1;
}
```

Evaluating the @summary_lines array inside a logical test gives the array a *Boolean context*, which is a *scalar context*, meaning it returns the number of elements it contains. If that number is greater than the limit stored in $summary_count, the if block is executed.

Something interesting is happening inside the if block. $#summary_lines is a special Perl variable that gives the *index* (that is, the offset) of the last element in the @summary_lines array. In other words, it is one less than the number of elements contained in the array (since array indices use a 0-based offset). You can use the same thing for any array variable; $#walnuts would be the index of the last element in the @walnuts array, and so on.

The clever Perlish thing about the $#summary_lines special variable is that it can be used as an *lvalue*. That is, you can assign to it, which is what you've done here. Assigning a number to it that is less than its current value causes the array to be shortened, with any extra elements at the end being thrown away. In this case, assigning $summary_count - 1 to $#summary_lines causes the @summary_lines array to be shortened so that it contains only $summary_count elements.

The next part of our rapidly expanding script is the initialization of the $report variable with the header from the report; we saw this previously. Now we open a filehandle for writing out to $summary_file and store the contents of @summary_lines there while also appending them to $report:

```
my $report = <<EndOfText;
$site_name Access Report -- $end_time

Summary of last $summary_count reporting periods:

        From                  To             Hits  Views Visits   Mb
==================== ==================== ====== ====== ====== ======
EndOfText

open SUMMARY, ">$summary_file" or
    die "couldn't open $summary_file for writing: $!\n";

foreach (@summary_lines) {
    $report .= $_;
    print SUMMARY;
}

close SUMMARY or die "couldn't close $summary_file after writing: $!\n";
```

Showing the Details of Each Visit

We're almost ready to test the fully functional version of the script. At the end of the report will be a "detail" section that describes each visit to the site, including the list of pages that were requested during that visit. As you might expect, this can make the report quite long (especially for popular sites), so the first thing to do in adding this feature is to put a configuration variable at the top of the script that lets us turn this feature off:

```
my $show_detail     = 1;   # (0 or 1) show detail?
```

Now, toward the end of the script proper, just before the part that prints out the $report variable, we'll add the following:

```
if ($show_detail) {
    $report .= <<EndOfText;

Detail for most recent reporting period:

EndOfText

    foreach my $visit_num (1 .. $total_visits) {
        $report .= &visit_detail($visit_num);
    }
}
```

As you can see, we're going to be using a separate subroutine called &visit_detail to return the formatted details for each visit. One interesting thing here is the use of the range operator (..) to produce the list of visit numbers to feed to that subroutine. Just as we were able to use ('a' .. 'b') to produce a list of all the lowercase letters of the alphabet in Chapter 6, we can use (1 .. $total_visits) to produce a list of all the integers between 1 and $total_visits.

To format the visit details so that they look nice, with the list of visited pages being given a hanging indent, we're going to take advantage of the standard Perl module Text::Wrap. To do that, we'll add the following up at the top of the script:

```
use Text::Wrap;
```

Then, in the configuration section below there, we'll add this line:

```
$Text::Wrap::columns = 60;
```

$Text::Wrap::columns is a scalar variable used by Text::Wrap to indicate the maximum number of characters we want to have on each line.

When we use a variable name like $Text::Wrap::columns, we are using something called a *package variable*. This is another approach to scoping, like using a my declaration to hide a variable from the outside world. Package variables are a somewhat more flexible approach than my variables, in that a package variable can be seen from outside its package, as long as you use a fully qualified variable name, like $Text::Wrap::columns, to refer to it. (You've actually been using package variables all along, since most of the variables you haven't explicitly scoped with a my declaration have been package variables in package main, which is the default package.) We'll be talking more about this in later chapters.

Now we'll go to the bottom of the script and create that &visit_detail subroutine:

```perl
sub visit_detail {

    # returns a formatted report for a particular visit.
    # assumes 'use Text::Wrap;'

    my $visit_num = $_[0];

    my $detail = <<EndOfText;
Visit Number: $visit_num
         Host: $host{$visit_num}
 First Access: $first_time{$visit_num}
  Last Access: $last_time{$visit_num}
EndOfText

    if ($log_format eq 'extended') {

        $detail .= <<EndOfText
    Referrer: $referer{$visit_num}
  User Agent: $agent{$visit_num}
EndOfText

    }

    # this uses Text::Wrap's wrap function
    my $page_sequence =
        wrap('', '                ', $page_sequence{$visit_num});

    $detail .= <<EndOfText;
Page Sequence: $page_sequence

EndOfText

    $detail;
}
```

That's all there is to it. The wrap function, which we get courtesy of using Text::Wrap, takes three arguments: the string to use for indenting the first line of the text we're going to wrap, the string to use for indenting all subsequent lines of the text we're going to wrap, and the text itself. The function returns the text wrapped accordingly, based on the arguments it was given and on the $Text::Wrap::columns variable you set earlier. In this case, the first argument is an empty string (meaning the first line of the wrapped text will be flush at the left margin). The second argument is a string consisting of 15 spaces (meaning all subsequent lines will get a hanging indent of that amount). Finally, the text to be wrapped is the sequence of pages requested, as stored in the %page_sequence hash and keyed by this $visit_num.

Thus, for each visit, the &visit_details subroutine should end up returning something like this:

```
Visit Number: 44
         Host: p49-max43.dialup.lies.com
 First Access: 06/Jul/1999:03:24:34
```

```
        Last Access: 06/Jul/1999:03:33:07
           Referrer: http://www.cgi-resources.com/search/index.cgi
         User Agent: Mozilla/4.0 (compatible; MSIE 5.0; Windows 98; DigExt)
      Page Sequence: /begperl/ 0:49, /begperl/guestbook.html 7:44,
                     /begperl/hello_command.html
```

Example 10-1 shows the entire script in its current form, building on the first two versions shown in Chapter 8. As with all the examples in this book, you can download this code from the book's web site at *http://www.elanus.net/book/*.

Example 10-1. The third version of log_report.plx

```perl
#!/usr/bin/perl -w

# log_report.plx

# report on web visitors. expects common or extended log
# format lines to be fed to it on STDIN.

use strict;
use Time::Local;
use Text::Wrap;

# configuration section:

my $log_format        = 'extended'; # 'common' or 'extended'
$Text::Wrap::columns  = 60;
my $site_name         = 'My Web Site';
my $expire_time       = 900; # seconds of inactivity to consider a
                             # "visit" ended (0 = forever)
my $summary_file      = './summary.txt';
my $summary_count     = 7;   # how many script runs to summarize
my $depth             = 20;  # how deep to go in reporting top N pages
my $show_detail       = 1;   # (0 or 1) show detail?

# script-wide my variable declarations:

my ($begin_time, $end_time, $total_hits, $total_mb, $total_views,
    $total_visits, %visit_num, %host, %first_time, %last_time,
    %last_seconds, %page_sequence, %referer, $agent);

# script proper begins

while (<>) {

    my ($host, $ident_user, $auth_user, $date, $time,
        $time_zone, $method, $url, $protocol, $status, $bytes,
        $referer, $agent);

    if ($log_format eq 'common') {

        ($host, $ident_user, $auth_user, $date, $time,
            $time_zone, $method, $url, $protocol, $status, $bytes) =
/^(\S+) (\S+) (\S+) \[([^:]+):(\d+:\d+:\d+) ([^\]]+)\] "(\S+) (.+?)
```

Example 10-1. The third version of log_report.plx (continued)

```
(\S+)" (\S+) (\S+)$/
        or next;

} elsif ($log_format eq 'extended') {

    ($host, $ident_user, $auth_user, $date, $time,
        $time_zone, $method, $url, $protocol, $status, $bytes,
        $referer, $agent) =
/^(\S+) (\S+) (\S+) \[([^:]+):(\d+:\d+:\d+) ([^\]]+)\] "(\S+) (.+?)
 (\S+)" (\S+) (\S+) "([^"]+)" "([^"]+)"$/
        or next;
} else {
    die "unrecognized log format '$log_format'";
}

++$total_hits;
unless ($bytes =~ /^\d+$/) {
    $bytes = 0;
}
$total_mb += ($bytes / (1024 * 1024));
unless ($begin_time) {
    $begin_time = "$date:$time";
}
$end_time = "$date:$time";

next if $url =~ /\.(gif|jpg|jpeg|png|xbm)$/i;
# don't care about these for visit-tracking purposes

++$total_views;
&store_line($host, $date, $time, $url, $referer, $agent);
}

# done processing log file. begin output.

my @summary_lines;

if (-e $summary_file) {
    open SUMMARY, $summary_file or
        die "can't open $summary_file for reading: $!\n";
    @summary_lines = <SUMMARY>;
    close SUMMARY or die "can't close $summary_file after reading: $!\n";
}

my $summary_line = sprintf
    "%s %s %6u %6u %6u %6u\n", $begin_time, $end_time,
    $total_hits, $total_views, $total_visits, $total_mb;
unshift @summary_lines, $summary_line;
if (@summary_lines > $summary_count) {
    $#summary_lines = $summary_count - 1;
}

my $report = <<EndOfText;
$site_name Access Report -- $end_time
```

Example 10-1. The third version of log_report.plx (continued)

```
Summary of last $summary_count reporting periods:

        From                  To             Hits  Views Visits   Mb
==================== ==================== ====== ====== ====== ======
EndOfText

open SUMMARY, ">$summary_file" or
    die "couldn't open $summary_file for writing: $!\n";

foreach (@summary_lines) {
    $report .= $_;
    print SUMMARY;
}

close SUMMARY or die "couldn't close $summary_file after writing: $!\n";

if ($show_detail) {
    $report .= <<EndOfText;

Detail for most recent reporting period:

EndOfText

    foreach my $visit_num (1 .. $total_visits) {
        $report .= &visit_detail($visit_num);
    }
}

print $report;

# end of script proper. subroutines follow.

sub store_line {

    # store one line's worth of visit data

    my($host, $date, $time, $url, $referer, $agent) = @_;
    my $seconds = &get_seconds($date, $time);

    if ($visit_num{$host}) {
        # there is a visit currently "working" for this host
        my $visit_num = $visit_num{$host};
        my $elapsed = $seconds - $last_seconds{$visit_num};
        if (($expire_time) and ($elapsed > $expire_time)) {
            # this visit has expired, so start a new one
            &new_visit($host, $date, $time, $url, $seconds,
                $referer, $agent);
        } else {
            # this visit has not expired, so add to existing record
            &add_to_visit($host, $date, $time,
                $url, $seconds, $elapsed);
        }
```

Example 10-1. The third version of log_report.plx (continued)

```
    } else {
        # there is no visit currently "working" for this host
        &new_visit($host, $date, $time, $url, $seconds,
            $referer, $agent);
    }
}

BEGIN {
    my %date_seconds;
    my %month_num = (
        Jan => 0,
        Feb => 1,
        Mar => 2,
        Apr => 3,
        May => 4,
        Jun => 5,
        Jul => 6,
        Aug => 7,
        Sep => 8,
        Oct => 9,
        Nov => 10,
        Dec => 11,
    );

    sub get_seconds {

        # this subroutine accepts a date string of the form
        # '06/Jul/1999' and a time string of the form '12:14:00'
        # and returns the number of seconds since the Unix
        # epoch, as determined by Time::Local's timelocal
        # function. the subroutine caches conversions of the
        # date part in %date_seconds in order to improve
        # performance.

        my ($date, $time) = @_;
        my $seconds;
        if ($date_seconds{$date}) {
            $seconds = $date_seconds{$date};
        } else {
            my ($day, $mon, $yr) = split /\//, $date;
            $mon  = $month_num{$mon};
            $yr = $yr - 1900;
            $seconds = $date_seconds{$date} =
                timelocal(0, 0, 0, $day, $mon, $yr);
        }
        my($hr, $min, $sec) = split /:/, $time;
        $seconds += ($hr * 3600) + ($min * 60) + $sec;
    }
}

sub new_visit {

    # record an entry for an access line that has been
```

Example 10-1. The third version of log_report.plx (continued)

```perl
    # determined to represent a new visit (either because
    # this is the first time this host has been seen,
    # or because the host's previous visit has expired)

    my ($host, $date, $time, $url, $seconds,
        $referer, $agent) = @_;
    my $visit_num              = ++$total_visits;
    $visit_num{$host}          = $visit_num;
    $host{$visit_num}          = $host;
    $first_time{$visit_num}    = "$date:$time";
    $last_time{$visit_num}     = "$date:$time";
    $last_seconds{$visit_num}  = $seconds;
    $page_sequence{$visit_num} = $url;
    if ($log_format eq 'extended') {
        $referer{$visit_num} = $referer;
        $agent{$visit_num}   = $agent;
    }
}

sub add_to_visit {

    # append to an existing visit record because it has been
    # determined that the current line contains more data to
    # be added to a currently "working" visit

    my($host, $date, $time, $url, $seconds, $elapsed) = @_;
    my $visit_num              = $visit_num{$host};
    $last_time{$visit_num}     = "$date:$time";
    $last_seconds{$visit_num}  = $seconds;

    my $elapsed_string =
        (int ($elapsed/60)) . ':' . sprintf "%.2u", $elapsed % 60;
    $page_sequence{$visit_num} .= " $elapsed_string, $url";
}

sub visit_detail {

    # returns a formatted report for a particular visit.
    # assumes 'use Text::Wrap;'

    my $visit_num = $_[0];
    my $page_sequence =
        wrap('', '                    ', $page_sequence{$visit_num});

    my $detail = <<EndOfText;
 Visit Number: $visit_num
         Host: $host{$visit_num}
 First Access: $first_time{$visit_num}
  Last Access: $last_time{$visit_num}
EndOfText

    if ($log_format eq 'extended') {
```

Example 10-1. The third version of log_report.plx (continued)

```
        $detail .= <<EndOfText
    Referrer: $referer{$visit_num}
  User Agent: $agent{$visit_num}
EndOfText


    }


    $detail .= <<EndOfText;
Page Sequence: $page_sequence


EndOfText


    $detail;
}
```

Reporting the Most Popular Pages

Our log_report.plx script will produce interesting output in its current form, but it could do more. One obvious thing to report on is which pages on the site are the most popular. To accomplish this we need to augment our data structure. First, we add a %views_by_page hash to the script-wide my variable declaration up at the top:

```
my ($begin_time, $end_time, $total_hits, $total_mb, $total_views,
    $total_visits, %visit_num, %host, %first_time, %last_time,
    %last_seconds, %page_sequence, %referer, %agent,
    %views_by_page);
```

Using the requested URL as the key, we can increment that hash value at the end of the while loop that processes log file lines, just before the invocation of the &store_line subroutine. Thus, the last part of the while loop will look like this:

```
    ++$views_by_page{$url};
    &store_line($host, $date, $time, $url, $referer, $agent);
}
```

Now that we've stored the data in that hash, it's time to modify the script to give us a report on the most popular pages. One question we need to think about first, though, is how far down the list of most-popular pages we wish to go in that reporting. We should probably make that a configuration variable up at the top of the script, which we can do with something like this:

```
my $depth        = 20;  # how deep to go in reporting top N pages
```

Now we can put the following immediately after the close SUMMARY line, toward the end of the script proper:

```
close SUMMARY or die "couldn't close $summary_file after writing: $!\n";

$report .= <<EndOfText;

Top $depth pages ($total_views page views total):

EndOfText
```

```
my $count = 0;
foreach my $page (sort
    { $views_by_page{$b} <=> $views_by_page{$a}
                    ||
                  $a cmp $b }
    keys %views_by_page) {
```

This code demonstrates something we haven't seen so far in this book: a sort block featuring a two-way sort operation. Before we try to make sense of that, let's take a minute and look at sorting in more detail.

Fancier Sorting

As you learned back in Chapter 6, we can customize how the sort function sorts things by giving it an explicit *sort block*, which is a curly-brace-delimited block containing instructions on how to sort two special variables, $a and $b.

Let's look at some examples, working from simple sorts to more complex ones:

```
@ary    = ('b', 'c', 'a');

@sorted = sort @ary;               # @sorted gets: a, b, c
@sorted = sort { $a cmp $b } @ary; # same thing
@sorted = sort { $b cmp $a } @ary; # reversed: c, b, a
```

This first example demonstrates something you already learned back in Chapter 6. Namely, that the cmp string-comparison operator, used in the sort block { $a cmp $b }, gives the same result as sort's default behavior, which is to sort a list into ascending ASCII order. It also demonstrates something you haven't seen before: how to sort in descending order. You do that simply by switching the places of the $a and $b variables in the sort block.

Since ASCII order gives case-sensitive sorting, with all the uppercase letters sorting first, here's a technique (also demonstrated back in Chapter 6) to overcome that behavior in situations where you actually want case-insensitive sorting:

```
@ary    = ('b', 'c', 'a', 'Y', 'X', 'Z');

@sorted = sort { $a cmp $b } @ary; # case-sensitive ASCII-order sort.
                            # @sorted gets: X, Y, Z, a, b, c

@sorted = sort { lc $a cmp lc $b } @ary; # case-insensitive sort, now.
                            # gives: a, b, c, X, Y, Z
```

All this is fine when you want to sort strings, but what about sorting numbers? The following examples demonstrate how to do that.

```
@ary    = (1 .. 20); # all the integers 1 - 20

@sorted = sort { $a cmp $b } @ary; # oops; string comparison via cmp.
                            # @sorted gets: 1, 10, 11, 12...

@sorted = sort { $a <=> $b } @ary; # numeric comparision via <=>.
                            # @sorted gets: 1, 2, 3, 4...
```

As you can see, we do numeric, as opposed to string, comparison by using a different operator: <=>, normally referred to in Perl circles as the *spaceship operator*. You have to love a language that has something with a name like that.

Now let's see how to sort hashes. The following example shows how to handle that, sorting by either the hash's keys or its values:

```
%hash = (a => 3, b => 2, c => 1);

@sorted = sort                     # sort by keys.
          { $a cmp $b }            # @sorted gets: a, b, c
          keys %hash;

@sorted = sort                     # sort by values.
          { $hash{$a} <=> $hash{$b} } # @sorted gets: c, b, a
          keys %hash;
```

We've folded the sort operation onto three lines and used the keys function to sort a list of the keys to our hash rather than an array, but otherwise these sorting operations look pretty much like the earlier examples. In the second example, notice how you can sort by value simply by taking $a and $b (which again are keys), and using them to access the corresponding hash values. Since those values are numbers, we have to switch to using the spaceship operator (<=>) to do the comparison.

For our final example, let's consider the case where we want to do a primary sort on one field and a secondary sort on another. In other words, we want to use the first field to determine the main sort order, but in cases where sorting on the first field results in a tie, we want to break the tie by sorting on the second field. Here's an example that demonstrates how to do that:

```
%age = (
    david   => 20,
    brenda  => 30,
    adam    => 20,
    carla   => 25,
);

# primary sort by age, secondary sort by name:

@sorted = sort
    { $age{$a} <=> $age{$b}
            ||
          $a cmp $b }
    keys %age;

# @sorted has adam, david, carla, brenda
```

We use the *logical or* operator (||) to separate the primary sort expression from the secondary sort expression, and put the whole thing inside our sort block. This works because comparison operators (like the <=> numeric comparison operator, and the cmp string comparison operator) do their magic like this: they compare the item on their left with the item on their right, and return -1 if the left item is less than the right item, 1 if the left item is greater than the right item, and 0 if the two items are equal. So in our two-way sort block, the primary sort expression normally gets to return the -1 or 1 that determines the sort order of the $a and $b currently being sorted. But in cases where those values are equal, the primary sort expression returns 0. That means that the || operator (which works something like the or you've been using in your or die... statements) causes the expression on its right to be evaluated, meaning the secondary sort expression gets to determine the sort order.

So, with all that under your belt, the two-way sort block that we were looking at from log_report.plx should be easy to understand. Here it is again:

```
foreach my $page (sort
    { $views_by_page{$b} <=> $views_by_page{$a}
                        ||
                    $a cmp $b }
    keys %views_by_page) {
```

In this case, we're reporting on the most popular pages from the most recent script run, as stored in the %views_by_page hash. That hash, you'll recall, has keys consisting of requested paths and filenames, and values consisting of the number of requests for those pages. We use a two-way sort, with the primary sort being a descending numeric sort on the number of page views (so that we get the most popular pages first), and the secondary sort being an ascending sort on the path-plus-filename.

Now that we have that fancy sort block out of the way, we can look at what happens to the sorted output in the remainder of the foreach block:

```
$report .= <<EndOfText;

Top $depth pages ($total_views page views total):

EndOfText

my $count = 0;
foreach my $page (sort
    { $views_by_page{$b} <=> $views_by_page{$a}
                        ||
                    $a cmp $b }
    keys %views_by_page) {
    ++$count;
    my $percentage = ($views_by_page{$page} / $total_views) * 100;
    $percentage = sprintf '%1.1f', $percentage;
    $report .= "$views_by_page{$page} ($percentage\%)\t$page\n";
    last if $count >= $depth;
}
```

As you can see, we increment our $count variable, then compute the percentage of the views for this page versus the total page views in the log file as a whole. We use sprintf to format that percentage, then append a line to the report describing this page's statistics in comparison to the other most-popular pages on the site. Finally, we check to see if $count has exceeded the limit specified in the $depth configuration variable. If it has, we bail out of the foreach loop using Perl's last function, which causes a script to stop executing the current while or foreach loop and go on with whatever comes after it.

Reporting the Referral and User Agent Information

Another interesting thing to report on is the most productive sources of off-site referrals, and the most popular user agents. To do so, we need to add two more hashes to our script-wide data structure: %referer_count and %agent_count. We can do that by adding them to that big top-of-script my variable declaration:

```
my ($begin_time, $end_time, $total_hits, $total_mb, $total_views,
    $total_visits, %visit_num, %host, %first_time, %last_time,
    %last_seconds, %page_sequence, %referer, %agent,
    %views_by_page, %referer_count, %agent_count);
```

The obvious place to record the referral and user agent information is in the &new_visit subroutine. At the end of that routine is a short if block that runs if the $log_format variable has been set to 'extended'; now we can modify that if block to include this new code:

```
if ($log_format eq 'extended') {
    if ($referer =~ m{^http://([^/]+)}i) {
        ++$referer_count{$1};
    } else {
        $referer = 'unknown';
        ++$referer_count{unknown};
    }
    $referer{$visit_num} = $referer;
    $agent{$visit_num}   = $agent;
    ++$agent_count{$agent};
}
```

The only tricky part of this is the use of a regular expression to match (and capture) the hostname part of the referring site so that we can keep track of which sites are the best sources of referral traffic. If we keyed the %referer_count hash by the entire $referer variable, we would end up with multiple entries for each search engine because the $referer reported by such sites typically includes a unique search string appended to the end of the URL.

Now that we've added the referral and user agent information to our data structure, we need to put it into the report. We can do that by adding the following just before the section where we append the detail section to the $report variable. This new section uses an if test to check whether we are using the extended log format, and if we are, it adds the referral and user agent information using the $count configuration variable to determine how deep to go. All of this should be pretty easy to follow:

```
if ($log_format eq 'extended') {

    # show referer and user agent information
```

```
    $report .= <<EndOfText;

Top $depth referer hosts ($total_visits total visits):

EndOfText

    my $count = 0;

    foreach my $referer (sort
        { $referer_count{$b} <=> $referer_count{$a} }
        keys %referer_count) {
        ++$count;
        my $percentage =
            ($referer_count{$referer} / $total_visits) * 100;
        $percentage = sprintf "%1.1f", $percentage;
        $report .=
            "$referer_count{$referer} ($percentage\%)\t$referer\n";
        last if $count >= $depth;
    }

    $report .= <<EndOfText;

Top $depth user agents ($total_visits total visits):

EndOfText

    $count = 0;
    foreach my $agent (sort
        { $agent_count{$b} <=> $agent_count{$a} }
        keys %agent_count) {
        ++$count;
        my $percentage = ($agent_count{$agent} / $total_visits) * 100;
        $percentage = sprintf "%1.1f", $percentage;
        $report .= "$agent_count{$agent} ($percentage\%)\t$agent\n";
        last if $count >= $depth;
    }
}
```

Tracking Robots

We've got log_report.plx in pretty good shape now. We're going to add just one more section to it: a section that reports on those visitors that request the largest number of pages. Typically, these represent *robots*: "spider" programs that wander a site to build offsite databases of its content.

Like their real-world counterparts, such spiders are usually harmless. Occasionally, though, a poorly written spider can cause problems, requesting so many pages so quickly that the server gets bogged down. Lincoln Stein, author of the CGI.pm Perl module, has come up with something he calls a *rudeness index* to measure how abusive such robots are. To compute that index, you divide the number of requests received from a particular host by the total number of requests received from all hosts, then multiply by 100 to get a percentage. Then you divide that percentage by the average interval (in seconds) between that particular host's requests, and the result is the rudeness index. A rudeness index greater than 1.0 is usually a sign of an abusive robot.

For this script, we'll be using page views rather than raw hits to compute the rudeness index. We begin by adding two more hash variables to the script-wide my variable declaration up at the top: %total_views and %total_elapsed, both of which will be keyed by $visit_num:

```
my ($begin_time, $end_time, $total_hits, $total_mb, $total_views,
    $total_visits, %visit_num, %host, %first_time, %last_time,
    %last_seconds, %page_sequence, %referer, %agent,
    %views_by_page, %referer_count, %agent_count,
    %total_views, %total_elapsed);
```

Next we modify the &new_visit subroutine to contain the following line:

```
$last_seconds{$visit_num}  = $seconds;
$page_sequence{$visit_num} = $url;
++$total_views{$visit_num};
if ($log_format eq 'extended') {
```

We also modify the &add_to_visit subroutine to contain the following lines:

```
my $elapsed_string =
    (int ($elapsed/60)) . ':' . sprintf "%.2u", $elapsed % 60;
$page_sequence{$visit_num} .= " $elapsed_string, $url";
++$total_views{$visit_num};
$total_elapsed{$visit_num} += $elapsed;
}
```

That will handle putting the necessary information into our data structure. Now we put the following in the configuration section at the top of the script:

```
my $show_rude      = 1;   # (0 or 1) track "rudest" hosts?
```

And now we add the following toward the end of the script proper, just before the section that adds the visit detail to the report:

```
if ($show_rude) {
    $report .= <<EndOfText;

Top $depth hosts by total page views (with "rudeness" index):

Vis #  Index  Views  % Vws  Avg Int              Host
=====  =====  ======  =====  =======  ==============================
EndOfText

    my $count = 0;
    foreach my $visit_num (sort
        {$total_views{$b} <=> $total_views{$a}}
        keys %total_views) {
```

```
        ++$count;
        unless ($total_elapsed{$visit_num}) {
            # avoid "uninitialized variable" warning and
            # divide-by-zero problems for 1-view visits
            # (if they manage to sort into top $depth)
            $total_elapsed{$visit_num} = 1;
        }
        my $avg_interval =
            $total_elapsed{$visit_num} / $total_views{$visit_num};
        my $percent_views =
            ($total_views{$visit_num} / $total_views) * 100;
        my $index = $percent_views / $avg_interval;

        $report .= sprintf "%5u  %5.2f  %6u  %5.2f  %3u sec  %-s\n",
            $visit_num, $index, $total_views{$visit_num},
            $percent_views, $avg_interval, $host{$visit_num};
        last if $count >= $depth;
    }
}
```

None of this should need much extra explanation at this stage in your Perl education,
except perhaps the part about uninitialized variable warnings and divide-by-zero
errors. If you take a second to think about it, though, that should be pretty easy, too.

If we have so few visits in our log file that we happen to have a one-request visit that
sorts into the top $depth visits, there will be nothing in that particular $total_
elapsed{$visit_num} hash value (since that only gets initialized with the visit's *sec-
ond* request, in the &add_to_visit subroutine). We will therefore get an "uninitialized value" warning when we try to use that hash value in the line where we assign
$avg_interval (because we've enabled warnings with the -w shebang line switch).
What's worse, that uninitialized value, when used in the division operation on the
righthand side of the assignment, will be interpreted by Perl as the number zero,
which means $avg_interval will be set to 0. That in turn means we will get a divide-
by-zero error when we try to divide $percent_views by $avg_interval two lines later,
and Perl, disgusted with our poor math skills, will bomb out of the script with a fatal
error.

In general, you should always be careful when dividing by some computed quantity.
If there's any chance you could end up trying to divide by zero, you should "program defensively" to avoid the problem. In this case, we handle the possibility by
testing for zero and replacing it with some reasonably sensible nonzero value.

Mailing the Report

The log_report.plx script is basically done. We're going to add just one more feature: a section that lets us specify a list of email addresses to receive a mailed copy of
the report every time the script is run.

We can just run the script manually from the command line whenever we get curious about what's going on in the log files, but it works best if we schedule it to run automatically at set intervals. A typical approach would be to have it run in the wee hours of the morning, building a report based on the previous day's log file. (Most web servers are configured to have their access logs rotated on a daily basis, so a particular filename like access.log.1 will always correspond to the previous day's log.) With this email feature, we can have the finished report sitting in our inbox ready for reading with our morning coffee.

In a moment we'll look at how we can use the Unix cron command to automate the running of log_report.plx. For now, let's add the emailed delivery option.

First, we need to figure out where our web server's copy of the sendmail program resides:

```
[jbc@andros jbc]$ which sendmail
/usr/sbin/sendmail
```

 Historically, the sendmail mail-delivery program has been the standard in the Unix world, but it is becoming less so. Still, even if your web server has some other mail delivery agent installed instead of sendmail, it is possible that that delivery agent features a sendmail-compatible emulation mode, such that you can use the following code unchanged. Contact your system administrator for details.

Now we add the following to the configuration section at the top of log_report.plx:

```
my $sendmail           = '/usr/sbin/sendmail'; # where is sendmail?
my @mailto_addresses = ('your@address.here');
my $from_line          = 'report@your.domain';
```

The @mailto_addresses array should contain a list of email addresses that you want to receive the report. If you don't want the report mailed to anyone, just set @mailto_addresses to the empty list, like this:

```
my @mailto_addresses = ();
```

The $from_line variable should get the address line that you want to show up in the From: header on the emails the script sends. You should probably pick one that will actually deliver to an appropriate place (like your own email address) in case someone replies to it.

Now, down at the bottom of the script proper, just before the subroutine invocations, we need to replace the print $report line with the following:

```
unless (@mailto_addresses) {
    print $report;
} else {
    foreach my $address (@mailto_addresses) {
        # send the email message
        open(MAIL, "|$sendmail -oi -t") or
```

```
            die "Can't open pipe to $sendmail: $!\n";
        print MAIL <<EndOfText;
    To: $address
    From: $from_line
    Subject: $site_name Access Report for $end_time

    $report
    EndOfText
        close MAIL or die "Can't close pipe to $sendmail: $!\n";
        }
    }
```

Take a careful look at what this code does. First off, it checks to see if @mailto_
addresses has been set to a true value, and if it hasn't, it just prints the report to
STDOUT like before. Otherwise, it sends a copy of the report to each address listed in
@mailto_addresses.

Here, as in the form-mailing CGI script you saw in Chapter 3, you are opening a pipe
to a command via an argument of "| commandname" to Perl's open function.

In this case you're piping the report you've just created, along with some suitable
mail header lines, to the sendmail program. The -oi command-line switch you supply to sendmail is important because it prevents sendmail from interpreting an input
line consisting solely of a period (.) as the end of the message to be sent. (It isn't particularly likely that your report will have a line consisting solely of a period, but it's a
good defensive-programming habit to include the -oi argument anyway.) The -t
command-line switch tells sendmail to expect the To: header to come in as part of the
piped input.

If you are going to be sending a *lot* of emails at one time from your script, by the way,
it would be a good idea to include an extra command-line switch of -odq, like this:

```
    open(MAIL, "|$sendmail -oi -t -odq") or
        die "Can't open pipe to $sendmail: $!\n";
```

This will cause sendmail to dump all the outgoing emails into a special holding area,
or *queue*, and send them out gradually rather than trying to send them all at once
and slowing down your server with a lot of simultaneous sendmail processes.

The log_report.plx script is finished! The final version of the script is given in
Example 10-2. Give yourself a clap on the back, then read the next section to see
how to set up a cron job to run it automatically.

Example 10-2. The fourth and final version of log_report.plx

```
#!/usr/bin/perl -w

# log_report.plx

# report on web visitors. expects common or extended log
# format lines to be fed to it on STDIN.
```

Example 10-2. The fourth and final version of log_report.plx (continued)

```perl
use strict;
use Time::Local;
use Text::Wrap;

# configuration section:

my $log_format      = 'extended'; # 'common' or 'extended'
$Text::Wrap::columns = 60;
my $site_name       = 'My Web Site';
my $expire_time     = 900; # seconds of inactivity to consider a
                           # "visit" ended (0 = forever)
my $summary_file    = './summary.txt';
my $summary_count   = 7;   # how many script runs to summarize
my $depth           = 20;  # how deep to go in reporting top N pages
my $show_detail     = 1;   # (0 or 1) show detail?
my $show_rude       = 1;   # (0 or 1) track "rudest" hosts?

my $sendmail        = '/usr/sbin/sendmail'; # where is sendmail?
my @mailto_addresses = ('your@address.here');
my $from_line       = 'report@your.domain';

# script-wide my variable declarations:

my ($begin_time, $end_time, $total_hits, $total_mb, $total_views,
    $total_visits, %visit_num, %host, %first_time, %last_time,
    %last_seconds, %page_sequence, %referer, %agent,
    %views_by_page, %referer_count, %agent_count, %total_views,
    %total_elapsed);

# script proper begins

while (<>) {

    my ($host, $ident_user, $auth_user, $date, $time,
        $time_zone, $method, $url, $protocol, $status, $bytes,
        $referer, $agent);

    if ($log_format eq 'common') {

        ($host, $ident_user, $auth_user, $date, $time,
            $time_zone, $method, $url, $protocol, $status, $bytes) =
/^(\S+) (\S+) (\S+) \[([^:]+):(\d+:\d+:\d+) ([^\]]+)\] "(\S+) (.+?)
 (\S+)" (\S+) (\S+)$/
            or next;

    } elsif ($log_format eq 'extended') {

        ($host, $ident_user, $auth_user, $date, $time,
            $time_zone, $method, $url, $protocol, $status, $bytes,
            $referer, $agent) =
/^(\S+) (\S+) (\S+) \[([^:]+):(\d+:\d+:\d+) ([^\]]+)\] "(\S+) (.+?)
 (\S+)" (\S+) (\S+) "([^"]+)" "([^"]+)"$/
            or next;
```

Example 10-2. The fourth and final version of log_report.plx (continued)

```perl
    } else {
        die "unrecognized log format '$log_format'";
    }

    ++$total_hits;
    unless ($bytes =~ /^\d+$/) {
        $bytes = 0;
    }
    $total_mb += ($bytes / (1024 * 1024));
    unless ($begin_time) {
        $begin_time = "$date:$time";
    }
    $end_time = "$date:$time";

    next if $url =~ /\.(gif|jpg|jpeg|png|xbm)$/i;
    # don't care about these for visit-tracking purposes

    ++$total_views;
    ++$views_by_page{$url};
    &store_line($host, $date, $time, $url, $referer, $agent);
}

# done processing log file. begin output.

my @summary_lines;

if (-e $summary_file) {
    open SUMMARY, $summary_file or
        die "can't open $summary_file for reading: $!\n";
    @summary_lines = <SUMMARY>;
    close SUMMARY or die "can't close $summary_file after reading: $!\n";
}

my $summary_line = sprintf
    "%s %s %6u %6u %6u %6u\n", $begin_time, $end_time,
    $total_hits, $total_views, $total_visits, $total_mb;
unshift @summary_lines, $summary_line;
if (@summary_lines > $summary_count) {
    $#summary_lines = $summary_count - 1;
}

my $report = <<EndOfText;
$site_name Access Report -- $end_time

Summary of last $summary_count reporting periods:

        From                 To            Hits   Views Visits   Mb
==================== ==================== ====== ====== ====== ======
EndOfText

open SUMMARY, ">$summary_file" or
    die "couldn't open $summary_file for writing: $!\n";
```

Example 10-2. The fourth and final version of log_report.plx (continued)

```perl
foreach (@summary_lines) {
    $report .= $_;
    print SUMMARY;
}

close SUMMARY or die "couldn't close $summary_file after writing: $!\n";

$report .= <<EndOfText;

Top $depth pages ($total_views page views total):

EndOfText

my $count = 0;
foreach my $page (sort
    { $views_by_page{$b} <=> $views_by_page{$a}
                         ||
                    $a cmp $b }
    keys %views_by_page) {
    ++$count;
    my $percentage = ($views_by_page{$page} / $total_views) * 100;
    $percentage = sprintf '%1.1f', $percentage;
    $report .= "$views_by_page{$page} ($percentage\%)\t$page\n";
    last if $count >= $depth;
}

if ($log_format eq 'extended') {

    # show referer and user agent information

    $report .= <<EndOfText;

Top $depth referer hosts ($total_visits total visits):

EndOfText

    my $count = 0;

    foreach my $referer (sort
        { $referer_count{$b} <=> $referer_count{$a} }
        keys %referer_count) {
        ++$count;
        my $percentage =
            ($referer_count{$referer} / $total_visits) * 100;
        $percentage = sprintf '%1.1f', $percentage;
        $report .=
            "$referer_count{$referer} ($percentage\%)\t$referer\n";
        last if $count >= $depth;
    }

    $report .= <<EndOfText;
```

Example 10-2. The fourth and final version of log_report.plx (continued)

```
Top $depth user agents ($total_visits total visits):

EndOfText

    $count = 0;
    foreach my $agent (sort
        { $agent_count{$b} <=> $agent_count{$a} }
        keys %agent_count) {
        ++$count;
        my $percentage = ($agent_count{$agent} / $total_visits) * 100;
        $percentage = sprintf '%1.1f', $percentage;
        $report .= "$agent_count{$agent} ($percentage\%)\t$agent\n";
        last if $count >= $depth;
    }
}

if ($show_rude) {
    $report .= <<EndOfText;

Top $depth hosts by total page views (with "rudeness" index):

Vis #  Index  Views  % Vws  Avg Int        Host
=====  =====  ======  =====  =======  ===============================
EndOfText

    my $count = 0;
    foreach my $visit_num (sort
        {$total_views{$b} <=> $total_views{$a}}
        keys %total_views) {
        ++$count;
        unless ($total_elapsed{$visit_num}) {
            # avoid "uninitialized variable" warning for
            # 1-view visits (if they manage to sort into
            # the top $depth)
            $total_elapsed{$visit_num} = 1;
        }
        my $avg_interval =
            $total_elapsed{$visit_num} / $total_views{$visit_num};
        my $percent_views =
            ($total_views{$visit_num} / $total_views) * 100;
        my $index = $percent_views / $avg_interval;

        $report .= sprintf "%5u  %5.2f  %6u  %5.2f  %3u sec  %-s\n",
            $visit_num, $index, $total_views{$visit_num},
            $percent_views, $avg_interval, $host{$visit_num};
        last if $count >= $depth;
    }
}

if ($show_detail) {
    $report .= <<EndOfText;
```

Example 10-2. The fourth and final version of log_report.plx (continued)

```
Detail for most recent reporting period:

EndOfText

    foreach my $visit_num (1 .. $total_visits) {
        $report .= &visit_detail($visit_num);
    }
}

unless (@mailto_addresses) {
    print $report;
} else {
    foreach my $address (@mailto_addresses) {
        # send the email message
        open(MAIL, "|$sendmail -oi -t") or
            die "Can't open pipe to $sendmail: $!\n";
        print MAIL <<EndOfText;
To: $address
From: $from_line
Subject: $site_name Access Report for $end_time

$report
EndOfText
        close MAIL or die "Can't close pipe to $sendmail: $!\n";
    }
}

# end of script proper. subroutines follow.

sub store_line {

    # store one line's worth of visit data

    my($host, $date, $time, $url, $referer, $agent) = @_;
    my $seconds = &get_seconds($date, $time);

    if ($visit_num{$host}) {
        # there is a visit currently "working" for this host
        my $visit_num = $visit_num{$host};
        my $elapsed = $seconds - $last_seconds{$visit_num};
        if (($expire_time) and ($elapsed > $expire_time)) {
            # this visit has expired, so start a new one
            &new_visit($host, $date, $time, $url, $seconds,
                $referer, $agent);
        } else {
            # this visit has not expired, so add to existing record
            &add_to_visit($host, $date, $time,
                $url, $seconds, $elapsed);
        }
    } else {
        # there is no visit currently "working" for this host
        &new_visit($host, $date, $time, $url, $seconds,
```

Example 10-2. The fourth and final version of log_report.plx (continued)

```
                $referer, $agent);
    }
}

BEGIN {
    my %date_seconds;
    my %month_num = (
        Jan => 0,
        Feb => 1,
        Mar => 2,
        Apr => 3,
        May => 4,
        Jun => 5,
        Jul => 6,
        Aug => 7,
        Sep => 8,
        Oct => 9,
        Nov => 10,
        Dec => 11,
    );

    sub get_seconds {

        # this subroutine accepts a date string of the form
        # '06/Jul/1999' and a time string of the form '12:14:00'
        # and returns the number of seconds since the Unix
        # epoch, as determined by Time::Local's timelocal
        # function. the subroutine caches conversions of the
        # date part in %date_seconds in order to improve
        # performance.

        my ($date, $time) = @_;
        my $seconds;
        if ($date_seconds{$date}) {
            $seconds = $date_seconds{$date};
        } else {
            my ($day, $mon, $yr) = split /\//, $date;
            $mon  = $month_num{$mon};
            $yr = $yr - 1900;
            $seconds = $date_seconds{$date} =
                timelocal(0, 0, 0, $day, $mon, $yr);
        }
        my($hr, $min, $sec) = split /:/, $time;
        $seconds += ($hr * 3600) + ($min * 60) + $sec;
    }
}

sub new_visit {

    # record an entry for an access line that has been
    # determined to represent a new visit (either because
    # this is the first time this host has been seen,
```

Example 10-2. The fourth and final version of log_report.plx (continued)

```perl
    # or because the host's previous visit has expired)

    my ($host, $date, $time, $url, $seconds,
        $referer, $agent) = @_;
    my $visit_num              = ++$total_visits;
    $visit_num{$host}          = $visit_num;
    $host{$visit_num}          = $host;
    $first_time{$visit_num}    = "$date:$time";
    $last_time{$visit_num}     = "$date:$time";
    $last_seconds{$visit_num}  = $seconds;
    $page_sequence{$visit_num} = $url;
    ++$total_views{$visit_num};
    if ($log_format eq 'extended') {
        if ($referer =~ m{^http://([^/]+)}i) {
            ++$referer_count{$1};
        } else {
            $referer = 'unknown';
            ++$referer_count{unknown};
        }
        $referer{$visit_num} = $referer;
        $agent{$visit_num}   = $agent;
        ++$agent_count{$agent};
    }
}

sub add_to_visit {

    # append to an existing visit record because it has been
    # determined that the current line contains more data to
    # be added to a currently "working" visit

    my($host, $date, $time, $url, $seconds, $elapsed) = @_;
    my $visit_num              = $visit_num{$host};
    $last_time{$visit_num}     = "$date:$time";
    $last_seconds{$visit_num} = $seconds;

    my $elapsed_string =
        (int ($elapsed/60)) . ':' . sprintf "%.2u", $elapsed % 60;
    $page_sequence{$visit_num} .= " $elapsed_string, $url";
    ++$total_views{$visit_num};
    $total_elapsed{$visit_num} += $elapsed;
}

sub visit_detail {

    # returns a formatted report for a particular visit.
    # assumes 'use Text::Wrap;'

    my $visit_num = $_[0];
    my $page_sequence =
        wrap('', '                    ', $page_sequence{$visit_num});
```

Example 10-2. The fourth and final version of log_report.plx (continued)

```
    my $detail = <<EndOfText;
 Visit Number: $visit_num
         Host: $host{$visit_num}
 First Access: $first_time{$visit_num}
  Last Access: $last_time{$visit_num}
EndOfText

    if ($log_format eq 'extended') {

        $detail .= <<EndOfText
     Referrer: $referer{$visit_num}
   User Agent: $agent{$visit_num}
EndOfText

    }

    $detail .= <<EndOfText;
Page Sequence: $page_sequence

EndOfText

    $detail;
}
```

Using cron

The Unix cron command is one of those things that makes you wonder how you ever got along without it. In brief, it lets you schedule a command or series of commands to be run periodically on the Unix server, whether you're logged in or not.

The instructions on what commands to run and when to run them are stored in a special *cron table*, or *crontab*. On many systems only the superuser can use the crontab command to modify the entries in that table. On other systems ordinary users can do so, but the exact method sometimes varies depending on what flavor of Unix the server is running.

> The following discussion assumes you are on a Linux server that has been configured to allow ordinary users to install their own crontab entries. If these instructions don't work in your case, you should contact your system administrator. You should also try consulting the cron and crontab documentation available on your server (via man cron, man 1 crontab, and man 5 crontab) because some of the features described here could well be different or absent in the case of your particular cron installation.

A *crontab* file is simply a text file. You edit it using any text editor you like, then install it on your server using the `crontab` command, like this:

```
[jbc@andros jbc] crontab mycronfile.txt
```

The format of the *crontab* file is very specific. Blank lines are ignored, as are lines beginning with a hash sign (#). All other lines need to consist of the following fields, separated by spaces:

- Minute of the hour (typically a number from 0-59)
- Hour of the day (typically 0–23)
- Day of the month (typically 1–31)
- Month of the year (typically 1–12)
- Day of the week (typically 0–7, with Sunday being 0 *or* 7, at least on the `cron` installation I use)

Everything after the fifth field, up until the end of the line, is considered the command to be run.

The numbers in the first five fields can be combined with dashes to give a range (4-6 would mean "4, 5, and 6"), or with commas to give a series (4,6,9 would mean "4, 6, and 9"). You also can combine ranges and series in one field, so you could use something like 4-6,8,10 to mean "4, 5, 6, 8, and 10". Finally, you can use an asterisk (*) to mean "everything"—that is, all possible values for that field.

Every minute the `cron` program wakes up and checks all the current *crontab* entries. If the minute, hour, and month of the year field for a particular entry all match the current values, and *either* the day of the week or day of the month fields matches, the command for that entry is executed.

This sounds pretty complicated when you hear it all at once, but it turns out to be pretty simple once you get the hang of it. Here is an example *crontab* file:

```
# run /home/jbc/bin/hello.plx at 3:17 a.m. every Tue, Thu, and Sat
17 3 * * 2,4,6 /home/jbc/bin/hello.plx

# output 'humbug!' every hour from 9:00 a.m. to 5:00 p.m., every
# weekday during December
0 9-17 * 12 1-5 /bin/echo 'humbug!'

# run /home/jbc/bin/monthly_report.plx 42 minutes past midnight on
# the first day of every month
42 0 1 * * /home/jbc/bin/monthly_report.plx

# run the log_report.plx script on access.log.1 at 2:17 a.m. each day
17 2 * * * /home/jbc/bin/log_report.plx < /w1/l/lies/.logs/access.log.1
```

Each *crontab* entry must fit onto a single line. That line can be as long as you like, but you need to be careful that your text editor doesn't wrap the line for you.

 If you are using the pico text editor under Unix, starting it up with the -w command-line option will turn off its automatic line wrapping.

Something else that often gives new users problems is the fact that the cron facility runs *crontab* entries with a *minimal environment*. That means things like your command path, or aliases you might have defined in a special shell startup file, will not be available when a *crontab* entry is executed. This in turn means that a command that works fine when you enter it manually at the shell prompt might not work properly when run as a *crontab* entry. In particular, you will probably need to specify the complete path to commands.

You can run multiple commands in sequence as part of one *crontab* entry by separating them with semicolons (;). This is not specific to *crontab* entries; it's just another shell metacharacter like the pipe (|) and redirection (<, >, and >>) symbols. When you use semicolons to separate two or more commands on a command line, first the leftmost command will be run, then the next, and so on, to the end of the line. For example, this command line:

```
[jbc@buffy jbc]$ cd /usr/bin; ls -l perl
-rwxr-xr-x   2 root     root          516828 Apr  6 20:36 perl
```

does the same thing as these two command lines entered one after the other:

```
[jbc@buffy bin]$ cd /usr/bin
[jbc@buffy bin]$ ls -l perl
-rwxr-xr-x   2 root     root          516828 Apr  6 20:36 perl
```

As you saw a minute ago, you install your *crontab* entries by creating a suitable *crontab* file, then running crontab *cronfile.txt* in the shell, with *cronfile.txt* being replaced by the name of the *crontab* file you have created. That file will then be installed, and will replace any previous *crontab* entries you might have had.

You can also invoke crontab with the -l option, which will cause it to print your current *crontab* entries to standard output. If you redirect that output to a file, you can then edit that file to make whatever changes or additions you like, then reinstall the modified file:

```
[jbc@andros jbc] crontab -l > mycronfile.txt
```

Edit *mycronfile.txt* to your satisfaction, save it, then reinstall it:

```
[jbc@andros jbc] crontab mycronfile.txt
```

Finally, you can bypass all this and just edit your *crontab* entries directly by invoking crontab with the -e option:

```
[jbc@andros jbc] crontab -e
```

This will put you in an editing session using whatever editor is defined in your account's VISUAL (or EDITOR) environment variable, with the current *crontab* already loaded and ready for modification. When you exit from that editing session, the modified *crontab* will be reinstalled.

So, again, with a *crontab* entry like this you can have your log_report.plx script process your web server's access log once each day:

```
17 2 * * * /home/jbc/bin/log_report.plx < /w1/l/lies/.logs/access.log.1
```

If you haven't configured log_report.plx to mail its output to you, though, it just prints its report to standard output. This is fine when you are running it from the command line because standard output just shows up on your screen. But what about a *crontab* entry, which runs when you are sound asleep, or at least not logged in? Where does the output go?

The answer is, it gets mailed to you anyway. By default, any output produced by a cron job is emailed to the *crontab*'s owner (you, in the case of your *crontab* entries). This is true whether the output is being sent to standard output or standard error; if anything is output, you'll be getting mail containing that output.

This is normally used as a means of notification in the case of broken *crontab* entries. Most *crontab* entries are designed to run silently, with the assumption that if something goes wrong it will start producing some sort of output on standard error, and the *crontab*'s owner will start getting mail about it so that he can fix the problem. In the case of a daily log analysis script that sends its report to standard output, though, it means you can just run the script as a cron job and you will should receive the reports via email.

When I say that cron will email you the output of your cron jobs, what I really mean is that cron will email that output to your user account on the machine where the cron jobs are running. If you have an email account on some completely different machine that you use as your primary mailbox, you may want to forward your mail from the machine running cron to that other mailbox. One common way to do that is to put a file called .forward in your home directory, with the file containing a single line consisting of the email address you wish to forward to. Contact your system administrator for more details on how to do this.

It can be intoxicating to be able to schedule jobs to run automatically. It's possible to get carried away, though. See the accompanying sidebar, "Playing Nice with cron," for suggestions on how to stay out of trouble.

Playing Nice with cron

When I first learned how to use the cron facility, I got so excited that I scheduled a *lot* of cron jobs. In some cases I was using cron inappropriately, having the computer perform the same operation over and over again even when it didn't need to, rather than taking the time to build a more efficient solution that would run only as needed.

Just because cron makes it easy to schedule some CPU-intensive task to run every hour on the hour from now to the end of time doesn't mean you should actually do that. Especially in a shared web-hosting environment, it is important to keep your cron jobs under control. Many ISPs limit users' ability to set up their own *crontab*s for just this reason. Others that do allow users to install their own *crontab* entries have policies limiting how often or during what times of day they can be run. You should make sure you are up-to-date on any policies your own ISP has in this area.

Besides making sure you don't run unnecessary cron jobs and making sure that big jobs run during the wee hours of the morning (or some other off-peak time), you can use another trick if you are running cron jobs in a shared environment. Instead of setting your *crontab* entries to fire off at the top of the hour, pick some strange time like 17 or 33 or 48 minutes after the hour. That way your cron jobs will be less likely to fire off at the same time as lots of other users' cron jobs.

## CHAPTER 11

Link Checking

This chapter introduces some very important Perl features that we'll be using in the rest of the book. For one thing, it shows how to use references to create a multilevel data structure. It also shows how to download and install CPAN modules. Finally, it offers a brief introduction to object-oriented Perl to help you take advantage of the many object-oriented modules available from CPAN. Even if you don't think you need a link-checking program, you should still take a look at the concepts introduced in this chapter.

Maintaining Links

One of the key factors in the success of the Web was Tim Berners-Lee's original decision to make links one-way. That is, anyone can construct a link connecting any web page to any other web page, and do so quickly and easily. There is no need to register with some central repository of links, no requirement that a return link be established and maintained, no need even to inform the people at the other end that you are linking to them. You just put an `<A HREF=...>` tag in your web page, and boom, you have a link. I still get a kick out of teaching people new to HTML how to do that. There is always that moment of shocked silence, usually followed by the question, "It's that easy?"

This was one of Berners-Lee's main goals when he invented the Web. He wanted people to be able to do with computers what they do so easily with their brains: make connections between seemingly unrelated things. The downside to this freedom, though, is that it is easy to create broken links, in which a typo or other error renders the link unusable. Worse, even if the link starts off in perfect working order, over time link rot will set in. As resources go away or are moved to new addresses, our web pages full of exciting connections become web pages full of broken links. It is our job, as maintainers of web resources, to police our own links. That job is hard enough when we're talking about a handful of links on a personal home page, but it swells to Herculean proportions when we're talking about sites containing hundreds or thousands of pages.

Perl to the rescue. This chapter presents three different versions of a Perl link checker. The first version runs very quickly, but processes only local links (that is, links that point to files in the local filesystem) and is fairly stupid about interpreting HTML. The second version adds the capability of checking remote (that is, off-site) links and still runs pretty quickly, but is also fairly stupid. The third version offers significantly enhanced cleverness, but at a cost of significantly slower operation.

Finding Files with File::Find

The first step in building our first link checker is to figure out a way for our script to get a list of all the HTML files on our site. Back in Chapter 4, we fed our script a list of filenames on the command line using the shell's ability to expand wildcard characters. Now, though, we're going to take a different approach, by using the standard File::Find module. We use it by putting use File::Find into our script, then invoking the module's find function. This will make it easy to construct a script that processes all the files under a given starting directory, including those in deeper subdirectories.

We'll start with the simple demonstration script, find_files.plx, shown in Example 11-1. (Like all the examples in this book, you can download it from the book's web site, at *http://www.elanus.net/book/*.)

Example 11-1. find_files.plx

```perl
#!/usr/bin/perl -w

# find_files.plx

# this script demonstrates the use of the File::Find module.

use strict;
use File::Find;

my $start_dir = shift
    or die "Usage: $0 <start_dir>\n";

unless (-d $start_dir) {
    die "Start directory '$start_dir' is not a directory.\n";
}

find(\&process, $start_dir);

sub process {
```

Example 11-1. find_files.plx (continued)

```
    # this is invoked by File::Find's find function for each
    # file it recursively finds.

    print "Found $File::Find::name\n";
}
```

Most of this script should look pretty straightforward at this point. It starts off by shifting off the first item in @ARGV (that is, the first argument supplied to the script when it was invoked on the command line) and putting it in the $start_dir scalar variable.

If $start_dir gets a false value, the script assumes that the user didn't supply a starting directory name, and dies with a *usage message*. A usage message is just a short message instructing the user how the script should be run; this one uses the $0 special variable, which gives the name of the current script being run. (We could also have just hard-coded "find_files.plx" into the usage message, but this way the message will automatically adjust itself if this code ends up being used in a script with a different name.)

The script then uses the -d file test operator, which you learned about in Chapter 6, to determine if $start_dir actually represents a directory, and (again) dies if it doesn't.

Next comes the heart of the script:

```
    find(\&process, $start_dir);
```

This find function has been pulled in by the use File::Find line earlier. As explained in the File::Find documentation (available via man File::Find, or perldoc File::Find), the find function takes two or more arguments, of which the second (and subsequent) arguments are the names of directories where we want to begin finding files. This file-finding process takes place *recursively*, which is a fancy way of saying that the find function will continue digging its way deeper and deeper through whatever subdirectories lie below (or are contained within, depending on how you look at things) the starting directory.

The Magic of References

So much for the second argument to the find function. What about the first argument? That's where the magic happens.

Yes, it's time for more magic. Look carefully at that first argument to the find function: \&process. It looks vaguely like a subroutine invocation, with that ampersand (&) at the beginning of &process, but what is that leading backslash (\) doing?

The backslash is creating a *reference*. Specifically, it is creating a reference to the &process subroutine. References are at the heart of some very useful and important

features in Perl. You haven't had to worry about them until now, but since the `Find:`
`:File` module makes use of them this is probably as good a time as any to bring them
up. A little later in this chapter you'll need to learn about them anyway, since you
will be using them to build a really nifty multilevel data structure.

For now, though, just concentrate on remembering this: a reference is a special sort
of way to refer to (and gain access to) some other thing that Perl knows about. That
other thing can be a value stored in a scalar variable, or the list of values stored in an
array, or the key-value pairs stored in a hash, or (as in this case) the code stored in a
subroutine. What makes this so useful is that a reference is always a *scalar* (that is to
say, a *singular*) thing, even if the thing it refers to isn't. This means you can do scalar
things with your references, like storing them as elements in an array, or as values in
a hash, or, as in this case, passing them as arguments to a function.

References are tremendously useful in Perl, but to take advantage of them you're
going to need to learn some new Perl syntax. As Mark-Jason Dominus explains in his
excellent `perlreftut` manpage, there are exactly four new pieces of Perl syntax you
need to learn in order to use references: two ways to create a reference, and two ways
to *dereference* a reference in order to gain access to the original thing it refers to.

You've already learned the first of those new pieces of reference syntax: the use of the
backslash in front of a variable or subroutine name in order to return a reference to
that variable's (or subroutine's) contents. You'll learn two of the remaining three
types of reference syntax later in this chapter. (You'll have to wait until Chapter 14
to learn the fourth one.)

It probably sounds like I'm carrying on about something that isn't all that important
or interesting. That's fine; you're allowed to think that. Just so you remember what's
going on with that first argument to the find function: we're passing a *reference* to
the &process subroutine. That is a very different thing from just putting &process
(that is, the subroutine invocation itself) as that first argument. That would cause the
&process subroutine to be evaluated for its return value (or values), with those values
in turn being passed to the find function. Passing the reference makes the subroutine itself available to the find function.

What does the find function want with a subroutine? As the File::Find documentation explains, the find function will run that subroutine once for each file it recursively finds. For each file it finds, the subroutine will be invoked and will get the
name of the current file passed to it in the special $_ variable. The subroutine will
also have access to the *package variables* $File::Find::dir, which gives the name of
the directory currently being processed, and $File::Find::name, which is the full
pathname of the file being processed. (In other words, $File::Find::name is the same
thing as "$File::Find::dir/$_", at least on systems that use the forward slash as the
path separator.)

This leaves it up to us to define that subroutine however we like. In this script, the &process subroutine has been written to simply print out the full path of each file it processes. If we run this script with a suitable directory name as its argument, we should see something like this:

```
[jbc@andros ora]$ find_files.plx /home/jbc/ora
found /home/jbc/ora
found /home/jbc/ora/find_files.plx
found /home/jbc/ora/walnuts
found /home/jbc/ora/walnuts/rutabagas
found /home/jbc/ora/walnuts/apples.html
found /home/jbc/ora/walnuts/oranges.txt
```

One of the interesting things this reveals is that for a Unix system, a directory is thought of as just another file. Both the ora directory and the walnuts directory contained within it show up in the list as found files.

Finding HTML Files Only

Let's say we want File::Find to ignore everything except files ending in .html. Nothing could be easier: we just use a regular expression to bail out of the &process subroutine if the current filename doesn't end that way. We can do that by adding the following line at the beginning of the subroutine:

```
return unless /\.html$/;
```

This will cause it to return immediately unless the filename (which you'll remember is stored by File::Find in the scalar variable $_ for each subroutine invocation) ends in .html.

Note how this line of Perl takes advantage of the fact that $_ is the default variable against which regular expressions try to do their matching. As a result, the line ends up being very concise and clear (assuming you know about $_). This is a very Perlish way to do this.

Note also how the backslash is used inside the regular exp+ression to escape the period (.), thus preventing it from being interpreted as a *metacharacter* matching "any single character." Finally, note the $ at the end of the expression, anchoring it to the end of the string being matched against, so that a file named walnuts.html.bak wouldn't match. Aren't regular expressions wonderful?

The modified subroutine should look like this:

```
sub process {

    # this is invoked by File::Find's find function for each
    # file it recursively finds.

    return unless /\.html$/;
    print "found $File::Find::name\n";
}
```

If we run the script now, we should get output that looks like the following:

```
[jbc@andros ora]$ find_files.plx /home/jbc/ora
found /home/jbc/ora/walnuts/apples.html
```

So, we now have a script that will descend recursively through a filesystem, processing all the files it finds that have names ending in `.html`.

Looking for Links

Now, let's use `find_files.plx` as the starting point for a new script, `link_check.plx`, that will do some simplistic checking for broken links in the HTML files it processes. The first step in doing that is to modify the &process subroutine so that instead of just printing out the names of the HTML files it processes, it opens up each one and reads its contents. We can achieve that by modifying the process subroutine as follows:

```perl
sub process {

    # this is invoked by File::Find's find function for each
    # file it recursively finds.

    return unless /\.html$/;
    my $file = $File::Find::name;
    unless (open IN, $file) {
        warn "can't open $file for reading: $!, continuing...\n";
        return;
    }
    my $data = join '', <IN>; # all the data at once
    close IN;
    return unless $data;
    print "found $file, read the following data:\n\n$data\n";
}
```

Looking at the new parts line by line, we can see that the *package variable* `$File::Find::name` is assigned to a `my` variable called `$file`. This is just for convenience. Since we'll be using that variable several times, typing `$file` is going to be easier than typing `$File::Find::name` over and over again.

Next we open the file for reading, associating the IN filehandle with it in the open statement. Notice how we're using warn rather than die to check for failed open operations. The idea here is that we probably want the script to continue its processing of files even if something strange happens in the middle and one of them can't be opened for reading.

Next comes a handy trick: grabbing all the data from that filehandle at once and storing it in a scalar variable, via this line:

```perl
my $data = join '', <IN>; # all the data at once
```

In the past we've usually put <IN> inside the parentheses of a while loop, which causes it to return a single line at a time. But putting it in an array context (which more properly would be termed a *list* context) causes the <IN> to return all its lines at once.

In Chapter 10 we accomplished this by assigning the return value of <FILEHANDLE> to an array variable, like this:

```
@walnuts = <IN>;
```

We could have done the same thing in this case, using two lines of code instead of one, like this:

```
my @data = <IN>;
my $data = join '', @data;
```

But since the second argument to the join function is (by definition) a list, we can just put the <IN> there, conferring a list context on it and causing it to return all its lines at once, without needing to use that intermediate @data array at all. Notice, by the way, how it's perfectly acceptable to specify the empty string (with the construct '') in join's first argument. This causes it to butt the joined strings right up against each other, with nothing in between (though they'll be separated by newlines in $data, since <IN> returns the terminal newline on each line).

The only real problem with this trick is that if we use it on a very large file, we're going to use a lot of memory as the whole thing gets assigned to the scalar variable in one big chunk. But web pages tend to be pretty manageable in size (at least compared to a modern computer's available RAM), so if we want to manipulate a file as a whole rather than line by line, this is a handy way to read it in.

When this version of the script is running properly, it will print out the complete text of every HTML file it finds.

Extracting

At this point, we are ready to move on to the next level: having the script extract just the links from those files, or more specifically, having it extract the values of all the SRC and HREF attributes.

As was discussed in Chapter 4, trying to parse HTML files with simple pattern matching is an inherently error-prone undertaking. The accompanying example fails in the face of several kinds of HTML markup that are perfectly valid as HTML, but break the simplistic assumptions in this script. For a "correct" link checker that will handle those variations more gracefully, see the example at the end of this chapter.

We begin by deleting the line from the end of the &process subroutine that prints out the current filename and the entire contents of the $data variable, and replacing it with the following chunk of code:

```
my @targets = ($data =~ /(?:href|src)\s*=\s*"([^"]+)"/gi);
print "In file $file, found the following targets:\n";
foreach (@targets) {
    print " $_\n";
}
```

Let's concentrate on that first line. It looks challenging, but assuming you've been doing your regular expressions homework it's really not that tough.

The first thing to focus on is the regular expression search pattern itself: /(?: href|src)\s*=\s*"([^"]+)"/gi. In order, from left to right, this pattern says to match a string that begins with either href or src, then has zero or more whitespace characters, then an equal sign (=), then zero or more whitespace characters, then a double-quote ("), then one or more characters that are anything but a double quote, then another double quote. After the pattern ends, the trailing /g and /i modifiers make the pattern match globally (that is, it keeps on matching after the first match) and case-insensitively, respectively.

The characters between the double quotes are captured into the special variable $1 courtesy of the parentheses surrounding that part of the expression. Significantly, though, the parentheses used at the beginning of the pattern to group the href|src alternatives have had their capturing role intentionally turned off. This was done by putting the special sequence ?: immediately after the opening parenthesis; with that in place, that pair of parentheses can perform their grouping function without doing any actual capturing.

Now take a look at the line as a whole, which is doing something interesting: it is assigning the return value of the regular expression to the array variable @targets. Assigning something to an array variable causes the right side of the assignment to be evaluated in a list context. Until now we have usually used regular expressions in a scalar context (more specifically, in a Boolean true/false context, which is still thought of by Perl as a scalar context). In other words, we have done things like this:

```
if (/pattern/) { do something; }
```

In this line the /pattern/ regular expression returns a true or false value based on whether it successfully matched. Putting the regular expression in a list context, though, causes it to behave differently. It still matches or doesn't match according to the same rules, but now its return value becomes a list of all the parts of the target string that matched the stuff inside the expression's capturing parentheses. (If the expression doesn't have any capturing parentheses, you get a list of all the parts of the target string that matched the entire expression, as if the expression had a pair of capturing parentheses surrounding the entire pattern.)

Again, this regular expression has a /g modifier at the end and continues to match the target string as many times as it can. Each time it matches, the part that matched inside the capturing parentheses gets added to the expression's return value. When it's finished, we get back a list of all the double-quote–delimited HREF and SRC values contained in the string stored in the $content variable.

The idea here is that we can extract all the destinations at which our HTML documents' <A HREF="...">`tags are pointing, and all the images being displayed via <IMG SRC="...">` tags, so that we can check them to make sure they actually exist. Again, though, this will work only for simple HTML examples.

Converting

By themselves, the values of our web pages' HREF and SRC attributes aren't much use for link-checking purposes. To see if they point to files that actually exist, we need to convert them into absolute filesystem paths.

Here again, we're going to be making some (possibly incorrect) assumptions, this time about how the web server is configured. In particular, we're going to assume that the web server's directory structure is in fact just a simple branch of the larger filesystem. In other words, we're going to assume that if the top of the web server's document tree corresponds to the directory /walnuts/rutabagas when viewed from the shell, paths pointing at local resources from the web server's perspective can be converted to filesystem paths by putting '/walnuts/rutabagas' in front of them.

We begin by adding a section like the following near the top of the link_check.plx script:

```
# configuration section:

# note: the first four configuration variables should *not*
# have a trailing slash (/)

my $start_dir   = '/w1/s/socalsail/expo';  # where to begin looking
my $hostname    = 'www.socalsail.com';     # this site's hostname
my $web_root    = '/w1/s/socalsail';       # path to www doc root
my $web_path    = '/expo';                 # web path to $start_dir
```

Now we add the following &convert subroutine at the bottom of the script:

```
sub convert {

    # This accepts the directory name of a file from
    # which a list of URLs was extracted (in the first argument)
    # and a list of URLs extracted from that file (in the
    # rest of the arguments). It returns a list of all the URLs
    # that did not point outside the local site, or were not
    # ftp:, mailto:, https:, or news: URLs, with those URLs
    # converted into local filesystem filenames.
```

```
        my($dir, @urls) = @_;
        my @return_urls;
        my $escaped_hostname = quotemeta $hostname;
        foreach (@urls) {
            next if /^(ftp|mailto|https|news):/i;
            if (/^http:/i) {
                # URL starts with 'http:'
                next unless /^http:\/\/$escaped_hostname/io;
                s/^http:\/\/$escaped_hostname//io;
            }
            if (/^\//) {
                # URL starts with '/'
                $_ = $web_root . $_;
            } else {
                # URL is a relative path
                $_ = $dir . '/' . $_;
            }
            s/#.*//;  # trim trailing #targets
            s/\?.*//; # trim trailing ?arguments
            push @return_urls, $_;
        }
        @return_urls;
    }
```

There isn't much new going on in this subroutine in terms of Perl. Basically, we hand it the name of a directory where we found an HTML file, and then we hand it a list of all the links extracted from that file. For each link, the script first checks to see if it begins with any of the following: ftp:, mailto:, https:, or news:. If it does the script forgets about this link and goes on to the next one.

Notice, by the way, how using the default index variable ($_) for the foreach loop lets us write the various regular expression matches in the subroutine very compactly, since they all match against the same $_ variable by default.

Next, the subroutine checks to see if this link begins with an initial http:. If it does, the routine either uses next to go to the next link (if the hostname is not the same as the $hostname configuration variable defined at the top of the script), or uses a search-and-replace variety of regular expression to replace the http://$hostname string with nothing.

Before it can do this, though, it has to prepare that $hostname string for use in the regex pattern by running the quotemeta function on it. quotemeta puts a backslash in front of every nonword character in the string you pass it, and then returns that backslashed string. ("Nonword character," in this case, means the same thing as the special \W regex sequence: any character that isn't an upper- or lowercase letter, a numeral, or the underscore character.) Since Perl's regexes are conveniently designed to always let you backslash any nonalphanumeric character in order to get that character's literal meaning for matching purposes, running quotemeta on $hostname will turn that string into something that can safely be used to match itself. If we tried to use $hostname in the regex pattern without running quotemeta on it first, we could run into trouble because of things like the dots in the hostname being interpreted as regex metacharacters.

Notice, by the way, how we've used the /o modifier on the end of the two regular expressions /^http:\/\/$escaped_hostname/io and s/^http:\/\/$escaped_hostname//io. This helps the script run more efficiently. As was mentioned in Chapter 7, the /o modifier is used to tell Perl that any variables contained in the search expression will not be changing during the life of the script. If an expression containing a variable is going to be evaluated many times, using /o makes the script run faster because Perl doesn't have to recompile the expression each time it is encountered.

We've bailed out on links pointing to other hostnames and stripped this site's hostname from the beginning of links that include it. Next, if the link begins with an initial slash (meaning it represents an absolute path on the web server), it is converted to a real filesystem path by sticking the contents of the $web_root configuration variable in front of it. Otherwise (that is, if the link is a relative path), the absolute path of the directory containing the HTML file from which it was extracted is stuck in front of it.

Putting It All Together

Let's take stock of what we've done so far. We've written a script that will descend recursively through a filesystem, reading in the contents of any HTML files it encounters and extracting all the <A HREF="..."> and <IMG SRC="..."> attributes from those files. We've also created a subroutine that will take a directory name and a list of links extracted from a file in that directory, identify which links point to local files, and convert them to full (that is, absolute) filesystem pathnames.

The fast-but-stupid version of our link-checker is almost finished. The main thing left is defining the data structure that will hold the information on the bad links it discovers.

For that, we go back to the top of the script, just below the configuration section, and add the following:

```perl
my %bad_links;      # A "hash of arrays" with keys consisting of URLs
                    # under $start_base, and values consisting of lists
                    # of bad links on those pages.

my %good;           # A hash mapping filesystem paths to
                    # 0 or 1 (for good or bad). Used to cache the results
                    # of previous checks so they needn't be repeated for
                    # subsequent pages.
```

Here we've declared two new hashes that are going to be used in our script: %bad_links and %good. %good is fairly straightforward; we're going to use it to store the result of testing the links our script processes. The keys of the %good hash are the local filesystem paths for the files we are checking (e.g., /w1/s/socalsail/index.html). A link that turns out to be bad (that is, that points to a nonexistent file in the local file-system) will be stored in the %good hash with a value of zero (0). A link pointing to a file that does exist will be stored with a value of one (1). A link that we haven't processed before will not have a key in the hash at all.

That way, we can do a quick lookup in the %good hash to tell if a particular link has already been checked, and what the result of that check was. Otherwise, we'd have to keep checking the filesystem (which is a relatively slow process) every time the same link showed up. Because web sites tend to have lots of navigational links pointing to the same files, using a hash to cache those lookups will make our script run much faster.

Creating a Hash of Arrays

What about that other hash we defined: %bad_links? That is where we are going to store the results of our checking. That is also going to be our first exposure to an incredibly cool and powerful feature of Perl: multilevel data structures. A *multilevel data structure* is something like an "array of arrays" or a "hash of hashes." Or a "hash of arrays," which is what the %bad_links hash is.

What do I mean when I say "hash of arrays"? I mean a normal hash with normal hash keys, but with values that consist of arrays rather than regular scalar values. (Sort of. More on this in a minute.) That is, we can use that hash to say "Give me the value corresponding to the key walnuts," and we'll get back a whole array rather than a single value. And we can have another, completely different array that is returned when we say "Give me the value corresponding to the key rutabagas." And so on.

In this case, the keys of the %bad_links hash will be the full pathnames of any HTML pages containing bad links. The corresponding value in each case will be an array containing a list of all the bad links on that page.

As it turns out, we can't actually store arrays as the values in our "hash of arrays" because the individual values in a hash can only be scalars. But we can store *references* to arrays in those values.

You remember at the beginning of the chapter, when we passed a subroutine reference to the Find::File module's find function? Instead of putting a subroutine invocation in the function's arguments (like function(&subroutine)), we put a *reference* to the subroutine in the function's arguments by using a backslash in front of the subroutine name (like function(\&subroutine)). As I explained then, a reference is a way of creating a scalar thingy that refers to the contents of some other thingy that Perl knows about. That other thingy can be a scalar, or an array, or a hash, or a subroutine, but the reference itself will always be a scalar.

So, to return to the %bad_links hash, what I've been calling a "hash of arrays" is not really a hash of arrays. It's a hash of array references. Once we've retrieved the reference, though, it's easy to access the array that it points to.

We'll need to learn some special syntax to work that particular magic, but it's definitely worth learning. Once we're comfortable creating and using multilevel data structures, many otherwise-difficult programming tasks will turn into the proverbial piece of cake.

Updating &process to Store Bad-Link Data

Enough of the sales hype. Let's see it in action. The next thing we need to do is to go back to the &process subroutine and modify it to look like the following:

```
sub process {

    # this is invoked by File::Find's find function for each
    # file it recursively finds. it extracts a list of HREF
    # and SRC attributes from an HTML file, converts those
    # to local filesystem paths using the convert subroutine,
    # checks them for "badness", then stores the bad ones in
    # the %bad_links "hash of arrays".

    return unless /\.html$/;
    my $file = $File::Find::name;
    unless (open IN, $file) {
        warn "can't open $file for reading: $!, continuing...\n";
        return;
    }
    my $data = join '', <IN>; # all the data at once
    close IN;
    return unless $data;

    my @targets = ($data =~ /(?:href|src)\s*=\s*"([^"]+)"/gi);

    @targets = &convert($File::Find::dir, @targets);

    foreach my $target (@targets) {

        if (exists $good{$target}) {

            # we've already seen this one

            if ($good{$target}) {
                # already known to be good
                next;
            } else {
                # already known to be bad
                push @{ $bad_links{$file} }, $target;
            }

        } else {

            # haven't seen this one yet
```

```
        if (-e $target) {
            $good{$target} = 1;
        } else {
            $good{$target} = 0;
            push @{ $bad_links{$file} }, $target;
        }
    }
  }
}
```

The first thing to notice is how we're now using the &convert subroutine to turn the list of extracted links into absolute filesystem paths:

```
@targets = &convert($File::Find::dir, @targets);
```

There's no problem using @targets on both sides of the assignment, by the way. Perl evaluates the right side of the assignment first, passing the original contents of the @targets array to the &convert subroutine, then sticks the &convert routine's return value back into @targets, replacing what used to be there.

The next thing to notice is how we're cleverly using the %good hash to control the flow of the program as each entry from @targets is being processed. First we check to see if this particular $target has been processed before, using the exists function. The exists function, you'll remember, checks a hash to see if a particular key exists in it, returning true if the key exists and false otherwise. (This lets you return true even for those keys that happen to have a false value, like 0 or undef, associated with them.)

If the exists function for this key returns true, it means we've already seen (and tested) this target, so we can just access the results of that prior test by getting the corresponding value using $good{$target}. If this $target has already been found to be good, we just skip to the next item in the foreach loop with next (because we don't care about good links, only bad ones). Otherwise (that is, if this target has already been found to be bad), we add it to the array of bad links for this particular file using the following extremely interesting line:

```
push @{ $bad_links{$file} }, $target;
```

This uses the push function, which you are already familiar with, to push $target onto the end of an array. But what a strange-looking array!

Take a moment to give that strange array a careful look. What we're seeing here is something called *dereferencing*, which means we are converting from a reference back to the original thingy the reference points to. In this case, the thing returned when we do a lookup of the key $file in the %bad_links hash is an *array reference*. (We'll see how that reference got there in just a minute.) Putting an array reference inside a pair of curly braces, with an array symbol (a @, that is) in front of the opening curly brace, gives us access to the original array that the reference points to, so we can do things like push entries onto the end of it.

To reiterate: if we have an array reference, we can dereference it, accessing the actual array that it points to, like this:

```
@{array_reference}
```

The same thing also works for dereferencing hash references. We just have to substitute the appropriate symbol (%) outside the curly braces:

```
%{hash_reference}
```

And that is the second of the four pieces of Perl reference syntax we will be learning. We now know one way to create a reference (putting a backslash in front of a variable or subroutine name, like \@walnuts or \&process), and one way to dereference a reference in order to get at the thing the reference points to (putting an appropriate symbol in front of a pair of curly braces containing the reference, like @{$ref}).

Let's return to the &process routine and look at the else branch of the loop, the one that fires off for files that we haven't tested before. That branch checks to see if the file exists in the local filesystem using the -e file test. If the file exists we store a true value (1) in $good{$target}. If the file doesn't exist, though, it means the current $target represents a broken link. In that case, we put a false value (0) in $good{$target}, and again push this target onto the end of the array whose reference is stored in $bad_links{$file}, like this:

```
push @{ $bad_links{$file} }, $target;
```

And that's it. When File::Find's find function has finished descending through the directories below $start_dir, the &process routine will have populated the script-wide hash called %bad_links with keys consisting of the names of all the HTML files containing broken links. The values corresponding to those keys will consist of array references, with each referenced array containing a list of the bad links in that particular HTML file.

Notice, by the way, that all those arrays don't have names, properly speaking. The only way to get at their contents is by dereferencing the array references that point to them. For this reason, you will sometimes hear such arrays referred to as *anonymous arrays*. The fact that you can have an anonymous array may seem confusing, until you understand that individual arrays (and hashes, and scalars, and subroutines) have their own independent existence within a Perl program, completely separate from any names that may or may not be associated with them.

You may also be a bit muddled on just how those references came into existence. We never actually "created" them by sticking a backslash in front of a conventional named array (like \@array), and we didn't use the second method for explicitly creating and returning a reference (which you haven't learned yet, but will be learning in Chapter 14). So, where did they come from? The answer is that they just sprang into existence, like Athena springing fully formed from Zeus' forehead, the first time you dereferenced those hash values with @{ $bad_links{$file} }.

Printing the Bad-Link Report

I know this reference-slinging seems like a lot of work. But now see how easily we can produce the report that is the link_check.plx script's final output. Let's add the following at the end of the script proper, just before the subroutine definitions:

```
my $time = localtime;

print "$hostname$web_path link_check report\n";
print "Report created at $time\n\n";

foreach my $file (sort keys %bad_links) {
    print "$file:\n";
    foreach my $target (sort @{ $bad_links{$file} }) {
        print "  $target\n";
    }
    print "\n";
}
```

See how simple that is?

When we run this version of the script from the shell, we get output that looks something like this:

```
[jbc@andros ora]$ ./link_check.plx | more
www.socalsail.com/expo link_check report
Report created at Sun Jan  9 13:14:11 2000

/w1/s/socalsail/expo/join/index.html:
  /w1/s/socalsail/search/search.gif
  /w1/s/socalsail/talk/
  /w1/s/socalsail/user_info/

/w1/s/socalsail/expo/nav/index.html:
  /w1/s/socalsail/search/search.gif
  /w1/s/socalsail/talk/

/w1/s/socalsail/expo/wx/buoy.html:
  /w1/s/socalsail/search/search.gif
  /w1/s/socalsail/talk/
```

Adding HTML Output

Let's add one additional feature to the script: HTML output. By producing the report as an HTML page, we can make it easy to review it in a web browser, clicking on links to visit the pages that have problems.

We begin by putting the following line near the top of the script, in the configuration section:

```
my $webify    = 1;                    # produce web-ready output?
```

Now, we modify the part that prints out the report to look like this:

```
if ($webify) {

    # print an HTML version of the report

    print <<EndOfText;
<HTML>
<HEAD>
<TITLE>$hostname$web_path link_check report</TITLE>
</HEAD>
<BODY>

<H2 ALIGN="center">$hostname$web_path link_check report</H2>

<P ALIGN="center"><STRONG>Report created at $time</STRONG></P>

<P>
EndOfText

    foreach my $file (sort keys %bad_links) {
        my $pretty_file     = $file;
        my $escaped_web_root = quotemeta $web_root;
        $pretty_file        =~ s/$escaped_web_root//o;
        $pretty_file        = "<P><STRONG><A HREF=\"$pretty_file\">$pretty_file</A>
</STRONG><BR>\n";
        print $pretty_file;
        foreach my $target (sort @{ $bad_links{$file} }) {
            $target =~ s/$escaped_web_root//o;
            print "<A HREF=\"$target\">$target</A><BR>\n";
        }
        print "\n</P>\n\n";
    }
    print "</BODY></HTML>\n";

} else {

    # just print a plain-text version of the report

    print "$hostname$web_path link_check report\n";
    print "Report created at $time\n\n";

    foreach my $file (sort keys %bad_links) {
        print "$file:\n";
        foreach my $target (sort @{ $bad_links{$file} }) {
            print "    $target\n";
        }
        print "\n";
    }
}
```

All that new code should be pretty straightforward to you at this point. If we now run the script with the $webify configuration variable set to a true value, it will produce an HTML page as its output. We could thus run it from the command line like:

```
[jbc@andros ora]$ link_check.plx > report.html
```

and view the results in a web browser, as shown in Figure 11-1.

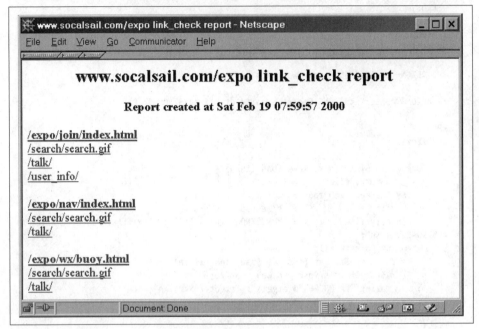

Figure 11-1. An HTML report produced by link_check.plx

The entire script as it should look at this point is given in Example 11-2.

Example 11-2. First version of a link-checking script

```perl
#!/usr/bin/perl -w

# link_check.plx

# this is a first version of an HTML link checker.
# it descends recursively from $start_dir, processing
# all .htm or .html files to extract HREF and SRC
# attributes, then checks all that point to a local
# file to confirm that the file actually exists.

use strict;
use File::Find;

# configuration section:
```

Example 11-2. First version of a link-checking script (continued)

```perl
# note: the first four configuration variables should *not*
# have a trailing slash (/)

my $start_dir = '/w1/s/socalsail/expo'; # where to begin looking
my $hostname  = 'www.socalsail.com';    # this site's hostname
my $web_root  = '/w1/s/socalsail';      # path to www doc root
my $web_path  = '/expo';                # web path to $start_dir
my $webify    = 1;                      # produce web-ready output?

# end of configuration section

my %bad_links;     # A "hash of arrays" with keys consisting of URLs
                   # under $start_base, and values consisting of lists
                   # of bad links on those pages.

my %good;          # A hash mapping filesystem paths to
                   # 0 or 1 (for good or bad). Used to cache the results
                   # of previous checks so they needn't be repeated for
                   # subsequent pages.

find(\&process, $start_dir); # this loads up the above hashes

my $time = localtime;

if ($webify) {

    # print an HTML version of the report

    print <<EndOfText;
<HTML>
<HEAD>
<TITLE>$hostname$web_path link_check report</TITLE>
</HEAD>
<BODY>

<H2 ALIGN="center">$hostname$web_path link_check report</H2>

<P ALIGN="center"><STRONG>Report created at $time</STRONG></P>

<P>
EndOfText

    foreach my $file (sort keys %bad_links) {
        my $pretty_file       = $file;
        my $escaped_web_root  = quotemeta $web_root;
        $pretty_file          =~ s/$escaped_web_root//o;
        $pretty_file          = "<P><STRONG><A HREF=\"$pretty_file\">$pretty_file</A></
STRONG><BR>\n";
        print $pretty_file;
        foreach my $target (sort @{ $bad_links{$file} }) {
            $target =~ s/$escaped_web_root//o;
            print "<A HREF=\"$target\">$target</A><BR>\n";
```

Example 11-2. First version of a link-checking script (continued)

```
        }
        print "\n</P>\n\n";
    }
    print "</BODY></HTML>\n";

} else {

    # just print a plain-text version of the report

    print "$hostname$web_path link_check report\n";
    print "Report created at $time\n\n";

    foreach my $file (sort keys %bad_links) {
        print "$file:\n";
        foreach my $target (sort @{ $bad_links{$file} }) {
            print "  $target\n";
        }
        print "\n";
    }
}

sub process {

    # this is invoked by File::Find's find function for each
    # file it recursively finds. it extracts a list of HREF
    # and SRC attributes from an HTML file, converts those
    # to local filesystem paths using the convert subroutine,
    # checks them for "badness", then stores the bad ones in
    # the %bad_links "hash of arrays".

    return unless /\.html$/;
    my $file = $File::Find::name;
    unless (open IN, $file) {
        warn "can't open $file for reading: $!, continuing...\n";
        return;
    }
    my $data = join '', <IN>; # all the data at once
    close IN;
    return unless $data;

    my @targets = ($data =~ /(?:href|src)\s*=\s*"([^"]+)"/gi);

    @targets = &convert($File::Find::dir, @targets);

    foreach my $target (@targets) {

        if (exists $good{$target}) {

            # we've already seen this one

            if ($good{$target}) {
                # already known to be good
                next;
```

Example 11-2. First version of a link-checking script (continued)

```
            } else {
                # already known to be bad
                push @{ $bad_links{$file} }, $target;
            }

        } else {

            # haven't seen this one yet

            if (-e $target) {
                $good{$target} = 1;
            } else {
                $good{$target} = 0;
                push @{ $bad_links{$file} }, $target;
            }
        }
    }
}

sub convert {

    # This accepts the directory name of a file from
    # which a list of URLs was extracted (in the first argument)
    # and a list of URLs extracted from that file (in the
    # rest of the arguments). It returns a list of all the URLs
    # that did not point outside the local site, or were not
    # ftp:, mailto:, https:, or news: URLs, with those URLs
    # converted into local filesystem filenames.

    my($dir, @urls) = @_;
    my @return_urls;
    my $escaped_hostname = quotemeta $hostname;
    foreach (@urls) {
        next if /^(ftp|mailto|https|news):/i;
        if (/^http:/i) {
            # URL starts with 'http:'
            next unless /^http:\/\/$escaped_hostname/io;
            s/^http:\/\/$escaped_hostname//io;
        }
        if (/^\//) {
            # URL starts with '/'
            $_ = $web_root . $_;
        } else {
            # URL is a relative path
            $_ = $dir . '/' . $_;
        }
        s/#.*//;  # trim trailing #targets
        s/\?.*//; # trim trailing ?arguments
        push @return_urls, $_;
    }
    @return_urls;
}
```

Using CPAN

As I previously pointed out, this first link-checking script is fairly limited. It only checks links that point to the local filesystem, and it will be confused by HTML pages containing things like <BASE HREF="..."> tags, which modify how the relative links on a page are resolved by a browser. Still, it runs quickly, and on a big site that doesn't violate its assumptions it makes short work of checking for at least the more obvious broken links.

A nice enhancement would be to make it check offsite links as well, using HTTP to request pages just like a web browser. We could write our own web browsing code to do this using Perl, but fortunately that work has already been done, and done better than you or I are likely to be able to do it. The person responsible for that is a very helpful member of the extended Perl community named Gisle Aas, author of the LWP module (short for libwww-perl).

Using LWP will save us vast amounts of time and headache. Since it is not currently included in the standard Perl distribution, though, we will need to download it from CPAN (the Comprehensive Perl Archive Network, at *http://www.cpan.org/*), and install it (assuming it isn't already installed as part of the copy of Perl we are using). Learning to do that will take some initial effort, but believe me, we'll be better off in the long run for having invested that time up front.

Checking for LWP

Before we jump in and start the download-and-install process, make the following quick check to see if you already have the LWP module installed in your copy of Perl:

```
[jbc@andros jbc]$ perl -MLWP -e 'print "LWP is installed!\n"'
```

The -M command-line switch followed by the name of a module (with no intervening spaces) causes our Perl one-liner to load the module in question. If the LWP module is already installed, we'll get the following output:

```
LWP is installed!
```

If it isn't, you'll get something like this:

```
Can't locate LWP.pm in @INC (@INC contains:
/usr/lib/perl5/i386-linux/5.00405 /usr/lib/perl5
/usr/lib/perl5/site_perl/i386-linux /usr/lib/perl5/site_perl .).
BEGIN failed--compilation aborted.
```

If LWP isn't installed in your case, the next section will show you how to go about downloading and installing it. If it is already installed with your copy of Perl, you can skip the next section (but be prepared to come back to it later, when you need some other CPAN goody that isn't installed in your server's Perl installation).

Installing LWP from CPAN

As was mentioned in Chapter 8, CPAN is so huge that it can be a bit overwhelming the first time you try to use it. After a while it will begin to make sense, however, and the time spent getting familiar with it will be paid back many times over.

There are a number of different ways to try to locate a particular module on CPAN. One way is to start at *http://www.cpan.org/README.html*.

From there, we can click the "Modules" link, which should take us to somewhere like: *http://www.cpan.org/modules/index.html*. From there, we can click on the "All Modules" link, which should take us somewhere like *http://www.cpan.org/modules/01modules.index.html*.

From there, we can look through the list of modules to find `LWP` and look for the download file for the latest version, which at the time of this writing was `libwww-perl-5.53.tar.gz`.

Another really handy tool we can use is the CPAN search engine, located at *http://search.cpan.org/*. By typing the name of a module into the search engine there, we can get a list of results that include links to the documentation for that module, as well as links to download the latest version of the module itself. Since I frequently find myself wanting to review the documentation for a module before taking the time to actually download and install it, this is very convenient.

However we come up with it, though, eventually we are going to locate a URL pointing to the latest version of `libwww-perl`. The next steps are for us to get that archive file onto our web server, decompress it, extract the files contained within it, and do the actual installation.

Getting the archive file onto the web server

There are several ways to get a CPAN file onto our web server. I typically locate a link to the archive file using my web browser, and copy the link location to my desktop computer's clipboard. (A right-click on the link in the Windows version of Netscape will pop up a menu allowing one to do this.) Then I switch to another window in which I'm running a telnet session on the web server. Once in that Telnet session, I switch to a temporary directory (like ~/tmp, a directory named `tmp` I created under my home directory), and type the command `lynx`, then paste in the URL on the command line after it using the Shift-Insert key combination. For example:

```
[jbc@andros tmp]$ lynx
http://www.perl.com/CPAN/authors/id/GAAS/libwww-perl-5.53.tar.gz
```

This puts me in the `lynx` browser, with a prompt to download the file to a local file. I do that and accept the default filename of `libwww-perl-5.53.tar.gz` to save it, and then quit out of `lynx`.

Decompressing the file

Back at the shell prompt, I use the gzip command (with the -d option) to decompress the downloaded file:

```
[jbc@andros tmp]$ gzip -d libwww-perl-5.53.tar.gz
```

This causes the libwww-perl-5.53.tar.gz file to be replaced by one that is not compressed called libwww-perl-5.53.tar. See the accompanying sidebar, "Tab Completion," for a useful trick to save you from developing repetitive-motion injuries while typing all these lengthy filenames.

Tab Completion

I spent years (literally) typing really long filenames at the Unix command line before a helpful guru told me about *tab completion*. In the bash shell, you don't need to type the entire filename when giving an argument to a command like gunzip. Instead, you only need to type enough of the filename to let the shell distinguish it from any other files that happen to be in the directory. Once you've typed that much of the name, just press the Tab key, and the shell will complete the rest of the name for you, after which you can press the Enter key to carry out the command.

Tab completion is just one of many useful command-line editing functions that bash makes available; read the section on the READLINE library in man bash for more details.

Extracting the files from the archive

Now we use the tar command (short for *tape archive*, a reference to the command's original function of helping to make tape backups) to extract the individual files from the tar file. (Actually, we're not just going to extract the individual files; we're going to extract a whole tree of directories and files.) The trickiest thing about tar is remembering all the appropriate switches to use. In this case, we'll want to use the x switch (to tell tar you're extracting from an existing archive), and the f switch (at the end, which is important) to tell it we're about to give it the name of the tar file we want to extract from. Put it all together and we get:

```
[jbc@andros tmp]$ tar -xf libwww-perl-5.53.tar
```

This will cause tar to extract all the original files and directories from the archive, placing them in a directory named libwww-perl-5.53. We use cd to switch into that directory (using tab completion, if we have any sense, rather than typing in the entire directory name), and then ls to list the directory's contents:

```
[jbc@andros libwww-perl-5.53]$ ls
ChangeLog  Makefile.PL  README.SSL  bin  lwpcook.pod
MANIFEST   README       TODO        lib  t
```

The actual installation

Once we have extracted the files contained in a Perl module's tar file, the first thing we should do is to read the accompanying README file. It will tell us, among other things, if there are any prerequisites for installing the module. In this case, it tells us the following:

```
We recommend that you have the following packages installed before you
install libwww-perl:
  URI
  MIME-Base64
  HTML-Parser
  libnet
  Digest::MD5
These packages should be available on CPAN.
```

It looks like we're going to get more downloading/decompressing/untarring practice. So, back we go to CPAN, and once there we locate the latest *.tar.gz files for all those modules and go through the steps listed above to download, gzip -d, and tar -xf them. When we're done, we have a bunch of directories under our tmp directory, with one for each of the recommended modules, plus one for the still-uninstalled libwww-perl module.

The trickiest part about this will be finding the libnet module because it is actually listed as Bundle-libnet.

At this point, an ls listing in our ~/tmp directory should look something like this:

```
[jbc@andros tmp]$ ls
Bundle-libnet-1.00       HTML-Parser-3.04       URI-1.04
Bundle-libnet-1.00.tar   HTML-Parser-3.04.tar   URI-1.04.tar
Digest-MD5-2.09          MIME-Base64-2.11       libwww-perl-5.53
Digest-MD5-2.09.tar      MIME-Base64-2.11.tar   libwww-perl-5.53.tar
```

Even though URI was the first module listed in LWP's list of dependencies, it turns out that the URI module wants us to have MIME-Base64 installed first, so that will be the first one that we will actually install. We cd into its directory and read its README. We'll find that it instructs us to perform the following four steps:

```
perl Makefile.PL
make
make test
make install
```

Each is a command we will need to enter at the Unix command line, and this same sequence of four commands is what we will use to install nearly every Perl module we ever install (unless we use the CPAN module; more about this in a few minutes).

Root Versus Regular User Installation

Installing a new Perl module is one of those times when it can be handy to have root access (or to have a cooperative system administrator who will employ it on our behalf). If we perform the installation (actually, just the final step, the make install) as the root user, the module we install can be installed with the server's core Perl installation, making it available to everyone who uses the server. We will also be able to use the module within our Perl scripts without manipulating the list of directories that Perl looks in for its module files.

If we don't have access to a root account, we can still install our own Perl modules, but we will have to install them in our own personal space on the server. Also, using those modules in our scripts will be just a little bit harder, requiring us to put an extra line into each script; we'll learn about that line in just a minute.

If we are installing as root, we can just go through the four steps described previously (perl Makefile.PL, make, make test, and make install), following the directions and answering any questions as they come up. (The final step, the make install step, is the only one for which we'll actually need to be the root user.) If we are installing using a regular user account, however, we will need to modify the perl Makefile.PL line slightly. In that case, we would enter that line like this:

```
[jbc@andros MIME-Base64-2.11]$ perl Makefile.PL PREFIX=/home/jbc/perl
```

where /home/jbc/perl corresponds to a directory we have write access to where we want to install our personal copies of Perl modules.

Then we would perform the make, make test, and make install steps as usual. After the last step, the make install, we should have a new module installed under the directory specified in the PREFIX parameter, with a path that looks something like:

```
/home/jbc/perl/lib/site_perl/5.005/i386-linux/MIME/Base64.pm
```

Now we just need to remember to put a use lib statement in our scripts before we try to use that MIME::Base64 module; something like:

```
use lib '/home/jbc/lib/perl5/site_perl/5.005/i386-linux';
```

This will tell Perl to add that directory to the list of directories in the special @INC array, which is checked for modules when we issue a use Some::Module statement.

So, we'll need to go through installing each module: Mime-Base64, URI, HTML-Parser, Bundle-libnet, and Digest::MD5. Once we've done each of those, we can go back to LWP and install it. (Installing LWP itself will be somewhat involved, as it asks a bunch of questions during the process so that it can configure various types of Internet services we might have reason to use. But even if we just skip past most of those questions, we should still get a version that works fine for our present purposes.)

All that downloading and unpacking and making and installing is pretty boring and repetitive. You'd think someone would have figured out a way to automate the process. Someone has: Andreas König, author of the CPAN.pm module (among others). See the accompanying sidebar, "Installing Modules with CPAN.pm," for details.

Installing Modules with CPAN.pm

The `CPAN.pm` module is tremendously useful for downloading, unpacking, and installing Perl modules. It offers a simple command-line shell that makes quick work of all those manual steps outlined in this chapter.

So, why did I bother explaining that whole process, if `CPAN.pm` lets you skip it? Because you may not have `CPAN.pm` installed already, in which case you will need to use the normal module-installation process to get it installed.

To test whether `CPAN.pm` is installed already with your copy of Perl, enter the following at the Unix command-line prompt:

```
[john@ithil john]$ perl -MCPAN -e shell
```

If `CPAN.pm` is available, you'll get something that looks like this:

```
cpan shell -- CPAN exploration and modules installation (v1.52)
ReadLine support enabled

cpan>
```

That last line is a shell prompt for the `CPAN.pm` shell. Try entering h or help, and it will list some of the available commands. Many times, all you will have to do is enter:

```
cpan> install Module_name
```

(where `Module_name` is replaced by the name of the module you wish to install), and `CPAN.pm` will perform the entire download/unpack/make/install sequence for you.

If `CPAN.pm` isn't installed, when you run that `perl -MCPAN -e shell` command you will get a message that looks like this:

```
[jbc@andros jbc]$ perl -MCPAN -e shell
Can't locate CPAN.pm in @INC (@INC contains: /usr/lib/perl5/alpha-linux/5.00404
/usr/lib/perl5 /usr/lib/perl5/site_perl/alpha-linux /usr/lib/perl5/site_perl .
).
BEGIN failed--compilation aborted.
```

In that case, go find the `CPAN.pm` module at CPAN, download it, and go through the manual module-installation process described earlier in this chapter. Then enter the `CPAN.pm` shell using that `perl -MCPAN -e shell` command. The first time that shell starts up, it will ask you a series of questions in order to configure itself. You can go ahead and accept the defaults for almost all of these, but one you should pay attention to: the one that asks you for any parameters you want to pass to `Makefile.PL`. Assuming you are not installing as root but need to install your modules into your own user space, you'll want to give a response like this when `CPAN.pm` asks you for those `Makefile.PL` parameters:

```
PREFIX=/home/jbc
```

With /home/jbc replaced by a directory you have write access to where you want `CPAN.pm` to install your personal Perl library.

Checking Remote Links

Example 11-3 shows link_check2.plx, an enhanced version of the link-checking script that gives us the option of checking offsite links. The parts of this script that differ from the previous version have been emphasized.

Example 11-3. Link-checking script with offsite checking

```perl
#!/usr/bin/perl -w

# link_check2.plx

# This is a modified HTML link checker.
# It descends recursively from $start_dir, processing
# all .htm or .html files to extract HREF and SRC
# attributes, then checks all that point to a local
# file to confirm that the file actually exists, and optionally
# uses LWP::Simple to do a HEAD check on remote ones for the
# same purpose. It then reports on the bad links.

use strict;
use File::Find;
use LWP::Simple;

# note: the first four configuration variables should *not*
# have a trailing slash (/)

my $start_dir    = '/w1/s/socalsail/expo'; # where to begin looking
my $hostname     = 'www.socalsail.com';    # this site's hostname
my $web_root     = '/w1/s/socalsail';      # path to www doc root
my $web_path     = '/expo';                # web path to $start_dir
my $webify       = 1;                      # produce web-ready output?
my $check_remote = 1;                      # check offsite links?

my %bad_links; # a "hash of lists" with keys consisting of filenames,
               # values consisting of lists of bad links in those files

my %good;      # A hash mapping absolute filenames (or remote URLs) to
               # 0 or 1 (for good or bad). Used to cache the results of
               # previous checks.

find(\&process, $start_dir); # this loads up the above hashes

if ($webify) {

    # print an HTML version of the report

    print <<EndOfText;
<HTML>
<HEAD>
<TITLE>$hostname$web_path link_check report</TITLE>
</HEAD>
<BODY>
```

Example 11-3. Link-checking script with offsite checking (continued)

```
<H2 ALIGN="center">$hostname$web_path link_check report</H2>

<P ALIGN="center"><STRONG>Report created at $time</STRONG></P>

<P>
EndOfText

    foreach my $file (sort keys %bad_links) {
        my $pretty_file      = $file;
        my $escaped_web_root = quotemeta $web_root;
        $pretty_file        =~ s/$escaped_web_root//o;
        $pretty_file        = "<P><STRONG><A HREF=\"$pretty_file\">$pretty_file</A></
STRONG><BR>\n";
        print $pretty_file;
        foreach my $target (sort @{ $bad_links{$file} }) {
            $target =~ s/$escaped_web_root//o;
            print "<A HREF=\"$target\">$target</A><BR>\n";
        }
        print "\n</P>\n\n";
    }
    print "</BODY></HTML>\n";

} else {

    # just print a plain-text version of the report

    print "$hostname$web_path link_check report\n";
    print "Report created at $time\n\n";

    foreach my $file (sort keys %bad_links) {
        print "$file:\n";
        foreach my $target (sort @{ $bad_links{$file} }) {
            print "  $target\n";
        }
        print "\n";
    }
}

sub process {

    # This is invoked by File::Find's find function for each
    # file it recursively finds. It extracts a list of HREF
    # and SRC attributes from an HTML file, checks them for
    # "badness", then stores the bad ones (keyed by filename)
    # in the %bad_links "hash of lists".

    return unless /\.html$/;
    my $file = $File::Find::name;

#    warn "processing $file...\n";

    unless (open IN, $file) {
```

Example 11-3. Link-checking script with offsite checking (continued)

```perl
        warn "can't open $file for reading: $!, continuing...\n";
        return;
    }
    my $data = join '', <IN>; # all the data at once
    close IN;
    return unless $data; # don't care about empty files
    my @targets = ($data =~ /(?:href|src)\s*=\s*"([^"]+)"/gi);
    @targets = &convert($File::Find::dir, @targets);

    foreach my $target (@targets) {

        next if $target =~ /\n/;

        if (exists $good{$target}) {

            # we've already seen this one

            if ($good{$target}) {
                # already known to be good
                next;
            } else {
                # already known to be bad
                push @{ $bad_links{$file} }, $target;
            }

        } elsif ($target =~ /^http:/) {

            # a remote link we haven't seen before

            if (head($target)) {
                $good{$target} = 1;
            } else {
                push @{ $bad_links{$file} }, $target;
                $good{$target} = 0;
            }

        } else {

            # a local link we haven't seen before

            if (-e $target) {
                $good{$target} = 1;
            } else {
                push @{ $bad_links{$file} }, $target;
                $good{$target} = 0;
            }

        }
    }
}

sub convert {
```

Example 11-3. Link-checking script with offsite checking (continued)

```
# this accepts the directory name of a file from
# which a list of URLs was extracted (in the first argument)
# and a list of URLs extracted from that file (in the
# rest of the arguments). It returns a list of all the URLs
# that did not point outside the local site absolutized into
# local filesystem pathnames. Optionally, if $check_remote
# is set to a true value, it also returns any links beginning
# 'http:' that *do* point outside the local site, left in their
# original form.

my($dir, @urls) = @_;
my @return_urls;
my $escaped_hostname = quotemeta $hostname;
foreach (@urls) {
    next if /^(ftp|mailto|https|news):/i; # skip these
    if (/^http:/i) {
        # URL starts with 'http:'
        if (/^http:\/\/$escaped_hostname/io) {
            # local link; convert to local filename
            # in preparation for further conversion below
            s/^http:\/\/$escaped_hostname//io;
        } else {
            # remote link
            push @return_urls, $_ if $check_remote;
            next;
        }
    }
    if (/^\//) {
        # URL starts with '/'
        $_ = $web_root . $_;
    } else {
        # URL is a relative path
        $_ = $dir . '/' . $_;
    }
    s/#.*//;  # trim trailing #targets
    s/\?.*//; # trim trailing ?arguments
    push @return_urls, $_;
}
return @return_urls;
}
```

Thanks to the work we did installing LWP (and all the other modules it needs), the modifications needed to allow this script to check remote web links are fairly minimal.

First, we need to invoke LWP::Simple, a module that gives us easy access to web transactions from within our script, via the following use statement at the top of the script:

```
use LWP::Simple;
```

Next, we've added a new configuration variable to control whether we want the script to bother with checking offsite links:

```
my $check_remote = 1;                    # check offsite links?
```

Finally, we've added a new elsif branch in the &process subroutine that handles remote links (that is, links starting with http:) that haven't been processed before:

```
} elsif ($target =~ /^http:/) {
    # a remote link we haven't seen before

    if (head($target)) {
        $good{$target} = 1;
    } else {
        push @{ $bad_links{$file} }, $target;
        $good{$target} = 0;
    }


}
```

Did you spot the place where we checked the remote link? It was in this line:

```
if (head($target)) {
```

which uses LWP::Simple's head function to do an HTTP HEAD request on the URL contained in $target. A HEAD request, as you may already know, is a web request that just asks for some metainformation about the remote document, rather than asking for the document itself. (If we wanted the whole document, we would use a GET request.) The HEAD request is nice because it lets us see if the document is there without having to actually download the whole thing.

LWP::Simple's head function is documented in the POD documentation included with the module. We can read that documentation from the shell like this:

```
[jbc@andros jbc]$ man LWP::Simple
```

or

```
[jbc@andros jbc]$ perldoc LWP::Simple
```

If we installed our copy of LWP in our own personal directory space, we may need to give man or perldoc some help finding the documentation. If your LWP installation is in:

```
/home/jbc/perl/lib/perl5/site_perl/5.005/i386-linux/
```

then we can try using:

```
[jbc@andros jbc]$ perldoc /home/jbc/perl/lib/perl5/site_perl/5.005/i386-linux/LWP/
Simple.pm
```

which will point perldoc at the module file itself, allowing it to extract the documentation directly from the embedded POD.

Finally, this version of the script has a bit more logic in the &convert subroutine to handle the remote links and stick them in the routine's returned array of links to check (assuming $check_remote has been set to a true value):

```
if (/^http:/i) {
    # URL starts with 'http:'
    if (/^http:\/\/$hostname/io) {
```

```
            # local link; convert to local filename
            # in preparation for further conversion below
            s/^http:\/\/$hostname//io;
        } else {
            # remote link
            push @return_urls, $_ if $check_remote;
            next;
        }
    }
}
```

And that's it! This version of the script will run somewhat slower than the first one, especially if it has to check a lot of offsite links, but it will still do a decent job of identifying our site's more-obvious broken links.

A Proper Link Checker

I've done a lot of badmouthing of the link-checking scripts we've developed so far in this chapter, so let's move on now and develop a "proper" link checker. This final version of our link-checking script gives up on the whole problematic notion of trying to extract SRC and HREF attributes from our HTML pages using simple regex patterns. It also throws out the practice of trying to use -e tests of the local filesystem to identify the presence or absence of local images and HTML files. Instead, it crawls through our site like a search engine's spider program, testing each link with a web request issued via LWP.

Without further ado, the script is given in Example 11-4. There's a lot going on here, in particular a lot of magic being performed via imported modules, but we'll cover it all in detail after taking a look at the script.

Example 11-4. A link-checking script that uses LWP to check for "badness"

```
#!/usr/bin/perl -w

# link_check3.plx

# This is a third version of an HTML link checker.
# Beginning with a URL (required as a command-line argument),
# it spiders out the entire site (or as much of it as it can
# reach via links followed recursively from the starting page),
# checking all HREF and SRC attributes to make sure they work
# using GET and HEAD requests from LWP::UserAgent. It then
# reports on the bad links.

use strict;
use LWP::UserAgent;
use HTTP::Request;
use HTML::LinkExtor;
use URI::URL; # required by HTML::LinkExtor, when invoked with base

my $from_addr  = 'your@address.here'; # email address for user_agent
```

```perl
my $agent_name = 'link_check3.plx';   # name that robot will report

my $delay      = 1;    # number of seconds between requests
my $timeout    = 5;    # number of seconds to timeout a request
my $max_pages  = 1000; # maximum number of pages to process
my $webify     = 1;    # produce web-ready output?
my $debug      = 1;    # produce debugging output on STDERR?

my %bad_links;    # A "hash of arrays" with keys consisting of URLs
                  # under $start_base, values consisting of lists of
                  # bad links on those pages.

my %good;         # A hash mapping URLs to
                  # 0 or 1 (for bad or good). Caches the results of
                  # previous checks so they needn't be repeated for
                  # subsequent pages.

my @queue;        # An array containing a list of URLs
                  # (under $start_url) to be checked.

my $total_pages;  # Contains the count of pages processed so far.

# Configuration ends. Script proper begins.

my $last_request = 0;    # Time of the last request, for $delay

# first, construct the user agent

my $ua = LWP::UserAgent->new;
$ua->agent("$agent_name " . $ua->agent);
$ua->from($from_addr);
$ua->timeout($timeout); # set timeout interval

# now process the command-line argument

my $start_url = shift or
    die "Usage: $0 http://start.url.com/\n";

my($success, $type, $actual) = &check_url($start_url);

unless ($success and $type eq 'text/html') {
    die "The start_url isn't reachable, or isn't an HTML file.\n";
}

$good{$start_url} = 1;
push @queue, $start_url;
my $start_base          = $start_url;
$start_base             =~ s{/[^/]*$}{/}; # trim everything after last '/'
my $escaped_start_base = quotemeta $start_base;

while (@queue) {
    ++$total_pages;
```

Example 11-4. A link-checking script that uses LWP to check for "badness" (continued)

```
    if ($total_pages > $max_pages) {
        warn "stopped checking after reaching $max_pages pages.\n";
        --$total_pages; # kludge so the count is correct in report
        last;
    }
    my $page = shift @queue;
    &process_page($page); # possibly adding new entries to @queue
}

# print the report

my $time = localtime;

if ($webify) {

    # print an HTML version of the report

    print <<EndOfText;
<HTML>
<HEAD>
<TITLE>$start_url $0 report</TITLE>
</HEAD>
<BODY>

<H2 ALIGN="center">$start_url $0 report</H2>

<P ALIGN="center"><STRONG>Report created at $time</STRONG></P>

<P>
EndOfText

    foreach my $file (sort keys %bad_links) {
        print "<P><STRONG><A HREF=\"$file\">$file</A></STRONG><BR>\n";
        foreach my $target (sort @{ $bad_links{$file} }) {
            print " <A HREF=\"$target\">$target</A><BR>\n";
        }
        print "\n</P>\n\n";
    }
    print "</BODY></HTML>\n";

} else {

    # just print a plain-text version of the report

    print "$start_url $0 report\n";
    print "Report created at $time\n\n";

    foreach my $file (sort keys %bad_links) {
        print "$file:\n";
        foreach my $target (sort @{ $bad_links{$file} }) {
            print " $target\n";
        }
```

Example 11-4. A link-checking script that uses LWP to check for "badness" (continued)

```
        print "\n";
    }
}

# script proper ends. subroutines follow.

sub check_url {

    # Check that this URL is valid, using the HEAD (and GET, if
    # HEAD fails) methods. Returns a 3-element array:
    # ($success, $type, $actual).

    my $url = shift;

    if ($debug) { warn " checking $url...\n"; }
    unless (defined $url) {
        return ('', '', '');
    }

    sleep 1 while (time - $last_request) < $delay;
    $last_request = time;
    my $response = $ua->request(HTTP::Request->new('HEAD', $url));
    my $success = $response->is_success;
    unless ($success) {
        # try a GET request; some hosts don't like HEAD
        sleep 1 while (time - $last_request) < $delay;
        $last_request = time;
        $response = $ua->request(HTTP::Request->new('GET', $url));
        $success = $response->is_success;
    }
    if ($debug) {
        if ($success) {
            warn "  ...good.\n";
        } else {
            warn "  ...bad.\n";
        }
    }
    my $type = $response->header('Content-Type');
    my $actual = $response->base; # in case we were redirected
    return ($success, $type, $actual);
}

sub process_page {

    # Invoked with a single argument of a page under
    # the $start_base that needs to be processed. That page
    # will be (1) retrieved via GET, (2) parsed for any links it
    # contains, and (3) have those links checked for validity themselves
    # (with any that fail being written to %bad_links, and any that
    # point to valid, unchecked HTML files under $start_base
    # being added to @queue). The subroutine has no return value.
```

```perl
my $page = shift;
return unless defined $page;

if ($debug) { warn "processing $page for links\n"; }

sleep 1 while (time - $last_request) < $delay;
$last_request = time;
my $response = $ua->request(HTTP::Request->new('GET', $page));
unless ($response->is_success
    and $response->header('Content-Type') eq 'text/html') {
    # strange, since it passed these tests
    # via HEAD request in order to get into @queue
    $good{$page} = 0;
    return;
}
my $base = $response->base;
unless ($base =~ /$escaped_start_base/o) {
    # looks like we were redirected away from $start_base
    return;
}
my $parser = HTML::LinkExtor->new(undef, $base);
$parser->parse($response->content);
my @links = $parser->links;
foreach my $linkarray (@links) {
    my ($tag, %links) = @{$linkarray};
    if ($tag =~ /^(a|img)$/) {
        TARGET: while (my($attr, $target) = each %links) {
            if ($attr =~ /^(href|src|lowsrc)$/) {
                # these $target entries are the ones we're
                # interested in.
                next TARGET unless $target =~ /^(?:https?|ftp):/;
                $target =~ s/#.*//; # lose trailing #targets
                if (exists $good{$target}) {
                    # have already seen this before
                    if ($good{$target}) {
                        # already known to be good
                        next;
                    } else {
                        # already known to be bad
                        push @{ $bad_links{$base} }, $target;
                    }
                } else {
                    # haven't seen this one before
                    my($success, $type, $actual)
                        = &check_url($target);
                    unless ($success) {
                        $good{$target} = 0;
                        push @{ $bad_links{$base} }, $target;
                        next TARGET;
                    }
                    $good{$target} = 1;
```

```
                    if (defined $type
                        and $type eq 'text/html'
                        and defined $actual
                        and $actual =~ /$escaped_start_base/o) {

                        push @queue, $target;
                    }
                }
            }
        }
    }
}
```

You're progressing enough in your Perl education to understand much of this script without needing it explained line by line. Here are the highlights.

The top of the script pulls in all the modules we will be using, including a few new ones (HTTP::Request, HTML::LinkExtor, and URI::URL) that will be used to do the heavy lifting, so to speak, of parsing our HTML pages and extracting the links. Our last link-checker did that with a simple regular expression, but these modules do it in a much more rigorous way, taking into account things like <BASE> tags in the head of the document.

The configuration section of the script assigns some scalar variables that will be used later on, among them a $delay that will be observed between successive web requests made by LWP (to avoid hammering the target web server with a large number of nearly simultaneous requests). We also define a $timeout after which our script will assume a link is broken and go on to the next. The $max_pages variable is there to prevent our script from getting stuck in an endless loop, which could happen if, for example, a CGI script on the server was generating an endless succession of links.

Object-Oriented Syntax

The first really new-looking part of this script comes when we construct a new user agent object with the following line:

```
    my $ua = LWP::UserAgent->new;
```

This odd-looking syntax, which you haven't seen before in this book, is characteristic of something called *object-oriented programming*, or *OOP*. The LWP::Simple module that we used in the second version of our link-checker let us do simple web transactions from within our Perl program without needing to know about OOP. In order to take advantage of the fancier features of LWP, though, we'll need to use the object-oriented interface of LWP::UserAgent.

You don't need to understand too much about object-oriented programming in order to use object-oriented modules created by others. It's probably worth your time, though, to try to learn at least a little before we continue. This will help you be more comfortable using other people's OOP, which in turn will let you take advantage of the many object-oriented Perl modules (like LWP::UserAgent) that you will find in CPAN. See the sidebar "Object-Oriented Perl" for a quick overview.

When we create a new user agent object with LWP::UserAgent->new, we need to stick that object in a scalar variable so that we can access it later on. In this case, we're sticking the user agent object in the scalar variable $ua.

You may be wondering how a scalar variable, which you already know only holds a single value, can hold something as complex and feature-filled as an object. If you think about it for a second, though, I'll bet you can guess how Perl does this. When was the last time you saw Perl turning something complex into a scalar so that it could be easily stored and manipulated? Right! References to the rescue!

The object returned from the LWP::UserAgent class's new method is actually a *reference*. To access the object's *methods* (that is, to store information in the object or get information back out of it), you have to dereference it. To do that, you use the third (and final) piece of Perl reference syntax you'll be learning in this chapter: the *dereferencing arrow*, or ->. (Don't get it confused with the => *comma-replacement operator* sometimes used to separate hash keys and values, by the way. It has nothing to do with => other than a coincidental resemblance.)

The next three lines from our link_check3.plx script demonstrate the use of the dereferencing arrow nicely:

```
$ua->agent("$agent_name " . $ua->agent);
$ua->from($from_addr);
$ua->timeout($timeout); # set timeout interval
```

The first line calls the $ua object's agent method to take the contents from the $agent_name variable (which you defined in the script's configuration section), concatenate those contents with the default return value of the same agent method, and store all those back in the object's agent property. The from method stores the $from_addr (likewise defined in the script's configuration section) in the object, and the timeout method sets the object's timeout value.

All these methods are described in the documentation that comes with LWP::UserAgent, which should be available to you by entering the command man LWP::UserAgent (or perldoc /path/to/local/copy/LWP/UserAgent.pm, if you had to install LWP in your own user space).

The script then shifts a starting URL off the @ARGV array (that is, it takes the first command-line argument supplied to the script and sticks it in $start_url), or dies with a usage message if an argument wasn't given. It then runs that $start_url through the &check_url subroutine, which returns a three-element list: ($success, $type, $actual). If we take a look at that &check_url routine, we'll see that it does some preliminary housekeeping, then has this interesting line:

```
sleep 1 while (time - $last_request) < $delay;
```

Object-Oriented Perl

Object-oriented programming, or OOP, is a relatively recent invention in the world of computer programming. Some people love it, some hate it, but regardless of how you feel about it, a lot of experienced Perl programmers have got the OOP religion in a big way, and use it when creating their modules. To be able to take advantage of those modules, it will help if you know a little bit about OOP.

At its heart, OOP is just another weapon in the programmer's perpetual war against complexity. Like subroutines that keep their internal variables private and pass all information in and out via their invocation parameters and return values, object-oriented programming helps programmers hide the complexities of their programs' low-level details. If a well-written subroutine is like a black box, though, object-oriented programming is like a black box with a lock on the lid and a little trapdoor on the side for passing notes in and out. In other words, OOP is much more rigorous about keeping you from messing around with the program's messy innards.

OOP accomplishes this by having an extra layer of abstraction that sits between you (the person using some piece of object-oriented code) and the code itself. In order to do something with an object-oriented Perl module, you use a special object-oriented interface, which is kept carefully separated from the behind-the-scenes implementation that does the actual work.

This process involves some new jargon. When you use an object-oriented program, you do so by *calling methods*. You call methods *on* things, and one of the things you call methods on is called a *class*. Calling a method on a class is called *calling a class method*. If you call a certain kind of class method, called a *constructor method*, it will return you an *object*. Once you have that object, you call *object methods* on it.

In Perl terms, classes look like the module names you've already seen (e.g., Some::Class). The objects returned by constructor methods are stored in scalar variables. Methods are called using a curious little arrow symbol (->) that connects the class name (or the object), on the left, with the name of the method being called, on the right. (You'll be learning more about this arrow symbol later on in this chapter.) Methods that take arguments get those arguments in a parenthetical list following the method name, much as a subroutine does.

Here are some quick examples of how object-oriented Perl actually looks, along with some comments giving the way programmers talk about it:

```
# call a class method to return a new object
my $obj = Some::Class->new;

# call an object method to assign an attribute
$obj->color('green');

# call an object method to return an attribute
my $color = $obj->color;
```

Just as we've previously created one-line versions of if blocks (by eliminating the curly braces and putting the if statement at the end of the line), we can do the same thing with a while loop. This line will cause our program to sleep for one second as long as the value returned by the time function (which returns the number of seconds since the Epoch) minus the value stored in $last_request (which holds the time of the script's most-recent request) is less than the configuration variable $delay. In other words, the script will pause here until $delay seconds have passed since the $last_request variable was updated with the current time. If we use the default value of 1 in $delay, this means our script will issue only one request per second, preventing the target web server from being inundated by hundreds or thousands of nearly simultaneous requests.

Checking Remote URLs

After our script is done sleeping and has replaced the contents of $last_request with the current time, the following very interesting line occurs:

```
my $response = $ua->request(HTTP::Request->new('HEAD', $url));
```

If we take a few seconds to digest this, it actually turns out to be pretty straightforward. We're issuing a HEAD request for the URL contained in the $url variable, and storing the response that we get in a new object called $response. Looking at the right side of the expression first and burrowing down inside the nested parentheses, we can see that we actually start off by creating a new object, calling the new method on the HTTP::Request class. We give that new method two arguments: the string 'HEAD' and the $url that was passed to the &check_url subroutine; this is how one creates an HTTP::Request object representing a HEAD request for that particular $url. (See man HTTP::Request for more specifics, if you're curious.)

We don't bother storing this HTTP::Request object in a variable, but instead pass it right on to the request method being called on the LWP::UserAgent object we created at the top of the script. That request method returns something that we store in $response, and that something (as mentioned previously) is another object. Once again, consult the relevant manpage (man LWP::UserAgent, in this case) if you want to know more about what's going on.

Whew. In one line, we've created one object, used it as the argument to a method called on another object, and returned a third object from that. As you may have gathered, object orientation is one of those in-for-a-penny, in-for-a-pound kinds of things. But that's okay: as long as we read the module documentation carefully and take pains to get our OOP syntax right, we can be reasonably sure that the code is doing what it's supposed to do.

Next we call the is_success method on our $response object:

```
my $success = $response->is_success;
```

The is_success method returns a true value if the request that produced this $response object generated a successful HTTP response code from the remote server, and false otherwise. In this case, if $success is false we execute an unless block, in which we redo the request but this time using method GET instead of method HEAD (because some web servers are configured to reject HEAD requests, even though they handle GET requests with no problem). After performing the GET request, we once again call the is_success method on the resulting $response object and store the result in $success. So, we now know if we can successfully request this particular URL.

Whether we performed the GET request or not, we now call the header method on our $response object, giving the method the argument 'Content-Type' to tell it that that's the header we wish to retrieve from the web server's response. We then stick that header in the $type variable:

```
my $type = $response->header('Content-Type');
```

We need to get that Content-Type header, by the way, and return it from the &check_url subroutine so that the code calling that routine knows if we got back an HTML page that needs to be parsed for other links to be checked.

Next we call the base method, which returns the base URL of the document returned to us. As the comment indicates, we do this because even though we know what URL we used in the &check_url subroutine's argument, we don't know if that's the page we actually ended up retrieving. One of the fancy things LWP::UserAgent does is to follow redirections for us, so the page we end up looking at might not be the page we initially requested. (This is an excellent example of the kind of thing we might not think of if we were trying to hand-code this LWP functionality ourselves.) We store the returned base URL in the $actual variable:

```
my $actual = $response->base; # in case we were redirected
```

Finally, we return the subroutine's three-element return value:

```
return ($success, $type, $actual);
```

Execution now continues back in the main part of the script, where we check the $success and $type returned from that first URL's having been run through &check_url, and die with an error message if they don't look right:

```
unless ($success and $type eq 'text/html') {
    die "The start_url isn't reachable, or isn't an HTML file.\n";
}
```

If our script is still there afterward, we put an entry for that starting page in %good. Then we push $start_url onto the @queue, which is an array of pages we are going to process:

```
push @queue, $start_url;
```

Processing the Queue

Next we assign that $start_url to a new scalar variable called $start_base, and use a substitution variety of regular expression to strip everything in $start_base after the last / character. In other words, $start_base will end up holding the URL of the directory containing our starting page. We also use quotemeta to escape any regex metacharacters in $start_base, storing the result in $escaped_start_base:

```
my $start_base         = $start_url;
$start_base            =~ s{/[^/]*$}{/}; # trim everything after last '/'
my $escaped_start_base = quotemeta $start_base;
```

We'll use this as we work our way through the pages in @queue in order to tell if we should follow the links that we find. The script will check all the links it finds for "badness," but it will look through the pages returned in a search for more links only if the page in question has a URL beginning with $start_base. (If our script didn't discriminate this way it could wind up wandering off on a link-checking excursion spanning the entire Web.)

Finally, the heart of the script simply processes each page in @queue:

```
while (@queue) {
    ++$total_pages;
    if ($total_pages > $max_pages) {
        warn "stopped checking after reaching $max_pages pages.\n";
        --$total_pages; # kludge so the count is correct in report
        last;
    }
    my $page = shift @queue;
    &process_page($page); # possibly adding new entries to @queue
}
```

This loop first checks to see if the script has reached the limit stored in the configuration variable $max_pages, and if it has we exit from the loop with the last command. Otherwise, it shifts the first page off the @queue array and runs the &process_page subroutine on it.

The potentially confusing thing is that the &process_page subroutine doesn't return any explicit return value, but possibly modifies the @queue array by pushing new entries onto the end of it, as we'll see in a minute. When used in moderation, such "action at a distance" is probably okay, though in general we should try to avoid it when we can in the interest of code comprehensibility and maintainability.

Turning to that &process_page subroutine, most of it should look pretty familiar by now. It sleeps for a suitable interval, creates a $response object by calling the request method on the $ua object, and checks that response to make sure the transaction was successful. Then it calls the base method on $response and checks to see if the base URL of the page we ended up on is actually outside of the path stored in $start_base. (It shouldn't have been, since we wouldn't have pushed the URL onto the

@queue array if it was, but again, we may have been redirected to another page some-where along the line.)

Notice, by the way, the use of the /o modifier in this line's regular expression:

```
unless ($base =~ /$escaped_start_base/o) {
```

As we previously learned, that /o modifier causes Perl to compile this regular expression only once, even though the search pattern contains a variable whose contents might change between invocations of the expression. In return for our promise to Perl that the contents of the search pattern won't change, the script will run somewhat faster than it would if the expression had to be recompiled each time it was run.

Next comes some more object-oriented razzle-dazzle courtesy of Gisle Aas' HTML::LinkExtor module. This is the code we'll be using to do a rigorous, "correct" extraction of links from the HTML documents being checked:

```
my $parser = HTML::LinkExtor->new(undef, $base);
$parser->parse($response->content);
my @links = $parser->links;
```

Try to keep up: we create a new $parser object by calling HTML::LinkExtor's new method. We pass it two arguments, although actually the first one is the undefined value, which is returned by Perl's undef function. We pass that first argument only for position. The second argument is the $base of the previously returned $response object.

Once we've created our new $parser object, we call its parse method, passing it the content of the page we retrieved (which we get from calling the content method on the $response object). Then we call the links method on the $parser object, which returns an "array of arrays" (which is really an array of array references) containing information about all the link tags in the document (that is, all the tags that link else-where via an SRC or HREF attribute).

Next we process each array reference by iterating over the @links array with a foreach loop:

```
foreach my $linkarray (@links) {
    my ($tag, %links) = @{$linkarray};
```

Inside the foreach loop, we dereference the current array reference (stored in $linkarray) with that dereferencing syntax we saw earlier in this chapter: @{$linkarray}. The array that we get back is actually a curious little data structure that looks like this: (tagname, attribute, value, attribute, value, ...). (You can read more about this with man HTML::LinkExtor.) By assigning this list to ($tag, %links), we create a scalar and a hash for the current tag that we can then use for fur-ther processing.

That processing begins by using a regular expression to see if this tag (which HTML::LinkExtor returns as lowercase) is either an <a...> or an <img...> tag:

```
if ($tag =~ /^(a|img)$/) {
```

If it is either of these, the following code kicks in:

```
TARGET: while (my($attr, $target) = each %links) {
```

A few new things are in this line. First off, we're using a *label* (that's what TARGET: is) to mark the beginning of a while loop. That will be useful in a minute because it will let us refer to this loop by name when we want to issue a next to go back to the top of the loop. The label can be whatever we want, though by convention it should be in ALL CAPS.

The second new thing in that line is our use of the each function. This is similar to the keys function we've already seen for constructing a list of all the keys for a particular hash, but it works a little differently. Instead of returning keys, each returns key/value pairs from the hash. Also, instead of returning the entire list of keys (as keys does), each just returns a single key/value pair (the "next" key/value pair, according to the hash's own internal more-or-less random ordering) each time we invoke it. If we put the assignment of each's return value inside a while loop's parenthetical test, as we've done here, we will eventually work our way through the hash.

Finally, here's the rest of the &process_page subroutine, in which we process each attribute from each link on the page being processed:

```
if ($attr =~ /^(href|src|lowsrc)$/) {
    # these $target entries are the ones we're
    # interested in.
    next TARGET unless $target =~ /^(?:https?|ftp):/;
    $target =~ s/#.*//; # lose trailing #targets
    if (exists $good{$target}) {
        # have already seen this before
        if ($good{$target}) {
            # already known to be good
            next;
        } else {
            # already known to be bad
            push @{ $bad_links{$base} }, $target;
        }
    } else {
        # haven't seen this one before
        my($success, $type, $actual)
            = &check_url($target);
        unless ($success) {
            $good{$target} = 0;
            push @{ $bad_links{$base} }, $target;
            next TARGET;
        }
        $good{$target} = 1;

        if (defined $type
            and $type eq 'text/html'
```

```
                        and defined $actual
                        and $actual =~ /$escaped_start_base/o) {

                    push @queue, $target;
                }
            }
        }
      }
    }
  }
}
```

This should all look pretty familiar by now; it does more or less the same thing as the previous version of our link-checker. Among the highlights are the use of the label to go back to the top of the while loop, like this:

```
next TARGET unless $target =~ /^(?:https?|ftp):/;
```

Also interesting is the way we use the &check_url subroutine to process each link that isn't already in the %good hash (that is, to process each link that hasn't been previously seen and tested). A final difference is the way we push URLs representing previously unseen links that are under $start_base into the @queue array for subsequent processing.

And that's pretty much it. The rest of the script simply prints out a report in the same way as our previous link checkers.

Congratulations! We have created a very cool link-checking script that can look for broken links on sites located anywhere on the Web, being fairly rigorous about correctly parsing HTML. We've learned how to download and install modules from CPAN and we've learned three of the four important pieces of Perl syntax for creating and using references. Finally, we know enough about Perl's object-oriented syntax to make effective use of object-oriented Perl modules. That's plenty for one chapter.

## CHAPTER 12

Running a CGI Guestbook

We're going to return now to the subject of CGI scripting, in order to create a guest-book script so that visitors to our web site can leave a pithy comment for others to read. Although some people view web guestbooks as vain and silly, I've chosen to present one here for two reasons. First, plenty of people (myself included) think the Web's greatest possibilities lie in the area of fostering two-way communication, and a guestbook is a nice (albeit simple) step in that direction. Second, a guestbook script will let us look at two issues that are very important to web programmers.

The first issue involves how to safely handle untrusted data. Letting outside users submit data that will be stored in a file on the web server and displayed to other visitors to our site creates several security-related problems. Fortunately, Perl has a feature called *tainting* that is very helpful in combating those problems.

The second issue involves multiple users trying to update the same data at the same time. In this chapter we'll see how to use something called *file locking* to solve that problem.

The Guestbook Script

The flowchart in Figure 12-1 shows the sequence of actions that our guestbook script, guestbook.cgi, will take.

As the flowchart shows, the program begins by printing the top of the guestbook page. Then it checks to see if this current invocation includes the submission of a new guestbook entry, and if it does, it formats that entry and adds it at the end of the entries stored in the external guestbook file. Then, regardless of whether this invocation involved submission of a new entry, it reads and displays all the entries stored in the external guestbook file. Finally, it finishes the HTML page it is displaying by adding a form that the visitor can use to add a new entry to the guestbook.

The guestbook script is shown in Example 12-1. As with all the examples in this book, you can download it from the book's web site, at *http://www.elanus.net/book/*.

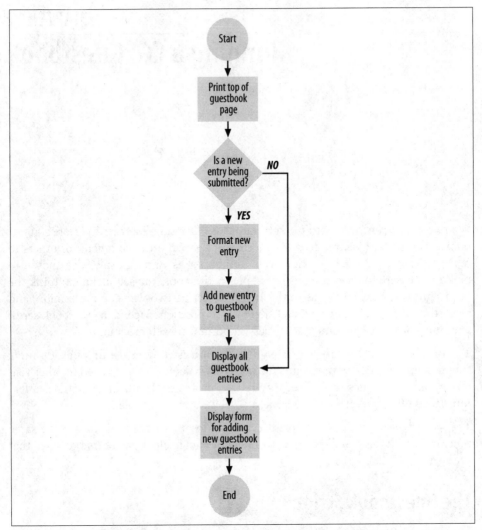

Figure 12-1. The sequence of actions taken by the guestbook.cgi script

There are a few new Perl features here, but don't worry. We'll be going through the whole thing, line by line, as usual.

Example 12-1. A simple CGI guestbook script

```
#!/usr/bin/perl -Tw

# guestbook.cgi - a simple guestbook script

use strict;

# configuration section
```

Example 12-1. A simple CGI guestbook script (continued)

```perl
my $data_file    = '/w1/l/lies/begperl/data/guestbook.txt';
my $max_entries = 50; # how many guestbook entries to save?
                    # set to '0' (zero) for infinite entries...

use CGI qw(:standard);
use Fcntl qw(:DEFAULT :flock);

print header, <<"EOF";
<HTML>
<HEAD>
<TITLE>My guestbook</TITLE>
</HEAD>
<BODY>
<H1>My guestbook</H1>

<P>Here's my guestbook. You can <A HREF="#form">add
your own comment</A> using the form at the bottom
of the page.</P>
<HR>
EOF

my $action = param('action');

if ($action and $action eq 'Add comment') {

    # process the form submission
    # and assemble the guestbook entry

    my @from_ary;
    foreach (qw(city state country)) {
        push @from_ary, param($_) if param($_);
    }

    my %sub = (
        name       => param('name'),
        from_where => join(', ', @from_ary),
        comment    => param('comment'),
    );

    # clean up $sub{name}

    unless ($sub{name}) {
        $sub{name} = 'Anonymous';
    } elsif (length $sub{name} > 50) {
        $sub{name} = 'Someone with a really long name';
    }

    # clean up $sub{from_where}

    if (! $sub{from_where} or $sub{from_where} =~ /^[,\s]+$/) {
        # empty, or nothing but commas and whitespace
        $sub{from_where} = 'parts unknown';
```

Example 12-1. A simple CGI guestbook script (continued)

```
    } elsif (length $sub{from_where} > 75) {
        $sub{from_where} = 'somewhere with a really long name';
    }

    # clean up $sub{comment}

    unless ($sub{comment}) {
        $sub{comment} = '...nothing to speak of.';
    } elsif (length $sub{comment} > 32768) {
        $sub{comment} = '...more than I feel like posting in my guestbook.';
    }
    $sub{comment} =~ s/\r\n?/\n/g;  # fix line-endings

    # disable HTML and do taint-mode laundering

    foreach (qw(name from_where comment)) {
        $sub{$_} =~ s/</&lt;/g;         # turn every '<' into '&lt;'
        if ($sub{$_} =~ /^([^<]*)$/) {
            $sub{$_} = $1;              # value is untainted now
        }
    }

    # assemble finished guestbook entry

    my $new_entry = <<"EOF";
<P><STRONG>$sub{name}</STRONG> <EM>from $sub{from_where} wrote:</EM><BR>
<BLOCKQUOTE>$sub{comment}</BLOCKQUOTE></P>
<HR>
EOF

    # open non-destructively, read old entries, write out new

    sysopen(ENTRIES, $data_file, O_RDWR)
                            or die "can't open $data_file: $!";
    flock(ENTRIES, LOCK_EX)  or die "can't LOCK_EX $data_file: $!";

    my $all_entries = join '', <ENTRIES>;
    $all_entries    .= $new_entry;

    if ($max_entries) {

        # lop the head off the guestbook, if necessary

        my @all_entries = split(/<HR>\n/i, $all_entries);
        my $entry_count = @all_entries;

        while ($entry_count > $max_entries) {
            shift @all_entries;
            --$entry_count;
        }

        $all_entries = join("<HR>\n", @all_entries);
```

Example 12-1. A simple CGI guestbook script (continued)

```
        $all_entries .= "<HR>\n";
    }

    # now write out to $data_file

    seek(ENTRIES, 0, 0)        or die "can't rewind $data_file: $!";
    truncate(ENTRIES, 0)       or die "can't truncate $data_file: $!";
    print ENTRIES $all_entries or die "can't print to $data_file: $!";
    close(ENTRIES)             or die "can't close $data_file: $!";
}

# display the guestbook

open (IN, "$data_file") or die "Can't open $data_file for reading: $!";
flock(IN, LOCK_SH)      or die "Can't get LOCK_SH on $data_file: $!";
print <IN>;
close IN                or die "Can't close $data_file: $!";

# display the form

print <<"EOF";
<A NAME="form"><H2>Add a comment to the guestbook (no HTML):</H2></A>

<FORM METHOD="POST" ACTION="guestbook.cgi">
<TABLE>

<TR>
<TD ALIGN="right"><STRONG>Name:</STRONG></TD>
<TD><INPUT NAME="name" SIZE=30></TD>
</TR>

<TR>
<TD ALIGN="right"><STRONG>City:</STRONG></TD>
<TD><INPUT NAME="city" SIZE=30></TD>
</TR>

<TR>
<TD ALIGN="right"><STRONG>State:</STRONG></TD>
<TD><INPUT NAME="state" SIZE=30></TD>
</TR>

<TR>
<TD ALIGN="right"><STRONG>Country:</STRONG></TD>
<TD><INPUT NAME="country" SIZE=30></TD>
</TR>

<TR>
<TD ALIGN="right" VALIGN="top"><STRONG>Comment:</STRONG></TD>
<TD>
<TEXTAREA NAME="comment" ROWS=5 COLS=30 WRAP="virtual"></TEXTAREA>
</TD>
</TR>
```

Example 12-1. A simple CGI guestbook script (continued)

```
<TR><TD COLSPAN=2> </TD></TR>
<TR>
<TD> </TD>
<TD><INPUT TYPE="submit" NAME="action" VALUE="Add comment"></TD>
</TR>
</TABLE>

</FORM>
</BODY>
</HTML>
EOF

# end of script
```

Taint Mode

As I mentioned already, security is going to be a big concern with this script. Right from the beginning, though, we've brought out the heavy artillery, courtesy of Perl's -T shebang-line switch:

```
#!/usr/local/bin/perl -Tw
```

This switch (which is lumped together with the -w warnings switch we've been using for a while now) is a very useful tool for making our CGI scripts more secure. The -T switch turns on Perl's built-in *taint mode*. Perl's taint mode is designed to make it easier to track which of the data our script is working with has come from an untrusted source, and fix that data so that it can't do anything we don't like. Specifically, taint mode has the following effects:

- Any data obtained by our script from the outside world (meaning anywhere other than the script itself) is considered *tainted*.

- Any variable that is modified in an expression that contains tainted data becomes tainted itself.

- Tainted data may not be used by our script to take certain kinds of actions that would affect the outside world (writing to a file, for example).

In essence, taint mode makes our script paranoid. It doesn't trust anything the outside world tells it, and it won't take certain kinds of actions based on that information. Instead, it will die with an error message if it catches us trying to do something it considers unsafe. The hoops we have to jump through to overcome this tainting process are a bit of a pain, but they are in fact a really good thing, since they force us to pay attention to the things bad guys could do with our script by feeding it bogus data.

In order for our scripts to run successfully under taint mode, we must *untaint* the data that comes from outside the script. (In some cases, though not in this script, we must do some other things, too, like explicitly setting the value in $ENV{PATH}.)

Untainting data turns out to be something of an exception to Perl's TMTOWTDI ("There's more than one way to do it") motto. There is, in fact, only one (1) official way to untaint data in Perl: by using a regular expression match to capture the data into the special $1 variable (or $2, $3, etc.). Once the data has been captured by a regex's capturing parentheses, Perl assumes that we've properly laundered it, and lets us do whatever we want to do with it. We'll see an example of how this works in just a moment.

Guestbook Preliminaries

Here's a guided tour of what's going on at the top of the guestbook script. First, we specify the name of the file where we will save the guestbook entries:

```
my $data_file = '/w1/l/lies/begperl/data/guestbook.txt';
```

(Your own guestbook file will probably reside somewhere else.) We'll be discussing appropriate permissions for this file toward the end of this chapter.

Next, we specify how many guestbook entries we want to save in that guestbook file:

```
my $max_entries = 50; # how many guestbook entries to save?
                      # set to '0' (zero) for infinite entries...
```

This is designed to prevent the guestbook from using up all our disk space. Even if we don't think our guestbook is likely to be that popular, we can't overlook the possibility that someone will attempt to use it maliciously. If $max_entries is set to a nonzero value, the script won't let the guestbook have more entries than that value; once that number is reached, the oldest entry will be deleted every time a new entry is added. If you really want to you can set $max_entries to zero (0) in order to disable this feature, but don't say I didn't warn you.

Next we pull in the CGI module, using the same line we saw back in Chapter 3's form-to-email-gateway example. We also pull in another module, Fcntl, which is going to help us do our file locking:

```
use CGI qw(:standard);
use Fcntl qw(:DEFAULT :flock);
```

Next, we print out the top of our HTML page:

```
print header, <<"EOF";
<HTML>
<HEAD>
<TITLE>My guestbook</TITLE>
</HEAD>
<BODY>
<H1>My guestbook</H1>

<P>Here's my guestbook. You can <A HREF="#form">add
```

```
your own comment</A> using the form at the bottom
of the page.</P>
<HR>
EOF
```

Here again, as with the form-to-email script in Chapter 3, we're using CGI.pm's header function as a convenient replacement for having to give the whole Content-type CGI header explicitly.

Next we use CGI.pm's param function to pull in the submitted form parameter named action (if it's there), assigning it to the scalar variable $action:

```
my $action = param('action');
```

This will store in $action the value of the Submit button named action that we're going to create in the form for submitting new guestbook entries later on in this script. We use that $action variable to tell if we're processing the submission of a new guestbook entry.

That actually happens in the next line, which begins an extended if block that fires off only if this script invocation represents the submission of a new guestbook entry:

```
if ($action and $action eq 'Add comment') {

    # process the form submission
    # and assemble the guestbook entry
```

Inside that if block, we take care of processing the submitted form elements: cleaning them up, untainting them, and assembling them into the new guestbook entry. The first part of that process involves taking the city, state, and country form fields and pushing them onto an array called @from_ary. We do that inside a foreach loop, adding each field to the array only if the field was actually submitted in the form:

```
my @from_ary;
foreach (qw(city state country)) {
    push @from_ary, param($_) if param($_);
}
```

You'll see why we're doing this in just a second. For now, though, I want you to notice the code inside the parentheses after foreach: qw(city state country). I can't believe I've gone this long without introducing something as useful as qw(). qw() is a special quoting operator whose function is to quote words. In other words, when we use qw(), anything inside the parentheses will be turned into a list of quoted strings, with the quotes being automatically applied wherever there is a word boundary. In still other words, the following two statements do exactly the same thing:

```
@stuff = ('walnuts', 'rutabagas', 'kumquats');
@stuff = qw(walnuts rutabagas kumquats);
```

Except that the second one is both easier to type and easier to read.

A *word*, for the purposes of the qw( ) operator, is defined as a string of consecutive nonwhitespace characters. This is slightly different from the behavior of the \w regular expression escape sequence, which defines *word characters* as letters, numbers, and the underscore character (_).

You needn't use ( ) to delimit the stuff that qw will act upon, by the way. You can use any delimiting characters you want, so you will occasionally see people using things like:

```
@stuff = qw/walnuts rutabagas kumquats/;
```

If you use one of the paired delimiters (( ), [ ], and { }) the closing delimiter is the appropriate closing member from the pair. Otherwise, the closing delimiter is the same as the opening delimiter, as in the preceding qw/ / example.

We've actually seen that qw( ) operator already, in the argument to some of the modules we've been using:

```
use CGI qw(:standard);
```

What it's doing there is providing a list of things to be imported from the module. In this case it happens to just be a one-element list, but it's handy to use the qw( ) operator anyway in case we might want to add more items to the list later.

Next, we create a hash, called %sub, containing the three pieces of submitted data we're going to be working with to assemble our new guestbook entry. Those three pieces of data are:

- The submitted name (from the form's name parameter)
- A string we assemble from the @from_ary by joining its elements together with the string ", "
- The submitted comment (from the form's comment parameter)

```
my %sub = (
    name       => param('name'),
    from_where => join(', ', @from_ary),
    comment    => param('comment'),
);
```

Now you can see why we wanted to put items into @from_ary only if they were actually submitted via the form. We're constructing a line like "Anytown, California, USA" to go with the from_where key in the hash, and we only want to stick the ", " string between elements that were actually submitted. Otherwise, we could end up with a string like "Anytown, , " if the user submitting the guestbook entry didn't bother filling out some of the fields.

Notice, by the way, how we've used parentheses to surround the arguments we're passing to join. Since the second argument to the join function is by definition a list, the function would go on greedily grabbing up the subsequent elements in the hash assignment if we didn't do that. With the parentheses there, though, join will get only the arguments we intended it to get.

Next comes a chunk of code to clean up the $sub{name} entry. Basically, we set the name to "Anonymous" if no name was submitted, or set it to "Someone with a really long name" if a name more than 50 characters long was submitted:

```
# clean up $sub{name}

unless ($sub{name}) {
    $sub{name} = 'Anonymous';
} elsif (length $sub{name} > 50) {
    $sub{name} = 'Someone with a really long name';
}
```

This code uses Perl's length function, which we haven't seen before. It returns the length (in characters) of the value given in its argument.

Next, we perform a similar cleanup operation on $sub{from_where}, which we assembled from the submitted form values for city, state, and country:

```
# clean up $sub{from_where}

if (! $sub{from_where} or $sub{from_where} =~ /^[,\s]+$/) {
    # empty, or nothing but commas and whitespace
    $sub{from_where} = 'parts unknown';
} elsif (length $sub{from_where} > 75) {
    $sub{from_where} = 'somewhere with a really long name';
}
```

Notice in the first line of the if-elsif block how we've used the exclamation point (!), which is Perl's logical not operator, to negate the expression that follows it. In other words, ! something will return true if something is false.

By putting *two* logical conditions in our logical test and joining them with or, we make it so that the overall logical test will evaluate to true if *either* of those logical tests conditions evaluates to true.

Next we clean up the actual submitted guestbook comment, via the following:

```
# clean up $sub{comment}

unless ($sub{comment}) {
    $sub{comment} = '...nothing to speak of.';
} elsif (length $sub{comment} > 32768) {
    $sub{comment} = '...more than I feel like posting in my guestbook.';
}
$sub{comment} =~ s/\r\n?/\n/g; # fix line-endings
```

The if-elsif block looks more or less like the cleanup operations we've already seen for the $sub{name} and $sub{from_where} values. The line that follows that if-elsif block is different, though: we're using a substitution-style regex to fix our guestbook submitter's line-ending sequences, making them conform to the Unix world's idea of how a line should end.

If the person submitting the guestbook comment enters newlines in the text area box that the form gives them, those submitted newlines will arrive in whatever form the submitter's computer thinks they should have. If the person submitting the new guestbook entry is on a Windows machine, each line will end with a carriage return character (\r) followed by a linefeed (\n). If the submitter is on a Mac, each line will end with a carriage return only. If the submitter is on a Unix machine, it will be a linefeed only. The s/\r\n?/\n/g substitution operation will make sure that the submission conforms to the Unix line-ending convention when it is stored in the guestbook file on the server.

This won't make any difference to a person viewing the guestbook because web browsers are smart enough to turn all these various line-ending sequences into a single space character. But it might make a difference to us because if we ever want to edit the guestbook file manually (say, to delete a comment we don't like, or add a response to a user's question), those various line-ending sequences will make things look ugly in our editor.

Next we're going to take care of that tainted-data problem we've been talking about. We're also going to disable any HTML tags our guestbook submitter might have tried to put in her entry. We do that with the following code:

```
# disable HTML and do taint-mode laundering

foreach (qw(name from_where comment)) {
    $sub{$_} =~ s/</&lt;/g;          # turn every '<' into '&lt;'
    if ($sub{$_} =~ /^([^<]*)$/) {
        $sub{$_} = $1;              # value is untainted now
    }
}
```

Since we need to do the same operation to each submitted element, we do it in a foreach loop, cycling through each of the three keys in the %sub hash. For each key, we take the associated value (accessed as $sub{$_}, since each item we're foreach'ing over is being stored in the special variable $_), and run the following substitution against it: s/</</g. This will have the effect of turning all less-than symbols (that is, left angle brackets) into <, the HTML entity that encodes that character.

Why are we doing this? Because turning all left angle brackets into entities will have the effect of disabling any HTML tags that the user entered into the form. If the submitting user can't put a literal left angle bracket into the displayed guestbook entry, she can't create any HTML tags (since they all begin with a left angle bracket). This will have the following effects:

- Our guestbook will be prettier this way because the script can format the entries consistently.

- Our script will be easier to write this way because disabling all markup is simpler than checking for user-supplied markup and passing only certain types through.

- Our guestbook will be safer this way because malicious users will not be able to use server-side includes to steal the web server's password file, or use JavaScript to do nasty things to visitors' browsers, or inline pictures of Barney from some other web site.

Untainting with Backreferences

Now that we've removed all the < characters from the submitted guestbook data, we're ready to untaint that data so that Perl's tainting mechanism won't cause the script to die when we write the new entry out to the guestbook data file. Here, again, is the chunk of code that does that untainting:

```
if ($sub{$_} =~ /^([^<]*)$/) {
    $sub{$_} = $1;              # value is untainted now
}
```

Looking carefully at that regular expression, the /^([^<]*)$/ search pattern says "Try to do a match in which we start at the very beginning of the string, match a whole bunch of characters that are anything except <, and end up at the end of the string. And while we're at it, let's save whatever gets matched in $1 for later backreferencing. " Or, to put it another way, this expression says "Match the whole string, but only if the string has no < characters in it. If it has any < characters, don't match anything."

We can be reasonably sure this expression *will* match because we previously used the substitution expression to replace all the < characters with <. Now we just take the captured string in $1 and assign it back to $sub{$_}, and voilá, we've laundered that particular hash value, and Perl's tainting mechanism no longer cares what we do with it.

 You'll notice that Perl's untainting mechanism doesn't actually stop us from doing insecure things. We could always use an all-inclusive pattern like /^(.*)$/ to match a piece of tainted data, then assign whatever the old value was back into the original variable via $1. The purpose of Perl's tainting mechanism is to help us avoid doing insecure things *by accident*; it doesn't stop us from doing such things *on purpose*. It's up to us to devise a restrictive-enough regex pattern to exclude dangerous elements from our data.

The next thing we do is to take our newly laundered data and use it to assemble the finished guestbook entry:

```
# assemble finished guestbook entry

my $new_entry = <<"EOF";
<P><STRONG>$sub{name}</STRONG> <EM>from $sub{from_where} wrote:</EM><BR>
<BLOCKQUOTE>$sub{comment}</BLOCKQUOTE></P>
<HR>
EOF
```

There's nothing tricky here. We simply interpolate our three laundered hash values into a here-document-quoted string, with some HTML formatting to make it look nice.

File Locking

Now that we've got our guestbook entry looking how we want it, we need to combine it with the earlier entries and save the whole kit and caboodle in a file on the server.

Which raises an interesting issue. Depending on how popular our site is, it's entirely possible that two people will try to view the guestbook—or worse, add new entries to it—at the same time. This could create a problem, causing us to end up with some really weird-looking guestbook entries.

We get around this problem by using something called *file locking*. This is a way of marking a file as "ours," at least temporarily. Assuming the other programs that want to access our file are written to respect file locking, they will wait patiently for us to finish what we're doing before they do whatever it is they want to do.

This is a pretty simple concept; anyone who has ever needed to keep two preschoolers happily playing with the same toy will understand the principle. That said, the actual implementation tends to be a bit more complicated than one might at first expect (which is also true for preschoolers, come to think of it).

There are two basic approaches to file locking. One way would be to use something called a *semaphore file*, which is a separate file, other than our data file, where we would do our actual locking. We use that technique for several file locking examples later in this book. For this example, though, we're going to do our file locking using the actual guestbook data file itself.

In order to do that, though, we'll need to use a different approach to opening our file than we've used so far in this book. Up until now, we've always used Perl's open function, whether opening a file for reading (via something like open IN, $file), or opening a file for writing (via something like open OUT, "> $file"). Unfortunately, that approach won't work here.

We can lock a file, it turns out, only after we've opened it and created a filehandle. In this case, we need to be able to read from the file (in order to get the old guestbook entries from it) and then write to the file (in order to add our new entry to it). But if we do that as two separate operations, we will lose our lock on the file during the interval between closing the first filehandle (used for reading) and opening the second filehandle (used for writing). Another instance of our program could slip in during that interval and make changes to the file, changes that would be overwritten and lost when our instance finally did its writing.

We need to be able to open the filehandle in a manner that allows both reading and writing. Then we can obtain our lock, read the old data, write out the new data, and only then release the lock. To do that, though, we have to use Perl's sysopen function, which is a higher-powered version of the open function. Using sysopen is a little more complicated than using open, but in this case it's really worth the extra hassle.

Here's the section of our code where we open the file using sysopen:

```
# open non-destructively, read old entries, write out new

sysopen(ENTRIES, $data_file, O_RDWR)
                    or die "can't open $data_file: $!";
```

Here we've opened a filehandle to the guestbook data file (the path and filename of which we defined at the top of the script). The O_RDWR argument to sysopen is a flag (provided courtesy of that Fcntl module we pulled in at the top of the script) that specifies that we wish to open this file for both reading and writing.

Next comes the part where we lock the file (which we actually do by locking the filehandle). We do that using Perl's flock function, passing it the filehandle and another flag (LOCK_EX, also obtained from the Fcntl module) that specifies that we wish to get an exclusive lock:

```
flock(ENTRIES, LOCK_EX)  or die "can't LOCK_EX $data_file: $!";
```

This reflects the fact that we normally request two kinds of locks via the flock function: *shared* and *exclusive*. Any number of scripts can have a shared lock at the same time; we use this when we're just going to be reading data from the file. An exclusive lock (which is the kind we got in this case) is what we want when we're going to be modifying the file. In order to get an exclusive lock, our script will have to wait until all other locks (shared or exclusive) on the file have been released.

That's what will happen at this point in the script if there are any other locks on that guestbook data file (perhaps because another instance of our guestbook script is currently reading from it or updating it). This instance of our script will wait, not doing anything, until that other lock is released and its own lock is granted.

Next come the following two lines, in which all the current guestbook entries are read in from the filehandle, joined into one long string, and have the newly submitted entry appended to them:

```
my $all_entries = join '', <ENTRIES>;
$all_entries    .= $new_entry;
```

Remember at the top of the script when we defined the $max_entries variable? Here's where we test whether it was set to a nonzero value. If it was, we check to see if we need to chop off some of the oldest guestbook entries. That checking and chopping off happens via the following if block, which is the next thing in the script:

```
if ($max_entries) {

    # lop the head off the guestbook, if necessary

    my @all_entries = split(/<HR>\n/i, $all_entries);
    my $entry_count = @all_entries;

    while ($entry_count > $max_entries) {
        shift @all_entries;
        --$entry_count;
    }

    $all_entries  = join("<HR>\n", @all_entries);
    $all_entries .= "<HR>\n";
}
```

Most of the code in this block should be self-explanatory. We split the guestbook entries on <HR>\n to turn them into an array of entries, and count how many entries we have by assigning that array to $entry_count, which puts it in a scalar context, causing it to return the number of elements it contains. (Since split does not return trailing null fields, the <HR>\n at the end of the last entry does not result in an extra field being returned, by the way.)

We then use a while loop that keeps shifting elements off the front of the @all_ entries array, and use Perl's auto-decrement operator (--) to reduce $entry_count by 1, until we've reduced our guestbook to the appropriate number of entries. Then we just use join to put those entries back together with the <HR>\n string we split it on earlier, taking care to append that trailing <HR>\n after we're done.

Now we do a little razzle-dazzle with the ENTRIES filehandle:

1. We use Perl's seek function to return the point where we're operating on the file-handle to the very beginning of the file.

2. We use Perl's truncate function to delete everything in the filehandle.

3. We print the $all_entries variable to the filehandle.

4. We close the filehandle (which is the step at which the file actually gets written out to disk).

```
    # now write out to $data_file

    seek(ENTRIES, 0, 0)      or die "can't rewind $data_file: $!";
    truncate(ENTRIES, 0)     or die "can't truncate $data_file: $!";
    print ENTRIES $all_entries or die "can't print to $data_file: $!";
    close(ENTRIES)           or die "can't close $data_file: $!";
}
```

The close statement also releases the exclusive lock we had on the file, so if other instances of the guestbook script have been waiting to get at it, now they can.

The closing curly brace (}) ends the block that began near the top of the script, where we tested whether the action parameter had been set to Add comment. That is, we're now done with the part of the script that runs only for cases in which someone invoked the script by submitting a new guestbook entry.

Next we need to display the guestbook, which we do with the following chunk of code:

```
# display the guestbook

open (IN, "$data_file") or die "Can't open $data_file for reading: $!";
flock(IN, LOCK_SH)      or die "Can't get LOCK_SH on $data_file: $!";
print <IN>;
close IN                or die "Can't close $data_file: $!";
```

This part opens $data_file for reading, using Perl's regular open function. We flock the filehandle, but this time using the argument LOCK_SH, meaning we are requesting a shared rather than an exclusive lock. Then we just print all the lines from the file by giving <IN> as the argument to print.

Once the current contents of the guestbook have been printed out, all that is left for the script to do is to print out the form for adding additional guestbook entries:

```
# display the form

print <<"EOF";
<A NAME="form"><H2>Add a comment to the guestbook (no HTML):</H2></A>

<FORM METHOD="POST" ACTION="guestbook.cgi">
<TABLE>

<TR>
<TD ALIGN="right"><STRONG>Name:</STRONG></TD>
<TD><INPUT NAME="name" SIZE=30></TD>
</TR>

<TR>
<TD ALIGN="right"><STRONG>City:</STRONG></TD>
<TD><INPUT NAME="city" SIZE=30></TD>
</TR>

<TR>
<TD ALIGN="right"><STRONG>State:</STRONG></TD>
<TD><INPUT NAME="state" SIZE=30></TD>
</TR>

<TR>
<TD ALIGN="right"><STRONG>Country:</STRONG></TD>
<TD><INPUT NAME="country" SIZE=30></TD>
</TR>
```

```
<TR>
<TD ALIGN="right" VALIGN="top"><STRONG>Comment:</STRONG></TD>
<TD>
<TEXTAREA NAME="comment" ROWS=5 COLS=30 WRAP="virtual"></TEXTAREA>
</TD>
</TR>

<TR><TD COLSPAN=2> </TD></TR>
<TR>
<TD> </TD>
<TD><INPUT TYPE="submit" NAME="action" VALUE="Add comment"></TD>
</TR>
</TABLE>

</FORM>
</BODY>
</HTML>
EOF

# end of script
```

I threw that `# end of script` comment at the end to solve a problem people kept reporting to me when I used this script as part of a web based Perl tutorial. By having the `EOF` here-document–terminating string at the very end of the file, I created a problem for people who edited the file using a text editor that left the trailing newline off on the last line of the file. A here-document terminator needs to have a trailing newline, so these people were getting errors about the EOF not being found. Adding the extra comment line to the script solved that problem for those people.

Guestbook File Permissions

Any time we want a CGI script to write to a file on the web server, we have some security-related issues to consider. Because the CGI script typically runs as `nobody` or `www` or some other unprivileged user, it can't normally make changes to a file owned by some other user (like our own user account, the one we've used for setting up the guestbook). There are at least three alternatives for solving this problem.

One solution is to have the guestbook file be owned by the same user as the web server process: `nobody` or `www` or whatever it is in this particular case.

If we have access to a helpful system administrator we could have him do this for us. Or we could make the directory in which the data file is going to be created world-writeable (using `chmod` to set its permissions to 777), then run a special CGI script to create the guestbook file. After that we would reset the directory's permissions to something more reasonable, like 755, which will still allow the guestbook script to add entries to the data file, but will prevent everyone else in the world from creating new files in the directory.

One problem with this approach is that it makes it harder for us to edit the guestbook file manually. We might want to add a reply to one of the guestbook entries, for example, or delete a specific entry. If the guestbook file is owned by the same account as the web server and isn't world-writeable, we won't be able to make changes to it easily.

Another approach would be to have the guestbook CGI script run in *setuid mode*.

By using chmod to set our script's permissions mode to 4755 rather than just 755, we turn on setuid mode, which means the script will run as if its owner (that is, our user account) were running it, even if it is started by some other user (like the web server; e.g., user nobody). The benefit of this is that the script will be able to make updates to the guestbook file even if that file is owned and writeable only by us.

Here's what that process would look like in the shell. Note the s in the permissions part of the ls -l listing; this is what tells us the script has been made setuid. That setuid setting probably will turn itself off automatically whenever we modify the script, by the way, which means we'll have an additional step to perform (using chmod to set it back to 4755) every time we make any sort of change to it.

```
[jbc@andros begperl]$ chmod 4755 guestbook.cgi
[jbc@andros begperl]$ ls -l guestbook.cgi
-rwsr-xr-x   1 jbc      jbc          4724 Oct 10 14:01 guestbook.cgi
```

Now we can create the directory that's going to hold the data file, use chmod to set the directory's permissions to 755, cd to the directory, and create a blank guestbook file with the Unix touch command (which is normally used to update the timestamp of a file, but which will create a blank file if the file whose name we give in its argument doesn't exist yet). After the guestbook file is created, we can chmod it to 644 (actually, we could chmod it to 600 if we were really paranoid), and we should be in business:

```
[jbc@andros begperl]$ mkdir data
[jbc@andros begperl]$ chmod 755 data
[jbc@andros begperl]$ cd data
[jbc@andros begperl]$ touch guestbook.txt
[jbc@andros begperl]$ chmod 644 guestbook.txt
[jbc@andros begperl]$ ls -l
total 0
-rw-r--r--   1 jbc      jbc             0 Oct 10 14:09 guestbook.txt
```

The downside to the setuid approach is that if someone succeeds in subverting our script, he will be able to do anything with it that we would have permission to do on the web server—e.g., delete or modify all our web pages, trash our home directory, and so on. A subverted script running as nobody probably would not be able to do as much damage. Another downside to the setuid approach is that our ISP may simply not allow it. On the other hand, some ISPs actually require such an approach, using script wrappers like the CGIWrap program, or using Apache server directives to make a particular virtual host run as a particular user.

For my money, having our scripts run as our regular user account is the best approach for a shared hosting environment, assuming we can use it.

Finally, we can make the guestbook file world-writeable.

This is pretty much the lowest-common-denominator approach. By making the guestbook file world-writeable, we allow the web server (that is to say, the guest-book CGI script) to write changes to it.

To do that, we would start by creating the directory where the data file will be stored, and using chmod to set its mode to 755:

```
[jbc@andros begperl]$ mkdir data
[jbc@andros begperl]$ chmod 755 data
```

Then we would cd to the directory and create a new, blank file to hold our guest-book entries by using the Unix touch command:

```
[jbc@andros begperl]$ cd data
[jbc@andros begperl]$ touch guestbook.txt
[jbc@andros begperl]$ ls -l
total 0
-rw-r--r--   1 jbc     jbc            0 Oct 10 14:09 guestbook.txt
```

Now we would chmod the guestbook.txt file to mode 666 (world-writeable):

```
[jbc@andros begperl]$ chmod 666 guestbook.txt
[jbc@andros begperl]$ ls -l guestbook.txt
-rw-rw-rw-   1 jbc     jbc            0 Oct 10 14:10 guestbook.txt
```

The main benefit of this approach is that it's easy. The downside is that anyone else with access to the web server's filesystem (that is to say, anyone else who has a shell account on the web server, or who can subvert our or someone else's CGI script) will be able to modify our guestbook file. They can delete it, add bogus entries, or stick in arbitrary JavaScript or server-side includes. It's not a pretty picture, which is why, on balance, I prefer the setuid approach outlined here.

There you have it: a simple guestbook script. As this chapter has demonstrated, even something as simple as that can have some complex issues associated with it. By using Perl, though, the solutions to the resulting problems are no more difficult than they need to be.

CHAPTER 13

Running a CGI Search Tool

As a web site grows, offering full-text searching of its contents becomes increasingly important. It just isn't possible (or desirable) to have a specific set of browseable links that will let every user find the content she is looking for.

SWISH (Simple Web Indexing System for Humans) is a freely available search tool, originally by Kevin Hughes, that has had a long history, featuring numerous incarnations. One of the current versions is SWISH-E, available from *http://sunsite.berkeley. edu/SWISH-E/*. This chapter demonstrates how to add keyword searching to a web site with SWISH-E and just a little bit of Perl CGI scripting.

The creation of this keyword-search capability will require a number of steps:

1. Downloading the SWISH-E software source code and documentation.

2. Uncompressing and expanding the downloaded SWISH-E source code and documentation.

3. Compiling the SWISH-E source code to make an executable version of the program.

4. Running the compiled SWISH-E program from the command line to create an index file.

5. Creating a Perl CGI script that can run the SWISH-E program to retrieve a set of results matching a set of search terms, then formatting and returning those results to the web user.

Downloading and Compiling SWISH-E

Within a few clicks of the SWISH-E home page is a downloads section where one can obtain the latest version of the software. At the time of this writing, that was *ftp:// sunsite.berkeley.edu/pub/swish-e/swish-efiles.1.3.2.tar.gz*. We'll begin by downloading the file into a new directory on our web server, perhaps by using the Lynx command-line browser, as shown in Figure 13-1.

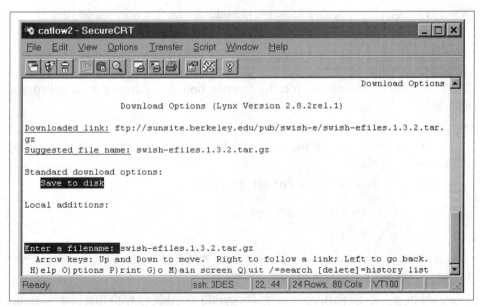

```
catlow2 - SecureCRT                                          _ □ ×
File  Edit  View  Options  Transfer  Script  Window  Help

┌─┐ ┌─┐ ┌─┐  ┌─┐┌─┐┌─┐  ┌─┐┌─┐┌─┐  ┌─┐┌─┐  ?
                                                  Download Options  ▲

                    Download Options (Lynx Version 2.8.2rel.1)

Downloaded link: ftp://sunsite.berkeley.edu/pub/swish-e/swish-efiles.1.3.2.tar.
gz
Suggested file name: swish-efiles.1.3.2.tar.gz

Standard download options:
   Save to disk

Local additions:



Enter a filename: swish-efiles.1.3.2.tar.gz
   Arrow keys: Up and Down to move.  Right to follow a link; Left to go back.
 H)elp O)ptions P)rint G)o M)ain screen Q)uit /=search [delete]=history list  ▼

Ready                              ssh: 3DES    22, 44   24 Rows, 80 Cols  VT100
```

Figure 13-1. Preparing to save a downloaded file in the Lynx web browser

Next, we uncompress the gzipped archive with a command like this:

```
[jbc@andros swish]$ gunzip swish-efiles.1.3.2.tar.gz
```

This will leave us with the original tar file, called swish-efiles.1.3.2.tar. Now we can use the tar command to extract the original files making up that archive. The x option to tar says to extract the original files from the archive, the v option says to do so verbosely (listing the extracted filenames as they are extracted), and the final f option says we are about to give the name of the tar file from which we want to do our extracting. Putting it all together, we get something like this:

```
[jbc@andros swish]$ tar xvf swish-efiles.1.3.2.tar
src/
src/Makefile
src/README-SWISH-E
src/check.c
src/check.h
src/config.h
```

And so on.

This creates a directory called src under the current directory, with that src directory containing the source code for the SWISH-E program. It's not ready to run, because it must first be compiled into an executable that can run on our machine. That sounds difficult, especially if you don't have any experience with compiling software, but the process is really not much different from installing proprietary software on a Windows or Macintosh computer, at least from the user's perspective. If everything goes right, it's easy. If there are problems, well, it may not work at all. But we can at least try it and see what happens.

Next we use the cd command to change to that src directory, and then use the more command to read the README-SWISH-E file. (It is common practice to distribute a README file with software in order to describe how the software is compiled and installed.)

This README file includes the following useful advice (after listing steps 1 and 2, which you've already performed in the course of downloading, ungzipping and untarring the gzipped tar archive):

```
3) In the Makefile change the path for the C compiler
        Change
        CC = /usr/local/bin/gcc
        to
        CC = {PATH}/gcc
```

This explains that we need to edit the file called Makefile in the src directory in order to specify where the gcc compiler can be found.

Using which gcc at the shell prompt will hopefully provide us with that information:

```
[jbc@andros src]$ which gcc
/usr/bin/gcc
```

It is then an easy task to use pico (or our editor of choice) to edit the Makefile in order to specify that location. In my case, that means editing the Makefile to replace this line:

```
CC = /usr/local/bin/gcc
```

with this:

```
CC = /usr/bin/gcc
```

Figure 13-2 shows a screenshot of what that looked like in my shell session, just after I'd made the change.

Next, the README-SWISH-E file advises that we need to make any "needed changes" in config.h to customize SWISH-E for our web site. The config.h file, which is another file extracted into the src directory from the tar archive, is a header file that will be used by the compiler during the compilation process. We don't need to know much about it, except to make our changes to it very carefully so as to avoid introducing problems in the parts that we don't understand.

In my case, I chose not to modify any of the default choices, so I was able to leave config.h as is. But you should feel free to look it over and read the embedded comments for instructions on making any changes you might want to make.

```
 catlow2 - SecureCRT                                    _ □ ×
 File  Edit  View  Options  Transfer  Script  Window  Help

 ┌──────────────────────────────────────────────────────────────┐
    UW PICO(tm) 3.5                    File: Makefile          ▲

 # Makefile for SWISH
 # Kevin Hughes, 3/12/95
 #
 # The code has been tested to compile on
 # Solaris and DEC   G.Hill  ghill@library.berkeley.edu 6/11/97
 #

 #CC= /opt/SUNWspro/bin/cc
 #CC= /usr/ccs/bin/ucbcc
 #CC = /vol/moby/moby_a/gnu/sun4_sunos5.1/bin/gcc
 CC = /usr/bin/gcc
 #CC = gcc

 #CFLAGS = -Xa
 CFLAGS= -O2
 #CFLAGS=-g

 LIBS=   -lm


 ^G Get Help  ^O WriteOut  ^R Read File ^Y Prev Pg  ^K Cut Text  ^C Cur Pos
 ^X Exit      ^J Justify   ^W Where is  ^V Next Pg  ^U UnCut Text^T To Spell ▼
 Ready                      ssh: 3DES   13, 11   24 Rows, 80 Cols  VT100
 └──────────────────────────────────────────────────────────────┘
```

Figure 13-2. Editing the Makefile in the pico text editor

> You'll notice, by the way, that the rules of how comments are speci-
> fied are different in C files than in Perl. The comments in config.h
> (which is a C file) are set off like this: /* this is a comment */. Also,
> the lines beginning with # symbols (like #define INDEXPERMS 0644) are
> *not* comments, but are very much "live" parts of the file. Don't remove
> the # symbols thinking you can thereby "activate" the configuration
> lines (like I did the first time I saw one of these files). Just modify the
> value at the end of the configuration line (if you need to), and leave the
> rest of the file alone.

The next step is for us to perform the compilation, by executing the make command
in the previously described src directory. Here's what I got when I ran that command in the shell:

```
[jbc@andros src]$ make
make CFLAGS="-g" check.o file.o index.o search.o error.o methods.o hash.o list.o mem.
o string.o merge.o swish.o stemmer.o docprop.o fs.o http.o httpserver.o
make[1]: Entering directory `/home/jbc/swish/src'
/usr/bin/gcc -c -g check.c
/usr/bin/gcc -c -g file.c
/usr/bin/gcc -c -g index.c
In file included from index.c:59:
```

```
docprop.h:30: warning: `struct metaMergeEntry' declared inside parameter list
docprop.h:30: warning: its scope is only this definition or declaration,
docprop.h:30: warning: which is probably not what you want.
/usr/bin/gcc -c -g search.c
/usr/bin/gcc -c -g error.c
/usr/bin/gcc -c -g methods.c
/usr/bin/gcc -c -g hash.c
/usr/bin/gcc -c -g list.c
/usr/bin/gcc -c -g mem.c
/usr/bin/gcc -c -g string.c
/usr/bin/gcc -c -g merge.c
/usr/bin/gcc -c -g swish.c
/usr/bin/gcc -c -g stemmer.c
/usr/bin/gcc -c -g docprop.c
/usr/bin/gcc -c -g fs.c
/usr/bin/gcc -c -g http.c
/usr/bin/gcc -c -g httpserver.c
make[1]: Leaving directory `/home/jbc/swish/src'
/usr/bin/gcc -o swish-e -g -O2 check.o file.o index.o search.o error.o methods.o
hash.o list.o mem.o string.o merge.o swish.o stemmer.o docprop.o fs.o http.o
httpserver.o  -lm
chmod 755 swish-e
```

Those warnings look scary, but apparently they didn't mean anything too bad, since
I was able to use the resulting binary (the swish-e file whose chmoding to mode 755 is
reported in the last line of make's output) without any problems.

The first test of that binary comes when we carry out the README file's next instruction: to run make test in the src directory:

```
[jbc@andros src]$ make test
./swish-e -i test.html -v -f index.swish
Indexing Data Source: "File-System"

Checking file "test.html"...
  test.html (48 words)

Removing very common words... no words removed.
Writing main index... 30 unique words indexed.
Writing file index... 1 file indexed.
Running time: Less than a second.
Indexing done!
./swish-e -f index.swish -w test
# SWISH format 1.3
# Swish-e format 1.3
#
# Name: (no name)
# Saved as: index.swish
# Counts: 30 words, 1 files
# Indexed on: 05/03/01 21:54:19 PST
# Description: (no description)
# Pointer: (no pointer)
# Maintained by: (no maintainer)
# DocumentProperties: Enabled
```

```
# Stemming Applied: 0
# Search words: test
# Number of hits: 1
1000 test.html "If you are seeing this, the test was successful!" 358
.
```

This test runs the swish-e binary in its *indexing mode*, in which it examines a sample data file and constructs a search index from it. It then runs the swish-e binary again, this time in *search mode*, meaning it takes a search phrase (the one-word query test, in this case) and searches through the index to see which of the files previously indexed contains the word or words making up that phrase. If everything worked properly, the test delivers the following successful-result message:

```
1000 test.html "If you are seeing this, the test was successful!" 358
```

Indexing with SWISH-E

The next step described in the README file is to copy the swish-e binary to a suitable location (like /usr/local/bin, a standard location for binary programs that you want to make available to every user on the server). The problem with that is, we will probably need root privileges on the server to write to that directory. What if we don't?

If we don't, we can just go ahead and stick the swish-e binary somewhere else. One obvious place to put it would be in a personal bin directory under our home directory. Just to keep things really simple, for this example we're going to stick it in the actual directory on the web server where the search CGI script is going to go. In this example, that directory turns out to be /w2/s/www.socalsail.com/html/search, which corresponds to the directory referenced by *http://www.socalsail.com/search* from the web server's perspective.

Besides copying the swish-e binary from the src directory to our search directory, we also need to copy the user.config file and edit it to reflect the parameters we want swish-e to use when creating its index of our site. This is different from the config.h header file we looked at a moment ago. That file told the make program some things it needed to know when creating the swish-e binary, which we have to do only once. The modified user.config file will tell the swish-e binary what to do when it is creating its search index, which is something it will need to do whenever the content on our web site changes.

In my case, I copied ~/swish/src/user.config to /w2/s/www.socalsail.com/html/search/scs.config, then edited the copied file to get lines that looked like this:

```
IndexFile /w2/s/www.socalsail.com/html/search/scs.index
# This is what the generated index file will be.

IndexName "SoCalSail search index"
IndexDescription "This is an index of the SoCalSail site."
IndexPointer "http://www.socalsail.com/search/"
```

```
IndexAdmin "John Callender (jbc@west.net)"

ReplaceRules replace "/w2/s/www.socalsail.com/html/" "/"
```

Most of these lines are pretty easy to figure out. The ReplaceRules directive is a little more complicated, however. It instructs swish-e that when creating its index, it should automatically transform the filenames in its record of the indexed files, converting them from Unix filesystem paths to web server paths. That way, when the CGI script is run to search the index, the returned results will be ready to go, without needing to be converted before being presented to the user. Realistically there isn't much difference between converting the filenames during indexing and converting them later in the CGI script that does the actual searching and returns swish-e's results, but it makes sense to do the work of converting those pathnames once, when creating the index, rather than doing it over and over again for each web search.

Anyway, I saved the scs.config file and ran the swish-e binary in index mode by following the instructions given in the SWISH-E web site's documentation:

```
[jbc@andros search]$ ./swish-e -c scs.config
Removing very common words... no words removed.
Writing main index... 5626 unique words indexed.
Writing file index... 486 files indexed.
Running time: 24 seconds.
Indexing done!
Running SWISH-E from the Command Line
```

Running SWISH-E from the Command Line

The way this chapter's web search tool is going to work is this: the user will type in some search terms in a web form and submit that form's contents to a CGI script. The CGI script will then execute the swish-e program, just as if we were running swish-e manually, from the command line. The CGI script will read the results back from swish-e, format those results in a suitable fashion, and display them back to the web user. It sounds complicated, but it all works out just fine.

To understand the part of the CGI script that executes the swish-e command-line query, we should now try running swish-e ourselves, from the command line. Here's an example that shows how such a command would look:

```
[jbc@andros search]$ ./swish-e -w "sails winches" -f ./scs_index
# SWISH format 1.3
# Swish-e format 1.3
#
# Name: SoCalSail search index
# Saved as: scs_index
# Counts: 5626 words, 486 files
# Indexed on: 25/02/01 15:57:07 PST
# Description: This is an index of the SoCalSail site.
# Pointer: http://www.socalsail.com/search/
# Maintained by: John Callender (jbc@west.net)
```

```
# DocumentProperties: Enabled
# Stemming Applied: 0
# Search words: sails winches
# Number of hits: 2
1000 /gear/category/sails.html "SoCalSail Gear Directory: Sailmakers and Sail Repair"
4987
982 /gear/category/winches.html "SoCalSail Gear Directory: Winches" 3430
.
```

We can see that the command, and the format of the returned results, are basically the same as they were when we ran make test after compiling the program. The swish-e command takes a -w command-line switch that is followed by the actual terms being searched for. Those terms are surrounded by quotation marks, either single or double quotation marks for the current purpose, which is just to mark the whole batch of words, however many there are, as a unit for associating with the -w switch. The command also takes an -f switch, followed by the name of the previously created index file we want to use for the actual searching.

The results consist of a number of comment lines, all of which begin with a # character, then the actual result lines, which take the form:

```
score path "page title" size
```

The *score* is a value from 0 to 1000 that is assigned by swish-e's internal relevence-ranking algorithm, which takes into account such things as the presence of search terms in the page's title, the proportion of search terms found on the page to the page's overall number of words, and so on. The *path* is the path and filename of the matching HTML page; in this case, it has already been modified to look like a web path rather than a filesystem path. Next comes the page's *title* (surrounded by double quotes), and then the page's *size* in bytes.

The final line returned by swish-e consists of a single period character. That is swish-e's way of telling you that it is officially finished returning its results.

Running SWISH-E via a CGI Script

As you can see, it's really pretty simple to run the swish-e program from the command line. As it turns out, running it as a CGI script isn't much harder. Example 13-1 shows a simple CGI script that does just that. This script, like all the other examples in this book, can be downloaded from the book's web site, at *http://www.elanus.net/book/*.

Example 13-1. A simple CGI script to do web site searching via SWISH-E

```
#!/usr/bin/perl -Tw

# search.cgi - simple web search script using swish-e

use strict;
```

Example 13-1. A simple CGI script to do web site searching via SWISH-E (continued)

```perl
use CGI qw(:standard);
$ENV{PATH} = '';

my $swish_program = '/w2/s/www.socalsail.com/html/search/swish-e';
my $index_file    = '/w2/s/www.socalsail.com/html/search/scs_index';

print header, <<"EOF";
<HTML>
<HEAD>
<TITLE>Search SoCalSail</TITLE>
</HEAD>
<BODY>
<H1>Search SoCalSail</H1>
EOF

my $search_words = param('search_words');

if (defined $search_words) {

    # run the external swish-e program to get the search results

    $search_words =~ s/[^\s\w\-\(\)]+//g; # lose naughty chars

    if ($search_words =~ /^([\s\w\-\(\)]*)$/) {
        # launder for taint-mode purposes
        $search_words = $1;
    }

    my $command = "$swish_program -w '$search_words' -f $index_file";

    my @results = `$command`;

    my $results = '';

    foreach (@results) {

        # process each line of the search results

        next if /^(#|\s|\.|err: )/; # skip comments, as well as space,
                                    # dot, and error lines

        my($score, $path, $title, $size)
            = /^(\d+)\s(\S+)\s"(.+)"\s(\d+)$/;

        $results .= <<"EOF";
<LI><STRONG><A HREF="$path">$title</A></STRONG><BR>
<EM>Score: $score, Size: $size</EM><BR>
EOF
    }

    close SWISH or die "can't close SWISH: $!";
```

Example 13-1. A simple CGI script to do web site searching via SWISH-E (continued)

```
    print "<H2>Results for '$search_words':</H2>\n";

    if ($results) {
        print "<UL>\n$results</UL>\n";
    } else {
        print "<P><STRONG>No results found.</STRONG></P>\n";
    }
    print "<HR>\n";
}

# print the form

print "<P><STRONG>Search terms:</STRONG><BR>\n",
    start_form,
    textfield(
        -name => 'search_words',
    ),
    "<BR>\n",
    submit(
        -name  => 'action',
        -value => 'Search',
    ),
    end_form,
    "\n</BODY></HTML>\n";
```

Like the guestbook CGI scripts we saw in Chapter 12, this one starts off with a -T in the shebang line, meaning it will run in taint mode. Because of that we will need to launder the user input before we can use it in certain types of potentially dangerous operations.

Next, the script pulls in the CGI.pm module with a use statement, and sets the command path to an explicit value (actually, to the empty string) with this statement:

```
    $ENV{PATH} = '';
```

That setting of the command path to an explicit value is one of the things required by the script's running in taint mode. The idea is that by requiring the script to set the command path, we make it harder for a malicious user to trick the script into running a command located somewhere on the system where we might not have been intending to run a command. Setting the command path to the empty string means that all external commands we wish to run will need the full pathname specified.

The script sets a few configuration variables, giving the location of the $swish_ program and the $index_file. We'll use those values when executing the external swish-e program from within the CGI script:

```
    my $swish_program = '/w2/s/www.socalsail.com/html/search/swish-e';
    my $index_file    = '/w2/s/www.socalsail.com/html/search/scs_index';
```

Obviously, your own copy of this script would need to be updated with the appropriate locations given for your copy of the swish-e program and its index file.

Next, we output the all-important CGI header and the top of the HTML page we are going to return.

Before continuing with the output of the HTML page the script is delivering, the script pauses to get the contents of the search_words form field that may (or may not) have been submitted to the script, and stores it in a scalar variable called $search_words:

```
my $search_words = param('search_words');
```

Now we test to see if that variable actually got anything, using Perl's defined function, which returns true if the thing that comes after it is anything other than the undefined value:

```
if (defined $search_words) {
```

This is almost, but not quite, the same thing as just saying:

```
if ($search_words) {
```

In the latter case, there are a few other values besides the undefined value that could cause the test to see a false value: the number 0, for example, or the string "0", or the empty string.

This is mostly just hair-splitting. But I thought it made more sense to use if (defined $search_words), instead of just if ($search_words), on the theory that we're really testing whether the user submitted something (anything) to the script via the search_words form element. If the user did, we should run this block, regardless of whether the submitted search_words happen to be one of those defined-but-false values mentioned previously.

In practice, it probably will never make much difference. It seems unlikely that this script would be used by someone wanting to search explicitly for the occurrence of the number 0 in a collection of web pages. But still, this is a good example of the kind of extremely literal thinking that programmers learn to cultivate. We should take the time to think carefully about how we want our script to behave when we are writing it because the script will never exhibit the sort of "common sense" that a human minion would display in the face of unanticipated circumstances. It will just do exactly what we told it to do, even if what we told it to do was not exactly what we would have wanted in this unforeseen situation.

So, having established via the logical test that this invocation of the search.cgi script is being executed in response to a user's submission of some search terms, the script proceeds to prepare those terms for handing off to the external swish-e program. The first step in that is a substitution variety of regular expression. It looks like this:

```
$search_words =~ s/[^\s\w\-\(\)]+//g; # lose naughty chars
```

This deletes any characters in $search_words that are anything other than whitespace characters, "word" characters (letters, numbers, and the underscore character), hyphens, or opening or closing parentheses. Among the "naughty" characters this will delete are semicolons, and left and right angle brackets (that is, the less than and greater than symbols, < and >). The thing that makes these characters naughty for the current script's purposes is this: in just a moment, we are going to pass the search words to a shell on the web server for interpretation as an external command to be executed. Without the deletion of the naughty characters, a malicious user could construct a $search_words string that fooled the shell into executing some other shell command of the malicious user's choosing. This would represent an extremely serious security problem.

The classic example of this would be a user managing to feed the following string to the shell via a CGI script:

```
some terms that don't matter; rm -rf /
```

Because the semicolon character tells the shell that we are ending one shell command and beginning another, whatever shell command gets this string as its argument will get as its argument only the stuff before the semicolon. Everything after that will be executed as a new, separate shell command, which in this case means that the shell will try to delete every file on the system. (The rm command deletes a file; the -rf argument says to do so recursively, deleting the contents of all subdirectories encountered, and to do so without prompting for confirmation; and the final / says to start the process at the top of the server's filesystem. Ouch.)

We definitely don't want to allow that. Anyway, once the dangerous characters have been removed, the following lines are used to launder the $search_words variable for taint-mode purposes. This time a conventional regular expression (a "regular" regular expression, if you will) is used instead of a substitution regular expression, but the search pattern is nearly identical. In this case, the pattern captures as much of the string as it can into the $1 backreference variable, capturing precisely those characters that we already know (because of the substitution operation just completed) will be the only characters left in the string. Then the captured string is stored back into $search_words, which completes the laundering operation and renders the string safe to use as far as Perl's tainting mechanism is concerned.

Next, the command line is constructed using the following line:

```
my $command = "$swish_program -w '$search_words' -f $index_file";
```

As we can see, this command line looks pretty much like the one we used to run a search with swish-e from the shell. We are using single quotes instead of double quotes to delimit the words stored in $search_words, but that's okay; for the current script's purposes the two types of quoting will work the same.

Next comes a very interesting line:

```
my @results = `$command`;
```

Those backward-leaning singlequotish characters are called *backticks*. Enclosing a string in them causes Perl to execute that string as an external shell command, and return the results. The command is subject to double-quote–style interpolation and interpretation before it is handed off to the shell, so this line executes the command stored in $command, rather than just giving the shell the literal string $command to execute, which obviously wouldn't be very helpful.

If we assign the results of a backtick operation to a scalar variable, we get all the output back as one big scalar, including any embedded newline characters (if the command returns more than one line of output). If we assign the results to an array variable, as we've done here, we get the results back as a list of lines.

Now we can process each line using a foreach loop, as shown here:

```
foreach (@results) {

    # process each line of the search results
```

In this case we're using the handy shortcut of not giving a scalar variable name after the foreach keyword, so the current item for each trip through the foreach loop will be stored in the default scalar variable, $_. We take advantage of that in the very next line, where we skip the current line and jump to the next trip through the foreach loop if the current line represents one of those extra lines returned by swish-e in addition to the actual results lines:

```
next if /^(#|\s|\.|err: )/; # skip comments, as well as space,
                            # dot, and error lines
```

This line uses the one-line form of an if statement, where the statement on the left of the if (the next function, in this case) will be executed only if the statement to the right of the if evaluates to true. In this case that statement is a regular expression, which, because it isn't tied to a variable with an explicit =~, does its matching against the default variable, $_. That variable conveniently contains the current line being processed by this trip through the foreach loop, so everything works out great.

So, the only lines returned from swish-e that will make it past this line in the foreach loop are the lines that represent actual search results. The script processes those results using another regex, which again matches against the default variable $_:

```
my($score, $path, $title, $size)
    = /^(\d+)\s(\S+)\s"(.+)"\s(\d+)$/;
```

This regex uses capturing parentheses to capture each of four items we're interested in from the search results into four different scalar variables: $score, $path, $title, and $size. Again, as we saw back in Chapter 8, putting a regular expression into a list context (by assigning its return value to a list of variables, as we've done here) causes the expression to return a list of the substrings that matched inside the pattern's capturing parentheses.

The actual pattern in this regular expression is something of a jawbreaker: ^(\d+)\ s(\S+)\s"(.+)"\s(\d+)$. This pattern starts by matching a series of one or more digits (via \d+) at the beginning of the string. These are captured into $1, or, as in this case, returned to the first variable in the list of variables on the left side of the assignment, courtesy of the parentheses surrounding the \d+. Then the pattern matches a single whitespace character, then one or more characters that are anything *other than* whitespace, capturing those nonwhitespace characters via a second pair of capturing parentheses. Next comes another whitespace character, then a pair of double quotes containing one or more of anything, with that anything being captured by the third set of parentheses. Finally, the expression matches another whitespace character, then captures one or more digits, with those digits needing to come at the very end of the string. If you figured all that out on your own just from reading the expression, good for you. If you didn't, don't sweat it.

In any event, now that we've captured the score, path, title, and size of this particular search result, we're ready to format it with some HTML markup and append it to our $results variable:

```
        $results .= <<"EOF";
<LI><STRONG><A HREF="$path">$title</A></STRONG><BR>
<EM>Score: $score, Size: $size</EM><BR>
EOF
```

Next we end the foreach loop begun earlier, and print the results (if any), or a "No results" message if there aren't any:

```
}

print "<H2>Results for '$search_words':</H2>\n";

if ($results) {
    print "<UL>\n$results</UL>\n";
} else {
    print "<P><STRONG>No results found.</STRONG></P>\n";
}
```

Next we print a horizontal rule tag (<HR>) to divide the search results from the part of the page that follows, and end the extended if block that was executed only if the user submitted some search terms:

```
    print "<HR>\n";
}
```

Finally, we print the actual HTML form used for searching. Notice how clever this is: if the user is invoking the script for the first time, without supplying any search terms, she just gets the search form (because there was nothing in the search_words parameter, so that whole part of the script that runs swish-e and returns the results gets skipped). If, however, the user is actually supplying some search terms to the script, she gets the results, followed by the original form, so the search can be modified and submitted again. Here's the part of the script that prints that form:

```
# print the form

print "<P><STRONG>Search terms:</STRONG><BR>\n",
```

```
        start_form,
        textfield(
            -name => 'search_words',
        ),
        "<BR>\n",
        submit(
            -name  => 'action',
            -value => 'Search',
        ),
        end_form,
        "\n</BODY></HTML>\n";
```

Several of the elements being printed here are `CGI.pm` functions that produce the various elements in the form. The end result is a form with a text field for entering search words, and a Submit button to execute the search. One nice thing about using the `CGI.pm` functions to produce our form is that the form elements are automatically made "sticky," meaning the previous search's search term will still be visible in the `search_words` text field in the form printed at the bottom of the results page. That's a handy feature for a user who wants to modify the search terms slightly and then run the search over again.

In a web browser, executing the same search seen earlier from the command line, this script produces a web page that looks like Figure 13-3.

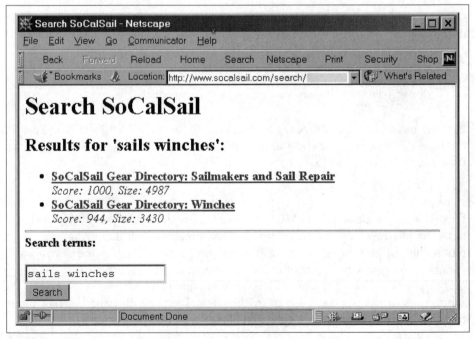

Figure 13-3. The search.cgi script in action

And there we have it: a simple CGI script which, in conjunction with SWISH-E, allows us to add full-text searching to our web site. Now we just need to remember to re-index our collection of documents whenever they change. If we have a frequently changing web site, one with a large numbers of contributors, perhaps, we can use the Unix cron facility to automate that task, as described previously in Chapter 10.

CHAPTER 14
Using HTML Templates

The next four chapters present an extended example from my own experience. A short time ago the principal of the local elementary school asked me to help with the school's entry in the International CyberFair, an event in which schools compete in creating web sites. The students had chosen to compete in the category "Local Leaders," meaning they would be creating a web site that profiled leaders from their local community. My contribution came in two forms: advising the students on basic HTML and web design issues, and building a set of Perl scripts to help simplify the process of creating and linking together a large collection of leader profiles and student pages.

This chapter begins that example by showing how to combine Perl with a simple template system in order to enforce design consistency across a large number of pages. Chapter 15 introduces the concept of using stored metainformation in a collection of HTML pages to automate the construction of links connecting those pages. Chapter 16 demonstrates how to pull out Perl code and place it in an external module file, so it can be shared across multiple Perl scripts. Finally, Chapter 17 shows how to build a CGI frontend to the system, helping inexperienced users add well-formed pages to it.

Using Templates

One of the first things I worked on for the Main School CyberFair project was a template system. Templates are a really obvious idea when you're creating a set of web pages. Even without knowing any Perl, most beginning web developers quickly realize that they can make their lives easier by using a set of predefined page templates as a starting point when creating a large site. It not only saves time for the developer, but it also helps ensure design consistency across multiple pages, enhancing the site's usability.

Tom Christiansen and Nathan Torkington's *Perl Cookbook* (my favorite O'Reilly book, out of the 30 or 40 I've obsessively collected over the years) features code to automate the filling in of a template with chunks of text to produce a finished HTML page. The following discussion borrows heavily (or if you prefer, "steals shamelessly") from that code, which you can find in their Recipe 20.9.

Let's start with a simple example. Suppose we have a template that looks like this:

```
<HTML>
<HEAD>
<TITLE>%%title%%</TITLE>
</HEAD>
<BODY>

<P><STRONG>Main School CyberFair: Local Leaders</STRONG></P>

%%content%%

</BODY>
</HTML>
```

In this template, %%title%% and %%content%% have been used as placeholders for the customized fillings that will eventually flesh out the template into a finished page. We could just use our text editor's copy-and-paste commands to fill in those fillings manually, but with just a little bit of Perl we can create a subroutine that will perform the task more quickly and reliably:

```
sub template {

    # fill in a template with custom fillings.
    #
    # $text is the template itself. $fillings is a reference to a
    # hash with keys consisting of the %%quoted%% placeholder
    # names, and values consisting of the actual text to plug
    # into those placeholders.

    my ($text, $fillings) = @_;

    $text =~ s{ %% ( .*? ) %% }
             { exists( $fillings->{$1} )
                   ? $fillings->{$1}
                   : ''
             }gex;

    return $text;
}
```

This might look a little daunting at first, but it's actually pretty simple once we figure out what's going on. First, let's see it in action. We would invoke the &template subroutine like this:

```
my $template = <<EndOfText;
<HTML>
```

```
<HEAD>
<TITLE>%%title%%</TITLE>
</HEAD>
<BODY>

<P><STRONG>Main School CyberFair: Local Leaders</STRONG></P>

%%content%%

</BODY>
</HTML>
EndOfText

my %params = (
    title   => 'This is my page title',
    content => <<EndOfText,
<H1>This is my main heading</H1>

<P>This is my actual content.</P>
EndOfText
);

my $finished_page = &template($template, \%params);
```

In this case, we would get this back from the &template routine:

```
<HTML>
<HEAD>
<TITLE>This is my page title</TITLE>
</HEAD>
<BODY>

<P><STRONG>Main School CyberFair: Local Leaders</STRONG></P>

<H1>This is my main heading</H1>

<P>This is my actual content.</P>

</BODY>
</HTML>
```

Now that we've seen what it does, let's dissect how the &template subroutine actually does it. There are only three statements in the whole subroutine (though the middle one has been broken up over five lines in an effort to make it more readable). The first statement is just the standard assignment of the subroutine's arguments to a pair of my variables: $text (which contains the text of our template), and $fillings, which is a reference to a hash. That hash has keys that correspond to the names of our template's placeholders, and values that correspond to the text we want to fill in in place of those placeholders. So far so good.

The last statement in the subroutine just returns the finished page.

But that statement in the middle is a thorny one. Here it is again:

```
$text =~ s{ %% ( .*? ) %% }
          { exists( $fillings->{$1} )
                  ? $fillings->{$1}
                  : ''
          }gex;
```

First off, we can see from the =~ that there is a regular expression match going on, with $text (which holds our template) being the thing matched against. The expression is actually the substitution variety of regular expression, as we can see from the initial s.

The expression uses paired curly braces to mark off the search pattern and the replacement string. If we rewrote it in one line it would have a form like this:

```
s{search pattern}{replacement string};
```

It uses the /x modifier, which lets us embed nonmeaningful whitespace inside the search pattern, as was discussed back in Chapter 8. It also uses the /g modifier, which you will recall causes it to keep matching repeatedly even after the first match has been made. Finally, it uses the /e modifier, which we haven't seen before.

The /e modifier is very powerful: it causes the replacement part of the pattern to be evaluated not as a double-quoted string (as it normally would be), but instead as a full-fledged Perl expression, which will be executed for its return value.

I've rarely had reason to actually use the /e regex modifier (probably because I find it vaguely scary), but I have to admit that in this case it provides a very elegant solution. Let's look now at what, exactly, this regular expression does.

In the first half of the expression, the search part, it's looking for things that match the pattern { %% (.*?) %% }. Bearing in mind that the whitespace isn't significant (courtesy of the /x modifier), this search pattern says to match any group of characters (including no characters at all) that are found between pairs of doubled percent signs (%%). (The "any group of characters" part comes via the .* because that, as you'll recall, means "match zero or more of anything".) The question mark (?) after the .* means to match minimally; that is, only match as much as we have to in order to make the entire expression match successfully.

A quick example: if we match against the string '%%first%% and %%second%%', this expression's capturing parentheses will get 'first', and then will get 'second' (courtesy of the /g modifier). If we didn't have the ? after the .* (that is, if the search part of the expression looked like { %% (.*) %% }), the greedy nature of the * quantifier would mean that the parentheses would capture as much as they could, or 'first%% and %%second', which wouldn't be very helpful.

So, the search pattern captures anything delimited by doubled percent signs. In other words, it matches the embedded placeholders in our template. But what does it do to them? Let's examine the replacement part of the expression.

That replacement part, if we remove the fancy line breaks and indenting, runs the following chunk of Perl code:

```
exists( $fillings->{$1} ) ? $fillings->{$1} : ''
```

This is our first exposure to Perl's fiendishly clever *conditional operator*. The conditional operator is something of a rite of passage for Perl programmers; once you start using it you'll have a harder time passing as an accidental programmer. The conditional operator performs a logical test, and depending on the outcome of that test, return either one value or another.

Here's a simplified view of the conditional operator:

```
logical test ? return value if true : return value if false
```

The conditional operator works a little like a compact if-else block. In this case, we're saying "If $fillings->{$1} exists, return it. Otherwise, return the empty string."

So, what is $fillings->{$1}? The $1, you already know, contains the name of this particular filling, captured from inside its doubled percent signs by the capturing parentheses in the search pattern. The -> symbol is a *dereferencing arrow*, to let us access an individual element in the hash whose reference is stored in $fillings. Just as we can dereference object references to access those objects' methods via something like $object->methodname (as we learned back in Chapter 11), we can access individual values in a hash reference with a construction like $hashref->{key}. The curly braces around {key} tell us this is a hash reference being dereferenced. If we happen to have an array reference we want to dereference, we use square brackets, like this: $aryref->[1].

Notice how the conditional operator lets us first check that the particular key we want to look up in the %{$fillings} hash exists (by using the exists function in the logical test). Then we can return either the value associated with it (if it does exist) or the empty string (if it doesn't). This is a clever way to avoid having our script generate a lot of "Use of uninitialized variable" warnings, if a particular %%name%% in our template doesn't have a corresponding entry in the hash referenced by $fillings.

So, this will let us merge a standard HTML page template with some custom fillings from within our Perl program. That HTML page template can be made as fancy as we like. We can even store the template as a separate file, and allow people who aren't Perl-literate to modify it. (The *Perl Cookbook*'s version of this &template subroutine works like this, taking a pathname pointing at a separate template file as its first argument, rather than taking the template itself.)

Reading Fillings Back In

This template system works great as long as we only wish to create template-based pages, either as output of a dynamic CGI script or as a one-way processing of some structured data into a set of finished web pages.

Better Template Systems from CPAN

This chapter's template-system example works fine as long as you only want to substitute simple scalar values into a template. As you work with templates more, though, you're going to find yourself wanting to do fancier things. For example, wouldn't it be cool to be able to pass an array variable to the template, and have the template loop over the values in that array, interpolating them into the finished document? Or to embed an actual Perl expression in the template, and have that expression evaluated for its return value?

Any time you find yourself saying, "Wouldn't it be cool if I had some Perl code to do X?", you should think of CPAN. If the thing you want to do is something that others might also want to do, there's probably already a CPAN module (maybe several modules) to do it.

In this case, the challenge isn't in finding a template module, but in choosing which of the several excellent template modules available on CPAN to use. One that I recommend highly is Mark-Jason Dominus' `Text::Template`, which lets you put arbitrary Perl expressions surrounded by curly braces into your template, then execute that code when the template is filled out.

Andrew Wardley's `Template-Toolkit` module collection is a more ambitious undertaking, which creates its own special-purpose template language, designed to be easy for non-Perl–literate users of your templates to understand, while still being powerful enough to perform nearly any nifty template trick you could think of.

Another variation on the template theme is Gerald Richter's `Embperl`. `Embperl` is an extension to the Apache web server that lets you embed Perl code inside your HTML documents, with the server executing that code for you and incorporating the result into the finished HTML document before returning it to the requesting web user.

But what happens if we want to make changes to the template, and then have those changes reflected in a bunch of HTML pages that have already been created? In the case of the Main School CyberFair project, I wanted to be able to have participating students post student pages describing themselves, and leader pages describing the leaders they had interviewed, even before the site's HTML design was finished. Later, I wanted to be able to update those pages to reflect the latest version of the site's template, without having to manually modify each page. What I needed was a way to read the fillings back in from a previously created page, separating those fillings (which I wanted to keep) from the HTML markup that was part of the original template (which I wanted to replace). To do that, I needed to add some additional structure to the HTML documents.

Some structure is built into every HTML page already, of course. For example, the page's title is easy to extract because it sits between the <TITLE> and </TITLE> tags.

The customized content on these pages, though, was harder because there was no structure in the page to separate that content from the template's standard HTML.

So, I added some structure. Let's do that now. With a few comment tags, we can create a container to hold the content filling, and make it easy to pluck out later on. We do that by modifying the template shown earlier to look like this:

```
<HTML>
<HEAD>
<TITLE>%%title%%</TITLE>
</HEAD>
<BODY>

<P><STRONG>Main School CyberFair: Local Leaders</STRONG></P>

<!--begin content-->

%%content%%

<!--end content-->

</BODY>
</HTML>
```

Now we can write a &read_page subroutine that will take a full pathname as its argument, and will return a hash of page fillings extracted from the page at that location. With this routine we're going to introduce a common Perl idiom: using shift to assign the subroutine's argument to a temporary variable. This works because inside a subroutine, shift operates by default on the special array @_, which holds the subroutine's arguments. Anyway, here's the subroutine:

```
sub read_page {

    # invoked with a full pathname as argument,
    # returns a hash of page fillings suitable
    # for feeding to &template

    my $pathname = shift;
    my %param;

    open IN, "$pathname"
        or die "Couldn't open $pathname for reading: $!";
    my $page = join '', <IN>;
    close IN;

    if ($page =~ m#<TITLE>(.*)</TITLE>#i) {
        $param{title} = $1;
    }
    if ($page =~ /<!--begin content-->\s*(.+?)\s*<!--end content-->/s) {
        $param{content} = $1;
    }

    return %param;
}
```

See how easy that is? First, we read the whole page into $page using the trick of join-ing each line read from <IN> with the empty string. Then we just use a couple of reg-ular expressions to pluck out the fillings. As long as the `<!--begin content-->` and `<!--end content-->` comment tags are there, the content filling will be plucked out just fine.

A problem will occur, though, if we write a script to traverse our site and rewrite its HTML pages to reflect the latest version of our template, and that script encounters an HTML page that wasn't based on the template. Without the `<!--begin content-->` and `<!--end content-->` tags, nothing will be captured into `$param{content}`, and when the page is written out its content will be empty.

We can solve this problem by having some embedded metainformation that flags the page as having been created from our template. The HTML spec already has a way to embed metainformation into an HTML page: the META tag. The first time I encoun-tered the META tag was when I wanted to make my web pages more search-engine friendly by putting tags like these into the pages' HEAD elements:

```
<META NAME="keywords" CONTENT="rutabagas, walnuts">
<META NAME="description" CONTENT="A page about rutabagas and walnuts.">
```

We can add additional META headers of our own devising. For example, we can use a META header named type to flag a page as having been created from the CyberFair template, using a CONTENT attribute of cf:

```
<META NAME="type" CONTENT="cf">
```

Now we can have our script check for the presence of the type META header, and rewrite a page using the new template only if the header has a CONTENT attribute of cf. We can also use this approach to have multiple templates for the same site, each with its own name.

In the CyberFair project I worked on, I wanted the option of storing several other pieces of information with the site's HTML pages for later extraction via the &read_ page subroutine. For a *student page* (that is, a personal page describing a particular student participating in the project), I wanted to be able to extract the student's full name (which we actually limited to first name and last initial, for privacy reasons). For *leader pages*, I wanted to be able to extract the leader's full name, as well as the identities of the students who wrote about and photographed that particular leader. I could then use that information to create links from leader pages to the pages of stu-dents who interviewed them, and from those student pages back to the leader pages for the leaders they interviewed. With a tight deadline and several hundred student pages and leader pages to cross-link to each other, this approach promised to save lots of time.

The full HEAD part of a student page ended up looking something like this:

```
<HEAD>
<TITLE>John C.'s Personal Page</TITLE>
```

```
<META NAME="type" CONTENT="cf">
<META NAME="name" CONTENT="John C.">
</HEAD>
```

Leaders' names were stored in the leader pages in a similar fashion, except that I used the leaders' full names, and the leaders got some extra META headers pointing to the pages of students who participated in that profile:

```
<HEAD>
<TITLE>Al Gore's Leader Profile</TITLE>
<META NAME="type" CONTENT="cf">
<META NAME="name" CONTENT="Al Gore">
<META NAME="writer" CONTENT="nakasone/johnc">
<META NAME="photographer" CONTENT="nakasone/johnc">
</HEAD>
```

The "writer" and "photographer" META headers here have CONTENT attributes that point to the appropriate student files for this particular leader: a student file in the nakasone directory (named for the student's teacher) and named johnc.html (for the student's first name and last initial). We'll come back to these META headers in the next chapter, where we'll see how they were used to automatically construct links connecting the site's pages to each other.

Rewriting an Entire Site

Now let's take a look at Example 14-1, which presents an early version of make_cf.plx. I wrote this script to descend recursively through the CyberFair site, reading in HTML pages and, for those that had the required <META NAME="type" CONTENT="cf"> header, rewriting them from the latest version of the site's template.

This is a pretty big script to be throwing at you all at once, but most of it consists of components we've seen already, either earlier in this chapter or in previous chapters. The new parts will be discussed in detail shortly. As with all the examples in this book, you can download it from the book's web site, at *http://www.elanus.net/book/*.

Example 14-1. Early version of make_cf.plx

```
#!/usr/bin/perl -w

# make_cf.plx

# rewrite all the pages on the CyberFair site that have 'type'
# META headers of 'cf', using the current template.

use strict;
use File::Find;

find(\&process, '/w1/s/socalsail/cyberfair');

sub process {
```

Example 14-1. Early version of make_cf.plx (continued)

```perl
    # this is invoked by File::Find's find function for each
    # file it recursively finds.

    return unless /\.html$/;
    my $filename  = $File::Find::name;
    my %page_hash = &read_page($filename);
    return unless defined $page_hash{type}
        and $page_hash{type} eq 'cf';
    &write_page($filename, &build_page(%page_hash))
        or die "couldn't write_page for file '$filename'\n";
}

sub read_page {

    # invoked with a full pathname as argument,
    # returns a hash suitable for
    # feeding to &build_page

    my $pathname = shift;
    my %return_hash;

    open IN, "$pathname"
        or die "Couldn't open $pathname for reading: $!";
    my $page = join '', <IN>;
    close IN;

    return unless $page;

    if ($page =~ m#<TITLE>(.*)</TITLE>#i) {
        $return_hash{title} = $1;
    }
    while ($page =~ m#<META\s+NAME="([^"]+)"\s+CONTENT="([^"]*)">#gi) {
        $return_hash{$1} = $2;
    }
    if ($page =~
        /.+<!--begin content-->\s*(.+?)\s*<!--end content-->/s) {
        $return_hash{content} = $1;
    }

    return %return_hash;
}

sub build_page {

    # given a suitable parameter hash, build a CyberFair page
    # and return it

    my %param = (
        type        =>    'cf',                  # these are
        title       =>    'Untitled Document',   # defaults...
        description =>    '',
        keywords    =>    '',
```

Example 14-1. Early version of make_cf.plx (continued)

```
        content      =>    '',
        @_,                 # supplied name-value pairs come in here
    );

    # translate the various META params into a merged $meta_block for
    # substituting into the template.

    my @meta_params = qw(type description keywords);
    my $meta_block = '';

    foreach my $meta_param (@meta_params) {
        if ($param{$meta_param}) {
            $meta_block .= <<EndOfText;
<META NAME="$meta_param" CONTENT="$param{$meta_param}">
EndOfText
            delete $param{$meta_param};
        }
    }

    $param{meta_block} = $meta_block;

    my $template = <<EndOfText;
<HTML>
<HEAD>
<TITLE>%%title%%</TITLE>
%%meta_block%%
</HEAD>

<BODY>

<TABLE BORDER=0 CELLSPACING=0 CELLPADDING=10>
<TR VALIGN="top">
<TD WIDTH=150 BGCOLOR="#99CC66">

<!--begin left navbar-->

<P ALIGN="center"><A HREF="/cyberfair/"><IMG
SRC="/cyberfair/shared/avo_sm4.gif" HEIGHT=100 WIDTH=100 BORDER=0 VSPACE=5></A><BR>
<A HREF="/cyberfair/"><STRONG>CyberFair 2000 Project</STRONG></A><BR>
<FONT SIZE="-1">Main School<BR>
Carpinteria, California, USA</FONT></P>

<P><STRONG>Carpinteria Valley Leaders<BR>
<FONT SIZE="-1">
<A HREF="/cyberfair/leader/government/">Government</A><BR>
<A HREF="/cyberfair/leader/environment/">Environment</A><BR>
<A HREF="/cyberfair/leader/school/">School</A><BR>
<A HREF="/cyberfair/leader/business/">Business</A><BR>
<A HREF="/cyberfair/leader/arts/">Arts & Entertainment</A><BR>
<A HREF="/cyberfair/leader/sports/">Sports & Recreation</A><BR>
<A HREF="/cyberfair/leader/medical/">Medical</A><BR>
<A HREF="/cyberfair/leader/community/">Community
```

Example 14-1. Early version of make_cf.plx (continued)

```
Services</A></FONT></STRONG></P>

<P><STRONG>About This Site<BR>
<FONT SIZE="-1"><A HREF="/cyberfair/student/">Who Made This
Site?</A><BR>
<A HREF="/cyberfair/avocado/">Why an Avocado Tree?</A><BR>
<A HREF="/cyberfair/narrative/">Project Narrative</A>
<A HREF="/cyberfair/sources/">Information
Sources</A></FONT></STRONG></P>

<!--end left navbar-->

</TD>

<TD>

<!--begin content-->

%%content%%

<!--end content-->

</TD>
</TR>
</TABLE>

</BODY>
</HTML>
EndOfText

    # replace %%quoted%% words with values in %param hash
    $template =~ s{ %% ( .*? ) %% }
                  { exists( $param{$1} )
                        ? $param{$1}
                        : ''
                  }gex;
    return $template;
}

sub write_page {

    # invoked with a full path and an HTML page,
    # writes the page to that file location.
    # will create directories as it goes, as needed.
    # issues a warning and returns undef (without
    # writing anything) if the page exists already
    # and is anything other than a regular text file.

    my($full_path, $made_page) = @_;
    unless ($full_path =~ /\.html$/) {
        warn "$full_path does not end with '.html'\n";
        return;
```

Example 14-1. Early version of make_cf.plx (continued)

```
    }
    unless ($full_path =~ /^\//) {
        warn "$full_path does not begin with a slash\n";
        return;
    }
    if (-l $full_path) {
        warn "$full_path is a symbolic link\n";
        return;
    }
    if (-B $full_path) {
        warn "$full_path is a binary file\n";
        return;
    }

    # still here? good. make any needed directories...

    my $dir_path = $full_path;
    $dir_path    =~ s{/[^/]+$}{}; # lose last '/' and ensuing filename

    &make_dirs($dir_path)
        or die "problem with &make_dirs on '$dir_path'...";

    open OUT, ">$full_path" or
        die "can't open $full_path for writing: $!";
    print OUT $made_page;
    close OUT or die "can't close $full_path filehandle: $!";

    chmod 0644, $full_path or
        die "couldn't chmod $full_path to 0644";
    1;
}

sub make_dirs {

    # invoked with an argument consisting of a full pathname,
    # split it on '/' and check each component to see if it
    # is a currently existing directory. If it isn't, create it
    # with permissions of 0755.

    # the last component is skipped if it contains any periods. this
    # is intended to avoid accidentally creating a directory out of
    # what should be a filename, e.g.: '/foo/index.html/'.
    # normally, though, the filename should not be passed to
    # the routine. note that this will cause the subroutine to fail
    # to create the last directory in a path if that directory's
    # name contains a dot.

    # for the sake of (minimal) security, this routine will abort
    # if the supplied argument contains two periods in a row ('..').

    my $full_path = shift;
    return if $full_path =~ /\.\./; # doesn't trust people passing '..'
```

Example 14-1. Early version of make_cf.plx (continued)

```
    my @dirs = split(/\//, $full_path);

    my $last_element = pop @dirs;
    unless ($last_element =~ /\./) {
        push @dirs, $last_element; # put it back on if no '.'
    }

    my $this_dir;

    umask 022;

    foreach (@dirs) {
        next unless $_; # empty element
        $this_dir .= "/$_";
        if (-e $this_dir) {
            unless (-d $this_dir) {
                warn "$this_dir path component exists but is not a
directory\n";
                return;
            }
        } else {
            mkdir $this_dir, 0777
                or die "couldn't mkdir $this_dir: $!";
        }
    }
    1;
}
```

In a certain sense, all the action in the script takes place in the following line:

```
    find(\&process, '/w1/s/socalsail/cyberfair');
```

This uses File::Find's find function, passing it a reference to the &process subroutine, as well as a starting directory of /w1/s/socalsail/cyberfair. That &process subroutine will then be executed for every file found by the find function as it recursively descends through the directories under that starting directory. The &process subroutine concludes with the following three statements:

```
    my %page_hash = &read_page($filename);
    return unless defined $page_hash{type}
        and $page_hash{type} eq 'cf';
    &write_page($filename, &build_page(%page_hash))
        or die "couldn't write_page for file '$filename'\n";
```

The first statement uses the &read_page subroutine (which we saw an example of already) to read the HTML page in question, storing its components in the %page_ hash variable. The second statement is a safety valve, of sorts. It returns from the &process subroutine without making any changes to the file unless the file has a META header of the form <META NAME="type" CONTENT="cf">.

Let's look at the third line, starting with the innermost pair of parentheses and working our way out. This line invokes the &build_page subroutine with the %page_hash

hash as its argument, then takes the result of that and uses it as an argument (along with the current file's $filename) to the &write_page subroutine.

The &build_page subroutine demonstrates a very interesting approach for receiving the arguments with which the routine was invoked:

```
sub build_page {

    # given a suitable parameter hash, build a CyberFair page
    # and return it

    my %param = (
        type        =>    'cf',                    # these are
        title       =>    'Untitled Document',     # defaults...
        description =>    '',
        keywords    =>    '',
        content     =>    '',
        @_,                     # supplied name-value pairs come in here
    );
```

This is letting us supply the arguments to the subroutine as a hash, with *named parameters*, instead of supplying those arguments as an array, with *positional parameters*, as we've done with our subroutines up until now. The named parameters are used as part of the initialization of the hash variable %param, which we will use later in the subroutine to access those parameters.

This solves a problem you may have noticed already. It can be a real pain to have to remember the proper order of our subroutine arguments, especially when we have more than two or three of them. The approach used here, which is described in the *Perl Cookbook*'s Recipe 10.7, lets us supply them in any order we like, as long as they are associated with the appropriate name. As a bonus, we can specify some default parameters in the subroutine's %param hash initialization, and those defaults will be overwritten by any supplied arguments with the same name. This works because the supplied parameters arrive in the hash assignment via the special @_ array, which is given last in that assignment. When we assign a key-value pair to a hash that already contains a value for that key, we simply overwrite the original with the new arrival. For example, the following code prints "last":

```
my %hash = (
    key => 'first',
    key => 'last',
);

print $hash{key}; # prints 'last'
```

The &build_page subroutine takes the various parameters in the %param hash and modifies them to create a meta_block parameter that is the result of merging all the parameters whose names are given in the array variable @meta_params. In other words, it takes a list of parameter names corresponding to the META headers in the page being built, and merges them all together into one big meta_block parameter:

```
# translate the various META params into a merged $meta_block for
# substituting into the template.

my @meta_params = qw(type description keywords);
my $meta_block = '';

foreach my $meta_param (@meta_params) {
    if ($param{$meta_param}) {
        $meta_block .= <<EndOfText;
<META NAME="$meta_param" CONTENT="$param{$meta_param}">
EndOfText
        delete $param{$meta_param};
    }
}

$param{meta_block} = $meta_block;
```

When I first built this script it didn't do this. I only added this capability later, when I realized I had a problem. If I wanted to support the 'description' META header used by third-party search engines to associate a brief description with a page, I needed to pluck that information out in the &read_page routine, and write it back out to the finished page with the &write_page routine. But I couldn't just have a section of the template that looked like:

```
<META NAME="description" CONTENT="%%description%%">
```

because then if a particular page didn't have any 'description' META header, the &template routine we saw earlier would produce a page with the following HTML:

```
<META NAME="description" CONTENT="">
```

This might cause a third-party search engine to display no description at all for the page, rather than displaying default text (i.e., an excerpt from the beginning of the page).

The workaround code given here loops through a list of potential META headers that might be in the %param hash, creating suitable META tags for any that do exist, appending those tags to a $meta_block scalar variable, and deleting them from the %param hash. Then, when it's all done looping, the $meta_block is stuck into the %param hash, keyed on the string meta_block. Then the template simply substitutes the whole string, containing all the appropriate META headers, in place of a %%meta_block%% placeholder.

The rest of the &build_page subroutine contains the definition of the $template scalar, the invocation of the same substitution code (more or less) that we previously saw in the &template routine, and the returning of the finished HTML page. (Simply embedding the page template into the &build_page routine was a shortcut that worked fine for this project, where I only needed a single template and didn't need to have non-Perl–literate people maintaining it. A more flexible approach is described in the accompanying sidebar, "What About Multiple Templates?")

What About Multiple Templates?

A useful enhancement to the &build_page routine described in the accompanying text would be to make it work more like the original version, which I stole from Recipe 20.9 in the *Perl Cookbook*, by having it support multiple page templates stored as a series of external text files. This would allow us to have one script using different templates for creating different types of pages, and would also let those templates be modified by any of the unfortunately large number of web developers who have yet to learn Perl.

Here's a modified version of the &build_page routine that works as a drop-in replacement for the original one, accepting the same arguments and producing the same output but supporting multiple external template files stored in a designated $template_dir:

```perl
sub build_page {

    # given a suitable parameter hash,
    # build a finished HTML page and return it

    my %param = (
        type        => 'cf',
        title       => 'Untitled Document',
        description => '',
        keywords    => '',
        content     => '',
        @_,# supplied name-value pairs come in here
    );

    my $template_dir  =
        '/w1/s/socalsail/maint/template';

    # translate the various META params
    # into a merged $meta_block for
    # substituting into the template.

    my @meta_params = qw(type description keywords);
    my $meta_block = '';

    foreach my $meta_param (@meta_params) {
        if ($param{$meta_param}) {
            $meta_block .= <<EndOfText;
<META NAME="$meta_param" CONTENT="$param{$meta_param}">
EndOfText
            delete $param{$meta_param};
        }
    }

    $param{meta_block} = $meta_block;
```

—continued—

```perl
    my $template_path = $template_dir . '/' .
        $param{type} . '.tem';

    open TEMPLATE, "$template_path"
        or die "can't open $template_path for reading: $!";
    my $template = join '', <TEMPLATE>;
    close TEMPLATE;

    unless ($template) {
        die "empty template loaded from '$template_path'";
    }

    # replace %%quoted%% words using %param hash
    $template =~ s{ %% ( .*? ) %% }
                  { exists( $param{$1} )
                        ? $param{$1}
                        : ''
                  }gex;
    return $template;
}
```

Now we can just keep a collection of template files in the location specified by $template_dir, with those files being named something like cf.tem (for the template of type 'cf') or walnuts.tem (for type 'walnuts').

Chapter 15 continues this example, showing the next stage in the make_cf.plx script's evolution. That version of the script goes beyond simply rewriting pages to make them fit the latest version of the site's template, and actually creates links linking the various pages in the site to each other.

CHAPTER 15

Generating Links

This chapter continues the example begun in Chapter 14, which describes a project I participated in that involved creating a template system for an elementary-school web site. At this point in the project, with a template system and a tool for automatically rebuilding pages when the template changed, students were able to begin creating the two types of pages that would make up most of the site:

- Personal pages for each participating student, with information about their favorite activities, their participation in the project, and so on
- Leader pages profiling local leaders in a variety of categories: school, government, business, and so on

This chapter describes the next stage in the project, in which I created a system to automatically generate links between the site's pages.

The Docbase Concept

The approach I took to building this feature was heavily influenced by Jon Udell's concept of a *docbase*. As described in his book *Practical Internet Groupware*, a docbase is something of a hybrid, having features of both a document collection and a database.

A *document collection*, from this point of view, is a largely freeform collection of information. Whatever relationships connect the various individual documents in the collection are apparent only to a human being, rather than being encoded in a way that can be understood by a computer. Most small web sites are document collections. As a side effect of their freeform nature, the links connecting the pages of such a site must be created and maintained by a human being.

A database, on the other hand, features a layer of *metainformation* (that is, information about the underlying information) that describes the database's content in terms meaningful to a computer. There is a great deal of structure to a database; information is arranged in columns and rows within separate tables, with explicit relationships connecting the tables to each other. Many large web sites are based on an underlying database. Because of the structural information in the database, the links connecting the various pages of such a site can be generated automatically.

A docbase, again, is a hybrid between these two approaches. Like a document collection, its information is stored in a collection of largely freeform files. Like a database, though, there is some metainformation embedded in those documents, structural information that is understandable by a computer. In the case of the Main School CyberFair site, most of that metainformation took the form of special META headers. (The rest of the metainformation was derived by the link-generating program from the pages' location in the site's directory structure.)

As we saw in the last chapter, the HEAD portion of a particular leader profile page on the site might look like this:

```
<HEAD>
<TITLE>Al Gore's Leader Profile</TITLE>
<META NAME="type" CONTENT="cf">
<META NAME="name" CONTENT="Al Gore">
<META NAME="writer" CONTENT="nakasone/johnc">
<META NAME="photographer" CONTENT="nakasone/johnc">
</HEAD>
```

This chapter demonstrates the Perl script I created to turn that metainformation into automatically generated links between the site's pages.

The CyberFair Site's Architecture

The architecture that our site's design team had worked out looked something like the diagram in Figure 15-1. Besides a few top-level pages, the bulk of the site was to consist of two kinds of pages: leader profiles, grouped into a number of categories (like "Government," "School," etc.), and student pages, grouped according to classroom.

So, in terms of automatically generated links, we needed to produce the following:

- Links from the "who made this site" page to each classroom page
- Links from each classroom page to each student page for that classroom
- Links from each student page to the classroom page for that class
- Links from each student's page to any leader pages that the student was involved in creating
- Links from each leader category page to the leader pages that fell under that category
- Links from each leader page to the category page that the leader fell under
- Links from each leader page to the pages of the students who were involved in creating it

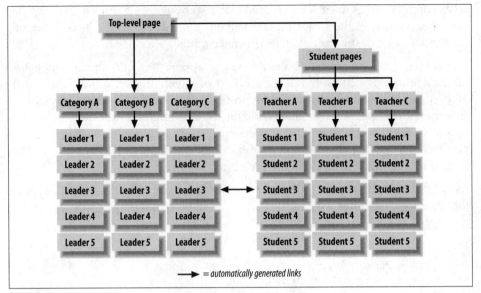

Figure 15-1. Site architecture for the CyberFair entry

To generate those links, the make_cf.plx script needed to traverse the site's pages twice: once to read all the pages and build up a data structure based on their metainformation, and the second time to rewrite each page with links to all the other pages in the structure.

Example 15-1 gives an updated version of make_cf.plx that can do that. There's a lot of script here, partly because of the many different kinds of links the script had to create, and partly because of all the copy-and-paste I used in developing it. For our current purposes, though, we need to look at only a small chunk of the script. I've highlighted that portion in the printed example, and will explain it in the following discussion. The rest of the script is mostly variations on the same theme; you're welcome to examine it, but we won't be discussing it in detail here.

Like all the examples in this book, you can download this script from the book's web site, at *http://www.elanus.net/book/*.

Example 15-1. A version of make_cf.plx that generates links to other parts of the site

```
#!/usr/bin/perl -w

# make_cf.plx

# re-creates the Main School 2000 CyberFair site,
# walking the site to rewrite all pages from the latest
# version of the templates, and re-creating the navigational
# links specific to each page.

use strict;
```

```perl
use File::Find;

my $fs_root         = '/w1/s/socalsail/cyberfair';
my $escaped_fs_root = quotemeta $fs_root; # for use in regex patterns
my $web_root        = '/cyberfair';

my %page_data;        # HoH w/ primary keys: path
                      #          secondary keys: page template params
                      #          values: corresponding content

my %teacher_students; # HoL, w/ keys of teacher short_name and values
                      # of arrays of student page paths.

my %student_profiles; # HoHoL, w/ primary keys of teacher/student
                      # string, secondary key of @attribute element,
                      # and values of leader page paths.

my %cat_leaders;      # HoL, w/ keys of leader cat short_names, and
                      # values of arrays of leader page paths.

my @attributes = qw(writer editor photographer illustrator);

my %verb = (
    writer       => 'written',
    editor       => 'edited',
    photographer => 'photographed',
    illustrator  => 'illustrated',
);

my %student_verb = (
    writer       => 'wrote',
    editor       => 'edited',
    photographer => 'photographed',
    illustrator  => 'illustrated',
);

# end configuration section

find(\&load_pages, $fs_root); # loads up %page_data

# use Data::Dumper;
# print Dumper(\%page_data);

# now, make all the pages

foreach my $path (sort keys %page_data) {

    my %build_hash = %{$page_data{$path}};
    my $made_page = &build_page(%build_hash);

    my $link_string = my $more_string = '';
    my($link_start, $link_end);
```

```
    if ($path =~ m{^$escaped_fs_root/leader/([^/]+)/index\.html$}o) {

        # this is the index page for a particular type of leader

        my $leader_cat = $1;
        $link_start = <<EndOfText;
<P><STRONG>All the leaders we profiled in this category:</STRONG></P>
<UL>
EndOfText
        $link_end = "</UL>\n";

        my %lc_lastname;

        foreach my $profile_path (@{$cat_leaders{$leader_cat}}) {
            next if $profile_path =~ /index\.html$/;
            my $name = $page_data{$profile_path}{name};
            my @name_ary = split /\s+/, $name;
            my $lc_lastname = lc (pop @name_ary);
            $lc_lastname{$profile_path} = $lc_lastname;
        }

        foreach my $profile_path (sort
            { $lc_lastname{$a} cmp $lc_lastname{$b} }
            keys %lc_lastname) {
            my $web_path = $profile_path;
            $web_path =~ s{$escaped_fs_root}{$web_root}o;
            $link_string .= <<EndOfText;
<LI><A
HREF="$web_path"><STRONG>$page_data{$profile_path}{name}</STRONG></A>
EndOfText
        }

    } elsif ($path =~ m{^$escaped_fs_root/leader/[^/]+/[^/]+\.html$}o) {

        # this is a leader profile page

        $link_start = "<P>";
        $link_end   = "</P>\n";

        my $cat_path = $path;
        $cat_path =~ s{[^/]+$}{index.html};
        my $cat_name = $page_data{$cat_path}{name};
        my $web_path = $cat_path;
        $web_path =~ s{$escaped_fs_root}{$web_root}o;
        $web_path =~ s{index\.html$}{};

        $more_string =
            "<P>View more <A HREF=\"$web_path\"><STRONG>$cat_name Leaders</STRONG></A></P>
\n";

        foreach my $attribute (@attributes) {
            my $verb = $verb{$attribute};
```

```
            if ($page_data{$path}{$attribute}) {
                $link_string .= "This page was $verb by ";
                my @params = split /\|/, $page_data{$path}{$attribute};
                my @links;
                foreach my $param (@params) {
                    my $page = "$web_root/student/$param.html";
                    my $path = "$fs_root/student/$param.html";
                    my $name = $page_data{$path}{name} || 'Unknown';
                    push @links,
                        "<A HREF=\"$page\"><STRONG>$name</STRONG></A>";
                }
                $link_string .= &join_list(@links);
                $link_string .= "<BR>\n";
            }
        }

    } elsif ($path =~ m{^$escaped_fs_root/student/([^/]+)/index\.html$}o) {

        # this is a teacher page

        $link_start = <<EndOfText;
<P><STRONG>The following students from this class participated
in the Main School CyberFair 2000 project:</STRONG></P>

<UL>
EndOfText
        $link_end    = "</UL>\n";

        if (my $aryref = $teacher_students{$1}) {

            my @student_paths = @{$aryref};
            foreach my $student_path (sort @student_paths) {
                next if $student_path =~ /index\.html$/;
                my $student_name
                    = $page_data{$student_path}{name} || 'Unknown';
                $student_path =~ s{$escaped_fs_root}{$web_root}o;
                $link_string .= "<LI><STRONG><A HREF=\"$student_path\">$student_name</A></
STRONG>\n";
            }
        }

    } elsif ($path =~ m{^$escaped_fs_root/student/([^/]+/[^/]+)\.html$}o) {

        # this is a student page

        $link_start = <<EndOfText;
<P><STRONG>I participated in the Main School CyberFair 2000 project
in the following ways:</STRONG></P>

<P>
EndOfText
        $link_end = "</P>\n";
```

Example 15-1. A version of make_cf.plx that generates links to other parts of the site (continued)

```
        my $student_string = $1;

        my $teacher_path = $path;
        $teacher_path =~ s{[^/]+$}{index.html};
        my $teacher_name = $page_data{$teacher_path}{name};
        my $web_path = $teacher_path;
        $web_path =~ s{$escaped_fs_root}{$web_root}o;
        $web_path =~ s{index\.html$}{};
        my $possessive = $teacher_name . '\'';
        unless ($possessive =~ /s'$/) {
            $possessive .= 's';
        }

        $more_string = <<EndOfText;
<P>View more students from
<A HREF=\"$web_path\"><STRONG>$possessive class</STRONG></A></P>
EndOfText

        if ($student_profiles{$student_string}) {

            # this student has leader profiles

            foreach my $attribute (@attributes) {
                if ($student_profiles{$student_string}{$attribute}) {
                    my @ary =
@{ $student_profiles{$student_string}{$attribute} };
                    if (@ary >= 2) {
                        $link_string .=
"I $student_verb{$attribute} the leader profiles for ";
                    } else {
                        $link_string .=
"I $student_verb{$attribute} the leader profile for ";
                    }
                    foreach my $elem (@ary) {
                        my $leader_name = $page_data{$elem}{name};
                        my $web_path = $elem;
                        $web_path =~ s{$escaped_fs_root}{$web_root}o;
                        $elem = "<A HREF=\"$web_path\"><STRONG>$leader_name</STRONG></A>";
                    }
                    $link_string .= &join_list(@ary);
                    $link_string .= "<BR>\n";
                }
            }
        }

    } elsif ($path =~ m{^$escaped_fs_root/student/index\.html$}o) {

        # this is the "Who made this site?" page

        $link_start = <<EndOfText;
<P><STRONG>You can browse a list of participants in the Main School
CyberFair 2000 project by following the teacher links
```

Example 15-1. A version of make_cf.plx that generates links to other parts of the site (continued)

```
below:</STRONG></P>

<UL>
EndOfText
        $link_end = "</UL>\n";

        foreach my $teacher (sort keys %teacher_students) {
            my $key = $fs_root . "/student/$teacher/index.html";
            my $teacher_longname = $page_data{$key}{name};
            my $possessive = $teacher_longname . '\'';
            unless ($possessive =~ /s'$/) {
                $possessive .= 's';
            }
            $link_string .= <<EndOfText;
<LI><STRONG><A HREF="$web_root/student/$teacher/">$possessive
Class</A></STRONG>
EndOfText
        }
    }

    if ($link_string) {
        $link_string =~ s/<BR>\n$//;
        $link_string = "$link_start$link_string$link_end";
    }

    $link_string .= "\n$more_string\n";

    $made_page =~
        s{(<!--\s*end\s+content\s*-->)}{$1\n\n$link_string}i;

    &write_page($path, $made_page) or die "&write_page failed";
}

# subroutines follow

sub load_pages {
    return unless /\.html$/;
    my $file = $File::Find::name;

    my %page_hash = &read_page($file);

    return unless $page_hash{type} and $page_hash{type} eq 'cf';

    $page_data{$file} = \%page_hash;

    if ($file =~ m{^$escaped_fs_root/student/([^/]+)/[^/]+\.html}o) {

        # it's a student page, so list it in the %teacher_students HoL

        my $teacher = $1;
        push @{$teacher_students{$teacher}}, $file;
```

Example 15-1. A version of make_cf.plx that generates links to other parts of the site (continued)

```perl
    } elsif ($file =~ m{$escaped_fs_root/leader/([^/]+)/[^/]+\.html}o) {

        # it's a leader page, so list it in the %cat_leaders HoL
        # and the %student_profiles HoL

        my $cat = $1;
        push @{$cat_leaders{$cat}}, $file;

        foreach my $attribute (@attributes) {
            if ($page_hash{$attribute}) {
                my @values = split /\|/, $page_hash{$attribute};
                foreach my $value (@values) {
                    push @{ $student_profiles{$value}{$attribute} },
                        $file;
                }
            }
        }
    }
}

sub join_list {

    # do a grammatical joining of a list into a string, and return it

    my @list = @_;
    my $string = '';
    while (@list) {
        $string .= shift @list;
        my $length = @list;
        if ($length > 1) {
            $string .= ', ';
        } elsif ($length == 1) {
            $string .= ' and ';
        }
    }
    $string;
}

sub read_page {

    # invoked with a full pathname as argument,
    # returns a hash suitable for
    # feeding to &build_page

    my $pathname = shift;
    my %return_hash;

    open IN, "$pathname"
        or die "Couldn't open $pathname for reading: $!";
    my $page = join '', <IN>;
    close IN;
```

```perl
    return unless $page;

    if ($page =~ m#<TITLE>(.*)</TITLE>#i) {
        $return_hash{title} = $1;
    }

    while ($page =~ m#<META\s+NAME="([^"]+)"\s+CONTENT="([^"]*)">#gi) {
        $return_hash{$1} = $2;
    }

    if ($page =~
        /.+<!--begin content-->\s*(.+?)\s*<!--end content-->/s) {
        $return_hash{content} = $1;
    }

    %return_hash;
}

sub build_page {

    # given a suitable parameter hash, build a CyberFair page
    # and return it

    my %param = (
        type        => 'cf',                # these are
        title       => 'Untitled Document', # defaults...
        description => '',
        keywords    => '',
        content     => '',
        @_,                     # supplied name-value pairs come in here
    );

    # translate the various META params into a merged $meta_block for
    # substituting into the template.

    my @meta_params = qw(type description keywords name writer editor
        illustrator photographer);
    my $meta_block = '';

    foreach my $meta_param (@meta_params) {
        if ($param{$meta_param}) {
            $meta_block .= <<EndOfText;
<META NAME="$meta_param" CONTENT="$param{$meta_param}">
EndOfText
            delete $param{$meta_param};
        }
    }

    $param{meta_block} = $meta_block;

    my $template = <<EndOfText;
<HTML>
```

```
<HEAD>
<TITLE>%%title%%</TITLE>
%%meta_block%%
</HEAD>

<BODY>

<TABLE BORDER=0 CELLSPACING=0 CELLPADDING=10>
<TR VALIGN="top">
<TD WIDTH=150 BGCOLOR="#99CC66">

<!--begin left navbar-->

<P ALIGN="center"><A HREF="/cyberfair/"><IMG
SRC="/cyberfair/shared/avo_sm4.gif" HEIGHT=100 WIDTH=100 BORDER=0 VSPACE=5></A><BR>
<A HREF="/cyberfair/"><STRONG>CyberFair 2000 Project</STRONG></A><BR>
<FONT SIZE="-1">Main School<BR>
Carpinteria, California, USA</FONT></P>

<P><STRONG>Carpinteria Valley Leaders<BR>
<FONT SIZE="-1">
<A HREF="/cyberfair/leader/government/">Government</A><BR>
<A HREF="/cyberfair/leader/environment/">Environment</A><BR>
<A HREF="/cyberfair/leader/school/">School</A><BR>
<A HREF="/cyberfair/leader/business/">Business</A><BR>
<A HREF="/cyberfair/leader/arts/">Arts & Entertainment</A><BR>
<A HREF="/cyberfair/leader/sports/">Sports & Recreation</A><BR>
<A HREF="/cyberfair/leader/medical/">Medical</A><BR>
<A HREF="/cyberfair/leader/community/">Community
Services</A></FONT></STRONG></P>

<P><STRONG>About This Site<BR>
<FONT SIZE="-1"><A HREF="/cyberfair/student/">Who Made This
Site?</A><BR>
<A HREF="/cyberfair/avocado/">Why an Avocado Tree?</A><BR>
<A HREF="/cyberfair/narrative/">Project Narrative</A>
<A HREF="/cyberfair/sources/">Information
Sources</A></FONT></STRONG></P>

<!--end left navbar-->

</TD>

<TD>

<!--begin content-->

%%content%%

<!--end content-->

</TD>
```

```
</TR>
</TABLE>

</BODY>
</HTML>
EndOfText

    # replace %%quoted%% words with values in %param hash
    $template =~ s{ %% ( .*? ) %% }
                  { exists( $param{$1} )
                        ? $param{$1}
                        : ''
                  }gex;
    $template;
}

sub write_page {

    # invoked with a full path and an HTML page,
    # writes the page to that file location.
    # will create directories as it goes, as needed.
    # issues a warning and returns undef (without
    # writing anything) if the page exists already
    # and is anything other than a regular text file.

    my($full_path, $made_page) = @_;
    unless ($full_path =~ /\.html$/) {
        warn "$full_path does not end with '.html'\n";
        return;
    }
    unless ($full_path =~ /^\//) {
        warn "$full_path does not begin with a slash\n";
        return;
    }
    if (-l $full_path) {
        warn "$full_path is a symbolic link\n";
        return;
    }
    if (-B $full_path) {
        warn "$full_path is a binary file\n";
        return;
    }

    # still here? good. make any needed directories...

    my $dir_path = $full_path;
    $dir_path    =~ s{/[^/]+$}{}; # lose last '/' and ensuing filename

    &make_dirs($dir_path)
        or die "problem with &make_dirs on '$dir_path'...";

    open OUT, ">$full_path" or
```

```perl
        die "can't open $full_path for writing: $!";
    print OUT $made_page;
    close OUT or die "can't close $full_path filehandle: $!";

    chmod 0644, $full_path or
        die "couldn't chmod $full_path to 0644";
    1;
}

sub make_dirs {

    # invoked with an argument consisting of a full pathname,
    # split it on '/' and check each component to see if it
    # is a currently existing directory. If it isn't, create it
    # with permissions of 0755.

    # the last component is skipped if it contains any periods. this
    # is intended to avoid accidentally creating a directory out of
    # what should be a filename, e.g.:
    # '/w1/s/socalsail/foo/index.html/'; normally, though, the filename
    # should not be passed to the routine.

    # for the sake of (minimal) security, this routine will abort
    # if the supplied argument contains two periods in a row ('..').

    my $full_path = shift;
    return if $full_path =~ /\.\./; # doesn't trust people passing '..'
    my @dirs = split(/\//, $full_path);

    my $last_element = pop @dirs;
    unless ($last_element =~ /\./) {
        push @dirs, $last_element; # put it back on if no '.'
    }

    my $this_dir;

    umask 022;
    foreach (@dirs) {
        next unless $_; # empty element
        $this_dir .= "/$_";
        if (-e $this_dir) {
            unless (-d $this_dir) {
                warn "$this_dir path component exists but is not a
                    directory\n";
                return;
            }
        } else {
            mkdir $this_dir, 0777
                or die "couldn't mkdir $this_dir: $!";
        }
    }
    1;
}
```

The Script's Data Structure

The first interesting thing in the script is the section at the top where the data structure that will hold the site's metainformation is defined:

```
my %page_data;          # HoH w/ primary keys: path
                        #       secondary keys: page template params
                        #       values: corresponding content

my %teacher_students;   # HoL, w/ keys of teacher short_name and values
                        # of arrays of student page paths.

my %student_profiles;   # HoHoL, w/ primary keys of teacher/student
                        # string, secondary key of @attribute element,
                        # and values of leader page paths.

my %cat_leaders;        # HoL, w/ keys of leader cat short_names, and
                        # values of arrays of leader page paths.
```

The comments here make use of a form of shorthand popular with Perl programmers when they are talking about multilevel data structures. *HoH* means "hash of hashes," *HoL* means "hash of lists" (another name for a "hash of arrays"), and the jolly-sounding *HoHoL* means "hash of hash of lists."

The %page_data hash of hashes is really the heart of the script. It is built up during the script's first cycle through the site's HTML pages. In effect, it is a little database that embodies all the META headers, TITLE tags, and comment-delimited content blocks of the site's HTML pages. That hash of hashes has a first-level key consisting of the page's path and filename, a second-level key of the name of the page attribute, and a value of the corresponding content. That is, for the Al Gore leader page whose META headers we looked at earlier, the entry in %page_data might have been created via a chunk of code looking something like this:

```
%hash = ( title        => 'Al Gore\'s Leader Profile',
          type         => 'cf',
          name         => 'Al Gore',
          writer       => 'nakasone/johnc',
          photographer => 'nakasone/johnc',
          content      => <<EOF,
<H2>Al Gore</H2>

<P>By: John C.</P>

<P>Al Gore was born on March 31, 1948, in Washington, D.C.</P>
EOF
);

$page_data{'/w1/s/socalsail/cyberfair/leader/al_gore.html'}
    = \%hash;
```

We'll see how that information is used to construct links between the site's pages in just a moment.

The next three hashes (%teacher_students, %student_profiles, and %cat_leaders) are little data structures used to collect the information for producing appropriate links at the bottom of the teacher pages, student pages, and leader category pages, respectively. I could probably have dispensed with these three hash variables and just extracted that data as needed from the %page_data hash, but doing it this way seemed easier to me at the time I was writing the script.

Once the configuration section ends, the script runs File::Find's find function, passing it the &load_pages subroutine to load up the %page_data hash, among others. Most of that &load_pages routine should look pretty familiar by now, since it's a variation on things we've seen in previous chapters, so we're not going to go over it in detail here. The main thing to understand about it is the routine's overall purpose, which is to assemble an in-memory data structure reflecting the structure of the site as a whole, as determined from the location of pages within the site's directory structure and from the contents of the pages' META headers. When the find function is finished recursing its way through the site, %page_data will allow us to build links connecting each page to the others in the site.

Using Data::Dumper

Next comes some interesting Perl archaeology:

```
# use Data::Dumper;
# print Dumper(\%page_data);
```

There, entombed by a layer of commenting, is a relic of a previous era in the life of this script. When I had developed it sufficiently far to have created the &load_pages subroutine, which populated the %page_data hash, I wanted to see what was being stuck in there. Enter the Data::Dumper module, a standard Perl module written by Gurusamy Sarathy. Data::Dumper turns a data structure (like that contained in the %page_data HoH) into a chunk of Perl code that would, if evaluated, re-create that original data structure. This turns out to be really handy for development and debugging because it lets us easily print out a snapshot of our script's data structure.

The Dumper function that Data::Dumper gives us takes as its argument a reference to the hash we wish to have represented as Perl code. In the example here, we produce that reference by sticking the backslash in front of the hash name, like \%page_data, as we learned how to do back in Chapter 11.

Here's an example of what the Dumper function might print out:

```
$VAR1 = {
          '/w1/s/socalsail/cyberfair/leader/government/al_gore.html' => {

'name' => 'Al Gore',

'title' => 'Al Gore's Leader Profile',
```

```
    'type' => 'cf',

    'content' => '<H2>Al Gore</H2>

    <P>By: John C.</P>

    <P>Al Gore was born on March 31, 1948, in Washington, D.C.</P>',

    'writer' => 'nakasone/johnc',

    'photographer' => 'nakasone/johnc'

    },
    (etc.)
```

Here's how to interpret that. If we took that output and ran it in a Perl script, the $VAR1 variable would end up holding a reference to a hash identical to the %page_data hash we fed to the Dumper function. That Data::Dumper output is thus another version of the example code we saw just a moment ago, which would populate the Al Gore section of the %page_data hash.

Creating Anonymous Hashes and Arrays

If we look at Dumper's output more closely, we can see that something interesting is going on. Here's a simplified version of it:

```
$HoH = {
    key1 => {
              key_a => 'value_a',
              key_b => 'value_b',
            },
    key2 => {
              key_a => 'value_a',
              key_b => 'value_b',
            },
};
```

What's up with the curly braces? We haven't seen them used like this before.

What's up is the fourth and final piece of reference magic we need to know: how to initialize an anonymous hash and return a reference to it at the same time. We do that by putting curly braces around it, where we would normally put the enclosing parentheses:

```
$hash_ref = {
              key1 => 'value1',
              key2 => 'value2',
            };
```

Here we have created an anonymous hash with two keys and two corresponding values, and returned a reference to it that we've then stuck in the scalar variable $hash_ref. If we take a bunch of those anonymous hashes and make the references that they return the values in an all-encompassing hash, and if we make that all-encompassing hash an anonymous hash and return a reference to it, we get a reference to a hash of hashes, or HoH. That's what Data::Dumper's Dumper routine printed out for us.

We can do similar reference magic with square brackets to create and return an anonymous array reference:

```
my $ary_ref = [ 'item1', 'item2', 'item3' ];
```

If we nest those we get a reference to an LoL, or List of Lists:

```
my $LoL = [
            [ 'item1', 'item2', 'item3' ],
            [ 'item1', 'item2', 'item3' ],
            [ 'item1', 'item2', 'item3' ],
          ];
```

And we can mix the two kinds of reference-returning bracketing as desired to produce HoLs and LoHs, like this:

```
$HoL = {
         key1 => [ 'item1', 'item2', 'item3' ],
         key2 => [ 'item1', 'item2', 'item3' ],
         key3 => [ 'item1', 'item2', 'item3' ],
       };

$LoH = [
         { key1 => 'value1', key2 => 'value2', key3 => 'value3' },
         { key1 => 'value1', key2 => 'value2', key3 => 'value3' },
         { key1 => 'value1', key2 => 'value2', key3 => 'value3' },
       ];
```

This seems a little complicated until you get used to it, but it's definitely worth the effort that goes into understanding it, since such an understanding will greatly simplify the task of creating and using complex data structures. Complex data structures, in turn, will greatly simplify the task of creating more powerful Perl scripts.

Anyway, once I was happy with the look of the data being stored in %page_data, I disabled Data::Dumper by commenting out the two lines where it was invoked. But I left the commented code in the script, in case I needed to uncomment it later for some quick debugging.

Automatically Generating Links

So, we now have covered the first part of the script, where we traverse the site and read the contents of all its pages into %page_data. Next, we're going to traverse that %page_data data structure itself and write those pages back out to the site, replacing the old versions of the pages with new ones. We're doing that for two reasons. First, we want to update those pages based on the latest (possibly updated) version of our template. Second, we want to add a section to each page, just after the "content" section, that features automatically generated links pointing to suitable pages elsewhere on the site.

The details of how all that gets done don't involve any new Perl features. But they provide a good example of the kind of work that Perl is perfectly happy to shoulder when we have a lot of HTML to manipulate.

That work begins with a foreach loop that iterates over all the keys of %page_data, storing the current key in $path:

```
foreach my $path (sort keys %page_data) {
```

The first thing that happens inside the loop is that the page is re-created from the template using the &build_page subroutine. You recall that that routine requires an argument consisting of a hash of page metainformation, and conveniently, such a hash (or rather, a reference to one) is what is stored at the top level of %page_data. So, we just use $page_data{$path} to get that reference and stick it inside %{ } to dereference it and get back the original hash. We feed that to &build_page and poof, we've got our rewritten page, stored in $made_page:

```
my $made_page = &build_page(%{$page_data{$path}});
```

Next comes the initialization of a bunch of variables that will be used to build up the links:

```
my ($link_string, $link_start, $link_end, $more_string);
$link_string = $link_start = $link_end = $more_string = '';
```

After that comes a long series of if-elsif tests that figure out if we're currently processing a page that will get automatically generated links attached to it, and if so, it creates those links by assigning the appropriate text to the appropriate variables.

I'm not going to bother going over all of this part of the script in detail because it's all just variations on the same theme. Here's a representative chunk, though, to help make sense of what the script is doing. This comes from the first branch of the if-elsif structure, which runs when the current page being processed is the top-level page for a particular leader category:

```
if ($path =~ m{^$escaped_fs_root/leader/([^/]+)/index\.html$}o) {

    # this is the index page for a particular type of leader

    my $leader_cat = $1;

    $link_start = <<EndOfText;
<P><STRONG>All the leaders we profiled in this category:</STRONG></P>
<UL>
EndOfText

    $link_end = "</UL>\n";

    my %lc_lastname;

    foreach my $profile_path (@{ $cat_leaders{$leader_cat} }) {
        next if $profile_path =~ /index\.html$/;
        my $name = $page_data{$profile_path}{name};
```

```
    my @name_ary = split /\s+/, $name;
    my $lc_lastname = lc (pop @name_ary);
    $lc_lastname{$profile_path} = $lc_lastname;
}
```

Again, here we're processing the top-level page for a particular leader category ("School Leaders", for example). While the find function was traversing all the pages in our site, the %cat_leaders HoL got loaded up with a list of all the pathnames corresponding to each leader category. So, now we can just loop through all the pages for this particular leader category, extracting each of the leaders' names, as stored in their individual pages' 'name' META headers, and accessible via the %page_data hash.

We get that list of leader pages for this category by dereferencing the array reference stored in the %cat_leaders HoL with the @{ $ary_ref } syntax. Because we're dealing with a hash of lists, we actually access the array with @{ $hash{key} }. Or, in this case, @{ $cat_leaders{$leader_cat} }.

Because that array in $cat_leaders{$leader_cat} includes not only the actual leader pages for that category, but also the main page for that category, we need to skip to the next path if this one ends in index.html. In other words, as we're cycling through all the pages stored in @{ $cat_leaders{$leader_cat} }, we need to skip over the page that corresponds to this leader category's top-level page, which is actually the page for which we're currently constructing this list of links.

Anyway, if we're still here after that line (that is, if we are processing an actual leader page), we extract the leader's name with the following very interesting line:

```
    my $name = $page_data{$profile_path}{name};
```

What is going on here? More curly-brace madness. We're dereferencing the %page_data hash of hashes to extract a particular value from the inner hash—in this case, the 'name' attribute obtained from the META headers of this particular page.

Doesn't this count as a fifth piece of new magical reference syntax? Well, technically, I suppose so. But conceptually it can fall under the heading of a special case of the dereferencing arrow syntax we already learned. That is, the previous line of code could have been written as:

```
    my $name = $page_data{$profile_path}->{name};
```

in which it is more clear that what we are doing is dereferencing the hash reference stored in $page_data{$profile_path}, extracting the value associated with the key 'name' in that inner hash. Perl lets us omit the arrow between two sets of subscripting brackets in the interest of clarity. The same thing works with square brackets, too. That is, we can do dereferencing to access elements from inside a multilevel data structure using syntax like $HoL{key}[1], $LoH[2]{key}, and $LoL[1][3].

The last thing we do in the foreach loop that is cycling over all the leaders for this category is to take this particular leader's last name and store a lowercase version of it in a hash called %lc_lastname. We do that by extracting the leader's name from

%page_data, splitting it on whitespace to create a @name_ary array, then popping off the last element of that array, lowercasing it with lc, and sticking it in %lc_lastname. We're doing that so that we can sort our list of leader links for this category according to each leader's last name. Here, again, is the code that does that:

```
my $name = $page_data{$profile_path}{name};
my @name_ary = split /\s+/, $name;
my $lc_lastname = lc (pop @name_ary);
$lc_lastname{$profile_path} = $lc_lastname;
```

Once we're done looping over all the leaders for this category, we just assemble the actual links. Specifically, we loop over the %lc_lastname hash we just created, sorting on the lowercase version of the leader's last name, and appending a link for that leader page to $link_string:

```
        foreach my $profile_path (sort
            { $lc_lastname{$a} cmp $lc_lastname{$b} }
            keys %lc_lastname) {
            my $web_path = $profile_path;
            $web_path =~ s{$escaped_fs_root}{$web_root}o;
            $link_string .= <<EndOfText;
<LI><A
HREF="$web_path"><STRONG>$page_data{$profile_path}{name}</STRONG></A>
EndOfText
        }
```

The only thing moderately sneaky here is the use of the /o modifier in the substitution regular expression. Since there is a variable in the search pattern, the expression will be recompiled every time it is seen, unless we include the /o. With it there, the expression will be compiled only once.

Inserting the Links

As mentioned earlier, the rest of that long if-elsif section simply repeats, with minor variations, the same process of creating a $link_string suitable for the page currently being processed by the enclosing foreach loop. Down at the bottom of that foreach loop, after the long if-elsif section, comes the following chunk of code:

```
if ($link_string) {
    $link_string =~ s/<BR>\n$//;
    $link_string = "$link_start$link_string$link_end";
}

$link_string .= "\n$more_string\n";
```

This does a cleanup on the $link_string variable, removing a trailing
\n it might have in the case of certain types of pages. It also appends another variable to it, called $more_string, that might have received some content in the case of certain kinds of pages. You can examine the if-elsif block to see how those cases work, if you're curious, but we won't be discussing them here.

Finally, we use a substitution operation to take the $made_page variable (which you'll recall contains the newly re-created version of the current page) and insert the cleaned-up $link_string variable into it just below the <!--end content--> comment. Then we use the &write_page routine to replace the actual version of the page on the web site with our new version of it:

```
$made_page =~
    s{(<!--\s*end\s+content\s*-->)}{$1\n\n$link_string}i;

&write_page($path, $made_page) or die "&write_page failed";
```

And that's it. By running this script when the site's collection of student and leader pages has changed, we can update all those pages with automatically generated links.

In Chapter 17, we'll look at a CGI frontend that makes it easy to add new pages to the site. But first, in Chapter 16, we're going to talk about creating our own Perl modules.

Writing Perl Modules

It's time we learned how to share code across more than one of our scripts by creating our own Perl modules. This sort of code sharing is a really good idea. We've already seen how helpful it can be to take some block of code that is going to be used multiple times in a script and put it into its own subroutine. In the same vein, it's helpful to take common code that is going to be used in multiple scripts and put it into a module that can be shared by all of them.

The typical beginner's approach to sharing code is to just use copy-and-paste, which is, of course, a problem waiting to happen. Eventually you'll want to update that code to fix a bug or add some new capability. When that happens, you'll have to choose between updating one copy and leaving others in the old state (which is bad), or making the same changes over and over again (which is also bad, though in a different way).

Modules are the solution. I felt kind of intimidated when I started writing my own modules. I'm not sure why; I guess in my newbiehood I had such a high opinion of Perl's standard and CPAN modules that I was reluctant to pry the lid off those black boxes and try to construct my own. But in retrospect, I didn't have anything to be worried about. Most of it is very straightforward, and the deeper parts can be safely ignored as long as you're careful to invoke the magic properly.

This chapter explains everything you need to know to start writing your own Perl modules. It starts with a very simple "Hello, world!" module, then shows a real module created to share code across the scripts associated with the Main School Cyber-Fair project, which was the subject of Chapters 14 and 15 and will be the subject of Chapter 17 as well.

A Simple Module Template

Example 16-1 gives a basic template that can be used as the starting point for creating a new Perl module. Like all the examples in this book, it can be downloaded from the book's web site, at *http://www.elanus.net/book/*.

Example 16-1. A template for creating a Perl module

```perl
package Walnuts::Rutabagas;

use strict;

BEGIN {
    use Exporter   ();
    use vars       qw(@ISA @EXPORT @EXPORT_OK $VERSION);
    $VERSION     = '0.01';
    @ISA         = qw(Exporter);
    @EXPORT      = qw();
    @EXPORT_OK   = qw(hello);
}

sub hello {
    print "Hello, world!\n";
}

1;
```

Let's go through this line by line. First comes the package declaration:

```perl
package Walnuts::Rutabagas;
```

An important goal when creating modules is to keep our namespace tidy. That is, the module shouldn't assign some value to a variable, or define some sequence of actions to be performed by a subroutine, if doing so will cause a conflict with a variable or subroutine of the same name somewhere else. Declaring a new package via the package declaration is the first step in keeping the namespaces of the main code and the module from interfering with each other.

Although we haven't had to think about it much before this, Perl uses the concept of a package to allow us to have multiple namespaces. All our named subroutines, and all our variables (except for those declared with my), reside in a particular package. If we never bother to put an explicit package declaration in a script (as we did in the previous example, with the line that says package Walnuts::Rutabagas), we're just in package main, the default package.

It's a bit like the directories in a filesystem. We can have a file called walnuts.txt in one directory and another, completely different file called walnuts.txt in some other directory, and our computer will never get them confused, as long as we're careful to switch to the appropriate directory before referring to it by its short filename. We also can give a full pathname, if we like, and refer to the file from somewhere else.

So far in our Perl scripts, we've always done everything in package main. That's like what a novice computer user does when he doesn't really understand the concept of directories, and just keeps everything in the same directory.

When we use a variable or subroutine name (like $walnuts or &rutabagas) in a Perl script, we are telling Perl to access the variable or subroutine of that name in the current package. We can access variables or subroutines in other packages by sticking the package name between the leading punctuation (the $ or &, that is) and the name itself. Thus, $kumquat refers to a scalar variable called kumquat in the current package (package main if we haven't declared another package), while $Walnuts::Rutabagas:: kumquat would access a scalar variable called $kumquat in the Walnuts::Rutabagas package. To continue the files/directories analogy, saying something like $Walnuts:: Rutabagas::kumquat is the equivalent of giving the full pathname to refer to a file in a particular directory.

When we use Perl's package function, we are declaring that henceforth in this script, every time we refer to a variable or subroutine without explicitly giving the package name, we are actually referring to the variable or subroutine of that name in that package. It's analogous to using cd to change to a different directory in the computer's filesystem, after which we can refer to files in that directory without giving a pathname.

 Normally, we declare a new package name at the beginning of our module file, and that declaration applies for the rest of the file. In fact, though, package declarations are scoped in the same way that my declarations are. If we issue a package declaration inside a curly-brace-delimited block, it applies only to the rest of that block. But again, most of the time we will just declare our package at the beginning of our module and have it apply to the whole file.

One more important thing about package names: I've been referring to the files-and-directories parallel as being strictly an analogy, but in one sense it goes a little further than that. If we are creating a Perl module and give its package declaration as package Walnuts::Rutabagas, we are saying that the module itself is going to reside in a file called Rutabagas.pm, and that that module file will be inside a directory called Walnuts. Further, that Walnuts directory in turn will need to be located in one of the library locations Perl knows about. That is, the double colon (::) in the middle of a two-part package name will be replaced with the directory separator used on our current system (e.g., a forward slash on Unix systems). A '.pm' will be appended to the end of the name, and the result will be the path and filename (relative to one of the library directories Perl knows about) of the actual module file.

In still other words, when we put package Walnuts::Rutabagas at the top of a Perl module file, we are making an implicit promise to Perl that that file will be named

Walnuts/Rutabagas.pm, with that Walnuts directory residing in one of the Perl library directories.

So much for the package declaration. The next item in our sample module is use strict, which should be pretty much a reflex for us by now. When creating a module, though, it's especially important to impose those use strict rules on ourselves so we don't do something silly that will lay a trap for someone who tries to use our module from within some other Perl script.

Next comes a BEGIN block, which you will recall is a block of code that executes as soon as possible, before any other non-BEGIN–blocked code in the script:

```
BEGIN {
    use Exporter   ();
    use vars       qw(@ISA @EXPORT @EXPORT_OK $VERSION);
    $VERSION      = '0.01';
    @ISA          = qw(Exporter);
    @EXPORT       = qw();
    @EXPORT_OK    = qw(hello);
}
```

What's going on here is a little bit of magic that I am officially telling you not to worry about for now. Just put it in there, just like that, and forget about it.

Actually, I suppose at this stage in your Perl education you deserve a little more explanation than that, so here it is. Eventually, when our module is finished, we are going to use it from within some other Perl script. When that happens, some variables and/or subroutines will be exported out of the module's namespace and into the namespace of the script doing the use-ing. (Unless we are creating an object-oriented module, which doesn't do that kind of exporting. But we won't be doing any of that in this book, so don't worry about it.)

The Exporter module is a standard module that we can use to help us do that exporting. Something like 95% of the Perl modules in existence use the Exporter module, so you should, too, until you learn enough to have some reason not to. The use vars qw( ) statement is where we declare the names of the global variables we are going to be using in this module. We need to do that to stay out of trouble with the strict pragma invoked earlier.

Having a $VERSION variable is a good practice, since even simple modules have a way of growing over time, and a version number is a good way of keeping track of which version of our module we're currently looking at. Also, it will help us feel a sense of accomplishment when we add some cool new feature and bump the version number up a notch. Finally, when we graduate to creating modules to be shared with other Perl users around the world via CPAN, those modules will need to have this variable.

The @ISA array is a magical thingy used by the Exporter module, and the @EXPORT and @EXPORT_OK arrays are where we stick the names of the variables and subroutines that we want to export into the namespace of the use-ing script.

The @EXPORT and @EXPORT_OK arrays each work slightly differently. @EXPORT contains a list of variables and subroutine names that will be automatically exported into the calling script's namespace. @EXPORT_OK contains a list of variables and subroutines that *may* be exported into the calling script's namespace, but only if the calling script explicitly asks for them. We'll see how the calling script does that in just a minute.

In general, it's better to use @EXPORT_OK than @EXPORT. Using @EXPORT to automatically export things into the calling script's namespace runs the risk of accidentally trampling something in the calling script. Better to have the calling script explicitly ask for the variables and subroutines it wants to use. As a bonus, by having the calling script explicitly ask for what it wants from the module, we make the interaction between the calling script and the module more obvious to someone who has to try to make sense of the calling script's code at a later date.

> You may have noticed that I left off the ampersand (&) at the front of the &hello subroutine's name when I mentioned it in the @EXPORT_OK array. That's okay; Perl still knows that we're referring to the subroutine of that name.

Next, our Walnuts::Rutabagas module has this subroutine that does the actual work:

```
sub hello {
    print "Hello, world!\n";
}
```

Finally, Walnuts::Rutabagas has the number 1 evaluated all by itself:

```
1;
```

We need that because when the module is used by a calling script, the script will fail to run if the module does not return a true value. By putting a lone 1 at the very end of the module, we ensure that the module will return a true value (since a module, when used, returns the value of the last expression evaluated in it).

Installing the Module

Now, to put this into action, we need to save this module file as Rutabagas.pm and stick it in a directory called Walnuts, which in turn is contained in one of Perl's library directories. If we don't have write access to the library directories for our server's Perl installation, we can stick it in our own personal library directory, making sure to stick an appropriate use lib statement in our script before trying to use the module, as described in Chapter 11.

Now we can create a script like the one shown in Example 16-2, and it will dutifully print Hello, world! to standard output.

Example 16-2. A sample script that uses the Walnuts::Rutabagas module

```perl
#!/usr/bin/perl -w

use strict;
use Walnuts::Rutabagas qw(hello);

&hello; # this will print "Hello, world!\n";
```

The Cyberfair::Page Module

Now that we know how to create our own module, let's take a look at Example 16-3. I created this module to allow me to take some of the subroutines out of the make_cf. plx script created for the Main School CyberFair project, and then share those subroutines across multiple scripts.

Example 16-3. A Perl module to allow easy re-use of the CyberFair project's subroutines

```perl
package Cyberfair::Page;

use strict;

BEGIN {
    use Exporter   ();
    use vars       qw(@ISA @EXPORT @EXPORT_OK);
    $VERSION       = '0.01';
```

```perl
    @ISA        = qw(Exporter);
    @EXPORT     = qw( );
    @EXPORT_OK  = qw(read_page build_page write_page);
}

sub read_page {

    # invoked with a full pathname as argument,
    # returns a hash suitable for
    # feeding to &build_page

    my $pathname = shift;
    my %return_hash;

    open IN, "$pathname"
        or die "Couldn't open $pathname for reading: $!";
    my $page = join '', <IN>;
    close IN;

    return unless $page;

    if ($page =~ m#<TITLE>(.*)</TITLE>#i) {
        $return_hash{title} = $1;
    }

    while ($page =~ m#<META\s+NAME="([^"]+)"\s+CONTENT="([^"]*)">#gi) {
        $return_hash{$1} = $2;
    }

    if ($page =~
        /.+<!--begin content-->\s*(.+?)\s*<!--end content-->/s) {
        $return_hash{content} = $1;
    }

    return %return_hash;
}

sub build_page {

    # given a suitable parameter hash, build a CyberFair page
    # and return it

    my %param = (
        type        =>  'cf',                    # these are
        title       =>  'Untitled Document',     # defaults...
        description =>  '',
        keywords    =>  '',
        content     =>  '',
        @_,                     # supplied name-value pairs come in here
    );

    # translate the various META params into a merged $meta_block for
```

```perl
    # substituting into the template.

    my @meta_params = qw(type description keywords
                         name writer editor illustrator
                         photographer);
    my $meta_block = '';

    foreach my $meta_param (@meta_params) {
        if ($param{$meta_param}) {
            $meta_block .= <<EndOfText;
<META NAME="$meta_param" CONTENT="$param{$meta_param}">
EndOfText
            delete $param{$meta_param};
        }
    }

    $param{meta_block} = $meta_block;

    my $template = <<EndOfText;
<HTML>
<HEAD>
<TITLE>%%title%%</TITLE>
%%meta_block%%
</HEAD>

<BODY>

<TABLE BORDER=0 CELLSPACING=0 CELLPADDING=10>
<TR VALIGN="top">
<TD WIDTH=150 BGCOLOR="#99CC66">

<!--begin left navbar-->

<P ALIGN="center"><A HREF="/cyberfair/"><IMG
SRC="/cyberfair/shared/avo_sm4.gif" HEIGHT=100 WIDTH=100 BORDER=0 VSPACE=5></A><BR>
<A HREF="/cyberfair/"><STRONG>CyberFair 2000 Project</STRONG></A><BR>
<FONT SIZE="-1">Main School<BR>
Carpinteria, California, USA</FONT></P>

<P><STRONG>Carpinteria Valley Leaders<BR>
<FONT SIZE="-1">
<A HREF="/cyberfair/leader/government/">Government</A><BR>
<A HREF="/cyberfair/leader/environment/">Environment</A><BR>
<A HREF="/cyberfair/leader/school/">School</A><BR>
<A HREF="/cyberfair/leader/business/">Business</A><BR>
<A HREF="/cyberfair/leader/arts/">Arts & Entertainment</A><BR>
<A HREF="/cyberfair/leader/sports/">Sports & Recreation</A><BR>
<A HREF="/cyberfair/leader/medical/">Medical</A><BR>
<A HREF="/cyberfair/leader/community/">Community
Services</A></FONT></STRONG></P>

<P><STRONG>About This Site<BR>
```

```
<FONT SIZE="-1"><A HREF="/cyberfair/student/">Who Made This
Site?</A><BR>
<A HREF="/cyberfair/avocado/">Why an Avocado Tree?</A><BR>
<A HREF="/cyberfair/narrative/">Project Narrative</A>
<A HREF="/cyberfair/sources/">Information
Sources</A></FONT></STRONG></P>

<!--end left navbar-->

</TD>

<TD>

<!--begin content-->

%%content%%

<!--end content-->

</TD>
</TR>
</TABLE>

</BODY>
</HTML>
EndOfText

    # replace %%quoted%% words with values in %param hash
    $template =~ s{ %% ( .*? ) %% }
                  { exists( $param{$1} )
                        ? $param{$1}
                        : ''
                  }gex;
    return $template;
}

sub write_page {

    # invoked with a full path and an HTML page,
    # writes the page to that file location.
    # will create directories as it goes, as needed.
    # issues a warning and returns undef (without
    # writing anything) if the page exists already
    # and is anything other than a regular text file.

    my($full_path, $made_page) = @_;
    unless ($full_path =~ /\.html$/) {
        warn "$full_path does not end with '.html'\n";
        return;
    }
    unless ($full_path =~ /^\//) {
        warn "$full_path does not begin with a slash\n";
```

```perl
        return;
    }
    if (-l $full_path) {
        warn "$full_path is a symbolic link\n";
        return;
    }
    if (-B $full_path) {
        warn "$full_path is a binary file\n";
        return;
    }

    # still here? good. make any needed directories...

    my $dir_path = $full_path;
    $dir_path    =~ s{/[^/]+$}{}; # lose last '/' and ensuing filename

    &make_dirs($dir_path)
        or die "problem with &make_dirs on '$dir_path'...";

    open OUT, ">$full_path" or
        die "can't open $full_path for writing: $!";
    print OUT $made_page;
    close OUT or die "can't close $full_path filehandle: $!";

    chmod 0644, $full_path or
        die "couldn't chmod $full_path to 0644";
    1;
}

sub make_dirs {

    # invoked with an argument consisting of a full pathname,
    # split it on '/' and check each component to see if it
    # is a currently existing directory. If it isn't, create it
    # with permissions of 0755.

    # the last component is skipped if it contains any periods. this
    # is intended to avoid accidentally creating a directory out of
    # what should be a filename, e.g.:
    # '/w1/s/socalsail/foo/index.html/'; normally, though, the filename
    # should not be passed to the routine.

    # for the sake of (minimal) security, this routine will abort
    # if the supplied argument contains two periods in a row ('..').

    umask 0000;
    my $full_path = shift;
    return if $full_path =~ /\.\./; # doesn't trust people passing '..'
    my @dirs = split(/\//, $full_path);

    my $last_element = pop @dirs;
    unless ($last_element =~ /\./) {
```

Example 16-3. A Perl module to allow easy re-use of the CyberFair project's subroutines (continued)

```
        push @dirs, $last_element; # put it back on if no '.'
    }

    my $this_dir;

    foreach (@dirs) {
        next unless $_; # empty element
        $this_dir .= "/$_";
        if (-e $this_dir) {
            unless (-d $this_dir) {
                warn "$this_dir exists but is not a directory\n";
                return;
            }
        } else {
            mkdir $this_dir, 0755
                or die "couldn't mkdir $this_dir: $!";
        }
    }
    return 1;
}

1;
```

There's really nothing new here. I simply combined the module template with the subroutines we saw in the make_cf.plx script from Chapter 15, and the result was a module that allows me to share those subroutines across multiple scripts.

To take advantage of that, I then needed to modify the make_cf.plx script in two ways. First, adding the following lines near the top of it:

```
    use lib '/home/jbc/lib';
    use Cyberfair::Page qw(read_page build_page write_page);
```

Second, deleting the copies of the &read_page, &build_page, and &write_page subroutines from make_cf.plx.

Then, I just saved my new Page.pm file in a directory called Cyberfair branching off from my personal /home/jbc/lib directory. That's it!

In Chapter 17, we'll complete this extended example by seeing how a CGI frontend made it easy for student participants to add new pages to the CyberFair project.

CHAPTER 17

Adding Pages via CGI Script

This chapter finishes the example begun in Chapters 14, 15, and 16. In this chapter, we'll see how a CGI frontend was used to simplify the process of adding new HTML pages to the Main School CyberFair site. Along the way, we'll see some new tricks for making multistage CGI scripts, executing external commands from within a Perl script, and doing file locking.

Why Add Pages with a CGI Script?

Back at the beginning of Chapter 15 I talked about Jon Udell's concept of a *docbase*, explaining that a docbase is a collection of documents that include some metainformation that a computer can understand. The HTML pages in the Main School CyberFair site are an example of a docbase, in that they contain important information in their META headers (and some other important information by virtue of where they are located in the site's directory structure). As we saw in Chapter 15, that metainformation allows a Perl program to automatically construct links connecting the site's pages to each other.

One of the drawbacks to this docbase approach is that it can be a challenge for fallible human beings to consistently adhere to the requirements it lays down for formatting new HTML pages correctly. Making that challenge even greater in this case was the fact that the people who were adding these pages were children under the age of 12, with most of them being relatively new to the task of creating HTML pages.

The solution was to use a CGI script as a frontend for creating new pages. This let our young content creators use a simple web browser interface to create the documents, with the CGI script that processed the submission taking care of formatting the metainformation correctly.

A Script for Creating HTML Documents

Example 17-1 shows the CGI script that we used. It's a long one, but I'll be explaining all the interesting Perl features it contains. Like all the examples in this book, you can download it from the book's web site, at *http://www.elanus.net/book/*.

Example 17-1. A CGI script to create new pages in the CyberFair docbase

```perl
#!/usr/bin/perl -Tw

# make_page.cgi

# gives a cgi frontend to allow users to
# create a new cyberfair student or leader page

use strict;
use lib '/home/jbc/lib';
use Cyberfair::Page qw(read_page build_page write_page);
$ENV{PATH} = '';

use CGI qw(:standard);
my $action = param('action');

my $fs_root         = '/w1/s/socalsail/cyberfair';
my $escaped_fs_root = quotemeta $fs_root;
my $web_root        = '/cyberfair';

my ($content, $err_msg);

use File::Find;

my @student_strings; # elements are strings of the form:
                     # 'teacher_short_name/student_short_name'

my %teacher_name;    # key: teacher short_name,
                     # value: teacher long_name

my %cat_name;        # key: cat short_name, value: cat long_name.

find(\&load_pages, $fs_root); # loads up the variables listed above

@student_strings = sort @student_strings;

# each of the subroutines below loads up the $content variable
# with the content to be delivered back to the user.

unless ($action) {
    &show_links;
} elsif ($action eq 'show_student_form') {
    &show_student_form;
} elsif ($action eq 'show_leader_form') {
    &show_leader_form;
} elsif ($action eq 'Create student page') {
```

Example 17-1. A CGI script to create new pages in the CyberFair docbase (continued)

```
        &post_student_page;
} elsif ($action eq 'Create leader page') {
        &post_leader_page;
} elsif ($action eq 'regenerate_site_links') {
        &regenerate_site_links;
} else {
        $err_msg = "<LI>Wacky 'action' param '$action'. Shouldn't be able
                    to get here.";
}

if ($err_msg) {
        $content = <<"EOF";
<H2>Hmmm. Something strange happened...</H2>

<P>The make_page.cgi script reported the following problem(s) when it
tried to process your request:</P>

<UL>
$err_msg
</UL>

<P>Please use your browser's "Back" command to return to the previous
page and try again. Thanks! If the problem persists, and you can't
solve it, please contact John Callender
(<A HREF="mailto:jbc\@west.net">jbc\@west.net</A>) and let him know.</P>
EOF
}

my $made_page = &build_page(
        title   => 'Make a Main School CyberFair page',
        content => $content,
);

print header, $made_page;

# script proper ends. subroutines follow

sub show_links {
        $content = <<"EOF";

<H1>Select an action:</H1>

<P><STRONG><A HREF="make_page.cgi?action=show_student_form">Make a
student page</A><BR>
<A HREF="make_page.cgi?action=show_leader_form">Make a leader
page</A><BR>
<A HREF="make_page.cgi?action=regenerate_site_links">Regenerate site
links</A>
</STRONG></P>
EOF
}
```

Example 17-1. A CGI script to create new pages in the CyberFair docbase (continued)

```perl
sub show_student_form {

    my @values = sort keys %teacher_name;
    my %labels = %teacher_name;
    push @values, 'choose';
    $labels{choose} = 'Please choose a teacher';
    my @letters = ('A' .. 'Z');
    unshift @letters, 'Please choose a letter';

    $content = join "\n",
        "<P ALIGN=\"center\"><STRONG><A HREF=\"$web_root/maint/make_page.cgi\">Return to
the maintenance page</A></STRONG></P>",
        '<H1 ALIGN="center">Make a student page</H1>',
        start_form,
        '<TABLE><TR><TD ALIGN="right">',
        b('Teacher:'),
        '</TD><TD>',
        popup_menu(
            -name    => 'teacher',
            -values  => \@values,
            -labels  => \%labels,
            -default => 'choose'
        ),
        '</TD></TR>',
        '<TR><TD ALIGN="right">',
        b('Student\'s first name:'),
        '</TD><TD>',
        textfield(
            -name      => 'student_first',
            -size      => 20,
            -maxlength => 50,
        ),
        '</TD></TR>\n<TR><TD ALIGN="right">',
        b('First letter of student\'s last name:'),
        '</TD><TD>',
        popup_menu(
            -name    => 'student_last',
            -values  => \@letters,
            -default => 'Please choose a letter'
        ),
        '</TD></TR>',
        '<TR><TD COLSPAN=2>',
        b('Page contents:'), br,
        textarea(
            -name    => 'content',
            -columns => 50,
            -rows    => 10,
            -wrap    => 'virtual',
        ),

        '</TD></TR>',
        '<TR><TD COLSPAN=2>',
```

Example 17-1. A CGI script to create new pages in the CyberFair docbase (continued)

```
            submit(
                -name => 'action',
                -label => 'Create student page',
            ),
            '</TD></TR></TABLE>',
            end_form;
}

sub show_leader_form {

    unshift @student_strings, 'Choose a student (optional)';

    my @values = sort keys %cat_name;
    my %labels = %cat_name;
    push @values, 'choose';
    $labels{choose} = 'Please choose a leader category';
    my @letters = ('A' .. 'Z');
    unshift @letters, 'Please choose a letter';

    $content = join "\n",
        "<P ALIGN=\"center\"><STRONG><A HREF=\"$web_root/maint/make_page.cgi\">Return to
the maintenance page</A></STRONG>",
        '<H1 ALIGN="center">Make a leader page</H1>',
        start_form,
        '<TABLE><TR><TD ALIGN="right">',
        b('Leader category:'),
        '</TD><TD>',
        popup_menu(
            -name    => 'leader_cat',
            -values  => \@values,
            -labels  => \%labels,
            -default => 'choose'
        ),
        '</TD></TR>',
        '<TR><TD ALIGN="right">',
        b('Leader\'s first name:'),
        '</TD><TD>',
        textfield(
            -name      => 'leader_first',
            -size      => 20,
            -maxlength => 50,
        ),
        '</TD></TR>',
        '<TR><TD ALIGN="right">',
        b('Leader\'s last name:'),
        '</TD><TD>',
        textfield(
            -name      => 'leader_last',
            -size      => 20,
            -maxlength => 50,
        ),
        '</TD></TR>',
```

```
'<TR><TD ALIGN="right">',

b('Writer:'),
'</TD><TD>',
popup_menu(
    -name    => 'writer',
    -values  => \@student_strings,
    -default => 'Choose a student (optional)'
),
'</TD></TR>',
'<TR><TD ALIGN="right">',

b('Editor:'),
'</TD><TD>',
popup_menu(
    -name    => 'editor',
    -values  => \@student_strings,
    -default => 'Choose a student (optional)'
),
'</TD></TR>',
'<TR><TD ALIGN="right">',

b('Photographer:'),
'</TD><TD>',
popup_menu(
    -name    => 'photographer',
    -values  => \@student_strings,
    -default => 'Choose a student (optional)'
),
'</TD></TR>',
'<TR><TD ALIGN="right">',

b('Illustrator:'),
'</TD><TD>',
popup_menu(
    -name    => 'illustrator',
    -values  => \@student_strings,
    -default => 'Choose a student (optional)'
),
'</TD></TR>',
'<TR><TD COLSPAN=2>',
b('Page contents:'), br,
textarea(
    -name => 'content',
    -columns => 50,
    -rows    => 10,
    -wrap    => 'virtual',
),

'</TD></TR>',
'<TR><TD COLSPAN=2>',
submit(
```

Example 17-1. A CGI script to create new pages in the CyberFair docbase (continued)

```perl
            -name => 'action',
            -label => 'Create leader page',
        ),
        '</TD></TR></TABLE>',
        end_form;
}

sub post_student_page {
    my $teacher        = param('teacher');
    my $student_first  = param('student_first');
    my $student_last   = param('student_last');
    my $student_content = param('content');

    $teacher =~ s/\W+//g;
    $teacher = lc $teacher;

    if (not $teacher or $teacher eq 'Please choose a teacher') {
        $err_msg .= <<"EOF";
<LI>No 'teacher' specified. Please choose a teacher.
EOF
    } elsif (not $teacher_name{$teacher}) {
        $err_msg .= <<"EOF";
<LI>The teacher you gave ('$teacher') is not recognized.
EOF
    }

    my $student_long = "\u\L$student_first";
    $student_long .= " \u$student_last.";

    $student_first =~ s/\W+//g;
    $student_first = lc $student_first;
    $student_last =~ s/\W+//g;
    $student_last  = lc $student_last;

    unless ($student_first) {
        $err_msg .= <<"EOF";
<LI>No 'student's first name' specified. Please give a first name.
EOF
    }

    if (not $student_last or $student_last eq 'Please choose a letter') {
        $err_msg .= <<"EOF";
<LI>No 'student's last initial' specified. Please give the student's
last initial.
EOF
    }

    $student_content =~
        s{<!--begin content-->\s*(.*?)\s*<!--end content-->}{$1}s;
    $student_content =~ s{\r\n?}{\n}g;

    unless ($student_content) {
```

Example 17-1. A CGI script to create new pages in the CyberFair docbase (continued)

```perl
        $err_msg .= <<"EOF";
<LI>No content was given. Please supply some content.
EOF
    }

    my $fs_path  = "$fs_root/student/$teacher/${student_first}${student_last}.html";
    my $web_path = "$web_root/student/$teacher/${student_first}${student_last}.html";

    if (-e $fs_path) {
        $err_msg .= <<"EOF";
<LI>The path I constructed for your page ('$fs_path') already exists.
That is, I've already created a file at that location, and don't
want to overwrite it. You'll have to give a different teacher and/or
student name, or ask Mrs. Cole to help you modify (or delete) the
existing file.
EOF
    } elsif ($fs_path =~ /\.\./) {
        $err_msg .= <<"EOF";
<LI>The path I constructed for your page ('$fs_path') contains
consecutive periods (..), which isn't allowed.
EOF
    }

    return if $err_msg;

    # still here? good!

    my $made_page = &build_page(
        title   => $student_long,
        name    => $student_long,
        content => $student_content,
    );

    # laundering variables to make taint-mode happy

    if ($fs_path =~ /(.+)/) {
        $fs_path = $1;
    }

    if ($made_page =~ /(.+)/s) {
        $made_page = $1;
    }

    &write_page($fs_path, $made_page);

    $content = <<"EOF";
<H2>Student page created for $student_long</H2>

<P><STRONG><A HREF="$web_path">View the $student_long page</A><BR>
<A HREF="$web_root/maint/make_page.cgi?action=show_student_form">Make
another student page</A><BR>
<A HREF="$web_root/maint/make_page.cgi">Return to the maintenance page</A></STRONG></P>
```

```perl
EOF
}

sub post_leader_page {

    my $leader_cat     = param('leader_cat');
    my $leader_first   = param('leader_first');
    my $leader_last    = param('leader_last');

    my $writer         = param('writer');
    my $editor         = param('editor');
    my $photographer   = param('photographer');
    my $illustrator    = param('illustrator');

    foreach ($writer, $editor, $photographer, $illustrator) {
        $_ = '' if $_ eq 'Choose a student (optional)';
    }

    my $leader_content = param('content');

    if (not $leader_cat or $leader_cat eq 'choose') {
        $err_msg .= <<"EOF";
<LI>No leader category specified. Please choose a leader category.
EOF
    } elsif (not $cat_name{$leader_cat}) {
        $err_msg .= <<"EOF";
<LI>The leader category you gave ('$leader_cat') is not recognized.
EOF
    }

    my $leader_name = "\u\L$leader_first";
    $leader_name .= " \u\L$leader_last";

    $leader_first =~ s/\W+//g;
    $leader_first = lc $leader_first;
    $leader_last  =~ s/\W+//g;
    $leader_last  = lc $leader_last;

    unless ($leader_first) {
        $err_msg .= <<"EOF";
<LI>No 'leader's first name' specified. Please give a first name.
EOF
    }

    unless ($leader_last) {
        $err_msg .= <<"EOF";
<LI>No 'leader's last name' specified. Please give the leader's
last name.
EOF
    }

    $leader_content =~
        s{<!--begin content-->\s*(.*?)\s*<!--end content-->}{$1};
```

Example 17-1. A CGI script to create new pages in the CyberFair docbase (continued)

```
    $leader_content =~ s{\r\n?}{\n}g;

    unless ($leader_content) {
        $err_msg .= <<"EOF";
<LI>No content was given. Please supply some content.
EOF
    }

    my $fs_path  = "$fs_root/leader/$leader_cat/${leader_first}_${leader_last}.html";
    my $web_path = "$web_root/leader/$leader_cat/${leader_first}_${leader_last}.html";

    if (-e $fs_path) {
        $err_msg .= <<"EOF";
<LI>The path I constructed for your page ('$fs_path') already
exists. That is, I've already created a file at that location, and
don't want to overwrite it. You'll have to use a different leader
category and/or leader name, or ask Mrs. Cole to help you modify (or
delete) the existing file.
EOF
    }

    return if $err_msg;

    # still here? good!

    my $made_page = &build_page(
        title       => $leader_name,
        name        => $leader_name,
        content     => $leader_content,
        writer      => $writer,
        editor      => $editor,
        photographer => $photographer,
        illustrator => $illustrator,
    );

    if ($fs_path =~ /(.+)/) {
        $fs_path = $1;
    }
    if ($made_page =~ /(.+)/s) {
        $made_page = $1;
    }

    &write_page($fs_path, $made_page);

    $content = <<"EOF";
<H2>Leader page created for $leader_name</H2>

<P><STRONG><A HREF="$web_path">View the $leader_name page</A><BR>
<A HREF="$web_root/maint/make_page.cgi?action=show_leader_form">Make
another leader page</A><BR>
<A HREF="$web_root/maint/make_page.cgi">Return to the maintenance page</A></STRONG></P>
EOF
}
```

```perl
sub regenerate_site_links {
    eval { system('./make_cf.plx') == 0 or die $? };
    if ($@) {
        $err_msg = <<"EOF";
<LI>The make_cf.plx script failed to run, possibly because another
copy of it was already running. You should try again in a minute
or so, and if you still get this message, send an E-mail to
<A HREF="mailto:jbc\@west.net">jbc\@west.net</A> to let
John Callender know there's a problem. Sorry about the inconvenience.
<LI>Here is the error number that was returned: $?
EOF
        return;
    }
    $content = '<H1>Site links regenerated</H1>';

    # now run the quick-and-dirty version of the link checker

    my $report = `$fs_root/maint/link_check.plx`;

    if ($report =~ /<BODY>(.+)<\/BODY>/s) {
        $content .= $1;
    }

    &show_links;
}

sub load_pages {
    return unless /\.html$/;
    my $file = $File::Find::name;

    my %page_hash = &read_page($file);

    return unless $page_hash{type} and $page_hash{type} eq 'cf';

    if ($file =~ m{^$escaped_fs_root/student/([^/]+)/index\.html}o) {

        # it's a teacher page, so stick the name in %teacher_name

        my $short_name = $1;
        my $long_name = $page_hash{name};
        $teacher_name{$short_name} = $long_name;

    } elsif ($file =~ m{^$escaped_fs_root/student/([^/]+/[^/]+)\.html}o) {

        # it's a student page, so list it in @student_strings

        push @student_strings, $1;

    } elsif ($file =~ m{$escaped_fs_root/leader/([^/]+)/index\.html}o) {

        # it's a leader category page, so list it in %cat_name
```

```
        my $short_name = $1;
        my $long_name = $page_hash{name};
        $cat_name{$short_name} = $long_name;
    }
}
```

Besides the usual -w warnings flag, our shebang line also features the -T option to turn on Perl's *taint mode*, which we learned about back in Chapter 12. As you'll recall from that discussion, taint mode makes our Perl script die with an error message if it catches us doing things it considers unsafe using data obtained from outside the program itself:

```
#!/usr/bin/perl -Tw
```

Next we turn on the strict pragma, declare a personal library directory with use lib, and pull in the Cyberfair::Page module we created in the previous chapter. We also set $ENV{PATH} (which controls the environment variable containing our script's search path) to an explicit value of the empty string (''), which will make Perl's taint mode happy later in the script when we try to execute some external commands:

```
use strict;
use lib '/home/jbc/lib';
use Cyberfair::Page qw(read_page build_page write_page);
$ENV{PATH} = '';
```

Next we pull in the CGI module, and use that module's param function to store the contents of the CGI form parameter named action into the scalar variable $action. In just a moment you'll see how we use that parameter to control which part of our script actually executes for this particular invocation:

```
use CGI qw(:standard);
my $action = param('action');
```

The next interesting thing in the script is where we define some configuration variables and declare some my variables, including the variables that will hold the script's data structures:

```
my @student_strings; # elements are strings of the form:
                     # 'teacher_short_name/student_short_name'

my %teacher_name;    # key: teacher short_name,
                     # value: teacher long_name

my %cat_name;        # key: cat short_name, value: cat long_name.
```

These look suspiciously like the data structures we saw already in the make_cf.plx script back in Chapter 15. If we look at the &load_pages subroutine that is run for each file recursively found by File::Find's find function in the next line:

```
find(\&load_pages, $fs_root); # loads up the variables listed above
```

we'll see that it looks very much like the same routine from make_cf.plx. You might be inclined to think that I just copy-and-pasted that routine from the other script into this one, and if you thought that, you'd be right. I did.

Which makes me out to be something of a hypocrite. First I admonish you to practice code-reuse, creating modules rather than creating a maintenance nightmare by copy-and-pasting multiple versions of your code. Then I turn around and break that commandment myself. What's going on?

What's going on is that I don't believe in letting a slavish adherence to consistency prevent me from taking shortcuts now and then. In this case, I needed a slightly different behavior from my &load_pages routine, and didn't want to invest the time in making a shared version that would behave one way in one set of circumstances and another way in another. I was working on a finite project, with a tight deadline and a narrow set of objectives. Perl gives us the flexibility to choose our own path, optimizing for whatever it is we want to optimize for. In this case, I optimized for development time, at a cost of future maintainability.

Controlling a Multistage CGI Script

The next interesting section of the script is a long chain of unless-elsif blocks that test the contents of the $action variable, and execute various subroutines based on what's in there. The idea here is to have a single CGI script that will carry out a whole sequence of actions as a user clicks his way through multiple dynamically generated pages, with the passed action parameter controlling which part of the script is run for each invocation:

```
unless ($action) {
    &show_links;
} elsif ($action eq 'show_student_form') {
    &show_student_form;
} elsif ($action eq 'show_leader_form') {
    &show_leader_form;
} elsif ($action eq 'Create student page') {
    &post_student_page;
} elsif ($action eq 'Create leader page') {
    &post_leader_page;
} elsif ($action eq 'regenerate_site_links') {
    &regenerate_site_links;
} else {
    $err_msg = "<LI>Wacky 'action' param '$action'. Shouldn't be able
            to get here.";
}
```

I've had people tell me that my use of unless-elsif is evil, but it makes sense to me when I read it out loud. Your mileage may vary.

The overall gist of this script is that each unless-elsif block will load up the $content variable with a different page to be delivered back to the requesting user. If anything goes wrong, a descriptive error message will be stuck in the $err_msg variable. After all the unless-elsif stuff is done, the script will check for the presence of anything in $err_msg, and if something is there, it will create an HTML error message incorporating it and stick it in $content. Whether there was an error message or not, the script will then use &build_page to turn $content into a finished HTML page formatted with the standard CyberFair page template, and deliver that page back to the user with the following line:

```
print header, $made_page;
```

Using Parameterized Links

Now let's take a look at those subroutines that are performed for the various unless-elsif blocks. The first one is the &show_links routine, which just sticks some HTML in the $content variable to display three links. When the user clicks on any of those links, the links will re-invoke the script to perform various actions:

```
sub show_links {
    $content = <<EndOfText;

<H1>Select an action:</H1>

<P><STRONG><A HREF="make_page.cgi?action=show_student_form">Make a
student page</A><BR>
<A HREF="make_page.cgi?action=show_leader_form">Make a leader
page</A><BR>
<A HREF="make_page.cgi?action=regenerate_site_links">Regenerate site
links</A>
</STRONG></P>
EndOfText
```

Note how using CGI.pm makes it easy to mix and match POST- and GET-method invocations of the script. In this case, we're using the GET method, creating links with parameters embedded in the URL. A question mark (?) separates the actual scriptname from the query string, which consists of name=value pairs. Using CGI.pm to retrieve the invocation parameters, our script can ignore the different mechanics involved in retrieving and decoding these parameters, as compared to how it would retrieve and decode parameters passed as part of a POST-method HTML form submission.

If you have multiple parameters to embed in a GET-method CGI script invocation, you use an ampersand to separate each pair. If you need to include characters that aren't legal in a URL, you need to *URL-escape* them, replacing a space character (for example) with the sequence %20. CGI.pm offers a handy method to URL-escape a string: the escape method, which you invoke as: $safe_string = escape($unsafe_string). You must explicitly ask for CGI.pm to import the escape method for you; you do this in the initial use CGI statement, by saying something like use CGI qw(:standard escape). Check the CGI.pm documentation for more details.

Building a Form

Now let's turn our attention to the &show_student_form routine. When this routine runs, it produces an HTML page that looks something like Figure 17-1.

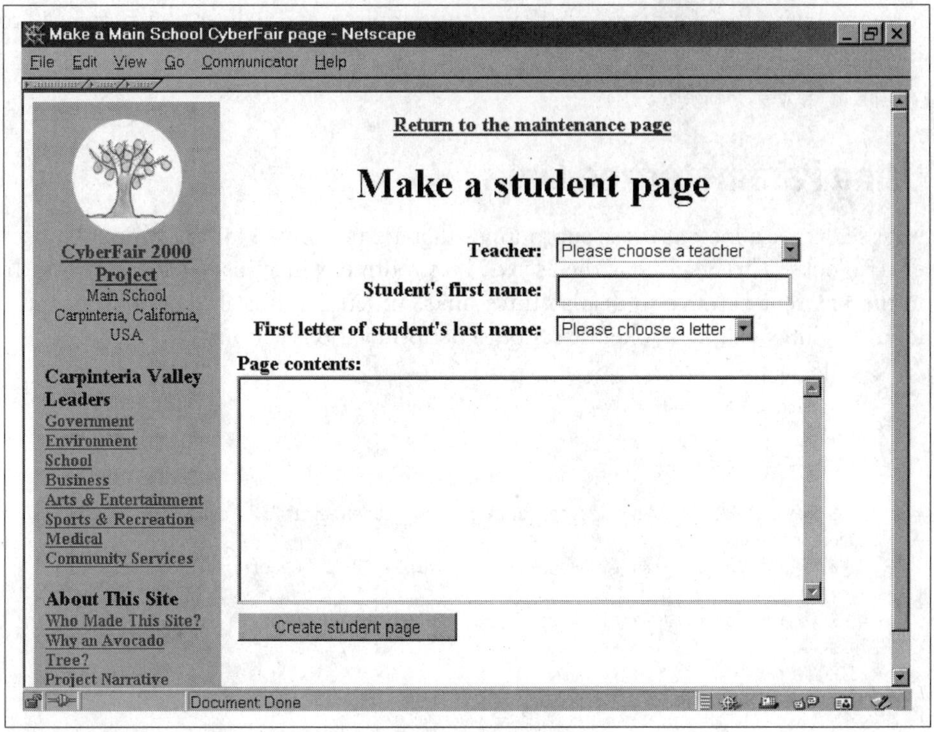

Figure 17-1. Form produced by the make_page.cgi script

Examining the subroutine code in more detail, we see that after some preliminaries it has the following:

```
$content = join "\n",
    "<P ALIGN=\"center\"><STRONG><A HREF=\"$web_root/maint/make_page.cgi\">Return
to the maintenance page</A></STRONG></P>",
    '<H1 ALIGN="center">Make a student page</H1>',
    start_form,
    '<TABLE><TR><TD ALIGN="right">',
    b('Teacher:'),
    '</TD><TD>',
```

And so on. This demonstrates another Perl idiom that seems to show up a lot in my CGI scripts: long chains of arguments to the join function. I often use long join statements, connecting (via \n, or some other suitable joining string) a long list of form elements and HTML embellishment. I tend to use single quotes to enclose the HTML, which saves me from having to backslash all the embedded double quotes surrounding the HTML attributes. This means I can't interpolate variables into the strings, but that's okay with me because I just terminate the single-quoted string, throw in a comma, and add the variable as another element in that long chain of join arguments. This works nicely for CGI.pm functions, which can't easily be interpolated inside double-quoted strings the way variables can.

I also sometimes use the *string concatenation operator* (a dot: .) to concatenate the strings together. So, for example, the previous chunk of Perl could also have been written as:

```
$content = '<P ALIGN="center"><STRONG><A HREF="'
   . $web_root
   . '/maint/make_page.cgi">Return to the maintenance
      page</A></STRONG></P>'
   . '<H1 ALIGN="center">Make a student page</H1>'
   . startform
   . '<TABLE><TR><TD ALIGN="right">'
   . b('Teacher:')
   . '</TD><TD>' # and so on...
```

This would have produced almost the same HTML output, except that it wouldn't have had the newlines between each chunk. That would make the resulting HTML page a tad smaller, at the cost of its source code being somewhat harder to view or edit if you found yourself wanting to do that. Another difference between the two approaches is that the dot-concatenation version actually runs somewhat faster, though the difference probably doesn't matter in this case because we're talking about a difference measured in very small fractions of a second. The join version is also noticeably easier to understand, at least to my eyes, which tips the scales very much in its favor. (If this sort of CPU efficiency *does* matter to you, see the accompanying sidebar, "Fun with Benchmarking," for a tool you can use to stage races between competing chunks of Perl code.)

This is more a question of personal style than anything else. Perl offers a half dozen different ways to do most things, and we're free to pick the one we like. Perhaps more important for the current discussion are the CGI.pm functions used to produce the form elements. Here's an example of a CGI.pm form-element-producing function from the &show_student_form routine:

```
popup_menu(
    -name    => 'teacher',
    -values  => \@values,
    -labels  => \%labels,
    -default => 'choose'
),
```

Check the CGI.pm documentation (available via man CGI or perldoc CGI) for all the details on this and other form-element–producing functions. One of the nice things about using CGI.pm to create our form elements is that the resulting form elements

Fun with Benchmarking

As you've probably realized by now, Perl offers many different ways to accomplish the same task. Most of the time we will choose an approach based on which one is easiest to write, or easiest to understand, or easiest to modify and maintain later on. In short, we will be interested in maximizing human efficiency. Occasionally, though, we will find ourselves dealing with a CPU-intensive task (a very big job the computer needs to perform, or a somewhat smaller job that needs to be performed a great many times), that causes us to be more interested in maximizing the computer's efficiency.

In such cases, the standard Benchmark module is useful. It lets us compare multiple ways of doing things to see which is faster, and by how much. I used the Benchmark module's timethese routine to test the two approaches described in the accompanying text for creating a long string from many shorter strings: the use of the dot-concatenation operator, and the use of the join function. Here's the code I used to run the test:

```perl
#!/usr/bin/perl -w

use strict;

use Benchmark;

timethese(1_000_000, {
    with_join => \&with_join,
    with_dot  => \&with_dot,
});

sub with_join {
    my $string = join "\n",
        'now', 'is', 'the', 'time', 'for',
        'all', 'good', 'men', 'etc.';
}

sub with_dot {
    my $string =  'now' . "\n" . 'is' . "\n"
        . 'the' . "\n" . 'time' . "\n"
        . 'for' . "\n" . 'all' . "\n"
        . 'good' . "\n" . 'men' . "\n" . 'etc.';
}
```

This script runs the two subroutines (&with_join and &with_dot) 1 million times each, after which it issues a report on how long it took for each one. (Running the routines a large number of times allows the timethese routine to generate better statistics.)

Notice the nifty use of the *underscore character* in the number 1_000_000. We can't use commas inside a large number in a Perl script because Perl will interpret them as the *comma operator*, which would break the number up into a list of smaller numbers.

—continued—

So, if we want to make the number more readable, we need to use the underscore in place of the comma.

Here's what I got when I ran this on a 500MHz Pentium III machine:

```
Benchmark: timing 1000000 iterations of with_dot, with_join...
  with_dot: 2 wallclock secs ( 2.21 usr + -0.01 sys = 2.20 CPU)
  with_join: 6 wallclock secs ( 6.07 usr + 0.00 sys = 6.07 CPU)
```

So there you have it: if you need to perform a string-joining (or dot-concatenation) operation like this 1 million times, you can save 4 whole seconds by doing it concatenation style.

are *sticky*, by which I mean that CGI.pm will automatically save and insert the same values in our form elements from one invocation of the script to the next.

Another nice thing about these CGI.pm form-producing functions is that they make it easy to generate groups of related form elements based on Perl data structures. In the previous example we've done that by feeding the popup_menu function arguments set to things like \@values (a reference to the array variable @values) or \%labels (a reference to the hash variable %labels). In this script, that popup_menu method returns a chunk of HTML that looks something like this:

```
<SELECT NAME="teacher">
<OPTION SELECTED VALUE="choose">Please choose a teacher
<OPTION  VALUE="bennettdavis">Mrs. Bennett-Davis
<OPTION  VALUE="buckelew">Miss Buckelew
<OPTION  VALUE="davis">Ms. Davis
<OPTION  VALUE="foley">Ms. Foley
<OPTION  VALUE="gravitz">Mrs. Gravitz
<OPTION  VALUE="kahler">Miss Kahler
<OPTION  VALUE="lopez">Ms. Lopez
<OPTION  VALUE="mireles">Mr. Mireles
<OPTION  VALUE="nakasone">Mrs. Nakasone &amp; Mr. Handall
<OPTION  VALUE="riley">Mr. Riley
<OPTION  VALUE="stout">Mrs. Stout &amp; Mr. Pigato
<OPTION  VALUE="wells">Mr. Wells
<OPTION  VALUE="white">Mrs. White
<OPTION  VALUE="young">Miss Young
</SELECT>
```

When rendered in a browser, it will produce a form widget that looks like Figure 17-2.

The rest of the &show_student_form routine is pretty much more of the same, as is the &show_leader_form routine. The trickiest thing about them is to make sure we supply all the right arguments to the various CGI.pm methods; Lincoln Stein's excellent documentation for the module explains everything we need to know about that.

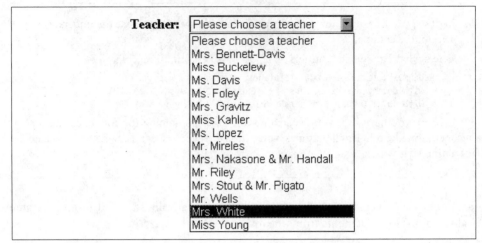

Figure 17-2. HTML pop-up menu produced by CGI.pm's popup_menu function

Posting Pages from the CGI Script

The next interesting part of the make_page.cgi script is the part where the script processes the submission of one of these forms. This is where the actual work occurs, that of taking the submitted form information, turning it into a finished HTML page, and writing that page out to the appropriate location on the site. This happens in the &post_student_page and &post_leader_page routines. In looking at the &post_student_page routine, the first new Perl trick we see is this:

```
my $student_long = "\u\L$student_first";
$student_long .= " \u$student_last.";
```

That takes the student's first name (as submitted in the form and stored in $student_first earlier in the routine) and uses the special string-escape sequences \u and \L to manipulate the case of the letters in the string. \u inside a double-quoted string makes the next character in the string uppercase, whether or not it started out that way. \L makes all subsequent letters in the string lowercase (up to the \E string escape if it's there, or to the end of the string if it's not). So, for example, if $student_first held the string 'john' or 'JOHN' or 'jOhN', interpolating inside double quotes with a leading \u\L would always return the string 'John'. I did this because I had noticed that the children using this tool tended to use many creative approaches to capitalization when typing their names into the form.

The downside to this approach was that if the student actually needed an internal uppercase letter in her name (e.g., LaShawn), this system would corrupt it (e.g., into Lashawn). Someone would have to go in and manually edit the resulting student page to correct the name META header created by the script. On balance, though, this approach seemed likely to save a lot of time, and in practice it worked out quite well.

The subroutine performs various other acts of cleanup on the submitted data, with all those acts being (hopefully) fairly easy for you to understand at this stage in your education. Among the more interesting ones is this:

```
$student_content =~
    s{<!--begin content-->\s*(.*?)\s*<!--end content-->}{$1}s;
```

This is there because most of the students created their student pages by editing a static template file on their local PC, and then, when they had it looking the way they wanted it, creating it on the public web server using the make_page.cgi script. That local page they had created was based on the same page template as the finished pages would be, and had <!--begin content--> and <!--end content--> comments setting off the content portion of the page. When it came time for them to copy and paste their content into the make_page.cgi form, I realized that it was significantly easier for them to just use a Select-All command, rather than trying to copy just the portion between the content-delimiting comment tags. So, this regular expression was thrown in to handle that situation: replacing an entire HTML file that had been submitted and stored in the $student_content variable with just the portion of it between those comment tags.

Another interesting bit is this:

```
$student_content =~ s{\r\n?}{\n}g;
```

Again, as we saw in the guestbook script back in Chapter 12, we need to deal with the variable line-ending sequences that Macintoshes and DOS/Windows machines put at the end of each line of text. This substitution operation makes those line endings conform to the Unix convention.

When the &post_student_page routine is finally ready to create the page, it does a few final checks for safety's sake. After constructing an appropriate path and filename (on my server, something like /w1/s/socalsail/cyberfair/student/nakasone/johnc.html), it checks to see if a file already exists there (with the -e file test operator), and if one does it generates an error message. It also generates an error message if the path of the file it is about to create contains two consecutive periods (..); this is intended to make it harder for a malicious user to trick the script into writing a file outside of the document tree of the web site.

If any of the previous error-message-producing checks actually produce an error message, the subroutine returns without creating the page. Otherwise, it builds the finished page with the &build_page routine, then does the following:

```
if ($fs_path =~ /(.+)/) {
    $fs_path = $1;
}

if ($made_page =~ /(.+)/s) {
    $made_page = $1;
}
```

Some extremely naive taint-mode laundering is occurring here. Again, as we learned in Chapter 12, the values stored in $fs_path and $made_page are considered tainted when running under the -T shebang line switch, because they contain elements that came from an untrusted source (the CGI form submission). To untaint them we need to replace them with the result of a regular expression-capturing operation (the $1 in the previous code). Perl assumes that once we've explicitly filtered the tainted data through a regular expression, it can be trusted.

Of course, these laundering operations are naive because we've used a regular expression of /(.+)/, which will match the entire string, regardless of what it contains, thus defeating the whole purpose of the tainting mechanism. The fact that Perl is perfectly willing to let us do such a silly thing is one of the things I really love about Perl.

Before you do something like this, please think carefully about how a malicious user might try to subvert your script. If you can craft a more-restrictive regular expression to do your laundering, you should try to do so. In this case, I ended up deciding that everything I could think of to be worried about had been taken care of already (by checking for the presence of .. in $fs_path, for example). In other circumstances, though, I would have been more careful with these untainting operations. In general, you should always try to launder tainted data using as strict a regular expression as possible. So, do what I say, not what I do (or at least did, in this case). More good advice about such security matters can be found in the perlsec manpage.

Because this CGI script must write HTML files to the server's filesystem, we need to address the resulting permissions issues. As described (again) in Chapter 12, we have a number of choices, including these:

- Make the directory where the HTML pages are going to be created writeable by the web server process.
- Make the web server run the CGI script under a different user account, like your own, either by making the script setuid or configuring the web server to run all your scripts under your account.

Assuming you choose to make the CGI script run in setuid mode, you'll need to be careful to restore the setuid bit every time the file is updated.

Running External Commands with system and Backticks

After a user had created a bunch of student and leader pages, I wanted him to be able to run the make_cf.plx script, which re-creates all the links at the bottom of all the pages, without my having to do it for him. For that reason, I created the Regenerate

Site Links choice on the default page delivered by make_page.cgi. Let's look now at what happens when the &regenerate_site_links subroutine is invoked.

```
eval { system('./make_cf.plx') == 0 or die $? };
```

This looks pretty scary, but it's not so bad once we pick it apart. As usual, we'll start on the inside of the statement and work our way out. First comes system('./make_cf.plx'). This uses the system function to have our script start up a separate process and run the function's argument in that process. Our script will wait for that other process to finish, then continue on. This is a lot like running an external command inside backticks (`), except that backticks return the output of that external command so that we can capture it into our program and do interesting things with it. system just runs the external command without returning its output.

It is important to check that nothing went wrong when the external command ran, which is what that == 0 or die $? part is doing. Unlike the way we normally check for success or failure in a Perl function, where the function returns a true value for success and a false value for failure, the system function does just the opposite. It returns the number 0 (which evaluates to false) if the external command ran successfully, and some nonzero error number if it failed. Therefore, we have to do the test as we have here, dying with an error message (which in this case is contained in the special variable $?) unless the system function's return value is numerically equal to zero (tested with == 0).

So much for the inside part of that line. What about the outside part? What does that eval { ... } construct do? It lets us trap fatal errors in our script, handling them in some more elegant way than just having the script die.

Allow me to jump ahead a bit. I knew that this &regenerate_site_links routine would take a long time (as much as 8 or 9 seconds) to run because as the site grew to include a large number of HTML pages, that's how long it took for make_cf.plx to run from the command line. I also knew that there was a good chance that in the final push to complete the project before the CyberFair competition's deadline, two or more users might try to regenerate the site's links at the same time. And that would be bad. I'll talk more about why it would be bad, and the steps I took to prevent it, in a minute. For now, though, it's enough for us to know that I modified the make_cf.plx script in such a way that it would die, rather than trying to rewrite all the pages on the site, if someone tried to run it while another copy of it was already running.

Because it was possible that users were going to have this &regenerate_site_links subroutine die on them, I wanted to have the make_page.cgi script give a more informative error message than the web server's "Internal Server Error" page. Using the eval function, I could do that.

eval { *something* } runs whatever is inside the curly braces as if it were its own miniature Perl script. If that mini Perl script dies, the program containing the eval doesn't die. Instead, the error message returned by the die is intercepted and placed in the special variable $@. Thus, we can stick some code that we suspect might die inside of an eval { } construct, then test to see if anything got stuck into $@. If it did, we know that the eval'd code died, and we can take whatever action we like.

 Be sure to stick a semicolon after the curly-brace–delimited block that is the argument to eval. It's not like the blocks used to set off logical if-then constructs, which don't get a semicolon there. I've often forgotten to include the semicolon after eval's block. Force of habit, I suppose.

Here's what comes immediately after the eval statement:

```
if ($@) {
    $err_msg = <<EndOfText;
<LI>The make_cf.plx script failed to run, possibly because another
copy of it was already running. You should try again in a minute or so,
and if you still get this message, send an E-mail to
<A HREF="mailto:jbc\@west.net">jbc\@west.net</A> to let
John Callender know there's a problem. Sorry about the inconvenience.
<LI>Here is the error number that was returned: $?
EndOfText
    return;
}
```

That just sticks my more-friendly error message into $err_msg, then returns from the subroutine immediately.

Race Conditions

Now let's jump out of the make_page.cgi script for a moment and see what I did to make_cf.plx to make it play nice in the presence of other copies of itself running at the same time. Before doing so, though, let's talk for a moment about what might have gone wrong if I didn't take those precautions.

The make_cf.plx script, you will remember, uses File::Find to descend recursively through the directories of the CyberFair site, reading in all the HTML files and storing their metainformation in a special data structure. Then it traverses that data structure, rewriting all the files to reflect the latest version of the site's design template and creating links to the other pages in the site.

Now, think for a moment about the following situation: one copy of make_cf.plx starts up, reads all the metainformation, and then begins rewriting pages. At that moment, a second copy starts up and begins reading metainformation. The first copy opens a file for writing, thereby clobbering everything that was previously in it. A moment later, it writes out the new version of that file, with everything updated nicely. But during that very short interval between the file being clobbered and the new version being completely written, the second copy of make_cf.plx comes along and reads the file. Maybe it gets no data because it reads the file while it is still clobbered. Maybe it gets corrupted data because it reads the file when it is only half-written. Either way will result in errors when that second copy writes out its version of the site.

This is a classic example of what programmers call a *race condition*. (Aside: I used to hear programmers speak of *race conditions* in fearful tones and assumed it must mean some horrible malfunction of the computer's circuits, with electrons spinning out of control like a steam engine with a broken governor. Once I figured out that it just means what it sounds like, a race between two programs, with the outcome depending on which one reaches the finish line first, it was quite a relief.) Race conditions are surprisingly easy to create when you have multiple copies of a script acting on the same data at the same time, which is precisely the situation you have when you use CGI scripts to update information on your site. Fortunately, we have a tool for dealing with this problem: *file locking*, as implemented by Perl's flock function.

File Locking

Back in Chapter 12, we instituted file locking for a guestbook CGI script using Perl's sysopen function, and some fancy magic involving rewinding and truncating the guestbook file to write to it after obtaining an exclusive lock. The approach to file locking that we'll be using in this case is different, in that it is based on the concept of a *semaphore file*. I first heard about semaphore files from Mark-Jason Dominus, one of the coolest Perl gurus around when it comes to explaining nifty Perl tricks in language even accidental programmers can understand.

The notion of a semaphore file sounded very familiar to me when I first heard about it, and after a few seconds I realized why: I had already been exposed to the concept back in kindergarten. All of us kids would sit in a circle, and when I wanted to say something I had to wait to be handed a special stuffed elephant that meant it was my turn to talk. Because there was only one stuffed elephant, there would (in theory) only be one child talking at any given time.

The semaphore file is the make_cf.plx script's stuffed elephant. Only one copy of the script gets to hold it at a time, and only the copy holding it gets to read from and write to the CyberFair pages.

Here's how it works. Up near the top of the make_cf.plx script (which was given as Example 15-1, back in Chapter 15), before any reading or writing has taken place, we add the following lines:

```
use Fcntl ':flock';
my $lock_file = '/my/private/dir/cyberfair.lock';
```

The first line uses the standard Fcntl module to import some magical file-locking constants. The second line specifies the location of the semaphore file, which is just a file that the script can read from and write to, and doesn't necessarily contain any other useful information. (For security reasons, though, it is important that this file *not* be in a world-writeable directory, like /tmp.)

Then, later on in the script but still before any reading or writing of files has taken place, we add the following:

```
open LOCK, "> $lock_file"
    or die "couldn't open $lock_file for writing: $!";
my $count = 0;
until (flock(LOCK, LOCK_EX | LOCK_NB)) {
    warn "PID $$ is sleeping with count $count...\n";
    sleep 1;
    ++$count;
    if ($count > 9) {
        die "couldn't get exclusive lock on LOCK for 10 seconds,
        quitting";
    }
}
```

In the first line, we are opening the semaphore file for writing. Then we initialize a counter variable to 0 and enter an until loop that tries to lock the file using the flock function. An until loop is exactly like a while loop, except it reverses the test in its conditional statement: the block following the condition will continue to execute until the condition returns a true value.

The flock function will return a true value when it successfully obtains a lock on the filehandle given in its first argument. The type of lock obtained is determined by the second argument to flock, which is where we use the constants imported with use Fcntl ':flock'. There are two main varieties of lock that flock can get: a *shared lock* (which means that any number of separate processes can hold the lock at one time), and an *exclusive lock* (which means that only one process at a time can hold the lock). In this case, we are applying for an exclusive lock on the semaphore file, courtesy of the LOCK_EX constant.

Except that we do something a little bit fancier: we use the bitwise-or operator (|) to add to that exclusive lock (LOCK_EX) constant the constant for a nonblocking lock (LOCK_NB). Since things like bitwise logic operations and binary arithmetic never seemed to get covered in the political theory classes I took in college, this sort of thing has always seemed somewhat deep and mysterious to me, but no matter; the magic works fine if you invoke it correctly.

Asking for a nonblocking lock causes flock to reverse its normal behavior, which is to *block* if the lock cannot at first be obtained. That means if we just use LOCK_EX as the second argument to flock, and another program already holds an exclusive lock on the semaphore file when our script tries to get it, the script will just sit there, patiently waiting for the lock to be granted. By using LOCK_EX | LOCK_NB as the second argument, though, the script will try to get the lock, fail, and go immediately on to whatever comes next. In this case, that means it will pause (because of the sleep 1, which makes the script go to sleep for 1 second), then increment the $count variable by one, and check to see if it has already cycled through the loop 10 times. If it has, the script will die. Otherwise, it will go through the loop again, trying to get the lock, sleeping if it fails, and so on.

The upshot of all this is that the make_cf.plx script will not go on to read in the information from the site and write out the revised pages until after it has successfully obtained an exclusive lock on the semaphore file. If it can't get that lock, it will keep trying to do so, once per second, for 10 seconds, at which point it will give up and die.

The only other thing the script needs to do is to release the lock when it is done rewriting the pages. We make it do that just by putting the following at the end of the script proper, before the subroutine definitions:

```
close LOCK;
```

That works because any locks on a filehandle are always released when the filehandle itself is closed.

 The file-locking system implemented by flock is merely *advisory* in nature. Having an exclusive lock on a file, for example, doesn't prevent another program from modifying it, unless that other program has been written to obtain a lock itself before doing so. This is actually a lot like the experience I had in kindergarten, when there always seemed to be someone who was willing to talk without waiting for the stuffed elephant. Such is life.

Adding Link Checking

We're going to put just one more little embellishment into the make_page.cgi script. At the end of the &regenerate_links process, it would be nice to run the quick-and-dirty version of the link-checking script we saw back in Chapter 11 (the one that just checked for breakage in links pointing to files in the local filesystem). The idea here is that the user has just added some pages to the site, with IMG and A tags pointing to other files on the site, and it would be nice to run a quick check to let the user know if any of those links were broken.

As it turned out, nothing could be easier. We can just stick a copy of that first version of the link checker in the same directory as make_page.cgi and modify its configuration variables to point it at the CyberFair site. We should also set it to output its results as HTML.

Then we add the following to the end of the &regenerate_site_links subroutine in make_page.cgi:

```
my $report = `$fs_root/maint/link_check.plx`;

if ($report =~ /<BODY>(.+)<\/BODY>/s) {
```

```
    $content .= $1;
}

    &show_links;
```

That just runs the link checker using backticks (`` ` ``), captures the output into $report, and then uses a regular expression to extract just the portion of the report between the <BODY> and </BODY> tags. That report is appended to the $content variable, so any broken links are reported to the user in the results page he sees after invoking &regenerate_site_links.

There are several things that the scripts described in these last four chapters don't do: they don't allow for browser-based content updates of existing pages, for example. Overall, though, they were very helpful in allowing contributions to the project by a large number of students, many of whom had only limited prior experience with web development. Using the tools shown here, we were able to maintain design consistency and appropriate internal linking while building a docbase containing several hundred HTML pages, and to do so during a relatively short span of time.

## CHAPTER 18

Monitoring Search Engine Positioning

The first commercial web site I worked on full time taught me many useful lessons. One of those lessons came about 18 months after the site's unveiling, when it suffered a sudden unexplained drop in visitor traffic. After a lot of research and a bit of hair-pulling, I finally figured out what had happened: I had invalidated a large number of offsite search engine links by changing the location of some pages on the site. The search engines eventually noticed all the resulting 404 errors at the destinations to which they were referring searchers and removed those pages from their databases. It took months to reestablish the site's "footprint" in the search engine databases and rebuild traffic to previous levels.

Needless to say, this brought home to me the importance of maintaining stable URLs for web resources. In a very real sense, your web site does not exist in isolation. It is simply a small component in a much larger, distributed system, and moving resources from one location to another breaks that larger system. It doesn't matter that you can update all the links on *your* site so that they work correctly with the new locations; offsite links will still be broken. The only really good way to avoid that is to make sure you maintain stable URLs for your web resources forever (or at least for as long as is practical).

The other thing that this incident brought home to me was the importance of third-party search engines as a source of visitors. This web site was the subject of an ongoing promotional campaign featuring mailings, print advertising, and trade show exhibit space, but despite all that, free referrals from search engines made up nearly half the site's incoming traffic.

This was true despite my having never pursued an active campaign of search engine "position enhancement." I'm not a big fan of trying to fool search engines into ranking a web page higher in search results than the page actually deserves. Tricks like loading up a page with keywords that don't relate to its actual content, or serving up one page to a search engine spider and another page to the site's actual users, may temporarily boost a site's traffic, but it's a bad idea. Such gains will be achieved only by degrading the effectiveness of the search engine in delivering targeted results, and thereby degrading the overall usefulness of the Web. In my view, that's immoral and counter to the traditions that built the Web in the first place. On a more practical level, it puts one in an ongoing, and ultimately unwinnable, arms race with the operators of the search engines, who will eventually notice the trickery and modify their indexing and ranking tools to counteract it.

A much better approach is to create pages that are as useful as possible, with specific, targeted content presented in an accessible manner, and then working to make sure that content is appropriately indexed by the search engines. In that context, a tool to analyze how your site stands in searches for particular phrases at particular search engines can be very useful. This chapter shows a pair of such tools: first, a simple Perl script that you can run from the command line to report the results of a particular search; and second, a more elaborate tool that creates HTML reports describing multiple searches at multiple search engines.

This might sound like a tall order, but in fact, by using some CPAN modules provided by helpful members of the extended Perl community, both scripts end up being really easy to create.

Installing WWW::Search

One of the cooler projects in the realm of web-related Perl modules is the `WWW::Search` module, created by Martin Thurn and available on CPAN. Along with the various add-on modules that work with it, it allows you to easily write Perl scripts that interface with third-party search engines, performing searches, returning results, and so on. Add-on modules exist for most of the major search engines (`WWW::Search::AltaVista`, `WWW::Search::Infoseek`, `WWW::Search::Google`, and so on), with some of those modules being maintained by Thurn himself, and others being maintained by other contributers in the extended Perl community. These modules tend to be fairly maintenance-heavy because in the absence of a real application programming interface (API) provided by the search engine vendors, `WWW::Search` modules must do their work by "screen scraping" (that is, simulating a user, submitting a query, and then parsing the HTML pages returned by the search engine to pluck out the relevant information). Whenever a search engine changes the format of its search form or its results page, it breaks the relevant `WWW::Search` module, which must be updated to reflect the changes.

I had a difficult time installing `WWW::Search` using the CPAN module, but it installed fairly easily using the traditional manual methods described in Chapter 11. Here is the sequence of steps I followed:

1. Using the search tool at *http://search.cpan.org/*, I located the latest version of the `WWW::Search` module (*http://www.cpan.org/authors/id/M/MT/MTHURN/WWW-Search-2.15.tar.gz*, at the time of this writing).

2. I downloaded that file to a temporary directory on my web server using the lynx command-line browser.

3. I untarred (and ungzipped) that file using the following command:

```
[jbc@ithil tmp]$ tar xhvzf WWW-Search-2.15.tar.gz
```

This is a modified version, by the way, of the unzipping and untarring operation shown in the earlier example. This time, I combined both operations into one step, courtesy of tar's -z command-line option, which causes it to unzip the tar file as part of the extraction process.

4. I used cd to go to the WWW-Search-2.15 directory that was created, and checked the README file for further instructions. That file told me I would need to install libwww-perl (the LWP module), the URI module, and the HTML::Parser module before installing WWW::Search. Fortunately I had installed all those modules previously, but if not, I would now have had to install each of them before continuing.

5. I then performed the following three steps from the shell, using the su command to become the root user before issuing the final make install command so that the module could be installed as part of the server's Perl installation. (The README file also contained helpful instructions on how I could have installed my own private copy of the module if I lacked root access):

```
perl Makefile.PL
make test
make install
```

And that was it. The make test phase complained about a few failed tests, but they appear not to have been significant for my purposes, since the module worked fine for me afterward.

Version 2.15 of the WWW::Search module comes with a bunch of add-on modules already, including ones for two of my favorite search engines (WWW::Search::AltaVista and WWW::Search::Infoseek), but it doesn't include one for my *very* favorite search engine. For that, I needed to search again at *http://search.cpan.org*, until I found the WWW::Search::Google module by Jim Smyser. It took me only a few minutes to install it using the steps outlined in its INSTALL file, once I had untarred and ungzipped it.

A Single-Search Results Tool

To give you an idea of how the WWW::Search module works, we'll start with a simple script that runs from the command line. This script will let us use arguments to specify which search engine to search, what query to submit to it, and so on. The script, called search_rank.plx, is in Example 18-1.

Example 18-1. Querying search engines from the command line with WWW::Search

```perl
#!/usr/bin/perl -w

# search_rank.plx

# using the WWW::Search module, compute the rank of the highest-ranked
# page for a particular site when searching a particular search
# engine for a particular query string.

use strict;

use WWW::Search;
use Getopt::Std;

my %opt;

getopts('s:u:q:m:', \%opt);

unless ($opt{s} and $opt{u} and $opt{q}) {

    die <<"EOF";
Usage: $0 [options]

Required options: -s search_engine
                  -u base_url
                  -q 'search query'

Optional options: -m max_#_to_retrieve (defaults to 50)

EOF

}

my $max = $opt{m} || 50;

my $search = new WWW::Search($opt{s});
$search->maximum_to_retrieve($max);

my $base_url = quotemeta($opt{u});
my $rank     = 0;
my $count    = 1;

$search->native_query(WWW::Search::escape_query($opt{q}));
while (my $result = $search->next_result()) {
    if (not $rank and $result->url =~ /$base_url/o.) {
        $rank = $count;
    }
    print "$count: ", $result->title || $result->url,
        ', ', $result->url, "\n";
    ++$count;
}

print "Rank: $rank\n";
```

Using the Getopt::Std Module

As you scan through this script, the first interesting thing you'll notice is the use of the Getopt::Std module. This is a standard module that comes with every Perl installation. It lets us easily use one-letter switches when invoking our program from the command line. We tell the program what switches we will be using via the getopts subroutine (which is imported automatically into the script by use Getopt::Std). In search_rank.plx, the line where that happens looks like this:

```
getopts('s:u:q:m:', \%opt);
```

This line says that the program will accept command-line switches named -s, -u, -q, and -m. All those switches will take arguments (which is what the colon after each switch name means), and the arguments will be stored in the %opt hash (whose reference was passed in the second argument to the getopts routine), keyed by the single letter used for the switch. For example, executing the program like this:

```
[jbc@andros search_rank]$ search_rank.plx -s AltaVista -u www.lies.com -q 'walnuts
rutabagas'
```

would have the same effect, once the program was up and running, as having the following lines in it:

```
$opt{s} = 'AltaVista';
$opt{u} = 'www.lies.com';
$opt{q} = 'walnuts rutabagas';
```

The idea behind using switches is that we can use the script in a very flexible fashion, altering its behavior by supplying appropriate command-line arguments. The -s option is used to specify which search engine to use (the name must correspond to an installed WWW::Search backend). The -u option gives a URL (or a partial URL) to look for in the results returned by the search engine. The search_rank.plx script will report where in the returned results that URL first appears. The assumption is that we are interested in how highly a particular site ranks in the results of a particular search engine query. The -u option is where we specify the site we are interested in.

Finally, the -q option is used to specify the query to be passed to the search engine. Note the single quotes surrounding the -q option 'walnuts rutabagas'. This quoting is necessary to avoid having only walnuts assigned to $opt{q}.

The next part of the script contains a test to see if the -s, -u, and -q options were all set. If they weren't, the script dies with a usage message.

Using || for Short-Circuit Assignment

Next comes the assignment of the -m option to the $max variable:

```
my $max = $opt{m} || 50;
```

This will be used to determine how many results to return from the search engine. If nothing was supplied in the -m option, $opt{m} evaluates to the undefined value, which is false, meaning the script's execution jumps over the || and 50 is assigned to $max instead. In other words, the script will default to returning 50 results, unless some other value is supplied explicitly via the -m switch.

This sort of *short-circuit* assignment behavior is commonly used in Perl scripts to specify a default value. It's important to use the || operator to achieve this effect, rather than the or operator, because the || has higher precedence than the assignment operator (=). Another way you often hear this expressed is that the || operator *binds more tightly* than the = operator. Using || in this case means the statement will be evaluated as shown by the explicit parentheses in the following example:

```
my $max = ($opt{m} || 50);
```

This is what we want: either $opt{m} is assigned to $max, or, if $opt{m} is false, 50 is assigned to $max. If we used the or operator (which has lower precedence, or *binds less tightly*, than the = operator), the statement would be evaluated as in the following example:

```
(my $max = $opt{m}) or 50;
```

That would assign $opt{m} to the $max variable, whether or not it contained a true value, and then, if it *did* contain a false value, the script would evaluate the number 50. It wouldn't actually *do* anything with the number 50; it would just evaluate it and throw away the result. In Perl terms, this is called *using a constant in a void context*. If we've enabled warnings in the script, we'll get a complaint about that.

Next come the following two lines:

```
my $search = new WWW::Search($opt{s});
$search->maximum_to_retrieve($max);
```

The WWW::Search module, you will notice, is object-oriented. The first of these lines creates a new WWW::Search object via the new method, storing that object in $search and initializing it with the value stored in $opt{s}. $opt{s}, again, is the value supplied after the -s switch on the command line. In other words, it is the name of the specific search engine back end we want to use with WWW::Search. The second line calls the maximum_to_retrieve method on that $search object (there's that nifty object-oriented terminology), setting it to the value in $max.

Next, the script initializes three more scalar variables:

```
my $base_url = quotemeta($opt{u});
my $rank     = 0;
my $count    = 1;
```

The $base_url scalar is initialized with the result of running Perl's quotemeta function on the contents of $opt{u}, which is the option where we specified the partial URL of the site whose position in the search results we are interested in. The quotemeta function, as you know already, takes a string and makes it suitable for literal matching inside a regular expression pattern.

The $rank scalar is initialized to 0. This scalar will be used to store the position in the search results of the highest result whose URL contains the string specified in $base_url. The $count scalar is initialized to 1; this will be incremented with each search result processed so that the appropriate position can be assigned to $rank when (and if) $base_url is encountered in a search-result URL.

Next comes the actual heart of the script, where the real action takes place. First there is the following line:

```
$search->native_query(WWW::Search::escape_query($opt{q}));
```

In this line, the native_query method is being called on the $search object to actually run a search using the specified search engine. The argument passed to the native_query method is the result of running the submitted query (in $opt{q}) through the WWW::Search::escape_query subroutine. Invoking a specific subroutine inside another package (which is what we are doing when we invoke WWW::Search::escape_query) is a rather unorthodox technique for a Perl program (and it's especially outré to find something like that in an object-oriented module like WWW::Search), but it works perfectly well, and that's what the WWW::Search documentation says to do, so that's how we do it. What escape_query actually does, by the way, is to convert our search query into the form suitable for transmission as a GET-method URL, turning spaces into plus signs (+) and so on.

Next comes a while loop to actually process the results of the search:

```
while (my $result = $search->next_result()) {
    if (not $rank and $result->url =~ /$base_url/o) {
        $rank = $count;
    }
    print "$count: ", $result->title || $result->url, ', ', $result->url, "\n";
    ++$count;
}
```

The next_result method returns the next result (naturally). The if block checks to see if $rank has been set, and if not, it uses a regular expression match to see if this result contains $base_url. (Note the use of the /o modifier to avoid needlessly recompiling the regular expression each time through the loop.) If the expression matches, $rank is set to the current value of $count. Finally, the current result is printed to STDOUT (using the title of the returned result, or, if it isn't available, the URL), and the $count variable is incremented by 1.

Finally, after the script is done printing all the results of the search, it prints the contents of $rank, and exits.

And there you have it: a script to query search engines from the command line. Here's an example of its output:

```
[jbc@andros search_rank]$ search_rank.plx -s AltaVista -u www.devicelink.com -q
'medical device' -m 3
1: Cancom:MediaKit:<EM>Medical Device</EM> Link, http://www.cancom.com/mediakit/md.
html
```

```
2: <EM>Medical Device</EM> Link, http://www.devicelink.com/
3: St. Jude Medical - <EM>medical device</EM> products for cardiac rhythm management,
http://www.sjm.com/
Rank: 2
```

Notice how the search terms are surrounded by <EM></EM> tags in the page titles returned with AltaVista's search results. That's just the way AltaVista does things, apparently.

Here's an example of the same search with a different search engine:

```
[jbc@andros search_rank]$ search_rank.plx -s Google -u www.devicelink.com -q
'medical device' -m 3
Found Total: 580,000
1: index, http://www.cancom.com/
2: Cancom:MediaKit:Medical Device Link, http://www.cancom.com/mediakit/md.html
3: Medical Device Link, http://www.devicelink.com/
Rank: 3
```

That Found Total: 580,000 line is interesting. It isn't being output by anything in the script. Some investigation turned up the following line in the WWW::Search::Google module:

```
print STDERR "Found Total: $n\n" ;
```

I guessed that that was a legacy of some debugging code the module's author had inserted at some point, so I commented it out in my copy of the module and sent an email to the author mentioning it. Isn't it wonderful having access to source code for the tools you use?

A Multisearch Results Tool

A logical way to extend the search_rank.plx script is to make it output its results in the form of web pages, and to let one specify multiple search engines and multiple query strings. The script in Example 18-2 (called search_rank2.plx) does just that.

Example 18-2. A script to submit multiple queries to multiple search engines

```
#!/usr/bin/perl -w

# search_rank2.plx

# more full-featured search-ranking script: multiple engines,
# multiple search queries, Web-based output.

use strict;
use WWW::Search;

# configuration:

my $max_results   = 50;
my $base_url      = 'http://www.devicelink.com/';
```

```perl
my @engines         = qw(AltaVista Google Lycos);
my $result_fs_path  = '/w1/e/elanus/search_rank';
my $result_web_path = '/search_rank';
my $index_file      = "$result_fs_path/index.html";

my %data; # HoH: primary key: engine name. secondary key: query string.
          # value: rank

# see end of script, after the __END__ token, for list of search queries

my $url_pattern = quotemeta($base_url);

chomp(my @queries = <DATA>);

foreach my $engine (@engines) {

    my $engine_dir = $result_fs_path . '/' . $engine;
    unless (-e $engine_dir) {
        mkdir $engine_dir or die "can't mkdir '$engine_dir': $!";
    }

    my $search = new WWW::Search($engine);
    $search->maximum_to_retrieve($max_results);

    foreach my $query (@queries) {

        my $query_dir  = clean_name($query);
        my $result_dir = $engine_dir . '/' . $query_dir;
        unless (-e $result_dir) {
            mkdir $result_dir or die "can't mkdir '$result_dir': $!";
        }

        my $detail_file = "$result_fs_path/$engine/$query_dir/index.html";
        my $detail_url  = "$result_web_path/$engine/$query_dir/";
        my $localtime   = localtime;

        open DETAIL, "> $detail_file"
            or die "can't open $detail_file for writing: $!";

        print DETAIL <<"EOF";
<HTML>
<HEAD>
<TITLE>$engine results for '$query'</TITLE>
</HEAD>
<BODY>
<H1>$engine results for '$query'</H1>

<P>Report run $localtime</P>

<P><A HREF="$result_web_path/">All results</A></P>

<TABLE BORDER=1 CELLPADDING=5>
```

```
<TR>
<TH>Rank</TH>
<TH>Site</TH>
</TR>
EOF

        $data{$engine}{$query} = my $rank = 'None';
        my $count = 1;

        $search->native_query(WWW::Search::escape_query($query));

        while (my $result = $search->next_result()) {
            if ($rank eq 'None' and $result->url =~ /$url_pattern/o) {
                $data{$engine}{$query} = $rank = $count;
            }
            my $url     = $result->url;
            my $title = $result->title || $result->url;
            my $description = $result->description || 'None provided';

            print DETAIL <<"EOF";
<TR>
<TD ALIGN="center">$count</TD>
<TD><A HREF="$url"><STRONG>$title</STRONG></A><BR>
$url<BR>
$description</TD>
</TR>
EOF

            ++$count;

        }

        print DETAIL <<"EOF";
</TABLE>
</HTML>
EOF

        close DETAIL;

    }
}

my $localtime = localtime;

open INDEX, "> $index_file" or die "can't open $index_file for writing: $!";
print INDEX <<"EOF";
<HTML>
<HEAD>
<TITLE>$0 results</TITLE>
</HEAD>
<BODY>
<A NAME="top"><H1>$0 results for $base_url</H1></A>
```

Example 18-2. A script to submit multiple queries to multiple search engines (continued)

```
<P>Report run $localtime</P>

EOF

my @engine_links = map { qq{<A HREF="#$_">$_</A>} } sort @engines;

print INDEX '<P>', join(' | ', @engine_links), "</P>\n";

foreach my $engine (sort keys %data) {

    print INDEX qq{<A NAME="$engine"><H2>$engine</H2></A>\n};

    print INDEX <<"EOF";
<TABLE BORDER=1 CELLPADDING=5>
<TR>
<TH>Query</TH>
<TH>Rank</TH>
</TR>
EOF

    foreach my $query (sort keys %{$data{$engine}}) {

        my $query_dir = clean_name($query);

        print INDEX <<"EOF";
<TR>
<TD><A HREF="$engine/$query_dir/">$query</A></TD>
<TD ALIGN="center">$data{$engine}{$query}</TD>
</TR>
EOF

    }

    print INDEX <<"EOF";
</TABLE>
<P><A HREF="#top">Return to top of page</A></P>
EOF

}

print INDEX "</HTML>\n";
close INDEX;

sub clean_name {

    # accept a string, turn whitespace to underscores and
    # remove non-alphanumeric chars, and return it.

    my $name = shift;
    $name =~ s/\s+/_/g;
    $name =~ s/\W+//g;
    $name;
}
```

```
__END__
medical device
medical manufacturing
medical manufacturing suppliers
stainless steel tubing
```

This script looks a lot like `search_rank.plx` (which shouldn't be surprising, since it started life as that script). The command-line options have been taken out, though, and have been replaced by a configuration section at the top of the script. Among the things that are specified there are `$result_fs_path` (the filesystem path to the directory where the script's results will be written), and `$result_web_path` (the same directory, as viewed from the point of view of the web server). There's also `$index_file`, which contains the path to the web page that will display the top-level results.

There's a `%data` hash of hashes (HoH), which should be pretty easy for you to figure out at this point. This is where the script stores the results of its queries for later summarizing in the `$index_file`. The primary keys of `%data` are search engine names, the secondary keys are the query strings executed on those search engines, and the corresponding values are the highest rank of the target site in the results from each search.

Then comes the following interesting comment:

```
# see end of script, after the __END__ token, for list of search queries
```

Turning dutifully to the end of the script, we see the following:

```
__END__
medical device
medical manufacturing
medical manufacturing suppliers
stainless steel tubing
```

What's going on there is a very useful trick that I never heard of in my early Perl days, but which I now use all the time. Basically, by putting `__END__` all by itself on a line in our script (that's two underscore characters, an uppercase END, and then two more underscore characters), we can tell Perl that our script is officially over. Everything after that `__END__` token will be ignored by Perl when it is parsing the script. But we can access whatever is stored there by reading from the special DATA filehandle. This is handy because we frequently want to have some sort of data file associated with a particular Perl script, but it can be awkward to have to always move that data file around with the script. By sticking the data after the `__END__` token, we can keep the whole kit and caboodle (program *and* data) in one place.

> If you want to store some data at the end of a module, by the way, you need to use a different token: `__DATA__`. But otherwise it works the same as the `__END__` token.

Next, the script turns the $base_url in the configuration section into a form suitable for use inside a regex using the quotemeta function:

```
my $url_pattern = quotemeta($base_url);
```

After that, the script reads all the lines from the DATA filehandle (that is, reads all those lines stored after the __END__ token), chomps them to remove their newlines (because each line has one at the end, just as if those lines were being read from an external file), and stores all those chomped lines in the @queries array, ready for processing later in the script. All this happens in a single line of Perl code:

```
chomp(my @queries = <DATA>);
```

Notice how the assignment to an array puts the <DATA> input operator into an array context, meaning all the lines are returned at once. In the past we've usually assigned from the input operator into a scalar variable, meaning we process one line at a time. Notice also how using chomp on a list chomps all the elements in the list, just as if we had chomped them individually. This chomping of all the elements being assigned to an array *en passant*, as it were, is a common shortcut used by experienced Perl programmers.

If you were paying close attention, you probably noticed that we invoked the clean_name subroutine without a leading ampersand (&):

```
my $query_dir  = clean_name($query);
```

Most experienced Perl programmers don't bother with using an ampersand when they invoke a subroutine. Now that you've had time to become familiar with most of Perl's important built-in functions, I figured it was okay if we started doing the same. For the rest of this book, then, I'll be omitting the ampersands when calling subroutines. Everything should work pretty much the same, as long as we remember this: if we are invoking a subroutine without supplying any arguments, we should give it a pair of (empty) trailing parentheses anyway. For example:

```
my @return_values = my_sub( );
```

If you want to learn more about the nitty gritty of invoking subroutines, you'll find everything you ever wanted to know (and more) in the perlsub manpage.

There isn't much that's new in the rest of this script. It simply iterates over all the engines in the @engines array (which we set in the configuration section), and for each engine it executes each query stored in @queries. Along the way it makes directories as needed in order to have a directory for each engine, and a subdirectory within each directory for each query. It saves the detailed results of each query in an index.html file in each query-specific directory, formatting the pages to look like the example in Figure 18-1.

Some object-oriented syntax is required for dealing with WWW::Search, but this part of the script works just like it did in the chapter's first example, where we ran the

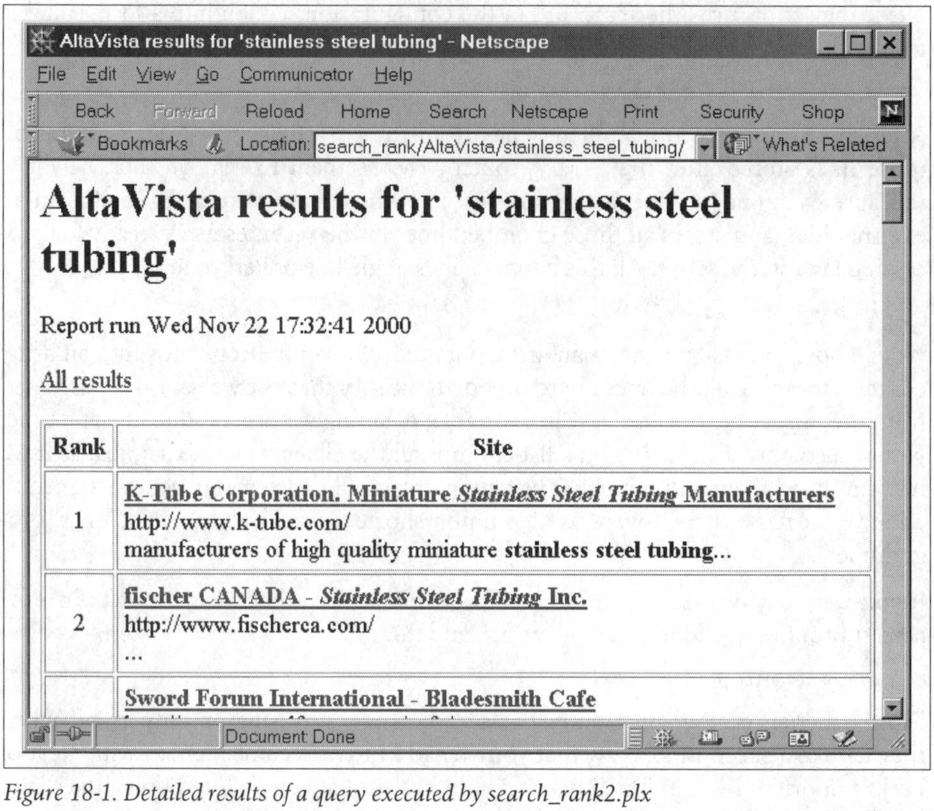

Figure 18-1. Detailed results of a query executed by search_rank2.plx

queries from the shell's command line. One thing I want to call your attention to is the assignment to the %data HoH, as in this line, where each value is initialized:

```
$data{$engine}{$query} = my $rank = 'None';
```

The same thing happens again, when the search pattern stored in $url_pattern is actually seen in the search results, triggering the storage of the current value of $count in $rank, and in $data{$engine}{$query}:

```
$data{$engine}{$query} = $rank = $count;
```

The $data{$engine}{$query} part is the same syntax we learned in Chapter 15. We are assigning a value to the "inner" hash of a hash of hashes. We could think of the expression on the left side of the assignment as being $data{$engine}->{$query}, where the hash reference stored in $data{$engine} is being dereferenced in order to access the original hash, and then a value is being assigned to it to go with the key $query. Perl lets us omit the dereferencing arrow between the pairs of curly braces, though, which makes the whole thing more readable.

The map Function

There's one more really cool thing in this script. Buried in its latter half, where the top-level page is being created to list all the results stored in the %data HoH, there is the following somewhat scary-looking line:

```
my @engine_links = map { qq{<A HREF="#$_">$_ </A>} } sort @engines;
```

This is our first use of Perl's map function. The map function is another one of those things, like the conditional operator (walnuts ? rutabagas : watermelons), that serves to separate the accidental programmers from the real ones. It took me years, literally, before I was comfortable enough with Perl to begin using the map function, but now that I'm familiar with it I can't imagine life without it. Larry Rosler, one of the nicest members of the extended Perl community when it comes to helping out beginners, called the map function "beautiful" in a session I attended at one of O'Reilly's Perl conferences, and after working with it for a while I can appreciate why he feels that way.

The map function is one of those Perl shortcuts, a diagonal path offering a more efficient route from point A to point B. In effect, it lets us take a foreach loop and squash it down into a single line. To be more specific, map lets us specify a block of code to be executed for each element in a list. The map function processes the list, running the block of code on each element, and returns a list consisting of the results of all those blocks' execution.

An example will clarify what I'm describing. Let's say we had a script containing the following array consisting of two-letter postal abbreviations for the 50 U.S. states. (This is intended only for demonstration purposes. Residents of DC, VI, and other locations, my apologies.)

```
my @states = qw(AL AK AZ AR CA CO CT DE FL GA
                HI ID IL IN IA KS KY LA ME MD
                MA MI MN MS MO MT NE NV NH NJ
                NM NY NC ND OH OK OR PA RI SC
                SD TN TX UT VT VA WA WV WI WY);
```

Let's further say that we wanted to turn that array into a hash in which each abbreviation was associated with the value 1. This would be useful if we wanted to do a quick hash lookup, for example, to tell if a particular two-letter abbreviation corresponded to one of those postal codes.

Now, we could do that with a foreach loop, like this:

```
my %is_state;

foreach my $state (@states) {
    $is_state{$state} = 1;
}
```

For the first several years of my Perl apprenticeship that's exactly how I would have done it. Once I got comfortable with map, though, I could write it like this:

```
my %is_states = map { $_ => 1 } @states;
```

See how simple and clear that is? This takes advantage of the fact that inside map's execution block, the current item from the list is represented by the default scalar variable, $_. That chunk of code inside the block turns each item from the @states array into a pair of elements, separated by the => comma-replacement operator, suitable for stuffing into the %is_states hash.

Let's go back now to the line that uses map in search_rank2.plx:

```
my @engine_links = map { qq{<A HREF="#$_">$_</A>} } sort @engines;
```

The list being fed to map's block in this case is the alphabetically sorted list of search engine names from the script's configuration section. For each engine, a link is constructed pointing at a location lower on the page where a <A NAME="engine_name"> target is going to be constructed in just a moment. The list of links is then stored in the @engine_links array.

Besides map, another cool trick is being used in this line: the qq{} alternate-quoting operator. You previously learned about the qw{} operator, which quotes a list of whitespace-separated words, returning the words as a list. The qq{} operator is similar; it serves as a clever way of double-quoting a string. What makes it clever is that, while a qq{}-quoted string does all the special things you would normally expect of a double-quoted string (variable interpolation, backslash interpretation), it *doesn't* need to have internal double quotes escaped with backslashes. In this case, that means the string inside the qq{} is significantly easier to type and to read than it would have been if all the internal " characters needed a leading \.

You'll also notice, by the way, how clever Perl is about keeping track of the nested curly braces. We never have to worry about Perl getting confused about which set of curly braces goes with the qq{}, and which set goes with the map function. (*We* may get confused if we're not careful, but Perl always keeps track accurately.)

The cleverer among you have doubtless speculated by now that if there is a qq{} quote-replacement operator for doing double quoting, there might well be a q{} operator for doing single quoting. And you'd be right. There is. For both of these, as for the qw{} operator you learned about previously, you can actually choose any character you like for the actual delimiter, so you'll see things like qq/here's a "doublequoted" string/. If you use one of the balanced delimiters (parentheses, square brackets, angle brackets, or curly braces), the closing delimiter is the corresponding closing version of the opening delimiter. Otherwise, the closing delimiter is the same as the opening delimiter.

And that's it! You can run this script to produce a web-based report of search results for multiple queries executed at multiple search engines. A top-level page will be produced with a summary of the results; it will look something like Figure 18-2. The links on that page will point to the detail pages described earlier.

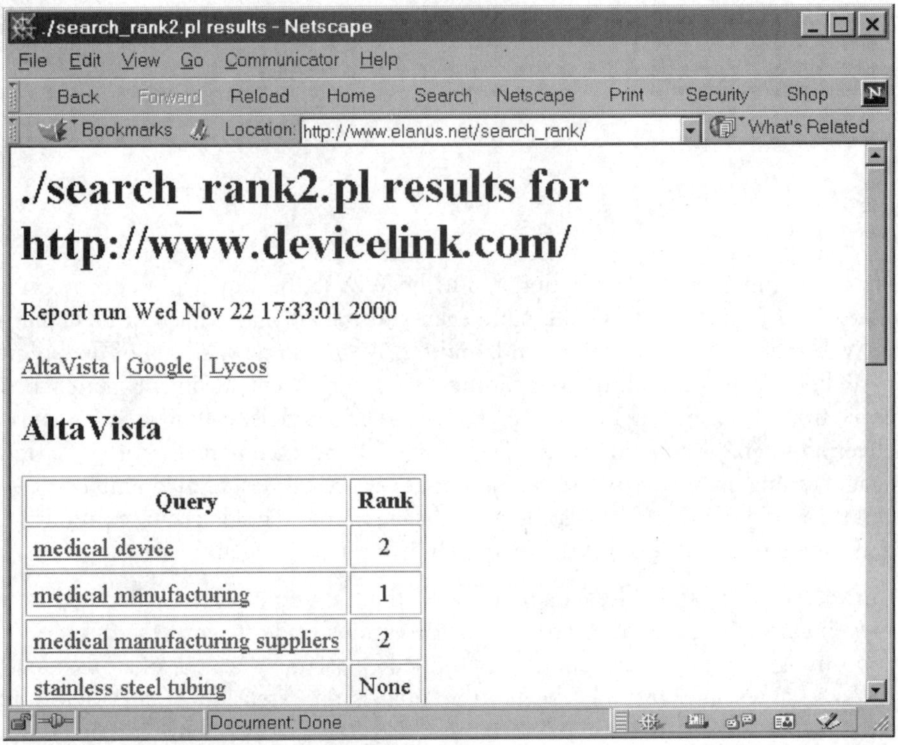

Figure 18-2. Top-level index page produced by search_rank2.plx

CHAPTER 19
Keeping Track of Users

One of the things I find fascinating about the Web is the way it presents a real-life version of the Hindu fable of the blind men and the elephant. Each of us comes to the Web from a different background, and the Web is so new, so full of unexplored possibilities, that we tend to see it through the filter of our previous experience. To people from the world of TV and movies, the Web's highest calling is as a means of delivering interactive video. To graphic designers and commercial artists, the most engaging thing about the Web is its potential as a visual design medium. To people from the world of printed books and periodicals, the Web holds promise primarily as a publishing tool, a way to get their words in front of a global audience.

Professionally I'm most closely aligned with that last point of view because in my pre-web career I was a writer and editor for various trade magazines. But I see the Web through another filter, one more compelling for me than the one provided by my professional background. To me, the Web is an extension of previous online communities. Interactive discussion groups, like the global Usenet, or the smaller worlds of hobbyist bulletin board systems, have been an intensely absorbing experience for me for many years. Real-time multiuser environments, MUDs and MOOs and various other incarnations of user-to-user chat, have similarly played a big part in my recreational computing. And it isn't all just fun and games. Much of what I've learned in making my career switch from writer/editor to web person has been learned from my online acquaintances, people I know as individuals and consider in many cases to be my friends, even though I could pass them on the street without recognizing them.

For me, then, the Web's most exciting possibilities involve bringing people together, providing a medium for two-way communication. And surprisingly, the Web has been relatively slow to deliver that kind of interactivity. A big part of the problem is that building an online community requires you to identify and keep track of individual users, and the Web, by virtue of its initial design philosophy, is not well-suited to that task. The next two chapters look at this shortcoming in more detail, and present a system that represents a first step in overcoming it.

This chapter covers the following:

- The stateless nature of web transactions, and the resulting difficulty in tracking individual users.
- HTTP's Basic Authentication as a tool for addressing that problem.
- A CGI-based user-registration system. The system presented here is composed of two parts: a registration script, which receives a new user's information and emails a verification code to the email address supplied by the user; and a verification script that lets that user supply the verification code in order to activate his account.

The next chapter takes this example further, replacing the flat-text-file storage scheme it uses with one based on DBM files, offering more efficient access to individual records as the number of records grows larger.

Stateless Transactions

Simplicity and efficiency were overriding concerns when Tim Berners-Lee was making the design decisions that led to the creation of the Web. HTTP, the protocol that governs web transactions, did not (at least in its original incarnation) waste computing resources by having the server maintain costly open connections while waiting for humans to make up their minds. Instead, a web server operates at the much faster pace of computerized decision-making. A request (for a particular HTML page, or a particular image, or the output of a particular CGI script) arrives at the server, the server responds immediately to that request, and then just as immediately it breaks the connection to the user and forgets all about him (or her). It is a *stateless* transaction because the server does not maintain any state information about who the user is or what the user is doing from one request to the next.

This works great when all we want to do is to deliver files to the world as quickly as possible. But it becomes a real pain as soon as we want to keep track of individual users. Maybe we want to let people put items into a virtual shopping cart, with those items being remembered at checkout time. Or maybe we want to let a community of users post comments in a web-based discussion forum, taking steps to ensure, within reasonable limits, that the person posting messages under a particular name today is the same person who posted messages under that name yesterday.

To do those kinds of things we need to add another layer of programming on top of garden-variety HTTP. That programming needs to do two things. First, it needs to identify individual users, tracking them as they interact with our web site. Second, it needs to maintain persistently stored information about those users. We'll look at each problem in turn.

Identifying Individual Users

The most obvious way to keep track of individual users is to look at the remote IP address from which requests originate and to which the server sends its responses. If our server gets a request from 209.151.241.118, and a few minutes later gets another request from the same address, we can assume that both requests came from the same user, correct?

Well, no, we can't. Although this was exactly the approach used in the log-analysis script in Chapter 10 to identify individual "visits" for statistical purposes, it can only give us an approximation rather than an exact count. The problem is that proxy servers often sit between our web server and our site's users. With proxy servers, one user can appear to be interacting with our site from multiple IP addresses, or, conversely, multiple independent users can all appear to be interacting with our site from the same IP address. The bottom line is, remote IP addresses are unsuitable as a way to track individual users.

What can we do? One promising tool is the browser cookie, introduced originally by Netscape in Version 1.1 of its browser, and supported by both Netscape Communicator and Internet Explorer these days. The cookie lets us use a CGI script to send a unique string to the user in a special HTTP response header, with the user's browser storing that string and submitting it back to the server on subsequent requests. Which is exactly what we want: a simple system that lets us tag an individual user ("You're user 'joe' from now on"), and have that user report his identity ("I'm 'joe'") in all subsequent transactions.

The main problem with using cookies for this purpose is that they don't work for everyone. Some people use browsers that lack cookie support. Other people intentionally disable cookies, or browse from behind proxies that strip them because of concerns about privacy or security.

But that may be good enough. If we are content to turn away 10%–15% of our site's users, we can just code up our user-tracking system with cookies, slap a "Cookies required" notice on the site, and be done with it. For most of the sites I've worked on, though, 10%–15% of the web population is too big a group to intentionally turn away. To track that group, something fancier is needed. The way you typically see such user tracking done is with some sort of system to deliver all pages dynamically, with the site's links and forms being rewritten on the fly to encode a unique identifier for each user. That identifier can appear either in the query string or the path info appended to a GET request, or in a hidden form field for POST requests. This method works fairly well, but it does so at the cost of an additional burden on the web server, which can bog down sooner in the face of high traffic levels because it is generating all those customized pages instead of simply delivering a static page stored on disk. Many of the shopping cart systems I see these days are implemented with a cookie/dynamic-page-generation hybrid: cookies for users who can use them, and dynamic page generation for those who can't.

Basic Authentication

As you can see, a user-tracking system based on dynamic page generation can be a fairly complicated undertaking. Rather than try to present something that complicated here, I'm going to explain a different approach to tracking web users' identities: using basic HTTP authentication. This is a system for enabling user logins on the Web. It isn't really suitable for e-commerce/shopping cart applications because it requires the user to enter a username/password combination before any user-tracking can take place, and it excludes any users who aren't already registered in the system. But it works fairly well for discussion-group applications, or any other application where you want to make some special part of your site available only to certain individuals. It's also relatively simple to implement, making it a good starting point for gaining some hands-on experience with tracking individual users on the Web.

Basic authentication is easy to implement because it's already built into the Apache server (because it was built into the NCSA server that Apache is based on). To set it up we just need to create three text files on the server:

- An .htaccess file, which goes in the web directory where we want to control users' access
- An .htgroup file, containing group names and user names
- An .htpasswd file, containing usernames and encrypted passwords

The .htaccess File

To turn on basic authentication, we need to put some Apache server directives somewhere. Typically, we put those in an .htaccess file in the web directory where we want the user tracking to happen. Those directives instruct the server to turn on basic authentication, and tell it where it can find the stored password information to verify users' identities. The .htaccess file is just a plain text file that looks something like this:

```
AuthUserFile /home/httpd/.htpasswd
AuthGroupFile /home/httpd/.htgroup
AuthName socalsail
AuthType Basic

<Limit GET POST>
require group socalsail_members
</Limit>
```

This gives the location of an .htpasswd file and an .htgroup file (both of which we'll be seeing in a moment), and a name (in this case, socalsail) to give in the authentication challenge that is sent to the user when a resource is requested from the directory containing the `.htaccess` file. This `.htaccess` file also contains an instruction to limit access to the directory to users whose names are listed in the `.htgroup` file in the section for the group `socalsail_members`.

The .htgroup and .htpasswd Files

The `.htgroup` file looks something like this:

```
socalsail_members: jbc yarbles martins hiro lucy
```

So far, all these files I've been describing are easily edited by hand, using `pico` or some other text editor. But the `.htpasswd` file, which is where the username/password combinations are stored, looks different:

```
jbc:c9OR6Rw.RCm82
yarbles:q/FOUzNWVwmZU
martins:ARLDIsofjC3sI
hiro:JCeJfcJeHYs6o
lucy:Ua4/heX7ajC9U
```

Each line of the `.htpasswd` file contains a username, then a colon (:), then a password. The passwords look wacky, though, because they are encrypted using a special one-way encryption technique. The idea is that we don't want to store users' passwords in plain text because that would mean that anyone with access to the password file could learn every user's password. Instead, we store encrypted versions of the passwords. When a user is challenged for a username/password pair, the submitted password is encrypted via the same one-way encryption method, and the encrypted version of the submitted password is compared to the encrypted version stored in the `.htpasswd` file. If the two match, the server knows that the submitted password was correct. This is the same method commonly used to handle the passwords associated with users' login accounts on a Unix server.

The only trick in populating that `.htpasswd` file is in generating those encrypted passwords. But that turns out to be fairly easy because of a utility program called `htpasswd` that comes with Apache and which we can run from the shell. (We can also do this sort of encryption from inside a Perl script using Perl's `crypt` function. Use `perldoc -f crypt` for more details.) To create the first entry in a new `.htpasswd` file we would do something like this:

```
[jbc@andros httpd]$ htpasswd -c .htpasswd jbc
New password:
Re-type new password:
Adding password for user jbc
```

We type in the password twice in order to confirm that we haven't accidentally made a mistake in entering it (since it doesn't display on our screen). The `-c` argument is what tells the `htpasswd` program that we are creating a new `.htpasswd` file.

To then add an additional entry, use a similar command, but without the -c option:

```
[jbc@andros jbc]$ htpasswd .htpasswd hiro
New password:
Re-type new password:
Adding password for user hiro
```

Once everything is set up correctly, with permissions allowing the .htaccess, .htgroup, and .htpasswd files to be read by the web server, a web user trying to reach the directory protected by the .htaccess file will receive a challenge dialog box that looks something like Figure 19-1.

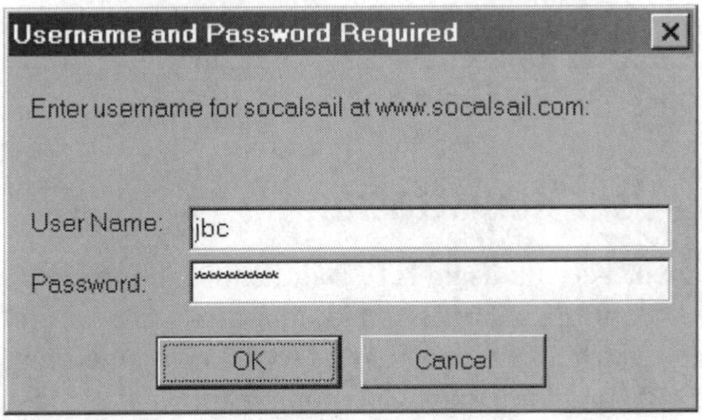

Figure 19-1. A password-challenge dialog delivered to a web user

Upon successfully entering a username and password that corresponds to one of the pairs entered in the relevant .htpasswd file, and for which the username also is represented in the appropriate manner in the .htgroup file, the user will receive the web resource originally requested. During the rest of that browsing session (that is, until the user exits from the browser), the browser will automatically submit the same username/password pair on the user's behalf, without the user needing to do so manually, every time something is requested from the protected directory. The username under which the user successfully authenticated will be available to CGI scripts by checking the environment variable stored at $ENV{REMOTE_USER}. Example 19-1 shows an extremely simple script that demonstrates this. Like all the examples in this book, you can download it from the book's web site, at *http://www.elanus.net/book/*.

Example 19-1. A CGI script demonstrating the $ENV{REMOTE_USER} variable

```
#!/usr/bin/perl -w

# who_am_i.cgi - print out authenticated username

print <<"EOF";
Content-type: text/plain

You authenticated as user '$ENV{REMOTE_USER}'.
EOF
```

What if the user fails to supply a valid username/password combination? In that case, the browser typically will present the user with a dialog box explaining that the username/password combination didn't work, and giving the user the option of either trying again or giving up. At the point when the user gives up, the server will deliver a 401 "Authorization Failure" error message.

More details on how to use basic authentication are in the htpasswd program's manpage, as well as in the venerable NCSA user authentication tutorial at *http:// hoohoo.ncsa.uiuc.edu/docs/tutorials/user.html*.

Assuming we are willing to enter username/password pairs manually in the shell using the htpasswd program, this basic HTTP authentication gives us a very useful tool. We can restrict access to a certain part of our site and, as a side benefit, track all users by name as they interact with it.

Automating User Registration

One of the big drawbacks with using HTTP authentication to keep track of web users is that we have to do all that manual updating of the .htpasswd and .htgroup files. A nice way to enhance such a system would be to automate the signup process, letting users create their own username/password combinations and updating the .htpasswd and .htgroup files accordingly.

Such an approach begs the following question, though: if users are signing themselves up for membership accounts in some automated fashion, what's the point of even bothering with a membership requirement? A malicious user of a web-based discussion forum could just create new membership accounts all day long, thwarting any effort to deny her access to the resource.

An approach taken by many membership-based web sites is to require users to demonstrate that they have supplied a real, working email address before granting them access. While such a system can still be subverted by a moderately motivated antagonist, in practice it is sufficient for many sites' authentication needs. In any event, that's the method that will be presented in this chapter's extended example.

Figure 19-2 diagrams the sequence of steps a user would follow to create a new member account using such a system:

1. The user fills out an initial form, supplying a username, a password, and an email address.
2. On the web server, the information supplied by the user is stored in a temporary holding area. Also stored with it is a random string of characters that will serve as the user's "verification code."
3. The web server sends a message containing the verification code to the email address supplied by the user.

4. The user receives the verification code.

5. The user fills out another form on the web site, supplying his username and verification code.

6. If the supplied username and verification code match, the web server completes the creation of the new account. It does that by removing the user's record from the temporary holding area, creating a new record for that user in the permanent user data, and adding appropriate entries to the relevant .htpasswd and .htgroup files.

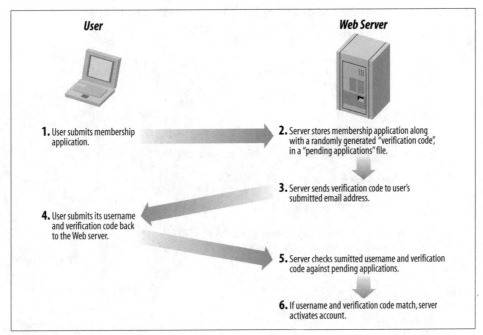

Figure 19-2. Steps in an automated web-user signup process

In practice, we can make this process a little simpler for the user by sending the email containing his verification code with a link in it that contains that code (and his username) in the query string. Then, when the user clicks on that link (assuming he uses an email client that activates such links), the username and verification code will be automatically supplied to the CGI script on the server, which can then complete the verification process without the user having to explicitly fill out the verification form.

Storing Data on the Server

One of the things this system must do is to store information on the server for later retrieval and manipulation. When the user applies for membership, his information must be stored in a special holding area, awaiting completion of the verification step.

When the verification has been done, that information must be retrieved and moved to its permanent home in the storage location for information about the site's verified users.

Flat Text Files for Data Storage

We can use a number of different approaches for this kind of data storage and retrieval. Perhaps the simplest approach is to use a flat text file, with one user record per line, and some sort of delimiter character separating the different pieces of information that make up each record. Consider the following subroutine:

```perl
sub write_register_queue {

    # invoked with an argument of a %HoH data structure, write
    # that data out to the $queue_file with one record per line,
    # and each record's fields separated by tabs.

    my %HoH = @_;

    open OUT, "> $queue_file"
        or die "couldn't open $queue_file for writing: $!";

    while (my($username, $href) = each %HoH) {

        my @record = ();

        foreach my $field ($username, $href->{verify},
            $href->{password}, $href->{real_name},
            $href->{phone}, $href->{email}) {

            # squash consec. whitespace into a single space char
            $field =~ s{\s+}{ }g;

            push @record, $field;
        }
        print OUT join("\t", @record), "\n";
    }
    close OUT;
}
```

This should all be pretty easy Perl for you to figure out by now. We invoke the subroutine by supplying it with a hash as its argument. Actually, we supply it with a hash of hashes (HoH), which you know by now actually means a hash of hash *references*. The primary keys of the HoH (that is, the keys of the "outer" hash, retrievable with something like keys %HoH), are usernames. The secondary keys (that is, the keys of the "inner" hashes, the ones stored as hash references) are verify, password, real_ name, phone, and email. Or at least they *should* be those because this routine expects to be able to access them under those names in order to store the corresponding values in the data file.

Serializing Data

In order to do that, the subroutine must first turn the randomly arranged key-value pairs of each inner hashref into a specific sequence of values. It does that with a foreach loop, pushing each field onto the end of a @record array in a specific order, and then, once the foreach loop has exited, joining the members of the @record array with tabs. It then tacks a newline on the end and prints that carefully constructed line of user data out to the disk file whose name was stored in $queue_file. This process of turning a data structure into a string is called *serializing*.

A seemingly minor, but actually very important, chunk of code inside the foreach loop is this:

```
# squash consec. whitespace into a single space char
$field =~ s{\s+}{ }g;
```

As the comment indicates, this substitution expression takes the current piece of data and, before it is pushed onto the end of the @record array, replaces any occurrence of one or more consecutive whitespace characters with a single space character. This substitution is important because without it, a field that happened to contain internal tabs or newlines would confuse the routine that reads the data back from the disk file and *deserializes* it in order to re-create the original data structure. Since the whitespace character class represented by \s includes both tabs and newlines, the substitution takes care of converting any of those found inside each field into spaces, which are "safe" characters that won't affect the serialization-deserialization process.

Let's take a look now at that deserialization routine:

```
sub read_register_queue {

    # invoked with no arguments, read all the membership
    # applications on the disk file, which must be formatted
    # like this:
    #
    # username\tverify\tpassword\treal_name\tphone\temail\n
    #
    # and return a HoH that looks like this:
    #
    # my %HoH = ( username => {
    #                 verify    => $verify,
    #                 password  => $password,
    #                 real_name => $real_name,
    #                 phone     => $phone,
    #                 email     => $email,
    #             },
    #             username => {
    #                 (etc.)

    my %HoH = ( );
```

```
    # note: okay to fail on open, if file doesn't exist yet

if (open IN, $queue_file) {

    while (<IN>) {
        chomp;
        my($username, $verify, $password,
            $real_name, $phone, $email) = split /\t/, $_;
        $HoH{$username} = {
            verify    => $verify,
            password  => $password,
            real_name => $real_name,
            phone     => $phone,
            email     => $email,
        };
    }
    close IN;   # close the data file
}

%HoH; # return the data structure
}
```

This routine should be easy to understand at this point. It simply reads the serialized records from the disk file and stores each one in an HoH data structure, re-creating the original HoH that the write_register_queue routine created in the first place.

Notice how the routine opens $data_file for reading without checking the return value of the open operation. That is, it doesn't use the usual or die... clause after the open statement. Using that or die... is such a strongly ingrained habit for me that it actually took me a minute to figure out how to set things up so this routine did what I wanted, which was to simply return an empty %HoH hash without complaining if the file whose name was stored in $data_file didn't exist. This way, the script wouldn't fail the first time it was run, if it happened to try to read $data_file with the read_register_queue routine before it had created that file with the write_register_queue routine.

So, we now have a subroutine to write pending user submissions (the ones that haven't been verified yet) out to a disk file, and another subroutine to read those submissions back in from the disk. We'll need a similar pair of routines to read and write the data for *verified* users (that is, for those who have completed the verification process).

When I created the user registration system that this chapter's example is based on, I created that pair of verified-user-handling subroutines by copying and pasting the pair that handled pending-submissions data and making a few minor changes. (Specifically, I needed to change the name of the variable holding the filename where the data would be stored, and I needed to alter the serializing and deserializing code to omit the verification code because there was no reason to store that once the user had completed the verification step.)

This was a quick approach, since it took only a few minutes to copy and paste the routines and make those few changes, but that benefit came at a cost: I created a future maintenance burden by having two parts of my program that were nearly identical. Any future enhancements or bug fixes made to the two pairs of subroutines would have to be made in two separate places. Normally it's best not to use copy-and-paste like this because the temptation to do so will often get you into trouble, especially when your code is going to end up growing longer and more complex over time—which code almost *always* ends up doing. But in this case, after considering the potential downside and balancing it against the added complexity I would need to put in in order to create one chunk of code that was smart enough to handle both sets of circumstances, I decided to go with copy-and-paste.

There's an interesting lesson here. As a beginner, you will usually get yourself into trouble by using copy-and-paste (which will always seem like the more attractive alternative in the heat of coding), rather than by creating a higher-order abstraction. But that doesn't mean you must *always* avoid copy-and-paste. Sometimes it's better to just give in to temptation. That's one of the joys of programming: getting to make those sorts of choices, to decide what path to take to accomplish a particular task, distilling a universe of possibilities down into a particular implementation that is a reflection of your individual values.

Updating the .htpasswd and .htgroup Files

This leads us to another, similar issue. Besides the data file that holds the pending user applications and the one that holds information on the verified users, this user-registration system needs to manipulate two other data files: the .htpasswd and .htgroup files that the web server will use to do its authentication. When users complete the verification step, both those files will need to be updated so that the newly verified user can access the site's password-protected features. Because manipulating these files from within a Perl script is such an obvious thing for someone to want to do, you'd think that there would be CPAN modules already written to do that. And there are: the Apache::Htpasswd and Apache::Htgroup modules.

The Apache::Htpasswd module worked fine for my purposes when I was writing this user registration system. But the Apache::Htgroup module presented a couple of problems. First, as its author acknowledged in the module's documentation, it didn't do any file locking. This was a real problem for me because I didn't want my code to be a ticking time bomb, waiting for the day when two users verifying their registrations at almost the same time caused the system to accidentally mangle the .htgroup file. Second, some of the .htgroup files I had created on my server had a slightly different structure than the Apache::Htgroup module assumed they would have.

Specifically, I had some .htgroup files on my server that looked like this:

```
group_name: user1 user2 user3
group_name: user4 user5 user6
```

Because it was sometimes inconvenient to manually edit files with really long lines, at some point in the past I had fallen into the habit of breaking up a particular group's entries across multiple lines. I did this without ever actually consulting the Apache server documentation to see if it was allowed, and even after spending some time looking through the documentation to try to figure out if it is kosher, I'm still not sure. But it seems to work, at least in the versions of Apache I've used until now. But the Apache::Htgroup module doesn't like .htgroup files of that form. It assumes that all of a particular group's entries are going to be given on a single line, and if it encounters the same group name on a subsequent line the later entries will overwrite any that were read previously.

That I even knew the module would have this problem with my data is a tribute to the strengths of the open source development model. All the modules on CPAN are distributed as source code, meaning I could answer the question of just how the module would deal with my data files in a few seconds, by inspecting the code directly.

But anyway, I had a problem. I wanted to "do the right thing," using the CPAN module rather than reinventing the wheel, but in this case I really needed a wheel slightly different from the one that was readily available. Rather than starting from scratch, though, I thought I'd just modify the existing module.

Updating the module to read group members across multiple lines in an .htgroup file was easy; I only had to change a few lines. But dealing with file locking was harder. The way I *wanted* to handle file locking in this case was to use a semaphore file. As explained in Chapter 17, a semaphore file lets you use a separate file as a gatekeeper to handle locking and unlocking of some other file. The nice thing about using a semaphore file is that it simplifies the locking operation considerably. You can use Perl's basic open function when you want to write to one of the files because even though opening the file for writing will clobber it, you can be sure (because you've already obtained the exclusive lock on the semaphore file) that it's okay for you to do that. Meanwhile, the semaphore file is being used only for locking purposes. Its contents don't matter at all, so clobbering them isn't a problem.

The alternative, if you don't want to use a semaphore file, is to do your locking using the data file itself. This requires you to open the file more carefully, using Perl's sysopen function, which gives you greater control. Using sysopen, you can open the file, obtain a lock on it, and only then replace its contents with your new data. But sysopen is a bit more complicated to use, which is why semaphore files are so nice.

But semaphore files are a less-portable choice, in that your script must be able to open and write to a semaphore file on any system where you want it to run. Choosing an appropriate filename for the semaphore file, and having that semaphore file spring into existence as needed, could conceivably pose a problem on some systems.

But why was I worrying about other systems? Because in looking through the Apache::Htgroup module and outlining the changes I needed to make to it, I decided that what

I *really* wanted to do was fix it so that it did file locking, and contribute the result back to the module's author. That way, everyone in the extended Perl community could benefit from my effort. This sort of generosity forms the fundamental basis of CPAN; helping out the rest of the Perl-using world was the least I could do for those helpful folks.

Alas, I ran out of time in my effort to rewrite the module robustly, and ended up falling back on some prewritten code of my own that worked fine for my immediate purpose but wasn't really CPAN-ready. Deadlines are like that sometimes. But enough of this hand-wringing. Here's the routine I ended up using to read .htgroup file entries:

```
sub read_htgroup {

    # read the htgroup file for Socalsail members.
    # returns a HoH of the following form:
    #
    # primary key: groupname. secondary key: membername.
    # value: 1.

    my %HoH = ();

    # okay to fail on open, since file may not exist yet

    if (open IN, $htgroup_file) {

        while (<IN>) {
            if (/^(\S+): (.+)/) {
                my $group = $1;
                my $rest  = $2;
                my @members = split /\s+/, $rest;
                foreach my $member (@members) {
                    $HoH{$group}{$member} = 1;
                }
            }
        }
        close IN;   # close data file
    }

    %HoH; # return data structure
}
```

There's nothing terribly clever here. While iterating over the lines of the .htgroup file with the while (<IN>) construct, the subroutine populates a hash of hashes (HoH) where the primary keys are the group names and the secondary keys are member names associated with values of 1. Why do it that way, by the way? Why not just have a data structure consisting of a hash of lists (HoL), in which each group name is associated with an array of member names? Wouldn't that more closely match the structure of the actual data contained in the .htgroup file?

Well, maybe. But it is easier (and faster, from Perl's perspective) to just iterate over all the members of each group once, when constructing the HoH. After that, lookups can be lightning quick (and easy): want to know if a particular username is in a particular group? Just do a hash lookup on $HoH{groupname}{membername} and test it for truth. If that member isn't in that group, you'll get the undefined value, which is false. Otherwise you'll get the stored value of 1, which is true.

Here's the corresponding write_htgroup subroutine, which takes the same %HoH data structure and creates a new .htgroup file from it:

```
sub write_htgroup {

    # invoked with a HoH: primary key:   groupname
    #                     secondary key: membername
    #                     value:         1
    #
    # writes the data out to $htgroup_file.

    my %HoH = @_;

    open OUT, "> $htgroup_file"
        or die "couldn't open $htgroup_file for writing: $!";

    while (my($group, $hashref) = each %HoH) {
        print OUT "$group: ", join(' ', keys %{$hashref}), "\n";
    }
    close OUT;
}
```

The trickiest line in this subroutine is this one, where the actual printing takes place:

```
print OUT "$group: ", join(' ', keys %{$hashref}), "\n";
```

It is tricky because we have both a print and a join in the same statement. Both of these functions take lists as their arguments, which means we need to be careful that one function doesn't accidentally grab some of the other function's arguments. In this case, the pair of parentheses that begin immediately after the join function tells join which of the arguments belong to it. Without those parentheses, the join function would go on sucking up arguments all the way to the semicolon at the end of the statement. Because of that the newline, which is intended to be an argument to the print function, would actually be handled by the join function, meaning we'd get an extra space after the last group member. That probably wouldn't hurt anything in this case, but it's still a subtle bug we need to watch out for when we get fancy with having multiple list functions in the same statement.

The Register Script

So, now that we have subroutines for reading and storing the various kinds of files we need to manipulate, we're ready to create the CGI scripts that our users will use to register on the site. Since the reading and writing subroutines will need to be shared by both the registration script (register.cgi) and the verification script (verify.cgi), we'll put those routines in a separate module file (Register.pm) that each script can pull in with a use statement.

Example 19-2 shows the finished Register.pm module.

Example 19-2. The finished Register.pm module

```perl
package Socalsail::Register;

# a module to contain routines for accessing and manipulating the
# various membership-related files on the Socalsail site.

use strict;

BEGIN {
    use Exporter;
    use Fcntl ':flock';

    use vars qw(@ISA @EXPORT @EXPORT_OK $VERSION
        $queue_file $queue_file_semaphore
        $member_file $member_file_semaphore
        $htgroup_file $htgroup_semaphore $htpasswd_file);

    $VERSION             = '0.01';
    $queue_file          = '/w1/s/socalsail/maint/data/pending_memberships.txt';
    $queue_file_semaphore = $queue_file . '.sem';
    $member_file         = '/w1/s/socalsail/maint/data/members.txt';
    $member_file_semaphore = $member_file . '.sem';
    $htgroup_file        = '/w1/s/socalsail/maint/data/.htgroup';
    $htgroup_semaphore   = $htgroup_file . '.sem';
    $htpasswd_file       = '/w1/s/socalsail/maint/data/.htpasswd';

    @ISA = ('Exporter');
    @EXPORT    = qw( );
    @EXPORT_OK = qw(read_register_queue write_register_queue
                    read_members write_members
                    read_htgroup write_htgroup);
}

sub read_register_queue {

    # invoked with no arguments, read all the membership
    # applications on the disk file, and return a HoH of
    # the following form:
    #
    # my %HoH = ( username => {
    #                 verify    => $verify,
    #                 password  => $password,
    #                 real_name => $real_name,
    #                 phone     => $phone,
    #                 email     => $email,
```

Example 19-2. The finished Register.pm module (continued)

```
#              },
#         username => {
#            (etc.)
#
# note that this routine counts on the caller to implement
# any file locking required. also, note that the routine
# counts on the $queue_file to be structured with one record
# per line, structured as follows:
#
# username\tverify\tpassword\treal_name\tphone\temail\n

my %HoH = ();

# note: okay to fail on open, if file doesn't exist yet

if (open IN, $queue_file) {

    while (<IN>) {
        chomp;
        my($username, $verify, $password,
            $real_name, $phone, $email) = split /\t/, $_;
        $HoH{$username} = {
            verify    => $verify,
            password  => $password,
            real_name => $real_name,
            phone     => $phone,
            email     => $email,
        };
    }
    close IN;    # close the data file
}

%HoH; # return the data structure
}

sub write_register_queue {

    # invoked with an argument of a %HoH data structure (see
    # read_register_queue), write that data out to the $queue_file
    # with one record per line, and each record's fields separated
    # from each other by tabs. Note that locking
    # must be taken care of by the caller.

    my %HoH = @_;

    open OUT, "> $queue_file"
        or die "couldn't open $queue_file for writing: $!";

    while (my($username, $href) = each %HoH) {

        my @record = ();
```

Example 19-2. The finished Register.pm module (continued)

```
        foreach my $field ($username, $href->{verify},
            $href->{password}, $href->{real_name},
            $href->{phone}, $href->{email}) {

            # squash consec. whitespace into a single space char
            $field =~ s{\s+}{ }g;

            push @record, $field;
        }
        print OUT join("\t", @record), "\n";
    }
    close OUT;
}

sub read_members {

    # invoked with no arguments, read all the member
    # records on the disk file, and return a HoH of
    # the following form:
    #
    # my %HoH = ( username => {
    #                    password  => $password,
    #                    real_name => $real_name,
    #                    phone     => $phone,
    #                    email     => $email,
    #              },
    #              username => {
    #                 (etc.)
    #
    # note that this routine counts on the caller to implement
    # any file locking required. also, note that the routine
    # counts on the $member_file to be structured with one record
    # per line, structured as follows:
    #
    # username\tpassword\treal_name\tphone\temail\n

    my %HoH = ();

    # note: okay to fail on open, since file may not exist yet

    if (open IN, $member_file) {

        while (<IN>) {
            chomp;
            my($username, $password, $real_name, $phone, $email)
                = split /\t/, $_;
            $HoH{$username} = {
                password  => $password,
                real_name => $real_name,
                phone     => $phone,
                email     => $email,
            };
```

Example 19-2. The finished Register.pm module (continued)

```
        }
        close IN;    # close the data file
    }

    %HoH; # return the data structure
}

sub write_members {

    # invoked with an argument of a %HoH data structure (see
    # read_members), write that data out to the $member_file
    # with one record per line, and each record's fields separated
    # from each other by tabs. Note that locking
    # must be taken care of by the caller.

    my %HoH = @_;

    open OUT, "> $member_file"
        or die "couldn't open $member_file for writing: $!";

    while (my($username, $href) = each %HoH) {

        my @record = ( );

        foreach my $field ($username,
            $href->{password}, $href->{real_name},
            $href->{phone}, $href->{email}) {

            # squash consec. whitespace into a single space char
            $field =~ s{\s+}{ }g;

            push @record, $field;
        }
        print OUT join("\t", @record), "\n";
    }
    close OUT;
}

sub read_htgroup {

    # read the htgroup file for Socalsail members.
    # return a HoH of the following form:
    #
    # primary key: groupname. secondary key: membername.
    # value: 1.

    my %HoH = ( );

    # okay to fail on open, since file may not exist yet

    if (open IN, $htgroup_file) {
```

Example 19-2. The finished Register.pm module (continued)

```
        while (<IN>) {
            if (/^(\S+): (.+)/) {
                my $group = $1;
                my $rest  = $2;
                my @members = split /\s+/, $rest;
                foreach my $member (@members) {
                    $HoH{$group}{$member} = 1;
                }
            }
        }
        close IN;   # close data file
    }

    %HoH; # return data structure
}

sub write_htgroup {

    # invoked with a HoH: primary key:   groupname
    #                     secondary key: membername
    #                     value:         1
    #
    # writes the data out to $htgroup_file.

    my %HoH = @_;

    open OUT, "> $htgroup_file"
        or die "couldn't open $htgroup_file for writing: $!";

    while (my($group, $hashref) = each %HoH) {
        print OUT "$group: ", join(' ', keys %{$hashref}), "\n";
    }
    close OUT;
}

1;
```

Next let's take a look at `register.cgi`, which is given in Example 19-3.

Example 19-3. A CGI script for submitting a membership application

```
#!/usr/bin/perl -Tw

# register.cgi - sign up for membership at the Socalsail site

use strict;
use CGI    qw(:standard);
use Fcntl qw(:flock);

$ENV{PATH} = '';

my $notify_email = 'register@socalsail.com';
```

Example 19-3. A CGI script for submitting a membership application (continued)

```perl
my $sendmail     = '/usr/lib/sendmail';

use lib '/home/jbc/lib';
use Socalsail::Make_page;
use Socalsail::Register qw(read_register_queue write_register_queue
                           read_members write_members);

my $action  = param('action');
my $content = '';

unless ($action) {

    # show the initial sign-up form

    my $form = make_form();

    $content = <<EndOfText;
<H2 ALIGN="center">Sign up for membership</H2>

<P>You may use this form to sign up for your free Socalsail membership.
Members are able to post messages in the site's discussion forums.</P>

$form

EndOfText

} elsif ($action eq 'Submit Membership Application') {

    # first, get an exclusive lock on the queue semaphore file.

    my $lockfile = $Socalsail::Register::queue_file_semaphore;
    open QUEUE_LOCK, "> $lockfile"
        or die "can't open $lockfile for writing: $!";
    flock QUEUE_LOCK, LOCK_EX
        or die "can't get exclusive lock on $lockfile: $!";

    # and get a shared lock on the member-data semaphore file

    $lockfile = $Socalsail::Register::member_file_semaphore;
    open MEMBER_LOCK, "> $lockfile"
        or die "can't open $lockfile for writing: $!";
    flock MEMBER_LOCK, LOCK_SH
        or die "can't get exclusive lock on $lockfile: $!";

    # now, check the submitted data for okay-ness.

    my $href = check_form();

    # still here? then it must be okay.

    close MEMBER_LOCK; # lose the shared lock on the member data
```

Example 19-3. A CGI script for submitting a membership application (continued)

```
    submit_application($href);

    close QUEUE_LOCK; # lose the exclusive lock on the queue file

    my $email = param('email');

    $content = <<EndOfText;
<H2>Membership application received</H2>

<P>Our membership system is now sending verification instructions
to the E-mail address you supplied ('$email'). You can activate
your account by following the instructions contained in that E-mail.
If you have questions or problems, you may contact us at
<A HREF="mailto:$notify_email">$notify_email</A>. Thank you!</P>

EndOfText

}

my $made_page = make_page(
    page_type => 'standard',
    title     => 'Membership Application',
    content   => $content,
);

print header, $made_page;

# script proper ends. subroutines follow.

sub check_form {

    # do some (minimal) checking of the submitted fields

    my($username, $password, $v_password, $real_name,
        $phone, $email) = (param('username'), param('password'),
        param('v_password'), param('real_name'), param('phone'),
        param('email'));

    my %QUEUE   = read_register_queue();
    my %MEMBERS = read_members();

    my @errors = ();

    push @errors, '<LI>No username supplied.' unless $username;
    push @errors, '<LI>Username can only contain letters, numbers,
        and the underscore character (_).'
        if $username =~ /\W/;
    push @errors, "<LI>Username '$username' is already taken."
        if $QUEUE{$username} or $MEMBERS{$username};
    push @errors, '<LI>No password supplied.' unless $password;
    push @errors, '<LI>Your two password fields do not match.'
        if $password and $password ne $v_password;
    push @errors, '<LI>No E-mail address supplied.' unless $email;
```

```
    push @errors, "<LI>E-mail address ('$email') doesn't look like
        a valid E-mail address."
        if $email and $email !~ /\w@\w+\.\w+/;

    if (@errors) {

        my $errors = join "\n", @errors;
        my $form   = make_form( );

        $content = <<EndOfText;
<H2 ALIGN="center">The following problem(s) were encountered
in trying to process your form:</H2>

<UL>
$errors
</UL>

<P>Please correct the error(s) in the form below, and re-submit.
We apologize for the inconvenience.</P>

$form

EndOfText

        my $made_page = make_page(
            page_type => 'standard',
            title     => 'Membership Application',
            content   => $content,
        );

        print header, $made_page;
        exit;

    }

    # no errors, so create the verification code, and
    # return a hash reference of submitted data suitable
    # for storing in the register_queue file.

    my $verify = join '',
        ('A'..'H', 'J'..'N', 'P'..'Z')
        [rand 24, rand 24, rand 24, rand 24, rand 24];

    my $hashref = {
        username  => $username,
        verify    => $verify,
        password  => $password,
        real_name => $real_name,
        phone     => $phone,
        email     => $email,
    };
}
```

```
sub make_form {

    # create and return the registration form

    my $form = join '',
        start_form,
        '<TABLE>', "\n",

        '<TR><TD ALIGN="right">',
        '',
        '<STRONG>Username</STRONG><BR>',
        '(No spaces or special characters allowed)',
        '</TD><TD>',
        textfield('username'),
        '</TD></TR>', "\n",

        '<TR><TD ALIGN="right">',
        '',
        '<STRONG>Password</STRONG>',
        '</TD><TD>',
        password_field('password'),
        '</TD></TR>', "\n",

        '<TR><TD ALIGN="right">',
        '',
        '<STRONG>Password</STRONG><BR>',
        '(enter again for confirmation)',
        '</TD><TD>',
        password_field('v_password'),
        '</TD></TR>', "\n",

        '<TR><TD ALIGN="right">',
        '',
        '<STRONG>Real name</STRONG>',
        '</TD><TD>',
        textfield('real_name'),
        '</TD></TR>', "\n",

        '<TR><TD ALIGN="right">',
        '',
        '<STRONG>Phone</STRONG>',
        '</TD><TD>',
        textfield('phone'),
        '</TD></TR>', "\n",

        '<TR><TD ALIGN="right">',
        '',
        '<STRONG>E-mail</STRONG>',
        '</TD><TD>',
        textfield('email'),
        '</TD></TR>', "\n",
```

```
            '<TR><TD COLSPAN=2 ALIGN="center">',
            submit(
                -name => 'action',
                -value => 'Submit Membership Application',
            ),
            '</TD></TR></TABLE>', "\n", end_form;
}

sub submit_application {

    # store this membership application in the application queue.
    # the supplied argument is a hashref of the form:
    #
    # my $hashref = {
    #     username  => $username,
    #     verify    => $verify,
    #     password  => $password,
    #     real_name => $real_name,
    #     phone     => $phone,
    #     email     => $email,
    # };

    my $href = shift;

    # store the user's information in the temporary holding area.

    my %QUEUE = read_register_queue();
    $QUEUE{ $href->{username} } = $href;
    write_register_queue(%QUEUE);

    # now send an email to the user

    my $mail_body = <<EndOfText;
You are almost finished registering for the Socalsail Web site. Please
click on the link below to complete your registration:

<http://www.socalsail.com/register/verify.cgi?username=$href->{username}&verify=$href->
{verify}>

If clicking on the link above does not automatically take
you to our verification Web page, you can also complete
your registration by going to the following address in
your Web browser:

<http://www.socalsail.com/register/verify.cgi>

and entering the following two items exactly as shown:

Username: $href->{username}
Verification code: $href->{verify}

Please note that these values are CASE SENSITIVE.
```

Example 19-3. A CGI script for submitting a membership application (continued)
```
EndOfText

    open MAIL, "|$sendmail -oi -t"
        or die "Can't open pipe to $sendmail: $!\n";

    print MAIL <<"EOF";
To: $href->{email}
From: $notify_email
Subject: Membership verification instructions

$mail_body
EOF

    close MAIL or die "Can't close pipe to $sendmail: $!\n";
}
```

One thing you'll notice about register.cgi is that it uses the same Make_page.pm module we saw in an earlier chapter to create a simple template system. That Make_page.pm module has been placed, along with the Register.pm module, inside a directory called Socalsail, which in turn is inside a user-specific library directory at /home/jbc/lib. A use lib statement at the top of the script specifies that library directory's location, and that, along with the addition of a Socalsail identifier at the beginning of the module name in the package declaration at the top of each module, makes everything work the way it's supposed to.

If we look over register.cgi, we'll see that the main part of the script consists of an extended unless-elsif construct. This section of the script tests the contents of the $action variable (which is read at the top of the script from the value stored in the CGI parameter called action, which is the name of the Submit button the user sees in the form delivered by the script). If the script sees no action parameter, it means the script is being invoked for the first time, via a GET request, so it delivers the initial new-member signup form, which we can see an example of in Figure 19-3. If the action parameter *is* present and contains the value Submit Membership Application, the script knows that it has been invoked by someone submitting a membership application form, so it processes that form.

Processing the form is a two-step process: checking the submitted information to make sure it is acceptable, and, if it is, storing that information in the pending-applications file. At that point, the user is shown a web page like the one shown in Figure 19-4.

The check of the submitted information, and the actual processing of that information, are handled by subroutines named check_form and submit_application, respectively. We'll look at those in just a moment, but first let's talk about the file-locking scheme that is employed to keep multiple simultaneous users of the system from fighting over the data files where the information is stored.

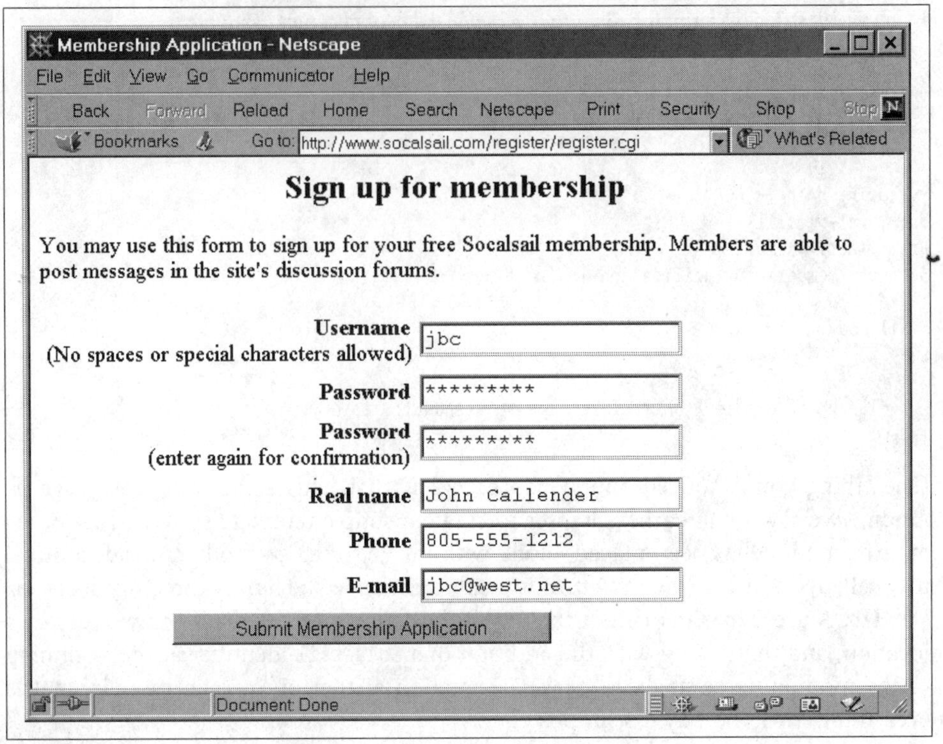

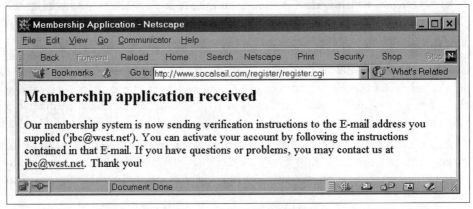

Figure 19-3. The new-user registration form delivered by register.cgi when no "action" parameter is present in its submitted parameters

![Membership application received screenshot]

Figure 19-4. The "thank you" screen displayed to a user after he has submitted a membership application

In broad terms, what happens during the processing of a submitted application is this: first, both the member file (containing the data on previously approved memberships) and the pending file (containing the data on previously submitted but not yet approved memberships) are checked to make sure the submitted username has not been used already. If it hasn't, and if the submitted information passes certain other checks (the two password fields must match each other, the supplied email address must look vaguely like an email address, and so on), the submission data is written out to the pending file.

Fixing a Race Condition

When I first wrote this script, I used what seemed to me like a straightforward approach to locking the data files. In the check_form subroutine, where I performed the check on the submitted information, I obtained a shared lock on both the member file and the pending file. If everything checked out okay I released those locks, and then, in the submit_application subroutine, I obtained an exclusive lock on the pending file in order to add the information about the new submission to it. Which was completely wrong, but is handy, nevertheless, because it offers an example of what can happen when one doesn't think carefully about file-locking issues.

Imagine that two users are trying to apply for new accounts using the same name at almost the same time. The first user gets the shared locks on the member and pending files, and verifies that the name isn't being used yet. Satisfied that it's okay to use the name, it releases the locks. Meanwhile, the second user has also obtained shared locks on these files, and also determined that the name is okay to use. As soon as the second user releases the lock on the pending file, the first user grabs it with an exclusive lock and writes the new application data to it. The second user waits dutifully for the exclusive lock to be released, then writes more data out to the pending file, using the same username and thereby overwriting the record just written out by the first user.

In effect, all that this particular (flawed) locking scheme accomplishes is to make sure that the pending file won't be corrupted by two copies of the register.cgi script writing to it simultaneously. But it fails to make sure that two copies of the script won't both think it's okay for them to use the same username. It creates a race condition by leaving a brief window of opportunity between the check for the previous existence of that username and the obtaining of the exclusive lock on the pending file in order to write the username out to it.

The solution to this problem is to hoist the locking procedure higher up into the script's logic, treating the check for a username's previous existence and the act of writing out the new data keyed on that username as a single, lockfile-controlled action. Rather than putting the locking and unlocking into the check_form and submit_application routines, I needed to put it into the code that calls those routines. Here is the sequence I ended up using:

1. The script obtains the shared lock on the member file and the exclusive lock on the pending file.

2. The check_form routine is run.

3. The shared lock on the member file is released.

4. The submit_application routine is run.

5. The exclusive lock on the pending file is released.

Generating a Random Verification String

The only other part of this script that requires additional explanation at this stage in your Perl education is the part where the random verification code is generated:

```
my $verify = join '',
    ('A'..'H', 'J'..'N', 'P'..'Z')
    [rand 24, rand 24, rand 24, rand 24, rand 24];
```

This is a clever little Perl idiom that constructs a list of uppercase letters using the range operator (..), then returns five randomly chosen members of that list and joins them together with the empty string. You should be on pretty familiar ground with the use of the range operator to construct a list of characters that are "between" (in terms of the standard ASCII sequence of characters) the characters on either side of the operator. The tricky thing here is that I've actually constructed *three* ranges of characters: those between A and H, between J and N, and between P and Z. I did this in order to exclude from my list the characters I and O because I've learned (through painful experience) that users are apt to confuse them with the numerals 1 and 0, respectively.

 The range operator lets us create lists of numbers, too, in which case we (obviously) don't need to quote the operands. For example, @nums = (3 .. 10) would populate the @nums array with the numbers 3, 4, 5, 6, 7, 8, 9, and 10.

Array and Hash Slices

So, that takes care of the trickiness in the construction of the list of possible characters that will be used to form the verification code. Another piece of trickiness here is the way I've enclosed the entire list of characters in parentheses to turn them into a list, and then subscripted that list with a pair of square brackets, just as if I was selecting a particular element from an array variable. Except in this case, I've put a *list* of subscripts inside the square brackets, which means I'm going to return a list of elements rather than a single element.

This works the same way whether we're using an explicit list of elements enclosed by parentheses, as we are here, or an array variable. So, for example, you might see some code that looked like this:

```
@ary = qw(
    white
    black
```

```
    red
    green
    blue
    purple
);
print join(', ', @ary[2, 3, 4]); # prints 'red, green, blue'
```

Notice how, when we are using an array variable to do this multiple-subscripting trick, we need an @ symbol in front of the array name, rather than the $ symbol we would normally use when accessing a single element of an array. This is called accessing a *slice* of the array variable. As long as I'm filling your head with useful bits of Perl arcana, you should know that you can also reference a *hash slice*, using code like this:

```
%color = (
    snow      => 'white',
    firetruck => 'red',
    grass     => 'green',
    ocean     => 'blue',
    plum      => 'purple',
);

# prints 'red, green, blue'
print join(', ', @color{'firetruck', 'grass', 'ocean'});
```

Notice that we don't use a % symbol just because the thing we're taking a slice of is a hash. The curly braces ({}) take care of letting Perl know we're dealing with a hash. Since the thing returned by our slice operation is a *list* of values, we use an @ symbol in front of the variable name, just like we did with the array slice.

The rand Function

But enough of this digression into slicing variables. In `register.cgi` we're slicing an explicit list enclosed by parentheses. And there's one more bit of trickiness we need to learn about in order to understand what's going on with the statement that constructs the verification code: Perl's `rand` function.

The `rand` function returns a random number between 0 and whatever number is given as `rand`'s argument. (If you just use `rand` by itself, you get a random number between 0 and 1.) To be very specific, the random number returned by the `rand` function will be a decimal fraction greater than or equal to 0, and less than but *not* equal to the number given as its argument (or 1, if no argument is given). It's not *really* a random number because random numbers are actually pretty hard to come up with, but it's random enough for the current script's purposes. (See the accompanying sidebar, "Random Versus Pseudo-Random," for more on this point.)

So, the `rand` function returns a random number between 0 and its argument. In the case of the `register.cgi` script, `rand` is invoked with an argument of 24 (because there are 24 letters in the list being subscripted). The `rand` function returns a decimal frac-

Random Versus Pseudo-Random

The number returned by Perl's rand function isn't *truly* random. It's what programmers call a *pseudo-random* number. In one of those interesting quirks about the way computers as distinct from human beings think, it's actually really hard for a computer to give you an unpredictable random answer every time you ask it for one. Instead, Perl's rand function picks a starting number, called a *seed*, and then runs that seed through a special mathematical transformation that produces a number randomly distributed between 0 and rand's upper bound (which is the number given in rand's argument, or 1, if you don't give it an argument). It uses the result of that operation to produce the seed for the next call to rand, and so on. The numbers produced aren't truly random because if you give another Perl program the same starting seed, it will generate exactly the same sequence of "random" numbers. So, assuming you know the starting seed, the output of Perl's rand function isn't random at all, but deterministic.

Since the randomness of the values returned by rand depends on your not knowing the starting seed, and since programs that use rand often depend on that randomness for security purposes, Perl tries fairly hard to make sure the starting seed isn't easily discoverable by bad guys. Still, that's not the same thing as saying it's completely undiscoverable. So, we shouldn't assume we can use the output of rand to produce a random password that will safeguard the gold in Fort Knox. For something like a web-user signup system, though, it's probably okay.

If we *are* trying to protect something valuable using a secret string produced with Perl's rand function, we also need to realize that successfully identifying the starting seed, and thereby identifying the nonrandom result of calling rand, is only one approach the bad guys might take to discovering our secret. A much more commonly used approach is the *brute-force attack*, in which the bad guys just try every possible combination until they guess the right one. The verification code used in this chapter to verify that a user has supplied a working email address, for example, uses a sequence of 5 characters, each of which can have 24 different possible values. This results in a *keyspace* of only about 8 million possible combinations, which wouldn't take all that long to plow through if someone were motivated to write a program to do so.

The bottom line is, when devising a system that depends on being able to generate a random string that cannot be guessed, we need to take the limits of our approach and the motivation and resources of those who might try to subvert it into account.

tion, meaning we will get a number between 0.00000 and 23.99999 (more or less), but in the square-bracketed subscript list the fractional part is ignored, meaning we will in effect get a random integer from 0 to 23, which is exactly what we want in order to select a random element from the list of 24 letters. Five calls to rand means five random letters returned from the list, which, when joined together using the empty string, gives us a random string of five uppercase letters for the verification code. The verification code is emailed to the address supplied by the user in the registration form, and the only way the user can activate the new account is by supplying that verification code back to the verify.cgi script.

I want to point out just one more clever thing about the register.cgi script: the way the submitted information is assembled into a hashref and returned from the check_form subroutine. Because that hashref is in the form that the submit_application routine expects to receive it in, having the data assembled into that particular data structure and then passed around that way makes the rest of the script relatively simple.

The Verification Script

We're almost finished with the user-registration system. All that's left now is the verify.cgi script, which is what allows users who have their emailed verification code to activate their account. That script performs the following steps:

1. Deleting the verification code from the user's submitted information (since it is no longer needed), and then storing that submitted information in the member data file.

2. Adding an entry for the user to the .htpasswd file, using the Apache::Htpasswd CPAN module mentioned previously.

3. Adding the user to the appropriate group in the .htgroup file.

4. Removing the user from the pending-applications file.

5. Emailing the user a copy of the username and password for future reference.

Example 19-4 shows the verify.cgi script that allows the final verification step to take place in the SoCalSail user-registration system.

Example 19-4. The verify.cgi script

```
#!/usr/bin/perl -Tw

# verify.cgi

# verifies receipt of the member's verification code, and activates the
# member's account by:
#
# 1) writing their information to the $member_file,
# 2) adding their username/password pair to the .htpasswd file,
# 3) adding their name to the .htgroup file, and
# 4) deleting their entry from the submission queue.

use strict;
use CGI    qw(:standard);
use Fcntl qw(:flock);
use Apache::Htpasswd;

use lib '/home/jbc/lib';
use Socalsail::Make_page;
```

Example 19-4. The verify.cgi script (continued)

```perl
use Socalsail::Register qw(read_register_queue write_register_queue
                           read_members write_members
                           read_htgroup write_htgroup);

$ENV{PATH} = '';

my $notify_email = 'email@example.com';
my $sendmail     = '/usr/lib/sendmail';

my $username = param('username');
my $verify   = param('verify');

my $content  = '';

unless ($username and $verify) {

    # they didn't come by clicking on the email link

    my $form = make_form();

    $content = <<"EOF";
<H2 ALIGN="center">Membership Verification</H1>

<P>In order to activate your membership at Socalsail,
you must give your username and the verification code that
was E-mailed to the address you supplied.</P>

<P><STRONG>Please note:</STRONG> The username and verification
code are <STRONG>case sensitive</STRONG>.</P>

$form

EOF

    my $made_page = make_page(
        title      => "Membership Verification",
        content    => $content,
        page_type  => 'standard',
    );
    print header, $made_page;
    exit;
}

# still here? then process their submitted information.

# first, get an exclusive lock on the queue semaphore file.

my $lockfile = $Socalsail::Register::queue_file_semaphore;
open QUEUE_LOCK, "> $lockfile"
    or die "can't open $lockfile for writing: $!";
flock QUEUE_LOCK, LOCK_EX
    or die "can't get exclusive lock on $lockfile: $!";
```

Example 19-4. The verify.cgi script (continued)

```
# and another exclusive lock on the member-data semaphore file

$lockfile = $Socalsail::Register::member_file_semaphore;
open MEMBER_LOCK, "> $lockfile"
    or die "can't open $lockfile for writing: $!";
flock MEMBER_LOCK, LOCK_EX
    or die "can't get exclusive lock on $lockfile: $!";

my %QUEUE   = read_register_queue();
my %MEMBERS = read_members();

if ($MEMBERS{$username}) {

    # they're already verified

    $content = <<"EOF";
<H2>Account already verified</H2>

<P>The account for user '$username' has already been
verified. You can use the account by supplying that
username, as well as the password you chose when you
created the account, when prompted for them.</P>

<P>If you have questions about this system, please contact
us at <A HREF="mailto:$notify_email">$notify_email</A>.</P>
EOF

} elsif (not $QUEUE{$username}) {

    # so they are in neither %MEMBERS nor %QUEUE

    my $form = make_form();

    $content = <<"EOF";
<H2>Unable to find membership application</H2>

<P>The username you supplied ('$username') is not in the list of
pending applications. It may be that there is a typo in the username
you supplied (usernames are case-sensitive, for example, such that
'myname' is different from 'MyName', which is different from 'MYNAME').
You can try again by completing, and re-submitting, the form below,
or you can start the process over again by
<A HREF="/register/register.cgi">submitting a new membership
application</A>. We apologize for the inconvenience.</P>

$form
EOF

} else {

    # they supplied a username that *is* in the pending-membership
    # queue, so check if they supplied the correct verification code.
```

Example 19-4. The verify.cgi script (continued)

```
    if ($verify eq $QUEUE{$username}{verify}) {

        # they successfully verified, so...
        # add them to the members file

        my $href = $QUEUE{$username};
        delete $href->{verify};          # don't need 'verify' now
        $MEMBERS{$username} = $href;
        write_members(%MEMBERS);

        # add their entry to the .htpasswd file

        my $htpasswd
            = new Apache::Htpasswd($Socalsail::Register::htpasswd_file);
        $htpasswd->htpasswd($username, $href->{password});

        # add them to the htgroup file

        my $lockfile = $Socalsail::Register::htgroup_semaphore;
        open HTGROUP_LOCK, "> $lockfile"
            or die "can't open $lockfile for writing: $!";
        flock HTGROUP_LOCK, LOCK_EX
            or die "can't get exclusive lock on $lockfile: $!";

        my %HoH = read_htgroup();
        $HoH{socalsail_members}{$username} = 1;
        write_htgroup(%HoH);

        close HTGROUP_LOCK;

        # remove them from the registration queue

        delete $QUEUE{$username};
        write_register_queue(%QUEUE);

        # send them an email with their access instructions

        my $mail_body = <<"EOF";
You have successfully activated your user account at Socalsail.
To access the site's membership features, you will need to
supply the following information when prompted at the site:

Username: $username
Password: $href->{password}

Please remember that your username and password are both
CASE-SENSITIVE.

We suggest you save this message for future reference.
```

Example 19-4. The verify.cgi script (continued)

```
If you have questions about this system, please contact
us at $notify_email.

Thank you.
EOF

        open MAIL, "|$sendmail -oi -t"
            or die "Can't open pipe to $sendmail: $!\n";

        print MAIL <<"EOF";
To: $MEMBERS{$username}{email}
From: $notify_email
Subject: Socalsail registration information

$mail_body
EOF

        close MAIL or die "Can't close pipe to $sendmail: $!\n";

        # give them the good news.

        $content = <<"EOF";
<H2>Congratulations</H2>

<P>Member account for '$username' has been successfully activated.</P>
EOF

    } else {

        # they supplied an incorrect verification code

        my $form = make_form( );

        $content = <<"EOF";
<H2>Unable to verify account</H2>

<P>The username you supplied ('$username') does not match the
verification code you entered ('$verify'). It may be that there
is a typo in the username or verification code. Both are
case-sensitive, for example, such that 'myname' is
different from 'MyName', which is different from 'MYNAME').
You can try again by completing, and re-submitting, the form below,
or you can start the process over again by
<A HREF="/register/register.cgi">submitting a new membership
application</A>. We apologize for the inconvenience.</P>

$form
EOF
    }
}

close QUEUE_LOCK;
```

Example 19-4. The verify.cgi script (continued)

```
close MEMBER_LOCK;

my $made_page = make_page(
    page_type => 'standard',
    title     => 'Membership Verification',
    content   => $content,
);

print header, $made_page;

# script proper ends. subroutine follows.

sub make_form {

    # create and return the verification form

    my $form = join '',
        start_form,
        '<TABLE>', "\n",

        '<TR><TD ALIGN="right">',
        '',
        '<STRONG>Username</STRONG><BR>',
        '(No spaces or special characters allowed)',
        '</TD><TD>',
        textfield('username'),
        '</TD></TR>', "\n",

        '<TR><TD ALIGN="right">',
        '',
        '<STRONG>Verification code</STRONG><BR>',
        '</TD><TD>',
        textfield('verify'),
        '</TD></TR>', "\n",

        '<TR><TD COLSPAN=2 ALIGN="center">',
        submit(
            -name => 'action',
            -value => 'Verify Membership',
        ),
        '</TD></TR></TABLE>', "\n", end_form;
}
```

There really isn't anything going on in verify.cgi that you can't figure out by reading the code. The script is designed to be run in one of two ways. The first way it can be run is by a user clicking on the URL embedded in his verification email, or by copying and pasting that URL into his browser. With this invocation method, the script receives the username and verification code in the query string that comes after the script name proper, as in the following URL:

```
http://www.socalsail.com/register/verify.cgi?username=jbc&verify=TKXCR
```

This is the easiest way for a user to invoke the script, especially if his email client supports the automatic activation of URLs embedded in the email body (that is, the turning of those URLs into clickable links that will call up the corresponding page in the user's browser). But for those users who don't want to or can't use this option, the script can also be invoked without the query string, in which case it will present a form into which the user can enter his username and verification code.

The rest of the script is unremarkable. It simply checks the user's input for a username and verification string that matches a pending application awaiting verification and, if it finds such an application, goes through the steps of approving it. As stated earlier, those steps are: deleting the verification code from the user's submitted information, adding entries for the user to the `.htpasswd` and `.htgroup` files, removing the user from the pending-applications file, and emailing the user a copy of his username and password for future reference.

Chapter 20 continues this example, explaining how the user-registration system can be improved by having it use DBM files, instead of flat text files, for data storage.

CHAPTER 20

Storing Data in DBM Files

This chapter continues the example begun in Chapter 19, in which we created an automated user-registration system for a web site. This chapter shows how to improve that system by converting it to using DBM files for its data storage.

Data Storage Options

The user-registration system described in Chapter 19 stores all the information it uses in flat text files. There are a lot of reasons why flat text files make really nice data storage locations:

- They're flexible.
- They're easy to use.
- They're easy to view and edit, which helps with debugging.
- They require no additional software libraries.
- They can be moved from one computer to another without becoming corrupted (assuming you take the appropriate care with line-ending conversions).

Flat-text-file storage has its limitations, however. For one thing, we have the hassle of serializing the data before we store it, and deserializing it when we read it back in. We need to make sure that the field- and record-delimiting characters we use don't occur in the data itself, or, if they do occur in the data, that they are appropriately escaped and unescaped as the data is stored and read back in from storage.

A more-serious limitation of flat-text-file storage is performance. In order to manipulate a particular record we must read the whole data file into memory, reconstruct the original data structure, modify it, and then write the whole thing back out again. For a few hundred or even a few thousand records that doesn't amount to much of a burden. If we need a system that can scale to the point of having tens of thousands or hundreds of thousands of records, however, or if we anticipate needing to access and update individual records frequently, something more efficient than a flat text file would be a good idea.

At the high end of the data-storage hierarchy in terms of efficiency and flexibility is the *relational database*. Discussion of how to set up and work with a relational database (such as MySQL or PostgreSQL) as the back-end data store for your web site is beyond the scope of this book, but it represents an excellent area for you to explore once you've mastered the material presented here. In the meantime, though, there is a set of tools that occupy a useful middle ground between flat text files and relational databases: *DBM files*.

DBM files are a group of software libraries that offer several different flavors of persistent data storage. DBM files are not Perl-specific, but Perl has convenient mechanisms for accessing and manipulating them. The principal feature of DBM files is that they allow us to access individual records efficiently via a unique key, just like a Perl hash. In fact, we can think of a DBM file as a sort of hash-on-a-disk, in which the key-value pairs of the hash are available from one invocation of the script to the next. What makes this so useful for persistant data storage is that we can access and manipulate one record at a time, rather than having to read and write our entire data file every time work with it. And our application can have hundreds of thousands, even millions of records, without suffering significant performance degradation.

Different flavors of DBM files have different strengths and weaknesses, but the two most generally useful DBM implementations are the GDBM and Berkeley DB libraries, which can be accessed from within Perl via the GDBM_File and DB_File modules, respectively. In the following discussion I will focus on the GDBM library, but either one should work fine for your web-related tasks.

The tie Function

We set up access to a DBM file from within our Perl script using the tie function, which ties a Perl hash variable to the DBM file on disk. From that point on, we work with the tied Perl hash just like we would with any other hash, adding, deleting, or modifying individual elements. As we perform those manipulations, Perl updates the DBM data on disk. When we are finished we use the untie function to sever the connection between the hash and the DBM file.

The only hard part is getting the syntax of the tie statement right. Here's how a typical tie statement looks for accessing a GDBM file for read-only access:

```
tie %HASH, 'GDBM_File', 'my_file.gdbm', &GDBM_READER, 0644;
```

To tie to a GDBM file in order to be able to read from, write to, or create the file, we would use a tie statement that looks like this:

```
tie %HASH, 'GDBM_File', 'my_file.gdbm', &GDBM_WRCREAT, 0644;
```

The individual arguments to the tie function are as follows:

- The name of the hash variable we're tying to the DBM file—in this example, %HASH. I fell into the habit of using all uppercase letters for my tied DBM file variable names early on; it's analogous to using all uppercase letters for filehandle names and is meant to indicate that there's an external file (the DBM file) involved with the variable. There's no law that says you have to use the all-uppercase convention for your tied DBM hash variables, but it has worked well for me.

- The name of the module that implements the tie operation we're performing—in this example, GDBM_File. We must have pulled in that module with a use GDBM_File statement somewhere earlier in the script in order to do this.

- The path to the actual DBM data file we're tying to—in this example, my_data. gdbm. This can include relative or absolute path information; in this example, we are telling Perl the file will be found in the current directory, whatever that is.

- The specific subroutine to use in setting up the tie operation—in this example, either &GDBM_READER (for read-only access) or &GDBM_WRCREAT (for reading, writing, and creating-the-file-if-it-doesn't-already-exist access). These arguments are specific to the GDBM_File module; other DBM implementations will require different arguments here. One nice thing about the GDBM flavor of DBM files is that it features its own built-in file locking. We will in effect be getting a shared lock on any GDBM file we tie with &GDBM_READER, and an exclusive lock on any GDBM file we tie with &GDBM_WRCREAT.

- The permissions we wish to give any new GDBM file that might be created by the tie operation—in this example, 0644.

A DBM Example Script

Let's take a look at a more complete example. Example 20-1 demonstrates how we might use GDBM_File in an actual script. Like all the examples in this book, it can be downloaded from the book's web site, at *http://www.elanus.net/book/*.

Example 20-1. A simple GDBM_File example

```
#!/usr/bin/perl -w

# color.plx - demonstrate GDBM_File

use strict;

use GDBM_File;
my $datafile = 'color.gdbm';

tie my %COLOR, 'GDBM_File', $datafile, &GDBM_WRCREAT, 0644
    or die "can't tie to $datafile for WRCREAT access: $!";

$COLOR{banana} = 'yellow';
$COLOR{apple}  = 'red';
$COLOR{orange} = 'orange';

untie %COLOR; # no longer tied to the DBM file
```

Example 20-1. A simple GDBM_File example (continued)

```
%COLOR = ( );  # empty the hash, to prove we're really storing
               # the data on disk.

tie %COLOR, 'GDBM_File', $datafile, &GDBM_READER, 0644
    or die "can't tie to $datafile for READER access: $!";

print "Here are all the records currently stored in $datafile:\n\n";

while (my($key, $value) = each %COLOR) {
    print "key: '$key', value: '$value'\n";
}

untie %COLOR;
```

If we run this script, it should produce output that looks like the following:

```
[jbc@andros jbc]$ color.plx
Here are all the records currently stored in color.gdbm:

key: 'orange', value: 'orange'
key: 'banana', value: 'yellow'
key: 'apple', value: 'red'
```

Suppose that we now add the following statement immediately after the first tie statement in color.plx, before the %COLOR hash has been untied:

```
tie my %ANOTHER, 'GDBM_File', $datafile, &GDBM_WRCREAT, 0644
    or die "can't tie to $datafile for WRCREAT access: $!";
```

At this point in the script we already have the DBM file whose location is given in $datafile opened for reading and writing and creating. This means that the GDBM library's built-in locking mechanism won't allow us to tie the %ANOTHER hash, causing the tie to return a false value, which makes the or die part of the statement fire off:

```
[jbc@andros jbc]$ color.plx
can't tie to color.gdbm for WRCREAT access: Resource temporarily
unavailable at ./color.plx line 23.
```

If we are building a web interface to a system that uses GDBM files for data storage, we need to think about how we want to handle the issue of concurrent users, just as we would if we were using flat text files for storage. GDBM's built-in locking mechanism, which allows only multiple readers, or a single writer, at any given time, will prevent us from accidentally corrupting our GDBM file, but it won't necessarily protect us from the other, more subtle sorts of race conditions that multiuser systems are prone to.

Blocking Versus Nonblocking Behavior

In the file-locking examples we've seen previously, using Perl's flock function and the Fcntl constants LOCK_SH and LOCK_EX, the default behavior has been to block on unsuccessful lock attempts. In other words, when a particular copy of our program fails to get a lock, it blocks, which means it sits there waiting for the lock to be granted. We can accomplish the same thing with a GDBM `tie` operation using an `until` loop, like so:

```
my %ANOTHER;

until (tie %ANOTHER, 'GDBM_File', $datafile, &GDBM_WRCREAT, 0644) {
    sleep 1;
}
```

This makes our script sleep for 1 second each time the `tie` fails, until it finally succeeds. (Notice how we had to take the `my %ANOTHER` declaration out of the `tie` statement, since we otherwise would be declaring `%ANOTHER` to be visible only inside the `until` block.)

We could omit the `sleep 1` statement inside the `until` loop if we wanted to, in effect having an empty loop that just spins continuously until the `tie` succeeds. That seemed to me like a lot of work to put our computer through, however, since it might run that loop a million times or more each second while waiting for the `tie` to succeed. If we did want to write a "continuous" loop like that, though, a common Perl idiom would be to remove the block altogether, using the one-line form shown here:

```
1 until tie my %ANOTHER, 'GDBM_File', $datafile, &GDBM_WRCREAT, 0644;
```

In that statement, the initial numeral 1 is just a true value, evaluated and thrown away by Perl after each failure by the `tie`.

But returning to the issue of blocking versus nonblocking `tie` operations, we also can create a block-for-a-little-while construct. With this approach, we give the script a certain amount of time during which it can try to get the lock, after which it will give up and die (or do whatever else we want it to do):

```
my %ANOTHER;
my $count = 0;

until (tie %ANOTHER, 'GDBM_File', $datafile, &GDBM_WRCREAT, 0644) {
    ++$count;
    if ($count > 5) {
        die "Couldn't tie $datafile in $count tries: $!";
    }
    sleep 1;
}
```

Of course, if we use a semaphore-file system for doing our locking, as we did in Chapter 19 with the `register.cgi` and `verify.cgi` scripts, we've got our file-locking bases covered and don't need to worry about tweaking GDBM's built-in file locking to achieve a particular kind of behavior. The shared and exclusive locks on our semaphore files will make sure that we never have a problem with two scripts contending over our data storage, whether that storage consists of flat text files or GDBM files.

Storing Multilevel Data in DBM Files

If we were to rewrite the user registration system given in this chapter using GDBM files for data storage, we would achieve some significant advantages. In particular, the system's performance would stay nice and snappy, even as the number of users grew larger. Rather than jumping right into a rewrite based on GDBM storage, though, let's take one more step.

A limitation of DBM files is that they store only key-value pairs. If we want to store a more-complex structure (like the HoH used in our registration system) we still have to go through the hassle of serializing and deserializing in order to create and read the hash values. This is really a pain, since it would be so cool to be able to treat the GDBM file like a real hash, capable of storing complex values. All it would take, really, is some standard code to do the serializing/deserializing. Someone really ought to write some software to do that and stick it in CPAN.

And of course, someone has. Two someones, in fact: Gurusamy Sarathy and Raphael Manfredi, authors of the MLDBM module. After installing it like any other CPAN module, a check of the documentation will reveal that, while it uses the Data::Dumper module to do its serializing by default, we will get better performance by installing Raphael Manfredi's Storable module. (Storable uses an extension to Perl written in the C language to do the serializing and deserializing, so it runs really fast.)

An MLDBM-Using Registration Script

Once we have downloaded and installed the MLDBM and Storable modules, we can take a look at Example 20-2, which is register.cgi rewritten as register2.cgi to work with the MLDBM, GDBM_File and Storable modules to store the member data.

Example 20-2. The revised register2.cgi script

```perl
#!/usr/bin/perl -Tw

# register2.cgi - sign up for membership at the Socalsail site

use strict;
use CGI    qw(:standard);
use Fcntl qw(:flock);
use GDBM_File;
use MLDBM qw(GDBM_File Storable);

$ENV{PATH} = '';

my $notify_email          = 'email@example.com';
my $sendmail              = '/usr/lib/sendmail';
my $queue_file            = '/w1/s/socalsail/maint/data/pending_memberships.gdbm';
my $queue_file_semaphore  = $queue_file . '.sem';
my $member_file           = '/w1/s/socalsail/maint/data/members.gdbm';
my $member_file_semaphore = $member_file . '.sem';
```

Example 20-2. The revised register2.cgi script (continued)

```perl
use lib '/home/jbc/lib';
use Socalsail::Make_page;

my $action  = param('action');
my $content = '';

unless ($action) {

    # show the initial sign-up form

    my $form = make_form();

    $content = <<"EOF";
<H2 ALIGN="center">Sign up for membership</H2>

<P>You may use this form to sign up for your free Socalsail membership.
Members are able to post messages in the site's discussion forums.</P>

$form

EOF

} elsif ($action eq 'Submit Membership Application') {

    # first, get an exclusive lock on the queue semaphore file.

    open QUEUE_LOCK, "> $queue_file_semaphore"
        or die "can't open $queue_file_semaphore for writing: $!";
    flock QUEUE_LOCK, LOCK_EX
        or die "can't get exclusive lock on $queue_file_semaphore: $!";

    # and get a shared lock on the member-data semaphore file

    open MEMBER_LOCK, "> $member_file_semaphore"
        or die "can't open $member_file_semaphore for writing: $!";
    flock MEMBER_LOCK, LOCK_SH
        or die "can't get exclusive lock on $member_file_semaphore: $!";

    # now, check the submitted data for okay-ness.

    my $href = check_form();

    # still here? then it must be okay.

    close MEMBER_LOCK; # lose the shared lock on the member data

    submit_application($href);

    close QUEUE_LOCK; # lose the exclusive lock on the queue file

    my $email = param('email');

    $content = <<"EOF";
```

Example 20-2. The revised register2.cgi script (continued)

```
<H2>Membership application received</H2>

<P>Our membership system is now sending verification instructions
to the E-mail address you supplied ('$email'). You can activate your
account by following the instructions contained in that E-mail. If
you have questions or problems, you may contact us at
<A HREF="mailto:$notify_email">$notify_email</A>. Thank you!</P>

EOF

}

my $made_page = make_page(
    page_type => 'standard',
    title     => 'Membership Application',
    content   => $content,
);

print header, $made_page;

# script proper ends. subroutines follow.

sub check_form {

    # do some (minimal) checking of the submitted fields

    my($username, $password, $v_password, $real_name,
        $phone, $email) = (param('username'), param('password'),
        param('v_password'), param('real_name'), param('phone'),
        param('email'));

    my @errors = ( );

    push @errors, '<LI>No username supplied.' unless $username;
    push @errors, '<LI>Username can only contain letters, numbers,
        and the underscore character (_).' if $username =~ /\W/;

    # tie to the queue and membership data files, check for an existing
    # account with the same username

    tie my %QUEUE, 'MLDBM', $queue_file,
        &GDBM_READER, 0644; # okay to fail, if it doesn't exist yet

    tie my %MEMBERS, 'MLDBM', $member_file,
        &GDBM_READER, 0644; # okay to fail, if it doesn't exist yet

    push @errors, "<LI>Username '$username' is already taken."
        if $QUEUE{$username} or $MEMBERS{$username};

    untie %QUEUE;
    untie %MEMBERS;

    push @errors, '<LI>No password supplied.' unless $password;
```

Example 20-2. The revised register2.cgi script (continued)

```
    push @errors, '<LI>Your two password fields do not match.'
        if $password and $password ne $v_password;
    push @errors, '<LI>No E-mail address supplied.' unless $email;
    push @errors, "<LI>E-mail address ('$email') doesn't look like a
        valid E-mail address." if $email and $email !~ /\w@\w+\.\w+/;

    if (@errors) {

        my $errors = join "\n", @errors;
        my $form   = make_form();

        $content = <<"EOF";
<H2 ALIGN="center">The following problem(s) were encountered
in trying to process your form:</H2>

<UL>
$errors
</UL>

<P>Please correct the error(s) in the form below, and re-submit.
We apologize for the inconvenience.</P>

$form

EOF

        my $made_page = make_page(
            page_type => 'standard',
            title     => 'Membership Application',
            content   => $content,
        );

        print header, $made_page;
        exit;

    }

    # no errors, so create the verification code, and
    # return a reference to an array, suitable
    # (once it gets the $username shifted off the front of it)
    # for storing in the register_queue file.

    my $verify = join '',
        ('A'..'H', 'J'..'N', 'P'..'Z')
        [rand 24, rand 24, rand 24, rand 24, rand 24];

    my $hashref = {
        username  => $username,
        verify    => $verify,
        password  => $password,
        real_name => $real_name,
        phone     => $phone,
        email     => $email,
```

Example 20-2. The revised register2.cgi script (continued)

```
    };
}

sub make_form {

    # create and return the registration form

    my $form = join '',
        start_form,
        '<TABLE>', "\n",

        '<TR><TD ALIGN="right">',
        '',
        '<STRONG>Username</STRONG><BR>',
        '(No spaces or special characters allowed)',
        '</TD><TD>',
        textfield('username'),
        '</TD></TR>', "\n",

        '<TR><TD ALIGN="right">',
        '',
        '<STRONG>Password</STRONG>',
        '</TD><TD>',
        password_field('password'),
        '</TD></TR>', "\n",

        '<TR><TD ALIGN="right">',
        '',
        '<STRONG>Password</STRONG><BR>',
        '(enter again for confirmation)',
        '</TD><TD>',
        password_field('v_password'),
        '</TD></TR>', "\n",

        '<TR><TD ALIGN="right">',
        '',
        '<STRONG>Real name</STRONG>',
        '</TD><TD>',
        textfield('real_name'),
        '</TD></TR>', "\n",

        '<TR><TD ALIGN="right">',
        '',
        '<STRONG>Phone</STRONG>',
        '</TD><TD>',
        textfield('phone'),
        '</TD></TR>', "\n",

        '<TR><TD ALIGN="right">',
        '',
        '<STRONG>E-mail</STRONG>',
        '</TD><TD>',
```

Example 20-2. The revised register2.cgi script (continued)

```
        textfield('email'),
        '</TD></TR>', "\n",

        '<TR><TD COLSPAN=2 ALIGN="center">',
        submit(
            -name => 'action',
            -value => 'Submit Membership Application',
        ),
        '</TD></TR></TABLE>', "\n", end_form;
}

sub submit_application {

    # store this membership application in the application queue.
    # the supplied argument is a hashref of the form:
    #
    # my $hashref = {
    #     username  => $username,
    #     verify    => $verify,
    #     password  => $password,
    #     real_name => $real_name,
    #     phone     => $phone,
    #     email     => $email,
    # };

    my $href = shift;

    # store the user's information in the temporary holding area.

    tie my %QUEUE, 'MLDBM', $queue_file, &GDBM_WRCREAT, 0644
        or die "couldn't tie $queue_file WRCREAT: $!";

    $QUEUE{ $href->{username} } = $href;

    untie %QUEUE;

    # now send an email to the user

    my $mail_body = <<"EOF";
You are almost finished registering for the Socalsail Web site. Please
click on the link below to complete your registration:

<http://www.socalsail.com/register/verify.cgi?username=$href->{username}&verify=$href->
{verify}>

If clicking on the link above does not automatically take
you to our verification Web page, you can also complete
your registration by going to the following address in
your Web browser:

<http://www.socalsail.com/register/verify.cgi>
```

Example 20-2. The revised register2.cgi script (continued)

```
and entering the following two items exactly as shown:

Username: $href->{username}
Verification code: $href->{verify}

Please note that these values are CASE SENSITIVE.
EOF

    open MAIL, "|$sendmail -oi -t"
        or die "Can't open pipe to $sendmail: $!\n";

    print MAIL <<"EOF";
To: $href->{email}
From: $notify_email
Subject: Membership verification instructions

$mail_body
EOF

    close MAIL or die "Can't close pipe to $sendmail: $!\n";
}
```

The first thing we'll notice here is that the `Register.pm` module has been done away with. With the switch to using the on-disk GDBM data hash for storage and the `MLDBM` module to do the serializing and deserializing, a lot of what was previously being done in the shared module was no longer necessary. Indeed, its only real remaining purpose was to serve as a central storage location for the package variables holding the names of the various data and semaphore files that the system manipulates. After thinking about it for a moment, I decided that I was better off using copy-and-paste to stick the names of the files at the top of both `register2.cgi` and `verify2.cgi`, rather than having to maintain a separate module just for that.

Up at the top of the script, we'll next notice the following new lines:

```
use GDBM_File;
use MLDBM qw(GDBM_File Storable);
```

The first pulls in the `GDBM_File` subroutines that will be used in `MLDBM`'s `tie` statements, and the second pulls in the `MLDBM` module itself, specifying `GDBM_File` as the type of DBM file to use and `Storable` as the serializer. We'll also see the following lines, taken from the old `Register.pm` module and rewritten slightly to work here:

```
my $queue_file = '/w1/s/socalsail/maint/data/pending_memberships.gdbm';
my $queue_file_semaphore = $queue_file . '.sem';
my $member_file         = '/w1/s/socalsail/maint/data/members.gdbm';
my $member_file_semaphore = $member_file . '.sem';
```

Aside from those differences, the only changes between `register.cgi` and `register2.cgi` are found in two subroutines: `check_form` and `submit_application`. In `check_form`, we see the following two `tie` statements, demonstrating how `MLDBM` ties work:

```
tie my %QUEUE, 'MLDBM', $queue_file,
    &GDBM_READER, 0644; # okay to fail, if it doesn't exist yet
```

```
tie my %MEMBERS, 'MLDBM', $member_file,
    &GDBM_READER, 0644; # okay to fail, if it doesn't exist yet
```

In each case, we give 'MLDBM' as the second argument, and then give the same arguments you would normally give to do a tie with GDBM_File. As the comments indicate, these particular ties are written to fail silently in case those particular queue and
member files don't exist. This could happen when our first user tries to register, for
example, when those files have never been tied to before with a &GDBM_WRCREAT argument, and hence don't exist yet. (We may actually see a warning from MLDBM showing up in the error log in that situation, but it won't hurt anything, and the
subsequent untie operation also should not cause a problem, even if we didn't actually tie anything.)

Once the script has tied to the two GDBM files (one for pending applications and one
for previously approved memberships), it's easy to check to see if the username currently being submitted has been used before. We simply check to see if the given hash
key is associated with a true value, just as we did in the previous version of the script:

```
push @errors, "<LI>Username '$username' is already taken."
    if $QUEUE{$username} or $MEMBERS{$username};
```

Since we're done reading from the GDBM files, we untie the two hashes right away:

```
untie %QUEUE;
untie %MEMBERS;
```

The rest of the check_form subroutine is identical to the first version of the script.

The changes to the submit_application subroutine are likewise straightforward. Having been invoked with a hashref containing the data for this particular membership
application, it uses MLDBM to tie to the GDBM-based queue file, stores that hashref as
a value keyed with $href->{username}, and unties the GDBM file:

```
tie my %QUEUE, 'MLDBM', $queue_file, &GDBM_WRCREAT, 0644
    or die "couldn't tie $queue_file WRCREAT: $!";

$QUEUE{ $href->{username} } = $href;

untie %QUEUE;
```

An MLDBM-Using Verification Script

The changes to the verify.cgi script are also simple, as the verify2.cgi script given
in Example 20-3 shows.

Example 20-3. The verify2.cgi script

```
#!/usr/bin/perl -Tw

# verify2.cgi
#
# verifies receipt of the member's verification code, and activates the
# member's account by:
#
```

Example 20-3. The verify2.cgi script (continued)

```perl
# 1) writing their information to the $member_file,
# 2) adding their username/password pair to the .htpasswd file,
# 3) adding them to the appropriate group in the .htgroup file, and
# 4) deleting their entry from the submission queue.

use strict;
use CGI    qw(:standard);
use Fcntl qw(:flock);
use Apache::Htpasswd;
use GDBM_File;
use MLDBM qw(GDBM_File Storable);

use lib '/home/jbc/lib';
use Socalsail::Make_page;

$ENV{PATH} = '';

my $notify_email          = 'email@example.com';
my $sendmail              = '/usr/lib/sendmail';
my $queue_file            = '/w1/s/socalsail/maint/data/pending_memberships.gdbm';
my $queue_file_semaphore  = $queue_file . '.sem';
my $member_file           = '/w1/s/socalsail/maint/data/members.gdbm';
my $member_file_semaphore = $member_file . '.sem';
my $htgroup_file          = '/w1/s/socalsail/maint/data/.htgroup';
my $htgroup_semaphore     = $htgroup_file . '.sem';
my $htpasswd_file         = '/w1/s/socalsail/maint/data/.htpasswd';

my $username = param('username');
my $verify   = param('verify');

my $content  = '';

unless ($username and $verify) {

    # they didn't come by clicking on the email link

    my $form = make_form( );

    $content = <<"EOF";
<H2 ALIGN="center">Membership Verification</H1>

<P>In order to activate your membership at Socalsail,
you must give your username and the verification code that
was E-mailed to the address you supplied.</P>

<P><STRONG>Please note:</STRONG> The username and verification
code are <STRONG>case sensitive</STRONG>.</P>

$form

EOF

    my $made_page = make_page(
```

Example 20-3. The verify2.cgi script (continued)

```
        title    => "Membership Verification",
        content  => $content,
        page_type => 'standard',
    );
    print header, $made_page;
    exit;
}

# still here? then process their submitted information.

# first, get an exclusive lock on the queue semaphore file.

open QUEUE_LOCK, "> $queue_file_semaphore"
    or die "can't open $queue_file_semaphore for writing: $!";
flock QUEUE_LOCK, LOCK_EX
    or die "can't get exclusive lock on $queue_file_semaphore: $!";

# and another exclusive lock on the member-data semaphore file

open MEMBER_LOCK, "> $member_file_semaphore"
    or die "can't open $member_file_semaphore for writing: $!";
flock MEMBER_LOCK, LOCK_EX
    or die "can't get exclusive lock on $member_file_semaphore: $!";

tie my %QUEUE, 'MLDBM', $queue_file, &GDBM_WRCREAT, 0644
    or die "couldn't tie $queue_file WRCREAT: $!";

tie my %MEMBERS, 'MLDBM', $member_file, &GDBM_WRCREAT, 0644
    or die "couldn't tie $member_file WRCREAT: $!";

if ($MEMBERS{$username}) {

    # they're already verified

    $content = <<"EOF";
<H2>Account already verified</H2>

<P>The account for user '$username' has already been
verified. You can use the account by supplying that
username, as well as the password you chose when you
created the account, when prompted for them.</P>

<P>If you have questions about this system, please contact
us at <A HREF="mailto:$notify_email">$notify_email</A>.</P>
EOF

} elsif (not $QUEUE{$username}) {

    # so they are in neither %MEMBERS nor %QUEUE

    my $form = make_form( );

    $content = <<"EOF";
```

Example 20-3. The verify2.cgi script (continued)

```
<H2>Unable to find membership application</H2>

<P>The username you supplied ('$username') is not in the list of
pending applications. It may be that there is a typo in the username
you supplied (usernames are case-sensitive, for example, such that
'myname' is different from 'MyName', which is different from 'MYNAME').
You can try again by completing, and re-submitting, the form below,
or you can start the process over again by
<A HREF="/register/register.cgi">submitting a new membership
application</A>. We apologize for the inconvenience.</P>

$form
EOF

} else {

    # they supplied a username that *is* in the pending-membership
    # queue, so check to see if they supplied the correct verification
    # code.

    if ($verify eq $QUEUE{$username}{verify}) {

        # they successfully verified, so...
        # add them to the members file

        my $href = $QUEUE{$username};
        delete $href->{verify}; # don't need the 'verify' code anymore
        $MEMBERS{$username} = $href;

        # add their entry to the .htpasswd file

        my $htpasswd
            = new Apache::Htpasswd($htpasswd_file);
        $htpasswd->htpasswd($username, $href->{password});

        # add them to the htgroup file

        open HTGROUP_LOCK, "> $htgroup_semaphore"
            or die "can't open $htgroup_semaphore for writing: $!";
        flock HTGROUP_LOCK, LOCK_EX
            or die "can't get exclusive lock on $htgroup_semaphore: $!";

        my %HoH = read_htgroup();
        $HoH{socalsail_members}{$username} = 1;
        write_htgroup(%HoH);

        close HTGROUP_LOCK;

        # remove them from the registration queue

        delete $QUEUE{$username};

        # send them an email with their access instructions
```

Example 20-3. The verify2.cgi script (continued)

```
        my $mail_body = <<"EOF";
You have successfully activated your user account at Socalsail.
To access the site's membership features, you will need to
supply the following information when prompted at the site:

Username: $username
Password: $href->{password}

Please remember that your username and password are both
CASE-SENSITIVE.

We suggest you save this message for future reference.

If you have questions about this system, please contact
us at $notify_email.

Thank you.
EOF

        open MAIL, "|$sendmail -oi -t"
            or die "Can't open pipe to $sendmail: $!\n";

        print MAIL <<"EOF";
To: $MEMBERS{$username}{email}
From: $notify_email
Subject: Socalsail registration information

$mail_body
EOF

        close MAIL or die "Can't close pipe to $sendmail: $!\n";

        # give them the good news.

        $content = <<"EOF";
<H2>Congratulations</H2>

<P>Member account for '$username' has been successfully activated.</P>
EOF

    } else {

        # they supplied an incorrect verification code

        my $form = make_form( );

        $content = <<"EOF";
<H2>Unable to verify account</H2>

<P>The username you supplied ('$username') does not match the
verification code you entered ('$verify'). It may be that there
is a typo in the username or verification code. Both are
case-sensitive, for example, such that 'myname' is
```

Example 20-3. The verify2.cgi script (continued)

```
different from 'MyName', which is different from 'MYNAME').
You can try again by completing, and re-submitting, the form below,
or you can start the process over again by
<A HREF="/register/register.cgi">submitting a new membership
application</A>. We apologize for the inconvenience.</P>

$form
EOF
    }
}

untie %QUEUE;
untie %MEMBERS;

close QUEUE_LOCK;
close MEMBER_LOCK;

my $made_page = make_page(
    page_type => 'standard',
    title     => 'Membership Verification',
    content   => $content,
);

print header, $made_page;

# script proper ends. subroutine follows.

sub make_form {

    # create and return the verification form

    my $form = join '',
        start_form,
        '<TABLE>', "\n",

        '<TR><TD ALIGN="right">',
        '',
        '<STRONG>Username</STRONG><BR>',
        '(No spaces or special characters allowed)',
        '</TD><TD>',
        textfield('username'),
        '</TD></TR>', "\n",

        '<TR><TD ALIGN="right">',
        '',
        '<STRONG>Verification code</STRONG><BR>',
        '</TD><TD>',
        textfield('verify'),
        '</TD></TR>', "\n",

        '<TR><TD COLSPAN=2 ALIGN="center">',
        submit(
            -name => 'action',
            -value => 'Verify Membership',
```

Example 20-3. The verify2.cgi script (continued)

```
        ),
        '</TD></TR></TABLE>', "\n", end_form;
}

sub read_htgroup {

    # read the htgroup file for Socalsail members.
    # return a HoH of the following form:
    #
    # primary key: groupname. secondary key: membername.
    # value: 1.

    my %HoH = ( );

    # okay to fail on open, since file may not exist yet

    if (open IN, $htgroup_file) {

        while (<IN>) {
            if (/^(\S+): (.+)/) {
                my $group = $1;
                my $rest  = $2;
                my @members = split /\s+/, $rest;
                foreach my $member (@members) {
                    $HoH{$group}{$member} = 1;
                }
            }
        }
        close IN;   # close data file
    }

    %HoH; # return data structure
}

sub write_htgroup {

    # invoked with a HoH: primary key:   groupname
    #                     secondary key: membername
    #                     value:         1
    #
    # writes the data out to $htgroup_file.

    my %HoH = @_;

    open OUT, "> $htgroup_file"
        or die "couldn't open $htgroup_file for writing: $!";

    while (my($group, $hashref) = each %HoH) {
        print OUT "$group: ", join(' ', keys %{$hashref}), "\n";
    }
    close OUT;
}
```

As with `register2.cgi`, `verify2.cgi` pulls in the `GDBM_File` and `MLDBM` modules with appropriate use statements:

```
use GDBM_File;
use MLDBM qw(GDBM_File Storable);
```

Also, it eliminates the use of the external `Register.pm` module, and instead has a configuration section at the top that gives the names of the various data and semaphore files. Obviously, it's important to make sure that these filenames match those in the registration script; the burden of making sure they match is the price we pay for the convenience of eliminating the shared module file. The `verify2.cgi` script also contains the subroutines for manipulating the `.htgroup` file (which previously resided in the `Register.pm` module, but didn't actually need to, since they weren't used by `register.cgi` anyway).

The next difference in the new version of the script is the part where, having determined that the user has supplied a username and verification code that need to be processed, the GDBM files holding the queue and member data are tied to:

```
tie my %QUEUE, 'MLDBM', $queue_file, &GDBM_WRCREAT, 0644
    or die "couldn't tie $queue_file WRCREAT: $!";

tie my %MEMBERS, 'MLDBM', $member_file, &GDBM_WRCREAT, 0644
    or die "couldn't tie $member_file WRCREAT: $!";
```

Notice the use of `&GDBM_WRCREAT`, rather than `&GDBM_READER`, in the `tie` statements, meaning we are now making a tie for reading, writing, and creating (if the GDBM file doesn't already exist). Notice also that we've used an explicit die statement in case either `tie` fails. Two copies of the script both trying to `tie` at the same time shouldn't be a problem, since the semaphore file locking will prevent that from happening. We will need to remember, though, that if we ever build other scripts that tie to these same GDBM files we will need to make sure that the new scripts use the same semaphore files for locking. Otherwise, we could experience unexpected `tie` failures when GDBM's built-in file locking prevents a script from tying to a GDBM file that is already tied to by another script.

The rest of the script ends up being pretty much the same as the old version, except that we don't have to worry about explicitly writing the modified %QUEUE or %MEMBERS HoHs back out to disk (since the changes we make are written to disk automatically via the DBM tie). Also, we *do* have to remember to untie the tied hashes when we are through with them.

One more chunk of code is worth mentioning, though, because it raises an interesting point about using MLDBM-tied data structures, and gives me a chance to mention a subtle limitation they are prone to.

In this section of `verify2.cgi`, the user-supplied verification code (in $verify) is compared with the one stored in the queue's data structure, and if the two match, the user's record is moved from the queue to the member file:

```
if ($verify eq $QUEUE{$username}{verify}) {

    # they successfully verified, so...
    # add them to the members file

    my $href = $QUEUE{$username};
    delete $href->{verify};         # not needed anymore
    $MEMBERS{$username} = $href;
```

Notice how in the condition of the if statement, we have directly accessed the "inner" hash of the HoH data structure stored in the MLDBM-serialized queue GDBM file. That works fine as long as we are *reading* from the tied multilevel data structure. Next, notice how we read the hashref for this particular user from the queue GDBM file, delete the verify key-value pair from it, and then write it out, again as a complete hashref, to the members GDBM file. This also works fine.

But suppose we tried to do the following, writing the complete $href data structure to the members file, and only *then* deleting the verify key-value pair from it:

```
my $href = $QUEUE{$username};
$MEMBERS{$username} = $href;
delete $MEMBERS{$username}{verify}; # won't work!!
```

As the comment indicates, this approach would fail. When we are *reading* from an MLDBM-tied data file, accessing individual elements nested inside the stored data structure is fine. When we are *modifying* that data structure, however, either by adding, changing, or deleting something stored at a level deeper than the top-level key-value pairs, we can't make the modification directly. Instead, we have to first make a temporary copy of the structure accessed by that particular top-level key, make the modification to that temporary copy, and then store the whole thing back in.

For example, let's say we wanted to let a user modify his or her password in the member file. Once we had used MLDBM to tie a %MEMBERS hash to the GDBM file, we could not use something like $MEMBERS{$username}{password} = $new_password. Instead, we would need to do something like this:

```
my $href             = $MEMBERS{$username};
$href->{password}    = $new_password;
$MEMBERS{$username}  = $href;
```

This limitation is described in the BUGS section of the MLDBM documentation, accessible via man MLDBM or perldoc MLDBM once we have installed the module. It's really not a problem once we get used to it, and it's a small price to pay for the power and flexibility offered by the MLDBM module.

## CHAPTER 21

Where to Go Next

Back at the beginning of this book, I spoke about the process of learning Perl for web development as being akin to mountain climbing. To return to that metaphor, you've now reached the summit and have hopefully picked up some useful tools and skills along the way. Looking back at your starting point, you should feel a nice sense of accomplishment. It's been a long ascent, with many challenges to overcome, and you've done a great job to come so far. Congratulations.

Now, as promised, it's time to look beyond the current peak and realize that what you've learned in this book is really just the beginning of the journey. There are many more peaks stretching beyond this one, higher peaks, with many new challenges.

This book took an eclectic approach. As a reflection of my own experience, it presented a little bit of everything. What path you take from this point is up to you. You might continue as you've started, picking up a little of this and a little of that on your way to becoming an ever-more-capable generalist. Or you might choose to specialize in a particular area.

With that in mind, here is a brief overview of where you might choose to go next.

Unix System Administration

Running Unix or Unix-like computer systems is a full-time task for many people. For many others it's an important component of their larger duties. Once you make the leap to having your own, dedicated web server, it's a task that might easily end up being yours. Even if you have outside help from a "real" system administrator, or *sysadmin*, there are some major benefits to be had from learning how to do your own system administration.

As a sysadmin, you will delve much deeper into the use of the shell. There are many shell commands that this book has not covered, and many advanced options of those that have been covered. To the system administrator these are essential tools, weapons, if you will, in a perpetual war against the forces of chaos. Not surprisingly, Perl is also a key weapon in that arsenal.

An excellent way to gain experience running a Unix-like machine is to install a copy of Linux on your personal computer. Using a piece of software called LILO, it is possible to configure your Intel-based PC to boot up either into Linux or Windows. Many people, myself included, use this approach to keep a foot in both worlds, as it were. I've had good experience running Red Hat Linux in this fashion, and the lessons I've learned have definitely helped me do a better job of taking care of the various dedicated web servers I deal with. See the Red Hat Linux web site at *http://www.redhat.com/* for more information.

The duties of a sysadmin are varied. A sysadmin must install software on the machine, and make sure that software runs properly. Disk, memory, and CPU usage must be monitored. A regular backup schedule must be established, and procedures put in place to recover from the inevitable hardware failures.

On your personal machine, where you are the only user, setting up and administering user accounts is a relatively simple task. Once you start dealing with multiple users, however, a whole new dimension of sysadmin duties rears its head. Prominent Perl celebrity and system administrator Elaine Ashton got a hearty laugh at a recent Perl conference when, as part of her introduction to the crowd, she was asked to name her least-favorite piece of computer technology, and she responded, "users." Kidding aside, setting up user accounts, answering users' questions, and cleaning up the messes they make is an important part of most sysadmins' daily responsibilities.

When the computer you are administering is connected permanently to the Internet, the number of users you must worry about expands dramatically. Instead of worrying only about those who are officially sanctioned to use the machine, you have to worry about the much larger population of malicious outsiders who would like to use the machine for their own, unsanctioned purposes. As a result, system security is a prominent concern for many sysadmins, who must be ever-vigilant, monitoring newsgroups and mailing lists, installing software patches to correct newly discovered vulnerabilities, and rolling quickly into action when an intrusion or a denial-of-service attack takes place.

Two books that have been very helpful for me in learning system administration are Æleen Frisch's *Essential System Administration* (O'Reilly), and Jerry Peek, Tim O'Reilly, and Mike Loukides' *Unix Power Tools* (O'Reilly).

Programming

One area where you certainly will never run out of things to learn is that of programming. The phenomenon of accidental programmers who use Perl as their 0th programming language is a relatively new one, but real programming is a complex and demanding discipline with a long history. To the extent you find yourself focusing more on programming than on other aspects of developing web sites, you will necessarily find yourself travelling farther and farther down the path of the programmer.

A Programmer's Editor

One of the first things you probably will find yourself doing in that case is learning to use a real programmer's editor. In the Unix world that traditionally has meant either vi or Emacs (mentioned briefly in a sidebar in Chapter 1). I can't advise you much in either case, since I've kept one foot firmly enough planted in the Windows world that my primary text editor is still a shareware Windows program called UltraEdit (*http://www.ultraedit.com/*). But having seen what someone well-versed in vi can do in terms of lightning-fast editing, I have no illusions about who would win a speed contest, and one of these days I really am going to learn vi, I swear. In the meantime, I normally get by when editing under Unix with jpico, the pico-flavored version of the joe editor.

Revision-Control Systems

Besides a good text editor, another essential tool of the programmer is a *revision-control system*. The standard revision-control system used in the Unix world is called RCS. A more full-featured tool that is commonly layered on top of RCS is CVS, which stands for "concurrent versioning system." About a year ago I begin using CVS to track all my important editing tasks, and now I can't imagine how I ever lived without it.

CVS allows you to maintain a history of all the prior versions of a file. It is most commonly used for tracking changes to computer source code, but it works well for any sort of text file, or even binary files. Using it for binary files is less efficient than using it for text files, though, because of the way the history of changes is stored.

Besides allowing you to track the history of changes you've made to a file, or roll back to any desired previous state in the file's history, CVS also allows multiple people to work on the same collection of files at the same time. It keeps track of who has made what changes, merging the changes made by different users or alerting them when they attempt to make changes that conflict with each other.

It typically works in this way. To begin with, a collection of files is uploaded to a repository on a CVS server. Users who wish to work with those files can then check out the repository, which means they make a copy of it in a working directory on their own machine, or in their own home directory on the same machine as the CVS server, or wherever they like. (I typically use a Windows CVS client called WinCVS, and keep my working directories on my Windows machine. See *http://www.wincvs.org/* for more about WinCVS.)

Once you have checked the files into your working directory, you are free to do whatever you want with them. When you reach a point that you might conceivably want to roll back to at some point in the future, you *commit* the modified version of your file, which means uploading it back to the CVS server, where it is merged with the previous version of the file.

Besides the initial checking out of a repository and the committing of modified versions of the file at periodic intervals, the other principal CVS action you can perform is an update, where you ask the CVS server to replace the current version of a file in your working directory with the most recent version of the file in the CVS server's repository, or with some other, older version of the file.

As I said, CVS excels at letting you keep track of the history of your changes to a file. With software source code, this is incredibly helpful because it lets you back out a change to a program, and revert to an earlier version, or identify the specific point when a particular bug appeared. This is useful even when you are the only person working on your files, but it becomes absolutely invaluable when you have more than one person working on them. I've lost track of the number of times that CVS has saved the day when I was trying to figure out just who did what and when they did it.

More Perl

Two excellent books on Perl that you should definitely try to own are Larry Wall, Tom Christiansen, and Jon Orwant's *Programming Perl, 3rd Edition* (O'Reilly) and Tom Christiansen and Nathan Torkington's *Perl Cookbook* (O'Reilly). A good beginner-friendly book that provides a more formal introduction to the language than I've given here is Simon Cozen's *Beginning Perl* (Wrox Press).

One thing that distinguishes real programmers from their accidental counterparts is that where accidental programmers typically know only one language, real programmers know lots of them. And as much as I love Perl and believe it is hands down the best choice if you can have only one language in your toolkit, there are many other languages that you will benefit from learning if you are going to progress very far down the programmer's path.

JavaScript

One of the first I should mention is JavaScript, the language Netscape introduced for embedding programming in web pages, and which Microsoft picked up and included in its Internet Explorer browser soon after. The idea with JavaScript is that you put some code in a web page, and it is parsed and executed in the user's browser. This is potentially a very powerful tool because it allows you to exercise much more control over the behavior of your web pages than you can with straight HTML. Also, it was designed to be relatively easy to learn, offering an easy upgrade path for users who want to move beyond HTML.

With that said, there are some inherent limitations to using JavaScript that have kept me from embracing it as completely as I otherwise might have. Differences in the behavior of the JavaScript runtime engine in different browsers, or different versions of the same browser, mean it can be difficult to create a JavaScript-dependent web application that will behave consistently for all users. Even today, some users still use JavaScript-incapable browsers, while others intentionally turn off JavaScript execution in their browser (or have it turned off for them by their corporate computing staff) because of security concerns. Still, for certain kinds of web enhancements (like graphical rollover effects on navigational buttons), or for environments where users' browser type and version are known quantities (like on corporate intranets), Java-Script has a definite role to play, even for a curmudgeon like me.

PHP

Another programming language that is very popular for web development is PHP (see *http://www.php.net/*). Like JavaScript, PHP is typically used as a scripting language whose code is embedded directly in web pages' HTML. Unlike JavaScript, though, which is downloaded and executed in the user's web browser, PHP code is parsed and executed by the web server itself, before delivering the page to the end user.

In effect, embedded scripting via PHP is the yin to the typical CGI script's yang. Both methods allow you to deliver web pages that feature dynamic content without having to rely on an inconsistent execution engine in the user's browser. But where a CGI script is a computer program that typically has some HTML embedded inside it, a PHP page is an HTML page with some programming embedded inside it. Depending on what you're trying to accomplish, this can be a very attractive alternative.

I've never spent much time with PHP, in part because it wasn't available when I started doing web development, and by the time it came along I was already proficient enough with Perl to do what I wanted that way. PHP gets high marks from my friends who use it, however. They like to point out that it is easier to learn than Perl, with its web-specific focus serving to reduce the complexities that go along with learning a more general-purpose language like Perl.

Embperl

One of these days I'll probably wind up buckling down and learning PHP. In the meantime, I've found that when I have a task that seems to call for the programming-embedded-in-HTML approach I've been able to use the Perl equivalent, Gerald Richter's Embperl (see *http://perl.apache.org/embperl/*). Like PHP, Embperl lets you embed code in your HTML pages for parsing and dynamic page generation by the web server, but with Embperl you get to embed Perl code rather than PHP code.

All the languages mentioned so far are special-purpose languages created specifically for web applications. There also are a number of other languages that compete more directly with Perl in terms of general-purpose programming.

Python

Python (*http://www.python.org/*) is probably Perl's closest competitor in the world of programming langauges. Like Perl, Python is an interpreted language and is designed to be relatively accessible for beginners. Indeed, its supporters like to claim that it is superior to Perl as a first computer language, citing its more rigid enforcement of whitespace formatting and its avoidance of Perl's three or four ways to do everything as factors making it easier for beginners to learn. Among other factors that argue in favor of learning Python is the central role Python plays in Zope (*http://www.zope.org/*), an open source web application server that is very popular for certain kinds of development.

Without descending into a Perl-versus-Python slugfest (of which there are plenty available already, if you search a bit on the Net), I have to say that for someone coming from my perspective, Perl still looks more attractive than Python. To my mind, it's a bit off-putting for an accidental programmer to have to contend with Python's insistence on precise whitespace usage, on using an object-oriented approach, or its preference for Just One Way to do things. Be that as it may, Python is very popular, and growing in popularity. Those who like Perl and wish to expand their horizons to other general-purpose languages should certainly give it a look.

Other Languages

Finally, at the high end of the real-programming-languages hierarchy are traditional, full-blown languages like C, C++, and Java. Learning these will definitely put you in the real-programmer camp, and will definitely take you well beyond the abilities of someone like me to offer you much advice and assistance. Good luck!

Apache Server Administration and mod_perl

At the point when you move beyond serving your web pages in a shared hosting environment, you will probably start dealing with web server configuration, which, for the large majority of those in a Unix-like environment, means Apache server configuration. Figuring out how the various Apache server configuration directives work is actually pretty easy, once you get the hang of it; you typically just need to make a change in the server's httpd.conf file, then restart the server for the changes to take effect. It's all fairly well documented in the comments contained in the httpd.conf file itself, and in the documentation reachable via *http://www.apache.org/*.

Once you've been using Perl and Apache for a while, you're going to start hearing about mod_perl (*http://perl.apache.org/*), which, for a Perl-using web developer, is one of the coolest things about having your own server to play with, rather than being in a shared hosting environment. Among other things, mod_perl solves the CGI-script performance problem.

That problem is this: suppose you have a moderately popular web site being served by an Apache server. As long as the large majority of the requests coming into the server are for static HTML pages, you will be fine. Apache will fork off a lot of child httpd processes, which will take turns handling the incoming requests. Apache's httpd processes are fairly small in terms of memory footprint, and they all typically share the memory that each starts off with, so that's even better. A server with a moderate amount of memory (say, 512MB) should have no problem forking off a few hundred httpd processes, which should be happy handling as many as several hundred requests for static HTML pages each second. No problem so far.

But let's say you get excited by the possibilities inherent in Perl CGI scripting and you decide to start delivering all the pages on your site dynamically, via Perl. Now the situation changes dramatically. Each request now results in the running of a separate CGI script process, which begins its life by loading up the megabyte-plus of the perl interpreter. Even if the CGI script doesn't put much strain on the CPU, trying to run a lot of them simultaneously is going to cause the server to run out of memory, at which point it will start swapping out memory to disk, at which point performance on the site is going to slow to a standstill.

The mod_perl Apache server module solves this problem by embedding a copy of the perl interpreter right into the httpd process. This is a somewhat mixed blessing, in that it makes those httpd processes bigger. Also, most CGI scripts need at least a bit of tweaking before they will run properly in the modified environment represented by mod_perl. But the performance improvement this delivers for Perl CGI scripts on busy sites is dramatic.

Relational Databases

In Chapter 20 I talked about using the GDBM library (optionally with Perl's MLDBM module) to maintain persistent data for a web site. A more full-featured way to achieve that kind of back-end data storage is to use a relational database and access the data using SQL (for "Structured Query Language"), a standard language for interacting with databases. A very popular free database engine used by many web sites for this purpose is MySQL (*http://www.mysql.com/*). Although some purists argue that MySQL isn't a "true" relational database management system (because it lacks certain features, like the ability to link a sequence of transactions together as a logical unit, such that if any individual transaction fails the whole series of transactions fails), it is fine for most web purposes. For those requiring the features missing in MySQL, PostgreSQL (*http://www.postgresql.org/*) is a competing free database engine that has them, at the cost of a bit more complexity and, perhaps, a bit slower performance (depending on who does the measuring).

Having a relational database to hold your web site's data both simplifies and complicates your life. It simplifies your life because the database engine solves many of the problems you would otherwise have to solve yourself. Various kinds of searches and updates to your data are easy to carry out using simple SQL queries. Multiple users trying to submit updates to the data at the same time are guaranteed not to mangle each others' data because the database engine will queue the incoming updates and handle them one at a time. Mixing and matching your data in various ways, even ways you didn't anticipate when you originally set up the database, is relatively easy, assuming you set up the database correctly. Procedures for backing up and/or replicating your data are straightforward.

Things are more complicated with a relational database because you are introducing a new component to the system, with its own quirks and its own learning curve to be surmounted. You must think carefully when setting up your database about just how it will be structured, deciding what tables you will use, what columns each table will contain, what datatypes will be used for each column, and how the various tables will be related to each other. You need to figure out how your data should be indexed to enable fast searching, while being careful not to use too much disk space by going overboard on indexing. The database ends up being like a miniature computer system in its own right, with its own administrative needs: user accounts to be established and maintained, backup procedures, and security concerns. In corporate computing environments, the database administrator is an important specialist with primary responsibility for these things.

Simplifying the task of integrating Perl programming with your relational database is Tim Bunce's very cool DBI module, available on CPAN. The DBI module provides an abstraction layer that you can use to connect to your database, issue SQL queries, and get back the results of those queries. What makes the DBI module so cool is that you can write your Perl code without having to worry (much) about the specific database engine you are using. You can even change from one database engine to another after your code is written, and assuming you haven't relied on any nonstandard features of the old database, all you will have to do is change one line in your Perl program. Specifically, you will only have to change the line where your program makes its connection to the underlying database.

The DBI module can do this because it doesn't talk directly to the database itself. Instead, it is layered on top of a lower-level DBD module that talks to the database engine. Every database has its own DBD module; there's one for MySQL, one for PostgreSQL, and so on, each maintained by a different volunteer maintainer. All the pesky, engine-specific details are handled in the various DBD modules, leaving the DBI module to sail serenely along on top of them, pretending that every database works in exactly the same way. It's all just terribly clever, and extremely helpful for lowly programmers, accidental or otherwise, who just want to get their work done.

Advocacy

"Advocacy" seems like an odd thing to be talking about in a book about web development and programming, but I wanted to make a brief plea before wishing you good luck and sending you on your way. The many tools and technologies I've talked about in this book, including Perl, Apache, Linux, and the various GNU utilities available in the shell, as well as the Web and the Internet itself, grew out of a certain culture. It is a culture that values openness and sharing. It fosters a sense of community, of contributing to the collective store of tools and information in a way that recognizes the contributions of those who came before, and builds a foundation that can be built upon by those who come after.

On many fronts, this traditional Internet culture is under attack. Get-rich-quick artists, or worse, legitimate but misguided businesses, pour millions of unsolicited commercial emails into the network each day, straining mail servers and stealing from individual Net users their most valuable commodity: their time. Companies take advantage of an antiquated patent system to obtain government-sanctioned monopolies for trivially obvious "innovations" like one-click ordering and name-your-price reverse auctions, then put teams of lawyers to work stopping others from using these techniques unless they are willing to pay license fees. Lobbyists for the film and music industries obtain passage of laws that restrict traditionally protected rights like free speech and fair use, treating Internet users as second-class citizens or presumed criminals, their rights subordinated to those of corporate owners of intellectual property.

It doesn't have to be this way. As you continue in your journey, learning from and making your own contributions to the amazing resource that is the Internet, please consider these issues. If you end up deciding, as I have, that the Internet's culture is worth defending, I encourage you to look into the activities of the following organizations, and to the extent that their aims agree with yours, supporting them. Thanks.

- Coalition Against Unsolicited Commercial Email (CAUCE) (*http://www.cauce.org/*)
- The Free Software Foundation (FSF) (*http://www.gnu.org/*)
- The Electronic Frontier Foundation (EFF) (*http://www.eff.org/*)

That's it! Have fun, and good luck with Perl!

Index

We'd like to hear your suggestions for improving our indexes. Send email to *index@oreilly.com*.

Dumper function, 358
dynamic page generation, 5, 422

E

-e file test operator, 82, 156
/e modifier in regular expressions, 329
each function, 289
echo command and $PATH shell
    variable, 32
EDITOR environment variable, 243
EditPad freeware program, 25
Electronic Frontier Foundation (EFF), 487
emacs editor, 23, 481
emailing
    log-analysis report, 230–232
    output of cron jobs, 243
embedding
    metainformation into HTML pages with
        META headers, 333
    programming in web pages, 482
Embperl (extension to Apache web
        server), 331, 483
encrypted passwords, generating, 424
encrypted web transactions, supporting, 5
__END__ token, 414
end-of-string anchor ($), 85, 170
$end_time scalar variable, 194
    formatting codes for, 212
ENTRIES filehandle in CGI guestbook
        script, 305
environmental stability and hosting
        providers, 6
$ENV{REMOTE_USER} environment
        variable, 425
Epoch seconds, 199–207
    converting into human-readable time
        strings, 199–201
eq (string equality) operator, 67
error messages
    die statements and, 69
    in make_page.cgi script, 389, 395
    paying attention to, 36
    &regenerate_site_links subroutine
        and, 397
    testing CGI scripts and, 47–49
escape method, importing, 389
escape_query subroutine (WWW::Search
        module), 409
escaping metacharacter (\) in regular
        expressions, 44, 170
eval statement in make_page.cgi script, 397

exclusive locks, 304, 400
    blocking vs. nonblocking behavior, 462
    on GDBM files, 460
execute permission, 33–35
exhibit.txt file, 100–102
    parsing, 118–121
    sanity checking in, 133
exists function, 258, 330
exit command, 18
expanding pathnames, 75–77
$expire_time configuration
        variable, 196–198
@EXPORT array, 368
@EXPORT_OK array, 368
Exporter module, 368
extended log format, 191–193
    reporting referral/user agent
        information, 227
extensions, regular expression, 169, 188
external commands, running with system
        function, 396–398
extracting
    files from archives, 268
    links, 251–255
    substrings from strings, 149

F

-f file test operator, 83
Fcntl module in guestbook script, 297
file locking
    CGI guestbook script and, 303–307
    CyberFair project and, 399–401
    lack of in Apache::Htgroup, 431–433
    race conditions in register.cgi script, 447
    (see also exclusive locks; shared locks)
file permissions
    in CGI guestbook script, 307–309
    in make_page.cgi script, 396
    umask function and, 155
    in Unix, 33–35
file test operators, 82, 156, 247
file transfers, encrypted protocols and, 22
File::Find module, 246–250
    in make_cf.plx script, 339, 358
filehandles
    creating, for writing to files, 95
    file locking and, 303–307, 399–401
    in form-to-mail gateway script, 68
    open function and, 89
filename extensions, 76
    using regular expressions to look for, 84

H

h2xs utility, making modules with, 370
hash of
 arrays, 357
  creating, 256
 hash of lists (HoHoL), 357
 hashes (HoH), 357, 414
  assigning values to inner hash of, 416
  invoking write_register_queue
   subroutine with, 428
  read_htgroup subroutine
   populating, 433
 lists (HoL), 357
hash references
 anonymous, creating, 359
 dereferencing, 259, 330
hash variables, 42–43
 accessing slices of, 448
 in log_report.plx script, 196
 in make_exhibit.plx script, 106, 147
 naming issues for, 107
 tie function and, 459
hashes, sorting, 225
hash-on-a-disk (DBM file), 459
head function (LWP::Simple module), 276
HEAD requests, 276
 checking remote URLs, 285
header function (CGI.pm module), 71, 298
header method, 286
headers, outputting CGI, 45
"Hello world!" script
 as a CGI script, 44–50
 creating, 27–31
 debugging, 35–38
here-document quoting, 46
 in regex.plx script, 174
HoH (hash of hashes), 357, 414
 assigning values to inner hash of, 416
 invoking write_register_queue subroutine
  with, 428
 read_htgroup subroutine populating, 433
HoHoL (hash of hash of lists), 357
HoL (hash of lists), 357
home directory, returning to with cd
  command, 17
host field in web logs, 180
%host hash variable, 196
hosting providers
 evaluating, 4–6
 hidden costs of, 5
$hostname configuration variable, 253, 254
 running quotemeta function on, 254

%hostname hash variable, 183
hostname lookups on IP addresses, 182–186
hostnames in web logs, 180
$hour scalar variable, 200
HREF attributes
 checking, via spider-like programs, 277
 converting values into absolute filesystem
  paths, 253–255
 extracting values of, via regular
  expressions, 251–255
 modifying, 87–97
.htaccess file, 423–425
.htgroup file, 424–426
 automating user registration, 426
 updating, 431–434
HTML documents
 adding structure to, 331–334
 alphabetical index, generating, 158–161
 embedding metainformation into, with
  META headers, 333, 345
 generating the top-level page, 165
 modifying HREF attributes in, 88–89
 outputting, 46, 135–166
 parsing with regular expressions, 87
HTML files
 finding, 249
 looking for broken links in, 250
HTML forms
 building with make_page.cgi
  script, 390–393
 creating, 53–56
 in web search script, printing, 323
HTML output, adding to report, 260–262
HTML pages (see web pages)
HTML tags, disabling in CGI guestbook
  script, 301
HTML templates, 326–343
 filling in text, 330–334
  copy-and-paste vs. subroutines, 327
 multiple templates, 342
 &template subroutine, 326–330
HTML::LinkExtor module, 288
HTML::Parser module, 87
.htpasswd file, 424–426
 adding entries to, using
  Apache::Htpasswd module, 451
 automating user registration, 426
 updating, 431–434
htpasswd utility, 424
HTTP authentication, 423–426
HTTP HEAD requests, 276
 checking remote URLs, 285

N

\n sequence in regular expressions, 171
named vs. positional parameters, 340
namespaces and package declarations, 366
native_query method, 409
NCSA user authentication tutorial, 426
ne (string inequality) operator, 67
negated character class, 78
networks
  outages/slowdowns and hosting
      providers, 6
  troubleshooting, 18–22
new method, 408
  HTML::LinkExtor module, 288
  HTTP::Request class, 285
newlines in regular expressions, 171
&new_visit subroutine, 198, 208
  recording referral and user agent
      information, 227
  tracking robots, 229
next function, 190, 322
next_result method, 409
nonalphanumeric characters in regular
      expressions, 84, 153, 169
nonblocking locks and flock function, 400
nonwhitespace characters in regular
      expressions, 171
nonword boundaries in regular expressions,
      matching, 171
nonword characters in regular expressions,
      matching, 172
not operator, 67
numbers
  random vs. pseudo-random, 450
  sorting, 224
numeric equality (==) operator, 67
numeric greater-than (>) operator, 67
numeric greater-than-or-equal-to (>=)
      operator, 67
numeric inequality (!=) operator, 67
numeric less-than (<) operator, 67
numeric less-than-or-equal-to (<=)
      operator, 67
numeric mode, supplying chmod arguments
      using, 34

O

/o modifier in regular expressions, 169, 255,
      288, 363
object methods, 284

object-oriented programming
      (OOP), 282–285
  HTML::LinkExtor module and, 288
  Perl and, 284
offline mode: message (CGI.pm debugging
      tool), 73
offsite links, checking, 272–277
one-or-more quantifier in regular
      expressions, 170
OOP (object-oriented
      programming), 282–285
  HTML::LinkExtor module and, 288
  Perl and, 284
open function, 89
  creating filehandles for writing to files, 95
  file locking in CGI guestbook script, 306
  vs. sysopen function, 304
open source vs. proprietary software, 1–3
or die statements in form-to-mail gateway
      script, 69
or next statements in log-analysis script, 190
or operator, 67
  vs. logical or operator, 408
O'Reilly, Tim, 480
Orwant, Jon, 482
OS X
  Darwin and, 3
  scp command-line program and, 22
output, piped, 68
output streams and more command, 120
outputting sample script data, 118–121

P

package declaration, 366–368
package function, 367
package variables, 216, 248
packet switching, introduction to, 20
%page_data hash of hashes, 357
  automatically generating links, 360–363
  dereferencing hash references in, 362
  &load_pages subroutine and, 358
  using Data::Dumper module, 358–360
Page.pm file, 375
pager programs, 11
  output streams and, 120
%page_sequence hash variable, 217
param function (CGI.pm module), 298, 387
%param hash variable, 340
parameterized links in make_page.cgi
      script, 389
parameters, named vs. positional, 340

parent directories, referring to with . . (dot dot), 16

parentheses ()
  grouping logical elements, 67
  grouping metacharacter in regular expressions, 170
  using capturing parentheses, 174, 177, 187, 297, 322, 329

parse method, 288

&parse_category subroutine, 124–127
  updating new variables in, 151

&parse_exhibitor subroutine, 109, 113–118
  adding sanity checks to, 121–124
  updating scriptwide variables, 148–151

parsing text files, 98–134

partial path of a directory, 15

password-challenge dialog box, 425

password-protected features, accessing, 431

passwords, encrypted, 424

path and directory structure, 14

PATH environment variable, 32

$path scalar variable, 156

$PATH shell variable, 32

pathname expansion, 75–77

pattern matching
  in HTML templates, 329
  operators, 83
    $ (dollar sign), 85
  parsing HTML files and, 251–253
  in regular expressions, 173–177, 187–191

Peek, Jerry, 480

pending users, reading/writing data for, 430

percent sign (%) and hash variables, 42

performance issues with flat-text-file storage, 458

Perl
  Apache server administration and, 484
  books on, 482
  debugger, 37
  evaluating statements as true or false, 64–68
  h2xs utility and, 370
  library directories in, 367
  locating on your system, 26
  modules, 51–53, 365–375
    installing, 266–271, 369
    installing with CPAN.pm, 271
    root vs. regular user installation, 269–271
    search engine add-ons, 404
    storing data at end of, 414
    template for, 366–369

object-oriented programming (OOP) and, 284
  running on a non-Unix computer, 28
  script vs. program, 31
  standard modules, 201
  taint mode for scripts
    in CGI guestbook script, 296, 301
    in make_page.cgi script, 387, 396
    in web site searching script, 319, 321
  turning on warnings feature, 36, 59, 80
  variables, 39–43
  vs. Python, 484

perl program
  compiling script without running it, 36
  determining version number of, 27
  running Perl debugger, 37

perldebug manpage, 38

permissions, file (see file permissions)

PHP for web development, 483

pico text editor, 23, 481
  creating "Hello world!" script, 27–31
  editing Makefile (SWISH-E), 312
  help screen, 30
  turning on special features with command-line options, 28

ping command, 19–22

pipe character (|)
  alternation metacharacter in regular expressions, 170, 177–179
  backslashed in regular expressions, 160

piped output
  in form-to-mail gateway script, 68
  open function and, 89

plus (+), used as quantifier metacharacter in regular expressions, 170

POD-based commenting, 154

pop function, 214

popup_menu function, 393

positional vs. named parameters, 340

postambles and brace expansion, 79

PostgreSQL and Perl, 485

&post_leader_page subroutine, 394

&post_student_page subroutine, 394–396

pragma, strict, 105, 387

preambles and brace expansion, 79

primary sorting, 225

print function, 30, 434
  chained together with join function, 190
  output streams and, 120
  printing to filehandles, 70, 96
  used in debugging, 37
  vs. filehandles, 69

WinCVS (Windows CVS client), 481
WinSCP (secure scp protocol), 22
&with_dot subroutine, 392
&with_join subroutine, 392
word boundaries in regular expressions,
        matching, 171
word characters in regular expressions,
        matching, 172
words, quoting with qw(), 298
working directory, 15
World Wide Web, 2
wrap function, 217
write permission, 33–35
&write_htgroup subroutine, 434
&write_page subroutine, 157, 162, 340, 364
    generating the top-level page, 166
&write_register_queue subroutine, 428
WWW::Search module
    creating new objects, 408
    installing, 404
    multisearch results tool,
        creating, 410–416
    single-search results tool,
        creating, 405–410

X

/x modifier in regular expressions, 169, 188,
        329

Y

$yday scalar variable, 200
$year scalar variable, 200

Z

-z option for pico command, 28
zero-or-more quantifier in regular
        expressions, 170
zero-or-one quantifier in regular
        expressions, 171
zero-width assertion, 173
Zope, 484

About the Author

John Callender currently works as an independent consultant specializing in web development. In previous stages of a somewhat erratic career he has worked as a teacher, writer, editor, and network administrator. He has been the beneficiary of an impressive amount of undeserved good fortune, including being selected as husband by his wife, Linda, and as father by his children, Julia and William. In his spare time he enjoys sailing, birdwatching, and learning about computers.

Colophon

Our look is the result of reader comments, our own experimentation, and feedback from distribution channels. Distinctive covers complement our distinctive approach to technical topics, breathing personality and life into potentially dry subjects.

The animal on the cover of *Perl for Web Site Mangement* is a proboscis monkey. The coastal rainforests and mangrove swamps of Borneo and the forests of the lower Kinabatangan River have the largest concentration of this species (*Nasalis larvatus*). Their fur is brick-red, and they have long tails and large bellies. The most obvious feature of Proboscis monkeys is the male's extremely long nose, which is shaped like a cucumber. The monkeys travel in groups of about five to fifteen. A group is usually made up of a dominant adult male with a harem of up to ten females as well as juveniles. They are vegetarians, eating primarily leaves, along with fruit, seeds, and flowers. Unusually among apes, they are very skilled swimmers and divers in the rivers that make up a large part of their habitat. The proboscis monkey's Malaysian name is Monyet Belanda, translated as "Dutchman Monkey." During the European colonial period, the Malaysians apparently thought the monkeys' red hair, pot bellies, and big noses resembled the European traders and colonialists.

This unique monkey is threatened with extinction through hunting and loss of habitat. The rainforests and swamps where they live are under severe threat from logging and land clearing. Attempts to keep this monkey in zoos have not been successful; the shy species does not survive. The only way to observe the proboscis monkey is in the rainforest, its natural habitat in the wild.

Colleen Gorman was the production editor, and Audrey Doyle was the copyeditor for *Perl for Web Site Mangement*. Sada Preisch and Leanne Soylemez provided quality control. Judy Hoer wrote the index.

Hanna Dyer designed the cover of this book, based on a series design by Edie Freedman. The cover image is a 19th-century engraving from the Dover Pictorial Archive. Emma Colby produced the cover layout with QuarkXPress 4.1 using Adobe's ITC Garamond font.

David Futato designed the interior layout. Neil Walls converted the files from Microsoft Word to FrameMaker 5.5.6 using tools created by Mike Sierra. The text font is Linotype Birka; the heading font is Adobe Myriad Condensed; and the code font is LucasFont's TheSans Mono Condensed. The illustrations that appear in the book were produced by Robert Romano and Jessamyn Read using Macromedia Free-Hand 9 and Adobe Photoshop 6. The tip and warning icons were drawn by Christopher Bing. This colophon was written by Colleen Gorman.

Whenever possible, our books use a durable and flexible lay-flat binding. If the page count exceeds this binding's limit, perfect binding is used.